Changing Seasons

A History of Cricket in England, 1945–1996

CHANGING SEASONS

A History of Cricket in England
1945–1996

David Lemmon

ANDRE DEUTSCH

First published in Great Britain in 1997 by
André Deutsch Limited
106 Great Russell Street
London WC1B 3LJ

André Deutsch is a subsidiary of VCI plc

CIP data for this title is available from the British Library

ISBN 0 233 99005 4

Typeset by Derek Doyle & Associates
Mold, Flintshire
Printed by
MPG Books, Bodmin, Cornwall

Contents

1   Prologue   1

2   The Long Road Out of Darkness, 1946–51   12

3   The Escape from the Wilderness, 1951–55   76

4   Supremacy and After, 1955–60   115

5   The Sad Sixties, 1960–69   150

6   Evolution and Revolution, 1969–77   221

7   Packer and After: The Age of Brearley
        and Botham, 1977–82   287

8   Fall from Grace, 1982–88   328

9   Profit and Loss, 1988–93   369

10 New Structures, 1993–96   405

Select Bibliography   439

Index   441

1
Prologue

On Friday, 1 September 1939, at Hove, Yorkshire beat Sussex by nine wickets and claimed the County Championship for the fifth time in seven seasons. Hutton and Yardley had scored centuries for Yorkshire on a rain-restricted second day, and, on the last, Sussex were bowled out for 33 with England's left-arm spinner Hedley Verity achieving one of the most remarkable performances of his distinguished career. In six eight-ball overs he took seven wickets for nine runs.

Two days later, Neville Chamberlain announced that Great Britain was at war with Germany, and what some referred to as 'the long hot summer', and others as 'the dishonest decade', was at an end. The poet Stephen Spender insisted that 'the thirties was being wound up like a company going into bankruptcy'.

The declaration of war was not unexpected, and Surrey had been unable to play their last match of the season at home because The Oval had been requisitioned. The game against Lancashire was rescheduled for Old Trafford, but when the teams arrived at the ground on the Friday with Lancashire needing 352 to win play was immediately abandoned because of the seriousness of the international situation. It was to be six years before first-class cricket reappeared in England and seven years before a full county programme was again possible.

What could not have been realised in September 1939 was that Hedley Verity's great bowling performance at Hove was the final act of his cricketing career. He was never again to appear in a first-class match. Commissioned in the Green Howards, he died of wounds received in the invasion of Sicily in July 1943.

Among other cricketers to be killed in action were three county captains, Maurice Turnbull of Glamorgan, Robert Nelson of Northamptonshire and Frederick Chalk of Kent, but, in contrast to what had happened in the First World War, cricket itself survived.

In 1915 cricket came to a standstill. *John Wisden's Cricketers' Almanack*, published the following year, offers tributes to Grace and Stoddart and eighty pages of obituaries. These pages contain the names of more than 300 young cricketers in their late teens or early twenties who had fallen during the first year of the First World War. Lord's was being used for military purposes, and cricketing activity was restricted to the public schools and to the schools' matches against MCC.

Twenty-six years on, the same annual, recording cricket in the first year of the Second World War, tells of the deaths of some twenty cricketing servicemen, but tells also of many entertaining matches that had been played in various parts of the country. The Oval had been commandeered by the military authorities, and Old Trafford had been damaged through enemy action, but there was a full programme of matches at Lord's, and the Bradford and Birmingham leagues thrived.

At the outbreak of war, Sir Pelham Warner was appointed as assistant deputy secretary, then deputy secretary of MCC in the absence on military service of Ronald Aird and R.S. Rait Kerr. It was almost entirely through Warner's efforts that cricket continued at Lord's throughout the Second World War. Initially, all matches except those between public schools were restricted to one day, and they invariably saw the appearances of some outstanding cricketers rich in Test experience, as well as retired veterans like Lord Tennyson, R.H. Twining and Percy Chapman. Sir Pelham Warner's XI which played a West Indian XI on 22 August 1940, for example, included Len Hutton, Denis Compton, 'Gubby' Allen, Walter Robins, Freddie Brown, S.C. Griffith, Bryan Valentine, and Ken Farnes, the Essex and England fast bowler who was to be killed in a flying accident just over a year later. The West Indian side numbered Constantine, Martindale, C.B. Clarke and E. St Hill in its ranks.

Martindale and Constantine appeared regularly in the Bradford League, as did Paynter, the Pope brothers and Smith of Derbyshire, Place, Arthur Mitchell, Barber and Norman Oldfield. Birmingham could boast Wyatt, Howorth, Palmer, Santall, Goddard and the New Zealander Merritt as well as Perks and Hollies who, in 1940, broke 'Tich' Freeman's league record when he took ninety-nine wickets.

There were two other enterprising organisations which did a tremendous amount to keep cricket alive during the Second World War, the London Counties and British Empire XI clubs, both of which were formed early in 1940. They operated primarily in the south of England and played mostly on club grounds. They raised much money for charities and gave enormous pleasure to many people. Their matches were played at weekends, and they fielded several Test and county cricketers. As Norman Preston wrote of London Counties, 'Some fifteen professional players, besides cricket enthusiasts in many parts of the country, were afforded the opportunity to assemble and for brief periods enjoy the delights of the summer game. The troubles of a war-ridden world seemed almost inconceivable during those sunny weekends.'

As the war moved into its second and third phases, many more than fifteen professionals turned out for London Counties, who were generally captained by Joe Hulme although the captaincy initially rotated, and the former Middlesex cricketer and Arsenal and England footballer contributed much to the team's popularity with his good humour and ready wit.

In 1940 a British Empire XI was led by Hugh Bartlett, the Sussex left-hander, but Ray Smith, the Essex all-rounder, captained them in the later stages of their existence. Their matches followed a pattern similar to that of London Counties, and they possessed an outstanding bowler in C.B. Clarke, the West Indian leg-spinner. He had toured with the West Indian side in 1939 and returned to England to study medicine. He was later to be a dominant force in club cricket with the BBC, and he played county cricket for both Northamptonshire and Essex. It is estimated that he took 746 wickets in wartime cricket.

Clarke played alongside such men as Denis Compton, Norman Yardley and J.G.W. Davies in his matches for the British Empire XI, for whom another regular entertainer was Reg Hayter, destined to become the doyen of Fleet Street sporting journalists.

The majority of those who played in these wartime matches were on active service and could appear only when they snatched weekend leave. Robert Nelson, for example, topped the British Empire XI batting averages in 1940. He and L.F. Parslow, who was later to play for London Counties and appeared once for Essex in 1946, shared an opening stand of 113 against London Counties, at Lord's, on 10 August 1940. A second lieutenant in the Royal Marines, Nelson was killed two months later.

Nor were matches themselves immune from the disruptions brought about by war. The game between Buccaneers and the British Empire XI on the last day of August 1940 saw later arrivals and an early finish because of the Battle of Britain. A week later, again at Lord's, an air-raid warning brought the game to a halt. The players waited long for the all-clear, but when it came Laurie Gray took four wickets in seven balls to win the game for a Middlesex XI with just a few minutes to spare.

The most remarkable incident occurred on 29 July 1944, when the Army were playing the R.A.F. at Lord's. Rain delayed the start until two o'clock, and the Army were 57 for one when a flying bomb, the notorious 'doodlebug', was heard and seen approaching Lord's from the south. The doodlebug flew at a low altitude and was powered by petrol and compressed air. It was steered by a gyroscope and designed to stall

3

when it ran out of fuel, exploding on impact. When the engine of the flying bomb approaching Lord's cut out the players and umpires flung themselves to the ground, but, miraculously, the bomb passed overhead and exploded harmlessly in Regent's Park. The players got to their feet and resumed the game. Two balls after the stoppage Jack Robertson, the Middlesex opening batsman, hooked Bob Wyatt for six in celebration.

The importance of these wartime matches cannot be overemphasised. For a young generation growing up in desperate circumstances, they created an everlasting love of the game, and they brought alive cricketers whose previous existences had only been as pictures on cigarette cards. For an older generation, they, like the concerts given by Myra Hess in the National Gallery, had a richer significance.

More than thirty years on, Stephen Spender, in his collection of essays *The Thirties and After*, gave eloquent voice to that significance.

> Looking back now, it seems to me that in England the war period was a little island of civilization in our lives. Civilized values and activities acquired a kind of poignancy because they were part of what we were fighting for and the reasons for which we were fighting.

A quarter of a million people watched cricket at Lord's in 1943, and, in spite of the threat from flying bombs, 170,000 people attended matches in 1944. Even more astonishing to contemplate today, perhaps, is the fact that, in 1942 and 1943, an Advisory County Cricket Committee met to consider the future of the game after the war. It must be remembered that these were the years of the fall of Singapore, of the Japanese conquests in the South Pacific, and of MacArthur leaving the Philippines for Australia with the words, 'I shall return.' These were the years of the defeats and then victories in North Africa, of the sieges of Stalingrad and Leningrad, and of the banning of the baking of white bread. Against that background, MCC had the optimism to consider 'cricket after the war'. As if in congratulation, the fortunes of the Allies began to prosper following the publication of the plan.

The plan itself reiterated the statements of the Findlay Commission of 1937 concerning attacking play, dynamic attitudes, the striving to win from first to last and the strict adherence to time-keeping in all aspects of the game.

The report covered two areas, the first season after the war and general post-war reconstruction. It recommended that county cricket should be resumed at the earliest possible date, for this was 'in keeping with the general feeling that entertainment must be an essential feature of the post-war social structure of the nation, and will be particularly valuable during demobilisation'. The MCC were to be asked to press the government to have cricket released from the payment of entertainment tax, and it should be left to the individual counties to decide whether to re-enter the County Championship.

In the light of proposals and agitations fifty years on, it is interesting to read that 'The revival of cricket in the widest field should be the main concern, and no compulsory elimination of Counties by amalgamation or any other method is recommended, nor any division into two Leagues, as this would spell financial disaster for those in the lower half of the table.'

The report also unanimously rejected the idea of playing first-class cricket on Sunday, but there was a more open view regarding the introduction of a knock-out competition. 'A scheme for a Knock-Out Competition to be played in addition to the normal Championship has been put before us, but for many reasons we do not consider it satisfactory in its present form. While we see many practical difficulties in the proposal, we suggest that should a satisfactory scheme be evolved later in which all matches are played under the Laws governing three-day cricket, the Advisory County Cricket Committee should examine the possibility of such a competition.'

In spite of the success and popularity of the one-day matches being played at Lord's and elsewhere, the committee totally rejected any idea of time-limit cricket:

Any departure from the existing method of three-day matches would be detrimental to First-Class County Cricket, and, therefore, the Committee do not recommend innings limited by time, or number of overs, or any system in which the result depends directly on the rate of scoring. It is not denied that such methods have proved useful in single-innings matches, and particularly half-day matches, but the following disadvantages appear to apply in the case of matches of longer duration:

(i) Detrimental to the art and character of the game, e.g. two-innings matches give the fullest scope for skilled captaincy to reap its reward; value of the all-rounder would be lessened and specialisation increased.

(ii) Captain will be drawn towards placing his field and using his bowler not to take wickets, but to keep down runs. If, on the other hand, he pursues aggressive tactics, he may well be assisting his opponents.

There is a mixture of perception and confusion here, but it was difficult for any of the committee to envisage anything other than the traditional

5

three-day game on which they had been nurtured and which they had played. Warner, joint-secretary of the committee, urged people not to be led away by the calls for brighter cricket. 'It is a leisurely, intricate game of skill. We live in an age of speed and people are apt to think that cricket must be speeded up; but my experience is that it is not necessary to have faster scoring to have interesting cricket.'

Warner was to die in January 1963, a few months before the first Gillette Cup match was played, but several other members of the committee lived long enough to see the advent of the Benson and Hedges Cup, the Sunday League and limited-over international cricket.

Ironically, as the report was being drafted in 1943, people were witnessing some of the most exciting cricket that it was ever going to be their pleasure to attend. The Bank Holiday matches at Lord's were a case in point. At Whitsun, Civil Defence scored 253 runs in 160 minutes to beat the Army by six wickets. Gimblett hit a century in eighty-six minutes, and he and Jim Parks senior put on 200 at two runs a minute. Two days later, on the Monday, playing for the R.A.F. against the Army, Austin Matthews, the Glamorgan pace bowler, had the first four batsmen caught behind by James, the immaculate New Zealand wicketkeeper who had played for Northamptonshire. The match was interrupted by a hailstorm, and, eventually, the R.A.F. were set to make 169 in 95 minutes. Brilliant batting by Cyril Washbrook, Les Berry and Bill Edrich saw them to victory with ten minutes to spare. Berry and Edrich hit the last 144 runs in 44 minutes.

At the August Bank Holiday, a two-day match was played between England and the Dominions. There was some wonderful cricket, with centuries from Ames and Dempster and some outstanding slow-left arm bowling from Denis Compton. England won by eight runs at quarter to seven on the second day. A crowd of 22,000 saw the match at Whitsun, and in excess of 38,000 watched the two days in August. On a generation of schoolboys, the game's potential post-war audience, cricket like this made an indelible impression.

On 6 June 1944 the Allied armies landed in Normandy, and as they pushed on through France and Belgium, the threat of flying bombs and of German air attacks began to recede, so much so that by November the lights were switched on in Piccadilly, the Strand and Fleet Street after five years of blackout. The presence in Britain of so many servicemen–cricketers from the dominions and colonies brought an added excitement to the matches played up and down the country. There were such fixtures as the Royal Australian Air Force and West Indies at Birmingham, and the Royal Australian Air Force and New Zealand Services at Maidstone while, at Lord's, 'England' played 'Australia'.

6

The Australian side was comprised of Australian servicemen in Britain, all of whom were unknown to the public, but men like wicket-keeper Sismey of New South Wales, batsmen Carmody and Stanford, and, above all, a thrilling all-rounder named Keith Miller became immensely popular. England fielded as many as eight Test players, while the novices in the side were Godfrey Evans, Trevor Bailey and A.W.H. Mallett.

Evans had kept wicket for Kent in five matches in 1939 when W.H.V. Levett was unavailable. Les Ames had given up wicket-keeping by that time because of a back problem. Evans, a sergeant in the R.A.S.C., became a favourite figure in matches at Lord's during the war, and, in fourteen seasons after the war, his popularity did not diminish.

Bailey and Mallett had just left Dulwich College where Bailey had broken all records. Mallett played occasionally for Kent in future years; Bailey became one of England's great all-rounders. Both men made their first-class debuts in 1945 when they played for Under-33 against Over-33, at Lord's, at the beginning of September.

The war in Europe came to an end in May 1945, and three months later the war in the Far East was at an end. This left no time even for MCC's emergency plans to come into operation, but a series of Victory Test matches between England and Australia hastily came into being.

The Australians were strengthened by the arrival of Lindsay Hassett, who took over the captaincy. He had made his Test debut on the 1938 tour of England when he had scored more than 1,500 runs and averaged more than 50. He proved to be a genial leader ideally suited to these celebratory matches. England were captained by Wally Hammond, who had been appointed captain of England in 1938 shortly after becoming an amateur. He had played for eighteen years as a professional and was recognised as the greatest English batsman of his generation.

Matches which had originally been scheduled as one-day fixtures were extended to three days, and the first 'Test' was played at Lord's over the Whitsun period. It resulted in a victory for Australia with Cec Pepper hitting the winning run off the fourth ball of the last over on the stroke of seven o'clock. Pepper, an exciting all-rounder, was later to give immense pleasure in the northern leagues and to serve as a first-class umpire for fifteen years. *Wisden* described the match at Lord's and Australia's manner of victory as 'true to the exhortation expressed in the post-war cricket plans'.

England levelled the series with a forty-one run win at bomb-scarred Bramall Lane, Sheffield, at the end of June. The match was played on what *Wisden* described as a 'natural wicket' and was, according to the same source, 'the finest match of the season'. Hammond scored a splendid hundred in difficult conditions on the opening day, and there was some fine bowling from George Pope and Dick Pollard, both of whom were of fast-medium pace and neither of whom had appeared for England in a pre-war Test match. Pope was to win his one and only Test cap in 1947, and by then he was thirty-six. He had been chosen for the tour of India, 1939–40, which was cancelled because of the outbreak of war. At least Pope gained a Test cap. Others selected for that tour – A.J. Holmes, H.T. Bartlett, J.M. Brocklebank, R.H.C. Human, Emrys Davies, John Langridge, and Parker and Mobey of Surrey – were never to be given another opportunity.

Perhaps suddenly conscious of the age of several of those who had brought victory at Sheffield – Hammond himself had celebrated his forty-second birthday four days before the game began – England chose three schoolboy cricketers for the third game, at Lord's. They were considered to be the best schoolboy cricketers of 1944, and they were D.B. Carr, J.G. Dewes and Hon. L.R. White. Donald Carr was to become a power in the game. He captained both Oxford and Derbyshire and was Assistant Secretary of MCC, 1962–73, and a popular secretary of TCCB for thirteen years. John Dewes was a rigidly coached left-handed batsman who played five times for England. He won his blue in all three seasons at Cambridge, and he appeared for Middlesex, but after the tour to Australia and New Zealand, 1950–51, he was rarely available because of his duties as a schoolmaster. Luke White's promising form at Eton was never to be translated into first-class cricket. He played only five more first-class games after his debut in the Victory Test, three of them for Middlesex, but never made a fifty.

The experiment of fielding three youngsters was not a success. They scored only forty-seven runs between them, and Carr sent down just nine overs. To add to England's woes, Hammond retired from the match with lumbago after the first day. England were beaten, and veterans like Fishlock and Pope were brought in for the fourth game, also at Lord's, which was drawn.

The final game in the series was played at Old Trafford six days after VJ Day. It was a triumph for the Lancashire medium-pacer Phillipson, who had match figures of nine for 130 on his first representative appearance, but, like many others, he was close to his thirty-fifth birthday and was to be denied an opportunity at Test level. England won by six wickets, and, to the contentment of all, the series was drawn.

Phillipson was one of twenty players that England used during the series, but there were notable absentees. Denis Compton was serving in India. Trevor Bailey was a lieutenant in the Royal Marines and was in Europe in the final stages of the military campaign, while Alec Bedser, having survived Dunkirk with his twin brother Eric, was again on active service.

Like Evans, who did not play in the Victory Tests, Griffith being the wicket-keeper, and Bailey, Alec Bedser was one of wartime cricket's great 'discoveries'. He had played for Surrey against Oxford and Cambridge Universities in 1939 without taking a wicket, but Surrey officials had predicted a great future for the twins, and that prediction was proved correct.

Unlike Bailey, who returned to England in time to make his first-class debut in the Under-33/Over-33 match mentioned above, Alec Bedser played no first-class matches in 1945, for MCC granted first-class status to Victory Tests and to six other matches, the most interesting of which was England v Dominions, at Lord's, at the end of August.

In the state of euphoria which pervaded its 1946 publication, *Wisden* referred to this encounter as 'one of the finest games ever seen'. Dominions won by forty-five runs with eight minutes to spare with Hammond hitting a century in each innings, Martin Donnelly, the New Zealand left-hander, scoring 133, and Keith Miller playing an innings which has remained long in the memory of all those privileged to see it.

In Dominions' second innings, Miller hit 185, the last 124 coming in ninety minutes. The power of his driving was astonishing, and one of his seven sixes, an on-drive off Eric Hollies, saw the ball lodge in the small roof above the England players' dressing room. More significant than Miller's great innings, however, was the fact that the Dominions' side was led by Learie Constantine.

Hassett should have captained the eleven but was unable to play because of illness. To a present-day reader, the choice of Constantine as captain seems obvious. He was the most experienced player in the side, a brilliant all-rounder of international standing, among the most popular cricketers in the world, and a month short of his forty-third birthday, but he was the only black man in the eleven. He had remained in England during the Second World War as a Ministry of Labour welfare officer with West Indian workers. Only a year before the historic match at Lord's he had fought a case against colour prejudice when he won damages from the Imperial Hotel in London for 'failing to receive and lodge him'. All his life, as C.L.R. James stated so memorably, Constantine 'revolted against the revolting contrast between his first-class status as a cricketer and his third-class status as a man'.

Biographer of both Constantine and Warner, Gerald Howat, claims that it was Warner who invited Constantine to lead the Dominions, but all other sources have always insisted that he was elected by the other players. Constantine was deeply moved and most appreciative, for, in a sense, this was the first sign of a liberalism that was to seep its way into the cricket establishment more slowly than into other parts of society in the years following the end of the Second World War.

Attitudes, like traditions, become deeply ingrained, and one cannot legislate for them. Certainly MCC found it difficult to conceive of playing cricket in any other than over a period of three days. An interim report, published in March 1945, again broached the subject of the knock-out competition. It was to embrace the seventeen counties and would consist of a bye round, a first round of eight ties, a second round of four ties, two semi-finals and a final at Lord's which would begin on the Friday immediately following the end of the County Championship. The matches would be of three days' duration, except the final which would be played over four days. The problems presented by the proposal were that no provision could be made for drawn matches and that the final would almost certainly take place after the start of the football season, considered unwise in 1945.

Although there was interest in the idea, it was decided that nothing should be done until county cricket was firmly re-established.

Having played forty-eight matches and travelled the length and breadth of the country, the Australian Services set sail for India. On their departure, their manager, Flight-Lieutenant Keith Johnson, waxed lyrical: 'You are putting your bats away here now, and in other parts of the world they are taking them out, the village greens of other countries are ringing with the joyous shouting of youth at play, for the grand game is always being played in some part of our Cricket Empire. We look back with pride and pleasure to the grand country where the game was born and nurtured.'

Excessive as Johnson's words and sentiments may seem by today's standards, they echoed the mood of patriotism which had been essential in war and the mood with which some now faced the peace. Wally Hammond had finished top of the first-class batting averages as he had done every season since 1933, and all, it seemed, would soon be back as it once was.

Throughout the country, street parties expressed the joy of deliverance from a terrible time, but amid the celebrations there was also a demand for change. In July the Labour Party had swept into office with a majority of 146 over all other parties, and the promised welfare state offered an end to the poverty and degradation which far too many people had suffered in the 1930s.

In India the Congress Party launched a campaign which demanded independence, and, in every continent, there was a cry for a brave new world. Few could anticipate the agonies and sacrifices that the desire for change would bring, but momentarily, at least, cricket felt safe in its own traditions, and plans went ahead for a full season of county matches and a visit from the Indians in 1946.

2

The Long Road out of Darkness, 1946–51

Whatever the difficulties, it was seen as important that first-class cricket be resumed on a normal basis as soon as possible. In the aftermath of war, there was fear of world famine, and food rationing was as severe as ever it had been in time of hostilities. The United Kingdom, like other countries in Europe, was exhausted and damaged, and it suffered a period of austerity as it struggled towards economic recovery and the rebuilding of the nation. In this climate, the reintroduction of a complete sporting calendar was a priority, for it would help to raise the morale of a population who, ravaged by war, were desperate for some joy and colour in their lives. This was the period in which more people went to the cinema than ever before, or since. This was the period in which a Third Division (North) soccer match between Hull City and Stockport County commanded a crowd of 46,000.

If cricket was welcomed back with slightly less enthusiasm, it was only because the weather was dreadfully unkind, cold and damp for much of the summer of 1946. In spite of this, there were record attendances at many grounds, and club membership rose to new heights in counties like Somerset and Hampshire.

In the County Championship the experimental eight-ball over was jettisoned and the six-ball over reinstated. As each county would now play the same number of games, twenty-six, there was no longer any need for percentages or averages. Twelve points were awarded for a win and four points for first innings lead in a match lost or drawn.

Such changes were not difficult to introduce, but the game was beset with problems for which legislation could provide no remedy. In 1946 several professional cricketers were still serving in the armed forces. Dawkes, the Leicestershire wicket-keeper, was a case in point. He was not demobilised until the summer of 1947 when he joined Derbyshire and played for them in the last four matches of the season. Others, like Bill Bowes of Yorkshire and Wilf Wooller of Glamorgan, had been prisoners-of-war and were in need of both mental and physical recuperation.

There were, too, the difficulties that faced counties whose grounds had been damaged in the war, not exclusively by the enemy. Old Trafford had suffered, but The Oval had been requisitioned in September 1939 for use as a searchlight base. It was then prepared as a giant prisoner-of-war camp for parachutists. The parachutists never came, and the historic old ground spent the duration of the war in a state of neglect and maltreatment.

Incendiary and high-explosive bombs had fallen round The Oval, but, apart from bomb blast damaging part of the perimeter wall, the ground itself survived amid the ruins around it. Incredibly, under the guidance of Bert Lock, the ground staff transformed the dilapidated site into a venue fit for Test cricket inside six months. The square had not been touched for six years. There were miles of barbed wire and a thousand poles set in concrete on the outfield, and there were pits, huts, weeds and an assault course to be removed. All was done so that the ground was ready for first-class cricket by April 1946, and within six weeks The Oval was scene to a world record.

Leicestershire had problems of a different nature. The Aylestone Road ground had been taken over by the National Fire Service, and then by the United States Pioneer Corps. When they vacated the ground the Leicestershire Corporation claimed it and built an extension to the neighbouring electricity works.

The County Cricket Club had foreseen this happening and had already entered into negotiations with the local education committee for the use of their former ground, Grace Road, which was used as a sports field for the City of Leicester School. The authorities still insisted that the ground should be used as a school playing field, and they wanted it to be used for country cricket only in the school holidays.

The County Cricket Club had visions of making Grace Road their permanent headquarters, but the ground itself had scarcely altered since 1900, and there was much work to be done to lift it to first-class standard. In 1946 Leicestershire took matches to Melton, Ashby and Barwell. Players and spectators faced rather primitive conditions at Leicestershire's home matches.

There were equally primitive conditions at Northampton where the ground was in a poor state after the war. The club was kept alive by the energetic secretary, Lieutenant-Colonel Alleyne St George Coldwell, who would convince ladies who complained that they should go to the lavatory before they went to the cricket. In effect, having spent the best part of six years sheltering from bombs or bullets, people were well adapted to discomfort and accepted conditions and facilities which would be scorned today.

One cannot overemphasise the fact that cricket was a major outlet for people seeking release from the privations around them. The year began with riots in France over the shortage of bread, and, by the summer, a loaf of bread in the United Kingdom had been cut by four ounces, and brewing by 15 per cent, in order to save grain. There were acute short-ages of coal, and, if one looks now at a film like *Hue and Cry*, made on location in London and the first of the Ealing comedies, one recognises that, in 1946, much of London was in ruins. Nor was London the only city to have suffered.

There were, of course, other difficulties that the game faced, not the least of which was counties fielding sides of adequate strength. Derbyshire found that the lure of the leagues had claimed Tommy Mitchell, Townsend and George Pope, although Pope was to return to county cricket in 1947. To balance these, E.W. 'Nobby' Clark, a left-arm pace bowler who had played for England, came back from league cricket to help out his old county, Northamptonshire, and, at the age of forty-three, was their leading wicket-taker. Lancashire were without Pollard for most of the season, for he was still in the services, as was Nottinghamshire's Bill Voce.

There were those who discovered, sorrowfully, that the war years had lessened their ability. Most notable among them was C.R. Maxwell, an amateur wicket-keeper who had played for Nottinghamshire in the late 1930s and who was considered to be on the verge of an England cap. He agreed to join Middlesex, but, after a handful of matches, it was appar-ent that he had lost his form, and he disappeared from the game. He was not alone.

There was also the question of captaincy. One of the traditions in which county cricket had found comfort was that the captain of a county club should be an amateur. Lord Hawke's comment at the Yorkshire AGM of 1925, 'Pray God, no professional shall ever captain England', was often quoted for reassurance although rarely in context and rarely doing justice to what his lordship had implied. There had been profes-sional captains of counties, but only in extraordinary circumstances and, even in the twentieth century, never for long.

It was not simply a question of background or breeding. Wally Hammond played as a professional for eighteen years, but when, in 1938, he announced that he would play in future as an amateur, he was appointed captain of England, and he became captain of Gloucestershire a year later. It was felt that the professional, bound by the need to earn his living, would not have the vision, the judgement or the necessary sense of bravado that was essential to good leadership. Paradoxically the war, while creating a desire for equality in society and socialism in politics, had reinforced the idea that men needed to be led by officers, and that officers were a special breed. What was not appreciated was that the number of 'officers' willing and able to give their time to first-class cricket was diminishing.

It is easy to sneer at the amateur and professional convention today. They stayed at different hotels, and the amateurs had their initials before their names or were referred to as 'Mister'. Certainly the system had its roots in a social order which has since been rejected, but, in the inter-war years, the very survival of certain counties was dependent upon the enthusiasm and commitment of a few amateurs. Often moderate players who would not have kept a place in a good county side, they gave up their summers to keeping their counties going. They captained the side and got an eleven together for each match. It was due to their efforts that no first-class county went out of existence in the inter-war years although some came close to it.

Somerset and Worcestershire were counties who had existed on a small band of professionals and as many amateurs who were willing to assist. In 1939 the number of Somerset professionals was seven, and this had increased to eight in 1946. In both seasons they were reliant on seventeen amateurs. Warwickshire fielded twenty-four amateurs as opposed to eight professionals in 1946, but the next few years were to see great changes.

Although 154 amateurs appeared in county cricket in 1946 compared to 109 in the last season before the Second World War, fewer were now able to commit themselves fully to the game or to the welfare of their counties. Talented amateurs were available on occasion, but many had been away from home for long periods during the war, and there were needs to repair both domestic and business lives. Others were young and had to look to fashioning careers other than cricket.

One is minded of men like John Bridger, who played in wartime Varsity matches in 1941 and 1943 and appeared in several other matches at Lord's during the war. He looked to be a batsman of considerable ability, but he took holy orders, was involved in the scholastic profession, and was able to play in only two matches for Hampshire in 1946, hitting 50 against Sussex and 39 and 142 against Middlesex. He was a player of class, but his career for Hampshire was restricted to thirty-eight matches which spanned nine seasons.

Michael Walford could surely have been an England cricketer had he been regularly available, but his career was restricted to fifty-two matches in eight seasons for Somerset. A magnificent all-round sportsman who had been a triple blue at Oxford in the 1930s and was to captain Great Britain at hockey in the 1948 Olympics, Walford was a master at Sherborne. He possessed that enviable quality of being able to pick up a bat in August and score runs at will. In 1947 he hit 942 runs in eight matches for Somerset. His innings of 264 against Hampshire at Weston-super-Mare was, at the time, the second highest innings ever played for Somerset.

Good as these and other players were, they had only a limited time to give to the game, and several counties found the task of appointing a captain for the first post-war season a difficult one. Indeed, when the time came for umpires to be chosen for the 1946 season so few counties had been able to decide upon a captain that the choice of umpires was made by MCC.

There were counties like Essex, Gloucestershire, Middlesex, Nottinghamshire, Somerset and Yorkshire who could turn to experienced pre-war leaders, while Glamorgan were indebted to J.C. Clay who was forty-eight years old and had assisted the county since 1921.

There were other counties who could find no one willing to take on the task. Leicestershire found themselves without a regular captain when the season started. The search for a suitable amateur had proved fruitless, and they turned to their senior professional, Les Berry. Berry, surely one of the best opening batsmen never to play for England, had been with Leicestershire since 1924, and he was asked to lead the side for the first six matches of the season. The committee still believed that a competent amateur would come forward. They were wrong, and Berry proved to be most capable. He was not the first professional to captain Leicestershire, for Astill had done the job in 1935. Under Berry, in 1946, the county enjoyed their most successful season 'since the record year of 1935'.

Les Berry was to captain Leicestershire until the end of the 1948 season, after which the county would again turn to an amateur.

In a time of austerity and economic recovery, business pressures precluded many men from taking up posts that they would have enjoyed. T.A. Higson, son of the Lancashire chairman, accepted the job as captain of the Red Rose county at the end of 1945, but, as the season approached, he announced that he would be unable to play because of business commitments.

Attention now turned to Jack Iddon, a fine all-rounder of the pre-war period. Iddon was forty-four years old and had played as a professional,

16

but it was generally accepted that he would become an amateur and lead the side. Tragically, he was killed in a road accident in April 1946, and the committee had to make a hasty appointment.

The choice fell upon Jack Fallows, son of the club treasurer. Fallows's cricket had been restricted to Minor County level, and there was a barrage of criticism at his appointment, particularly from people outside the club who were unaware of the qualities and experience that Fallows possessed. He had a fine military record, had frequently captained the Manchester side in the 1930s and was steeped in the Lancashire tradition. Although he had severe limitations as a player – he finished with a batting average of under 9 and with a highest score of 35 – Fallows was something of an inspired choice. He led a side which contained only four players with regular experience of pre-war cricket to third place in the County Championship.

Fallows was a team man, an unselfish leader blessed with wisdom and common sense and the common touch. The most famous story told of him was how, when Lancashire played Surrey at The Oval, they found only four eggs were available between twelve players and a scorer, such were the stringencies of rationing. Fallows settled the argument as to who would have the eggs by deciding, 'We are in the field this morning. Let the bowlers have the eggs . . . the batsmen can have them tomorrow.'

He was immensely popular with his side, and with the supporters, but his reward was to be sacked by the committee at the end of the year. Two other county skippers were to be sacked at the end of the season, one, indeed, before the end of the season, but with more justification.

Having overcome the physical damage inflicted on the club, Surrey found themselves with a side which, although boasting an average age of thirty-six, was relatively inexperienced and to which there was no heir apparent as captain. Monty Garland-Wells, captain in 1939, had been badly wounded in the war and did not feel that he could cope with a season of first-class cricket. His predecessor, Errol Holmes, was giving all his time to the attempt to raise the funds necessary for the restoration of the ground. It would have been something akin to sacrilege for Surrey, a mighty power in the cricket establishment, to have broken with tradition and appointed a professional, although Laurie Fishlock probably had the credentials.

With neither Garland-Wells nor Holmes willing or able to take on the task, Surrey named N.H. Bennett as their captain for the 1946 season. The reasons for this appointment will for ever remain shrouded in mystery, but, fifty years on, it is generally accepted that the choice of Nigel Harvie Bennett was due to a clerical error and that the committee had intended to offer the captaincy to A.C.L. Bennett.

Leo Bennett was a renowned club cricketer who had been educated at Dulwich College and was qualified for Surrey by residence. In 1947 and 1948 he was to appear for Northamptonshire and captained that county on occasions.

Initially, nothing was known of N.H. Bennett. It then transpired that he had batted well at Stowe and had played for the Young Amateurs of Surrey in 1929 and 1930. He had played five innings for Surrey Second XI in 1936 after which he had gone to New Zealand on business. He had returned to England on the outbreak of war, was commissioned in the Royal Engineers and served in the Far East. With the war over, he walked into the Surrey offices and asked if he might be given some Second XI games in 1946. The case of mistaken identity followed, and Nigel Bennett was offered the captaincy, which he accepted.

The tale may be fictitious, but it has never been denied, and no alternative explanation has been offered as to how this strange appointment came about.

Bennett's one year in first-class cricket was not a happy one although his 688 runs, average 16, suggest that he was not totally devoid of ability. The greatest problem was that he did not know his players, and they did not know him. Surrey had lost its complete stock of towels and other equipment during the war, and each player was given a bonus of fifteen clothing coupons in an effort to help replace the lost kit. These were hardly sufficient for the purpose of buying flannels, blazers, shirts and other essentials, and it did not help team spirit when seasoned professionals noted that Bennett, who was instantly capped, was wearing a pre-war Surrey blazer. It had belonged to Roger Winlaw, a Cambridge blue and Surrey batsman of distinction, who had been killed in the war. His family had given it to the club in the belief, one presumes, that it would be exhibited in the Long Room. The sight of Bennett wearing it was not likely to make the new captain popular in the eyes of a team who were having great difficulties in trying to kit themselves out.

Surrey did not have a good season, and *Wisden*'s final verdict on Bennett was that 'want of knowledge of county cricket on the field presented an unconquerable hindrance to the satisfactory accomplishment of arduous duties. This prejudiced the general work of the side, and several bad spells culminated in consecutive defeats in the last six Championship matches.' Errol Holmes, forty-one years old, returned to the side and took over the captaincy in 1947.

Bennett had been allowed to see out the season, which was a privilege denied to Peter Murray-Willis, captain of Northamptonshire. The death in the war of Robert Nelson had been a terrible blow for the Midlands

18

county, for the young captain had been immensely popular and had led Northamptonshire out of the darkest of times. In every sense it was a most difficult task to find a successor, and eventually the selection rested on Peter Murray-Willis, who was to be remembered for his sportsmanship, enthusiasm and total naivety. He had played for both Worcestershire and Northamptonshire on a few occasions before the war and was quite obviously well short of county class with the bat as well as being something of a liability in the field. It was reported that he once went in pursuit of the ball only to stop to reclaim his cap when he lost it in the chase.

As the season progressed, the dissatisfaction with Murray-Willis's captaincy grew. There was constant criticism in the press, and the players themselves conveyed their disquiet to the committee, who summoned the captain and put pressure on him to resign. Murray-Willis was reluctant to concede the leadership, but he was forced to bow to the pressure, and he resigned at the end of July. The affair was shrouded by the announcement that he was going 'for business reasons', which was cricket's equivalent of the soccer manager who just received 'a vote of confidence' leaving by 'mutual consent'.

Northamptonshire could release Murray-Willis abruptly because Jack Webster, a Cambridge blue in 1939 and a master at Harrow, was available to take over the captaincy on a temporary basis during the school holidays.

The career record of Peter Murray-Willis was 467 runs at an average of 10.37. It is easy to respond to such figures with contempt and ridicule, but he deserves sympathy. He was a victim, a man who was asked to do a job that was beyond his capabilities. Cricket was still in search of its 'officers' and 'gentlemen', but the well was already running dry.

There was, however, a problem that affected everyone and that transcended the damage to grounds, the distinction between Gentleman and Player, and the choice of captain. A cessation of all serious cricket for six years was bound to have a disastrous effect upon the standard of the game. However gifted a cricketer, he will never reach the highest level without a long and arduous apprenticeship, and when he has reached the top flight he will remain there only with constant practice and application. This is, perhaps, especially true of bowlers.

Sir Stanley Jackson, President of Yorkshire, echoed these sentiments at the end of the 1946 season when he said, 'I think last season's results showed very clearly a lack of bowlers of real merit throughout the counties. Too many runs were made, not through improved skill in batting, but because of deterioration in bowling.' Jackson, it must be remembered, was one of the four England selectors in 1946, the other three being Brian Sellers, Walter Robins and Group Captain A.J. Holmes.

One must have some sympathy for these men. Their task was not an easy one. Wally Hammond was top of the averages. Seven batsmen, including Denis Compton, Washbrook, Fishlock of Surrey and Gimblett of Somerset exceeded 2,000 runs. Yorkshire won the County Championship, with Middlesex second and Lancashire third. All, it seemed, was as it had always been. Cricket was continuing as if there had been no break, unless, that is, one looked closely at the first-class bowling averages.

With the wasted years of war behind them, counties could only turn to veterans, and, for the most part, England had to do the same. The first four places in the bowling averages were filled as follows:

Booth	111 wickets, average 11.61
J.C. Clay	130 wickets, average 13.40
Matthews	93 wickets, average 14.29
Robinson	167 wickets, average 14.95

Of these bowlers, Booth was forty-four, Clay forty-eight, Matthews forty-one and Robinson the youngest at thirty-five.

Yorkshire had consistently founded their success on a slow left-arm bowler of the highest class, men like Peel, Rhodes and Verity, and with Verity dead in the war, in 1946 they turned to Arthur Booth. He had first been tried in 1931, but the greatness of Verity left him few opportunities. He moved to Northumberland and found favour in the Bradford League. There was experience in a few of the matches recognised as first class in 1945, and then a regular place in the Championship side and a county cap in his forty-fourth year.

Compared to others, Booth was a junior. Tom Goddard bowled his off-spin for Gloucestershire and captured 177 wickets at the age of forty-six, and Arthur Wellard, forty-three years old, was leading wicket-taker for Somerset.

Of the front-line bowlers in the country, only Alec Bedser and Cliff Gladwin were under thirty although Eric Hollies, who took more wickets than anyone else, was a mere thirty-four.

Eric Hollies was a leg-spinner of considerable merit, and his 184 wickets in the season included all ten wickets for 42 runs against Nottinghamshire at Edgbaston. Seven of his victims were bowled and three were leg-before so that he managed the remarkable feat without the aid of his fielders. In spite of this, he was not selected to play against India, nor was he chosen in the party to tour Australia. He did play in the first of two Test trials, but, as was learned in the years to come, such matches have little or no meaning.

The leg-spinners preferred to Hollies, both against India and for the tour to Australia, were Doug Wright and Peter Smith. Wright was to thrive in Australia, but it was the medium pace of Alec Bedser that was to dominate the Indians.

The Indian side of 1946 was more successful than its predecessors of 1932 and 1936 in that it won eleven and lost only four of its twenty-nine first-class matches. The team arrived in England at a time when the politicians were debating the future of their country, and they were, in effect, the last *All India* team to play England. The pre-war tourists had tended to be fractious and had been led by men of considerable social standing but of a cricketing ability that was really below first class let alone Test class. The 1946 side was led by the Nawab of Pataudi, who had scored centuries for Oxford University, Worcestershire and England and who was now given dispensation to play for and to captain India. He had the qualities long sought in a captain of India; he was both an aristocrat and a talented cricketer, although he was no longer in the best of health. He could also call upon players of experience and ability like Merchant and Amarnath. The tour was to reveal the genius of cricketers such as Hazare, and Mankad, an outstanding all-rounder who completed the 'double'.

Above all, the Indian side was courteous, modest and gentle. They fell short of their own aspirations in the Test series, but they knew that the tour was one of rehabilitation for all concerned. Their attitude and demeanour were admirably suited to the time. Sadly, instead of sunshine and hard wickets, they met with rain, storm, cold and wet turf.

They began in the cold at Worcester, which, traditionally, was the starting point for all tourists, and they were welcomed by a crowd of 8,000, one of the biggest ever seen on the ground. They fell to a century by Dick Howorth, who also claimed seven wickets in the match, and were beaten by sixteen runs. Martin Donnelly, the New Zealand Test player, scored another century against them in the drawn game at Oxford, and then they travelled to The Oval.

The Indians batted first on the Saturday, and, with Alec Bedser in good form, they were reduced to 205 for nine. Banerjee now joined Sarwate, and the pair added 249 in three hours ten minutes. This remains the highest last-wicket stand ever recorded in England and the only occasion on which numbers ten and eleven have both scored centuries in the same innings. The tourists won, and they continued successfully until the first Test match, at Lord's, towards the end of June. One should now consider the England team with which they were confronted.

There had never been any doubt that Hammond would captain the side. He was an amateur and had led England since 1938. He remained dominant in English cricket and was to top the first-class averages by a margin of more than sixteen runs from his nearest rival. He was still considered by many to be the best batsman in the world. The liabilities were ignored. He was forty-three a few days before England's first post-war Test, was troubled by arthritis, had virtually ceased to bowl and was no longer the exceptional slip fielder he had been in his youth. He was also, as was to become increasingly apparent, unpopular with his team, most of whom found him distant, arrogant and, at times, contemptuous.

The only other amateur in the side, and therefore, by definition, vice-captain, was the wicket-keeper Paul Gibb, who had played in the five Test matches when England toured South Africa in 1938–39. He had opened the innings in each of those Tests and had scored 93 and 106 on his debut as well as 120 in the fifth, the famous 'timeless' Test. He was played purely as a batsman in that series as Les Ames was still keeping wicket, and when Ames dropped out in 1939, Gibb's Yorkshire colleague Arthur Wood took over the gloves.

Gibb had actually been selected to keep wicket for England in the Old Trafford Test against Australia in 1938, but the game was abandoned without a ball being bowled, which deprived another Yorkshireman, Tom Smailes, of his first Test cap.

Smailes was a useful all-rounder, a medium-pace right-arm bowler and a left-handed hard-hitting batsman. He had taken all ten Derbyshire wickets at Bramall Lane, Sheffield, in 1939, but he remained on the fringes of the England side. He was to say later that throughout the war, when he was a captain with the Central Mediterranean Forces in the Italian campaign, the one thing that made him determined to survive was his ambition to win the Test cap of which rain had robbed him in 1938. His ambition was realised at Lord's in 1946 when he was thirty-six years old. It was to be his only Test cap.

For another Yorkshireman, Bill Bowes, it was a fifteenth and last. Bowes was a month short of his thirty-eighth birthday, and he had been one of the most consistent, aggressive and quick England bowlers in the pre-war period. His Test debut had been against India in 1932, and, on the 'Bodyline' tour, he had played in one Test and bowled Bradman for a duck. He would certainly have appeared in more Tests had he been a better batsman and fielder, but he had been an integral part of the great Yorkshire side of the 1930s and was the most intelligent of bowlers. His selection for Test cricket in 1946, however, was at best sentimental. Commissioned in the war, he had been taken prisoner at Tobruk, and,

22

after three and a half years in a prison camp, he was four and a half stone lighter in weight. Yorkshire nursed him carefully, but he never recovered physically to the extent where he was really fit for first-class cricket. His pace was reduced and, even in normal circumstances, a bowler of his type was likely to be beyond his best at the age of thirty-eight.

Bowes was given a benefit in 1947, played in most of Yorkshire's Championship matches and topped the county's bowling averages. Then he retired and became an outstanding journalist.

The fourth Yorkshireman in the side was Len Hutton, who already had Test centuries against New Zealand, Australia and the West Indies to his credit. He held the world record in Test cricket with his 364 against Australia at The Oval in 1938 and, with five hundreds in thirteen Tests by the age of twenty-three, he had the cricket world at his feet when war broke out. Seven years on, with one arm shorter than the other following an injury suffered during the war, he was about to restart his international career and to open the innings with the Lancastrian Cyril Washbrook, a year his senior and with one Test appearance nine years earlier behind him.

Like Hutton, Denis Compton, two years younger than the Yorkshireman, was restarting a career that had flourished excitingly in the seasons immediately preceding the war. He was a handsome, glamorous figure who had played in wartime soccer internationals for England and was to play in a Cup Final, but, unfortunately, when the first Test against India arrived he was in the middle of his worst run of scores in first-class cricket.

Completing the batting line-up was Joe Hardstaff junior, the most elegant batsman of his generation. The Nottinghamshire cricketer had played sixteen times for England between 1935 and 1939 and delighted with his attacking cricket. Twenty-nine years old when war broke out, he was at his prime, and, as in the case of so many others, one can only conjecture what he might have achieved but for those lost years.

Doug Wright was the main spin bowler. He had first played for Kent in 1932 at the age of eighteen and had won his first Test cap in the 1938 series against Australia. In the post-war period, he tended to bowl his leg-breaks quicker than he had done in 1939, which he later admitted he considered a mistake. His run to the wicket was an eccentric series of kangaroo hops, and he was, to say the least, erratic and unpredictable, but there were days when he was unplayable as seven hat-tricks in a career testifies, and he was much favoured by selectors.

The two players in the side who were new to Test cricket were Alec Bedser, the wartime discovery whom all had expected to be chosen, and

Jack Ikin whose selection had surprised nearly everyone because little was known of him.

Ikin was twenty-eight and had played for Staffordshire at the age of sixteen. He had appeared four times in the Lancashire side in 1939 and won a regular place in the side in 1946, although, when picked for England, he was an uncapped player. He was a solid left-hander who could, and did, bat anywhere, a useful leg-break and googly bowler, and a brilliant fielder close to the wicket. He was to play in eighteen Tests for England over a period of nine years, but, in truth, he was short of Test class and selectors seemed to return to him again and again as a stop-gap when there was an emergency.

The public interest in this first post-war Test match was immense. (A match played between Australia and New Zealand in Wellington three months earlier was not accorded Test status until 1948.) As was the custom until 1950, only three days were given to Test matches against all save Australia and South Africa, and the gates of Lord's were closed by noon on the Saturday and the Monday with nearly 30,000 people crammed inside. There were 15,000 present on the final day. This was before the age of corporate hospitality when spectators were willing to sit on the grass at the boundary edge, separated from the play only by a rope which they never ventured to cross.

India batted when the Nawab of Pataudi won the toss, but batting first proved to be anything but an advantage as the pitch gave some assistance to the bowlers after much rain, and the outfield remained sluggish. Using his height to the full, maintaining an admirable length and delivering every ball with an energy that made it zip off the pitch, Alec Bedser gave a glimpse of things to come with a magnificent debut performance of seven for 49 as India were bowled out for 200.

England quickly lost Hutton, and Compton was bowled first ball, while Hammond and Washbrook were both out as the score reached 70. Gibb then joined Hardstaff, and they took the score to 135 by the end of the day.

On Monday, the pitch played more easily following Sunday sunshine, and Hardstaff and Gibb hit 117 in under two hours before the Yorkshire wicket-keeper fell to a slip catch. Hardstaff completed the highest and last of his four Test centuries, and the innings remains the only double century made against India at Lord's. *Wisden* said of this first post-war Test hundred:

> During five and a quarter hours at the wicket Hardstaff maintained
> close concentration on every ball. Bareheaded, as usual, he stood erect,
> holding the bat at full length, defending or forcing the ball away with

wristy strokes; amidst the cheers that greeted his 200 he remained unruffled and as watchful as ever until the last wicket fell. He trusted to perfect timing for every kind of scoring stroke with the ball kept down, and one lifted drive from Amarnath to the pavilion rails caused surprise calling for special comment.

The teams were presented to King George VI before India began their second innings, and the war was becoming a distant memory. The visitors were 162 for four on the Monday evening, and they fought tenaciously to the end, but England claimed victory at one-thirty on the final day.

One interesting statistical comparison emerges from this match. It was completed in two days and one session, and during that time 343.5 overs were bowled. When West Indies beat England at Headingley at the start of the 1995 series the victory was achieved at around tea time on the fourth day. A total of 236.4 overs were bowled in the match and only one more wicket fell than in the game at Lord's in 1946.

In the second Test of the 1946 series England brought in Voce and Pollard for Bowes and Smailes. As was then customary at Old Trafford, rain interfered with play, and England, having dropped two vital catches, saw India, needing 278 to win, draw the match with their last pair defending stoutly for thirteen minutes. Bedser, who reached a hundred wickets for the season during the game, again took eleven wickets, this time at a cost of 93 runs. Pollard marked his Test debut with a spell of four for 7 and a first innings analysis of five for 24 in 27 overs.

By the time the third Test arrived in late August, most thoughts were on the selection of the side to tour Australia, and Fishlock, Edrich, James Langridge, Peter Smith and Godfrey Evans, all to gain selection, played against India. So, too, did Alf Gover, who was appearing in his fourth and last Test ten years after his first.

Gover was a good, wholehearted, unlucky fast bowler with Surrey who was closer to his thirty-ninth than his thirty-eighth birthday when he played at The Oval in August 1946, and why he was chosen is a mystery, for he was not too secretive about his reluctance to tour Australia under Hammond's captaincy. As it transpired, the Oval Test was ruined by rain. There was no play until five on the first day and none at all on the last, but the game was graced by a century from Vijay Merchant, one of the great Indian batsmen. He scored 2,385 runs, average 74.53, in this wet summer, a remarkable achievement.

Gover did not go to Australia; the others in the side did. Laurie Fishlock was a left-hander who generally opened for Surrey. He had toured Australia and New Zealand in 1936–37, but he had a very

disappointing Test record in contrast to his consistency at county level.
He would celebrate his fortieth birthday on the Australian tour.

First Post-war Test Match
England v India at Lord's
22, 24 and 25 June 1946

India First Innings		Second Innings	
V.M. Merchant c Gibb b Bedser ...	12	lbw b Ikin	27
M.H. Mankad b Wright	14	c Hammond b Smailes .	63
L. Amarnath lbw b Bedser	0	(8) b Smailes	50
V.S. Hazare b Bedser	31	c Hammond b Bedser	34
R.S. Modi not out	57	(3) lbw b Smailes	21
Nawab of Pataudi (capt) c Ikin			
b Bedser	9	b Wright	22
Gul Mahomed b Wright	1	lbw b Wright	9
Abdul Hafeez b Bowes	43	(5) b Bedser	0
†D.D. Hindlekar lbw b Bedser	3	c Ikin b Bedser	17
C.S. Nayudu st Gibb b Bedser	4	b Bedser	13
S.G. Shinde b Bedser	10	not out	4
Extras (b 10, lb 6)	16	(b 10, lb 2, nb 3)	15
Total	200	....	275

BOWLING	Overs	Mdns	Runs	Wkts	Overs	Mdns	Runs	Wkts
Bowes	25	7	64	1	4	1	9	–
Bedser	29.1	11	49	7	32.1	3	96	4
Smailes	5	1	18	–	15	2	44	3
Wright	17	4	53	2	20	3	68	2
Ikin	–	–	–	–	10	1	43	1

fall of wickets
1–15, 2–15, 3–44, 4–74, 5–86, 6–87, 7–144, 8–147, 9–157
1–67, 2–117, 3–126, 4–129, 5–174, 6–185, 7–190, 8–249, 9–263

England First Innings		Second Innings	
L. Hutton c Nayudu b Amarnath ..	7	not out	22
C. Washbrook c Mankad b Amarnath	27	not out	24
D.C.S. Compton b Amarnath	0		
W.R. Hammond (capt) b Amarnath	33		
J. Hardstaff, jnr not out	205		
†P.A. Gibb c Hazar, b Mankad	60		
J.T. Ikin c Hindlekar b Mankad ...	16		
T.F. Smailes c Mankad b Amarnath	25		

A.V. Bedser b Hazare   30
D.V.P. Wright b Mankad   3
W.E. Bowes lbw b Hazare   2
   Extras (b 11, lb 8, nb 1)   20   (lb 1, w 1)   2

   Total   428   48

BOWLING	Overs	Mdns	Runs	Wkts	Overs	Mdns	Runs	Wkts
Hazare	34.4	4	100	2	4	2	7	–
Amarnath	57	18	118	5	4	–	15	–
Gul Mahomed	2	–	2	–	–	–	–	–
Mankad	48	11	107	2	4.5	1	11	–
Shinde	23	2	66	1	–	–	–	–
Nayudu	5	1	15	–	4	–	13	–

fall of wickets
1–16, 2–16, 3–61, 4–70, 5–252, 6–284, 7–344, 8–416, 9–421
umpires – H.G. Baldwin and J.A. Smart
England won by 10 wickets

Bill Edrich was the last member of the party to be chosen for the tour, and he was named as senior professional. In 1938 he had scored a thousand runs before the end of May, but he had failed in all four Tests against Australia. The failures had continued in South Africa as he moved up and down the batting order until, in the second innings of the final Test, he scored 219. Nevertheless, he did not play against the West Indies in 1939. He enjoyed a splendid season for Middlesex in 1946, was very popular, not least on account of his fine war record and his dashing approach to the game, and deserved selection, but doubts prevailed in the minds of the selectors as to whether he was of Test quality. When one reflects on Edrich's subsequent career such doubts seem strange, particularly as he was an outstanding slip fielder and among the quicker of the England bowlers available at the time. At the end of the tour he announced that he would in future play as an amateur. If he had hopes of gaining the England captaincy, he was to be disappointed. He was too wild a character for the cricket establishment of those immediate post-war years.

Of the fast bowlers in the party, Bill Voce was the senior. He had celebrated his thirty-seventh birthday in August 1946, and had been able to play in only a few matches towards the end of that season because he was still in uniform. The left-arm Voce had partnered Larwood on the 'Bodyline' tour of 1932–33 and, before his recall to the England side in

1946, had not played Test cricket since 1937. In selecting him, the panel must have been swayed by historical reminiscences rather than by the evidence of form.

Like Pollard, Voce was able to tour Australia only because he was given special leave. He played in the first and third Tests without taking a wicket. He was off the field for much of the third Test because of a groin strain. He played five matches for Nottinghamshire at the beginning of the following season, took ten expensive wickets and announced his retirement.

Keeping fit was one of the most difficult tasks that faced the party. James Langridge, forty years old, had played in seven Tests between 1933 and 1936 before being brought back for the Oval Test ten years later and chosen as the all-rounder, left-handed bat and slow left-arm bowler, for the Australian tour, on which he appeared in only four first-class matches. He was one of the twelve chosen for the third Test, but he suffered a groin strain during fielding practice before the match, and his Test career was at an end.

Hardstaff, not selected until the fourth Test, was unfit for the fifth. Like Langridge and Gibb, he did not accompany the party to New Zealand. Gibb had played in the first Test and then gave way to Evans, one of the successes of the tour. Gibb, a strange and solitary character, faded from cricket only to reappear dramatically in 1951.

An ageing side, all of whom had suffered privations of some kind during six years of war, arrived in Australia to find glorious sunshine and excellent food. These delights came at the end of a relaxing sea trip, and it was natural that the players should put on weight. Voce and Pollard, suddenly freed from army disciplines, put on more than most, but weight problems did not help anyone to maintain peak fitness.

Certainly Hammond was far from fit, and he was stricken with fibrositis during the fourth Test and did not play again until the side reached New Zealand. On his return to England, he announced his retirement from first-class cricket. A glittering career had ended with a whimper. In truth, there were few among his party who were sorry to see him go. As Ray Robinson wrote in the *Cricketer*:

> To Australian eyes the chief defect in his captaincy was that away from the grounds he did not mingle with his men more. A motor firm's provision of a car for his use meant that he often travelled apart from the main body of the team.

It meant, too, as some shrewdly observed, that Hammond expended

28

energy on driving from city to city which could have been better spent on the cricket field.

As Hammond bowed out, the positive gain from the tour was the advance of Norman Yardley as both a cricketer and a leader. Yardley, a Yorkshireman and ex-Cambridge captain, had won one Test cap on the tour of South Africa, 1938–39, and had been a late and somewhat surprising choice as vice-captain to Hammond for the Australian tour. A cheerful cricketer and a good mixer, 'he won the team's liking as well as their admiration for his capacity for rising to the occasion as batsman and bowler'.

A stylish and enterprising right-handed batsman and a slow medium-pace bowler both underrated and underused, Yardley learned much in Australia where, in the fifth Test, he led England for the first time. He was to play a significant role as England sought to rebuild in the years that followed.

As well as the problems caused by injury and age, MCC were hampered by some bad weather at crucial times, and it was suggested kindly that they did not enjoy the best of luck. In fairness, MCC had been most reluctant to send a team to Australia so soon after the end of the war. They were acutely conscious that English cricket was far from ready for a series against the old enemy, but the Australians pressed their case hard, pleading that the Australian people would be bitterly disappointed if England did not tour. The fact that nearly 850,000 attended the five Tests certainly gave proof to the popularity of the tour and of the game itself. Where MCC erred was in underestimating the strength of the Australian side, a far less experienced combination than England. Six Australians made their Test debuts during the series, and six others – Johnson, Lindwall, McCool, Miller, Tallon and Toshack – had played only against New Zealand in March 1946, a game that was not to be recognised as a Test until eighteen years later. Bradman, Hassett and Barnes were the only seasoned Test players for Bill Brown was not available because of a hand injury; and doubts existed about Bradman.

At the start of the season Bradman was far from well, and it was generally believed that if he did not succeed in the first Test match, he would retire from international cricket. He won the toss, and Australia batted. England began well, for Bedser had Morris caught at first slip in his second over. Bradman seemed nothing like the great batsman of the pre-war years, and he floundered against Bedser. In forty minutes, he made only 7, and he lost Barnes at 46, splendidly caught at square-leg at the second attempt by Bedser.

With the score at 74 for two shortly before lunch, Bradman chopped a ball from Voce to second slip where Ikin claimed the catch. Bradman stood his ground, and the umpire ruled not out. Many saw this as the turning point of the tour. Had Bradman gone, it was believed, he would have left the Test scene forever. As it was, he went on to make 187 and share a record third-wicket stand of 276 with Hassett. On top of this Bedser suffered a stomach upset, a legacy of war service, and the Australian batsmen scored heavily.

Rain and bad light limited play to ninety-five minutes on the third day when Australia lost their last five wickets for forty-nine runs. Hutton was bowled when he played back to Lindwall, and three hours were lost on the fourth day. A violent thunderstorm and high winds turned the pitch into a treacherous surface. The ball turned and lifted, and England lost fifteen wickets in three and a half hours to give Australia a record margin of victory.

England brought in Peter Smith and Godfrey Evans for the second Test. Smith, the Essex leg-break bowler, was another veteran cricketer, thirty-eight years old when the tour began. He had been the victim of a cruel practical joke in 1933 when, watching a film in a Chelmsford cinema, he saw a message flashed on the screen that he had been picked for the Oval Test against the West Indies and was to report immediately. When he arrived at the ground he discovered that the call had been a hoax, and he had to wait another thirteen years for his Test debut. He played in two Tests in Australia and one in New Zealand, suffered an injured hand and met with little success, but he did establish a record when he took nine for 121 against New South Wales and became the first England touring bowler to perform such a feat in Australia.

Smith did not play Test cricket again after that tour, but he did the 'double' in 1947 and took 172 wickets in the season, an Essex record. He set up another record in that season when he hit 163 against Derbyshire at Chesterfield. As he was batting at number eleven, he established a record for the highest score for a batsman going in last. He and Vigar added 218 for the tenth wicket.

Evans marked his debut against Australia by not conceding a bye while 659 runs were scored. Barnes and Bradman scored 234 apiece, and, in spite of a brave century from Edrich, England were again crushed by an innings.

Even though they avoided defeat in the third Test, mainly because of Cyril Washbrook's second-innings century, England were made acutely aware of the great strength of the Australian eleven. Morris, emerging as a fluent left-handed batsman of grace and reliability, hit a century, as did McCool, a colourful all-rounder and Lindwall, a fast bowler of the highest quality, while wicket-keeper Tallon made 92.

Compton had begun the tour uncertainly, but before the fourth Test, played in Adelaide, he hit centuries against a Combined XI and against Tasmania. A century in each innings of the Adelaide Test meant that he had completed hundreds in four consecutive first-class innings. On top of this achievement, Hutton and Washbrook began both England innings with three-figure partnerships, and Alec Bedser bowled Bradman for nought. In response, Morris, too, hit a century in each innings and Miller became the seventh Australian to score a hundred in the series, a series which he had begun by taking seven for 60 at Brisbane.

Hammond's declaration on the last day left Australia three and a quarter hours in which to score 314 to win. They settled for 215 for one, and the match was drawn.

Ill fortune followed England to the end, for, in the final Test at Sydney Hutton played supremely well to score 122 on a damp pitch before being forced to retire ill. He defied the pace of Ray Lindwall who, in a magnificent display of fast bowling, had swept aside the rest of the English batting, taking seven for 63 in the process.

Thanks to Wright's exploitation of the responsive pitch, England took a first innings lead of 27. The Kent leg-spinner returned the best figures he was to achieve in his thirty-four Tests, seven for 105, and England had a chance of victory. Colin McCool, a more conventional leg-spinner than the medium-pace Wright, had other ideas, and Australia ran out winners by five wickets.

Hutton, unable to bat in the second innings, was flown home to England, and it is interesting to note that Norman Preston, in *Wisden*, suggested that MCC should employ this form of transport between the Australian capitals on future tours.

Battered and bruised at the end of the series, England licked their wounds and sombrely considered the seemingly limitless resources of the Australians. Of the Services' side that had opposed England in the Victory matches, only Miller had found a place in the Test team, and only six others had won places in state sides. One excludes Hassett in these calculations, for he was an established Test cricketer before the war and had been flown to England in order to captain the Services party.

Lindwall and Miller had emerged as a pair of quick bowlers worthy of comparison to McDonald and Gregory in 1920–21. History, it seemed, was repeating itself. Don Tallon was immediately recognised as one of the finest wicket-keepers that the game had known, and there was balance, organisation and control in all that the Australians did. In contrast to the gentle and courteous cricket played by the Indians in 1946, England found Australia under Bradman tougher in every respect. H.L. Collins, a former Australian captain, complained that cricket as a

31

game had disappeared and that the only policy of the Australian side was that it must not lose. It did not, and, in the process, England were outwitted in every department, not least in Bradman's tactical use and non-use of the roller within the legal boundaries of the game. A new, harder age was beginning and England, as yet, were several years behind in grasping this fact. As Pelham Warner remarked in the *Cricketer*, external forces were posing a threat to the game.

> Modern Test cricket is played in a blaze of publicity and is in danger of being sensationalised; and much of the ill-considered writing during the recent series was due to the craving for what is called 'a news-story'. In future tours we must have the highest possible standard of cricket description; any deviation from that standard is detrimental to the game.

Warner could have no idea what lay in store in years to come, but E.W. 'Jim' Swanton of the *Daily Telegraph* and a BBC commentator, ever perceptive, ever the sage, did much to lessen the damage done by constant criticism of the Australian umpires by pointing out that a player's reactions and demeanour are no guide to the correctness or incorrectness of an umpire's decision.

Once debate or controversy had calmed, England could reflect that not all was gloom and doom. Hutton and Washbrook had performed admirably as an opening pair. Edrich had been an outstanding success and had proved himself a great battler. Compton was maturing into one of the world's great Test batsmen and Yardley, captain-elect, was warm, intelligent and well respected. Evans had confirmed that he was a wicket-keeper of the highest quality and that he had the temperament for Test cricket. In sweltering heat at Adelaide, he had batted for two hours thirteen minutes and scored 10 as he aided Compton in a wonderful rearguard action which rescued England from a precarious position. Lively and cheerful, Evans was to prove to be a man for all seasons and all occasions.

The bowling presented less cause for optimism than the batting, wicket-keeping and captaincy. The clear atmosphere and the Australian pitches had rendered Voce and Pollard innocuous, and Alec Bedser, accompanied throughout the tour by his twin brother Eric, was forced to work tremendously hard, for he had no support and little luck. His sixteen Test wickets cost him 54.75 runs each, but Bradman was one of many who was quick to recognise Bedser as an adversary touched by greatness.

England's leading wicket-taker in the series was Doug Wright, who claimed twenty-three victims. The Test match in New Zealand was to mark the halfway point of Wright's international career. He was to continue to enjoy the confidence of the selectors for the best part of another five years, but he was to remain an enigma for the rest of his career. He captured 108 Test wickets, but they were bought at a high price. He caused doubts in the minds of the very best of batsmen, but he bowled at a pace that meant that the leg-break would lift and turn so sharply that it would miss both bat and stumps. In striving for the unplayable ball, this gentle man bowled too many bad ones. Like Bedser, Wright was asked to do an immense amount of work in the series. Between them, they sent down 486.5 eight-ball overs; Miller and Lindwall bowled 244.4.

Above Wright in the Test bowling averages was Norman Yardley, a revelation with the ball, whose ten wickets cost 37.20 runs each. This would have put him sixth in the Australian averages while Hutton's batting average of 51.12 would have ranked him sixth among the Australian batsmen. The gap between the two sides was considerable.

To make matters worse, there was no ready-made fast bowler waiting back in England and pressing for a place in the side. The two cricketers who had most reason to feel disappointed at not being chosen for the Australian tour were Charlie Barnett, of Gloucestershire, and Eric Hollies. Barnett was a thrilling, unconventional opening batsman who had met with success at Test level but whose style and technique were not appreciated by his former county colleague Wally Hammond, while Hollies was a successful leg-spinner with Warwickshire whose record we have already noted.

However badly the MCC touring party had fared in Australia, its members could consider themselves fortunate compared to those who remained in England's winter, which was of a severity not experienced since and which, coupled with the economic situation, caused the greatest of hardships.

In January steel works were forced to close through lack of coal, and freezing weather (temperatures were as low as minus 16 degrees fahrenheit) caused chaos and power cuts everywhere. A hauliers' strike brought a shortage of food supplies, and the meat ration was cut from one shilling and twopence to one shilling a week. Wheat stocks were so low that a cut in the bread ration was predicted and beer production was reduced by 50 per cent.

In February fifty-nine soccer matches had to be cancelled because of the weather, and this was in a period when it was quite customary to play on a carpet of snow and mark the lines in red or blue.

Heavy snowstorms and sub-zero temperatures brought fuel short-ages, and 4 million people were made idle by power cuts. More than 300 roads were blocked, trains were at a standstill and fifteen towns were completely cut off. In an attempt to boost productivity and increase exports, a ban on mid-week sport was introduced in March.

In April came the thaw and the floods after the freeze. More than 2 million sheep were killed, a week's meat ration for the whole popula-tion, and 500,000 acres of wheat were destroyed, the equivalent of a month's bread ration. Coal and gas fires were banned until September, and the milk allowance was reduced to two and a half pints a week. As the food crisis worsened, rationing became more severe than it had been in wartime.

There are those who complain that the 1947 season has been extrava-gantly overpraised, that it has been bathed in a romance which it does not deserve. To believe this is to fail to understand the background against which the cricket was played.

When, in May, the sun finally shone – and Eros came back to Piccadilly Circus – it was as though, in spite of the turmoil in the rest of the world, Britain had finally found peace. One dared to look forward for the first time for over a decade, and the cricket reflected this spirit. It was carefree and touched by joy.

South Africa provided the opposition for England in 1947. They were an experienced side with an average age of thirty, and three of the bats-men, Mitchell, Nourse and Viljoen, had toured England with the 1935 team. The captain, Alan Melville, a man of great charm, had led both Oxford University and Sussex, and he had captained South Africa against Hammond's team in 1938–39. The batting was solid, but the bowling lacked pace and, although Athol Rowan and 'Tufty' Mann worked hard as off-spinner and left-arm spinner, respectively, the attack was not of high quality. For England, it would be a calm after the storms of facing Lindwall, Miller, McCool and Toshack, but, like South Africa, England were still in search of an attack. Indeed, they were to employ fourteen front-line and three occasional bowlers in the five Test matches.

The search for bowlers was a priority from the start of the season, and there was great excitement when Somerset beat Middlesex by one wicket in the opening county match of the year at Lord's.

With Edrich scoring his first century of the season, Middlesex made 231 in the first innings, and then bowled out Somerset for 134, Edrich capturing four wickets for 5 in six overs on the second morning. That Somerset, trailing by ninety-seven runs on the first innings, clawed their way back into the game was due almost entirely to Maurice Tremlett, a 24-year-old who was making his county debut. He took five wickets for

8 in five overs and finished with match figures of eight for 86. Needing 176 to win, Somerset lost nine wickets before completing the task, and once more it was Tremlett who was the hero. He finished the match by hitting a six and two threes. 'The Middlesex team lined up and cheered as their successful opponents went to the pavilion.'

Later the same month, Tremlett took six for 84 against Essex at Ilford, and he was compared to Maurice Tate. He bowled fast–medium with an economical action, and, in the words of Norman Preston in the *Cricketer*, he had strength and perseverance and relied 'more on old-fashioned "break-back" than on the comparatively modern fetish of swerve for his unplayable ball'. He finished the season with 656 runs, average 17.72, and sixty-five wickets at 30.50 apiece. He was chosen to go to the West Indies where he played in three Tests, and he was also selected to tour South Africa in 1949–50, but, while his batting developed, his bowling did not prosper as had been anticipated. He never claimed a hundred wickets in a season, and he was not the answer to England's prayers; nor were J.W. Martin, Mallett or 'Sam' Cook, who bowled encouragingly for MCC against the South Africans at Lord's.

Somerset were Middlesex's bogey side in 1947, for they beat the Metropolitan county in the return match at Taunton in mid-July, but these were rare setbacks for Middlesex in a season when they won nineteen and drew two of their twenty-six Championship games. At last, under Walter Robins, they deposed Yorkshire as champions, and the White Rose county showed an alarming decline, dropping to seventh in the table and, at one time, being just three off the bottom.

For the followers of Middlesex, and for lovers of the game in general, the season will always be remembered for the doings of the 'twins', Compton and Edrich. Rarely, if ever, have two batsmen of such quality and excitement come together in one side at the same time. They were different in style. Edrich had not the easy grace and fluency of Denis Compton – he was more of a tenacious and rugged batsman – but they shared the same lust for life, and it showed in their batting.

Middlesex also had a fine opening pair in Robertson and Brown, who would prepare the ground for the 'twins' in a brisk and admirable manner, and George Mann, wicker-keeper Leslie Compton and Walter Robins himself could all contribute useful runs. Thirty-seven hundreds were scored for the county in Championship matches, and there seemed to be a wealth of batting talent waiting in the wings. Thompson provided able support, and the left-handed Fairbairn scored centuries in his first two first-class matches.

Uniquely perhaps for a Championship-winning side, the Middlesex attack was very limited. Laurie Gray was an honest, fast-medium-pace

35

bowler who was asked to do a great deal of work. Edrich, the quickest bowler in the country in the opinion of many, was a 'shock' bowler who captured sixty-seven wickets in the season and might well have completed the 'double' had he not been forced to give up bowling after injuring his shoulder at the beginning of August. This meant that Jack Young, the left-arm spinner, had to open the bowling in the closing stages of the season. He and Jim Sims, the 44-old leg-spinner, were the backbone of the attack, and both captured a hundred wickets. There was also the left-arm spin of Denis Compton, who captured seventy-three wickets in the season with his somewhat eccentric blend of chinamen and long-hops.

Nearly all of Middlesex's matches were attended by huge crowds who responded to the dynamic attitude that Robins, a genial cricketer but a hard man, demanded of his players. He sought victory from the first ball of the match, and his batsmen scored at so brisk a rate that it left the bowlers ample time in which to dismiss the opposition. Robins himself had scored at a rate of 58.3 runs an hour in 1946, was a fine leg-break bowler, although now past his best, and an outstanding fielder. More than one of his players was to say in later life, 'I would have died for that man on the cricket field.'

Two matches epitomised Middlesex's approach to the game. The first was against Leicestershire, at Leicester, in mid-July; the second was against Gloucestershire, at Cheltenham, a month later.

At Leicester Edrich, leading Middlesex for the first time, won the toss and asked the home county to bat. They responded by scoring 309. Middlesex lost Brown when he was struck in the eye, but Robertson and Edrich put on 159, and Edrich and Compton scored 277 in 130 minutes. Denis Compton reached a hundred at a run a ball, and Bill Edrich hit 257 in 285 minutes with four sixes and twenty-six fours. In the 140 minutes between lunch and tea on the second afternoon, Middlesex scored 310 runs.

Middlesex led by 328 on the first innings, but at lunch on the third and final day Leicestershire were seventeen runs ahead with six wickets standing, and only one hour and twenty minutes of play remained. In thirty-five minutes after lunch, Middlesex, mainly through the unpredictable spin of Denis Compton, captured the remaining Leicestershire wickets while forty-eight runs were scored. This left Middlesex twenty-five minutes in which to score the sixty-six runs needed to win.

With Brown and Robertson padded up and sitting behind the sight-screen ready to run to the middle if a wicket fell, Compton and Edrich opened the innings. Brown and Robertson were not needed, for Compton and Edrich hit the runs required off seven overs.

A month later, Middlesex went to Cheltenham. Gloucestershire, now led by Basil Allen, who had resumed the captaincy he had relinquished to Hammond in 1939, were level with Middlesex at the top of the table. The match coincided with the fifth Test at The Oval, but the county game drew as much attention and interest as the Test, for it was seen as the Championship decider. The match at The Oval had deprived Middlesex of Denis Compton and Jack Robertson, but Edrich was not in the England side as he was unable to bowl.

The wicket at Gloucestershire's headquarters at Bristol had become noted as a spinner's paradise. It had been specially treated by the Bingley Government Research Station, and it had certainly become a delight for the veteran off-spinner Tom Goddard who finished the season with 238 wickets. Cook, slow left-arm, took 144. The Cheltenham wicket proved to be no less conducive to spin, and the match against Middlesex was over in two days with nineteen wickets going to the slow bowlers.

Edrich and Brown began the Middlesex innings with a stand of 50 before a record crowd of 14,500 on whom the gates had been closed long before the start. Goddard brought about a collapse, but Sims, Sharp, in his first game of the season, and Young scored invaluable runs at the close. Middlesex, bowled out for 180, were batting again before the end of the day. Backed by brilliant fielding, Sims and Young dismissed Gloucestershire for 153.

Goddard, fifteen for 156 in the match, trapped Edrich leg before on the Saturday evening and, with Middlesex 33 for two, the game was in the balance. Harry Sharp joined Robins in a stand of 70 which virtually decided the game in favour of Middlesex. Robins hit 45, and Sharp, who played Goddard particularly well, scored 46 which included eight leg-side fours off the master off-spinner. The last six wickets went down for 16 runs.

This was to be the game that Sharp remembered for the rest of his life, which was spent with Middlesex as coach, scorer and mentor to Mike Gatting. An unpretentious, honest county cricketer never really sure of a place in the side, he added three for 39 to his 60 for once out, and Middlesex won by 68 runs and went on to take the title.

At The Oval, news of the game was relayed at intervals to Denis Compton. He celebrated by hitting 113. It was his fourth century in eight innings in the series, in which he totalled 753 runs, average 94.12. He also hit centuries against the tourists for Middlesex and for the South of England. Edrich made two hundreds in the four Tests in which he appeared, and he averaged 110.40 from five completed innings. He also took sixteen wickets.

England won three of the Tests while the first and the last were drawn slightly in favour of South Africa. Initially, the signs were not good for England. For the first Test, they omitted Wright from the chosen twelve, brought in Dollery of Warwickshire to bat at number five on his first appearance in international cricket, and chose Hollies, Martin and Cook to complete a new-look attack with Alec Bedser. Hollies had played Test cricket before, and was to play again, but 'Sam' Cook, the Gloucestershire left-arm spinner, and J.W. Martin, a fast bowler from Kent, were playing their one and only Test.

Jack Martin was a noted club cricketer who played as an amateur for Kent in thirty-three matches over a period which spanned fourteen years. He was quick by club standards, and he was also recognised as a batsman, but at Test level, on a placid Trent Bridge pitch, he was out of his depth. He finished with match figures of one for 129, bowling Melville when the South African skipper had scored 189. Cook failed to take a wicket in thirty overs which cost him 127 runs. He was unlucky, though, not to be given another chance in the years to come.

Bruce Mitchell square-cut Martin's first ball of the match for four, and by the end of the day South Africa were 376 for three. Melville was out early on the second morning, but Nourse made 149, and England faced a total of 533. Hollies had justified his selection by taking five for 123.

Hutton and Washbrook were out with 48 scored, but Edrich, 44, and Compton, 65, took England to 154 by the close of the second day, and all seemed right with the world. This was a delusion. Compton was out without addition to his score on the third morning, caught at slip off a rash stroke to the second ball of the day. Tuckett struck a purple patch. The England tail was long, and the last six wickets went down in twenty-five minutes for ten runs. England followed on 325 runs in arrears.

There were immediate problems for England in their second innings when Tuckett, his inspired day continuing, knocked back Hutton's off stump. Edrich and Washbrook showed resolution, but when Dollery was fourth out and Yardley joined Compton England were still 155 runs away from an innings defeat.

In 199 minutes before the close, Compton and Yardley added 108. Compton, 83, had completed a thousand runs for the season – it was 10 June – and Yardley was on 45.

The following morning, Yardley ordered that Evans, Bedser, Cook, Martin and Hollies, those of the England side yet to bat, should have an hour's concentrated net practice before the start of play. It was an effort that was to bring dividends.

Yardley was to be dropped at slip when 51, but, that apart, neither he nor Compton offered the semblance of a chance as they added 237, a record fifth-wicket stand for England against South Africa. Compton was finally caught at slip for 163 after four and three-quarter hours at the crease, but Yardley now found an excellent partner in Evans, who hit a lusty 74 in seventy-five minutes, an innings full of good shots. Yardley's fighting innings ended when he was caught at slip off Dawson with the new ball. The England skipper had made 99, and never again was he to get so close to a Test match hundred.

South Africa's problems were not at an end, for Martin and Hollies scored 51 for the last wicket and occupied a valuable forty-eight minutes in doing so. Left 140 minutes in which to get 227 to win, South Africa finished on 166 for one, with Melville completing his second century of the match.

When South Africa lost their grip on the first Test they lost their chance in the series. At Lord's, where Wright and Barnett returned and George Pope, having resumed county cricket with Derbyshire, made a belated Test debut, South Africa became the victims of Compton and Edrich at the height of their halcyon days. The pair scored 370 for England's third wicket, which was, at the time, a record for all Test cricket. The gates were closed on capacity crowds for the first two days of the match, and they thrilled to see Edrich hit 189 in just under six hours and Compton make 208 in five hours fifty minutes. Barnett played a glorious cameo of 33, and Yardley declared sixty-five minutes after lunch on the second day when his side had scored 554 for eight. Doug Wright then took ten wickets, and England won by ten wickets. Edrich had set up the victory by bowling Nourse with the first ball of the last day and by taking a stunning slip catch to dismiss Mitchell.

England's fielding was not good, and still they searched for a quick bowler. Bedser, who had suffered by having several catches dropped at Lord's, and Pope gave way to Cranston and Gladwin. As a medium-pacer of unflagging zest, Gladwin's cause had been espoused in the press – he was one of a long line of Derbyshire bowlers to have come from a mining background – but the selection of Ken Cranston took all by surprise.

Cranston had been appointed captain of Lancashire in place of Fallows at the start of the season, a decision which caused anger. When he appeared for England he had played in just thirteen first-class matches and had only two months of first-class cricket behind him. He acquitted himself quite will on his home ground, but the honours in England's seven-wicket victory again went to Edrich and Compton, who scored 191 and 115 respectively and shared a third-wicket partnership of 228 in 196 minutes.

39

Cranston came into his own in the Headingley Test where there were two more Test debutants, Young, the Middlesex left-arm spinner, and Butler, the Nottinghamshire pace bowler, replacing Hollies and Gladwin. Butler, thirty-four years old and somewhat overweight, did well, but he had a constant battle to keep fit. Young was less successful, but he was to come again. Cranston, however, enjoyed his best moment when he took four wickets in six balls to end South Africa's second innings. Hutton had earlier hit a century and finished the match by hitting Mann for six. England won by ten wickets in three days.

Edrich had opened the England bowling in all the Tests but the first, and when he was deemed unfit to bowl he was omitted from the final Test. Gladwin returned to share the new ball with his county colleague Copson, and Howorth, the Worcestershire all-rounder who bowled slow left-arm, came in for Young. The match was drawn, thanks mainly to a century in each innings from Bruce Mitchell, the South African opener, who was on the field for all but eight minutes of the game. He was a wonderfully durable batsman. England ended the series with a sense of self-satisfaction. They had given Test debuts to ten players during the summer, and eight of them had been bowlers. The series had been won comfortably against a side who batted well, bowled tidily and fielded brilliantly. Above all, county cricket was thriving.

It was so popular that a decision was taken in June to revive the end-of-season fixture between the Champion county and the Rest of England, which had not been played since 1935. Traditionally, the match was played at The Oval and, although there were misgivings, particularly with regard to a match in mid-September vying with football for the public's interest, it was decided to go ahead.

Four days were allocated to the game, but it was all over after five minutes' play on the fourth day. Middlesex won by nine wickets, and Edrich and Compton finished their glorious summer with innings of 180 and 246. This meant that the pair had established batting records which one is confident to say will never be broken. In 1906 Tom Hayward, the Surrey and England batsman, had scored 3,518 runs; and in 1925 Jack Hobbs, also of Surrey and England, made sixteen centuries. In 1947 Denis Compton scored 3,816 runs, average 90.85; and Bill Edrich hit 3,539 runs, average 80.43. Compton made eighteen centuries, Edrich twelve.

It is difficult for a reader today to conceive the grasp that these two had on the public's imagination. They were a physical expression of the country's new-born hope and light. Compton, in particular, popularised by his good looks and his picture in Brylcreem advertisements, was idolised in a manner which had previously been reserved for American

40

film stars. He received hundreds of letters which offered gifts of money and proposals of marriage. But he was never a businessman. His casual, forgetful air was part of his charm. Forty years on, in the days of personal appearances, television chat shows and the opening of super-markets, he would have become a multi-millionaire.

The triumphs of the 'Middlesex twins', the opportunities at Test level afforded to a batch of new bowlers, the successes at the universities of cricketers like Pawson, Mallett, Willatt, Insole and Bailey, and the praise being heaped upon younger players like Coxon of Yorkshire, Broderick of Northamptonshire, and Bedford of Middlesex, a schoolboy who had enjoyed outstanding achievements with his leg-breaks and googlies in his few county matches, all combined to create, as we have said, a feeling of self-satisfaction; although some may call it complacency.

There was an impatience to encourage young players, which was forgivable, but the judgements were not always sound for the very reason that they were hasty. A tour of the Caribbean was made in the winter of 1947–48 and, for a variety of reasons – mostly connected with long absences from home during the war followed by the tour of Australia – Hutton, Edrich, Compton, Yardley, Bedser, Wright and Washbrook said that they would not be available for the trip. This caused little concern, for these were the days when only Australia were considered to be of real strength to test England. MCC and those respon-sible for the game in Britain were slow to recognise that the world, and cricket with it, had moved on since 1939.

With Yardley unavailable for business reasons, MCC had to find a new captain of England. Although not a selector – a task undertaken by A.J. Holmes of Sussex, Walter Robins and J.C. Clay – Pelham Warner was an influential figure in the higher circles of administration, and he approached Tom Pearce, who had been a joint-captain of Essex in the 1930s and had been sole captain in the first two post-war seasons, and asked him if he would lead the side to the West Indies. Pearce said that he would be delighted if he could arrange to be released from his work in the wine trade. He set about making arrangements immediately and was given leave of absence with the wholehearted backing of his firm. A few weeks later, he bought an evening newspaper and read that G.O. Allen was to captain the side in the Caribbean. Such weaknesses in man-management and irresponsible codes of behaviour in basic communi-cation were to follow the administrators of cricket in England even when they became known as the Test and County Cricket Board.

The choice of Allen as captain of England for the 1947–48 tour is impossible to justify or explain. He was past his forty-fifth birthday, had

41

not played for England since he captained the side in Australia, 1936–37, and had played only once for Middlesex in 1947 without taking a wicket. A fast bowler with a classic action, and a hard-hitting batsman of technique and determination, Allen's best years were long in the past, and his selection brought amazement and proved to be a disaster. He was named as both captain and manager, with 'Billy' Griffith, the Sussex wicket-keeper, as assistant manager, and Ken Cranston, veteran of three Tests and one season, as vice-captain.

Butler, Evans, Howorth and Robertson, who had played against South Africa, were in the party, as were Ikin and Hardstaff, who had toured Australia under Hammond the previous winter. Two opening batsmen, Winston Place of Lancashire and Dennis Brookes of Northamptonshire, were chosen. Both won Test caps on the tour but were never to appear in international cricket again. The party was completed by four young players, Tremlett, Wardle, Laker and Smithson.

Maurice Tremlett, the Somerset all-rounder, had virtually been assured of a place since his fine start to the season at Lord's. Johnny Wardle, left-arm spinner, and Jim Laker, off-break bowler, were both Yorkshiremen although Laker was playing for Surrey. Both had shown considerable promise in 1947 when many others had struggled, but to cast such inexperienced spinners in a leading role was demanding too much, and it was generally felt that Howorth, with 164 wickets to his credit in the English season, would have to undertake a considerable amount of work. However, it was the selection of Smithson that was most interesting and most publicised.

Gerald Smithson was a twenty-year-old left-handed batsman who had scored 887 runs for Yorkshire in 1947, including a highly attractive 169 against Leicestershire. In this era of compulsory National Service, he had been conscripted to go down the mines as a 'Bevin Boy'. He was selected for the tour by MCC and, after his case had been debated in the House of Commons, he was released from the mines and given permission by the government to go on the tour. The decision showed how much importance was placed on sport, but Smithson must have later regretted that permission had ever been granted.

The tour was a disaster even before the team got off the boat. Allen pulled a calf muscle while skipping on the ship deck on the way out, and he was unable to play in the first of the four Test matches,which was the third game of the tour. He was never really fit for the entire three months.

In sending an inexperienced, virtually an 'A' side, MCC had grossly underestimated the strength of the opposition. It was known that

Worrell was a fine batsman, but the reports from Barbados that Weekes was his equal and Walcott not far behind were scorned. Cranston was leading the side against Barbados within three days of arriving in West Indies, and Weekes, Walcott and Taylor plundered centuries.

Not only was Allen unfit, but Butler, the other opening bowler, pulled a muscle in the first match, suffered an attack of malaria and broke down again in Jamaica. Laker learned much on the tour and, alongside Howorth, was the most successful of the bowlers, but he was handicapped by strained stomach muscles for most of the tour. Ikin was weakened by carbuncle trouble, and Brookes chipped a finger bone in the first Test and took no further part in the tour. Hardstaff tore a leg muscle, Place bruised a knuckle and ruptured a groin muscle. Towards the end of the tour Smithson injured an arm so badly that he was unable to play throughout the 1948 season. He never re-established himself in the Yorkshire side and joined Leicestershire in 1951, but he did not fulfil the promise he had shown in 1947.

The accumulation of disasters led to 'Billy' Griffith being pressed into service as an opening batsman in the second Test. He scored 140 on his Test debut, his maiden first-class century, a feat which no other Englishman has accomplished. Wardle, too, made his Test debut in this game, but he was given only three overs while the West Indies scored 497 and 72 for three.

A beleaguered team sent for reinforcements, and Len Hutton agreed to fly out to bolster the side. He hit 138 and 62 not out against British Guiana in his first match and he made a century against Jamaica, but it was all to no avail. England lost two of the four Tests and, for the first time in history, MCC went through an overseas tour without a single victory.

Norman Preston sounded a warning in *Wisden*: 'After these experiences it is essential that MCC treat a West Indies tour as seriously as one to Australia.' He should have added India, New Zealand and South Africa, for it was several years before the lessons of that Caribbean tour were truly learned.

There were other events at this time, causes for concern, which could not be fully comprehended when they occurred. Denis Compton had ended the 1947 season with the first signs of a troublesome knee injury, but none then could be expected to foresee that the 'Compton knee' would become a feature of public debate for the next few years. He played in the last fourteen soccer matches of the season as Arsenal won the First Division Championship in 1948 and, indeed, he was to make appearances for the famous London club up to and including the Cup Final of 1950. It was possible in those days to combine football and cricket as professions. Arsenal's final league game in 1948 was on 1 May; Middlesex began their programme on 8 May.

Politically, the collapse of collaboration between the four great powers in Berlin, the air-lift which followed, the ever-increasing tensions of the Cold War, and the supremacy of communism in China and North Korea were to lead to the increase in the period of National Service, first from one year to eighteen months, then from eighteen months to two years, yet the political event which was to have the most direct influence on cricket was the defeat of Jan Smuts in the elections in South Africa and the coming to power of Douglas Malan and his Nationalist Party. Ultra right-wing, Malan's party was segregational and dedicated to the ideal of separate development, or 'apartheid'.

In 1948 these were faraway shadows. For those who had lived through six years of *hot* war, the Cold War was a minor irritant, and, as L.P. Hartley might have said, South Africa was a foreign country. They did things differently there. For the majority of the population, wishing to escape the gloom, the most important happenings of 1948 were that the Olympic Games were to be staged in London in July and August and Bradman was to lead an Australian team to England for the last time. The enthusiasm for the Olympics did nothing to diminish the enthusiasm for cricket or, indeed, for such sports as speedway, which was enjoying a boom time. The appetite for sport, it seemed, was unquenchable.

Bradman had not been seen in England for ten years. There was a half-generation for whom he was a legend of whom they had had only a chance to read. There have been others since who have laid claim to greatness as batsmen, but none has reached the pinnacle that Bradman achieved, whether that pinnacle is measured statistically or simply by his very presence. For nearly twenty years he bestrode the cricket world. Slight of build he may have been, but on the cricket field he was a colossus. One did not have to ask for him to be identified. Like the greatest of actors he illuminated any stage upon which he performed.

He celebrated his fortieth birthday during that final tour of England, and he celebrated much else, for he led what was arguably the finest side that has ever toured England. Their record would give proof to that assertion for they were the first side ever to go through an English tour unbeaten, and they won the Ashes series by four Tests to nil. Bradman's own contribution on the tour was 2,428 runs, including eleven centuries, at an average of 89.92.

He had said at the outset that this was to be a goodwill tour, and when he began at Worcester with an innings of 107, he was taken at his word. In his three previous tours of England, he had begun with a double century. More significant, perhaps, were the facts that Lindwall had Don Kenyon leg before with the second ball of the match and Arthur Morris hit 138 on his first appearance in England. The Australians won by an innings, but Worcestershire were comforted by record attendances and receipts.

In the second match, at Leicester, Keith Miller scored a double century,;and at Bradford, with Bradman absent, the Australians won narrowly as Bill Johnston claimed ten for 40 and Miller nine for 91. England had not encountered Johnston when they played the 1946–47 Ashes series. He had made his Test debut against India a year later. Left-arm medium-pace, he proved the perfect supplement to the speed of Miller and Lindwall and was to take 102 first-class wickets at under 17 runs apiece on that 1948 tour.

There was an innings victory over Surrey, followed by an innings victory over Cambridge University. Trevor Bailey scored 66 not out for Cambridge in that match, which finished on the Friday, and on the Saturday he was in the Essex side which played the Australians at Southchurch Park, Southend. He later felt that he was rather fortunate in that, having dismissed Brown and Miller with successive deliveries, he damaged a thumb and could take no further part in the match. Other Essex bowlers were less lucky. Bradman hit 187 in 125 minutes and, with Brown who also scored a century, added 219 in ninety minutes for the second wicket. Loxton and Saggers were other centurions, and they put on 166 in sixty-five minutes for the sixth wicket. In six hours' play in the day, the Australians scored 721 runs, a record, at 5.58 an over. It is worth noting that, although the ball was being struck to all parts of the field, the Essex bowlers sent down 129 overs in the six hours and, as Tom Pearce, the Essex captain, used to boast, 'We were the only side to bowl out Bradman's Australians in a day.' Essex were bowled out twice on the Monday, and the Australians won by an innings and 451 runs.

There was a relentless efficiency in all that they did, and their first real test came at the end of May when they met MCC at Lord's. The matches between MCC and the touring side were preludes to the Test matches and were very much trials of strength. The MCC side against the Australians was led by Yardley and included Hutton, Edrich, Compton, Cranston, Robertson, Griffith, Laker and Donnelly, the New Zealander who had been playing for Oxford University and now Warwickshire, all of whom had played Test cricket. Morris was out early to Edrich, but Barnes and Bradman then added 160. When two runs short of his century Bradman edged a ball from Captain J.H.G. Deighton to Edrich at slip.

The match at Southend had attracted record crowds and brought

45

record receipts, and the three days of the MCC game saw 60,000 people pass through the turnstiles at Lord's. The gates were closed on a capacity crowd on the first day, the Saturday, and when Bradman was out the crowd exploded. To dismiss him for less than a hundred was a momentous event.

Deighton was a regular army officer whose county cricket was restricted to seven matches in three seasons for Lancashire. He was selected for MCC as part of England's constant search for a fast bowler, and his capture of the wicket of Don Bradman was still being recorded in newspaper advertisements nearly half a century later.

For a few overs after that wicket, he bowled more quickly and there was a spring in the step of the MCC fielders, but Keith Miller scored 163. The MCC twice fell to the spinners and were beaten by an innings.

The Australians could only draw against Lancashire and Nottinghamshire, and Hampshire led them on the first innings before losing by eight wickets. Any glimmer of success by an Englishman was seized upon avidly. There was no play on the first day at Old Trafford, and the Australians had the better of the draw, but a nineteen-year-old left-arm spinner, Malcolm Hilton, bowled Bradman for 11 in the first innings and had him stumped for 43 in the second. The press was almost united in demanding that Hilton should be in the England side for the first Test. He was, in fact, uncapped and played only occasionally for Lancashire until claiming a regular place in 1950.

Australia's progress towards the Test series was triumphant; England had problems, one of which was of their own making. The first problem concerned Norman Yardley, England's captain-elect. Business was demanding more and more of his time. Although captain of Yorkshire, he was unable to play in the county's first four fixtures. In his first county match of the season he was out for a 'pair' against Warwickshire. Leading MCC against the Australians, he made 17 and 24, and he did not bowl a ball in either of these matches. He had been troubled by lumbago, and his inactivity caused much debate as to whether he should captain England. At the beginning of June, two days before the first Test, he brought Yorkshire to play Middlesex at Lord's, and with Len Hutton added 141 in 105 minutes for the third wicket. Yardley scored a quite beautiful 90, with a six and thirteen fours, and outshone his partner. He pulled Denis Compton for what would have been his fourteenth four when it was noticed that a bail was lying on the ground, dislodged as the stroke was made. He left the field to rapturous applause, and Walter Robins shook his hand before he climbed the pavilion steps. One problem had been solved; another was insurmountable.

46

In one of those perpetual tamperings with the laws and regulations of the game, it had been decreed that, for an experimental period, the bowling side could take a new ball every fifty-five overs. The Australians, with Lindwall and Miller the finest opening attack in world cricket, with Johnston as able support, and Toshack, a slow-medium left-arm spinner capable not only of taking wickets but of closing an end with his relentless accuracy, had been presented with a potent, additional weapon to their armoury, and they were to use it to good effect.

Before the Second World War, Tests in the Ashes series had been limited to four days, with the final Test sometimes being decreed 'timeless'. In 1948 Tests in England were allocated five days for the first time. Misfortune followed England to the last. Doug Wright had been suffering from lumbago, so the selectors called up George Pope of Derbyshire, but neither he nor Wright was chosen to play, and Reg Simpson of Nottinghamshire was named as twelfth man on his home ground at Trent Bridge. Yardley won the toss and, rightly, chose to bat although play began late in damp and gloomy weather.

Miller and Lindwall bowled at a considerable pace, a pace far above anything that English batsmen had encountered in county cricket since the war. Even a fine player of fast bowling like Hutton was beaten by the speed of Miller, and in the afternoon session seven wickets went down, and England faced tea at 74 for eight. There had been a downpour in the lunch interval, and thereafter the ball tended to skid through. Even though they lost Lindwall with a groin-muscle injury, the Australian bowlers exploited the conditions to such an extent that the England innings was in ruins and the game virtually decided before tea on the first day.

Edrich was beaten for pace; Compton, attempting his renowned sweep, missed a straight ball; and Hardstaff was brilliantly caught at slip second ball by Miller, who ended up almost standing on his head. The Australian fielding was brilliant, with Tallon outstanding behind the stumps, and Bradman's tactics and manipulation of his bowlers could not be faulted. England faced total humiliation before Laker, the one positive gain from the series in the Caribbean, and Bedser added 89 in seventy-three minutes.

England bowled well, often frustrating Australia with a leg-stump attack to a packed leg-side field. Bradman was contained for long periods. Laker produced a spell of three for 22 before, unwisely, he was taken off to make way for the second new ball. Evans was as lively and agile as ever, Yardley again proved his worth as a change bowler, and, on the Saturday, Young bowled eleven consecutive maidens and eventually conceded only 79 runs from sixty overs, but Australia still took a first innings lead of 344.

When England batted a second time Hutton and Compton came together on the Saturday evening. Hutton, surviving a barrage of bumpers from Miller which angered the crowd, reached a delightful 50, but he was out on the Monday morning after the partnership had realised 111. Compton now proceeded to play what was his highest innings in a Test match against Australia and probably the finest Test innings he ever played. It ended on the Tuesday morning shortly before lunch. The conditions were never easy, the bowling always hostile, but for ten minutes under seven hours he was master. His innings was interrupted nine times by rain, bad light and the scheduled intervals, but his concentration never wavered. He hit nineteen fours and, with Evans giving brave and patient support in a seventh-wicket stand, he even gave hope that England might be saved. The end was an anti-climax. He shaped to hook a bumper from Miller, changed his mind, slipped on the damp surface and fell on his wicket.

Bedser dismissed Bradman for nought, but Australia strolled to victory by eight wickets. The might of Australia was obvious, but equally obvious were the deficiencies in the England side. At Trent Bridge, Australia could call upon Lindwall, until injured, Miller and Johnston as their new-ball attack; England's strike force was Bedser, Edrich and Barnett. Edrich and Barnett were primarily batsmen who were beginning to bowl less and less. Barnett took thirty-six wickets in 1948, Edrich thirty-seven rather expensive ones. Alec Bedser, 115 wickets, was desperately in need of a partner, someone else to help carry the burden. The selectors turned to Yorkshire's Alex Coxon. Barnett and Hardstaff, both of whom were nearing the veteran stage, were omitted and never again played Test cricket. Wright returned at the expense of Young, and Dollery of Warwickshire, who had played in the first Test against South Africa the previous year, was asked to boost the middle order.

The Lord's Test lasted until just before lunch on the fifth day. It broke all previous records for attendances and receipts, and the result underlined the gap that existed between the two sides. The first day belonged almost entirely to England. Bradman won the toss for the only time in the series, and Australia batted. They were handicapped in that Miller was unable to bowl because of a bad back, but they made no change from the side that played at Trent Bridge. Four bowlers proved sufficient.

In his second over of what proved to be his only Test match, Coxon had Barnes taken at short fine-leg by Hutton. This was the first of three catches that Hutton took in this position, which some call leg-slip. The second accounted for Bradman, who had made 38. He was the victim of Bedser's late in-swinger, and Bedser had claimed his wicket twice at Trent Bridge in a similar fashion. Arthur Morris, an elegant left-hander, scored a most pleasant century, but Australia closed the day on 258 for seven, and there was joy in the English camp.

It did not last long. In the first seventy minutes of the second day, Tallon led a spree which brought ninety-two runs, thirty of them, frustratingly, coming from a last-wicket partnership between Johnston and Toshack which hovered between high comedy and low farce.

The England despair increased when, in the fourth over bowled by Lindall, Washbrook was caught behind. Hutton totally misjudged an off-break from Ian Johnston, and Edrich, painfully ill at ease for overs on end, and Dollery were both beaten by Lindwall's pace and bowled within the space of three balls. Compton and Yardley now combined in the one significant stand of the innings, worth 87, but after tea Lindwall and Johnston again had the new ball available to them.

An event now occurred which was of little significance but well remembered. Johnston held the new ball and waved it at Yardley to indicate that it was being taken. Yardley shielded his eyes and turned away in mock horror. Bradman would have stared back with a lack of emotion that bordered on contempt, but he was a hardened professional with a mind that conceived only thoughts of victory. That was one of the differences between the two sides.

Almost immediately, Johnston had Compton beautifully taken at slip by Miller, and Lindwall knocked back Yardley's off stump with the first ball of the next over. The England innings edged into the Saturday and ended when Lindwall bowled Bedser to claim his fifth wicket of the innings. Australia led by 135 and plundered runs eagerly and entertainingly. Barnes scored the century in a Lord's Test which had been his ambition. He took 21 off one over from Laker, including two successive sixes, and was caught on the boundary off Yardley for 141. Yardley took the wicket of Hassett in the same over, but there was no other respite for England. Bradman and Barnes scored 174 for the second wicket, and the declaration on the fourth day left England a target of 596. They were bowled out for 186.

There was now cause for more debate and reconstruction. In came Young, Pollard and the Gloucestershire pair, Emmett and Crapp, an opener and a left-handed batsman respectively. Both were making their Test debuts. Out went Wright, Coxon, Laker and, dramatically and controversially, Hutton. In retrospect, this seems an astonishing omission, but there were critics at the time who believed that Hutton returned refreshed after being rested from the Old Trafford Test.

The match was ruined by rain. There was no play on the fourth day and less than two hours' play was possible on the last day. This was hard on England, who led by 142 on the first innings and declared at 174 for three in their second.

Emmett, one of ten England players to be used just once in the series, found the pace of Lindwall too much for his capabilities and was out for 10 and nought. He was never again to appear in a Test match, but, like Dollery, who had one more Test to come, he was a victim more of the time in which he was called to make his debut than of his own limitations.

The main features of this drawn match were the bowling of Bedser and Pollard, seven wickets between them, an injury to Barnes, and a brave and brilliant century from Denis Compton. Compton had scored four when he mishooked a ball from Lindwall and deflected it on to his forehead. He was led bleeding from the field, had stitches inserted in the wound and returned when the fifth wicket fell at 119. Seemingly unruffled by his injury, Compton withstood the lightning pace of Lindwall, hit sixteen fours and scored 145 not out in five hours twenty minutes.

Barnes's injury was sustained while fielding. One of the features of the series had been Barnes standing at silly mid-on, very close to the bat. He took only one catch in four Tests, but his presence was a constant menace to the batsmen and seemed to symbolise Australia's dominance. At Old Trafford a strongly hit pull-drive by Pollard hit Barnes under the ribs. He was carried from the field, but he came in to bat at number six. He was obviously in much pain and collapsed after half an hour. He spent the next ten days in hospital.

The injury to Barnes gave Neil Harvey his first chance against England in the fourth Test at Headingley. Saggers also came in for the injured Tallon while Loxton, a medium-pacer and attacking batsman, retained the place he had won from Bill Brown at Old Trafford.

England went through their usual permutations, and, as it proved, with disastrous results. Hutton returned for Emmett, Laker for Young and Cranston for Dollery. The omission of Young, a member of the original party, left England short of spin on a wicket where spin was expected to play an important part.

For the better part of four days, all went well for England. Hutton and Washbrook scored 168 for the first wicket; Edrich and Washbrook 100 for the second. Washbrook and Edrich, whose determination and resolve had brought him through a sticky period, both scored centuries, and night-watchman Alec Bedser hit 79. If the rest of the batting disappointed (England lost their last seven wickets for 73 after Edrich and

50

Bedser had added 155), England still reached 496, their highest score of the series.

The highlights of the Australian innings were a thrilling 112 by Neil Harvey on his debut against England, and an innings of 93 by Loxton which included five sixes.

Leading by 38, England scored briskly and consistently when they batted a second time. Hutton and Washbrook again opened with a century partnership, and no one could be said to have failed. Yardley batted two overs into the last morning so that he could use the heavy roller in an attempt to break up the pitch, which was already showing considerable signs of being conducive to spin. Australia were left a target of 404 runs in 344 minutes. No side had ever reached such a fourth-innings total to win a Test match.

The ball lifted and turned sharply, but Laker's greatness was still a few years ahead. In 1948 he was still honing his craft, and his length was erratic. In the field, England were fallible. Evans should have stumped Morris; Crapp dropped Bradman at slip. The bowler to suffer both times was Compton, whose only success was when he caught and bowled Hassett at 57.

Morris and Bradman scored 64 before lunch, and in the afternoon there was a cascade of runs against some poor bowling which was further distressed by missed chances. Behind the stumps, Evans had one of his worst days.

Quality spin would have brought victory, but quality spin was lacking. Hutton, a reasonably successful leg-break bowler at county level a decade earlier, was pressed into service. His four overs cost 30 runs. The partnership between Morris and Bradman had realised 301 before Yardley, who could well have bowled himself more in the series, accounted for Morris when he had made 182. Miller went cheaply, but when Harvey made the winning stroke there were still fifteen minutes of play remaining. Bradman was unbeaten on 173, the last of his twenty-nine Test centuries. It was his fourth century in six innings in Tests at Leeds and his nineteenth hundred against England. His 301-run stand with Morris had lasted just 217 minutes.

If England believed that they had suffered the ultimate humiliation, they were wrong. They gave two more new Test caps at The Oval. Dewes, the Cambridge blue who was capped by Middlesex in this year, replaced the injured Washbrook, and Watkins, the Glamorgan all-rounder, came in for Cranston. Watkins was a strange choice. Glamorgan were winners of the County Championship, but Watkins had had only a moderate season with bat and ball and had so far failed to justify the expectations his county had of him. Other changes saw

51

Laker and Pollard replaced by Young and Hollies.

The selection of Watkins, a brilliant fielder, Dewes and Hollies brought the number of players used by England in the series to twenty-one, five whom were new caps.

The final Test of the series was decided within two and a half hours of the start of the match. Heavy rain during the preceding week – the game began on a Saturday – had left The Oval very damp, and play could not start until midday. Even then, there were vast amounts of sawdust needed to help batsmen and bowlers gain footholds, although Lindwall, Miller and Johnston seemed little troubled by the conditions and enjoyed considerable movement in the humid atmosphere.

Miller immediately bowled Dewes, whose pedigree as a Test player remained ever in doubt. In the post-lunch period, Lindwall, a magnificent bowler in any conditions, took five for 8 in 8.1 overs. He varied his pace and attacked the stumps. He who hesitated was bowled. Watkins was struck on the shoulder, which nullified what use he might have been as a bowler. Only Hutton showed the necessary technique and application. He was last out, brilliantly caught one-handed down the leg side, having made 30 of England's pitiful 52, their lowest score in the first half of the twentieth century.

Nor was the drama over for the day. Barnes and Morris scored 117 for Australia's first wicket on a pitch which now seemed to have lost all venom. Shortly before six, Barnes was caught behind off Hollies, and Bradman came down the pavilion steps. The crowd stood and applauded him all the way to the wicket, where Yardley shook his hand and called the England players into a circle to give him three cheers. The crowd joined the players in the salute.

Playing forward to the second ball he received, Bradman was beaten by a googly and was out for nought. He left the field to applause as loud and as warm as the ovation that had greeted him. As one newspaper headline alliteratively described the occasion: 'In a Day of Ducks Don's was the Saddest of them all.'

Morris was last out for 196, and Australia duly won in four days. They had totally outplayed England in the series, and yet the complaints and whinges that would be heard in years to come were not in evidence then. The game itself meant more than the result, and the greatness of Bradman and the supreme qualities of his team had captured the public imagination. The attendances at the rain-ruined Old Trafford Test were greater than they had been at Lord's, and, at Leeds, more people watched the Test than had ever watched a cricket match in England before. Cricket was flourishing.

The Lower Depths
England v Australia at The Oval
14, 16, 17 and 18 August 1948

England First Innings		Second Innings	
L. Hutton c Tallon b Lindwall	30	c Tallon b Miller	64
J.G. Dewes c Miller	1	b Lindwall	10
W.J. Edrich c Hassett b Johnston . .	3	b Lindwall	28
D.C.S. Compton c Morris b Lindwall	4	c Lindwall b Johnston . .	39
J.F. Crapp c Tallon b Miller	0	b Miller	9
N.W.D. Yardley (capt) b Lindwall .	7	c Miller b Johnston	9
A.J. Watkins lbw b Johnston	0	c Hassett b Ring	2
†T.G. Evans b Lindwall	1	b Lindwall	8
A.V. Bedser b Lindwall	0	b Johnston	0
J.A. Young b Lindwall	0	not out	3
W.E. Hollies not out	0	c Morris b Johnston	0
Extras (b 6)	6	(b 9, lb 4, nb 3)	16
Total	52	. . . .	188

BOWLING	Overs	Mdns	Runs	Wkts	Overs	Mdns	Runs	Wkts
Lindwall	16.1	5	20	6	25	3	50	3
Miller	8	5	5	2	15	6	22	2
Johnston	16	4	20	2	27.3	12	40	4
Loxton	2	1	1	–	10	2	16	–
Ring	–	–	–	–	28	13	44	1

fall of wickets
1–2, 2–10, 3–17, 4–23, 5–35, 6–42, 7–45, 8–45, 9–47
1–20, 2–64, 3–125, 4–153, 5–164, 6–167, 7–178, 8–181, 9–188

Australia First Innings	
S.G. Barnes c Evans b Hollies	61
A.R. Morris run out	196
D.G. Bradman (capt) b Hollies	0
A.L. Hassett lbw b Young	37
K.R. Miller st Evans b Hollies	5
R.N. Harvey c Young b Hollies . . .	17
S.J.E. Loxton c Evans b Edrich	15
R.R. Lindwall c Edrich b Young . . .	9
†D. Tallon c Crapp b Hollies	31
D.T. Ring c Crapp b Bedser	9
W.A. Johnston not out	0
Extras (b 4, lb 2, nb 3)	9
Total	389

BOWLING	Overs	Mdns	Runs	Wkts
Bedser	31.2	9	61	1
Watkins	4	1	19	–
Young	51	16	118	2
Hollies	56	14	131	5
Compton	2	–	6	–
Edrich	9	1	38	1
Yardley	5	1	7	–

fall of wickets
1–117, 2–117, 3–226, 4–263, 5–265, 6–304, 7–332, 8–359, 9–389
umpires – H.G. Baldwin and D. Davies
Australia won by an innings and 149 runs

Cricket was also touched with romance. Glamorgan, who had not entered the County Championship until 1921, who had spent most of the inter-war years languishing among the bottom three, and who had never finished higher than sixth, in 1946, won the title for the first time. The romance did not end there, for, in the closing stages of the competition when the challenge of Yorkshire, Derbyshire and Surrey was finally beaten off, J.C. Clay, a member of the original 1921 side, virtually won two matches with his off-breaks. He could not play more regularly, not because he was in his fifty-first year, but because he was a Test selector.

One of Glamorgan's strengths was that they were able to field the same side for most of the season. Wooller and Muncer appeared in the Gentlemen and Players match, and Watkins was picked for the last Test, but otherwise Glamorgan were free from calls upon their players. Muncer was an off-break bowler who had begun his career with Middlesex and who was asked to do a huge amount of work. He was the ideal county cricketer, strong in loyalty and values, and he was head coach at Lord's for many years. There were two other recruits from Middlesex, Hever and Eaglestone; the former, an opening bowler who was used intelligently, was particularly effective.

The season also saw Glamorgan give a debut to a talented and elegant batsman, Gilbert Parkhouse, and there were runs galore from the left-handed Willie Jones, but the real strength of the side lay in team-work under the dynamic leadership of Wilf Wooller.

Wooller had been a prisoner-of-war in Japanese hands and did not feel able to take over the captaincy until 1947. He lived and breathed Glamorgan cricket and Welsh rugby. He was forthright in expressing his views, and he bowed to no man. He was a hard-hitting batsman, a medium-pace bowler and an exceptional fielder close to the bat where he made some breathtaking catches. He led from the front and he was ruthless and often a law unto himself, but he never asked a player to do anything he was not willing to do himself. Like Watkins, he was invited to go with the MCC side to South Africa in 1948–49, but he was unable to accept the invitation for business reasons.

Neither Yardley nor Edrich could accept invitations for the same reason, and George Mann, who had succeeded Walter Robins as captain of Middlesex, was asked to lead the side. His father Frank had led England in South Africa in 1922–23 and, like his father, George Mann was to captain England on his Test debut. He proved to be a fine captain, on and off the field, intelligent, enthusiastic, fair and respected in his man-management. He raised the level of the side in the field, and he used his bowlers with good judgement. The *Cricketer* was fulsome in its praise: 'he got the best out of his men. Never for one moment did he allow any sort of slackness or lethargy. He kept his side at concert pitch and his own fielding was admirable. He won golden opinions on all sides.'

The party to tour South Africa included six players, as well as Mann, who had not appeared against the Australians: Simpson, Charles Palmer, Gladwin, Tremlett, Roley Jenkins and Griffith. Of these, Tremlett and Griffith had made their Test debuts on the tour of the West Indies the previous winter, and Reg Simpson had been twelfth man for the Trent Bridge Test against Australia. Simpson, an elegant opening batsman and fine fieldsman, played in the first Test in South Africa, but neither Palmer nor Tremlett featured in the series.

The problem with Tremlett was that England had seen in him the quick bowler whom they desperately needed, but the tour verdict on him was, 'He is a natural straight-bat hitter and if his bowling has been disappointing, he should develop into a dangerous batsman.'

Jenkins and Gladwin played in all five Tests in South Africa and finished first and second in the bowling averages for the series. Cliff Gladwin, the Derbyshire medium-pace bowler, had earned his place on the tour by capturing 128 wickets at low cost in 1948. He was accurate, enthusiastic, a good team man and a lion for work, and he was to become a national hero on his Test debut. Roley Jenkins, the Worcestershire leg-spinner, was a late replacement for Eric Hollies, who had been forced to withdraw from the chosen party. He was the outstanding bowling success of the tour, capturing seventy-one wickets in first-class matches, sixteen of them in the Tests. A rich and likeable character, he listened and learned on the tour and was a better bowler at the end of it than he had been at the beginning. In spite of this, one feels that the selectors never really believed in him, accepting the opinion that he was not effective against the best batsmen.

MCC played nine matches of assorted quality before the first Test match. They won six of them and drew three. In these matches, Hutton, Compton, Simpson and Washbrook had excelled, and the match at Benoni, against North Eastern Transvaal a fortnight before the first Test, produced some sensational cricket. The home side lost their last four wickets in five balls on the opening day as Gladwin completed the first hat-trick of his career. At the close of play Denis Compton was 120 not out, having reached three figures in sixty-six minutes. On the second day he thrashed the bowling from the start. He and Simpson put on 399 for the third wicket, and when Compton was finally caught off Funston he had scored 300 in 181 minutes. His innings included five sixes and forty-two fours, and his third hundred had come in thirty-seven minutes. Compton's triple hundred remains the fastest ever recorded. When the home side batted again Jenkins took seven wickets, and MCC won in two days.

The love affair between Denis Compton and South Africa began in 1947 and was consummated on this tour. He has ever remained a hero in South Africa, and he never ceased to extol the virtues of that country.

England's new-ball partnership remained constant for the series – Bedser and Gladwin – and the pair performed well on the first day of the first Test, taking seven wickets between them as South Africa were bowled out for 161. Rain and bad light were perpetual irritants, and England's first innings, an inconsistent one, extended into the third day. The England wickets were shared by spinners Mann and Athol Rowan while eight of the South African second-innings wickets were captured by spin. When Jenkins bowled McCarthy England were left with 135 minutes in which to score 128 to win.

The chase had no sooner begun than rain caused a ten-minute interruption, and on the resumption Hutton was caught. Washbrook was leg-before 24 runs later, and Mann fell to a brilliant slip catch by Bruce Mitchell off Cuan McCarthy, who returned his best Test bowling figures in this innings. The fast bowler dismissed Watkins, Simpson and Evans in quick succession, and, at 70 for six, England were in grave danger of defeat.

Compton, 28, and Jenkins, 22, added 45 before Compton was bowled by McCarthy, and Jenkins was caught behind off the same bowler one run later. Gladwin, dropped before he had scored, and Bedser batted stoically, and when the last (eight-ball) over arrived eight runs were needed for victory. There was a leg-bye and Gladwin struck a four, but with three balls left any one of four results was possible. Bedser levelled the scores by taking a single off the sixth ball of Tuckett's over, but

Gladwin's heave at the seventh failed to make any contact. A mid-wicket conference between the two batsmen determined that they would run at any cost on the last ball. Gladwin swung at the final delivery, missed, and the ball rebounded a few yards in front of him off his thigh. 'Tufty' Mann at short-leg pounced on the ball, but both batsmen had made their ground, and England had won a famous victory.

There was great jubilation and celebration, and it seemed as if the memory of that humiliating defeat by Australia at The Oval three months earlier had been expunged.

South Africa could never claw their way back into the series. In the second Test at Ellis Park, Johannesburg, Hutton and Washbrook established an English first-wicket record for Test cricket with a partnership of 359. Both batsmen scored hundreds, as did Compton; and Eric Rowan, who had just learned that he had been dropped for the third Test, batted throughout the final day to save South Africa from defeat.

The home country led on the first innings in the match at Newlands and were eventually set a target of 229 in 125 minutes, which they did not attempt. Compton took five for 70 in the first innings, the only time he was to take five wickets in a Test innings.

The fourth Test, again in Johannesburg, saw Hutton, who grew in stature and confidence as the tour progressed, hit his second century of the series and South Africa ignore a challenge to score 376 runs in 270 minutes.

This unwillingness to accept any challenge was the marked difference between the two sides. England adopted a positive approach; South Africa, solid in defence, lacked a real stroke-player, not least because Melville could play only in the third Test.

At Port Elizabeth, George Mann scored his one and only Test hundred, a typically enterprising affair at a critical juncture in the match. The England innings did not end until the fourth and final morning with the skipper 136 not out. For once, the South African batting was quite adventurous, and Nourse was able to throw down the gauntlet at tea, asking England to score 172 in ninety-five minutes if they wanted to win the match. Allowing for the fact that eight-ball overs were bowled in the series, this was an asking rate of nearly seven an over.

Hutton responded to the challenge by hitting the first ball he received for four, and Washbrook hooked the first delivery he received for six. The pair scored 58 in twenty-seven minutes for the first wicket. In the next twenty-six minutes, Compton and Washbrook added another 46. Four wickets fell for 21 runs, and when the score reached 152 Gladwin and Griffith were out in the space of three deliveries. Watkins now joined Crapp, who finished the game by hitting 'Tufty' Mann for ten runs off three successive balls with just one minute remaining.

George Mann's side had gone through the tour unbeaten, and they had won the Test series by two matches to nil. Both Test victories had been thrilling affairs. There was a general state of euphoria, and many believed that the recovery in post-war English cricket was well under way. Wiser voices cautioned that England had beaten a rather poor side, that the return of Edrich was needed to bolster both the batting and the slip fielding, and that 'a fast bowler is essential to our full complement and such a one must be found before we tackle Australia, during the winter of 1950–51'.

It must have been rather galling for the selectors when they sat down to choose the party for the South African tour to glance at the averages and see that the two leading bowlers in the country were Tom Pritchard, the Warwickshire pace bowler, with 172 wickets, and Jack Walsh, the Leicestershire left-arm spinner, with 174 wickets. Pritchard was a New Zealander and Walsh an Australian. *Plus ça change . . .*

Whatever reservations some may have held, it was generally accepted that Mann had returned from South Africa with the nucleus of a worthy side. There had been positive gains from the tour in the shape of Jenkins and Gladwin, and in what amounted to the rebirth of Len Hutton as one of the greatest batsmen. Having been dropped for the third Test of the Ashes series, Hutton had returned revitalised. He had batted bravely at The Oval as all around sank, and his form in South Africa had approached the sublime, the fusion of perfectly executed attacking strokes and an unmatched defensive technique.

On the debit side, Bedser was being asked to do a tremendous amount of work with inadequate support and was looking jaded, while Evans so lost form as to give way to Griffith in the last two Tests of the series.

The form that Hutton had shown in South Africa continued into the English summer. He enjoyed his greatest ever domestic season, hitting 3,429 runs, including twelve centuries. Only Compton, Edrich and Hayward have scored more runs in a season. His heavy scoring enabled Yorkshire to share the Championship with Middlesex. It was the first time in the twentieth century that the Championship had been tied.

Middlesex, still operating with a limited attack, set the early pace, but Yorkshire won their last six matches to earn their share of the title. Yardley was available for most of the season and scored a thousand runs in the Championship, while Coxon, Wardle and a young all-rounder named Brian Close took most of the wickets.

In his first season in county cricket, Close completed the 'double', the youngest player ever to achieve this feat. He also played in the third Test match, at Old Trafford, and, at the age of 18 years 149 days, was the youngest ever to play for England. He had a fine physique, would open the bowling with pace and swerve and later turn to off-breaks. He batted left-handed and was a magnificent fielder close to the wicket. Great things were prophesied for his cricketing future, but he never quite realised his immense potential.

Another Yorkshire debutant who received less publicity was a fast bowler named Fred Trueman. He first played in the Whitsun Bank Holiday Roses match at Old Trafford but failed to take a wicket. A fortnight later, he appeared against Middlesex at Lord's. Robertson and Brown put on 198 for the first wicket before Trueman, who had bowled a wild opening spell, had Brown caught by Hutton. His enthusiasm knew no bounds, and it was apparent to those watching that here was a bowler with fire in his heart. In his four county matches, he took thirteen wickets and did not score a run. None prophesied what lay in store for him.

For Middlesex, the strength was in batting. They contributed five players to the England side for the second Test, at Lord's, and two of them, Compton and Robertson, scored centuries. It did not save Robertson, an elegant and graceful batsman, from being omitted from the remaining two matches of the series. His answer was to hit 300 in a day against Worcestershire, who were leading the Championship at the time, at Worcester while England were engaged in the third Test.

Edrich was as reliable as ever with the bat, but his bowling was no longer a force. Sims and Young both took a hundred wickets in the Championship, but Sims, a jovial and witty leg-break bowler, was forty-five and Jack Young was thirty-seven. It was easy to recognise that at the height of the Middlesex success there were already the seeds of decline.

Age was certainly becoming a concern for the England selectors. Louis Duffus, the South African journalist, had described Mann's party as 'rather elderly', and England were engaged in a perpetual search for youth. Gilbert Parkhouse had caught the eye for Glamorgan in 1948, and Tom Graveney, Arthur Milton, Roy Tattersall, Hubert Doggart, Dick Spooner and Peter May were among those to make their first-class debuts in that year, but none had yet established himself. Close was to burst upon the scene and was to play in the Test trial at Edgbaston at the beginning of June and later, as we have noted, in the third Test at Old Trafford. Another to play in that trial was Alan Wharton, a left-handed batsman and right-arm medium-pace bowler who had done well for Lancashire. He was twenty-six years old, and there were expectations that he would do well, but he played in the first Test without success (he was not called upon to bowl), was chosen for the second but withdrew through injury and was not selected again. Another all-rounder made his Test debut in the same match as Wharton, Trevor Bailey, and he was to prove to be the first cricketer without first-class experience before the Second World War to win a permanent place in the Test side and to play a significant role in the revival of England's fortunes.

He had come down from Cambridge expecting, like so many other amateurs, to follow a career in teaching and to assist Essex in the summer holidays, but he was offered the job of county secretary, and this enabled him to play regularly. He was, in 1949, quicker than any other bowler at England's disposal, as he soon demonstrated against the New Zealand tourists. He was also a most capable batsman with a sound defence and, when the occasion warranted, a full range of shots. He was the first man to complete the 'double' in 1949, and he was to achieve the feat seven more times in his career. Only four other cricketers have more than Bailey's eight doubles to their credit.

In 1949 Bailey bowled more quickly than he was to do in years to come, and he moved the ball both ways. Against Lancashire, at Clacton in August, he took all ten wickets for 90 runs, but, rather typically for the time, Essex were beaten in two days.

New Zealand first played Test cricket at the beginning of 1930. By the time they arrived in England in 1949 they had played eighteen Tests in all, fifteen of them against England, and had never had even a scent of victory. They were considered the weakest of Test-playing nations, and, as with India and the West Indies, only three days were allocated for England's meetings with them in England.

At the start of the 1949 season they surprised people with their results. They drew with Yorkshire and Leicestershire and beat Worcestershire, Surrey and a strong Cambridge University side. Their batting, with Sutcliffe, Donnelly, Wallace, skipper Walter Hadlee and the young Reid was strong. The attack had limitations, but Cowie, fast-medium, and Burtt, slow left-arm, were fine bowlers.

The first real test for them was against MCC towards the end of May. Edrich, Simpson, Watkins and Compton hit fifties, and MCC made 379 in spite of some excellent bowling by Burtt, who took six for 98 in 59.5 overs. More than 28,000 people saw the first day's play, and there was another large crowd on the Monday to see the end of MCC's innings and the New Zealanders bat.

Robertson, Simpson, Carr, Broderick (an all-rounder from Northamptonshire) and Bailey were all 'on trial' in this match. Bailey passed with flying colours. He bowled at a considerable pace, had Hadlee caught behind and Donnelly at slip, and knocked back the stumps of Sutcliffe and Reid. In addition, he took a brilliant right-handed catch at forward short-leg off a full-blooded hit by Wallace as the tourists slumped to 96 for six. He finished with five for 83, but thanks to a defiant stand from Mooney and Rabone the match was drawn. Bailey's place in the England side for the first Test was assured.

Mann continued as England captain, and he won the toss in the first three Tests. At Headingley, Hutton and Compton hit centuries as England made 372. Cowie and Burtt shared the wickets, and it is interesting to note that, although both Hutton and Compton were praised for style and technique, they were criticised for taking four hours to score 101 and three hours thirty-five minutes to score 114 respectively.

The pace of Bailey and the lift he obtained immediately troubled the New Zealand batsmen. With his eighth ball in Test cricket, he had Scott caught at fourth slip. He finished with six for 118. Washbrook hit a century in the second innings, and the match was drawn.

For the second Test, Robertson and Watkins came in for Washbrook and Wharton, who were injured, and Bedser was dropped in favour of Gladwin. The *Cricketer* aired the view of many when it doubted the wisdom of discarding Bedser after one match of the series. Readers were reminded how highly Bedser was regarded by Bradman and it was lamented that neither Bedser nor Wright, the two most successful bowlers on the last tour of Australia, was in the current England side. Jenkins, too, following his successful tour of South Africa, had found no place in England's plans, and the chosen spinners, Hollies and Young, were 'getting on in years'.

There was another concern, and it was centred on Bailey. Fear was being expressed that he would be overworked in county cricket. He was the quick bowler and all-rounder of whom England had need, but it was felt that he should be spared the daily rigours of the county game as much as possible. There was, it was suggested, too much cricket. This belief was to whistle down the wind for the next half-century.

The Lord's Test was watched by 81,000 people and, inevitably, on a good pitch in fine weather with limited bowling resources on both sides and the match restricted to three days, it was drawn. Mann made history by breaking the existing law and declaring on the first day to leave New Zealand a quarter of an hour batting. A wicket did not fall in this time and Donnelly hit a double century on the Monday.

Bailey did not take a wicket in the match, but he joined Compton when England were struggling in their first innings at 112 for five. He hit 93 in two and a half hours with sixteen fours, and the pair added 189, Compton making a century.

English cricket was still troubled by the problem of captaincy. Among the counties, Derbyshire had turned to David Skinner to lead them in 1949. A genial and popular accountant who had been educated at The Leys, Cambridge, he handled the side quite well and set a good example in the field, but, as an off-spinner, he was no more than club standard and his ability as a batsman was very limited. He did a commendable job in difficult circumstances, but he stood down at the end of the year and took charge of the second eleven.

Leicestershire found an amateur replacement for Les Berry in the form of Stuart Symington. At the age of twenty-two, he was Leicestershire's youngest-ever captain and the youngest captain in post-war county cricket. His reign lasted just one season before Charlie Palmer came from Worcestershire to take over as secretary/captain.

Warwickshire followed a path that went the opposite way from Leicestershire's. Ron Maudsley was officially the captain in 1948, but as he was teaching Law at Oxford University until mid-June, the senior professional 'Tom' Dollery led the side in the first half of the season. Such a situation was not good for the team, and Maudsley stood down in 1949 and backed the idea that Dollery should become captain.

The appointment was not well received in the higher chambers of cricket, but the Warwickshire committee was wise and unanimous. Dollery himself was to say that fellow professionals saw his appointment as being a giant step towards 'removing the last great disability of professionalism'.

The *Birmingham Post* fully supported Dollery's appointment, believing that 'we have advanced far since the days the amateurs and professionals left the pavilion by different gates. It is the game which counts and if a man is a good sportsman, a first-class cricketer, a born leader and appeals to the crowd, then he is the man to skipper the team.'

Dollery was an instant success, with Warwickshire climbing to fourth in the table, but he was a wise man and he knew that the weight of establishment opinion was still heavily against the idea of a professional captain. He knew that he must tread warily. When Reg Simpson became captain of Nottinghamshire he bowled an over of lobs as a protest against Glamorgan's slow scoring. Marlar at Sussex and Wooller at Glamorgan were responsible for displaying similar gestures of protest (or contempt), but Dollery was aware that what was considered 'humour' or 'eccentricity' in an amateur would be damned as 'bad taste' in a professional. Dollery's strength and a reason for his success was that the committee that appointed him allowed him to get on with the job without interference. The same could not have been said of the Lancashire committee at the time.

After two seasons of first-class cricket in which he had captained

Lancashire and England, Ken Cranston left the game to concentrate on his dental practice. The obvious man to succeed him was Cyril Washbrook, but he had no desire to turn amateur, a prerequisite for the job, so the committee turned to N.D. Howard.

Nigel Howard was a promising and attractive right-handed batsman who had scored a thousand runs in 1948. He was twenty-four years old, and he was to be the recipient of much unkind criticism during his period of office. In many ways this was unfair. He worked hard, encouraged young players and did much for Lancashire cricket, but he was never his own master. He was inexperienced and ill-equipped for the job and was constantly instructed what to do by senior committee members. John Kay, the Lancashire historian and journalist, related one of the many rumours, probably true, which became associated with Howard's time as captain. He would frequently receive messages or telegrams instructing him what to do if he won the toss and when to make bowling changes: 'On one occasion a careless telephonist misheard and Howard received a telegram advising him to "put Greenwood in first". He duly did so, when what was meant was "put Greenwood on first". A distinction with a difference, and a state of affairs that could not help any cricketing cause.'

Howard, once so promising, inevitably declined as a batsman. Lancashire cricket lost a sense of purpose, but, to their credit, Howard's players stood by him, knowing where the real fault lay.

In 1951–52 Howard was selected to captain MCC on the tour of India, and this underlined the problem that was facing England with regard to maintaining the tradition of amateur captaincy.

Norman Yardley had been unable to lead the side to South Africa, nor, now, could he see his way to captaining England against New Zealand. Mann had stepped nobly into the breach, but the Lord's Test in which he had broken the law by declaring on the first day was his last. Business claimed him. Where could England turn now? Apart from Mann, there were two other amateurs in the side, Bailey, veteran of two Tests, and Edrich, who had been senior professional on the last tour of Australia and who had turned amateur after that tour, hoping, it was generally believed, to become England captain. He was sure of his place in the side on merit, he had a fine war record and was a popular public figure. It would seem that he was the obvious choice, but it is doubtful that he was ever seriously considered.

Even Middlesex were reluctant to name Edrich as captain, and when he did lead the side he never appeared to have the full backing of the committee. A most lively and warm companion, Edrich tended to become uncharacteristically cold and formal when he spoke publicly or was engaged in business. This chilly façade was in total contrast to the real man whose lust for life was unquenchable. At Edrich's memorial service in 1986, Denis Compton told how, at Sydney in 1946, Edrich had disappeared for the night on the eve of the fourth day. He returned for breakfast not looking in the best of shape, and Compton had done all in his power to keep him out of Hammond's sight. He was successful, and Edrich went out that day and scored a hundred. That was the way Edrich lived his life, but there were those who would not have accepted it as a model for an England captain.

So where were the selectors now to turn? They looked to Northamptonshire and invited Freddie Brown to become captain of England.

A Cambridge blue, Brown had played for Surrey intermittently between 1931 and 1948. He had gone on the 'Bodyline' tour as a leg-break bowler and hard-hitting batsman but had not appeared in a Test match. He had played against India and New Zealand, but when called upon to lead England against New Zealand at Old Trafford in July 1949, he was approaching his thirty-ninth birthday and the last of his six not very successful Test appearances was twelve years in the past. In fairness, Brown had captured the public imagination with his achievements for Northamptonshire.

His business had moved to the county in 1949, and he was granted special registration to play for Northamptonshire. He was appointed captain, and his zest helped lift a side that had spent more than a decade wallowing at or near the bottom of the Championship to sixth place. His contribution as a player was to complete the 'double', in all matches. Brown was no great tactician as a captain, and his judgement of players was not always sound, but he was an enthusiast ever ready to lead the charge himself.

Like Mann and Gladwin, Jack Young had seen his international career end with the Lord's Test. The young Close made his Test debut at Old Trafford, scored nought and took a wicket after Brown had won the toss and put the New Zealanders in. Simpson, for whose inclusion there had been a clamour all summer, made 103 not out and Bailey scored 72 and took six for 84 in the first innings. Most interestingly, England gave a first international cap to Les Jackson, the Derbyshire bowler.

Jackson was tall and wiry and bowled off a comparatively short run, but he was decidedly quick and hostile. He could move the ball either way and make it rear from a length. He did not possess a model action, but he was relentlessly accurate and totally committed. His career brought 1,733 wickets at 17.37 runs each, a very impressive record, and in his first Test he had match figures of three for 72 from thirty-nine

64

overs. In spite of England's search for quick bowlers, Jackson had to wait another twelve years for his second Test appearance and that was his last. His omission at a time of need will for ever remain a mystery.

Bedser, Laker and Wright returned for the fourth and final Test against New Zealand. Bedser, refreshed no doubt after missing most of the series, took seven wickets in the match, Hutton scored 206, Edrich 100, and the pair added 218 for the second wicket. New Zealand were in some danger on the third day, but the match, like the three before it, was drawn.

This was the last time that three days were thought to be sufficient for a Test match in England. The pattern was set for the forthcoming series against the West Indies when five days were scheduled for each of the four Tests. What was also apparent from the series against New Zealand was that there was no longer *weak* opposition in a Test match. The New Zealanders had shown themselves more than capable of dealing with all that England had to offer.

There were, however, signs that English cricket was stirring. The advent of Bailey had been a distinct gain. Evans had recovered his form and held his place behind the stumps, although he was often disappointing at county level. Simpson had proved his worth, and there was a glimpse of promise from Close. Other aspects of selection, in addition to the treatment of Les Jackson, remained erratic and often incomprehensible. Following Jenkins's success in South Africa, he had shown his considerable improvement by becoming the country's leading wicket-taker with 183 wickets. He had also scored 1,183 runs, and, at thirty years old, he was one of the younger bowlers; yet he did not appear in a single Test.

For those with vision, there was gratification that, in his second season with Gloucestershire, Tom Graveney had hit four centuries and been chosen to represent the Players against the Gentlemen, an honour which always hinted that the selectors had a player in mind.

It was evident, too, that there was considerable talent at Oxford and Cambridge. In 1950 the first four in the Cambridge batting order were Dewes, Sheppard, Doggart and May, and Warr was opening the bowling while Insole had come down and was taking over the captaincy of Essex. Peter May, the former Charterhouse captain, had made a deep impression in 1949 by scoring 695 runs in eleven completed innings for the Combined Services. Only Hardstaff and Hutton finished above him in the first-class batting averages.

In spite of these seemingly encouraging signs, writers like Ian Macartney in the *Cricketer* could identify little sign of recovery for the English game, except in Yorkshire. The 'sterile series of Test matches with the New Zealanders' gave little encouragement for the distant future and none at all for the tour of Australia in 1950–51. He pleaded the perennial argument that the leading players played too much cricket, yet the leading players of that time like Alec Bedser would argue today that players do not play enough and that he rose to the heights he did because of the amount that he had to bowl.

These were changing times. The MCC made a significant gesture when they elected twenty-six former professionals of distinction to life membership of the club. In the General Election of February 1950, a record number of candidates stood, and when Labour was returned with a reduced majority the new parliament included twenty women members. Never had there been so many.

More significantly for cricket, the BBC and various sporting representatives met towards the end of May and agreed to the televising of a hundred sporting events a year. This agreement was made at a time when the production of television sets had risen by 250 per cent in the year. An avalanche had been set in motion which was to have a profound influence upon cricket and all other sports.

If there had been optimism after the series with New Zealand that a stable England side was taking shape, the series with the West Indies shattered that idea. In the four Tests, England called upon twenty-five players, and not one cricketer appeared in every Test. Eight men were introduced to Test cricket – Berry, Doggart, Parkhouse, Insole, Shackleton, Hilton, McIntyre and Sheppard. Of those, Berry and Doggart played in the first two Tests and never played for England again.

There were problems in that a variety of injuries deprived England of the services of Hutton, Bailey, Washbrook and Evans. The side that took the field for the fourth and last Test showed eight changes from the side that played in the third Test.

The most serious loss for England was that of Denis Compton. The injury to his right knee which had been giving cause for concern for more than three years became critical, and an operation was deemed necessary. Compton played no cricket in June and did not reappear until Fishlock's benefit match at The Oval on 29 July. He hit 115 not out and 48,530 people watched the three days' cricket. Such was his drawing power.

Edrich, too, was forced to rest for a long period because of a back strain, and he missed the last two Tests and the tour of Australia, for which he was fit. Edrich was quite clear in his own mind as to why he was not chosen. During the Lord's Test against the West Indies, he went in search of jollity as was his wont and returned to his hotel in the early hours of the morning. He was walking along the corridor to his room when one of the selectors, R.E.S. Wyatt, appeared on his way to the bathroom. Nothing was said, nor was Edrich ever reprimanded, but he believed until the end of his life that he was sentenced to three years'

66

exile from Test cricket for his misdemeanour. Certainly, it was three years almost to the day before he again played for England.

The weather had been unwelcoming to the West Indians. They arrived as a side known to be strong in batting with an attack that was limited and inexperienced. In mid-May at Cambridge, the university hit 507 for three against them on the first day and declared at 594 for four. Dewes, 183, and Sheppard, 227, scored 343 for the first wicket, and Doggart made 71. The tourists replied with 730 for three with Weekes making 304 not out. The wicket was perfect and the weather cold, and when MCC, with an attack that was not the strongest, beat the West Indians by 118 runs it was generally felt that they would not provide the most taxing of opponents in the coming series.

The first Test seemed to support that opinion. England were 88 for five and had lost Hutton with a hand injury before Bailey and Evans added 161. Evans hit 104, his first century in major cricket. The bowler to cause England most trouble was Valentine, a left-arm spinner, who had match figures of eleven for 204. He took the first eight wickets to fall in the first innings. The West Indies were twice bowled out by Hollies and Berry, who was another slow left-arm bowler.

Yardley had returned to captain the England side, and the victory was heartening and boded well for the winter tour although it had to be admitted that the West Indians were, in strong contrast with what was to come some years later, virtually totally lacking in a pair of opening bowlers. The second Test suggested that pace men were not needed.

The West Indies won a famous victory through the spinners Ramadhin and Valentine. Neither had appeared in more than two first-class matches before the tour began, and even by the end of the tour no one had been able to determine what type of bowler Ramadhin was. Jenkins returned to Test cricket and took nine wickets in the match, and Washbrook scored a second-innings century, but the West Indies won by 326 runs and the famous calypso was sung at Lord's.

Rae and, massively, Walcott had scored centuries in the second Test; Worrell, 261, and Weekes, 129, shared a fourth-wicket partnership of 283 in 210 minutes in the third. For the first time in Test history, the England team consisted of eleven players from eleven different counties. Washbrook and Simpson began the second innings with a record part-nership of 212, and Washbrook hit his second century in successive Tests, but England lost by ten wickets.

The West Indies went through the series using only twelve players; England, as we have said, made eight changes for the final Test. Compton was welcomed back, but Yardley had announced that he was unavailable for the tour of Australia, and the selectors turned again to

Freddie Brown. Two leg-spinners, Jenkins and Hollies, had played in the third Test, but Brown was a leg-spinner and with Wright recalled neither of them was required for The Oval, where West Indies claimed an innings victory. Hollies's Test career was over.

The return of Compton gave hope that the series would be drawn, but when he went to the crease England, facing a total of 503, were 120 for two. He and Hutton added 109 before Compton ran himself out, not a rare occurrence. Hutton carried his bat for 202, a wonderful achievement. He hit twenty-two fours and batted for 470 minutes, but England lost their last six wickets for 34 runs and followed on 159 runs in arrears. Valentine and Ramadhin bowled them out for 103 in their second knock.

Plans and predictions were in tatters. The County Championship again ended in a tie, Lancashire and Surrey sharing the honours. In spite of being constantly advised by the Lancashire committee, Nigel Howard kept his side together on the field and encouraged the young. Lancashire relied heavily on spin, for the wicket at Old Trafford was so helpful to the spinners as to draw from one opposing *professional* captain, James Langridge, the comment that he thought it was not really fit for three-day cricket. Certainly, the off-spinner Roy Tattersall ended the season with 193 wickets and was top of the averages. At one time Malcolm Hilton was opening the bowling, and then, as *Wisden* commented, 'just as everyone wondered how long the attack could be sustained without real pace, along came Brian Statham to provide a real tonic'.

It would not be long before Statham provided a tonic for England, too, but as yet the name of Trueman, who took thirty wickets in his few appearances for Yorkshire, was scarcely mentioned.

In finishing level with Lancashire, Surrey owed much to Jim Laker, who was rapidly developing his art and finished the season with 166 wickets to his credit. Johnny Wardle had 174, and his team-mate Coxon, with 131, was an infinitely better bowler than he had been when picked for England in 1948, but none of these players was picked to tour Australia under Freddie Brown in 1950–51.

The selection committee consisted of Sellers, Wyatt, Pearce and Ames, the first professional to be elected to the committee as opposed to players like Hobbs and Rhodes who had been co-opted on occasions. As captain, Brown, of course, was also a member of the committee. Their final selection offered one of the most bizarre parties ever to represent MCC and England in Australia or anywhere else. One journalist described it cruelly as 'spivs and schoolboys'. The more restrained language of Norman Preston suggested that the selectors had 'gambled on five or six young men who had accomplished nothing in Test cricket'. Among them was Brian Close.

Close had spent the summer in the Army. He had played only two innings for Yorkshire and had taken seven wickets. Preston felt sensibly that 'constant match practice is necessary for youth to develop, and on the few occasions that Close appeared in 1950 it was obvious that he had gone back'.

Preston's opinion that Brown was the best England captain since Jardine is very hard to support, but he struck a right chord when he observed that the selectors had been too influenced by batting averages and that runs scored on featherbed pitches like Fenner's or Trent Bridge should be discounted.

As well as Brown, there were five other amateurs in the party – Simpson, Bailey, Dewes, Sheppard and Warr – yet Compton was named as vice-captain. Edrich, as noted, was not picked. His view that he was under suspension may be true, but he was not liked by Brown, who had no wish to have him in the side. Trevor Bailey, however, holds the firm opinion that, with Edrich in the side, England could well have won the first two Tests.

Hutton, Parkhouse and Washbrook completed the batting, Evans and McIntyre, of Surrey, were the wicket-keepers, and the rest of the bowling contingent was Bedser, Hollies, Wright and Berry, the slow left-arm spinner from Lancashire.

To this day, the inclusion of quick bowler John Warr in the party leaves one in a state of shock. Warr had done well in his second year at Cambridge and had done useful work for Middlesex, but, in the context of a representative match like Gentlemen and Players in which Brown had scored a thrilling century, his limitations and lack of experience were cruelly exposed. Trevor Bailey remembers that Essex were playing Derbyshire at Southend when the news came through that Warr had been chosen ahead of Les Jackson and that the looks on the faces of Jackson's colleagues were unforgettable.

A witty man, and one who was to do much for the game, Warr played in two Tests on the tour and finished with one for 281, which makes him the most expensive wicket-taker in the history of Test cricket. One cynic commented that Warr's figures flattered him, but he deserved a better cricketing epitaph.

England's motley crew needed some luck; they got none. In this first post-Bradman series, they staggered towards the first Test with some unconvincing performances. None of the batsmen save Compton had made runs consistently, but he averaged over 100 from seven innings. The bowling and the fielding were moderate, and the catching was poor. For the Brisbane Test Hutton was asked to drop to number six (he batted eight in the second innings because of the state of the wicket after a thunderstorm) and McIntyre was included as a batsman and to improve the fielding.

Australia batted first on a good pitch, and no one gave England any chance. With the fourth ball of the day, Bailey had Moroney caught at backward short-leg by Hutton. The catch was a good one, and it had the effect of lifting the England side. Bedser and Bailey bowled magnificently. Evans was inspirational behind the stumps with brilliant catches to account for Harvey and Loxton, and the fielding rose to great and unexpected heights. Australia were bowled out for 228 before bad light ended play for the day with England totally in command.

That evening the England party went to the theatre, and there they heard a storm break. No play was possible on the second day, nor until half an hour before lunch on the third day when England found themselves batting on a notorious Brisbane 'gluepot'. Simpson and Washbrook began the innings with great skill and application to score 28, but in the post-lunch period twenty wickets fell. Medium-pace bowling of good length rendered batting impossible. Brown declared with England on 68 for seven, and Bailey and Bedser reduced Australia to 32 for seven before Hassett declared. Needing 193 to win, England were 30 for six at the close. Their splendid work in bowling out Australia on a good pitch inside one day had been nullified by the weather.

In England's second innings, Simpson had been yorked first ball by Lindwall, and although Washbrook and Dewes offered sound defence for half an hour, they were out in quick succession. Worse was to come as three wickets went down in the last ten minutes of the day; those of Bailey, Bedser and McIntyre, who was run out going for a fourth run at a time when preservation should have been all.

There was a hint on the fourth morning that the pitch had lost some of its venom. Evans helped Hutton to add 16 before he and Compton pushed successive balls from Johnston into the hands of forward short-leg. At 46 for eight, England were doomed, but Hutton proceeded to play one of the great Test innings. He treated the fast bowlers with majestic contempt, and he played the turning, lifting ball with a skill at which others could only wonder. Brown stayed with him while 31 were added, and Wright supported him for half an hour while 45 runs were scored. On the stroke of lunch, Wright, losing patience and concentration, hooked at Iverson, the mystery bowler, and was caught. England were out for 122: Hutton was 62 not out.

In the state games Compton continued to bat well, but his knee began to prove a problem, and he was unable to play in the second Test. His place went to Parkhouse while Close replaced McIntyre.

In Melbourne, as in Brisbane, all began well for England. Bailey and Bedser again bowled outstandingly well after Hassett had won the toss.

The pitch was tame, but the atmosphere was heavy, and both bowlers exploited the conditions to the full. In the last ten minutes of the day four wickets fell, three in five balls, and Australia were out for 194.

Bailey and Bedser each had four wickets. Brown and Close, both bowling medium pace, had a wicket each, but Wright's eight eight-ball overs cost 63 runs. He was woefully inaccurate, and, as it transpired, this inaccuracy proved to be the difference between the two sides.

Well as England played on the first day, they frittered away their advantage on the second. Conditions were easier for batting, but a sustained attack from Lindwall, Miller, Johnston and Iverson proved too much for some weak defence and lack of application. Six wickets went down for 61 before Bailey gave a glimpse of things to come. Offering a straight bat to all that was bowled to him, he lasted for seventy minutes and scored 12 while the total was increased by 65. Brown hit mightily in scoring 62, and Evans followed his example, but a first innings lead of 3 was a bitter disappointment.

Australia quickly wiped off the arrears and were 82 for one at lunch on the third day. In two and a half hours after the break they lost their last nine wickets for 99 runs. Bailey and Bedser again bowled well, and Brown, bowling medium pace of a good length and gentle movement, took four for 26 in twelve overs. No captain could have done more with bat and ball.

England required 179 to win, and they lost Washbrook and Bailey before the close of the day with 28 on the board. Hutton and Simpson took the score to 52 before Simpson was bowled by Lindwall. Dewes, who had spent much of the match confined to bed with a chill, lasted until just before lunch when England were 84 for four.

The departure of Hutton after making 40 was really the end of the challenge in spite of worthy efforts by Parkhouse and Bedser, who looked totally at ease making 14 not out at number ten. England lost by 28 runs. With three days in which to score 179, England had been over-cautious and totally lacking in self-belief. Bradman had gone, but his ghost lived on.

At Sydney, Compton returned in place of Dewes; Warr made his debut at the expense of Close. Hutton returned to his rightful place at number one. For England, the match was a disaster.

> When sorrows come, they come not single spies,
> But in battalions.

Brown won the toss for the only time in the series and England batted. Washbrook fell to a brilliantly spectacular one-handed catch at slip by

71

Miller, who had a tremendous influence on the game with bat, ball and in the field. Brown made 79, Hutton 62 and England were bowled out for 290. Bailey had his thumb fractured by a ball from Lindwall, and Wright tore a tendon in his leg when he was run out. Brown was left with three bowlers, including himself.

In extreme heat, Brown, forty years old, sent down 44 overs, Bedser 43 and Warr 36. Compton contributed six overs. Brown rotated his bowlers wisely, and he and Bedser each took four wickets. It was a brave rearguard action, but the cause was lost. Australia won by an innings and retained the Ashes.

With the injury list growing and with Compton's knee suspect, England sent for reinforcements. They arrived in the form of the Lancashire pair, Statham and Tattersall. Hollies and Berry had found no form in Australia, and Tattersall went straight into the side for the fourth Test. He replaced the injured Bailey while Sheppard came in for Parkhouse.

Bedser had Archer taken by Compton in the leg-trap off the third ball of the match in Adelaide, but Morris hit a double century. In Australia's second innings, Burke scored a century on his Test debut and Miller made 99. Hutton became the only England batsman to carry his bat through a completed Test innings twice. He made 156 in the first innings, and 45 in the second, but once more his wonderful batting went practically unsupported, and Australia won by 274 runs. This was England's seventh successive Test defeat, and it was hard to see when the clouds would ever be lifted. Australia had won 20 and drawn 5 of their last 25 Tests.

The fifth Test at Melbourne saw Bailey return in place of Warr, and Hole made his debut for Australia at the expense of Archer. Hassett won the toss for the fourth time in the series, and Australia batted.

At 23, Burke fell to Bedser, but Bailey twisted his ankle when bowling his third over and was out of the attack for the rest of the day. Brown, who had been involved in a car accident during the fourth Test and had injured his shoulder, had hoped not to have to bowl, but Bailey's injury meant revised tactics.

Hassett and Morris took the score to 111 shortly before tea when Brown returned for a second spell. He trapped Morris leg-before when the batsman tried to turn a straight ball to leg. In his next over Brown had Harvey caught behind as he tried to cut, and he deceived Miller with the first ball of his next over. The batsman played too soon and was caught and bowled. In seventeen balls Brown had captured three major wickets without conceding a run.

Hole averted the hat-trick and helped steady the innings, but he fell to Bedser at 156 and Johnson went ten runs later. Hassett was playing beautifully, but he became Brown's fourth victim, superbly caught at slip by Hutton, who then took another fine catch to get rid of Tallon. Australia closed on 206 for eight, and England could be well pleased with their day's work.

Rain prevented any play on the second day, but the last two Australian wickets fell quickly on the third morning. England began with a flourish and 40 runs came in half an hour. Washbrook edged an out-swinger to the wicket-keeper, and Australia might have had more success had they not been guilty of uncharacteristic lapses in the field.

At tea England were 160 for one, most happily placed. Surprisingly, Hutton was beaten by one of Hole's occasional off-breaks. Compton was taken at slip off Miller, which heralded a disastrous period for England as Lindwall and Miller tore out the middle order with the second new ball. Sheppard, Brown and Evans were beaten by the sheer pace of the attack, and England closed at 218 for six, a lead of 1 and the game in the balance.

Australia continued to claw back the initiative on the fourth morning as Bedser, Bailey and Wright were brushed aside while the score reached 246. When Tattersall joined Simpson the Nottinghamshire batsman was on 92. In the next hour he scored 64 while Tattersall scored 10. The partnership was worth 74, and England took a lead of 103. No praise can be too high for Simpson, who flayed the spinners and the fast men alike while keeping Tattersall away from the bowling as much as possible. Six of Simpson's twelve fours came in his last 56 runs, and his innings lasted five hours forty minutes. His only century against Australia came on his thirty-first birthday.

Bedser immediately accounted for both openers in a fine opening spell. Harvey threatened before being leg-before to a ball which kept low. Miller again failed against Brown so that Australia had lost four wickets before clearing the arrears. Hassett and Hole took them to 129 by the end of the day.

The stand between Hole and Hassett was beginning to take on menacing proportions when Wright, as unpredictable as ever, produced a magnificent over in which he bowled Hassett with an unplayable leg-break, which pitched outside leg stump and hit middle-and-off, and without addition to the score had Johnson caught.

This was the breakthrough that England needed, though Lindwall helped Hole to add 50. Decisively, Bailey bowled Hole, and the last four wickets fell for 5 runs; three of the wickets, deservedly, went to Bedser.

England needed 95 to win and soon lost Washbrook. Hutton was once more in majestic form, and although Simpson was run out, England seemed sure of victory as long as the great Yorkshireman remained. It was appropriate that Hutton and Compton, the only survivors from

73

England's last victory over Australia, at The Oval in 1938, should be at the crease when the game was won.

It may seem excessive to lavish praise on a single victory in a series where the opponents won four matches, but it was an event equivalent to the sound barrier being broken in other fields or the mile being run in under four minutes.

In New Zealand England won one Test and drew one, and they returned home happy. Bedser had taken thirty wickets in the Ashes series at 16.06 runs apiece, and Bailey had proved that he had acquired stamina to complement his aggression. No leader could have set a better example than Brown by his personal achievements, and Hutton stood supreme among world batsmen. Evans's wicket-keeping had touched new heights in skill, agility and passion.

In spite of the victory and the advances that had been made in various quarters, problems remained. Brown's fitness and form had been remarkable, but he had spent several years in a prisoner-of-war camp and was forty-one years old. Yardley and Mann were hardly likely to return, so who would captain England?

What, too, of Compton? He had scored more than a thousand runs on the tour, but his average in the Test series was 7.57. He refused to offer his damaged knee as an excuse, but there was the realisation that the real glory days of the most entertaining batsman the game has known were at an end. He still had a few surprises ahead for his admirers, but nothing was ever quite to be as it had been in those golden years immediately after the Second World War.

For the time being, however, the clouds had lifted. The success in Melbourne had had a liberating effect on England's cricket.

England's First Post-war Victory over Australia
Australia v England at Melbourne Cricket Ground
23, 24, 26, 27 and 28 February 1951

Australia First Innings		Second Innings	
J.W. Burke c Tattersall b Bedser ...	11	c Hutton b Bedser	1
A.R. Morris lbw b Brown	50	lbw b Bedser	4
A.L. Hassett (capt) c Hutton b Brown	92	b Wright	48
R.N. Harvey c Evans b Brown	1	lbw b Wright	52
K.R. Miller c and b Brown	7	c and b Brown	0
G.B. Hole b Bedser	18	b Bailey	63
I.W. Johnson lbw b Bedser	1	c Brown b Wright	0
R.R. Lindwall c Compton b Bedser	21	b Bedser	14
†D. Tallon c Hutton b Bedser	1	not out	2
W.A. Johnston not out	12	b Bedser	1

74

J.B. Iverson c Washbrook b Brown	0	c Compton b Bedser ...	0
Extras (b 2, lb 1)	3	(b 2, lb 8, w 1, nb 1)	12

| Total .... | 217 | .... | .197 |

BOWLING	Overs	Mdns	Runs	Wkts	Overs	Mdns	Runs	Wkts
Bedser	22	5	46	5	20.3	4	59	5
Bailey	9	2	29	–	15	3	32	1
Brown	18	4	49	5	9	1	32	1
Wright	9	1	50	–	15	2	56	3
Tattersall	11	3	40	–	5	2	6	–

fall of wickets
1–23, 2–111, 3–115, 4–123, 5–156, 6–166, 7–184, 8–187, 9–216
1–5, 2–6, 3–87, 4–89, 5–142, 6–142, 7–192, 8–196, 9–197

England First Innings		Second Innings	
L. Hutton b Hole	79	not out	60
C. Washbrook c Tallon b Miller ...	27	c Lindwall b Johnston ..	7
R.T. Simpson not out	156	run out	15
D.C.S. Compton c Miller b Lindwall	11	not out	11
D.S. Sheppard c Tallon b Miller ...	1		
F.R. Brown (capt) b Lindwall	6		
†T.G. Evans b Miller	1		
A.V. Bedser b Lindwall	11		
T.E. Bailey c Johnson b Iverson ...	5		
D.V.P. Wright lbw b Iverson	3		
R. Tattersall b Miller	10		
Extras (b 9, lb 1)	10	(lb 2)	2

| Total .... | 320 | .... | 95 |

BOWLING	Overs	Mdns	Runs	Wkts	Overs	Mdns	Runs	Wkts
Lindwall	21	1	77	3	2	–	12	–
Miller	21.7	5	76	4	2	–	5	–
Johnston	12	1	55	–	11	3	36	1
Iverson	20	4	52	2	12	2	32	–
Johnson	11	1	40	–	1	–	1	–
Hole	5	–	10	1	1	–	3	–
Hassett	–	–	–	–	0.6	–	4	–

fall of wickets
1–40, 2–171, 3–204, 4–205, 5–212, 6–213, 7–228, 8–236, 9–246
1–32, 2–62
umpires – A.N. Barlow and H. Elphinston
England won by 8 wickets

3

The Escape from the Wilderness,
1951–55

Brown follows the tradition of the great amateurs who made this
game of cricket as we know it in the first-class sense. There is
always room for the talented professional but the amateur brings
the essential spirit of adventure.

So wrote Norman Preston in *Wisden* in his comments on the 1951 season.
With the victories at Melbourne and in New Zealand, and a triumphant
3–1 series win over South Africa, it was expected that the cricket boom
would continue, but the public's post-war honeymoon with the game
was over. In the year of the Festival of Britain, people were beginning to
expect more glitter in their entertainment, and cricket was growing list-
less and complacent.

Attendances at the Test matches generally stood up well although the
South Africans did not match the glamour and excitement of the West
Indians. Their batsmen offered stolid defence in contrast to the range of
exotic strokes offered by those from the Caribbean in 1950.

South Africa won the first Test at Trent Bridge in spite of centuries
from Simpson and Compton, but England won comfortably at Lord's
and Old Trafford, less comfortably at The Oval, and drew a high-scoring
match at Headingley. From the England point of view, the series was a
great success. Bedser took thirty wickets in a rubber for the second time
within a few months; Laker and Tattersall bowled admirably; Hutton's
masterful form continued; and Compton put the gloom of the Ashes
behind him. More importantly, five young cricketers made their Test
debuts during the summer. Three of them, the left-handed Watson, who
had played soccer for England, wicket-keeper Don Brennan and opening batsman Lowson were from Yorkshire; Tom Graveney was from

Gloucestershire; and there was Peter May, Cambridge University and Surrey.

May made his debut in the Headingley Test. He scored 138 and shared a second-wicket partnership of 129 with Hutton. May's arrival on the international scene at the age of twenty-one was a revelation for the general public. Reg Hayter wrote of his maiden Test innings, 'His equanimity from first to last, his subordination of self for side even after completing his century, and his sound technique stamped him as a player well above the ordinary.' Indeed, he was. May was the first *great* post-war England batsman and, arguably, the country has not produced a better one since. He finished top of the Test-match batting averages, and his 2,339 runs, average 68.79, put him top of the national averages ahead of Compton.

As an amateur, May already had the mark of a future England captain about him, but for the present Brown continued in the job following his achievement in Australia, and Yardley was now chairman of selectors. There was no sign of an heir-apparent for the captaincy of England, and leadership was an increasing problem in county cricket where the number of drawn games was increasing and attendances were dropping dramatically.

The Select Committee had demanded of cricketers in the immediate post-war years that they show a dynamic attitude, but that attitude, like the selfless passion to build a new Britain, was lapsing into apathy and self-satisfaction. Pad play had begun to dominate the game, and there was the question of the early finish, matches in which there were extended hours of play on the first two days so that the game could be brought to an end in mid-afternoon on the third day, for whatever reason. There was the growing belief that what went on in the middle was of concern only to those involved and had nothing to do with the paying customer. That is, of course, fatal and a cure is still being sought.

Wisden considered poor captaincy the main reason for the decline of the appeal of the game, yet, in spite of evidence to the contrary, it was still wedded to the ideal of the amateur captain. There was even the suggestion that too much cricket was being played and that the game should be restricted until August when more amateurs would be available.

What cricket had yet to come to terms with was that others had joined the market place where once cricket had had a monopoly. Increasingly, alternative summer pursuits were becoming available to ordinary people. There were more car-owners, and tennis and golf had become more accessible. The death of King George VI in 1952 led to an increased demand for television sets from the millions who wanted to watch the coronation of Queen Elizabeth II.

77

Ernie Gregory, who played 381 times in goal for West Ham United and who has served the club for more than fifty years, recalled, 'When I was a kid you played football in the winter and cricket in the summer. I hated cricket, but I played for London Schools and got a hundred. Play cricket was what you did in the summer. Now?'

By its very nature, cricket is a conservative game reluctant to recognise or absorb change. Problems were arising in the 1950s: suspect bowling actions, sustained short-pitched bowling, drab cricket and the continuing divide between amateur and professional, which few wanted to face. At the start of the 1951 season, one problem had to be confronted.

Paul Gibb, graduate of Cambridge University, representative of the Gentlemen against the Players and an England cricketer until the end of the 1946–47 tour of Australia, had not appeared in first-class cricket since that tour, an unhappy one for him. He had taken up a position with Charles Barker Ltd., a gentleman's outfitting firm in Tottenham Court Road. He tired of the job and, in 1951, with the retirement of Tom Wade, he accepted an offer to keep wicket for Essex as a *professional*. This placed MCC in a difficult position, for he was still a playing member of the club. The problem was resolved by MCC temporarily suspending his membership while he was in paid employment as a cricketer.

From this distance it is difficult to understand how acute the embarrassment for the cricket establishment was at the time. Paradoxically, Gibb proved to be a better wicket-keeper and a freer batsman as a professional with Essex than he had been as an amateur with Yorkshire and England. He even forced his way into a Test trial in 1953 and did not retire until 1956 when injury, and the fact that he was nearing forty-three, caused him to cease playing and take up umpiring. He was on the first-class list until 1966.

The insistence that only an amateur with his 'spirit of adventure' was the ideal captain for a county side was against all the evidence. In 1951 the County Championship was won by Warwickshire, an all-professional side led by 'Tom' Dollery. They were, too, a team of imports with only Grove and Gardner of the regular side born within the county. There were no 'stars' in the side. No one was chosen for any of the Tests or representative matches. But they were a *team*, totally committed to each other and most intelligently and warmly led. While there was concern that in importing so many players, three of them from New Zealand, in order to bring success Warwickshire were encouraging a soccer-style transfer system, the praise for Dollery was unstinted. He was 'able to get the best out of his team both on and off the field'. He 'showed that a paid player can become a captain in the real sense of the word' and he had 'raised the status of the professional'.

The words were written by Leslie Smith as *Wisden* named Dollery one of the five cricketers of the year. The Warwickshire captain did not see himself as a messiah – he was a balanced man – but he did realise the significance of his side's achievement. 'Professionals still feel some inferiority,' he wrote, 'as was made clear when we had won the Championship by the many professionals, whether still in active cricket or retired, who hailed the victory as a great vindication of professionalism.'

Perhaps most deserving of praise was the Warwickshire committee who had appointed Dollery, backed him totally in face of veiled criticism and set winning the title as their sole purpose. They were rewarded with the biggest membership and gate receipts in the club's history.

Not all counties were so visionary. To follow Wally Hammond and Basil Allen as captain, Gloucestershire appointed Sir Derrick Bailey as captain in 1951. The son of a wealthy South African businessman, Bailey had won the DFC when serving with the Royal South African Air Force during the war. Studying at the Royal Agricultural College at Cirencester, he played a few games for Gloucestershire in 1949 and was asked to captain the side in 1951. He was not a bad cricketer and, in the first of his two seasons as skipper, he scored more than a thousand rather dour runs, but his period of captaincy delayed the inevitable. It was with great reluctance that the Gloucestershire committee agreed to the management committee's recommendation that a professional should succeed Bailey as captain. Jack Crapp led the side in 1953 and 1954, and he was succeeded by George Emmett. Tom Graveney took over in 1959 and Gloucestershire were runners-up in the Championship. The following year was a little disappointing, mainly due to a crop of injuries, including one to Graveney himself. In November 1960 an astonished cricket world heard that Graveney was being relieved of the captaincy and that the Old Etonian Tom Pugh would take over. The Gloucestershire committee old guard believed that a professional captain was causing unrest in the dressing room. In consequence, the county lost the services of one of the most graceful and powerful of batsmen. Wounded by his treatment, Graveney went to play for Worcestershire, which he served with great distinction.

Kent's problems were greater and more immediate. In the years after the Second World War they were one of the weaker counties. For three difficult seasons they were led by David Clark, later to be a tour manager and the author of a famous report. He stood down at the end of the 1951 season and was succeeded by Bill Murray-Wood. The captaincy was offered to Les Ames, but at the age of forty-six and troubled by fibrositis and a slipped disc, he declined. It was later learned that Ames had been offered the captaincy some years earlier, but only on the condition that he play as an amateur, which he refused to do.

Murray-Wood had won his blue at Oxford in 1936 and had scored a century against Gloucestershire on his first-class debut. He was a good fielder, but his leg-breaks lacked control and were expensive. Moreover, he had tended to play less and less since his first year at university. Knowledge of the game and his ability to manage the men he was to captain were not his strong points.

In fairness, the captaincy of Kent at this period was no sinecure. Tony Pawson recalled that Arthur Fagg was constantly moaning that, although he was senior professional, Clark never consulted him. Pawson tactfully approached Clark on that point, and Clark readily agreed to seek Fagg's advice on occasions. Later, Pawson passed Fagg in the field only to hear him muttering, 'Always asking me what to do. He's supposed to be the bloody captain.' Clark could handle such a situation and relationship with humour; Murray-Wood could not.

In 1952 Kent were fifteenth in the Championship; the following year, they slipped one place lower. From the start of the season things went badly, and there was great unrest among the players. In July the Kent committee asked Murray-Wood to resign. He refused on the grounds that he had been appointed for the season. By Canterbury week, the first week in August, the situation had become critical and, during the second match of the week when Kent met Middlesex, the tension had become such that it was believed that the Kent players would refuse to take the field if Murray-Wood remained as captain. The Kent committee was faced with the most difficult of problems, and they took the unprecedented step of dismissing Murray-Wood in mid-season.

Sadly, the agony did not end there. The press learned of the decision before Murray-Wood or the Kent players, and the vendors of evening papers were shouting the news at Canterbury before any official statement had been made. Having hoped for quiet and diplomacy, the Kent committee was subjected to the glare of publicity and to a period of bitterness.

Doug Wright, whose Test career had ended with the 1950–51 tour of Australia and New Zealand, was the reluctant caretaker captain.

With the county game beset by such problems, it was becoming obvious that the question as to who would succeed Freddie Brown as captain of England must soon be faced. Compton had been vice-captain in Australia and, with more than two thousand runs and eight centuries to his credit in 1951, had seemed to have regained all his old form. Hutton was not far behind him, and, appropriately at The Oval, a ground with which he was always to be associated, he had made his hundredth hundred. It was testament to Hutton's reputation and to the continued drawing-power of the truly great players that 15,000 people went to The Oval on the Monday to see him score the 39 runs he needed to complete the historic century.

Peter May, an amateur, had blazed upon the scene, but he was still at university, and the selectors turned to Nigel Howard.

Howard, of course, had bravely handled the difficult problems he encountered as captain of Lancashire. As captain of England in India in 1951–52, he faced challenges of a different nature but no less demanding. The selectors, Yardley, Wyatt, Brown and Ames, chose a party which was immediately labelled an 'England Second XI'. Of the sixteen players, only nine had appeared in Test cricket. Tattersall had played in nine Tests, Watkins seven and Robertson six. Nobody else had played in more than three. Carr, Kenyon, Howard himself, Poole, Ridgway, Spooner, and the Yorkshire leg-spinner Leadbeater, who was flown out as a replacement when Rhodes, the Derbyshire leg-spinner, had to undergo a hernia operation, all made Test debuts during the series. Of these, only Kenyon, a magnificent batsman, and Spooner played in a Test match again.

As in the first post-war tour of the Caribbean, the quality of the opposition was underestimated. From the England point of view, the main value of the tour was shown in the development and class of Graveney and in the experience given to Statham. The fourth Test match was won by the spin of the Lancashire pair Tattersall and Hilton, but neither of them took the opportunity that the Indian pitches gave them to display their craft. Hilton never played Test cricket again after this tour, while Tattersall made only two more appearances in international cricket with Laker being confirmed as England's premier off-spinner.

Watkins enjoyed a fine tour and played an innings of heroic proportions to save the first Test match. Robertson, following his outstanding domestic season in 1951, also did splendidly on the tour, but he was ever competing with Hutton, Simpson, Washbrook and now a younger generation of openers so that the Middlesex batsman, a player of great charm, passed from the international stage. So, too, virtually did Lowson, the Yorkshire opener, of whom much had been expected.

Howard developed pleurisy towards the end of the tour, and Donald Carr captained England in the final Test. India won by an innings and 8 runs. It was their twenty-fifth Test match and their first victory, yet they must have viewed drawing the rubber with mixed feelings, for they were unquestionably the stronger side throughout the series.

81

Two bowlers who might have expected to make the tour were the Yorkshiremen Bob Appleyard and Fred Trueman. Appleyard was twenty-seven years old when he made his first-class debut in 1951, and in that debut season he caused a sensation by taking 200 wickets at 14.14 runs each, a record. He bowled brisk in-swingers and off-breaks, and he disguised his pace to a marked degree. Here, surely, was a bowler to test the Australians, but illness kept him out of the game for all but one match in 1952, and he was unable to play at all in 1953. Remarkably, he returned in 1954 when he won the first of his nine Test caps.

Trueman took ninety wickets at just over 20 runs apiece in 1951 and was catching the eye of good judges of the game. 'He showed promise of developing into an unusually good fast bowler', although he often 'sacrificed accuracy and direction by not bowling within himself'. From the start, he was a character, a personality that the game needed, but for the immediate present National Service called, and a tour of India was hardly the best preparation or incentive for an up and coming fast bowler.

For the main part, the series in India had been no more than a holding action. The party was devoid of star names and 'contained few personalities'. Moreover, said Leslie Smith in the *Cricketer*, 'N.D. Howard led the side capably, despite his own disappointing form with the bat, but he did not solve one of England's most difficult problems – a leader who can hold a place on personal ability.'

India followed England back to the United Kingdom for a four-match series, but they knew that this time they would be faced by no second string. They were also having to face the fact that Mankad, one of the world's leading all-rounders, was under contract to Haslingden in the Lancashire League and would not be available for much of the tour. In the event, he played in the last three Tests.

Trevor Bailey captained MCC against the Indians, but he had lost favour with the selectors, and Watkins was the chosen all-rounder for the first three Tests with Ikin returning for the fourth after a long absence. There was concern not only regarding the captaincy, but as to the quality of cricket being played. There were constant demands for *brighter* cricket, and one national newspaper even went so far as to publish its own 'Brighter Cricket League Table' and to make awards accordingly based on how quickly counties scored their runs. Essex were frequently high in the table, but never got anywhere near winning the Championship.

Wiser heads believed that what was desperately needed was for England to be consistently successful, particularly against Australia, to recapture the Ashes and so rekindle interest in the game as Chapman's side had done in 1926.

It was generally believed that the selectors had two choices in selecting a captain of England. They could choose an experienced cricketer as captain simply for the series against India, or they could choose a younger man with a view to blooding him to lead the side against Australia the following year. Once again, this was asking for history to repeat itself, to find another Chapman. There were two candidates for the second option: Peter May and, most consistently lobbied for, David Sheppard, now in his last year at Cambridge where he was captain.

It transpired that both Compton, vice-captain under Freddie Brown though junior to Hutton in years and experience, and Hutton himself had been sounded out at the beginning of 1951 as to whether they would consider playing as amateurs with the prospect of the England captaincy as bait. Different in temperament they may have been, but they were both good, honest professionals and saw no reason for changing their status.

The selectors really now had no alternative and invited Len Hutton to captain England against India at Headingley in June 1952. Even so, the hierarchy of the game saw this as a temporary arrangement until Sheppard was ready to lead the side against Australia or even later in the series against India. Certainly, the appointment of Hutton as captain was not to the liking of all.

In *The Times* Geoffrey Green gave a balanced and realistic response:

For the first time a professional player has been chosen to captain England. Though there are many who will look back with anxious eyes and with sorrow at the passing of an age, there are yet those who will welcome the ending of an anachronism. The amateur, in the older meaning of the word, no longer truly exists. He has largely been destroyed by the economic circumstances of the mid-twentieth century. Further, to find such a man, both with the character to lead and also the quality to hold indisputably a place in an England team, has progressively become more difficult. When F.R. Brown was called on by the selectors two years ago the writing was on the wall. Brown's unqualified success, heartening though it was, solved nothing. It merely postponed the hour that was to come.

The selectors, who for some time have been struggling to balance the requirements of tradition with the needs of the moment, are to be congratulated on the action they have taken.

The pressure on Hutton must have been enormous. The eyes of the cricketing world were upon him, and he was conscious that not all were wishing him well. Many were ready to seize upon the first error of judgement, the first signs of failing in his own performance and the first hint of a breach of etiquette. He had the comfort of making his debut as captain on his home ground, and he had with him in the side a Yorkshire fast bowler making his Test debut.

Freddie Trueman was from a mining family and was twenty-one years old. He had played in a Test trial in 1950, but this had been more of a fillip to him and to give batsmen some practice against fast bowling than a real consideration of him as a Test cricketer. His cricket in 1952 was limited because of his service in the RAF, but he played in Yorkshire's earlier matches with devastating effect. He had match figures of eight for 109 against Somerset, eight for 85 against Worcestershire, five for 107 against Derbyshire and four for 86 in the Roses match at Headingley in the first month of the season. He was a quicker developer than Statham; he was quick and he was aggressive; he was chosen for the first Test. The match was a triumph for both Yorkshiremen.

Hutton lost the toss, and India batted. They were soon in trouble at 42 for three as Hutton never allowed any batsman to settle and changed his bowling intelligently, using Trueman in short bursts. India recovered nobly through Hazare and Vijay Manjrekar, who added 222. They seemed to be cruising to a big score when, suddenly, within a few minutes, three wickets fell. Evans, who always stood up to the brisk medium pace of Alec Bedser, took a brilliant catch off the under-edge of the bat as Hazare attempted to cut at the Surrey bowler. In the next over, part of Trueman's sixth spell of the day, two wickets fell. Manjrekar was splendidly caught at slip by Watkins diving low to his left, and Gopinath edged the second ball he received into his stumps.

The pitch was affected by overnight rain, and when he was finally brought into the attack Laker took the last four wickets in nine balls as 2 runs were scored.

The conditions when England batted were considerably worse than they had been for India, and Ghulam Ahmed, the off-spinner, bowled beautifully to send back Hutton, Simpson and Compton. May fell to Shinde, and England owed much to Graveney, Watkins, Evans and Jenkins, who gave the middle order a substance which had been absent for some years. England took a first innings lead of 41 for which they had had to work very hard. What followed was one of the most sensational few minutes that Test cricket has known.

Beginning their second innings on the Saturday afternoon, India lost four wickets in the first fourteen balls without a run being scored. The second ball of Trueman's opening over from the Kirkstall Lane end was

84

short, but it was fast, and Roy, attempting to hook, was caught at slip off the back of the bat. The fourth ball of Bedser's first over lifted off a length and Gaekwad was caught in the gully. The first ball of Trueman's next over, fast and straight, left Mantri floundering, and Manjrekar edged the next ball into his stumps. The crowd were stunned and elated.

Umrigar fell to Jenkins at 26, but Hazare and Phadkar then added 105 in a manner which mocked what had gone before. Ten minutes before the close of play, Hutton recalled Trueman, and he beat Hazare for sheer pace. Jenkins's leg-breaks soon brought the innings to an end on the Monday, and England won their first Test under Hutton shortly after three o'clock on the fourth day.

Trueman took eight wickets in the Lord's Test, which England won comfortably on the last morning in front of a small crowd who had been admitted free. Hutton scored 150, and Evans scored 104 out of 159 put on with Graveney for the sixth wicket in 130 minutes. Evans had earlier made his hundredth Test dismissal when he stumped Shinde off Watkins, a spectacular piece of wicket-keeping. Mankad played heroically for India, but England won by eight wickets.

Eight days before the second Test, at Lord's on Wednesday 11 June 1952, Denis Compton hit 107 for Middlesex against Northamptonshire. It was his hundredth first-class hundred. Thereafter his form declined, and he asked to be omitted from the last two Tests of the series against India. It is interesting to recall what loss of form was for Denis Compton for he finished the season with 1,880 runs and 77 wickets. He also held twenty-six catches.

England made several changes for the Old Trafford Test. Sheppard came in for Simpson, Ikin for Compton and Lock, making his debut, for Jenkins.

Showers limited play on the first day, and the weather was cold and drab on the second, at the end of which England were 292 for seven, Hutton having completed his second century in successive Tests. May and Evans, in contrasting styles, were also impressive, and Hutton declared thirty-five minutes into the third morning.

In the three and three-quarter hours that followed, India were bowled out twice, the first Test side to be dismissed twice in a day. They were shattered by the pace of Trueman in the first innings. Not only had he now found more control, but he was quicker and more inventive than he had been at the beginning of the series. The search was over. England had found a fast bowler.

They had found, too, a fielding side that exceeded in quality any eleven that they had selected since the war. Lock's first contribution to Test cricket was to hold a magnificent catch at short-leg to dismiss

85

Mankad off Bedser. The next six wickets went to Trueman, who was supported by some outstanding close catching. The second innings saw Trueman take the first wicket and Bedser and Lock do the rest.

At The Oval Hutton and Sheppard scored 143 for England's first wicket, Sheppard making 119, and Bedser and Trueman took five wickets each as India, now totally demoralised by the pair, were shot out for 98. Rain prevented Hutton from leading England to four victories in four matches. He had finished the series as leading batsman, 399 runs, average 79.80, and his captaincy had won plaudits from unexpected quarters. 'Billy' Griffith felt that he had 'handled the team with admirable skill both on and off the field, and there is no doubt that his tactical appreciation is exceptionally sound.'

Trueman had twenty-nine wickets at 13.31, and Bedser twenty at 13.95 in the four-match series. England had not felt so confident about meeting Australia for many years.

Hutton Leads England for the First Time
England v India at Headingley
5, 6, 7 and 9 June 1952

India First Innings		Second Innings	
P. Roy st Evans, b Jenkins	19	c Compton b Trueman	0
D.K. Gaekwad b Bedser	9	c Laker b Bedser	0
P.R. Umrigar c Evans b Trueman	8	(4) c and b Jenkins	9
V.S. Hazare (capt) c Evans b Bedser	89	(6) b Trueman	56
V.L. Manjrekar c Watkins b Trueman	133	b Trueman	0
D.G. Phadkar c Watkins b Laker	12	(7) b Bedser	64
C.D. Gopinath b Trueman	0	(8) lbw b Jenkins	0
†M.K. Mantri not out	13	(3) b Trueman	0
G.S. Ramchand c Watkins b Laker	0	st Evans b Jenkins	0
S.G. Shinde c May b Laker	2	not out	7
Ghulam Ahmed b Laker	0	st Evans b Jenkins	14
Extras (b 1, lb 7)	8	(lb 5, w 1, nb 1)	7
Total	293		165

BOWLING	Overs	Mdns	Runs	Wkts	Overs	Mdns	Runs	Wkts
Bedser	33	13	38	2	21	9	32	2
Trueman	26	6	89	3	9	1	27	4
Laker	22.3	9	39	4	13	4	17	–
Watkins	11	1	21	–	11	2	32	–
Jenkins	27	6	78	1	13	2	50	4
Compton	7	1	20	–	–	–	–	–

fall of wickets
1–18, 2–40, 3–42, 4–264, 5–264, 6–264, 7–291, 8–291, 9–293
1–0, 2–0, 3–0, 4–0, 5–26, 6–131, 7–143, 8–143, 9–143

England First Innings		*Second Innings*	
L. Hutton (capt) c Ramchand,			
b Ghulam	10	b Phadkar	10
R.T. Simpson c Ramchand b Ghulam	23	c Mantri b Ghulam	51
P.B.H. May b Shinde	16	c Phadkar b Ghulam	4
D.C.S. Compton c Ramchand			
b Ghulam	14	not out	35
T.W. Graveney b Ghulam	71	not out	20
A.J. Watkins lbw b Ghulam	48		
†T.G. Evans lbw b Hazare	66		
R.O. Jenkins c Mantri b Ramchand	38		
J.C. Laker b Phadkar	15		
A.V. Bedser b Ramchand	7		
F.S. Trueman not out	0		
Extras (b 15, lb 11)	26	(b 4, lb 3, nb 1)	8
Total	334		128

BOWLING	Overs	Mdns	Runs	Wkts	Overs	Mdns	Runs	Wkts
Phadkar	24	7	54	1	11	2	21	1
Ramchand	36.2	11	61	2	17	3	43	–
Ghulam								
Ahmed	63	24	100	5	22	8	37	2
Hazare	20	9	22	1	3	–	11	–
Shinde	22	5	71	1	2	–	8	–

fall of wickets
1–21, 2–48, 3–62, 4–92, 5–182, 6–211, 7–290, 8–325, 9–329
1–16, 2–42, 3–89
umpires – H.G. Baldwin and H. Elliott
England won by 7 wickets

Trueman's Match
England v India at Old Trafford
17, 18 and 19 July 1952

England First Innings	
L. Hutton (capt) c Sen b Divecha	104
D.S. Sheppard lbw b Ramchand	34
J.T. Ikin c Divecha b Ghulam	29
P.B.H. May c Sen b Mankad	69

T.W. Graveney lbw b Divecha 14
A.J. Watkins c Phadkar b Mankad . 4
†T.G. Evans c and b Ghulam 71
J.C. Laker c Sen b Divecha 0
A.V. Bedser c Phadkar b Ghulam .. 17
G.A.R. Lock not out 1
F.S. Trueman
    Extras (b 2, lb 2) 4

    Total for 9 wickets dec. 347

BOWLING	Overs	Mdns	Runs	Wkts
Phadkar	22	10	30	–
Divecha	45	12	102	3
Ramchand	33	7	78	1
Mankad	28	9	67	2
Ghulam Ahmed	9	3	43	3
Hazare	7	3	23	–

fall of wickets
1–78, 2–133, 3–214, 4–248, 5–252, 6–284, 7–292, 8–336, 9–347

India	First Innings		Second Innings	
M.H. Mankad c Lock b Bedser	4	lbw b Bedser	6
P. Roy c Hutton b Trueman	0	c Laker b Trueman	0
H.R. Adhikari c Graveney b Trueman	0	c May b Lock	27
V.S. Hazare (capt) b Bedser	16	c Ikin b Lock	16
P.R. Umrigar b Trueman	4	c Watkins b Bedser	3
D.G. Phadkar c Sheppard b Trueman	0	b Bedser	5
V.L. Manjrekar c Ikin b Trueman ..	22	c Evans b Bedser	0
R.V. Divecha b Trueman	4	b Bedser	2
G.S. Ramchand c Graveney b Trueman	3	c Watkins b Lock	1
†P. Sen c Lock b Trueman	4	not out	13
Ghulam Ahmed not out	1	c Ikin b Lock	0
Extras (lb 1)	1	(b 8, nb 1)	9
Total	58	....	82

BOWLING	Overs	Mdns	Runs	Wkts	Overs	Mdns	Runs	Wkts
Bedser	11	4	19	2	15	6	27	5
Trueman	8.4	2	31	8	8	5	9	1
Laker	2	–	7	–	–	–	–	–
Watkins	–	–	–	–	4	3	1	–
Lock	–	–	–	–	9.3	2	36	4

fall of wickets
1–4, 2–4, 3–5, 4–17, 5–17, 6–45, 7–51, 8–53, 9–53
1–7, 2–7, 3–55, 4–59, 5–66, 6–66, 7–66, 8–67, 9–77
umpires – D. Davies and F.S. Lee
England won by an innings and 207 runs

There has long been a view that England are strong only when Yorkshire are strong. One would dispute that belief and suggest that England are strong when one particular county is strong and dominant. In 1942 Stuart Surridge was appointed captain of Surrey.

Surridge was an amateur, but he was not an Oxbridge man. He was in a family business famous for making bats and cricket equipment. He had learned his trade the hard way, for although his grandfather had founded the firm in the nineteenth century, and it had been passed from father to son, Stuart was expected to start at the bottom and to learn every aspect of the firm's work. He had been brought up on the creed that you do not know how to give orders until you have learned how to take them.

He had played for Young Surrey before the Second World War and made his first-team debut in 1947. By 1950, he was a regular in the side, and he had earned his place on merit. He was a tall medium-pace bowler who could swing the ball appreciably, a very hard-hitting batsman and a brilliant fielder. He took 506 wickets in his career, and if he had not been so unselfish, he would have taken many more, but he believed that those who played the game to earn a living needed encouragement, and when there was a chance of cheap wickets it was the professionals who were given that chance.

Surridge always insisted that he learned much from Brian Sellers, another 'professional amateur', who led Yorkshire through their glorious period in the 1930s. Of Sellers, he said, 'He was tough. He was hard. He stood no nonsense, and he led by example. He wouldn't ask anyone to field closer to the bat than he was prepared to field himself.' The same description aptly fitted Surridge himself, as did Sellers's maxim that you got nothing for being second.

He had grown up with most of the Surrey players, and when he was asked to captain the side he told the committee that Surrey would win the Championship for the next three years. He was wrong. They won it for five years under Surridge, a record that is never likely to be equalled, and two under Peter May. Is it merely coincidental that during that period England did not lose a Test series?

89

The Surrey fielding had been considered competent, but Surridge transformed it until it reached a standard which few sides have been able to emulate. *Wisden* remarked on his own contribution in the field. His dynamism resulted 'in the acceptance of some catches which might be regarded by many cricketers as impossible'. He, Lock and the others 'exerted an unnerving effect upon opposing batsmen'. They became afraid to hit the ball, succumbing to the pressure, the feeling of being attacked on all fronts.

The bowling, of course, was magnificent, and it is true to say that no county has ever fielded a better attack. Alec Bedser, Peter Loader (who played regularly from 1952 onwards, first as replacement when Bedser was on Test duty) and Surridge shared the new ball. Laker, Lock and Eric Bedser did the spinning. In the five-year period under Surridge, this sextet captured 2,163 wickets at little over 17 runs each. These are phenomenal figures for six bowlers in the same side, and they relate only to the Championship. Alec Bedser, Loader, Lock and Laker also took wickets for England.

The dynamic approach in the field gave Surrey a true team spirit. Surrey players enjoyed their cricket, and they enjoyed playing for each other. The batsmen were never required to get big scores, simply the amount that was required, one run more than the other side. There was flair, personality, dedication, hard work and an instinct for the game. The Oval bubbled, and the crowds came to see them. Cricketers in other counties all wanted the Surrey match for their benefit match.

There were some sensational victories, most notably one over Worcestershire at The Oval in August 1954. Rain had affected the wicket and the start was delayed until two o'clock when Surridge won the toss and asked the visitors to bat first. Lock took five for 2 in thirty-three balls and they were bowled out for 25 in 100 minutes. Surrey lost three wickets for 77, but Worcestershire had no spinners of the class of Laker and Lock, and when Barrington joined May it seemed that Surrey would build a big lead. To the amazement of batsmen and spectators, Surridge declared before five-thirty with the score on 92. Surrey captured two wickets before the close, and the game was over within an hour on the second morning as Laker and Alec Bedser were principally responsible for dismissing Worcestershire for 40.

Surrey had won by an innings and 27 runs a match in which they had only scored 92. There were those who thought Surridge was mad, but then that is an opinion that many have of those who are visionaries.

Surridge played three times for the Gentlemen against the Players, but it was not a fixture he enjoyed or supported. His heart was with Surrey, and he left representative cricket to others. He believed the

Hutton and Washbrook, England's post-war opening pair. Hutton went on to become England's first professional captain. His record as Test batsman and England captain were second to none.

The Middlesex Marvels, Edrich and Compton, broke all records in 1947. No batsmen have given people more pleasure.

Don Bradman waves his hat as his Australian team of 1948 arrive at Tilbury. Arguably, Bradman led the strongest side ever to come to England.

The Australian tour of 1948 begins. Bradman and A.F.T. White, the Worcestershire captain, toss in front of the Pavilion at Worcester.

Australia take the field. Bradman, Hassett and Toshack lead the way in the opening match at Worcester, April, 1948.

Charlie Palmer, later an England player and manager, and Edwin Cooper go out to face the music for Worcestershire against the Australians, 1948. The pair shared a brave second wicket stand of 137.

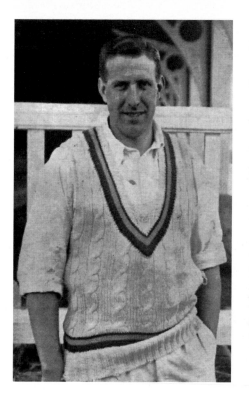

Arthur Fagg, a sound opening batsman for Kent before and after the Second World War, and later a controversial Test umpire.

George Mann, Middlesex, followed in his father's footsteps in becoming captain of England. A popular skipper, he led the side in South Africa and at home to New Zealand in 1949.

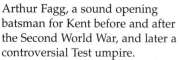

England's final indignity, all out for 52 against Australia and The Oval, 1948. Hutton was last man out for 30. He fell to a brilliant catch by Tallon off Lindwall. Hollies is the batsman at the non-striker's end.

Edrich is caught by Gomez off Valentine in the first Test between England and West Indies at Old Trafford, 1950. Valentine took 11 wickets in this match, but England won, only for West Indies to take the remaining three matches in the series.

Doug Wright, Kent and England, an erratic genius as a leg-break bowler. Wright later stated that he believed he tried to bowl too fast in the post-war period.

Back injury prevented Les Ames from keeping wicket after the war, but he reached 102 centuries before retiring in 1951. He was the first professional to become a Test selector.

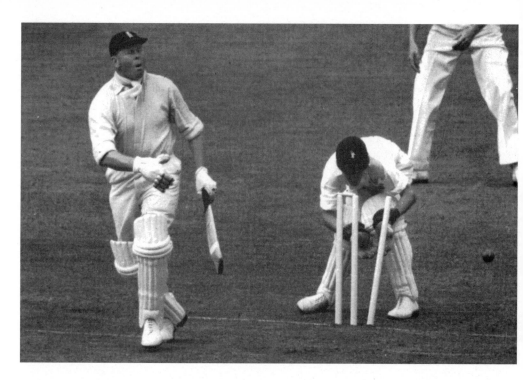

Veteran Freddie Brown led England in Australia in 1950-51, and won one Test match, England's first victory over Australia since 1938. He led England to success in the series against South Africa in 1951, but here he has his stumps shattered by a ball from Chubb, at Lord's.

The County Championship was dominated by the great Surrey side in the 1950s. Jack Young of Middlesex is bowled by Jim Laker. McIntyre is the wicket-keeper.

The Surrey side of the 1950s was always capable of scoring 'enough' runs according to skipper Stuart Surridge. Tom Clark gets a ball away against Middlesex. Leslie Compton is the keeper, Edrich is in pursuit and Jack Robertson turns and looks. Peter May is the non-striking batsman.

Godfrey Evans, England's great wicket-keeper of the immediate post-war period, stumps Morris off Laker in the fourth Test of the 1953 'Ashes' series.

England regain the 'Ashes', 1953. Compton pulls Morris to the boundary.

The emergence of Trevor Bailey as an all-rounder of international quality was a vital factor in England's success in the 1950s.

Gentlemen and Players match to be an anachronism.

Surprisingly, May and Alec Bedser were the only Surrey players in the side for the first Test when the Australians arrived in 1953. Tattersall was the off-spinner and Wardle the left-arm spinner. The selectors remained the same – Ames, Wyatt, Yardley and Brown – but Brown had taken over as chairman. Suddenly, it was as if the triumphs of the previous season were being discounted. Hutton was named as captain for the first Test only, and Trueman was not included in the side.

Still serving in the RAF, Trueman played a little at the start of the season and failed to take a wicket in the Test trial, where his bowling was erratic. In spite of this, there were many who felt that his record against the Indians should have been enough to convince the selectors that he was the fast bowler so much needed by England.

The first Test at Trent Bridge was ruined by bad weather. A truncated first day ended with Australia on 157 for three. Hassett completed his century on the Friday, but Australia lost their last seven wickets for 12 runs. Bedser finished with seven for 55; Bailey had two for 75. By the end of the day, Bailey was at the crease as England had crashed to 92 for six. Lindwall remained a force.

England finally trailed by 105, but some outstanding bowling by Bedser, who finished with match figures of fourteen for 99, gave every hope of victory. Needing 229 to win, England ended the Saturday with 42 for the loss of Kenyon, but rain prevented any further play until 4.30 on the Tuesday. Hutton and Simpson scored 78 more runs and the match was drawn.

Perhaps the selectors were too much in awe of Australia, for they made three changes for the Lord's Test, and one of them was to bring in Watson for May. May had come through his trial period as a Test-match batsman with flying colours. He had proved himself technically and temperamentally, and it was a travesty that he should be dropped after one failure. He had batted in near darkness on the Friday evening and had been given out caught behind for 9 although, as he was to claim years later, he did not touch the ball. Another change saw Statham replace Simpson while the third brought in Brown for Tattersall.

It was announced that his fellow-selectors had persuaded Brown to play on the grounds that Australia could be susceptible to leg-spin. Certainly, leg-break bowling in England was becoming a dying art as the talents of Jenkins, Hollies and Wright began to fade. There had been a time when to send an England side into the field without a leg-spinner was unthinkable.

The problem regarding Brown's inclusion was that it was seen in some quarters as a vote of no confidence in Hutton or at least as a way in which a senior could keep an eye on the England captain. This view was not weakened by Brown's statement that he was happy to play under Hutton or by Hutton's statement that he was content to have Brown in the side.

There was another century for Hassett on the opening day at Lord's and, on the second day, Bedser became the first England bowler to take 200 Test wickets, while the pressure on Hutton became obvious. He missed three straightforward chances, and one of his dropped catches brought him a bruised thumb which needed dressing-room repairs. Redemption came by the end of the day: having lost Kenyon for three, England were 177 for one, Hutton 87, Graveney 78.

The Saturday was as bathed in sunshine as the first two days had been, but the day began disastrously for England with Lindwall yorking Graveney before a run had been scored. Compton, anxious to prove himself after a series of failures, joined Hutton to face Lindwall and Miller at their best with the new ball. Hutton and Compton triumphed. They added 102 before Hutton, having batted with classical elegance and command for five and a quarter hours, hitting sixteen fours, was caught in the leg-trap by Hole off Johnston for 145. It was his fifth and last hundred against Australia.

At lunch England were 287 for three and riding high. Only 59 runs separated the two sides. Disappointment followed. Watson was stumped when the ball rebounded off the wicket-keeper's pads. Compton misjudged a leg-break from Benaud, and the pace of Lindwall was too much for the remainder as the last five wickets went down for 44 runs. England's lead had been restricted to 26.

Hassett was soon caught behind off Statham, but Morris and Miller took Australia to 96 on the Saturday evening. The batsmen continued in their adopted roles on the Monday. Morris played the strokes; Miller, uncharacteristically, offered solid defence alone. Hutton's misery in the field followed him into Australia's second innings. With his score on 82, Morris cut Wardle into the hands of the England captain, who put down the easy chance. It proved not to be too costly, for Compton was tried for a couple of overs before the new ball was taken and Morris skied him to leg where Statham took a fine tumbling catch.

At lunch Australia were 209 for two, but England captured five wickets in the afternoon session as 96 were scored. One of the wickets to fall was that of Miller, bowled by the accurate Wardle for 109. In the final session of the day, Lindwall hit 50 out of 63 in three-quarters of an hour. Brown finished with four wickets, and England faced a target of 343.

An hour of the fourth day remained when England began their innings, and it was to be a dreadful hour for them. Lindwall had Kenyon caught at mid-on and Hutton taken at slip. Langley took a thrilling diving catch off Johnston to get rid of Graveney, and England were 12 for three. Compton and Watson added 8 runs before the close, but there was gloom over England. Defeat seemed imminent, and Watson could have been caught off Ring in the closing minutes of the day.

Thousands of people had been turned away on the first four days; the final day saw a crowd of 14,000 to watch the last rites. There was a strange lack of urgency about Australia's early play as neither Lindwall nor Johnston seemed at their most aggressive. The weather was fine, the pitch dusty and helpful to leg-spin. Ring bowled well, as did Benaud, a cricketer new to England.

Compton seemed to be settling. He put the 50 up, and he twice drove Benaud through the covers to the Tavern boundary, but ninety-five minutes into the morning he was leg-before to Johnston. Bailey joined Watson at 12.43. At lunch, 1.30 in those days, England were 116 for four: Watson, who had enjoyed some luck, 54 and Bailey 10.

Bailey batted with the straightest of bats and the most vigilant of defences, nose right over the ball. Watson, too, met the ball with the full face of the bat. Lindwall and Miller attacked them fiercely with the second new ball in mid-afternoon. Three times Bailey was hit on the hand. He paused only to shake the hand before taking his guard again. Watson swayed to avoid a Miller bouncer and the danger was passed. Forty minutes of hostile bowling had allowed only 12 runs, but Watson and Bailey were still together.

The defiance of the batsmen had infected the crowd, who began to cheer every defensive stroke. Bailey, in particular, had imposed a discipline upon himself by which he treated the ball as if it were an offending wasp, smothering it with anger and contempt.

Having batted for five and three-quarter hours, Watson's innings of 109 came to an end. It was 5.50, forty minutes before the close, and he and Bailey had added 163 in one of the greatest rearguard actions Test cricket has ever known. Watson was to play in twenty-three Tests and average under 26, yet he stamped his name indelibly on the history of the game by his innings at Lord's on the last day of June 1953.

Five minutes after the fall of Watson, Bailey, to his own annoyance, lost concentration and drove at Ring only to give a simple catch to Benaud. He had batted for more than four and a quarter hours and hit 71. Defence was not his natural game in county cricket, but he gave England whatever was needed, and that day he earned the sobriquet 'Barnacle'. At 246 for six, with thirty-five minutes left, England still had

93

problems, for the ball was lifting and turning sharply. Brown threw caution to the wind and hit lustily, making 28 before falling to Benaud with four balls remaining. Wardle played rigid forward defence to those four balls, and England had earned a draw that was greeted as a national victory.

Watson and Bailey were acclaimed everywhere. Brown returned to his duties as a selector and announced that he would retire from first-class cricket at the end of the season. Hutton was subjected to a subtle press campaign which suggested that too much was being expected of him. He was being asked to open, to be England's leading run-getter and to captain the side. Was that not too great a responsibility? Sheppard was scoring a host of runs for Sussex, but he was not in the side. Bailey and Simpson, now captain of Nottinghamshire, could also be considered as contenders for the leadership.

The strange thing was that Australia had expected to have to face a brave new England, but they were confronted by the old guard. After three years in 'exile' Edrich, like Hutton himself now thirty-seven years old, was recalled for the Old Trafford Test in place of Kenyon while Simpson and Laker came in for Brown and Statham. The match was ruined by rain. There was another five-wicket haul for Bedser and a century by Harvey as Australia made 318 which spread into the third day. There was no play on the fourth day, and England were bowled out for 276. One hour remained when Australia began their second innings on a treacherous pitch which saw the ball jumping and turning spitefully. When stumps were drawn they were 35 for eight, Wardle having taken four for 7 in five overs. The Australians had revealed their weakness against good bowling in adverse conditions. England no longer had anything to fear. The supermen had vanished.

Wardle lost his place for the Headingley Test, for Lock, who had missed much of the season through injury, was fit again. Hassett won the toss for the fourth time, but he asked England to bat first. They scored only 142 runs off ninety-six overs on the opening day, which was shortened by twenty-five minutes. The last three wickets realised another 25 runs on the second morning. In contrast, Australia scored briskly and were all out for 266 just before the close of the second day, which ended with Bedser dismissing Langley to give him figures of six for 95 and the record number of wickets in Test cricket, surpassing Grimmett's 216.

Only 100 minutes' play was possible on the Saturday, and rain cut a large chunk out of Monday's play when Compton and Edrich added a valuable 77 in 135 minutes. England began the last day on 177 for five, but Compton could not resume his innings because of an injured hand.

Evans was soon out, but Laker hit some crisp drives in his 48 out of 57 in 110 minutes.

Compton, having received an injection, did not have to bat until after lunch when he came in at the fall of Laker's wicket. He scored only one more run, but he lasted another twenty-five minutes, an invaluable contribution. Once more, the batting hero was Trevor Bailey, who was last out, caught at slip off Davidson, for 38. He had occupied 262 minutes and done much to frustrate Australia's chances of victory, for when they batted a second time they needed 177 runs in 115 minutes.

To their credit, they went for the runs. Lock opened the bowling with Bedser and 20 runs came in nine minutes. Hassett chopped on to Lock, and Morris, having scored 38, was stumped off Laker with the score on 54, made in forty-eight minutes. Hole and Harvey added 57 in half an hour, and when Davidson joined Hole 66 were wanted in forty-five minutes, a seemingly simple task. Bailey, who had been kept out of the attack after his batting vigil, was brought on to save England. He adopted leg theory, had Hole caught at square-leg by Graveney, stifled the batsmen and conceded only 9 runs in six overs. Australia finished 30 short of their target, and the sides went to The Oval all square. A sixth day was added to the final Test in the hope that a result could be obtained.

Hutton had survived the series as captain, and the selectors adopted a more liberal policy for the deciding Test. Peter May came in for Simpson, and Freddie Trueman played his first match of the series in place of fellow Yorkshireman Watson. The inclusion of May and Trueman to join Lock and Laker immediately raised the standard of the fielding, and it was apparent from the outset that Trueman's pace gave Australia problems that they had not encountered earlier in the series. Hasset won the toss and Australia, who went into the match without a genuine spinner in their side, went in to bat.

It took England an hour to break the opening partnership. Morris, totally deceived by Bedser's movement, offered no stroke and turned his back on the ball to be leg-before. Bailey immediately captured the valuable wicket of Miller who, like Morris, was deceived and offered no stroke. At lunch, Australia were 98 for two, and light rain in the interval seemed to enliven the pitch. Hassett groped forward to Bedser and was caught behind, and in the next over Harvey hooked Trueman for Hutton to take a good catch running back from short square-leg.

There was a brief shower, and on the resumption de Courcy, a batsman of great charm who did not do himself justice in this his only series, flashed at Trueman and was well caught by Evans. Hole was

95

positive, and Archer defensive, but both fell at the same score. Hole gave Evans his third catch, and Archer gave Bedser a gentle return catch. This proved to be Bedser's last wicket of the series, but it was his thirty-ninth and so he established a record for England–Australia series. By mid-afternoon, Australia were 160 for seven on an easy-paced pitch.

Lindwall gave a fine display of hitting as he made 62 in 110 minutes with eight fours before being last out. The last three wickets realised 115 runs, but England could still be content with their day's work. Australia had been bowled out on the first day for 275.

In two overs before the close, England scored 1 run, and Hutton had his cap dislodged by a Lindwall bouncer.

With thousands locked outside, England began well on the Monday. Edrich fell to Lindwall at 37, but Hutton and May, the present and the future, scored 100 in 140 minutes. All seemed to be going well, but May was out and Hutton suddenly lost his way before succumbing to Johnston, who bowled slow left-arm to good effect. Tea arrived with England on 165 for three, and the new ball due.

It had not been taken when Compton, who batted poorly, was caught down the leg side. When it was taken, Graveney went to a brilliant slip catch. Evans chose to attack, and he twice hooked Lindwall for four, but Davidson surprisingly stopped a vicious pull off Johnston, and Evans slipped as he was sent back and was run out. Bailey had been defensive in the main, but he now cut loose and hit 11 in an over from Johnston. Laker fell to Miller, and the day ended with Bailey 33, Lock 4, and England 235 for seven.

The fourth ball of Lindwall's second over on the third morning ended Lock's innings, caught off his glove at short-leg, and Australia were very much in control. Trueman gave Bailey good support as 25 were added, but England still trailed by 13 when Bedser joined the Essex all-rounder. The last pair stayed together until the stroke of lunch and added 44, so giving a first-innings lead of 31 which was a totally unexpected bonus. Bailey, finally bowled when he went forward to Archer, had played another masterly innings which lasted three and three-quarter hours and was as valuable to England as had been his knocks at Lord's and Headingley.

Hutton read the pitch well. It had been subjected to the heavy roller at Hassett's instruction, and it was of no encouragement to pace. With the score on 19, Hutton turned to his spinners. Laker bowled round the wicket and trapped Hassett leg-before with the last ball of his first over. After another hour's play Australia had slumped to 61 for five. In the last fourteen minutes of that hour, four wickets went down as 2 runs were scored. Hole was leg-before as he attempted to attack Laker, and Lock, bowling with supreme accuracy, knocked back Harvey's off stump and had Morris leg-before, while Laker had Miller taken at short-leg.

Typically, Australia responded with aggression, but de Courcy was brilliantly run out by Bailey from mid-wicket. Archer hit Lock for six, Davidson took four and six off successive balls from Laker, and Australia went to tea at 131 for six.

After the break Laker concentrated on a leg-side attack, and Lock on an off-side attack. Bedser bowled a steadying spell. When Lindwall was caught on the pavilion fence off Laker the last four wickets had fallen for 31 after tea, and England needed 132 to regain the Ashes.

There were fifty minutes of the third day left when Hutton and Edrich began England's task. Perhaps under tension with his goal in sight, Hutton ran himself out when he went for a second run, unwisely, as de Courcy fumbled the ball. There were no more alarms, and England ended the day on 38 for one as the nation held its breath.

Progress was slow on the fourth day. There was no need for hurry, and 24 runs came in the first hour. Lindwall, bowling mostly to contain, was twice hooked for four by Edrich when he tried bouncers while May cover drove with great authority. May was taken at leg-slip after a second-wicket stand worth 64, and the 'twins' were now together. At lunch England were 101 for two.

At seven minutes to three, Compton played his famous sweep and sent a ball from Morris to the boundary to give England victory and to recover the Ashes after a period of three days under nineteen years. Never had they been away from England for so long, and there were scenes of jubilation. This was the year of the Coronation, the conquest of Everest and, incidentally, the birth of Graham Gooch. England had come out of the wilderness.

There were many heroes, not least Bedser, Bailey and Hutton himself, but the immediate task was to face the West Indies in the Caribbean. Sir Pelham Warner chaired the MCC committee which chose the party for the winter tour, and although he was known to be hostile to the idea of a professional captain, there was no option but to invite Hutton to lead the party in view of the recent success of the England side under his leadership. The side virtually chose itself. Of those who had appeared against Australia, Tattersall, Kenyon, Simpson, Edrich and, of course, Brown did not make the trip. Alec Bedser, too, was omitted, but this was in order to give the great bowler a rest after several years of considerable endeavour.

England Regain the Ashes
England v Australia at The Oval
15, 17, 18 and 19 August 1953

Australia First Innings		Second Innings	
A.L. Hassett (capt) c Evans b Bedser	53	lbw b Laker	10
A.R. Morris lbw b Bedser	16	lbw b Lock	26
K.R. Miller lbw b Bailey	1	(5) c Trueman b Laker ..	0
R.N. Harvey c Hutton b Trueman .	36	b Lock	1
G.B. Hole c Evans b Trueman	37	(3) lbw b Laker	17
J.H. de Courcy c Evans b Trueman	5	run out	4
R.G. Archer c and b Bedser	10	c Edrich b Lock	49
A.K. Davidson c Edrich b Laker ...	22	b Lock	21
R.R. Lindwall c Evans b Trueman .	62	c Compton b Laker	12
†G.R.A. Langley c Edrich b Lock ..	18	c Trueman b Lock	2
W.A. Johnston not out	9	not out	6
Extras (b 4, nb 2)	6	(b 11, lb 3)	14
Total	275	....	162

BOWLING	Overs	Mdns	Runs	Wkts	Overs	Mdns	Runs	Wkts
Bedser	29	3	88	3	11	2	24	–
Trueman	24.3	3	86	4	2	1	4	–
Bailey	14	3	42	1	–	–	–	–
Lock	9	2	19	1	21	9	45	5
Laker	5	–	34	1	16.5	2	75	4

fall of wickets
1–38, 2–41, 3–107, 4–107, 5–118, 6–160, 7–160, 8–207, 9–245
1–23, 2–59, 3–60, 4–61, 5–61, 6–85, 7–135, 8–140, 9–144

England First Innings		Second Innings	
L. Hutton (capt) b Johnston	82	run out	17
W.J. Edrich lbw b Lindwall	21	not out	55
P.B.H. May c Archer b Johnston ...	39	c Davidson b Miller	37
D.C.S. Compton c Langley b Lindwall	16	not out	22
T.W. Graveney c Miller b Lindwall	4		
T.E. Bailey b Archer	64		
†T.G. Evans run out	28		
J.C. Laker c Langley b Miller	1		
G.A.R. Lock c Davidson b Lindwall	4		
F.S. Trueman b Johnston	10		
A.V. Bedser not out	22		
Extras (b 9, lb 5, w 1)	15	(lb 1)	1
Total	306	....	132

BOWLING	Overs	Mdns	Runs	Wkts	Overs	Mdns	Runs	Wkts
Lindwall	32	7	70	4	21	5	46	–
Miller	34	12	65	1	11	3	24	1
Johnston	45	16	94	3	29	14	52	–
Davidson	10	1	26	–	–	–	–	–
Archer	10.3	2	25	1	1	1	0	–
Hole	11	6	11	–	–	–	–	–
Hassett	–	–	–	–	1	–	4	–
Morris	–	–	–	–	0.5	–	5	–

fall of wickets
1–37, 2–137, 3–154, 4–167, 5–170, 6–210, 7–225, 8–237, 9–262
1–24, 2–88
umpires – D. Davies and F.S. Lee
England won by 8 wickets

A tour of the Caribbean has never been an easy task for any team.
There has always been inter-island rivalry, and West Indies are united
really only in cricket. There was an insistence that local umpires
should officiate in the Tests, which meant that Burke and Ewart stood
in both Tests at Sabina Park, but six different officials stood in the
other three matches. The pressure on these umpires was enormous.
The wife and son of Burke were physically attacked after he had given
out Holt, a Jamaican batsman, leg-before when six short of his century
at Sabina Park. When McWatt was given run out after sharing an
eighth-wicket stand of 99 with Holt in the third Test in Georgetown, a
section of the crowd bombarded the England fielders with bottles and
other missiles.

With umpires facing such intimidation, it was only human that they
should err in favour of the home side in their decisions, and it was
equally human that the England players should resent what they saw as
bias. Unfortunately, one or two of the less experienced England cricketers made their discontent all too obvious.

The man to receive most criticism was Fred Trueman, arguably the
'Gazza' of his day. In his review of the tour Reg Hayter put the blame for
much of Trueman's behaviour at Hutton's door:

Earlier and firmer handling of the most recalcitrant member, the fiery
Trueman, might have avoided several situations, but, anxious not to
dim the spark of Trueman's hostility and aggressiveness, Hutton
probably waited too long before calling his lively colt to heel.
Potentially Trueman remained a fast bowler of whom England could

99

expect stirring deeds, but first he required to harness his temper solely to his fast bowling.

There were other pressures and problems for the England captain. There was a growing movement towards independence among the Caribbean colonies, and English residents in the West Indies were constantly impressing upon the MCC party the need to win at all costs. The series was stupidly labelled in some areas of the press as the 'cricket championship of the world'.

Against this backdrop, Hutton had to lead England on tour for the first time. To add to his burden, the appointed manager for the party was C.H. Palmer, a man of intelligence and charm, who was, however, acting as a tour-manager for the first time and was asked to be player-manager. As Hayter commented, the idea was not one to be commended: 'In such trying circumstances as existed in 1954 the manager required to know exactly where his authority and duties began and ended.'

When one considers the organisation and events of the tour, Hutton's achievements at the end of it were quite remarkable. He was ably assisted by his vice-captain Bailey, as reliable as ever, by Compton, who showed a good return to form, and by the maturing May.

There were two newcomers in the party, Alan Moss, the Middlesex pace bowler, and Ken Suttle, the Sussex left-hander. Moss played in the first Test, but Suttle, who might have solved the problem as to who was to open with Hutton, was never to appear in Test cricket. It was strange in view of previous and later tour parties that Hutton was the only recognised opener in the sixteen.

The tour began with a very good victory over Jamaica. Watson opened with Hutton, scored 161, and was selected for the first Test. England collapsed in their first innings and were beaten by 140 runs although, needing 457 to win after Stollmeyer did not force the follow on, they began the last day at 227 for two. Watson had hit 116.

Statham bowled very well, but there was concern about Lock, who became the first bowler for fifty-six years to be no-balled for throwing in a Test match. When the side moved to Barbados Lock was no-balled three times in a day. It was Lock's faster ball that was the offending delivery, and he discarded it for the rest of the tour, thereby reducing his effectiveness, for he had lost an element of surprise.

In the Barbados Test Palmer, in his only Test appearance, replaced Trueman, and England were crushed for a second time. Walcott hit a double century, Ramadhin and Valentine again perplexed England, who, with Compton scoring 93, came close to saving the game until the last seven wickets went down for 55 runs.

Wardle came in for Palmer when the sides met for the third time, at Bourda. Hutton won the toss for the first time in eight Tests, and he himself hit 169 and shared a third-wicket stand of 150 with Compton. Statham bowled well, and England won by nine wickets, Watson finishing the match with a six. The match became notorious for the cascade of missiles after umpire Menzies, who was also the groundsman, had ruled McWatt run out.

Some of the players were fortunate to escape injury, and the President of the British Guiana Cricket Association came on to the field and suggested to Hutton that he and his players should retreat to the pavilion. Hutton declined, preferring to remain on the field and try to capture another wicket. His bravery was rewarded, and the next morning England were able to enforce the follow-on.

The fourth Test match, in Trinidad, brought a feast of runs. Trueman was back for Wardle, Spooner came in for the injured Evans and Bailey moved up to open the innings with Hutton. West Indies made 681 for eight, with Weekes, 206, Worrell and Walcott, the three Ws, all scoring centuries. The highlight of the England innings was a third-wicket stand of 166 between May and Compton, both of whom scored centuries. With Graveney scoring 92, the follow-on was saved and the match was drawn, but England paid a price. Laker was hit in the eye by a bouncer and was forced to retire hurt for a while, and Watson, too, sustained injury. Most serious of all, however, was that Statham pulled a rib muscle on the first day, did not bowl again and could not play in the final Test. He had taken sixteen wickets at 28.75 runs each in the series and had emerged as a fast bowler of the highest quality, intelligent, accurate and controlled. His spell of three for 10 at the start of the West Indian innings in the third Test had played a major part in establishing victory, and it was to Statham rather than to Trueman that England would turn in the immediate future.

Like the first Test, the fifth was played in Kingston, Jamaica. The West Indies, who won the toss and batted, were without Valentine, the left-arm spinner, and brought in a seventeen-year-old Barbadian who also bowled left-arm, Gary Sobers. For England, Evans returned for Spooner, and Wardle replaced the injured Statham.

The pitch looked perfect, but there had been rain and overcast weather in the days before the Test, and the pitch had sweated under the covers to provide some moisture as help to the bowlers. To be offered assistance is one thing; to use it to the full is another. Bailey exploited every drop of help that was possible.

He had Holt caught in the leg-trap by Lock off the fifth ball of the match. Maintaining a relentlessly accurate length, he was able to swing the ball either way and to cut it back off the seam. One such delivery knocked Weekes's off stump out of the ground, and late movement saw Stollmeyer caught behind off a bad stroke. When Worrell stabbed Trueman to short-leg the West Indies were 13 for four, and there was to be no effective recovery. They were bowled out for 139, and Bailey finished with seven for 34, which, at that time, was the best bowling analysis an Englishman had produced against the West Indies.

Play began late on the second day, and Hutton and Bailey took the score to 41 by lunch time. Two runs after lunch, in Sobers's second over in Test cricket, Bailey was caught behind. May and Compton both promised more than they achieved, and England ended the day on 194 for five, Hutton 93.

The third day, 1 April 1954, was one of the finest days of Hutton's brilliant career. Reporting for the *Cricketer*, Philip Thomson wrote:

> In one of the greatest innings ever played against the West Indies in her Test history, Hutton, with solid support from Evans and support of a more dashing nature from Wardle, put England well on the road to victory and the squaring of the rubber. In his faultless innings which lasted eight hours and 52 minutes Hutton, this day, as the score mounted became freer and in addition to his superb cover driving once drove Atkinson straight back for 6.

There is a ring of *Henry V* and St Crispin's day in Thomson's eulogy, but, undeniably, Hutton played a very great innings, the first double century by an England captain in an overseas Test. His 205 took England to a first-innings lead of 275, and, with Trueman bowling better than he had done in any previous match of the tour, victory was achieved by nine wickets.

To come from two Tests down to level the series against the West Indies in the Caribbean was an astonishing performance, but the euphoria and the congratulations were muted. Reg Hayter, one of the most balanced and perceptive of commentators, spoke of the responsibility placed upon all cricketers who were honoured by selection for MCC and said that, whatever the provocation, only harm could follow when MCC cricketers fell from the highest standards of conduct on the field:

> As many loyal West Indies people pointed out, the foundation of their own task in instilling the principles of sportsmanship into the rising generations in the islands was to cite English cricketers as the models. They said that if the models lowered their code, the effect could be far-reaching and depressing.

Some saw the lapses in behaviour, of course, as the inevitable price one paid for having a professional as captain. The knives were drawn.

Hutton had been reared in a Yorkshire tradition of non-fraternisation with the opposition, and this attitude had told against him when first leading England and particularly on the tour of the West Indies where he had been accused of slighting the Chief Minister of Jamaica, Alex Bustamente. This, together with the alleged misdemeanours of members of his side – many of the stories were unsubstantiated – meant that he returned home under considerable pressure. He had averaged 96.71 in the Tests and topped the tour batting averages as well as the Test averages. He had led his side back from the brink of defeat in the most difficult of circumstances. He was mentally and physically exhausted.

Harry Altham had become chairman of selectors. Brown had retired from the panel, and Wyatt had been replaced by Walter Robins, an inspiring captain and a very hard task-master. Hutton was appointed captain for the first Test only, and it was announced that 'Gubby' Allen and Charlie Palmer would join the selectors later in the season to choose the side to tour Australia. The immediate series was against Pakistan, who had been admitted to the Imperial Cricket Conference in 1952 and were not being taken too seriously.

Hutton was cheered all the way to the wicket when he played for Yorkshire against MCC at the start of the season, but he was bowled by Surridge for 1. The first Test was ruined by rain, and he was bowled by Khan Mohammad for nought. It was apparent that all was not well, and on the advice of his doctors Hutton took a few weeks' rest.

This brought to the boil the question of the England captaincy which had been simmering below the surface. As vice-captain in the Caribbean, Bailey was the obvious choice to lead the side while Hutton was regaining his health, but Bailey had upset the establishment by a newspaper article (in which he had been misquoted) and he was judged guilty of a breach of rules. Nearly half a century earlier, he would have succeeded to the England captaincy under the existing system of automatic succession as the senior amateur, but the only time Bailey was to captain England was in a computer game. When the white heat of technology arrived the names of the great England cricketers of the period, together with statistics and relevant information, were fed into a computer which was asked to select the best eleven. The computer named Bailey as captain. In 1954 the selectors turned to David Sheppard.

It is surprising how little credit was given to the achievements in the Caribbean. It seemed that only the negative aspects of the tour interested some sections of the public. May, a vital part of the England side and of Surrey's dominant county team, was overlooked, and there was even a

103

lobby against Compton being in the England side. Compton answered his critics by averaging more than 90 in the Pakistan Tests and he made his highest Test score, 278, when England won by an innings at Trent Bridge. This was the first Test in which Sheppard led England, opening the innings with Simpson.

Sheppard was an enterprising captain of Sussex, a batsman at that time at the height of his powers and a very fine fielder close to the wicket. He had played for Sussex while still at school, Sherborne, and for England while still at Cambridge. To the traditionalists, he appeared to have all the necessary attributes for leadership. Ironically, he was a far from establishment figure, and his pronouncements on social and political issues were outspoken. In years to come, some of those who had advocated that he should replace Hutton as England's captain were the very same people who castigated him for his stand against sporting links with South Africa and its apartheid regime, but by then he was Bishop of Liverpool.

Public opinion and the press were strongly in favour of Hutton even though his position had been weakened by illness, but Robins was a strong supporter of Sheppard, and Pelham Warner, whose opinions could now be voiced only in the *Cricketer* and in the inner sanctums of the game, continued to plead for the amateur captain. Subtly, he claimed that, by popular demand, he was reprinting in the *Cricketer* 'Some Thoughts on Captaincy', which had first been seen in one of his books published three years earlier.

The third Test was drawn, very much in favour of England, and Hutton was fit to return for the fourth and last Test. Whatever the strength of the opposition set against him, Hutton had the indestructible weapon of his own record as England captain. The public and the press won the day, and Hutton was named as captain for the final Test against Pakistan and for the tour of Australia.

Pakistan gained a famous victory in The Oval Test, with Fazal Mahmood taking twelve for 99 in the match, and became the first country to win a Test in their first rubber in England. Some may find it hard to believe but, at the time, this defeat was not taken too seriously. In a series almost ruined by rain England had totally outclassed the newcomers to Test cricket in the first three matches, and the main concern was to blood players at international level prior to the tour of Australia.

Lock and Trueman played no part in the series. Lock was coming to terms with reshaping the way in which he bowled his quicker ball and was vying with Wardle, a better bowler overseas; Trueman was still the naughty schoolboy standing in the corner. Bob Appleyard, fit again after

104

two years, Jim McConnon, and Jim Parks junior were introduced to Test cricket at Trent Bridge and Old Trafford, and Peter Loader and Frank Tyson played at The Oval.

Appleyard showed no sign of having suffered from his two years' absence, and he had season's figures of 154 wickets, at 14.42 runs each. Loader had become a potent force as Alec Bedser's new-ball partner in the all-conquering Surrey side. He did not move the ball as sharply as Bedser, but he was quicker and very accurate. Parks was a stylish bats-man and a magnificent fielder who later, to the regret of many, took up wicket-keeping. McConnon and Tyson were virtually unknown.

McConnon had first played for Glamorgan in 1950, and his selection ahead of Laker caused an outcry. He took three for 19 and held four fine catches on his Test debut. He was tall with long, strong fingers, and he turned the ball appreciably. Highly strung, he was in constant need of encouragement, and he was seldom able to show his true worth. Following his two Tests against Pakistan, he went to Australia but was injured and returned home early without appearing in a Test.

The speed of Tyson had been noted when he was at Durham University, but he was considered raw and untutored. In 1954 Trueman took 134 wickets at 15.55; Tyson, playing for Northamptonshire, had 78 at 21.38. The omission of Trueman, it was argued, was an example of the social divisions that persisted in the first-class game, but 'Viator' in the *Cricketer* balanced that view with the comment that 'the selectors have information and facts at their disposal which are not available to the general public'.

Tyson was twenty-four years old and, at the time of his selection, few followers of the game realised how quick he was. Loader, Statham and Bedser completed the selection of the quicker bowlers for the Australian tour while the spin was in the hands of McConnon, Wardle and the versatile Appleyard. Keith Andrew of Northamptonshire, a quiet, unfussy wicket-keeper, was named as Evans's understudy while Bailey was the only true all-rounder in the side.

Bailey, however, was no longer vice-captain. That post had gone to Peter May who, at the age of twenty-four, had become the heir-apparent. David Sheppard was not in the party, for the rest of the batting was comprised of Compton, Edrich, Graveney, Simpson, never a consistent selection but ever in mind, Hutton himself and a 21-year-old named Colin Cowdrey.

If the omission of Laker, Lock and Trueman had caused concern, the inclusion of Cowdrey caused a sense of bewilderment and even anger in some quarters. He had proved an admirable captain at Oxford University, but centuries against Sussex and Kent, his own county, and

1,577 runs, average 35.84, was hardly a recommendation that placed him ahead of batsmen like Kenyon, who had had a marvellous season, Lowson, Sheppard or Insole. The scepticism of the public turned out to be unfounded; the selectors proved to be men of vision.

The prestige of the side was weakened by the defeat at the hands of Pakistan at The Oval where Bailey and Bedser were absent, Evans was at number six and Tyson, who took five wickets in the match, looked neither the fastest bowler in the world nor of Test quality.

The worries did not end there. Compton suffered a recurrence of his knee trouble and remained in England for treatment while the others set sail from Tilbury.

Compton flew out to join the party just before the end of October and hit a century against South Australia within two days of his arrival. As a precaution, Vic Wilson, the Yorkshire left-hander, became the eighteenth member of the squad.

Nothing in the early stages of the tour gave a hint of what was to come. Statham, in particular, took wickets, and Cowdrey scored a century in each innings against New South Wales. MCC won three and drew five of the matches played before the first Test.

Rarely has a side been confronted by such disasters as befell England in that first Test at Brisbane. On the eve of the match Evans became ill with sunstroke and was unable to play. For the first time in Australia, the pitch was fully covered and Hutton, after careful inspection and believing that the pitch would be at its liveliest on the first day, asked Australia to bat first.

To put the other side in when winning the toss has become a more common occurrence in recent years, but in the mid-1950s it was the equivalent of sacrilege, a denial of one of the principles of the game. England had banked on an all-out speed attack; there was no spinner in the side save Compton, and his effectiveness in the match ended early. On the first morning he chased a ball to the boundary, ran into the palings and broke a bone in the back of his left hand. He batted at number eleven in the first innings and number ten in the second and was unfit for the second Test.

The pitch proved to be perfect, and England's cause was not helped by lapses in the field. Before he had scored, Morris was dropped by Andrew off Bedser in the third over of the match. He went on to score 153, offering more chances along the way. Harvey, too, was reprieved on his way to 162 and, all in all, it was estimated that England put down more than a dozen catches. When Ian Johnson, captaining Australia for the first time, declared on the third day Australia had made 601 for the loss of eight wickets. The runs had come at more than 40 an hour. Tyson finished with one for 160 from twenty-nine eight-ball overs.

With Lindwall fresh and lively, England lost their first four wickets inside an hour for 25 runs. In his first Test Cowdrey showed admirable temperament and sound technique in scoring 40 and, inevitably, Bailey played a chanceless innings which lasted for four hours twenty minutes and produced 88. He was only out when partnered by Compton, who was batting against medical advice and who could scarcely hold his bat.

England followed on 411 in arrears. Edrich and May batted bravely, but defeat came at ten minutes past four on the fifth day. The margin was an innings and 154 runs.

The invective to which Hutton was subjected for having asked the Australians to bat first bordered on the outrageous, and one can only conjecture what effect it had on the man, for he was far from an insensitive being. The England side must have moved to Sydney and the second Test in a state of siege as, in England, the cries for Laker, Lock and Trueman were renewed.

England made four changes for the second Test. Evans, Graveney, Wardle and Appleyard came in for Andrew, Compton, Simpson and Bedser. Bailey moved up to open the innings. With Johnson and Miller injured, Australia brought in Burke and Davidson. The main controversy was that, on the morning of the match, Hutton omitted Bedser from the final eleven. It was a brave act and a hard decision to make, and once more Hutton faced condemnation. The truth was that Bedser had suffered from shingles shortly after the side arrived in Australia, and he was never really fully fit thereafter. It was not known at the time, but the great bowler had played his last game against Australia.

Morris followed Hutton's example in the first Test and put England in when he won the toss, but he met with more success than Hutton. After half an hour with the breeze at his back Lindwall changed ends and immediately yorked Bailey. May was soon caught in the leg-trap, and England struggled to lunch at 34 for two. Worse was to follow. Hutton was out to a magnificent diving catch at leg-slip, the first of five wickets to go down in the afternoon, and at tea England were 94 for seven. The only joy came in a last-wicket stand of 43 in twenty minutes which left Wardle as top scorer.

The Australians bowled and fielded well. A chastened England got some comfort from dismissing Morris off the last ball of the day.

Exploiting what moisture was left in the pitch, Bailey, Tyson and Statham bowled England back into the match on the second day. The Australians started briskly enough, but as soon as Bailey was switched to the end from which Lindwall had operated so well, a wicket fell. Favell was caught at second slip, but Australia still lunched comfortably at 88 for two.

Bowling in harness, Bailey and Tyson caused much discomfort to the Australian batsmen, who were forced on the defensive. Four wickets went down between lunch and tea as 70 runs were scored. The attack was directed on or outside the off stump, and although the occasional ball reared off a length, like the one that got Harvey, it was the persistent accuracy and aggression which troubled Australia. Archer chanced his arm and hit six fours and a six, a massive pull off Appleyard, to add 52 in an hour with Davidson, but Australia were out before the close, their lead restricted to 74.

Hutton and Bailey looked secure at the start of the third day, and it was something of a surprise when Bailey was caught behind. Worse followed, for, in his second over, Johnston accounted for both Hutton and Graveney. Australia looked set for a comfortable victory, but the next three and a quarter hours changed the complexion of the match. In that period, May and Cowdrey added 116. They were totally assured, sound in defence, positive in attack. A new, young generation of English batsmen had now taken centre stage. With just twenty-five minutes of the day remaining, Cowdrey attempted a big drive off Benaud and was caught at deep mid-off. He had given a taste of things to come, and the selectors had been vindicated.

May played a wide range of shots, and his mastery forced Morris to remove his leg-trap and to go on the defensive. England ended the day on 204 for four, May 98, Edrich 16.

With the outfield a little damp on the fourth morning, Morris delayed taking the new ball. May duly completed a magnificent century, but a shower interrupted play for twenty minutes. Half an hour after the resumption, Morris felt confident to take the new ball, and Lindwall immediately ended May's innings with a yorker. May's innings had lasted five hours and contained ten fours.

His dismissal heralded trouble. Tyson turned his back on a Lindwall bumper and was hit on the head. He was knocked out and had to be helped off the field. On the stroke of lunch, Edrich dragged a ball into his stumps, and although Tyson bravely returned, England slipped to 250 for nine. Once more, the last-wicket stand was crucial, and Appleyard and Statham hit 46 in fifty minutes. This brought the difference between the two sides to 222.

Tyson had worked on his bowling since the first Test. He had shortened his run, gained in accuracy and generated more pace. He was the fastest bowler world cricket had seen since Larwood more than twenty years earlier. Statham was not far behind and beat Morris four times in the last over before tea before having him leg-before.

On the resumption, Tyson devastated Favell for pace and had him taken at slip. Burke and Harvey were not comfortable, but they survived. Australia ended the day at 72 for two and looked set to win.

Tyson had other ideas. The pitch had lost some of its fire, but in his first over of the fifth day, the second of the morning, Tyson beat both Burke and Hole, spreadeagling their stumps with yorkers of terrific pace. Hutton did not overbowl Tyson or Statham, but when he turned to Appleyard and Bailey, Benaud skied the Yorkshire spinner to deep square-leg. At lunch Australia were 118 for five, and the game had tilted slightly in favour of England.

In the fifty minutes after the break, the tilt became a landslide. Tyson and Statham removed Archer, Davidson, Lindwall and Langley as 27 runs were scored. The bowling had lifted the fielding, and Evans took a spectacular diving catch in front of first slip to get rid of Davidson. Harvey remained defiant, and Johnston helped frustrate England in a last-wicket stand which lasted forty minutes. Harvey monopolised the strike, and Johnston was asked to face only sixteen balls, but the sixteenth proved decisive. Johnston flashed at a leg-side ball from Tyson and was caught behind. England had won by 38 runs and levelled the series.

The pace of Tyson, who bowled for ninety minutes with the breeze at his back in the final act to finish with six for 85, had set the cricket world aglow, but Statham's contribution was not forgotten. He bowled into the wind with unflagging zest and accuracy for eighty-five minutes. He finished with five wickets in the match to Tyson's ten, but they complemented each other.

England went happily into the New Year and to Melbourne for the third Test, yet the pressures on Hutton were increasingly evident. Memoirs of senior members of the side published in the years to come revealed that Hutton had not wanted to play in the Melbourne Test, believing himself to be too unwell. Only at the last minute had the counsel of Compton and others prevailed and Hutton agreed to play. He won the toss, and England, who welcomed back Compton for Graveney, batted.

What advantage there had been in batting first disappeared when Miller, in a pre-lunch spell lasting ninety minutes, dismissed Hutton, Edrich and Compton at a personal cost of 5 runs, two scoring shots, in nine eight-ball overs, eight of which were maidens. With May caught off his glove, four wickets had fallen for 41 runs.

Bailey now joined Cowdrey in another match-saving stand. In two hours they added 74, and the partnership was only broken when Bailey hit a long-hop on to his pads from which it lobbed gently to the wicket-keeper Maddocks, making his debut in place of the injured Langley. Evans stayed while 54 runs were added and Cowdrey neared his hundred. A straight drive off Archer and a delicate flick to leg for three brought him his maiden Test century. He was bowled round his legs ten minutes later, but his four-hour innings, which included fifteen fours, was a memorable effort, and it had salvaged England. The last four wickets fell for 22 runs, and Australia began the second day afresh and confident in what their bowlers had achieved.

Compton could not field on the second day because of a bruised thumb, and, in intense heat, Hutton used his bowlers in short spells. They toiled manfully and compensated for the batting lapses by reducing Australia to 151 for eight. This brought Johnston in to join Maddocks and by the end of the day they had taken the score to 188, just 3 runs behind England's total.

The rest day, the Sunday, provided one of the unresolved scandals of Test cricket. Over the first two days the pitch had been, to say the least, 'sporting', and large cracks were evident on the Saturday evening. By the Monday these had closed, and the pitch played more easily. A report in the *Age* alleged that the pitch had been illegally watered on the Sunday, but the Victorian Cricket Association and the Melbourne Cricket Club emphatically denied the allegations, claiming that they had made exhaustive enquiries and that no tampering or doctoring had taken place.

Be that as it may, Australia's last two wickets held out for an hour on the third morning, and Australia gained a lead of 40.

It was imperative that the England batsmen did not fail for a second time, and the arrears had just been cleared when Edrich was bowled by a ball which pitched on leg stump and hit the off. May now joined Hutton and was immediately impressive, strong in the drive, compact in defence.

Hutton had shown masterly defence for two and a half hours before he fell to a ball which moved in sharply from outside off stump, and Cowdrey played on to Benaud. At the close of play, with May and Compton together, England were 159 for three.

May's valuable innings was ended by Johnston, who bowled the England vice-captain off his pads. Compton soon followed, gliding the ball to the wicket-keeper, and Bailey was now obliged to drop anchor once more as Evans and Wardle offered belligerence. Wardle was particularly effective, hitting 38 out of 46 in forty minutes. For once the tail flopped, and Australia faced a target of 240.

110

They began as if they intended to score the necessary runs that evening. Favell cut and hooked, Morris fell to a diving catch at forward short-leg. Benaud was promoted to continue the aggression, but Favell was yorked by Appleyard, and Australia ended the day on 75 for two, 165 runs short of victory but in a sound position.

England's hopes, it appeared, rested with Appleyard and Wardle, for the pitch was worn and likely to aid spin, particularly the brisk off-spin of Appleyard. It all turned out very differently.

Harvey glanced the seventh ball of the fifth day and Evans took a fine catch. Benaud hooked ambitiously, and Miller, having survived a couple of shooters, got a ball that lifted and was caught at slip. In the first half-hour, Tyson had taken three wickets in twenty-one balls, and Australia were 87 for five.

Tyson was rampant, and Statham as reliable and probing as ever. Frustrated, Hole flashed at him and was caught behind. In one over Tyson forced Maddocks to play on and beat Lindwall as he went to drive. Statham bowled Archer with a fast full toss, and Evans ended the match when he caught Johnston one-handed high to his left off Tyson.

In seventy-five minutes' play on the fifth morning, eight Australian wickets had gone down while 36 runs were scored. Rarely has there been such a collapse in Test cricket. Never had there been such a blistering spell of fast bowling. Tyson, now 'Typhoon', had taken six for 16 in 6.3 overs; Statham two for 19 in six.

There was nearly a month between the third and fourth Tests, but Australia remained shattered. Consistent batting took them to 323 at Adelaide – Bailey, Tyson and Appleyard took three wickets each – but England, with Hutton scoring 80 and Cowdrey 79, took a first-innings lead of 18. Tyson and Statham produced another devastating spell of fast bowling, causing six wickets, three each, to fall for 34 runs before lunch on the fifth day, and England won by five wickets to take the rubber and retain the Ashes. It was their first series win in Australia since the 'Bodyline' tour of 1932–33.

The fifth Test was ruined by torrential rain, and play could not begin until after lunch on the *fourth* day. Graveney made a century, Compton 84, May 79 and Bailey 72. Bailey went down the wicket and allowed himself to be bowled by Lindwall, who thereby claimed his hundredth wicket in England–Australia Tests. Bailey, believing that the fast bowler would never again play in Tests between the two countries, walked down the pitch and was the first to shake hands with Lindwall. Events were to prove that Bailey was premature in his assumption, but the all-rounder had learned his first-class cricket in a chivalrous age. His one double century, for Essex against Sussex at Eastbourne in 1949, had been made with the encouragement of the opposition. At the outset of his career, cricketers came down to breakfast wearing a tie and never went to lunch without wearing a blazer. By the end of his career, things had changed.

England made 371 for seven declared, and Australia did not begin their innings until the penultimate day, but they were forced to follow on and were 118 for six, still 32 runs adrift, when the match ended. Wardle had eight wickets in the match, and, ironically, it was this draw which convinced people of the total superiority of the England team.

All that remained of the tour were two Tests in New Zealand, both of which were won by England. The first attracted record crowds, and Tyson and Statham excelled. Appleyard starred in the second. England won by an innings and bowled out New Zealand for 26, the lowest score in Test cricket, in the second innings. Appleyard had four for 7, Statham three for 9. Batting at number five, Hutton was top scorer in England's innings with 53. It was his last Test match. Simpson and Edrich, too, had ended their Test careers.

Hutton had captained England in twenty-three Tests, eleven of which were won and eight drawn. He had regained and held the Ashes and had never lost a series. He had scored five centuries as captain and had averaged 52.14 with the bat.

He was to play occasionally for Yorkshire in 1955, but he announced his retirement from Test cricket because of back trouble. Those close to him would suggest that he was finally defeated by weariness after receiving more than his fair share of criticism. His approach was seen as being too professional, and he was guilty of slowing down the over-rate.

At Melbourne Ray Robinson, the Australian journalist, suggested that the only blot on the cricket was 'the amount of time taken up between overs by numerous confabulations and dilatory crossing over, which irritated the crowd and accounted for the fact that only 54 overs were bowled compared with 67 the previous day.' In modern, six-ball-over, terms, this means that England bowled 72 overs in a day as opposed to the 90 bowled by the Australians. Hutton apologised for this after he had won the series, but said it was necessary.

England's debt to him as captain and batsman is incalculable. He had led England out of the wilderness. Perhaps he had also led cricket into a new age.

Tyson and Statham, the Time of the 'Typhoon'
Australia v England at Melbourne Cricket Ground
31 December, 1954, 1, 3, 4 and 5 January 1955

England First Innings		Second Innings	
L. Hutton (capt) c Hole b Miller ...	12	lbw b Archer	42
W.J. Edrich c Lindwall b Miller ...	4	b Johnston	13
P.B.H. May c Benaud B Lindwall ..	0	b Johnston	91
M.C. Cowdrey b Johnson	102	b Benaud	7
D.C.S. Compton c Harvey b Miller	4	c Maddocks b Archer ..	23
T.E. Bailey c Maddocks b Johnston	30	not out	24
†T.G. Evans lbw b Archer	20	c Maddocks b Miller ...	22
J.H. Wardle b Archer	0	b Johnson	38
F.H. Tyson b Archer	6	c Harvey b Johnston ...	6
J.B. Statham b Archer	3	c Favell b Johnston	0
R. Appleyard not out	1	b Johnston	6
Extras (b 9)	9	(b 2, lb 4, w 1)	7
Total	191	279	

BOWLING	Overs	Mdns	Runs	Wkts	Overs	Mdns	Runs	Wkts
Lindwall	13	–	59	1	18	3	52	–
Miller	11	8	14	3	18	6	35	1
Archer	13.6	4	33	4	24	7	50	2
Benaud	7	–	30	–	8	2	25	1
Johnston	12	6	26	1	24.5	2	85	5
Johnson	11	3	20	1	8	2	25	1

fall of wickets
1–14, 2–21, 3–29, 4–41, 5–115, 6–169, 7–181, 8–181, 9–190
1–40, 2–96, 3–128, 4–173, 5–185, 6–211, 7–257, 8–273, 9–273

Australia First Innings		Second Innings	
L.E. Favell lbw b Statham	25	b Appleyard	30
A.R. Morris lbw b Tyson	3	c Cowdrey b Tyson	4
K.R. Miller c Evans b Statham	7	(5) c Edrich b Tyson	6
R.N. Harvey b Appleyard	31	c Evans b Tyson	11
G.B. Hole b Tyson	11	(6) c Evans b Statham ..	5
R. Benaud c sub (Wilson) b Appleyard	15	(3) b Tyson	22
R.G. Archer b Wardle	23	b Statham	15
†L.V. Maddocks c Evans b Statham	47	b Tyson	0
R.R. Lindwall b Statham	13	lbw b Tyson	0
I.W. Johnson (capt) not out	33	not out	4
W.A. Johnston b Statham	11	c Evans b Tyson	0
Extras (b 7, lb 3, nb 2)	12	(b 1, lb13)	14
Total	231	111	

113

BOWLING	Overs	Mdns	Runs	Wkts	Overs	Mdns	Runs	Wkts
Tyson	21	2	68	2	12.3	1	27	7
Statham	16.3	–	60	5	11	1	38	2
Bailey	9	1	33	–	3	–	14	–
Appleyard	11	3	38	2	4	1	17	1
Wardle	6	–	20	1	1	–	1	–

fall of wickets
1–15, 2–38, 3–43, 4–65, 5–92, 6–115, 7–134, 8–151, 9–205
1–23, 2–57, 3–77, 4–86, 5–87, 6–97, 7–98, 8–98, 9–110
umpires – C. Hoyand and M.J. McInnes
England won by 128 runs

4

Supremacy and After, 1955–60

Hutton was appointed captain of England for all five Tests against South Africa in 1955, but for reasons already discussed he declined, and he virtually disappeared from first-class cricket after that season. He was made an honorary member of MCC, the first professional to be elected while still playing, and, a year later, he was knighted for his services to cricket.

All rationing had ended in 1954. Winston Churchill resigned as Prime Minister in 1955, the first floodlit soccer international took place at Wembley and, with commercial television creeping into existence, the BBC was given exclusive rights to televise Test matches. The war was finally over.

There remained the question of Cowdrey's feet. England's new, young hero returned from Australia in April 1955, ready for his two years' National Service in the RAF. He had long suffered from stiffening of the joints in both big toes, had undergone a manipulative operation while at Tonbridge and played cricket in specially made boots. It was presumed that a young athlete who had recently scored a Test century and had proved agile in the field in sweltering heat in Australia was at the height of fitness, and Cowdrey entered the RAF.

The service doctors immediately queried Cowdrey's health because of the state of his feet. They deemed him unfit to drill, for fear of permanent injury, and, within weeks, he was invalided out and was back playing cricket for Kent. He finished second in the national batting averages.

Cowdrey's feet became front-page news, and questions were asked in the House of Commons, the implication being that he was let out of the RAF simply to play cricket for England while young men of other professions were forced to serve. The debate was soon supplanted by less trivial matters.

In fact Cowdrey appeared in only one Test in 1955. He was unable to play until June and appeared in the Old Trafford Test against South Africa at the beginning of July. He badly damaged a finger and missed the matches at Leeds and The Oval.

England were in search of an opening pair. Kenyon and Graveney opened in the first three matches, Bailey and Lowson in the fourth, and the left-handers Ikin and Close at The Oval.

There were problems, too, relating to Tyson, whose cricket was restricted by a foot injury. This quiet and modest man bowled England to victory in the first Test with figures of six for 28 in the second innings, finishing the match with a spell of five for 5 in 7.3 overs. He missed the second Test when Trueman was paired with Statham, who brought a glimpse of Australian glories with seven for 39 in the second innings, his best performance for England.

Tyson's only other appearance was at Old Trafford, where he had match figures of six for 179. He opened the bowling with Bedser, who was playing in his fifty-first, and last, Test match. He left the international scene with a record 236 wickets to his credit. He was to continue to serve English cricket in other ways for many years to come.

Having lost the first two Tests, South Africa fought back to draw level, but Laker and Lock bowled England to victory at The Oval. May had won his first series as England captain in what was the first rubber in England to produce five clear results.

Badly hit by injuries against a very keen and competent side who hit six centuries in the Tests and had three first-rate bowlers in Tayfield, Goddard and Heine, England used twenty-five players in the series. May, Compton, Bailey and Graveney were the only men to play in all five Tests while Barrington and Titmus were the two newcomers. May scored centuries at Lord's and Old Trafford, where Compton also hit a hundred in what was England's first defeat in Manchester for fifty-three years.

If that represented a change, so, too, did the general pattern of county cricket. There were those who felt that run-rates were too slow while others, like Wilf Wooller, considered that games were becoming more competitive. Surrey took the Championship for the fourth year in succession, leaving Yorkshire sixteen points in their wake. Significantly, six of the seventeen counties were now captained by professionals. More significantly, there were now more than twenty 'overseas' cricketers playing in the Championship.

Most notable of these were Roy Marshall, George Tribe and Bruce Dooland. Marshall, a free-scoring opening batsman who endeared himself to English crowds, had toured England with the West Indian party in 1950. He was later to admit that, batting at the other end to

116

Weekes, Worrell and Walcott made him realise his limitations, and he remained in England to qualify for Hampshire.

George Tribe was a left-arm spinner who had played three times for Australia shortly after the war and had qualified for Northamptonshire. He did the 'double' seven times, including every year from 1952 to 1957. In 1955 he took 176 wickets.

In the same season Bruce Dooland took 150 wickets. The previous year he had been the leading wicket-taker in the country with 196 wickets and had performed the 'double' for the first time. He was to do it again in 1957. Like Tribe, Dooland, a leg-break and googly bowler, had played three times for Australia in the late 1940s, but had qualified for Nottinghamshire and served them nobly for five seasons.

Overseas cricketers had been assisting English counties for well over half a century, but, almost unnoticed by followers of the game, the numbers were increasing every season. Within the next three years Somerset were to engage two formidable Australians, Alley and McCool.

In the winter of 1955–56, an MCC 'A' team was sent on a tour of Pakistan. The object of the tour was twofold: to help develop and keep alive interest in cricket in Pakistan and to give experience to promising English cricketers, future Test prospects. Indeed, Carr, the captain, Watkins, Barrington, Lock, Moss, Close, Parks and Titmus had already appeared in Test cricket. Cowan, Sutcliffe, Sainsbury, Swetman and Richardson were seen as up and coming. Tompkin, the Leicestershire batsman, and Stephenson, the Somerset wicket-keeper, were being rewarded for consistently good form in county cricket over a number of years. Swetman, strangely beloved by selectors, was, at the time, the Surrey reserve wicket-keeper and was to play for two other counties.

The tour was successful in its aim of furthering the careers of Barrington, Richardson, Titmus and Close, while the experienced Lock had a wonderful time, capturing eighty-one wickets in eleven matches. That Pakistan had the better of the representative matches did not matter; the incidents that caused diplomatic friction did. Perhaps we were seeing the shape of things to come.

The first eruption came during the third representative match, in Peshawar. Some of the MCC party, acting in the manner of a student rag week, subjected umpire Idris Begh to the 'water treatment'. Unfortunately, the timing was as bad as the dousing was inappropriate, for Pakistani onlookers saw it as some sort of revenge for umpiring decisions which the tourists had not liked. The President of MCC, Lord Alexander of Tunis, offered to call off the rest of the tour.

Apologies were graciously accepted, and the politicians and administrators handled the incident with considerable diplomatic skill although there were complaints about 'sledging' in the final match which did not help them. The scars were to last long, and one wonders if an insensitivity among cricketers to the manners and customs of Asian countries has ever been truly expunged.

Such speculation, of course, was in the future. The immediate concern was the Ashes series against Australia. English cricket was in the ascendancy. May had served an apprenticeship under Hutton, and the transition from one leader to the next had been smooth. As Hutton had passed from the scene and Compton's mighty powers had shown signs of diminishing, new talents like Cowdrey had arisen. Men like Bailey, Evans and Graveney provided a sense of continuity. There was, too, competition. Should it be Lock or Wardle? Laker, Tattersall or Titmus? Trueman or Tyson or Statham or Loader?

In contrast Australia had never truly recovered from the departure of Bradman, the man who had so dominated their game as batsman and captain. The side that Ian Johnson led to England in 1956 was, unquestionably, one of the weakest to come to these shores, and the miracle was that they only lost the Test series by two matches to one, for they were outplayed in four of the five Tests.

They arrived at The Oval in mid-May to play the county champions without a first-class victory to their credit, and they were beaten by ten wickets. Surrey were the first county for forty-four years to defeat an Australian touring side. The match was a triumph for Jim Laker, who, on the first day, came on to bowl at the pavilion end at 12.20. He bowled until 5.45 when he had Wilson caught behind to give him figures of ten for 88 from forty-six overs. The only other bowler to have taken all ten wickets against the Australians was Edward Barratt, a slow left-armer and another Surrey man, who had accomplished the feat for the Players in 1878. Laker, wonderfully accurate, had allied variation of flight to his considerable ability to spin the ball.

The Australians were bowled out for 259 and, with the ever reliable Bernard Constable hitting 109, Surrey took a first-innings lead of 88. Interestingly the Australian captain and off-spinner took six wickets in the Surrey innings, but they cost him 168 runs and took him 60.3 overs.

When the Australians batted a second time they were bowled out for 107, and Lock took seven wickets. Their vulnerability to spin was obvious. Laker took 132 wickets in 1956, and 63 of them were Australian.

The visitors showed quite well against MCC with Harvey getting a double century, but they had injury problems. Those problems were as nothing compared to England's when it came to the first Test. Compton

118

had undergone an operation for the removal of his right kneecap, could not play until June and appeared in only eight matches for Middlesex. Tyson and Trueman were unfit, and on the morning of the first Test Statham, too, broke down. On top of that, Moss had bowled only four overs when he pulled a groin muscle and had to be helped from the field.

In effect, all this mattered little, for more than twelve hours were lost to rain, including all of the second day, and the match was drawn. There were some aspects of the game from which England could draw comfort. Laker and Lock took ten of the twelve Australian wickets to fall, and the new opening partnership of Peter Richardson and Colin Cowdrey began the second innings with a stand of 151.

Trueman and Statham were back for the Lord's Test, but England were beaten as Keith Miller took ten wickets in a Test for the only time in his career, and Gil Langley had nine dismissals behind the stumps, which, at the time, was a Test record.

The defeat at Lord's caused great concern, for it was apparent to all that England had a far stronger side than Australia. Trueman had taken seven wickets at Lord's, Bailey six. They had been thwarted in the second innings by Richie Benaud, who scored 97 out of a seventh-wicket stand of 117 with 'Slasher' Mackay. Even so, the real weakness in the England side was the middle-order batting. Watson had failed at Lord's and so, too, had Tom Graveney.

A most elegant batsman and prolific scorer at county level, Graveney had been a consistent under-achiever in Test matches since his century at Sydney at the beginning of March 1955. In fairness, he had been forced into opening for a period, which was not his position, but, at the highest level, he had also developed a weakness outside the off stump. In the second innings at Lord's, Miller had gone round the wicket to him and had immediately induced a flick and a catch behind off a ball that was leaving the batsman. Even the most ardent of Graveney fans believed that the Gloucestershire man must go.

The selectors for 1956 were 'Gubby' Allen, Les Ames, Wilf Wooller and Cyril Washbrook. As captain, Peter May joined them and had the casting vote. It appears that Allen and Wooller had met before the official selection meeting and had agreed that Washbrook should be asked to play in order to bolster the middle order. They found that Ames, too, was of their persuasion. May, a young captain anxious to build a new, young side, was not. Washbrook was asked to leave the selection meeting while Allen, Wooller, Ames and May debated. May, reluctantly one feels, was persuaded by the three older men.

Washbrook was forty-one and had not played Test cricket for five years. He was now captain of Lancashire and not having the happiest of times. When the news of his recall to the England side broke there was an uproar in the press, who were adamant that, in future, no selector should be allowed to choose himself as a player.

The selectors made three other changes as Oakman came in for Watson, Lock for Wardle and Insole for Statham, who was left out on the morning of the match when it was decided that spin would be the major weapon on the Headingley pitch.

For England, who won the toss, the start was disastrous. Within the first hour, they lost three wickets, all to Archer, and Richardson, Cowdrey and Oakman were back in the pavilion with just 17 scored. Washbrook joined May and, in 287 minutes, the pair took the score to 204 before May was caught ankle-high by Lindwall backward of square. The bowler was Johnson, the ball a full toss. There was no further scoring before the end of the day and Washbrook finished on 90 not out.

The selectors had been vindicated. Washbrook was a hero, and there was genuine sadness when he was out, leg-before to Benaud, two short of his century the following morning. The stand with May had turned the game, and Bailey and Evans batted well so that England reached 325. Australia, in disarray, were 81 for six by the close, and although there was no play on the third day, they followed on 182 in arrears on the Monday.

Rain threatened on the final day so that England, with eight Australian wickets still to capture, needed to hurry. Laker and Lock obliged, and the match was won shortly after lunch. Laker had match figures of eleven for 113; Lock had seven for 81. Better was to come.

England had levelled the series by beating Australia by an innings and 42 runs. It was England's first Headingley victory over the old enemy. Sheppard for Insole and Statham for Trueman were the only changes for Old Trafford. The choice of Sheppard was a surprise. He had given up regular first-class cricket and taken holy orders. He had, at the time of his selection, played only four first-class innings for Sussex during the season. One of these had brought him 97 against the Australians a few days before the first Test.

The pitch at Old Trafford deserves some comment. Bill Bowes, once of England and now a distinguished journalist, gave his assessment:

In over 25 years, playing and watching, at Old Trafford I have never seen the playing strip so barren and such a reddy-brown in look. The absence of grass meant no help of any kind for fast bowlers. The colour meant that marl had been used in the preparation of the pitch, and spin bowlers generally agree they would rather see marl than anything else. When wet it will give the perfect 'sticky' wicket. When dry it has a tendency to powder.

Accusations were to be made later that the pitch had been specially prepared for the England spinners, and the Australians reacted bitterly and angrily. The Lancashire authorities denied the accusations, and the truth of the matter lay somewhere in the fact that Laker and Lock were far better bowlers than Johnson, rarely impressive at Test level, and Benaud, whose great days were yet to come, when he had fully learned his craft.

So easy-paced was the pitch on the first day that Richardson, who hit a maiden Test century, and Cowdrey scored 174 for the first wicket. At lunch they had made 111 in two hours. Both batsmen hit eleven fours. Cowdrey was the first to go, giving a faint edge as he moved to drive Lindwall. Richardson did not last much longer and was out when he lost concentration and dabbed at a widish delivery. Sheppard was soon into his stride, and May looked in magnificent form until he edged Benaud to slip. Bailey came in and carried on the brisk scoring. England closed on 307 for three, Sheppard 59, Bailey 14. In the growing professional age the first five English batsmen had been amateurs.

The mutterings of complaint at this stage were that the pitch had nullified the Australian pace bowlers and that it would turn viciously as the game progressed. From this distance, it would seem that the Australians were beaten in the mind long before Laker or Lock took the ball in their hands. Much of cricket at any level is played in the mind.

Sheppard's absence from first-class cricket had in no way affected his capabilities as a batsman. He hit a six and fifteen fours in moving to a chanceless and graceful 113. There was panache from Evans, and England were bowled out for 459. The last six England wickets realised 138, so that what followed was a little difficult to comprehend.

McDonald and Burke began steadily, but Laker and Lock were soon into the attack. The Australian innings began at 2.30, and after seven overs had been bowled for 9 runs Laker replaced Bailey. With 17 scored, Lock took over from Statham. There was no sign of viciousness in the pitch, and 43 runs came in eighty minutes. At this point, May changed his spinners round, and Laker operated from the Stretford End. The change brought almost immediate results, for McDonald pushed at a straight ball from Laker and was taken in the leg-trap. Without addition to the score, Harvey allowed for non-existent turn and was bowled.

Australia went to tea at 62 for two. On the resumption the last eight wickets went down in thirty-five minutes for 22 runs. Burke was caught at slip off the first ball after the break. The first ball of the next over, from Laker, had Craig leg-before, and Mackay went third ball, taken at slip. Miller hit Lock for a towering six and then was taken at slip when he lunged at Laker. Benaud was taken on the boundary, and Archer gave Laker the charge and missed. Maddocks hit Lock through the covers for four before getting in a tangle against Laker, who then bowled Johnson with a full toss.

The Australians had convinced themselves that they were batting on an unplayable pitch. The pitch was dry, and England had scored 152 runs in 140 minutes on it before the Australian innings began. In twenty-two balls after tea, Laker had taken seven wickets for 8 runs, and his nine for 37 was the second-best analysis in Test match history, the best against Australia.

May had pressured the Australians into disintegration, and he maintained the pressure when he asked them to follow on. The composed batting of Burke and McDonald served to emphasise how dreadful had been the batting of their colleagues. They took the score to 28, at which point McDonald retired with an injured knee which needed examination and treatment. This brought in Harvey, who ran down the pitch to the first ball he received from Laker and hit it on the full into the hands of Cowdrey. Twice in the match Harvey had thrown his wicket away without scoring. Craig and Burke offered more sense, and Australia closed on 53 for one, facing an innings defeat after just two days' play.

Rain offered them a reprieve. Play could not begin until ten minutes past two on the Saturday, and a downpour, which left the pitch under water and great pools on the outfield, ended play at five to three. During that period Australia scored 6 runs and lost Burke, taken at leg-slip.

The weather on the Sunday was horrendous, and it was only a little better on the Monday when there were two sessions of play, one of fifteen minutes and one of forty-five minutes. McDonald, who had returned, and Craig advanced the score to 84.

The dreadful conditions of the Monday eased somewhat, and play was able to start only ten minutes late on the final morning. The cloud was still heavy and the pitch damp. There was little to help the bowlers, and solid defence could easily save the day for Australia. At lunch McDonald and Craig were still together, and the score was 112.

Just before the interval there had been a suggestion of sun, and now the pitch began to dry. Bailey bowled one over after the break so that Laker could move to the Stretford End again, and from then on he and Lock operated in tandem. In his third over of the afternoon, Laker ended

122

Craig's brave four-and-a-quarter-hour knock. McDonald went to his 50 off Lock, but Mackay was taken at slip in Laker's next over. Miller defended grimly until he was drawn forward and bowled, but the admirable McDonald and Benaud batted sensibly, and Australia went to tea at 181 for six.

Crucially, Laker took two wickets immediately after tea. McDonald's 337-minute vigil was ended when he was taken in the leg-trap, and Benaud was bowled. That left England ninety minutes in which to capture the last two wickets. Lindwall and Johnson held the bowlers at bay for twenty minutes. Lock, like Laker, often beat the bat, but it was not his day, and his next contribution was to catch Lindwall at short-leg off his Surrey partner.

The tension had mounted every over, for the crowd was now anticipating not only an England victory but an historic achievement.

Maddocks was struck on the pad. Laker wheeled to the umpire in appeal, and the finger went up. For the first time, a bowler had taken ten wickets in a Test innings. For the first time, a bowler had taken ten wickets in an innings twice in a season. For the first time, a bowler had taken 19 wickets in a match. Unquestionably, this was the most phenomenal piece of bowling that first-class cricket had ever known.

'Laker's Match' captured the public imagination. It also meant that England had beaten Australia twice in a home rubber for the first time since 1905, which was the last time there had been a definite result between the two countries at Old Trafford, and it was also the first time since five-match series had been introduced at the end of the previous century that England had held the Ashes for three series.

The Oval Test was ruined by rain, over twelve hours being lost, but it went very much in favour of England. The selectors, seemingly, could do nothing wrong. There were doubts as to Bailey's fitness, so Tyson returned and, in place of Oakman, Denis Compton was recalled.

The operation to remove Compton's right kneecap, it had been believed, had ended his Test career. Allen and his committee thought otherwise. He was cheered to the wicket, and he and May took England from 66 for three to 222 before Compton was caught at short fine-leg for 94. Washbrook, Sheppard, Compton – the selectors had performed a hat-trick.

The last seven England wickets went down for 25 runs, but Laker and Lock ensured a first-innings lead of 45. Eventually, May declared at tea on the final day, leaving Australia two hours to score 228 on a soft pitch. They finished on 27 for five. Laker took three for 8 in eighteen overs. He had established a new record for an Ashes rubber with forty-six wickets at 9.60 runs each. Superlatives were exhausted.

123

Laker's Match
England v Australia at Old Trafford
26, 27, 28, 30 and 31 July 1956

England	First Innings	
P.E. Richardson c Maddocks b Benaud		104
M.C. Cowdrey c Maddocks b Lindwall		80
Rev. D.S. Sheppard b Archer		113
P.B.H. May (capt) c Archer b Benaud		43
T.E. Bailey b Johnson		20
C. Washbrook lbw b Johnson		6
A.S.M. Oakman, c Archer b Johnson		10
†T.G. Evans st Maddocks b Johnson		47
J.C. Laker run out		3
G.A.R. Lock not out		25
J.B. Statham c Maddocks b Lindwall		0
Extras (b 2, lb 5, w 1)		8
Total		459

BOWLING	Overs	Mdns	Runs	Wkts
Lindwall	21.3	6	63	2
Miller	21	6	41	–
Archer	22	6	73	1
Johnson	47	10	151	4
Benaud	47	17	123	2

fall of wickets
1–174, 2–195, 3–288, 4–321, 5–327, 6–339, 7–401, 8–417, 9–458

Australia First Innings		Second Innings	
C.C. McDonald c Lock b Laker . . .	32	c Oakman b Laker	89
J.W. Burke c Cowdrey b Lock	22	c Lock b Laker	33
R.N. Harvey b Laker	0	c Cowdrey b Laker	0
I.D. Craig lbw b Laker	8	lbw b Laker	38
K.R. Miller c Oakman b Laker	6	(6) b Laker	0
K.D. Mackay c Oakman b Laker . .	0	(5) c Oakman b Laker . .	0
R.G. Archer st Evans b Laker	6	c Oakman b Laker	0
R. Benaud c Statham b Laker	0	b Laker	18
R.R. Lindwall not out	6	c Lock b Laker	8
†L.V. Maddocks b Laker	4	(11) lbw b Laker	2
I.W. Johnson (capt) b Laker	0	(10) not out	1
Extras	0	(b 12, lb 4)	16
Total	84	205	

BOWLING	Overs	Mdns	Runs	Wkts	Overs	Mdns	Runs	Wkts
Statham	6	3	6	–	16	10	15	–
Bailey	4	3	4	–	20	8	31	–
Laker	16.4	4	37	9	51.2	23	53	10
Lock	14	3	37	1	55	30	69	–
Oakman	–	–	–	–	8	3	21	–

fall of wickets
1–48, 2–48, 3–62, 4–62, 5–62, 6–73, 7–73, 8–78, 9–84
1–28, 2–55, 3–114, 4–124, 5–130, 6–130, 7–181, 8–198, 9-203
umpires – D.E. Davies and F.S. Lee
England won by an innings and 170 runs

Laker was, of course, a member of the Surrey side that, under Stuart Surridge, won the Championship for the fifth year in succession. It was an attack of international class – the Bedser twins, Lock, Laker, Loader and Surridge himself – that was Surrey's most potent weapon, but the county had unearthed two batsmen of considerable talent in Stewart and Barrington, the second of whom had already won Test caps.

At the end of the campaign Surridge announced that he would retire and hand over the captaincy to May. It was not that, after five titles in his five years as captain, he felt like Alexander the Great with no more worlds to conquer. It was that, contrary to today's beliefs, he considered it right and proper that as May was captain of England he should also be captain of Surrey.

No captain had served a better apprenticeship than May, who was tutored by the two outstanding leaders of the period. By nature, he was more akin to Hutton than to Surridge. He lacked Surridge's ebullience, and there was a hard vein of professionalism and determination in May, who was a little reticent in himself. Some of the press interpreted this, wrongly, as aloofness, and he did not always enjoy the best of relations with them. He was admired and respected by his players, and he was to enjoy their companionship to the end of his all too short life.

Before taking over Surrey, his immediate challenge was to lead the MCC side to South Africa in the 1956–57 season. He began the tour with five centuries, but he endured a poor run in the Tests, and South Africa came back from two down to draw the rubber. Jim Parks developed eye trouble almost as soon as he arrived in South Africa and took no part in the tour after appearing in just one match. Tyson, his speed reduced, played in only two Tests, and Lock spent most of the tour as understudy to Wardle, who had twenty-six wickets in four Test matches and once again proved himself to be the better bowler on foreign soil. Laker, too,

125

was disappointing, particularly in view of the fact that Tayfield, the South African off-spinner, had an outstanding series.

Bailey had a fine tour, opening the batting in all five Tests, with Cowdrey giving substance to the middle order. Cowdrey was one of three England batsmen to score Test hundreds, the others being Richardson and Insole, the vice-captain, who topped the Test batting averages.

Neither Trueman nor Graveney was on the tour, and this was the last series in which Denis Compton played Test cricket for England. He had been one of the last three to be invited to tour, but this was simply because MCC wanted clarification as to his fitness. Doubts were expressed as to whether his knee would stand up to a full tour, but he played in fourteen matches, including all five Tests, and if not the force of old, he acquitted himself well. He topped the Middlesex batting averages in 1957 and scored more than 1,500 runs, but announced that he would retire from professional cricket on a regular basis, assisting Middlesex occasionally as an amateur if required.

Edrich, too, was to disappear within a couple of years, and with the passing of this pair the lustre of the game was diminished. They lit a beacon which illuminated the game and brought a multitude of followers to cricket.

A strange selection for that tour to South Africa was Brian Taylor, who had just won a regular place as wicket-keeper and hard-hitting left-handed batsman in the Essex side. Swetman, it will be remembered, had gone on the MCC 'A' tour of Pakistan as wicket-keeper while John Murray was earning glowing praise as wicket-keeper/batsman for Middlesex. Indeed, in 1957, Murray was to become only the second wicket-keeper after Les Ames to score a thousand runs and claim a hundred dismissals in a season.

Taylor had come to first-class cricket through the *Evening News*'s colts scheme. The now defunct London evening paper had established a plan shortly after the war to discover and help to develop talented youngsters. Alan Moss, the Middlesex pace bowler, was another of their protégés. Unlike Moss, Taylor never played for England, and the tour of South Africa was the nearest he got to international honours, but he served the county game nobly.

In the late 1950s there was a growing concern about the county game. The Test series in South Africa had been marked by slow scoring of deadly intensity, and it had been felt for some time that the rate of scoring in the Championship was not what it should be. Accordingly, it was decided that, in 1957, two points should be awarded to the side who, in winning or drawing a match, had the faster run-rate in the first innings. The rate was calculated on runs per over. It made no difference to Surrey, of course, who took the title under the captaincy of Peter May; Northamptonshire were runners-up, ninety-four points behind.

The tampering with the points system suggested that cricket was becoming marginally aware of what was happening in the world, of events and practices which would give cricket far more competition than it had ever known before in the clamour for people's interests and for their cash. 'Lucky Jim' and the Angry Young Man had given way to *Rebel without a Cause* and *The Blackboard Jungle*. Fewer and fewer people listened to the radio as more and more homes had television sets, and Elvis Presley and Tommy Steele had become household names. Shortly after the MCC party had left for home, South Africa had declared that *God Save the Queen* was no longer to be the country's national anthem, and, in Rome, six ministers signed a treaty which began the process for a united Europe.

In any period of history it is difficult for man to comprehend fully the significance of political decisions or social changes. For the time being, cricket went on its innocent, traditional way.

England were unconquered and unconquerable, the holders of the Ashes, the Champions of the World. To assume that title was rather presumptuous on the part of England since their challengers in 1957, the West Indies, had convincingly won the series on their last visit seven years earlier. They had not lost a series to England since 1939 and still possessed Weekes, Worrell, Walcott, Ramadhin and Valentine.

The path to the first Test match suggested nothing had changed. Ramadhin bemused batsmen wherever he went, thirty-eight wickets in eight innings at low cost by 24 May, and the much praised Sobers, new to England, had hit 101 not out against MCC at Lord's and 219 not out against Nottinghamshire at Trent Bridge. His record Test score was only some ten months away.

England were still confronted by the problem of who was to open with Peter Richardson and recalled Close for the first Test at Edgbaston. This was Close's fourth Test. His first had come in 1949, and he was yet to play two Tests in succession. Recalled, too, was Freddie Trueman, who opened the attack with Brian Statham.

Valentine was not in the West Indian side, but it did not matter. Having won the toss, England batted. They left out Wardle and Graveney from the chosen thirteen, preferring Insole and Lock. Bowling as ever with his shirt sleeves buttoned at the wrists and with a flick of the hand at the moment of delivery which helped to disguise intention, Ramadhin bowled out England in four hours on a perfect pitch, his seven for 49 being his best figures in Test cricket. Gilchrist, tall, wiry and fast, gave admirable sustained support and England were out for 186.

The champions were rocked. The history of 1950 was repeating itself.

Trueman yorked Pairaudeau in his second over, but there were no more successes that evening as the West Indies closed contentedly on 83 for one.

Kanhai was leg-before to Statham without addition on the second morning, and Walcott pulled a leg muscle as he attempted to take a quick single and had to bat with a runner. England kept in the game for much of the day. Bailey held a wonderful catch at slip off a full-blooded cut from Sobers, and by mid-afternoon, with the second new ball due, the West Indies were 197 for five. England scented success, but 'Collie' Smith and Frank Worrell stopped the rot. By the end of the day, the tourists were 316 for five.

On the third day Smith went to the highest score he was to make in Test cricket (he was killed in a road accident two years after this Test) and he and Worrell made their partnership worth 190. This was the first Test match to be played at Edgbaston for twenty-eight years, and a record crowd of 32,000 people on the Saturday saw the West Indies take total command. The Smith/Worrell stand had begun at 3.20 on the Friday, and it was not broken until Statham bowled Worrell with the last ball before lunch on the Saturday, five hours' playing time later. Like Walcott, Worrell had batted with a runner; that runner was Pairaudeau on both occasions.

Smith and Goddard added 79 in eighty-five minutes, but once they were separated the end came quickly. The West Indies led by 288, and England faced an innings defeat.

Worrell was unable to bowl, and the West Indies fielded two substitutes. Richardson and Close scored 63 in ninety minutes before Ramadhin deceived Richardson and had him caught. In his next over Ramadhin beat and bowled Insole, and a familiar pattern seemed about to take shape. Close stood firm, and May was assured from the start, so that the pair took the score to 102 for two on the Saturday evening.

Twenty minutes into the fourth day, again fine and sunny, Close fell to Gilchrist, and Cowdrey now joined May. What followed was the greatest rearguard action by a pair of English batsmen in Test history. At the close England were 378 for three, May 193, Cowdrey 78.

May and Cowdrey had analysed and discussed Ramadhin and had decided to play him as an off-spinner. Frequently, they would thrust the front pad well outside off stump or far down the wicket and smother the ball without offering a shot. Ramadhin became as exhausted by the endless appeals to which he got no response as he did from the mammoth stint that he was asked to bowl. The partnership lasted eight hours and twenty minutes and realised 411 runs, which remains

England's highest stand for any wicket. Cowdrey hit sixteen fours and sixty-three singles before driving to long-on. When May declared at 3.30 on the last day he had batted five minutes short of ten hours and hit two sixes, twenty-five fours and 111 singles. They had batted virtually without blemish and had driven with power and elegance, but it was the pad play which had nullified the spinners and which had, in effect, ended Ramadhin's career as a potent force in Test cricket.

The little spinner whose bowling had been one of the delights of post-war Test cricket established records of his own in the match. He sent down 588 balls (98 overs) in the second innings, and 774 balls (129 overs) in the match. In the second innings the West Indies used only two balls. Goddard did not take the second until 96 overs had been bowled, and 162 were bowled with the second. By the time of the declaration, Ramadhin could barely amble to the wicket.

Set a target of 296 in 140 minutes, a totally demoralised West Indian side soon lost both openers to Trueman. Laker and Lock were brought into action, and wickets tumbled. Finally, Goddard, having watched May and Cowdrey, constantly thrust his pads to the ball and played out the last forty minutes.

England had drawn the match and, psychologically, May and Cowdrey had won the series.

May and Cowdrey Destroy Ramadhin
England v West Indies at Edgbaston
30, 31 May, 1, 3 and 4 June 1957

England First Innings		Second Innings	
P.E. Richardson c Walcott		c sub (Asgarali)	
b Ramadhin	12	b Ramadhin	34
D.B. Close c Kanhai b Gilchrist	15	c Weekes b Gilchrist	42
D.J. Insole b Ramadhin	20	b Ramadhin	0
P.B.H. May (capt) c Weekes			
b Ramadhin	30	not out	285
M.C. Cowdrey c Gilchrist b Ramadhin	4	c sub (Asgarali) b Smith	154
T.E. Bailey b Ramadhin	1		
G.A.R. Lock b Ramadhin	0		
†T.G. Evans b Gilchrist	14	(6) not out	29
J.C. Laker b Ramadhin	7		
F.S. Trueman not out	29		
J.B. Statham b Atkinson	13		
Extras (b 3, lb 3)	6	(b 23, lb 16)	39
Total	186	for 4 wickets, dec.	583

BOWLING	Overs	Mdns	Runs	Wkts	Overs	Mdns	Runs	Wkts
Worrell	9	1	27	–	–	–	–	–
Gilchrist	27	4	74	2	26	2	67	1
Ramadhin	31	16	49	7	98	35	179	2
Atkinson	12.4	3	30	1	72	29	137	–
Sobers	–	–	–	–	30	4	77	–
Smith	–	–	–	–	26	4	72	1
Goddard	–	–	–	–	6	2	12	–

fall of wickets
1–32, 2–61, 3–104, 4–115, 5–116, 6–118, 7–121, 8–130, 9–150
1–63, 2–65, 3–113, 4–524

West Indies First Innings		Second Innings	
B.H. Pairaudeau b Trueman	1	b Trueman	7
†R.B. Kanhai lbw b Statham	42	c Close b Trueman	1
C.L. Walcott c Evans b Laker	90	(6) c Lock b Laker	1
E. de C. Weekes b Trueman	9	c Trueman b Lock	33
G. St A. Sobers c Bailey b Statham .	53	(3) c Cowdrey b Lock . .	14
O.G. Smith lbw b Laker	161	(7) lbw b Laker	5
F.M.M. Worrell b Statham	81	(5) c May b Lock	0
J.D.C. Goddard (capt) c Lock b Laker	24	not out	0
D. St E. Atkinson c Statham b Laker	1	not out	4
S. Ramadhin not out	5		
R. Gilchrist run out	0		
Extras (b 1, lb 6)	7	(b 7)	7
Total	474	for 7 wickets	72

BOWLING	Overs	Mdns	Runs	Wkts	Overs	Mdns	Runs	Wkts
Statham	39	4	114	3	2	–	6	–
Trueman	30	4	99	2	5	3	7	2
Bailey	34	11	80	–	–	–	–	–
Laker	54	17	119	4	24	20	13	2
Lock	34.4	15	55	–	27	19	31	3
Close	–	–	–	–	2	1	8	–

fall of wickets
1–4, 2–83, 3–120, 4–183, 5–197, 6–387, 7–466, 8–469, 9–474
1–1, 2–9, 3–25, 4–27, 5–43, 6–66, 7–68
umpires – D.E. Davies and C.S. Elliott
Match Drawn

England made three changes for the Lord's Test. Neither Laker nor
Lock was fit, and Wardle and Graveney returned while D.V. Smith, the

Sussex left-hander, came in for Insole and opened the innings, as he did at Trent Bridge and at Headingley, but with no success and never again.

At Lord's England won in three days, the game ending on the Saturday afternoon. Batting first on a fast track, the West Indies were torn apart by Trevor Bailey and lost their last five wickets for 42 runs. Cowdrey hit 152 out of England's 424 and, batting a second time 297 runs in arrears, the West Indies again fell to the England pace bowlers. Bailey took four wickets, Statham three, Trueman two, and England won by an innings and 36 runs.

Derek Richardson, younger brother of Peter, played at Nottingham where Graveney got 258, Peter Richardson 126 and May 104 in England's 619 for six, the highest total against the West Indies in a home Test. Trueman took nine wickets in the match and, in spite of the fact that Worrell, who opened with Sobers, carried his bat for 191, the West Indies followed on 247 runs behind. At 89 for five in their second innings, they looked well beaten, but 'Collie' Smith saved his side with his second century of the series, 168. England needed 121 but, with *only* seventeen overs bowled in the last hour, they finished on 64 for one.

England won the last two Tests. The hero at Headingley was Peter Loader, who took nine for 86 in the match, including a hat-trick which brought West Indies' first innings to an abrupt end. It was the first hat-trick by an England bowler in a home Test match since 1899. Evans became the first wicket-keeper to claim 200 victims in Test cricket, and Trueman was warned for intimidatory bowling when he sent four bouncers in an over to Kanhai.

Laker and Lock did their usual double act at The Oval. Facing an England total of 412, the West Indies were bowled out for 89 and 86, and for the third time in the series England had won in three days. David Sheppard had returned at Headingley and scored 68 at number six in England's 279 (still enough to win by an innings). At The Oval, he opened with Peter Richardson and made 40 out of a first-wicket partnership of 92. Richardson and Graveney then added 146 and both scored centuries.

Graveney finished the series with 472 runs in four completed innings, boosted, of course, by his career best 258 at Trent Bridge. May, Cowdrey and Peter Richardson all scored over 400 runs. Trueman took twenty-two wickets, and five other bowlers had more than ten wickets in the series.

Unquestionably, England remained supreme, and the visit of New Zealand in 1958 gave not even the slightest hint that the supremacy could be challenged. Reid's side was weak, lacking depth and substance in batting and, the enthusiastic and hard-working medium pace of MacGibbon apart, quality in bowling. England won the first four Tests by massive margins, and the fifth was ruined by rain with England again on top. Lock took thirty-four wickets in the series at under 8 runs apiece, and five other bowlers captured their wickets at less than 20 runs each. New Zealand's batsmen struggled to average 20 and could not manage a Test century between them.

England batsmen hit four centuries, one of them coming from Arthur Milton on his Test match debut at Headingley. England omitted Peter Richardson from that match because they wished to try out opening batsmen in preparation for the forthcoming tour of Australia. Milton opened with M.J.K. Smith, captain of Warwickshire, once of Leicestershire, who had made his debut in the first Test. There was something unique in the Milton–Smith pairing in that Milton, an Arsenal footballer, had won a soccer international cap playing for England against Austria while Smith had won an England cap at rugby. Smith was out for 3 at Headingley, but Milton, a brilliant fielder and a stylish batsman from Gloucestershire, hit 104 not out and shared an unbroken third-wicket partnership of 194 with May, who also made a century. England's 267 for two was enough to help them to an innings victory in three days.

They also won the next Test, at Old Trafford, by an innings and gave first Test caps to Ted Dexter, Ray Illingworth and Raman Subba Row. Dexter, captain of Cambridge, had enjoyed a good season with bat and ball; Illingworth had done the 'double' for Yorkshire the previous year. The left-handed Subba Row had first assisted Surrey when coming down from Cambridge but had followed Freddie Brown's path to Northamptonshire where he became captain in 1958. That season, against his old county at The Oval, at the beginning of June, he had scored 300, a landmark sure to be noticed by the selectors. He was also to make the party to tour Australia, as did Milton and, ultimately, Dexter. That lay in the future. There were immediate issues in the present.

Surrey won the Championship for the seventh year in succession, yet the signs that their magnificent reign was nearing its end could be recognised by the observant. In surveying the season, *Wisden* commented:

> The latest triumph was not all plain sailing. Illness, injury and heavy representative calls presented many difficulties and they needed all their high skill, resource, team spirit and determination to preserve their standing. With each passing season of success the strain increases. Everywhere there is a growing resolve to end Surrey's stranglehold on the title. The going is hard, particularly because, as in previous years, Surrey made a large-size contribution to England's Test teams. Peter May, the captain, Lock, Laker and Loader played in

132

all, or part, of the series with New Zealand. To enable them to be fit for a five-day Test Lock's knee and Laker's finger had to be given periodical rest, which meant that Surrey's contribution extended beyond the span of the Test matches.

Illness had struck before the season began. Alec Bedser went down with pneumonia and could not play until July. In the absence of May and Bedser, McIntyre, in his last season before becoming county coach, led the side capably. Swetman, his deputy, was selected as Evans's under-study for the tour of Australia, a choice not received with universal glee.

If there were indications that Surrey's star was dimming, the county was still able to unearth talent. Ken Barrington and Micky Stewart were now well established, and 1958 saw the appearance in one match of a stocky left-hander, John Edrich, cousin of Middlesex and England's Bill Edrich.

Surrey took the title by a margin of twenty-six points from Hampshire, who had never before finished so high. Hampshire owed a tremendous debt to Desmond Eagar, who had led the side from 1946 to 1957 and who, as secretary, had transformed the club. He had brought substance, financial stability and enthusiasm and, in 1958, he handed over the captaincy to Colin Ingleby-Mackenzie.

Under Eagar, Hampshire had climbed to third in the Championship in 1955, but with Ingleby-Mackenzie, 'Young Cricketer of the Year' in 1958 and one of the great characters of the game, the side was nearing its peak. Derek Shackleton, a relentlessly accurate medium-pacer, was the focal point of the attack. Like Derbyshire's Les Jackson, he was given scant attention by the England selectors. Roy Marshall, the West Indian opening batsman, was among the most attractive batsmen in the coun-try. He, May and M.J.K. Smith were the only three batsmen to top 2,000 runs in 1958. Marshall played for the Players against the Gentlemen at Lord's and one rocket-like cover drive will ever remain in the memory of those who saw it.

Hampshire dominated the Championship from the middle of June until the middle of August, and they looked likely to depose Surrey, but they won only one of their last eight matches. From start to finish, they played their cricket with enterprise and daring, and they caught the imagination of the public.

Another county to do so, but in a very different way, was Yorkshire. It had been apparent in 1957 that all was not well with the White Rose county even though they finished third in the Championship. The captain, Billy Sutcliffe, son of the great Herbert, stated that he would not be able to lead the side in 1958, and he did not play for Yorkshire again.

133

In addition Yorkshire agreed to allow Watson to take up an appointment with Leicestershire, where he was made captain. There was considerable speculation as to who would succeed Sutcliffe, but none had suspected that Yorkshire's new captain would be J.R. Burnet. The announcement was not made until November 1957, and a few outside Yorkshire had the slightest notion who he was.

John Burnet had been captain of Yorkshire second eleven since 1952. He was thirty-nine years old when he first led the Championship side. Few captains can ever have been faced with such problems and traumas. Watson had left; Lowson and Appleyard had lost form and fitness and neither was re-engaged after the 1958 season, when Yorkshire, in Burnet's first year in office, declined to an unacceptable eleventh in the table. The weather was awful, and Yorkshire's receipts went down by £5,000, a considerable amount of money in 1958. Over all this was the Wardle Affair.

Johnny Wardle was a slow left-arm bowler in the great Yorkshire tradition. His ability to spin the ball was exceptional and, in his twenty-eight Tests, he took 102 wickets at 20.39 runs each, and this at a time when England were rich in spin and he was vying with Tony Lock for a place in the Test side.

To the public, Wardle was a comic, a jovial entertainer who could bring laughter. To his colleagues, he was often caustic and was given to expressing forceful opinions to his captain and to his team-mates.

During the match against Somerset at Sheffield at the end of July, the Yorkshire secretary, J.H. Nash, announced that the county would not be calling on the services of Wardle after the end of the 1958 season. Yorkshire beat Somerset by an innings, and Wardle had figures of six for 46 and two for 29.

The statement shattered the cricket world who, unaware of the events behind the scenes, pointed an accusing finger at Burnet, beginning a first-class year at an age when others had long retired and claiming a career best score of 54 against Sussex at Bradford.

Wardle was selected for the next match, the Roses match at Old Trafford, but rain caused a delayed start and while the players were waiting for the game to commence Burnet issued a statement. 'J.H. Wardle has requested that he stand down from the match because of comments he intends to make about his colleagues in a newspaper article to be published while the match is in progress. He has been given permission to stand down and has left the ground.'

The *Daily Mail* duly published articles under Wardle's name which made unflattering comments about the Yorkshire players, captain, coaches and committee.

These attacks came to the attention of MCC, who announced that they felt that, since the articles had appeared in the *Daily Mail*, the affair between Wardle and Yorkshire was now public rather than domestic and the MCC committee would discuss the situation at their meeting on 19 August. The Yorkshire committee's response was dignified:

> The Yorkshire County Cricket Club Committee regret the unpleasant publicity given to their decision to dispense with the services of J.H. Wardle after the present season. In past years Wardle has been warned on several occasions that his general behaviour on the field and in the dressing rooms left much to be desired. As no improvement was shown this year, the decision to dispense with his services was made, as it was unanimously considered that it was essential to have discipline and a happy and loyal team before any lasting improvement could be expected in the play of the Yorkshire XI.
>
> It is felt that recent articles published in the *Daily Mail* fully justify the committee's decision. Wardle broke his contract when he wrote these articles without first obtaining permission, and the committee are therefore terminating his engagement forthwith. The committee emphatically reaffirm their high regard for the services of Mr J.R. Burnet and his predecessors in the captaincy, for the loyalty and restraint shown by players in the trying circumstances and for the valued work the former players give so helpfully in acting as cricket coaches.

Wardle was interviewed by the MCC committee at their meeting on 19 August, and the committee also considered a report sent to them by Yorkshire County Cricket Club. The *Daily Mail* articles had appeared after Wardle had been invited to tour Australia as a member of Peter May's side in the winter of 1958–59. MCC felt that what Wardle had done was a 'grave disservice to the game', and they believed that 'the welfare of cricket as a whole in terms of loyalty and behaviour must override all other considerations'. The invitation to Wardle to be a member of the side to tour Australia was withdrawn.

Wardle was later quoted as saying that he had been sacked because he 'refused to accept the authority of the hopeless old man appointed captain'. If he looked for support, it was not forthcoming. Unsolicited, the Yorkshire players issued a statement pledging their loyalty to Burnet and their confidence in him.

Inevitably, other counties made offers to Wardle to join them, and he accepted an invitation to play for Nottinghamshire. Some weeks later, he announced that he was finished with county cricket, and he went into the Lancashire League. He made some scathing comments on the 1958–59 tour for the *Daily Mail*, but he never played Test or county cricket again.

None of this, of course, was any help to Burnet. He began his second season of captaincy in 1959 with discontent bubbling among Yorkshire members who believed that the problem could lie with the committee's desire to preserve a fading tradition that the captain must be an amateur. What was overlooked was that Burnet had led the second eleven for five years and that he had encouraged and helped develop cricketers like Binks, Bolus, Bird, Sharpe, Birkenshaw and Don Wilson. He knew his men, and they knew him.

A defeat at the hands of Lancashire at Old Trafford and a mid-table position by mid-June did nothing to placate the members, but then came wins against Sussex, Warwickshire and Essex. Yorkshire went top, and they were never out of the first three for the rest of the season.

By the end of August Surrey needed to win their last two matches to retain the title they had held for seven years. Surrey were entertaining Middlesex at The Oval while Yorkshire were playing Sussex at Hove. Middlesex forced a draw against Surrey, but Yorkshire won a sensational victory.

Ray Illingworth, who completed the 'double', hit 122 and helped give Yorkshire a first-innings lead of 97. Sussex cleared the arrears for the loss of two wickets, and Parks batted excitingly to frustrate Yorkshire, who could not take the last Sussex second-innings wicket until half an hour after lunch on the final day. This left Yorkshire, playing their last county game of the season, 105 minutes in which to score 215 runs if they were to win the Championship. This was a rate of approximately 7 runs an over.

Thomson's first over went for 15 runs, Stott getting 13 of them, and the 50 came up in twenty minutes, but Taylor and Close were gone. Padgett joined Stott, and the pair added 141 in just over an hour. Padgett was out for 79 and Stott for 96 in eighty-six minutes, but they had provided the runs and the impetus for a famous victory. At 4.23, Bolus deflected a ball from Dexter to the fine-leg boundary, and Yorkshire had won with seven minutes to spare. Their batsmen had played a shot at every ball, and they had scored at 7.64 runs an over. Having achieved more than any could have expected, Burnet, 'the hopeless old man', stood down, and Vic Wilson became Yorkshire's first professional captain of the twentieth century. Surrey's supremacy had come to an end.

When, at the end of the previous season, MCC named a party of seventeen under Peter May to tour Australia and New Zealand in the winter

136

of 1958–59 the general consensus was that this was one of the strongest sides to have left these shores. This view persisted even after the party had been reduced to sixteen by the withdrawal of the invitation to Wardle.

The batting was in strong hands. May, with two Test hundreds against the New Zealanders, and Cowdrey were at the height of their powers. Watson was reliable and experienced. Graveney had matured into a Test batsman of high quality, and Richardson's career at international level had begun with a flurry of centuries. Milton had already proved himself with a Test century on his debut, and much was expected of Subba Row, who could bat anywhere in the order.

Statham, Trueman, Loader and Tyson comprised a quartet of fast bowlers that was the envy of the world, as were the spin duo Lock, a much improved batsman, and Laker. Bailey, a seasoned campaigner and a great all-rounder, could and would fill any role that he was asked to play. Evans remained supreme among wicket-keepers.

Despite the optimism, nothing seemed to go right. Initially, Laker had declined the invitation to tour but had later changed his mind. He celebrated his thirty-seventh birthday on the tour, and, as his career drew to a close, he appeared to become less enamoured of the game. He had rubbed his fingers raw in spinning the ball – Les Ames was to say that he was the last man really to spin the ball as opposed to rolling his fingers over the top – and he was to leave Surrey in somewhat acrimonious circumstances at the end of the 1959 season. He did not play Test cricket after the 1958–59 tour of Australia.

The Test careers of Tyson and Bailey were others which were to come to an end on this tour although Bailey, one feels, was jettisoned a little prematurely. Tyson's form for Northamptonshire had been indifferent in 1958, and his selection was based on remembrance of things past rather than on current form. He had been the fastest in the world, but four years can be a long time for a pace bowler.

The problems did not end with selection. Watson hurt himself on board the boat, SS *Iberia*, and had to undergo a knee operation, while Subba Row broke his wrist just before the first Test. Mortimore, the Gloucestershire off-spinner, and Dexter were flown out as reinforcements to the party.

If the construction of the MCC party could be blamed on selection and the injuries on bad luck, there was another factor which put strain on the tourists and soured the series – the suspect actions of four members of the Australian attack, Burke, Meckiff, Rorke and Slater. None of these bowlers was 'called' for throwing, and the Australian Board of Control denied the existence of any problem, but most people

137

felt that they were blinding themselves to what was happening.

Meckiff was a left-arm bowler with a strong physique and a deceptive, quick pace. He took nine for 107 to help Australia win the second Test in Melbourne. Criticisms of his action were loud and long. He did not tour England in 1961 because of injury and loss of form, and his action escaped censure until December 1963. Playing for Australia against South Africa at Brisbane, he was no-balled four times in his opening over by umpire Colin Egar, and he announced his immediate retirement from all forms of first-class cricket.

Keith Slater bowled both off-spin and medium pace and had success for Western Australia against MCC at the start of the tour. The Englishmen were very critical of his action, but he played in only one Test and was no-balled only once for throwing, and that was in his final season, 1964–65. Like Slater, Burke was an off-break bowler, but he was used only occasionally in Test matches. Nevertheless, his action was notoriously that of a 'chucker'.

Rourke's problem was different. Massive, blond-haired and handsome, he bowled the ball from a great height, but he also dragged his rear foot well over the bowling crease and was intimidating. It was his action that had a considerable influence on the alterations in the no-ball law, which judged no-balls on the front foot in relation to the batting crease for the first time in 1963.

Whatever the concerns over actions and the excuses that could be offered regarding injuries, nothing could alter the fact that the Australians were a far better side than May's men, and that no stigma was attached to the two bowlers who did most to win back the Ashes, Benaud, the new captain, and Davidson.

Both of these bowlers, like Meckiff, moved the ball from leg to off, and the England batsmen were ill at ease against such movement – one could suggest that they have remained so ever since. England had sought to counter the Australian form of attack by choosing three left-handers, but Watson and Subba Row were handicapped by injury – Subba Row did not appear in a single Test – and Richardson had a disappointing series and tour. Milton, too, had a less than happy tour, and England were again faced with an openers problem. The ever-faithful Bailey was asked to open in the last four Tests.

Bailey was one of those accused of making this the dullest of Test series. In the first Test he batted 458 minutes for 68, but Burke was to manage an even slower rate with 28 in 250 minutes. In the third Test Cowdrey's unbeaten century occupied 362 minutes and was the slowest hundred in the history of the Ashes series until Woolmer's innings at The Oval sixteen years later. Mackay was always painfully slow, but he did not bat on the fourth day of the first Test when England scored 106 runs, the fewest ever recorded in a day's Test cricket in Australia. One writer on the tour was to comment later that, had he not been paid to report on the cricket, he would not have crossed the road to watch it.

There were other areas in which the series brought criticism. The judgements of veteran Test umpire McInnes proved to be controversial. He stood in the first four Tests and retired when not invited to officiate in the fifth. The disgruntled manner in which decisions were received brought credit to neither side, and there were instances of gamesmanship, of running on the pitch and rubbing the ball on the ground, which did nothing to advance the reputation of the game.

Aside from the abysmal rate of scoring, the deliberate slowing of over-rates was deplorable. On the second day of the fourth Test at Adelaide England bowled only fifty-one overs, and on the fourth day Australia restricted their quota to fifty-six.

It was in this fourth Test that Australia regained the Ashes, winning by ten wickets. McDonald scored a fine 170, and Benaud took nine wickets. Australia had won the first two Tests and drawn the third at Sydney, where Swetman made his Test debut in place of the injured Evans. Swetman also played in the final Test at Melbourne when McDonald got another hundred and Australia won by nine wickets.

Statham and Laker bowled well for England, and May and Cowdrey scored England's only centuries in the series. They stood head and shoulders above their colleagues as batsmen, and none argued with the assessment that May was the finest batsman in the world. As a captain, however, he seemed strained, lacking in positiveness and often surrendering the initiative to the dynamic and innovative Benaud. May failed to communicate to his men as once he had done, while Benaud, thirty-one wickets in the series, made a side of average ability feel that they were supermen.

As with all sides that struggle, England changed their personnel frequently, and of the eighteen players in the party only Subba Row failed to appear in a Test and only Cowdrey, May, Graveney and Bailey appeared in all five. Dexter played in the third and fifth Tests, raw and untried, and, in the opinion of one critic, 'very upright and very vulnerable'. His late summoning to the tour had captured the public's imagination, for he had been holidaying in Paris with his beautiful wife, a fashion model, when the call came. Mortimore played in the last Test, but he had become immortalised before setting foot in Australia. About to board his flight, he had responded to reporters' questions by replying, 'I am under contract to MCC and am not empowered to say anything about cricket.'

Laker stated that he was unfit for the New Zealand leg of the tour and returned to England. Bailey, too, did not play in New Zealand, and in his last Test he was out for a 'pair', twice falling to Lindwall, to whom, four years earlier, he had surrendered his wicket, believing that Lindwall was playing his last Test.

Lock took eleven wickets and Dexter scored a maiden Test hundred as England beat New Zealand by an innings at Christchurch. Years later, Dexter was to pay tribute to May who, he said, talked him through the first part of his innings. May himself hit a century in the second, rain-ruined Test, which saw the end of Tyson's brief but memorable international career.

Looking back on events, it seems now that cricket was beginning to suffer from a malaise of which it was blissfully unaware. Not for the first time, the game was insensitive to the social changes that were taking place and which were sure to have an effect on it. The arrival of yellow lines, parking meters, the M1 and traffic wardens gave indication of the ever-increasing number of cars that were now on the roads; and the fact that nearly a hundred cinemas had shut down and more were scheduled for closure showed clearly that people were able to pursue a variety of entertainments, many more than had once been available to them. Television was becoming a dominant force, and the swallowing of the *News Chronicle* by the *Daily Mail* was the first sign that the newspaper world was beginning to shrink.

England were conscious that they had to rebuild. The 1959 series against India saw Greenhough, Horton, Taylor, Pullar and Rhodes introduced to Test cricket, and Parkhouse, after eight years, Barrington, Close, Moss, Mike Smith, Illingworth and Subba Row recalled. The series was won, spectacularly, by five Tests to nil, but there were misgivings.

Godfrey Evans played in the first two Tests, hit 73 in the first and brought his total of dismissals to 216 in ninety-one matches. This total included forty-six stumpings, which remains an English record. It was obvious, though, that a spark had gone. He was thirty-nine, and Swetman replaced him after the Lord's Test.

Martin Horton, the Worcestershire all-rounder, and Ken Taylor, the Yorkshire opener, were never to establish themselves in the England side, although Taylor was to be recalled for one match five years later.

Geoff Pullar was to play in twenty-eight Tests for England as a left-handed opening batsman, but his Lancashire colleague, the leg-spinner Tommy Greenhough, was less fortunate. Benaud's tremendous success had only served to underline England's lack of a top-class leg-spinner. Where England had once gone into a Test match with as many as three

140

leg-spinners in the side, they now had none. Leg-spinning was a dying art. The use of artificial fertilisers, the increased lushness of outfields in an effort to keep the ball 'new' for longer and so aid the pace bowlers, and the loss of natural wickets were telling, particularly against the leg-spinner, who was to become virtually extinct in English cricket.

The case of Harold 'Dusty' Rhodes was very different. With Tyson and Bailey having ended their Test careers, England were in search of a fast bowler to support the now firmly established pair of Trueman and Statham. Loader was still in good form, but the selectors had turned their back on him, and Moss played in the first three Tests against India, sharing the new ball with Trueman at Headingley. Rhodes made his debut in that Test, took four good wickets in the first innings, and followed this with match figures of five for 159 at Old Trafford. His victims were all top-order batsmen, but he never played Test cricket again. He was twenty-three years old, quick and a wicket-taker, but his action was suspect.

The problem, as had been the case with Lock, arose especially when Rhodes attempted to deliver a quicker ball. At Derby in 1960 umpire Paul Gibb called him six times for throwing, and Rhodes was later called by Syd Buller. MCC investigated the affair and concluded that Rhodes had a 'hyper-extended arm', and he was officially cleared, but Rhodes was guilty until proved innocent. Although consistently near the top of the first-class bowling averages and with England crying out for a quick bowler, he was never selected; even when, in 1965, he captured 119 wickets at 11.04 runs each.

The first Test against India, played at Trent Bridge, was won by an innings. Trueman and Statham proved to be too much for the Indians, but the main feature of the match was a faultless century by Peter May. It was his thirteenth and last in Test cricket. He led England in the next two Tests, both won convincingly, Cowdrey getting 160 at Headingley, but then stood down at Old Trafford and The Oval. An internal problem necessitated surgery, and Cowdrey captained England in the last two games, which, again, were resounding victories.

For May, it was a difficult season. He could not take his place in the Surrey side until the end of May. In mid-July he was laid low by illness and the operation followed. In all he played only seven Championship matches for Surrey, who, as we have seen, lost the Championship title. But there were compensations for Surrey in that John Edrich enjoyed a wonderful first full season in county cricket and hit five centuries. Micky Stewart, too, batted splendidly, and Ken Barrington earned a recall to the England side. He played in all five Tests and averaged 59.50 although he did not make a century.

The two centurions, apart from May and Cowdrey, were Geoff Pullar and Mike Smith. Pullar's 131 at Old Trafford was, surprisingly, the first Test hundred scored by a Lancashire batsman on the famous old ground. Smith scored exactly 100 in the same match. Both men had outstanding seasons. Smith hit 3,245 runs and finished top of the national averages with Watson second, Pullar, 2,647 runs, third and Barrington, 2,499, fourth. Jim Parks, who had turned to wicket-keeping and claimed ninety-one victims, John Edrich and Trevor Bailey were also high on the list. With more than 2,000 runs and 100 wickets, Bailey had a right to feel that he would earn a place in the party to tour the West Indies, but the selectors, G.O. Allen, Herbert Sutcliffe, Doug Insole and Wilf Wooller, had announced that they were embarking on a three-year plan aimed at producing a side capable of regaining the Ashes in 1961 and Bailey, Graveney, Richardson and Evans were among those, temporarily at least, no longer part of their plans. The side that went to the Caribbean, with Walter Robins as manager, was 'new' England.

May led the side, Cowdrey was his lieutenant, and Subba Row, Pullar, Barrington and Smith completed the batting. Trueman, Statham and Moss were the pace men; Greenhough, Illingworth and Allen, an off-spinner lately discovered by Gloucestershire, were the spinners. Andrew and Swetman were the wicket-keepers while Dexter was cast in the role of all-rounder although his seam bowling could never seriously be considered as in a class approaching Bailey's.

When they set sail for the Caribbean on the *Camito* this side was given no chance of winning the rubber by most observers of the game, yet they returned four months later with an historic victory to their credit.

There was little indication of such success early on when MCC lost to Barbados just before the first Test, in which Allen made his debut. It was an unfortunate Test for a bowler to make his first appearance, for it was dominated by the bat. Barrington and Dexter scored centuries for England; Sobers, 226, and Worrell, 197 not out, added 399 in 579 minutes for the West Indies' fourth wicket. They batted together for two days, and the match was drawn.

Two victories over Trinidad between the first and second Tests raised spirits which were heightened even more when, in Port of Spain, May won the toss in the second Test. Statham, who had been unfit for the first encounter, came in for Moss, the only change to the England side, while the West Indies included Solomon and C.K. Singh in place of McMorris and Scarlett. Singh was making his debut, and he was to be at the centre of an unfortunate incident for which, one should add, he was totally blameless.

142

The pitch was lightning fast, and Hall and Watson were in their element. Hall conceded 12 runs in his opening over, but thereafter the batsmen were subjected to a fierce barrage. England had not solved their openers problem, and Cowdrey, reluctantly but bravely and successfully, took on the burden in all five Tests.

For half an hour Pullar and Cowdrey repelled all that Watson and Hall could muster, but the bowlers then changed ends. They proceeded to unleash a furious attack of short-pitched balls and bumpers. Pullar was out from a fine leg-glance after forty-five minutes, and Cowdrey, hit painfully twice in four balls, played on to Hall. May, clearly below his best, edged to slip in the last over before lunch, which came with England on 57 for three.

The afternoon session belonged entirely to England as Dexter and Barrington batted with assurance and belligerence. Dexter had come of age in Test cricket. His imperious bearing had won him the nickname of 'Lord Ted', and his powerful cover-driving, regal in manner, confirmed the epithet. If more reflective, Barrington was equally effective and offered a solidity to the England batting which was much needed. At tea the pair had taken the score to 170.

The stand was worth 142 in 157 minutes when Dexter gave Singh a return catch. Dexter had batted magnificently and had been almost contemptuous of the barrage of short-pitched deliveries. Both Hall and Watson were cautioned under Law 46 of the 1947 code, and there were fewer short balls on the third day, but the matter was not at an end.

Barrington and Smith took England to 220 by the close, Barrington having reached 97. He duly completed his second successive Test century the next morning and was not dismissed until shortly after lunch, falling to a fine diving catch by the wicket-keeper Alexander. He had batted ten minutes under six hours and he had provided England with a concrete base after a disastrous start. With Barrington gone, Smith decided to attack and hit sixes off both Singh and Ramadhin. He was ninth out, caught close in by Worrell off a hard hit, and his 108 had come in under five hours.

The West Indies' Hunte and Solomon survived the last twenty-six minutes of the day, scoring 22, but nothing prepared the spectators for what was to happen on the third day.

Hunte was caught off bat and boot without addition to the overnight score, and Kanhai was leg-before to a ball of very full length nine runs later. Sobers – who had made the highest Test match score of 365 not out against Pakistan in 1957–58 – entered to a tremendous ovation but left almost in silence as he flashed wildly at Trueman. The ball flew to May who knocked it up for Barrington to complete the catch.

The West Indies disintegrated before the fast bowling of Trueman and Statham, who were hostile and controlled. Solomon was run out by Allen's fine throw from cover while Worrell fell to an excellent catch by Swetman. At lunch the West Indies were 45 for five.

Butcher and Alexander had no option but to concentrate exclusively on defence. At one stage Barrington bowled twelve overs of his occasional leg-breaks for 3 runs. Butcher had batted 106 minutes for his 9 when he was leg-before to Statham, and Alexander was leg-before offering no stroke to Trueman just after tea. A fast return from Dexter at cover ran out Singh.

Then came the eruption

There was a crowd of almost 30,000, and Singh was the local hero making his Test debut. On top of this, the West Indies had collapsed to 98 for eight. A section of the crowd took the running-out of Singh as a signal to show their disapproval, although Singh did not question the umpire's decision. He knew and accepted that he was out. Bottles, beer cans and a variety of missiles were thrown, and soon the crowd was milling on the playing area with the England team marooned in the middle. Alexander came on to the field and spoke with May who, after about ten minutes, led his side off the field. The police were unable to restore order, and they needed the assistance of the mounted police, riot squad and fire brigade before the ground could be cleared.

On the rest day a conference was held between police, ground authorities, managers and captains, and it was agreed that half an hour should be added to the remaining three days to compensate for the time lost. The game restarted on 1 February in an atmosphere of calm.

The West Indies' innings soon came to an end, but May chose not to enforce the follow-on although England had a lead of 270. Cowdrey attempted to force the pace and was caught behind. Pullar found scoring difficult before, in frustration, hitting out at Ramadhin and suffering the consequence. Barrington again looked solid until edging a catch as he drove at Hall, who struck again when he bowled Dexter 4 runs later.

May was at the crease for two hours, but it was apparent that all was not well with the England captain. Smith and Swetman failed, but the Yorkshire pair, Trueman and Illingworth, hit 63 in the last forty-five minutes of the day. Trueman hit Singh for two sixes in an over which brought 18 runs, and England were in command.

Trueman was out 5 runs into the fourth morning, and when May declared after forty-five minutes' play which had brought 34 runs, the West Indies had ten hours in which to score 501. Solomon and Hunt were comfortable until lunch, but immediately after the break Allen claimed his first Test wicket when he had Solomon caught behind as he tried to cut.

Caution was now the policy, and two hours produced only 48 runs. Hunte's patience finally broke and he was out at 107, but Kanhai, 55, and Sobers, 19, added 27 before the close of play and looked quite capable of saving the game, even though May had the option of the new ball at the start of the sixth and last day.

It was nearly an hour before England got the vital breakthrough on the last morning, Sobers falling leg-before to a ball from Trueman which kept low. Decisively, Worrell was out 1 run later, and England scented victory.

Butcher was never happy against the quick bowlers, but Kanhai and Alexander gave solid resistance for forty-five minutes. Kanhai's innings lasted 378 minutes and included a six and nineteen fours. He excited the crowd after lunch on the final day by hitting Trueman for 15 in an over, but he hit a full toss from Dexter straight into the hands of mid-wicket. With his next ball, Dexter had Ramadhin leg-before. The last three wickets fell at the same total, Barrington claiming two of them, and England had won a fine, but unexpected, victory.

England Win a Series in the West Indies for the First Time
West Indies v England at Queen's Park Oval, Port of Spain, Trinidad 28, 29, 30 January, 1, 2 and 3 February 1960

England First Innings		Second Innings	
G. Pullar c Alexander b Watson . . .	17	c Worrell b Ramadhin . .	28
M.C. Cowdrey b Hall	18	c Alexander b Watson . .	5
K.F. Barrington c Alexander b Hall	121	c Alexander b Hall	49
P.B.H. May (capt) c Kanhai b Watson	0	c and b Singh	28
E.R. Dexter c and b Singh	77	b Hall	0
M.J.K. Smith c Worrell b Ramadhin	108	lbw b Watson	12
R. Illingworth b Ramadhin	10	not out	41
†R. Swetman lbw b Watson	1	lbw b Singh	0
F.S. Trueman lbw b Ramadhin	7	c Alexander b Watson . .	37
D.A. Allen not out	10	c Alexander b Hall	16
J.B. Statham b Worrell	1		
Extras (lb 3, w 1, nb 8)	12	(b 6, lb 2, w 4, nb 2)	14
Total	382	for 9 wickets, dec.	230

BOWLING	Overs	Mdns	Runs	Wkts	Overs	Mdns	Runs	Wkts
Hall	33	9	92	2	23.4	4	50	3
Watson	31	5	100	3	19	6	57	3

Worrell	11.5	3	23	1	12	5	27	–
Singh	23	6	59	1	8	3	28	2
Ramadhin	35	12	61	3	28	8	54	1
Sobers	3	–	16	–	–	–	–	–
Solomon	7	–	19	–	–	–	–	–

fall of wickets
1–37, 2–42, 3–57, 4–199, 5–276, 6–307, 7–308, 8–343, 9–378
1–18, 2–79, 3–97, 4–101, 5–122, 6–133, 7–133, 8–201, 9–230

West Indies First Innings		Second Innings	
C.C. Hunte c Trueman b Statham .	8	c Swetman b Allen	47
J.S. Solomon run out	23	c Swetman b Allen	9
R.B. Kanhai lbw b Trueman	5	c Smith b Dexter	110
G. St A. Sobers c Barrington			
b Trueman	0	lbw b Trueman	31
F.M.M. Worrell c Swetman b Trueman	9	lbw b Statham	0
B.F. Butcher lbw b Statham	9	lbw b Statham	9
†F.C.M. Alexander (capt) lbw			
b Trueman	28	c Trueman b Allen	7
S. Ramadhin b Trueman	23	lbw b Dexter	0
C.K. Singh run out	0	c and b Barrington	11
W.W. Hall b Statham	4	not out	0
C.D. Watson not out	0	c Allen b Barrington . . .	0
Extras (lb 2, w 1)	3	(b 11, lb 6, w 2, nb 1) . . .	20
Total	112	. . . .	244

BOWLING	Overs	Mdns	Runs	Wkts	Overs	Mdns	Runs	Wkts
Trueman	21	11	35	5	19	9	44	1
Statham	19.3	8	42	3	25	12	44	2
Allen	5	–	9	–	31	13	57	3
Barrington	16	10	15	–	25.5	13	34	2
Illingworth	7	3	8	–	28	14	38	–
Dexter	–	–	–	–	6	3	7	2

fall of wickets
1–22, 2–31, 3–31, 4–45, 5–45, 6–73, 7–94, 8–98, 9–108
1–29, 2–107, 3–158, 4–159, 5–188, 6–222, 7–222, 8–244, 9–244
umpires – E.N. Lee Kow and E.L. Lloyd
England won by 256 runs

The task now was to hold the lead and secure the rubber, but this hardly looked possible after the first day at Sabina Park, which saw

Cowdrey fight a lone battle, ending the day with 75 out of a total of 165 for six. He completed a fine hundred on the second day, and the tail wagged well, but a Sobers century gave the West Indies a first-innings lead of 76. Pullar and Cowdrey brought England right back into the game with an opening stand of 177. They both fell at the same total, with Cowdrey following his first-innings 114 with an equally fine 97.

A mid-order collapse followed, and England ended the fifth day on 280 for nine. Crucially, Allen and Statham held out for forty-five minutes on the final morning and added 25. The West Indies needed 230 in 245 minutes on a pitch which was showing signs of wear and on which the ball tended to keep low.

McMorris was soon bowled by Trueman, but Hunte was off with a flourish. He hit 20 runs in the last two overs before lunch and had scored 40 out of 48 in an hour when Trueman bowled him. Kanhai and Sobers began to score freely, and the run-rate seemed to be presenting no problems. The turning point came when Sobers was needlessly run out. Nurse was bowled by Trueman almost on the stroke of tea, and the West Indies needed 115 in ninety minutes in the last session with six wickets standing.

Kanhai was seized with cramp, and Alexander requested a runner, which May refused. Kanhai was, in fact, quite entitled to a runner, and there was no need to have asked May's permission on the point. When Kanhai was bowled hitting out the West Indies called off the chase.

The fourth Test was in British Guiana, but a week before the Test itself MCC played the colony. May had stood down from the previous match in Antigua, but he led the side in Georgetown. British Guiana declared at 375 for six. Pullar and Cowdrey scored centuries and put on 281 for the first wicket. May was unable to bat through illness.

Following the operation which had kept him out of the last part of the English season, May had declared himself fit to lead the side to the Caribbean. It was obvious from his form in the Tests that he was not himself, and his action of refusing to allow Kanhai a runner was uncharacteristic. The reasons for May's form and attitude became clear when it was revealed that the wound from the operation had reopened before the second Test, a fact which he had kept to himself. In spite of his physical condition, he scored a century against Jamaica between the second and third Tests, and one can only conjecture what this must have cost him. He was in extreme discomfort, and when his state of health became known he was advised to fly home for treatment, which he did, missing the last two Tests. His courage in continuing to play cricket at such a high level while under severe handicap can only be admired.

Jim Parks was coaching in Trinidad and was released from his contract so that he could bolster the MCC party after May's departure. He was not the last to be in the right place at the right time when an England party was on tour.

Subba Row took May's place in the England side for the fourth Test, with Cowdrey taking over the captaincy. Sobers hit a century, his third of the series, and took the West Indies into a first-innings lead of 107. Dexter and Subba Row scored hundreds, and the match was drawn, but it was noted for some tediously slow cricket.

Swetman's wicket-keeping had been disappointing, and Andrew, for long the best technical keeper in England, was never really considered for a Test place because of his limited ability as a batsman. That was to be his fate for his unobtrusive, neatly efficient thirteen-year career in first-class cricket. Parks was given a game against Berbice, the only match which separated the fourth and fifth Tests. He scored 183 and replaced Swetman for the final encounter back in Port of Spain. Poor Keith Andrew played in just four first-class matches and had but one innings on the whole tour, yet he still led the fielders with twelve dismissals, five of them stumpings.

England won the toss for the fifth time in the series in Port of Spain, and Cowdrey and Dexter scored 191 for the second wicket, with Cowdrey hitting his second hundred of the rubber. Even without Statham, who, like May, had been forced to fly home to England, the English bowlers contained the West Indian batsmen, and Alexander declared 55 runs in arrears. His action seemed proved right when England slipped to 148 for six. Parks now joined Smith in a record stand of 197. Parks batted three and a half hours for his maiden Test century. He had grasped the opportunity that fate had given him. Cowdrey's declaration set the West Indies a target of 406 in under three hours. The match was drawn, and England had won a series in the West Indies for the first time.

There was much to be grateful for. Cowdrey scored a thousand first-class runs on the tour and he was now recognised throughout the world as a great batsman. Dexter had developed to such an extent as to rival both May and Cowdrey. He was tall, upright and commanding and no man played short-pitched bowling better. Barrington looked less happy against such bowling, but he had shown that he was a batsman of tremendous grit and determination. Allen had justified his selection as an off-break bowler, and Trueman and Statham had carried the attack splendidly.

Trueman had matured to the extent that he took over as senior professional when Statham flew home to England. Trueman's twenty-one wickets were more than any other England bowler had taken in a Test series in the Caribbean, and he had become a clown prince, very popular with the crowds.

If these were positive points, there were areas of disquiet which concerned the game as a whole. Several of the West Indian bowlers encountered on the tour had actions which were suspect, yet they went uncensured, mainly because umpires felt that if they no-balled a bowler for throwing, they would not receive the necessary backing. As Leslie Smith noted in *Wisden*, 'One leading umpire in West Indies resigned because he intended to call a certain bowler for throwing and knew he would not get the support from his authorities.'

Umpires were also reluctant to apply Law 46: 'The persistent and systematic bowling of fast short-pitched balls at the batsman is unfair.' Perhaps the law, as it stood, was too imprecise, but it was generally felt that the use of the bumper had reached epidemic proportions.

If these criticisms were applied mainly at the West Indies, England took most of the blame for the dreadfully slow play that characterised the series. Having won the second Test, they adopted tactics which they hoped would minimise the chances of defeat. They employed negative bowling tactics, maintaining a line outside off stump to defensive field placings. If frustrating for the spectators, such tactics were legitimate, but the time-wasting was not. The field changes between overs, and when left-handed and right-handed batsmen were at the wicket together, became laborious. Where once twenty overs an hour had been the norm in Test cricket, the rate plummeted to fourteen in this series.

These were problems that the Imperial Cricket Conference were to be forced to address, but, for the time being, as Leslie Smith so aptly stated, 'Authorities everywhere must take the blame for the decline in cricketing ethics and the breaking of laws. In the majority of cases they know what is happening but shut their eyes, particularly if it suits them to do so.'

The sixties had begun to swing.

5

The Sad Sixties, 1960–69

News from Africa dominated the early part of the 1960s. There was, Harold Macmillan had said, 'a wind of change' sweeping through the continent. Countries were gaining independence from colonial rule. The map of Africa was being redrawn. In South Africa, where all black political organisations were outlawed, attitudes were hardening. People in Britain who had remained ignorant of, or indifferent to, what had been happening there were outraged at the news of the Sharpeville massacre and the suppression that existed in the state of emergency that followed. At the United Nations only Britain refused to condemn South Africa.

For the most part, the cricket community tried to pretend that nothing was amiss, that the commonwealth of cricketing nations was unaffected by these political events, but the first salvo in what was to be a long battle was fired by David Sheppard. Recently appointed to a committee that had been set up to investigate the financial state of the game, Sheppard announced publicly that he would not tour South Africa for political and moral reasons. The announcement was made just before the South African side under McGlew arrived in England.

It was a poor side, and the tour was to be a far from happy one for a variety of reasons. For the fourth consecutive summer a visiting Test side failed to extend England. The rubber was decided after the first three matches. The Tests were generally poorly attended, although it was unclear whether this was due to the one-sidedness of the contests, the dullness of the South Africans' play or the first rumblings of political boycott.

On his return to England from the Caribbean, Peter May had undergone a second operation and spent the summer recuperating. He played no cricket, and Cowdrey retained the England captaincy. Parks was kept as wicket-keeper, and the series saw Bob Barber, Peter Walker and Doug Padgett win England caps.

As Barrington missed the first Test, England took the field without a Surrey player in the eleven for the first time since 1949.

In 1951 South Africa had toured England with a quick bowler in their side, Cuan McCarthy, about whose action there was considerable concern. Nine years on they returned with Geoff Griffin, another pace bowler.

Griffin had suffered an accident at school which left him with an inability to straighten the right arm properly because of a crooked elbow. Naturally, this cast grave doubts upon his action as a fast bowler, particularly at a time when 'throwing' had become a major subject of concern and debate. When the South Africans drew with MCC in May Griffin was called for throwing by both umpires, Frank Lee and John Langridge. A week later, at Trent Bridge, he was called by umpires Copson and Bartley.

Alf Gover, the former Surrey fast bowler and a most respected coach who ran his own cricket school, gave Griffin a three-day intensive course in an attempt to rectify the faults in the bowler's action. Griffin played at Cardiff without mishap, and in the first Test at Edgbaston where he took four wickets.

England won that Test by 100 runs. Five county captains were in the England side; one of them, Barber, was making his debut. A left-handed batsman and a leg-break bowler, Barber was leading Lancashire through a particularly tempestuous period. By completing the double over Yorkshire, Lancashire looked set to win the title, but they fell apart in August and finished second. Yorkshire, under the professional Vic Wilson, took the Championship for the second year running.

Barber was openly critical of Cowdrey following Lancashire's drawn match with Kent at Old Trafford. The Lancashire committee immediately dissociated themselves from Barber's statement, and there were further altercations with Dyson and Clayton. The latter was dropped and Dyson, a fine soccer player with Manchester City, was sacked, although he did reappear a couple of years later, by which time Barber had moved to Warwickshire.

Barrington returned in place of Barber for the second Test match at Lord's, which England won by an innings. Griffin was called eleven times for throwing by umpire Lee. This was the first time a bowler had been no-balled for throwing in a Test in England, and the no-balling of Griffin in the MCC match at Lord's earlier had been the first instance of a member of a touring party being called for the offence.

Griffin's contribution to history did not end there, for, in dismissing Smith with the last ball of one over and Walker and Trueman with the first two balls of the next, he became the first bowler to perform the hat-trick in a Test at Lord's and the first South African to claim a Test hat-trick.

Facing a total of 362, South Africa were bowled out for 152 and 137, and the match was over a quarter of an hour after lunch on the fourth day. Statham had match figures of eleven for 97, his best in Test cricket.

It was agreed to play an exhibition game as the Test had ended early, and what followed could best be described as tragic farce. Griffin bowled one over which consisted of eleven balls. He was no-balled four times in five balls by umpire Syd Buller, who scrutinised Griffin's action from both square-leg and point. McGlew, the South African captain, spoke to Buller and told Griffin to finish the over bowling underarm. As soon as Griffin bowled underarm, umpire Lee no-balled him for not informing the batsman in advance. The over was duly completed, and Griffin did not bowl again on the tour, nor did he ever appear in another Test match. South Africa won the fifteen-over exhibition by three wickets, scant compensation.

The South Africans refused to accept Buller as an umpire for future Tests in the series on the grounds that he had applied the law in a friendly match. In effect, they were confirming the umpires' view that they were under intense pressure not to apply the law at all.

Buller was one of the best half-dozen umpires ever to have stood in a Test match: honest, fearless and clear. His action helped to force an ICC debate which brought an end to the controversy, albeit with a compromise period of amnesty. The ICC also considered the questions of bouncers, leg-side fielding limitations and slow play. Changes were also made to the Championship for 1961 when the follow-on was abolished and the new ball could only be taken after eighty-five overs.

Meanwhile, England won the third Test to clinch the rubber and drew the fourth and fifth matches. In the fifth Test at The Oval Pullar, 175, and Cowdrey, 155, shared an opening stand of 290. McLean had hit a century in the rain-ruined Test at Old Trafford; these were the only hundreds in a series dominated by the pace bowlers. Statham took twenty-seven wickets for England; Trueman twenty-five. Moss had nine in two Tests, and all three captured their wickets at under 21 runs each. Adcock took twenty-six wickets at under 23 for South Africa.

The summer was a poor one, but this did not totally explain attendances at cricket matches falling to their second-lowest figure since the war. They were down on every day of the week, and the finances of counties suffered.

There were some ideas put forward as to how finances could be improved, but often they were based on spending money which was not available. Charles Jones, who had organised the London Counties side

152

during the Second World War, put forward the plan for a 'festival of cricket' which would involve England, Australia, New Zealand, Pakistan, India and the West Indies playing thirty three-day Tests during an English summer, with each county staging at least one Test. The County Championship would be reduced to sixteen matches to accommodate the tournament. To ease pressure on the counties, no county would be asked to contribute more than one player to the England side for each match.

The estimated cost for all this was £180,000, and it was one of the schemes put to a new Committee of Inquiry, the fourth such committee set up in a period of twenty-five years to discuss and determine the future structure and conduct of first-class cricket in England. It was not only falling attendances that concerned MCC and the cricket public in general, but the controversies and scandals which seemed to be attending the game. As well as those concerning slow play and bouncers, there were domestic issues such as Graveney's rift with Gloucestershire over captaincy and Laker's break with both Surrey and MCC following the publication in 1960 of the book *Over to Me* which bore his name as author.

The Committee of Inquiry under the chairmanship of Colonel R.S. Rait-Kerr comprised past and present players and administrators. When Rait-Kerr died, Walter Robins was invited to take over the chair and the committee immediately identified the importance of increasing spectator interest while remaining sensitive to the traditions of the game.

The subcommittee whose task it was to report on the structure of the game made very clear that their report would have been very different had it been possible to play cricket on Sundays.

At the time, when cricket was played on Sundays the matches in which first-class cricketers were involved were benefit games. The beneficiary would take his county colleagues to play a local club side. No admission could be charged, but programmes were sold and there were collections. These games were generally well supported and were a good public relations exercise, drawing players and spectators closer together. They were, however, not universally welcomed, and even Denis Compton's record benefit, £12,200, in 1949 had been subjected to protest from the Lord's Day Observance Society.

The subcommittee, keenly aware that in 1961 attendances at Championship matches had fallen to their lowest since the war and threatened to fall further, sought to offer more varied cricket which would reawaken interest in followers of the game. They suggested a County Championship in which each first-class county should play every other first-class county in one three-day match and two one-day

153

matches (on consecutive days). It was hoped that these one-day games, played under the existing rules for such matches, would be *recognised as first-class*.

It was also suggested that a knock-out competition should be introduced which could include some Minor Counties. The knock-out cup matches would be decided over sixty-five overs per innings, but three days should be set aside for each game to ensure a result.

Much of the thinking behind this report came from the counties' desire to concentrate cricket at the weekend when amateurs would be available to play. This would enable them to reduce the number of professionals on the staff and so save money.

The professionals were very much under fire. There was the perennial cry that the game was devoid of personalities, and Norman Preston warned the professional batsman that he 'should remember he is a paid entertainer and if he fails or makes no attempt to keep the onlookers interested, the time will surely come when he will have to seek a living elsewhere'.

In contrast, Ted Dexter was held up as a model. He was captaining Sussex and had brought an increase in attendances at the county's matches through his enterprising batting. There were implied criticisms that Hutton, May and Cowdrey, all winners of Test series, had led England into a dull period, and that another Freddie Brown was needed. There is something peculiarly English in lusting for success and then denigrating the heroes who achieve it.

The section of the subcommittee's report that was accepted was the suggestion that a sixty-five-over knock-out tournament should be inaugurated, and the date was set for 1963. At the same meeting at which this decision was taken, MCC revealed that a letter had been received from the Home Office inviting views on Sunday cricket. The Lord's Day Observance Act would have to be amended if the public were to be charged for admission.

The world was suddenly running very quickly, and cricket was panting to keep up. More than half the population was now watching television. There was a growing air of liberalism in the discussion of subjects which had once been taboo. The publication of *Lady Chatterley's Lover* by Penguin Books had led to a court case, but 200,000 copies were sold on the first day of publication. The BBC ended its ban on mentioning sex, politics, royalty and religion in comedy shows, and this was the era of *That Was the Week That Was* and the launch of *Private Eye*. The Beatles exploded into a phenomenon. Beeching slashed the railways, for the car was taking over, and there was bribery in football, scandal in Parliament and a massive robbery from a train.

Some may see these, and such momentous events as the first man in space, as peripheral to cricket, yet they were indications of the speed and the direction of the world. They were manifestations, good and bad, of a society from which cricket could not remain immune for ever.

Ronnie Aird, the retiring secretary of MCC, was acutely aware of this. He warned that other attractions had drawn people away from the county game and that cricket could never hope to recapture all of the audience it once had. To survive, cricket had to explore every possible avenue from which income could be derived: 'It seems strange that the very existence of a cricket club should have to depend on income from outside sources, but I honestly believe that the time has arrived when this is so and that this fact has got to be faced.'

Aird's vision was a significant contribution to the survival of professional cricket. Within two years Gillette were sponsoring the first knock-out competition.

What Aird did not foresee was that within four years of vehemently defending the preservation of amateur status and the distinction between the amateur and the professional, the Advisory County Cricket Committee would meet at Lord's on 26 November 1962 and announce that the first-class counties had decided by a clear majority to abolish amateur and professional status and call all players 'cricketers'. Like many historic or momentous decisions, it was evolutionary rather than revolutionary.

Cricket was being carried along by events. In 1961 South Africa declared itself to be a republic. The following year Jamaica and Trinidad gained independence. Inevitably, this would make a difference when England and the West Indies met on the cricket field, for if independence means anything, it is that you no longer live and play in the shadow of another man's history. For the time being these things lay in the future. The immediate task was Richie Benaud's Australians and the 1961 Ashes series.

Australia arrived on the back of a victorious rubber against the West Indies which included a tied Test, extolled by many as the greatest Test in history. There were no 'chuckers' or 'draggers' in the Australian side, and there was a new opening bowler in Graham McKenzie and a new left-handed opening batsman in Bill Lawry. They arrived at the first Test unbeaten, but they had not enjoyed the best of weather.

There were uncertainties about the composition of both teams in the days prior to the first Test at Edgbaston, but Peter May had indicated that he did not yet feel fit, and Cowdrey led the side. As it transpired, May hit 153 not out for Surrey at Taunton on the Wednesday before the

Test. England gave a first Test cap to John Murray of Middlesex. Parks had held the wicket-keeping spot since being an emergency choice in the Caribbean, but he was far from being the best keeper in the country. The majority felt that since he had taken up keeping his exciting batting had declined and that, in any case, Murray was a stylish and accomplished batsman.

Murray was a cricketer incapable of an inelegant gesture. He was to claim eighteen dismissals in the series, at that time a record, and he must rank alongside Evans and Knott as one of England's great post-war wicket-keepers, although he was never treated as kindly and as fairly as the two Kent men.

Cowdrey won the toss, and England opened with the two left-handers Pullar and Subba Row. With rain interruptions enlivening the pitch, England were bowled out on the second morning for 195. Harvey then hit his twentieth Test century and shared a third-wicket stand of 146 with O'Neill. With Benaud at nine and Grout at ten, Australia had virtually no tail, and Benaud was able to declare at 516 for nine.

England began the final day on 106 for one, still 215 in arrears, but the pitch was now playing easily and the weather was fine. Subba Row completed his century, and Dexter went on to make 180. He hit thirty-one fours and played some magnificent strokes. England ended on 401 for four, and the match was drawn.

Australia beat England at Lord's, the game ending on the fourth afternoon. This was the Test match in which batsmen became suspicious that there was a ridge on the Lord's pitch at the Nursery End from which the ball lifted uncomfortably at times. Benaud's shoulder injury kept him out of the match and Harvey led Australia while May returned for England. Cowdrey retained the captaincy in order to allow May to ease his way back into Test cricket following his long illness.

Cowdrey won the toss for the ninth time in succession, and England were bowled out on the first day as the ball leapt and jumped from the quicker bowlers. Statham struck immediately by bowling McDonald to take his two hundredth Test wicket. Facing a total of 206, Australia were 6 for two and 88 for four, but Bill Lawry, to be a thorn in England's side for some years to come, hit a most courageous century. Battered and bruised, he made 130 out of 238 and was seventh out. Grout went for a duck, and England were right back in the game.

They were thwarted by the ungainly Mackay, and by McKenzie and Misson. The ninth wicket realised 53, and the tenth 49. Australia batted into the third day and took a lead of 134. For the first time since the West Indies' visit in 1957, the gates at Lord's were closed on the Saturday. The capacity crowd saw England have another rocky time. May showed great determination, and Barrington remained steadfast until the end of the day, but Cowdrey was totally out of form and Dexter was out in bizarre fashion when he swivelled and dropped the ball on to his own stumps.

Barrington and Murray added 47 for the seventh wicket before being separated on the fourth morning. The last four wickets fell for 11 runs, and Australia needed 69 to win. Trueman and Statham reduced them to 19 for four, and Harvey was out at 58 before Burge steered Australia to victory.

At the end of the match, MCC stated that they would call in a team of experts to examine the pitch. Several depressions were discovered, and MCC announced that they would attempt to put things right before the start of the 1962 season.

Controversy over pitches did not end with the Lord's Test. The pitch at Headingley had been chemically treated, was pale green and did not play true.

Peter May took over again as captain, and, with Statham unfit, England called up Les Jackson, the Derbyshire seam bowler, now forty years old, for his second Test appearance. His first had been against New Zealand twelve years previously. Australia welcomed back Benaud, who won the toss.

This was to be Trueman's match, but the first two wickets went to Lock, and, after eighty-seven overs, Australia were 183 for two at tea. Jackson took the new ball at the Pavilion end and was square-cut for four by Harvey, but Trueman's first delivery had O'Neill splendidly taken low in the gully by Cowdrey, so breaking a stand which had realised 74 in seventy minutes. Trueman was on fire, bowling at his fastest. He had Harvey taken at backward short-leg and removed Simpson and Benaud with successive deliveries. He also had Grout caught behind, and Jackson sent back Burge and Mackay in successive overs before Allen took the last wicket. The last eight wickets had gone down for 50 runs.

Cowdrey hit 93, and England took a first-innings lead of 62, somewhat disappointing as they had reached 190 before losing their third wicket, only to fall to 299 all out.

When Australia batted a second time Jackson immediately flattened McDonald's leg stump, but Harvey was again in supreme form. He and Cowdrey were the only batsmen to negotiate the difficulties of the pitch.

May varied his bowlers, and Allen's first delivery accounted for the left-handed Lawry, who was beaten by the turn and edged to Murray. The return of Trueman brought an end to Harvey, who played too soon and lobbed to cover. This was the first of five wickets to fall to

Trueman in twenty-four balls without his conceding a run. He finished with six for 30, match figures of eleven for 88, and Australia were out for 120. England won the match at 6.17 on the Saturday evening. May had captained the side with intelligence and aggression. Trueman had been lethal, and Cowdrey had batted magnificently. All, it seemed, was again right with England's world. Then came the Old Trafford Test.

England decided to play three fast bowlers at Manchester. Lock was omitted to accommodate Flavell, the Worcestershire seamer, who was preferred to Jackson. The Derbyshire man took four for 83 at Leeds, but the selectors never smiled kindly upon him, one of the great unsolved mysteries of post-war cricket. Statham was fit again, but Cowdrey, who had a throat infection, was replaced by Close. Australia had lost McDonald through injury, and Booth came in for his first Test cap.

Benaud won the toss, and when rain brought play to an end at 2.40 they were 124 for four with Lawry unbeaten on 64. He added only 10 to his score next morning as the last six wickets fell for 66 runs. Statham had five wickets, Dexter three. By the close of play on Friday England were 187 for three, just 3 runs short of Australia's total, and May was 90 not out.

He was caught at first slip for 95 on the Saturday morning and Close, his overnight partner, fell with no addition to the score. Barrington and Murray stopped a collapse with a stand of 60, and Barrington and Allen continued the repair work with a partnership of 86. Simpson ended England's innings with a spell of four for 2 in twenty-six balls, but the England lead was a commanding 177.

Lawry and Simpson took Australia to 63 by the end of play on the Saturday, and on the Monday the gates were shut upon a capacity crowd. The opening partnership was worth 113 when Murray took a good catch low to his right to dismiss Simpson off the bowling of Flavell. Murray also caught Harvey off Dexter, but Australia lost only those two wickets in clearing the arrears.

Lawry completed the second century of his first Test series, but almost immediately was brilliantly caught at leg-slip by Trueman off Allen. O'Neill, an adventurous batsman who never quite reached the heights expected, and Burge put on 64 in quick time, but Murray caught them both to claim seven catches in the match and equal Evans's record against Australia. Booth went cheaply, and Australia started the last day on 331 for six, a lead of 154. England were still slightly ahead on points.

They seemed to have clinched the match on the final morning when

Allen took three wickets in fifteen balls without cost, and Australia slumped to 334 for nine. At this point McKenzie joined Davidson. Surprisingly, the left-handed Davidson elected to take what to him were the leg-breaks of Allen on a pitch that was offering turn. His tactics became obvious when he hit the Gloucestershire man for two sixes and two fours. Perhaps unwisely, May immediately took Allen off and brought back Trueman. The last-wicket stand became worth 98 before Flavell bowled McKenzie for 32. Davidson's heroic belligerence had brought him 77. England needed 256 in 230 minutes to take the lead in the rubber.

Pullar and Subba Row scored 40 against some accurate bowling before Pullar hit tamely to mid-wicket. Dexter arrived to play an innings which was glorious but too short. He cut, drove and pulled with total majesty. Subba Row took what runs came his way, and the hundred went up in ninety-four minutes. Three times Dexter crashed Simpson through the covers, and he raced to 50 in under an hour. He lifted Mackay for six, and 150 was on the board in just over two hours. England were comfortably ahead of the clock.

Dexter and Subba Row had scored 110 in eighty-four minutes, of which Dexter had made 76 with a six and fourteen fours, when Benaud, bowling round the wicket and pitching into the rough outside the leg stump, had him caught behind as he attempted to cut. Dexter had dominated the innings with one of the most magnificent displays of controlled hitting that Test cricket has known, but now Benaud moved centre stage. He bowled May round his legs for nought, and one can still recall the Australian captain's delight as his customary modest composure exploded in a moment of self-congratulation.

Close's innings was incomprehensible. He swung wildly, hit a six but missed more often than he connected and was caught at square-leg. Subba Row's solid knock was ended when Benaud bowled him, and England went to tea at 163 for five; 93 runs were needed in the last eighty-five minutes. Barrington was the main hope, but he was leg-before to Mackay for 5. Murray was caught at slip off Benaud for 4. England were 171 for seven.

Allen and Trueman allowed the tempo and the temperature of the match to drop. They played sensible cricket and scored 18 in half an hour. Benaud had bowled unchanged since lunch and taken five wickets. His sixth came when Simpson took a spectacular one-handed catch at slip to dismiss Allen. Simpson replaced the economical Mackay and had Trueman caught at slip by Benaud. Australia claimed the extra half-hour, and Benaud rested in favour of Davidson, who knocked back Statham's stumps. Australia had won a great victory by 54 runs with twenty minutes extra time remaining.

Arguably, Benaud's performance stood comparison with Laker's on the same ground five years earlier, for he had brought a victory where none had seemed possible. Nursing an injured right shoulder, he concentrated more on pitching the ball into the rough than trying to spin it prodigiously. He bowled with great intelligence and relentless accuracy – thirty-two overs, eleven maidens, six wickets for 70 runs. Australia had retained the Ashes.

What of England? There are always incidents or events of which the public knows nothing but which can influence the outcome of a match, and there are those England cricketers who played in that Old Trafford Test who would suggest that comments made by some in high authority to Ken Barrington in particular regarding 'brighter cricket' did little to help England's cause.

For England, there was no way back. Rain interfered with the match at The Oval, but Australia scored 494 to England's 256 and 370 for eight so that the draw was very much in their favour. O'Neill scored 117 and Burge 181, and the pair added 123 for the fourth wicket. Burge and Booth then added 185 for the fifth wicket. Subba Row hit a century for England in the second innings, but the significance of this Test was that it was Peter May's last.

After captaining England in 41 of his 66 Tests, a record, May announced that he would not be able to take part in any more major tours abroad. Accordingly, he felt it would be wrong to make himself available for the captaincy. He said that he hoped to play for Surrey for many years to come. He captained Surrey in 1962, but he handed over to Micky Stewart for 1963, when he appeared in only two Championship matches. That marked the end of the first-class career of the greatest batsman England had produced since the Second World War.

The reason given for his relinquishment of the England captaincy was the inevitable pressure of business, yet the general feeling was that the intense pressures of international cricket allied to his serious illness had taken their toll. A deeply sensitive man, he had been subjected to criticism that was totally unjust and, often, he had had to restrain his natural free-flowing style as a batsman for the sake of England. To retire from the England captaincy and from Test cricket at the age of thirty-one was a sadness that was both personal and national.

In contrast, the time was much happier for another captain, Colin Ingleby-Mackenzie of Hampshire. In 1961 he led his county to the first Championship title in their history. They had a wonderfully reliable seam bowler in Shackleton, a brilliantly exciting batsman in Marshall and some superbly consistent performers in 'Butch' White, Henry Horton and Jimmy Gray. Their path to the top was fraught with danger. They lost two more matches than Yorkshire, who finished second, but Ingleby-Mackenzie was a shrewd gambler and his enterprise brought victories where others would not have dared.

He was a throwback to the Edwardian amateur, but he had a sympathetic understanding of the professionals he led, and he was an excellent man-manager. As a captain and a swashbuckling left-handed batsman, he cut a romantic figure. He lived well and liked a gamble, and he was credited with saying that the only rule he had laid down for his Championship-winning side was: 'Be in bed by breakfast time.'

This all helped to create an image, with Hampshire taking their first-ever title, which was both romantic and attractive, but it tended to obscure the fact that Ingleby-Mackenzie had determination and a sharp brain. His subsequent business career in the city is testimony to that.

He was never under consideration for an England place, and his name was not mentioned when a captain was needed to take the MCC side to India and Pakistan in the winter of 1961–62. May had resigned and Cowdrey was unavailable. The choice, inevitably, lighted on Dexter, with Mike Smith as his vice-captain. Both held regular places in the England side, both were county captains and both were seen as establishment figures. Dexter, as has been noted, was very much the batsman set up as a model to others. He batted with aggression and freedom, and was the one to be emulated if cricket were to recapture popular appeal.

The party that Dexter led to the Indian subcontinent lacked some of the leading players who had appeared against Australia, notably Trueman and Statham, and seven members of the side lacked Test experience: Alan Brown, the Kent pace bowler; Barry Knight, the Essex all-rounder; Geoff Millman, the Nottinghamshire wicket-keeper; Peter Parfitt, the Middlesex left-hander; Eric Russell, his team-mate and opening batsman; 'Butch' White of Hampshire; and David Smith, the Gloucestershire quick bowler. Both Smith and Knight had been named in sides during the Ashes series, but neither had made the final eleven. Smith had been particularly unlucky. He generated considerable pace off a shortish run and got through a tremendous amount of work.

Perhaps most interesting of the newcomers were the Middlesex pair, Parfitt and Russell. Parfitt was a chunky left-hander capable of sound defence or blistering attack. He was also an outstanding fielder. Russell had come down from Scotland to join the Middlesex staff and was the natural heir to the Hearne and Robertson line. He was elegant in all that he did. He scored an emormous number of runs, and his off-drives and leg-glances were among the delights of the game. With England still in search of an established opener, the tour offered him a great opportunity, but he appeared in only two Tests and in one of those he batted at number six.

This was a confused and dismal tour. There was a Test match against Pakistan in October 1961, followed by a five-match Test series against India before the side returned to Pakistan for two more Tests in January and February 1962.

Against Pakistan at Lahore, Barrington and Mike Smith put on 192 after Richardson and Pullar had gone with the score on 21. Barrington was run out for 139 and Smith for 99. England won by five wickets. Having had a dearth of openers, England had four in this side, with Russell at six and Barber at seven.

This victory in Lahore was to be England's only success in the eight Tests. When they returned to Pakistan, England drew at Dacca and at Karachi, so taking the series, but this was anything but a happy tour. Pullar made 165 at Dacca; Dexter, 205, and Parfitt, 111, added 188 for England's fourth wicket at Karachi; yet these were limited rewards for what had gone before.

Leslie Smith, the perpetual tourist, was uncompromising in his criticism in his reports for the *Cricketer*. He first identified the problem which saw only *reserve* sides making tours of the subcontinent, where enthusiasm for the game was unbounded:

> Two or three of the leading players in England said that they were not available to tour, and their presence might have made just that difference, for over all the sides were evenly matched. It is to be hoped that the authorities find a way of bringing more pressure on reluctant tourists instead of allowing them to pick and choose which visits they will accept. Several of this MCC team resented the fact that through financial reasons, or concern about their future in the game, they could not afford to say 'no' to the tour, whereas others could, and did. Both outlooks should be condemned. They are part of the unfortunate attitude helping to ruin cricket.

It was to be several years before those in authority responded completely to Leslie Smith's correct and important observations.

He was also highly critical of the way in which cricket was played on the tour, where the emphasis in batting, bowling and field-placing was on defence. There was something understandable in bowlers who were

162

expected to operate on placid pitches concentrating on a tight line and hoping for mistakes by the batsmen, but it made for poor cricket, and the disease is with us still. Less forgivable was batsmen being content to occupy the crease in an attempt to build an impregnable total. Whatever his own attitudes, Dexter did not transmit them to his team. There was an 'absence of keenness and inspiration and an almost total disregard for the public'. These were identified as the very reasons why crowds in England were dwindling.

The twenty-four matches played on the MCC tour of Pakistan, India and Ceylon were watched by nearly 2 million people, double the number that had attended all the matches played in the first-class season in England in 1961.

The tour did have its successes, notably the batting of Parfitt and Barrington, and the continued enthusiasm of Lock, but there were also disappointments. Following his highly impressive series against Australia, John Murray lost form. It was discovered that he was suffering from varicose veins, and he was flown back to England for an operation. Binks, the Yorkshire wicket-keeper, was flown out as replacement, but Millman kept wicket in the last four Tests.

The greatest disappointment and humiliation was that England lost a rubber to India for the first time. The first Test saw Barrington score a century and bat for over nine hours in the match without being dismissed. The match was drawn, as was the second when, forced to follow on, England were indebted to a second-wicket stand of 139 between Pullar and Barrington, who both scored centuries, as did Dexter.

Rain ruined the third Test, but Barrington scored his fourth hundred in four Tests, three of them against India. This was the end of his run spree and the end for England. India, who had introduced an exciting young wicket-keeper-batsman, Farokh Engineer, won the fourth and fifth Tests by comfortable margins to take the series.

Barrington averaged 99 in the five Tests and Lock and Allen took forty-three wickets between them, but the quicker bowlers had struggled and Barber suffered from lack of control.

When the party returned to England they were confronted by a new panel of selectors – Robins, Insole, Watson and Alec Bedser, who was beginning a long stint. Walter Robins, the chairman, immediately caused a rumpus by calling a press conference at which he stated that the selectors would give preference to players of enterprise and courage, that there was no place for defensive tactics in the England team and that he 'would not mind losing all five Tests in Australia if we played the right way.' The last statement drew some vehement criticism from former Test cricketers, notably Trevor Bailey.

Robins's remarks reflected a state of paranoia that existed concerning English cricket, particularly in relation to what was happening in Australia. The dynamic leadership of Benaud had revitalised the Australian side. They had enjoyed the wonderfully exciting series against Worrell's West Indians, and India had gone to the West Indies immediately after beating England and had been trounced 5–0. The trauma of England's seemingly strong and invincible side being beaten by Benaud's team was still being felt, and all the blame was being attached to slow batting. Former heroes like Bailey were now accused of being the root cause of the paralysis that had gripped the game. Memories were very short.

In fact, the greatest problem was slow play. England scored their runs as quickly as Australia, but the number of overs being offered per hour was ever decreasing. Time-wasting and gamesmanship were rampant, and the emphasis was on attrition rather than attack.

Robins was right when he said, 'The cricketing public expect some-thing more in this day and age than in the years gone by.' In John Woodcock's words, the spectator had 'come to demand a fuller flavour for his money'. The trouble was he was getting something which was increasingly lacking all flavour. Many, however, were worried that Robins's words meant that, whoever was appointed captain of England, it was Walter Robins, as chairman of selectors, who would be deciding tactics and pulling the strings.

That there should be any debate as to who would succeed May seems incredible. Cowdrey had been May's lieutenant and had led England with success. He had taken on every role that had been asked of him, including that of opener which he did not relish. In his perceptive response to Robins's press statement, Woodcock had written, 'In any side the Cowdreys of this world, the greatly gifted stroke-players, are worth their weight twice over if they lead the way aggressively.' Cowdrey had served an apprenticeship under the two captains who had brought more success to England than anyone since Douglas Jardine. He was a man for all seasons. So why the doubt?

Cowdrey had caused consternation when he captained England for the first time in 1959 against India. He had taken over with England three Tests up in the series. Two of the matches had finished in three days and the third midway through the fourth afternoon. At Old Trafford Cowdrey had announced, with England in an unassailable position, that, given the opportunity, he would not enforce the follow-on because he felt that the match should be prolonged over the weekend for the benefit of the spectators. This caused outrage in some corners of the inner sanctum of cricket where it was argued that the captain's first duty was to win the game irrespective of all other considerations.

Another criticism often laid against Cowdrey was that he was too nice a person. Indeed, he was and is a gentle man, but, like May, the kindly exterior hid a strong desire to win and a shrewd tactical sense.

Cowdrey's strongest challenger for the captaincy was Dexter. He fitted Robins's image of the cavalier leader. Lord Ted was a batsman of majestic power who scored runs in a quick and regal manner, but his captaincy in India and Pakistan had singularly failed to lift his men. Appearances were deceptive. Whatever the public image of the mighty Dexter smiting bowlers to all parts of the ground, the reality was that Dexter was not a good captain. He was not liked by those he led, some of whom went so far as to say that if they never played under him again, it would be too soon. His threshold of boredom was low, and although he thought much about the game, his greatest service in leadership was to be apparent in years to come, and for that he was not to receive the praise he deserved.

Suddenly, a third contender appeared for the captaincy as the name of David Sheppard was resurrected. He was doing missionary work at the Mayflower Centre in East London and played little cricket, but E.M. Wellings suggested he be considered in an article in the *Evening News*, and Robins acted on the suggestion. Sheppard was persuaded to take a sabbatical and to play some games for Sussex with a view to going to Australia with the MCC party, probably as captain.

That there were three contenders was made public knowledge although why Cowdrey should have been subjected to this farce is beyond reasoning. No captain was appointed for the series against Pakistan in 1962, for the Tests were to be used as a trial and error process to decide who would inherit May's crown in the forthcoming Ashes series. That Dexter had just captained England in eight Tests, that Cowdrey had taken over from the wounded May in the Caribbean and had led England ten times, and that Sheppard had been in this position, unsuccessfully, eight years earlier seemingly counted for nothing.

Dexter led in the first Test, which England won by an innings. Cowdrey hit 159, opening the innings with Pullar; Parfitt made the first of three centuries he was to hit in the series; Graveney, recalled to the colours, made 97; and Dexter and Allen hit 70s. Pakistan were not a strong side and succumbed meekly.

At Lord's Dexter was again captain. Graveney hit 153, and Len Coldwell, enjoying great success with Worcestershire as a pace bowler, took nine for 110 in the match, which was his debut in Test cricket. Trueman also had nine wickets, and there was another debutant in

Micky Stewart. England won by nine wickets.

Cowdrey was made captain for the Headingley Test, which England again won by an innings. Ted Dexter took four for 10 in the first innings, his best bowling performance in Test cricket. Cowdrey handled the side astutely. Titmus had taken two wickets for 3 runs, but Cowdrey took him out of the attack so that Trueman could bowl at Burki, who was considered vulnerable to pace. The ploy worked. Dexter captained in the last two Tests and took the side to Australia.

Sheppard hit a century for the Gentlemen against the Players, the last time that this historic fixture was played, and also hit hundreds against Oxford University and Middlesex. He took Cowdrey's place in the fourth Test when the Kent captain reported unfit, and he opened with Cowdrey in the final Test at The Oval.

It was in that Test that David Larter made his international debut. Like Tyson, he played for Northamptonshire, and he was welcomed as if he were a new Tyson. He stood six feet seven-and-a-half inches and bowled briskly off a comparatively short run. He had good control and could vary his pace, but he could never generate that of Tyson, and his physique was not ideal for a fast bowler. Against Pakistan he had match figures of nine for 145 in a ten-wicket victory, and he won a place in the party to go to Australia.

Dexter, captain, and Cowdrey, vice-captain, joined in a record stand for the second wicket against Pakistan in the fifth Test. Cowdrey hit 182, the highest of the twenty-two hundreds he made for England, and Dexter scored 172. Together they put on 248.

Both men finished high in the first-class batting averages, as did the rejuvenated Graveney who, having served the necessary qualification period, was now excelling with Worcestershire. Also among the premier batsmen of the year was the Surrey trio, Barrington, Stewart and Edrich.

Barrington was an established rock in the England side, and Stewart had appeared in two Tests against Pakistan, scoring 39, 34 not out and 86. An all-round sportsman, he had missed appearing in a Wembley Cup Final because he preferred to play cricket in the Caribbean with Jim Swanton's side. He was not only a capable opening batsman who topped two thousand runs in 1962, but a brilliant fielder who had established a world record some five years earlier when he held seven catches in an innings against Northamptonshire. In spite of such credentials, he was not selected to tour Australia under Dexter. Nor was John Edrich.

The praises of the left-handed Edrich had been sung since he first made his mark in county cricket in 1959. England were in search of an opener, and why they did not turn to Edrich is a mystery. In 1962 he was the leading run-scorer in the country with 2,482 runs, but the call still did not come. In Australia, England would rue their neglect of him.

Graveney was recalled. He had enjoyed a wonderful season for Worcestershire, who had lost Peter Richardson to Kent for personal reasons. Inspiringly led by Don Kenyon, arguably the best batsman the county ever produced and a man worth many more than the eight England caps he won, Worcestershire were top of the Championship when they beat Nottinghamshire in their last match of the season. Kenyon scored an unbeaten century in that match, and Len Coldwell took eight wickets to give him 132 in Championship matches alone. He was ably supported by Flavell, who missed the last part of the season through injury, Standen, Carter, Gifford and Horton. Worcestershire were exciting in the field, a major factor in helping them to climb to a position that they had never attained before.

They were denied the title by Yorkshire, who played Glamorgan on the three days following Worcestershire's last match. Vic Wilson put Glamorgan in on a drying pitch and, with Don Wilson taking six for 24, the Welshmen were bowled out for 65. Yorkshire struggled in their turn and were saved from total ignominy by Ken Taylor, who was eighth out having hit 67 out of 100. Trailing by 36 on the first innings, Glamorgan reached 13 without loss on the Wednesday evening. The loss of Thursday's play to rain heightened the tension, but on the Friday the triple spin attack of Don Wilson, Illingworth and Close caused another Glamorgan collapse. They were bowled out for 101, and Yorkshire needed 66 to win. Jeff Jones bowled Taylor with the first ball of the second innings, so completing the hat-trick, for he had dismissed Don Wilson and Binks with the last two balls of the first innings. Yorkshire had no further alarms and won the match and the Championship with two hours to spare.

This was a triumphant end to Vic Wilson's first-class career and his period as captain. He was succeeded by Brian Close.

Two of the Championship-winning side, Trueman and Illingworth, were named in the party to tour Australia. Trueman, Coldwell, Larter and Statham formed the pace attack, and these four were supplemented by Barry Knight, the Essex all-rounder, a seam bowler. Illingworth, with Titmus and Allen were the three off-break bowlers in the side. Even allowing for the fact that Illingworth and Titmus were classed as all-rounders and that Allen, was a more than useful bat, three off-spinners left the attack unbalanced.

Dexter, Cowdrey, Barrington, Graveney, Parfitt, Sheppard and Pullar were the batsmen, so that there remained still the uncertainty over the openers. Pullar opened regularly for Lancashire, but Cowdrey did not like the job and Sheppard had made only a limited return to first-class cricket, was thirty-three years old and, before his return against Pakistan, had been out of Test cricket for five years. His selection was not universally popular and confused many.

The most puzzling selection, however, was that of the second wicket-keeper. When Murray had gone down with varicose vein trouble in India Millman had taken over, and the Nottinghamshire wicket-keeper had kept in the first two Tests against Pakistan in England before Murray returned when fit. Yet A.C. Smith was chosen as the second wicket-keeper in the party to tour Australia, an incomprehensible selection, particularly in view of the alternative options available.

Smith had claimed eighty-two dismissals in 1962 and scored more than a thousand runs, but he was never more than a keen county player. He had captained Oxford University two years in succession, a most unusual honour and one which was testimony to his popularity and enthusiasm. He could also bowl medium-pace and was brimful of confidence, but none of these things justified his selection ahead of some half-dozen more qualified candidates.

The announcement of the party was coolly received, and the dominant influence of Robins and Dexter in the selection was generally recognised. Even before the players flew to Aden, where they were to board the *Canberra* and complete the rest of the journey by sea, there were misgivings.

At a cricket dinner in the Midlands shortly before the start of the tour, I spoke to Ray Hitchcock, Warwickshire's New Zealand-born all-rounder, and proffered the opinion that England had a major asset in that Murray was the best wicket-keeper in the world. Hitchcock agreed, but he added the postscript that Murray would not play in the Tests because Dexter did not like him. This did not augur well for the future, and it was to prove all too painfully true.

Murray was not chosen for the first two Tests and was injured taking a spectacular catch in the third. When the party reached New Zealand, where two Tests were to be played, Murray was sitting drinking with colleagues when Dexter walked past and said, 'You're playing in the first; A.C.'s playing in the second.' And that was the extent of the information that was given him regarding his last Test appearance for three years.

It seems almost sacrilegious to level such criticism at Dexter. He is a good man who has done much for the game. Whenever he came out to bat a shiver of excitement and expectancy would go round the ground, and spectators were rarely disappointed. But as a captain and a communicator with his men, he was a different person from the Dexter with a bat (or a golf club) in his hand. Later he admitted that he was not good with wicket-keepers. He had been persuaded that keepers like Keith Andrew were technically the best available, and yet he saw them miss as many snicks standing up as lesser keepers (but better batsmen) did standing back. The debate has continued long since then.

There were surprises other than the playing contingent when the MCC side was announced, the most newsworthy being that the Duke of Norfolk would manage the side. Socially, the Duke was an asset. He was forceful at receptions and press conferences where he consistently promised bright, attacking cricket. Realistically, however, the burden of the duties of management fell on Alec Bedser, the assistant manager, for the Duke had had little experience of handling money or signing cheques. In any case the Duke had to return to England to deal with other matters. His absence was to have been for four weeks, but illness turned it into six, and 'Billy' Griffith, secretary of MCC, deputised for a period.

MCC's performances before the first Test were indifferent, and Cowdrey took some weeks to find his form. It was apparent that the wicket-keeping spot had been settled, for Smith played in four first-class matches to Murray's two before the Brisbane Test.

With Trueman in good form, England started well on the first day, but a century of charm from Booth, stern defence from Mackay and some aggression from Benaud took Australia to 404. Barry Knight, later to settle in Australia, finished with a spell of three for 10, but Australia's last four wickets added 210.

Dexter, Barrington and Parfitt batted well for England, but it was consistency rather than individual brilliance which took the score to 389 in spite of Benaud's six wickets.

On a pitch which was becoming slower, Australia found it difficult to force the pace, and Benaud's declaration at the end of the fourth day on 362 for four left England the final day, six hours, in which to score 378 to win.

Pullar and Sheppard began with a partnership of 114, and Dexter hit 99 in 167 minutes. He and Barrington added 66 in just over an hour, but England were never up with the required run-rate for any lengthy period. They ended on 278 for six, and the match was drawn.

The draw and the evenness of the contest as a whole gave England a fillip, but there were concerns arising from the match and from the early part of the tour. Statham, though still accurate, seemed to have lost something of his cutting edge, and Sheppard was certainly not the crick-eter he once had been. He was to be one of four batsmen to reach a thou-sand runs on the tour, and his century in the second Test helped bring an

England victory, but a man who was once a very fine fielder close to the wicket was now something of a liability in a side whose standard in the field had dropped considerably since the days of Hutton and May.

The draw at Brisbane was followed by a win over Victoria, as Coldwell took six for 49 in the second innings, and a draw with South Australia at Adelaide. It was in this match that Colin Cowdrey and Tom Graveney put on 344 in under four hours for the fifth wicket. Batting six and a half hours, Cowdrey hit four sixes and twenty-nine fours in scoring 307, the highest innings played by an Englishman in Australia.

It put him in good heart for the Melbourne Test where Parfitt, having been pressed into opening against Victoria and South Australia, was omitted for Graveney, and Coldwell replaced Knight to bring an emphasis on pace. Ironically, it was the off-spin of Titmus that caused the greatest concern to Australia's strong middle order.

Australia did not bat well on the opening day, losing their first six wickets for 164, but Davidson and Mackay rallied them, adding 73, and the last three wickets realised 79. By the end of the second day England, 210 for three, were in a strong position. This had been brought about by Dexter and Cowdrey after both openers had gone for 19. Captain and vice-captain added 175 in 198 minutes. Dexter was caught at slip off Benaud for 93, but Cowdrey batted into the third morning and followed his triple century at Adelaide with 113, which was to be the highest of his five Test centuries against Australia. He and Barrington fell in successive overs from McKenzie, and although Graveney played well, the last seven wickets went down for 77. England led by just 15.

If England were disappointed by the smallness of their lead, they were soon uplifted by Trueman. In his fourth over, bowling very fast, he bowled Simpson and with his next ball had O'Neill caught at slip. Harvey was run out when, unwisely, he attempted a fourth run, and Statham bowled Burge to leave Australia floundering at 69 for four. Booth joined Lawry to take the score to 105 by the close.

They were not separated until the last ball before lunch on the fourth day when Lawry was bowled by Dexter. Lawry and Booth had added 92, but it had been grim stuff. Lawry batted more than six hours for his 57, and the assertion that brighter, attacking cricket would be played was looking rather hollow. Trueman caused havoc among the tail with the new ball. The last five wickets fell for 55 runs, and Booth was last out, caught by Trueman off Statham for 103.

Needing 234 to win, England lost Pullar to a spectacular catch by wicket-keeper Jarman in the second over of the innings, and the day ended with the score 9 for one.

By lunch on the final day, England were much happier, with

Sheppard and Dexter still together and 96 on the board. In the afternoon, Dexter was run out by Benaud's fine throw from cover, and Cowdrey and Sheppard were dropped in successive overs. Had these chances been taken, the result might have been different, for Sheppard went on to complete his hundred and Cowdrey finished on 58 not out.

Sheppard showed great determination and batted for 301 minutes for 113. With the scores level, he attempted to take the winning single and was run out. His match-winning century redeemed his first-innings duck and two dropped catches. England had won a Test match in Australia for the first time in eight years.

The question that was now asked was, what attitude should England adopt after taking a lead in the series? As often before, philosophies had not so far been translated into practice. In the Test arena fear of defeat was still paramount. Nevertheless, England did lose at Sydney.

They won the toss and batted badly, with only Cowdrey and Pullar showing any form. Facing a total of 279, Australia lost Lawry at 14 to a magnificent diving catch by Murray, who had been recalled in place of A.C. Smith. Unfortunately, Murray injured his shoulder in taking the catch, and Parfitt had to take over behind the stumps. Simpson and Harvey added 160 for the second wicket before Titmus took four wickets for 5 runs in fifty-eight balls. He finished with seven for 79, his best analysis in Test cricket, but Australia took a first-innings lead of 40 thanks to Shepherd's 71 not out on debut.

By the end of the third day England were a beaten side. They had collapsed before Davidson and were 86 for six. Murray, batting virtually one-handed, survived for 100 minutes to finish with 3 not out, but England's last three wickets fell for 4 runs. They were out for 104, and Australia had won soon after lunch on the fourth day.

With the series level and two matches to play, there was a belief that the series would now come alight. England had to win to regain the Ashes, and Benaud was not thought to be defensively minded. Once again the philosophy of attack received a setback when it came to be practised. As *Wisden* commented on the fourth Test, 'Several factors contributed to the stalemate in this match, but to some extent it was due to a fear by either side of losing.'

In fairness, three hours' play was lost on the third day, and Australia did make 322 for five on the opening day, with Harvey and O'Neill making centuries. Davidson broke down with a pulled muscle in his fourth over, and this injury dictated Australian policy for the rest of the match. The wicket was fast and true, and Australia, 393, led by 62 on the first innings. They batted into the last day, being all out at lunch, and left England a target of 356 in four hours. Barrington made a century after

Pullar and Sheppard had gone cheaply.

If the fourth Test match was something of a disappointment, the last match, played at Sydney like the third, was a disaster, 'a dull, lifeless game which did immense harm to cricket, particularly in Australia'. The pitch was too slow for both batsmen and bowlers, and the outfield was too long. This led to slow scoring, but the batsmen must take most of the blame for the dreary encounter. They had neither the ability nor the inclination to overcome the conditions.

With Pullar unfit, Cowdrey moved up to open the innings, and England played three off-spinners. Dexter won the toss, Barrington hit another century, but England scored only 195 for five in six hours' play. They were all out for 321 on the second day and had Australia in some trouble at 71 for three, but Burge, who had been dropped from the side for the third and fourth Tests, scored a hundred, and England trailed by 28 on the first innings.

They had turned that to a 137-run advantage by the end of the fourth day when Barrington and Sheppard put on 97 in 112 minutes. Barrington was out on the last morning, 6 runs short of his second century of the match. His 94 had occupied 263 minutes and contained only two fours. The onus was on England to press for runs and for victory. Dexter declared at lunch, leaving Australia four hours in which to score 241. They ended on 152 for four, with Lawry unbeaten on 45, which had occupied seventy-two overs, four hours.

'The end arrived,' wrote Leslie Smith, 'with the small crowd slow handclapping and booing the players off the field, as no attempt had been made to entertain them even when the game was an obvious draw. So the tour finished on a dismal note, and with this final memory all that had gone before was forgotten.' For the first time, three matches in an Ashes series in Australia had been drawn.

There had been successes for England, notably Barrington, Titmus and Trueman, who had taken twenty and twenty-one Test wickets respectively. Barrington made 1,763 runs in Australia and New Zealand.

Allen, Graveney, Pullar and Statham did not go on the New Zealand part of the tour, but England totally dominated there, winning all three Tests, the first two by an innings. In Auckland Barrington hit his third century in successive Tests, while Parfitt, 131 not out, and Knight, 125, shared a record sixth-wicket stand of 240.

At Wellington, Cowdrey, batting at number eight, hit 128 and A.C. Smith made 69 to share an unbroken ninth-wicket partnership of 163 in 161 minutes. It was a world Test record for the ninth wicket and remains England's highest.

Fred Trueman became the first bowler in the world to take 250 Test wickets when he had match figures of nine for 91 in the third match at Christchurch, where New Zealand led on the first innings and England won by seven wickets without any of their batsmen reaching 50.

These triumphs in New Zealand could not compensate for the drab performances in Australia. The gap between Dexter the batsman and Dexter the captain still existed. Summarising the tour in *Wisden*, Leslie Smith commented on Dexter, 'He did not always bring his dashing approach into his captaincy and in general his leadership lacked inspiration, but he made few mistakes and did his best to set a high standard of fielding by his enthusiastic work either in the covers or close to the bat.'

Ray Robinson, the Australian commentator, was of the opinion that the cricket played by the MCC tourists was losing friends by the drove and that the game's controllers must act.

The 'controllers' already had their hands full. They were debating Sunday cricket, had eased the qualification demands on overseas players appearing in county cricket, and had to contend with the arrival of a strong West Indian side under Frank Worrell. There was no longer a distinction between amateur and professional, and the new sixty-five-over knock-out competition was to begin, but without the inclusion of any Minor Counties. The inaugural competition, with each bowler allowed fifteen overs, proved to be too long, and sixty overs became the innings allocation in 1964 when the bowlers' limitation was reduced to thirteen overs and five leading Minor Counties competed. Later, the bowlers' ration became twelve overs and the competition was expanded. The *Daily Express* organised a 'better cricket' competition. The public demanded overseas cricketers, limitations on the length of the first innings, and Sunday cricket after church. There was also a suggestion that disciplinary action be taken against those who deliberately wasted time to prevent the other side winning. The fact that has consistently thwarted administrators of all sports is that you cannot legislate for attitudes, and attitudes were what cricket most needed to change.

The first Gillette Cup was a success, although there were teething troubles. The preliminary-round match saw Lancashire beat Leicestershire at Old Trafford, the game going into a second day. Peter Marner laid claim to the first Man of the Match award. He hit 121 and took three for 49. Maurice Hallam, the Leicestershire skipper, also hit a century. Hallam had put Lancashire in when he won the toss, but the Red Rose county scored at 4.67 runs an over against mainly defensive fields. Such a rate of scoring was a rarity in the County Championship.

Bowlers could bowl up to fifteen overs, and there were no fielding restrictions other than those applied in the first-class game. Attendances were good, although there were several matches which did not go the full distance. This was especially the case in the semi-final when Worcestershire bowled out Lancashire in 31.1 overs for 59. Flavell took six for 14 in thirteen overs.

In the final, played before a crowd of 25,000 at Lord's in weather that was cold, dreary and often damp, Worcestershire lost to Sussex by 14 runs. Two slow left-arm bowlers, Gifford and Slade, restricted Sussex to 168 in 60.2 overs. Gifford took four for 33 and won the Man of the Match award. The all-seam attack had not yet become fashionable although Sussex relied on their quicker bowlers in the closing stages when Snow took three wickets. Dexter held the cup aloft, and a new form of cricket had been launched. Sussex had never won the County Championship.

With Close as captain for the first time, Yorkshire retained the title that they had won under Vic Wilson. The county was well served by Trueman, Nicholson and Don Wilson in attack and by a young bespectacled opening batsman, Geoffrey Boycott. He was the only Yorkshireman to score a thousand runs in Championship matches, and, in a wet summer, he finished second to M.J.K. Smith in the national averages. The Cricket Writers' Club voted him Young Cricketer of the Year.

Close proved himself to be a good leader. He knew his men and their capabilities, and he was a first-rate tactician. He was tough, led by example and was imbued with the Yorkshire philosophy: 'You get nowt for being second.' His own form was good and for the first time he held a regular place in the England side.

The West Indies presented very different opposition from that which they had offered in recent years. They arrived in England having won their last Test series 5–0 against India. For the first time in England, they were led by a black West Indian, Frank Worrell, and their strength in attack was in the electrifying pace of Hall and Griffith rather than in the subtle spin of Ramadhin and Valentine, although they did possess a great off-spinner in Lance Gibbs. There was also Sobers, who could, and did, bowl everything from slow left-arm spin to considerable left-arm pace.

Led by Worrell, the West Indies had won eternal fame and glory in a magnificent series in Australia two years earlier, and they symbolised all that England searched for in better, brighter cricket. Kanhai was now a wonderful batsman, and the sight of him landing on his backside in the crease as he pulled the ball over the square-leg boundary will linger ever with those lucky enough to see him. Hunte was an opening batsman of the highest order, Butcher a fine attacking player, and Worrell and

174

Sobers were already cricketing legends. Robins maintained that England would match them in excitement, and Dexter was appointed captain for the first two Tests.

John Edrich at last made his Test debut in the first encounter, at Old Trafford. He opened the innings with Stewart, and with Barrington at number three Surrey provided the first three in the England order. For the third Test, Peter Richardson was recalled at the expense of Edrich, and Bolus who, having moved from Yorkshire to Nottinghamshire, was enjoying a splendid season, was Stewart's opening partner in the fourth Test. The axe fell on Stewart for the fifth when Edrich returned.

The first Test was over in four days. Conrad Hunte hit 182 out of 501 for six declared, and Gibbs took eleven wickets as England were bowled out for 205 and 296, which left the West Indies needing 1 run to win.

England made two changes for the second Test at Lord's. Shackleton, the backbone of Hampshire, took over from Statham. Shackleton was a surprise choice, for he was thirty-eight years old, but he was in form and took seven wickets in the match. The other change saw Parks brought back in place of Andrew, who had played at Old Trafford. Parks came in to strengthen the batting, and the argument was to rage for the next few years as to who should keep wicket for England. All coaching manuals stated that the best wicket-keeper should be chosen irrespective of all other considerations, but that dictum was never followed by MCC or the selectors.

The 1963 Test match at Lord's was one of the great international games in cricket history. It was very much what England needed to lift the sagging spirits of the game. When the last over arrived any one of four results was possible: a win for England, a win for the West Indies, a tie or a draw.

Worrell won the toss, and the West Indies began on a high note. Hunte drove the first three balls of the match, bowled by Trueman, to the boundary. Psychologically, the first round had gone to the West Indies, but Shackleton was naggingly accurate, Trueman found his length, and, at lunch, the score was only 47.

Trueman dismissed McMorris straight after the break, and he also accounted for Hunte. Sobers and Kanhai added 63 in sixty-five minutes. Butcher went cheaply, but Kanhai and Solomon added 74, and the West Indies moved towards a commanding position. Trueman changed the complexion of the game when he had Kanhai caught, and then bowled Worrell for nought. The West Indies ended the day on 245 for six. England were well satisfied.

Shackleton had troubled batsmen on the first day but had not taken a wicket. On the second day, after Trueman had had Murray taken at slip,

Shackleton finished the innings by dismissing Solomon, Griffith and Gibbs in the space of four balls.

John Edrich's Test career began disastrously (but then so had Hutton's) when he was caught behind off the first ball he received. Stewart also fell to Griffith, and England had an uneasy lunch at 20 for two. What followed was another of those breathtaking Dexter minia-tures, an even better innings, perhaps, than the one he had played against Australia at Old Trafford two years earlier. In eighty minutes he made 70, flaying Hall and Griffith to all parts of the field. He faced only seventy-three balls and made his runs at a time of crisis. Barrington supported him in a stand of 82 in sixty-two minutes and took command when Dexter was dismissed, but Cowdrey and Close failed. Parks helped Barrington halt a collapse, and Titmus batted admirably to take England to a tremulous 244 for seven by the close.

On the Saturday the gates were closed at Lord's for the first time in seven years. Titmus manoeuvred England to within 4 runs of the West Indies' total, and Charlie Griffith finished with five wickets. For most of his Test career, Griffith had his action under scrutiny. His build was massive and his action chest on. His yorker was vicious, and no batsman relished facing him. He was twice no-balled for throwing, and his volatile temperament earned him a reputation as a fearsome opponent. He and Hall formed one of the finest and fastest of new-ball combina-tions in Test cricket.

Trueman and Shackleton gave England a magnificent start when the West Indies batted a second time, reducing the visitors to 104 for five. The bowlers were wonderfully supported by Cowdrey at slip, where his catching made the most difficult of chances look pedestrian. It was not only Cowdrey's catching which was of such assistance to the bowlers, but his captaincy.

Dexter was off the field with an inflamed knee and Cowdrey took over the reins. He used Trueman in short bursts, and the Yorkshireman thrived on being used as an out-and-out attacker. The *Cricketer* commented:

> England were under two captains, Dexter in the first West Indian innings, Cowdrey in the second. In their first innings West Indies, with the luck befriending them, made 301. Titmus, the taker of 21 wickets against Australia last winter, did not bowl. Dexter concentrated almost entirely upon the seam. Cowdrey was more flexible, as he needed to be, being short of a seamer. But for his injury, which may keep him out for the rest of the season, Cowdrey might have had the captaincy before the end of the series. As it is, Dexter has been appointed for the three remaining matches.

Butcher and Worrell halted the England advance and took the score to 214 for five by the close. In twenty-five minutes on the Monday morning, the last five wickets went down in six overs for 15 runs. Trueman, ably supported by Shackleton, took five for 52, bringing his match figures to eleven for 152, one of his best performances in a most distinguished career.

England needed 234 to win and hopes were high. They sank when Edrich, Stewart and Dexter were out for 31. Barrington and Cowdrey now batted heroically against some very hostile bowling. Both Hall and Griffith consistently pitched short, and the batsmen were struck on the body and the fingers. Eventually, with the score on 72, Cowdrey was struck on the arm by a ball from Hall and was forced to retire with a broken bone just above the left wrist. His arm was put in plaster and he did not play again that season.

Barrington and Close continued the fight-back in poor light. Barrington hit Gibbs for two sixes in one over, but, after two stoppages, play was finally abandoned for the day at 4.45. England were 116 for three and needed another 118 to win, but the fates were against them. Rain and bad light delayed the resumption on the final day until 2.20. This left England just 200 minutes in which to score the necessary runs.

The pitch was lively and the bowling fierce. Only 15 runs came in the first hour, Barrington having scored 5 in fifty-five minutes before falling to Griffith. Close and Parks added 28, and Titmus gave Close commendable support. At tea England were 171 for five, with Cowdrey injured and 63 needed in eighty-five minutes. The problem confronting England was that the West Indies were bowling their overs at no more than fourteen an hour.

Close, a mass of bruises from constantly being hit about the body, changed his tactics and gave Hall 'the charge'. He met with some success, but, with twenty minutes remaining and the score on 219, he advanced down the pitch, swung and touched the ball to the wicket-keeper. His innings lasted ten minutes under four hours, and although his later tactics were criticised, he defended them by saying that the West Indians were taking so long to bowl their overs that he felt he had no option but to do what he did. Certainly, desperate measures had been needed after Titmus and Trueman had fallen to successive deliveries.

Close's advance on Hall had caused Hall to rick his back slightly, but he bowled throughout the 200 minutes of the last day. By the end his eyes were rolling in his head, but he maintained a formidable pace.

When Shackleton joined Allen 15 runs were needed, but they fell behind the clock, and when Hall began the last over England were 8 runs short of victory. Singles were taken off the second and third balls,

177

but the fourth ball saw the end of Shackleton. The ball was played to Worrell; he picked it up, raced to the bowler's end and removed the bails before Shackleton could get home. It was instinctive and inspired.

Eyes now turned towards the pavilion where Cowdrey appeared, his left arm in plaster. This was no time for heroics, and Allen defended the last two deliveries. Cowdrey did not have to face a ball. When questioned later he confirmed that he would have turned round and batted left-handed to protect his broken arm.

The climax of the game gripped a huge audience. The BBC television news was due as the last over was being bowled. There was a return to the studio for the news, but no sooner had the newsreader started than the cameras returned to Lord's to see the end of the match. That was an unprecedented action on the part of television administrators.

Drama at Lord's
England v West Indies at Lord's
20, 21, 22, 24 and 25 June 1963

West Indies First Innings		Second Innings	
C.C. Hunte c Close b Trueman	44	c Cowdrey b Shackleton	7
E.D.A. St J. McMorris lbw b Trueman	16	c Cowdrey b Trueman . .	8
G. St A. Sobers c Cowdrey b Allen .	42	(5)c Parks b Trueman . . .	8
R.B. Kanhai c Edrich b Trueman . .	73	(3)c Cowdrey b Shackleton	21
B.F. Butcher c Barrington b Trueman	14	(4) lbw b Shackleton . . .133
J.S. Solomon lbw b Shackleton	56	c Stewart b Allen	5
F.M.M. Worrell (capt) b Trueman . .	0	c Stewart b Trueman . . .	33
†D.L. Murray c Cowdrey b Trueman	20	c Parks b Trueman	2
W.W. Hall not out	25	c Parks b Trueman	2
C.C. Griffith c Cowdrey b Shackleton	0	b Shackleton	1
L.R. Gibbs c Stewart b Shackleton .	0	not out	1
Extras (b 10, lb 1)	11	(b 5, lb 2, nb 1)	8
Total	301	229

BOWLING	Overs	Mdns	Runs	Wkts	Overs	Mdns	Runs	Wkts
Trueman	44	16	100	6	26	9	52	5
Shackleton	50.2	22	93	3	34	14	72	4
Dexter	20	6	41	–	–	–	–	–
Close	9	3	21	–	–	–	–	–
Allen	10	3	35	1	21	7	50	1
Titmus	–	–	–	–	17	3	47	–

fall of wickets
1–51, 2–64, 3–127, 4–145, 5–219, 6–219, 7–263, 8–297, 9–297
1–15, 2–15, 3–64, 4–84, 5–104, 6–214, 7–224, 8–226, 9–228

England First Innings		Second Innings	
M.J. Stewart c Kanhai b Griffith ...	2	c Solomon b Hall	17
J.H. Edrich c Murray b Griffith ...	0	c Murray b Hall	8
E.R. Dexter (capt) lbw b Sobers ...	70	b Gibbs	2
K.R. Barrington c Sobers b Worrell	80	c Murray b Griffith	60
M.C. Cowdrey b Gibbs	4	not out	19
D.B. Close c Murray b Griffith	9	c Murray b Griffith	70
†J.M. Parks b Worrell	35	lbw b Griffith	17
F.J. Titmus not out	52	c McMorris b Hall	11
F.S. Trueman b Hall	10	c Murray b Hall	0
D.A. Allen lbw b Griffith	2	not out	4
D. Shackleton b Griffith	8	run out	4
Extras (b 8, lb 8, nb 9)	25	(b 5, lb 8, nb 3)	16
Total	297	for 9 wickets 228	

BOWLING	Overs	Mdns	Runs	Wkts	Overs	Mdns	Runs	Wkts
Hall	18	2	65	1	40	9	93	4
Griffith	26	6	91	5	30	7	59	3
Sobers	18	4	45	1	4	1	4	–
Gibbs	27	9	59	1	17	7	56	1
Worrell	13	6	12	2	–	–	–	–

fall of wickets
1–2, 2–20, 3–102, 4–115, 5–151, 6–206, 7–235, 8–271, 9–274
1–15, 2–27, 3–31, 4–130, 5–158, 6–203, 7–203, 8–219, 9–228
umpires – J.S. Buller and W.E. Phillipson
Match Drawn

The drawn Test produced a surge in advance bookings for the Edgbaston Test. England did not disappoint. In his first Test Phil Sharpe made 85 not out in the second innings, and England went on to win by 217 runs. The man they had to thank most was Trueman. He had taken five for 75 in the first innings. In the second, with the West Indies chasing 309 to win in 280 minutes, he brought about an astonishing collapse. They were bowled out for 91, and Trueman took seven for 44. His last six wickets were taken in the space of twenty-four balls at the cost of a boundary by the last man, Gibbs. The West Indies lost their last six wickets for 13 runs.

The fact that England had levelled the series further stimulated public interest, but the West Indies gained resounding victories at Headingley and at The Oval to take the series by three matches to one. Although Sharpe played well on three occasions, there were concerns about the England batting. No English batsman hit a century in the series, and the vulnerability to great pace was apparent.

The bowling offered more encouragement. In spite of being able to bowl only one over in the second innings of the final Test, Trueman captured thirty-four wickets in the series. The problem was that he was now in search of a new-ball partner. The decline in Statham that had been apparent in Australia proved to be no temporary loss of form. He took three wickets for 68 runs in the first innings at The Oval, but this was to be his penultimate Test.

The most disquieting aspect of the series, however, had nothing to do with England's batting or bowling. Particularly at Headingley, fierce competitiveness sometimes degenerated into rank bad feeling. This was one of the indications that, in the second half of the twentieth century, cricket did not always bring nations closer together.

Equally disturbing was the fact that, irrespective of the success of the Test series and the Gillette Cup, the domestic game was still limping along. In the years immediately after the war, the Whitsuntide match at Lord's between Middlesex and Sussex would attract near-capacity crowds. Now the ground was nearly empty for such matches. There seemed to be a lethargy in many counties.

There was a bizarre and unique incident in the match between Kent and Middlesex at Tunbridge Wells in June. Middlesex bowled out Kent for 150 on the Saturday and reached 121 for three in reply. At 11.30 on the Monday morning when the game was due to recommence, only three Middlesex players were at the ground. They were White, one of the not out batsmen, Sid Russell, already out, and Clark, the twelfth man. The umpires waited a generous two minutes, the statutory time, and then declared the Middlesex innings closed under Law 17. The Kent second innings began with six Kent men fielding for Middlesex. Within three overs, the whole Middlesex side had arrived and were fielding. It appears that they had gone home for the weekend and had been delayed by the Monday morning traffic on their return. It was not the kind of incident that would convince followers of the game that county cricket was being taken seriously.

This match at Tunbridge Wells was Cowdrey's final game for Kent before he suffered his broken arm in the Lord's Test. The injury took a considerable time to heal. He agreed to lead MCC to India where, in a period of eight weeks, five Test matches were to be played.

Unfortunately, as the time for departure drew closer, Cowdrey did not feel fit enough to undertake the tour. Mike Smith of Warwickshire, appointed as Cowdrey's vice-captain, took over the leadership. Smith had not appeared in the series against the West Indies. Stewart had, and had not fared too badly, but he was not selected for the tour of India, which left England with only Bolus and Edrich as opening batsmen. When Cowdrey dropped out Stewart was brought in. Ironically, Stewart fell ill and had to be flown home while Barrington also had to return home because of a broken finger. The men flown out to replace them were Parfitt and Cowdrey.

Once more Trueman did not make the trip to India, and the fast bowlers were Larter, Jeff Jones, Price of Middlesex, and the all-rounder Knight, about whom selectors seemed to be rather undecided.

The five Tests in eight weeks itinerary was the first attempt to cut down the length of overseas tours. However, the brevity tended to increase rather than reduce the pressure on players with one Test following upon another.

Interestingly, Cowdrey named sixteen young players from the 1963 season whom he believed would become Test cricketers. One of them, Sharpe, had already played for England, and Price and Jeff Jones were chosen for the tour. Among the others were Boycott, Fletcher, Milburn and Underwood. Roger Harman and Nicholas Majendie were two Surrey players Cowdrey named. Harman, a slow left-arm bowler, had immense talent, but he never lived up to expectations after enjoying a wonderful year in 1964. Majendie kept wicket for Oxford University, but eight games for Surrey in 1963 was the extent of his county cricket. He was one of many gifted players who chose paths other than cricket.

M.J.K. Smith had come to the England captaincy by default. Dexter was unavailable for the tour, and Cowdrey had withdrawn initially through injury. However, Smith won high praise for his handling of the team in India. He instilled a team spirit, and there was a harmony and courtesy off the field which made the party very popular. E.M. Wellings went so far as to say that the conduct of the tour should serve as a model for all such ventures.

An outstanding success as a batsman at Oxford, Mike Smith had first played for Leicestershire before joining Warwickshire, where he was captain from 1957 to 1967. Tall and bespectacled, he was a prolific scorer in county cricket with great powers of concentration. He was a slow starter, but he could hit strongly and effectively when set – particularly on the leg side. As befitted a man who played rugby for England against Wales, he was a brilliant fielder, a short-leg specialist. He was also very popular with his players, who found him kind and fair and responded to him. Unfortunately, he was to become less popular with the public who, at a crucial time for the game of cricket, associated his period of stewardship with one of the dullest periods in Test history.

For all the praise showered upon him by Wellings and others, 'M.J.K.' led England to five draws in five Tests in India. Most English critics blamed India's reluctance to risk defeat in front of their adoring millions, but the fact remains that, in the first Test, England's scoring rate was 1.5 runs per over in the first innings. Even allowing for illness to Stewart and Parks, this was defence taken to the extreme. 'Bapu' Nadkarni, the slow left-arm bowler, sent down twenty-one consecutive maidens, and his first-innings figures were nought for 5 from thirty-two overs, twenty-seven of them maidens.

England gained what was considered a brave draw in the second Test in spite of several players being unwell, but again they scored at under 2 runs an over in both innings. In Calcutta England took a first-innings lead of 26, but their 267 runs came off 66.3 more overs than India's 241.

England took a first-innings lead of 107 in the fourth Test, but as India's second innings did not begin until the fourth afternoon, no result looked possible.

Knight and Parfitt both hit centuries in the final Test, at Kanpur, but India scored only 136 in five and a half hours on the third day, and the game died.

There were some positive points from the tour for England. Fred Titmus was once more an outstanding success, taking twenty-seven wickets in the Test series. His Middlesex colleague John Price had also done well on pitches which were of no help to a bowler of his pace.

Cowdrey had been out of cricket for seven months. He had not played a competitive game since the Lord's Test when he had suffered his broken arm. As Wellings wrote:

> To resume playing in the heady atmosphere of international cricket and then to score centuries in the next two Tests represented a remarkable feat. But Cowdrey continues unaware of his vast potential, and, even after the first century had restored his touch, he stood suspiciously aloof in Delhi and left others to attempt the scoring rate his side needed.

Wellings was voicing a concern which was to gain common currency in the next few years: that Cowdrey was one of the greatest of batsmen was unquestioned, yet he appeared to lack self-belief. The treatment he had received at the hands of the selectors could not have helped, but

2,000 runs per season never seemed to assure him that his technique was correct. There was a constant search for a better grip, a different stance.

Inevitably, certain worries followed the series in India. The greatest failing was that England still searched for an opening pair. Brian Bolus and Mike Smith had opened in the first two Tests, Bolus and Binks, the reserve wicket-keeper, in the third, and Bolus and Edrich, who had been unwell, in the last two. Bolus, like Micky Stewart, was never called upon again, and England had five different pairings in the Ashes series of 1964.

This was one of the least memorable of encounters between the old enemies. The emphasis remained firmly on the determination not to lose and much of the cricket was joyless. It was also Robins's last year as chairman of selectors, and his period of office ended with the lack of success that had marked his reign. He had been one of the best of captains, but as a selector he was, like Illingworth thirty years later, too close to the players, too prone to make public criticism, too eager to voice his disapproval to an individual while a match was in progress. He certainly did not help Dexter's cause, but, as Dexter has said forgivingly since, 'We did not know then that he was a sick man.'

In his search for brightness before winning, Robins used twenty players against Australia in 1964, and M.J.K. Smith was not one of them. In an age when the *Daily Herald* had closed, to be replaced by the *Sun*, when the Rolling Stones had begun to shock, and when the Windmill, once the bastion of nudity and comedy, closed because it had become an institution overtaken and rendered obsolete by permissiveness, the emphasis on brightness was inevitable. One cannot help but feel, however, that the philosophy must have had an unsettling and unhelpful effect on a generation of cricketers who had been reared on the idea that one played to win and whose models were Hutton and May.

Luck did not smile upon England during the series. The first Test, at Trent Bridge, was much reduced by rain. England chose a new opening pair in Boycott and Edrich, but the Surrey left-hander was injured shortly before the match. There was no reserve batsman, so England played five bowlers – Flavell, Coldwell, Allen, Trueman and Titmus – and Titmus improvised as an opening batsman. Boycott broke a finger while fielding and could not bat in the second innings, when Dexter opened with Titmus. The match was drawn.

Dexter and Edrich opened in the second Test, which saw the debut of Norman Gifford, the left-arm spinner. John Edrich hit a century, but rain decimated play and the match was drawn.

The third Test match, at Headingley, was the only one of the five to produce a result. England won the toss and batted first. They were bowled out on the first day for 268, Hawke and McKenzie doing the damage. Cowdrey was absent through injury, and Taylor, his replacement, Flavell and Parfitt all suffered injuries during the match.

Australia began well enough, but fine bowling from Titmus and Gifford reduced them to 178 for seven. Both Burge and Hawke were struggling against the spinners, but Dexter chose to take the second new ball, a move for which he was strongly criticised, and the first seven overs from Trueman and Flavell, neither of whom had been impressive earlier, brought 42 runs. The tension was broken. The Australian pair took their partnership to 105 on the third day, and it needed a third new ball to bring Burge's great innings of 160 to an end.

Following Dexter's decision to take off Titmus and Gifford on the second day, Australia scored 202 runs and took a first-innings lead of 121. If England could set Australia a target of 200 or so, they still had a chance of victory, but Simpson, an excellent captain in this series, handled his bowlers well. In spite of Barrington's 85, England were out for 229, and Australia needed 109 to win.

In the absence of the injured Flavell, Titmus opened the bowling and took two for 25 in twenty-seven overs, but Australia won by seven wickets on the fourth day; the result was enough to see them keep the Ashes.

The Old Trafford Test was a statistician's delight and a nightmare for lovers of the game. Having won at Headingley, Simpson adopted the strategy of avoiding defeat in the last two Tests and so holding on to the Ashes. He won the toss, and he and Lawry scored 201 for the first wicket before Lawry was run out for 106. Simpson's innings did not end until the third day when he was caught by Parks off Price for 311. His innings lasted 762 minutes and remains the longest ever played against England. He declared at 656 for eight. Tom Cartwright, making his Test debut, bowled seventy-seven overs and took two for 118. Fred Rumsey took two for 99 on his debut.

England made 611. Barrington scored 256 and Dexter 174, and Tom Veivers bowled 95.1 overs to take three for 155. He bowled fifty-one overs unchanged. It was the type of match that would threaten a slow death for cricket.

For the fifth Test, at The Oval, England brought in Trueman, Cowdrey and Barber for Rumsey, Mortimore and Edrich. This was to be an historic match, but one of only moderate interest. Having won the toss, England squandered the advantage when they were bowled out for 182 on the opening day. Their main destroyer was Neil Hawke. Top-scorer Ken Barrington passed 4,000 runs in Test cricket.

Australia reached 245 for five on the second day. Lawry batted five and a quarter hours for his 94. They forged ahead towards lunch, losing only Grout, until, with the break imminent, Trueman knocked back Redpath's middle stump. Next ball he had McKenzie caught at slip. There was no time for Hawke to begin his innings, so there was eager anticipation throughout the interval as to whether Trueman would complete the hat-trick.

He did not, but 24 runs into the afternoon, he found the edge of Hawke's bat and Cowdrey took the catch at first slip. Fred Trueman had become the first bowler to take 300 wickets in Test cricket. He added Corling a few overs later to bring his total to 301. There were two good seasons ahead for him in county cricket, but, at thirty-three, his Test career as a fast bowler was drawing to a close.

By the end of the third day England were 132 for two and on the fourth day Geoff Boycott completed his first Test match hundred. His innings lasted five hours and was 'full of splendid strokes, particularly drives and square-cuts'. England had found an opener.

Barrington joined Cowdrey at 255 for four and by the close they had advanced the score to 381 and Cowdrey had completed 5,000 runs in Test cricket. There were faint hopes of an English victory, but there was no play on the fifth day because of rain, and a limp series had come to an end. So had Dexter's reign as England's captain.

Trueman's 300th Test Wicket and Boycott's First Test Hundred
England v Australia at The Oval
13, 14, 15, 17 and 18 August 1964

England First Innings		Second Innings	
G. Boycott b Hawke	30	c Redpath b Simpson	113
R.W. Barber b Hawke	24	lbw b McKenzie	29
E.R. Dexter (capt) c Booth b Hawke	23	c Simpson b McKenzie	25
M.C. Cowdrey c Grout b McKenzie	20	(5) not out	93
K.F. Barrington c Simpson b Hawke	47	(6) not out	54
P.H. Parfitt b McKenzie	3		
†J.M. Parks c Simpson b Corling	10		
F.J. Titmus c Grout b Hawke	8	(4) b McKenzie	56
F.S. Trueman c Redpath b Hawke	14		
T.W. Cartwright c Grout b McKenzie	0		
J.S.E. Price not out	0		
Extras (lb 3)	3	(b 6, lb 4, nb 1)	11
Total	182	for 4 wickets	381

185

BOWLING	Overs	Mdns	Runs	Wkts	Overs	Mdns	Runs	Wkts
McKenzie	26	6	87	3	38	5	112	3
Corling	14	2	32	1	25	4	65	–
Hawke	25.4	8	47	6	39	8	89	–
Veivers	6	1	13	–	47	15	90	–
Simpson	–	–	–	–	14	7	14	1

fall of wickets
1–44, 2–61, 3–82, 4–111, 5–117, 6–141, 7–160, 8–173, 9–174
1–80, 2–120, 3–200, 4–255

Australia   First Innings
R.B. Simpson (capt) c Dexter
  b Cartwright 24
W.M. Lawry c Trueman b Dexter . . 94
N.C. O'Neill c Parfitt b Cartwright 11
P.J.P. Burge lbw b Titmus 25
B.C. Booth c Trueman b Price 74
I.R. Redpath b Trueman 45
†A.T.W. Grout b Cartwright 20
T.R. Veivers not out 67
G.D. McKenzie c Cowdrey b Trueman 0
N.J.N. Hawke c Cowdrey b Trueman 14
G.E. Corling c Parfitt b Trueman . .   0
  Extras (b 4, lb 1)   5

  Total 379

BOWLING	Overs	Mdns	Runs	Wkts
Trueman	33.3	6	87	4
Price	21	2	67	1
Cartwright	62	23	110	3
Titmus	42	20	51	1
Barber	6	1	23	–
Dexter	13	1	36	1

fall of wickets
1–45, 2–57, 3–96, 4–202, 5–245, 6–279, 7–343, 8–343, 9–367
umpires – J.F. Crapp and C.S. Elliott
Match Drawn

    The lack of success brought criticism where once there had been nothing but praise. In *Wisden* Norman Preston identified England's problems as lack of a settled team and choice of captain. That England suffered

Colin Cowdrey, untried and untested when he went to Australia in 1954, proved to be an outstanding batsman and was to serve England faithfully and well for many years in many ways.

The way we were. Titmus and Evans batting for England against South Africa at Lord's, 1954. The spectators on the grass were separated from the playing area by only the boundary rope, yet none would have contemplated crossing that boundary.

Tom Graveney is caught behind by Waite off Heine, England v South Africa, Lord's, 1955. England won the series 3–2. One felt that Graveney, one of the most stylish players in the game, was never quite trusted by the England selectors.

Trevor Bailey, one of six openers tried by England in the 1955 series, is caught and bowled by Tayfield in the fourth Test, which South Africa won.

One-time contender with Hutton for the England captaincy, David Sheppard, later Bishop of Liverpool.

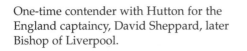

The power of Typhoon Tyson. Winslow's leg stump is broken.

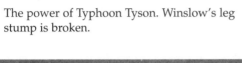

Jim Laker – 19
wickets in a Test
match.

Mackay is caught
Oakman bowled
Laker, Old Trafford,
1956. *Laker's Match.*

For many judges, Peter May remains England's greatest post-war batsman. He captained England on a record 41 occasions.

Ken Barrington, an England rock. The fielder is Colin Bland.

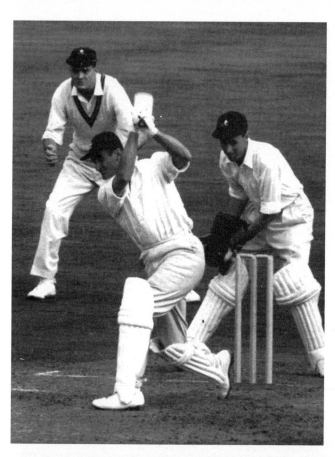

'Lord Ted' – Ted Dexter's majestic drive.

M.J.K. Smith is caught by Goddard off the bowling of Tayfield at The Oval in the final Test between England and South Africa, 1960.

England v Australia, Headingley, 1961. Harvey is caught Lock bowled Trueman who took five for 58 in the first innings. He followed this with six for 30 in the second innings.

Sheppard just makes his ground as Jarman whips off the bails, Australia v England, Melbourne, 1963. Sheppard was eventually run out for 113 as England won by seven wickets.

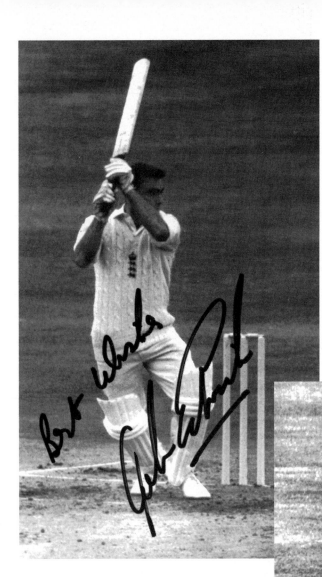

John Edrich cuts a ball from Brian Yuile to the boundary during his innings of 310 not out, England v New Zealand, Headingley, 1965.

Bob Barber is bowled by Neil Hawke for 185, Sydnay, January, 1966. Barber and Boycott scored 234 for the first wicket. Barber's outstanding innings was his only century in Test cricket. John Edrich, who also scored a century, is at the non-striker's end.

from the absence of a top-class all-rounder and that no adequate replacements for Trueman and Statham had been found were true, but, Preston asserted, 'Dexter is a grand natural cricketer; indeed, a fine all-round sportsman, but has he managed to get the best out of his men? He has now led England in losing rubbers against India, Australia and West Indies.'

The knives were out for Dexter, but there was no need to sack him. For reasons he himself has never quite understood, he agreed to stand as Conservative candidate against Jim Callaghan in Cardiff at the October General Election. It was the election that brought Labour, under Harold Wilson, back into power, and as Callaghan was a senior member of Wilson's front-bench team, Dexter was never considered to have a real chance of unseating the Labour politician.

The side to tour South Africa in 1964–65 was chosen and Mike Smith, who had not played against Australia, was named as captain. The selectors announced that Dexter would join the party in South Africa if he was unsuccessful in the election, which he was.

Like Smith, Graveney had not been chosen to play against Australia. He scored more runs, 2,385, than any other batsman in the country, and his 132 against Northamptonshire at Worcester in August was the hundredth hundred of his career. A batsman of effortless grace and balance, Graveney was not only an aesthetic delight, he was a massive accumulator of runs. In 1964 he was a vital member of the Worcestershire side which took the County Championship for the first time in its history. They fought hard most of the season against neighbouring Warwickshire, but Mike Smith's county faded towards the close, and Worcestershire won by a margin of forty-one points, winning eighteen of their twenty-eight matches. Kenyon, a calm, intelligent captain, Ron Headley, son of the great West Indian batsman, 'Dick' Richardson, Martin Horton and Graveney provided a formidable and consistent batting combination. Coldwell, Flavell and Gifford bowled for England while Carter, Slade and Standen were reliable in support. Booth enjoyed a magnificent year behind the stumps, and the fielding and catching were of the highest quality.

In this respect one should single out Jim Standen. A professional goal-keeper with Arsenal and West Ham United, Standen displayed an athleticism which shamed many cricketers on the circuit. On top of that, his sixty-four wickets at 13 runs each put him first in the national bowling averages. Coldwell was second, emphasising that bowlers win titles. Flavell and Gifford were also in the top twelve.

Graveney finished fourth in the batting averages with Barrington, Cowdrey and another Worcestershire player ahead of him: that cricketer was not eligible to appear in the Championship, for he was still qualifying. His name was Basil D'Oliveira. He hit centuries against the Australians and Oxford University. Within a few years he would move centre stage.

Warwickshire were not only runners-up in the Championship, they were the beaten finalists in the second Gillette Cup. Sussex retained the trophy with a resounding victory by eight wickets. They bowled out Warwickshire for 127. The Man of the Match was Ian Thomson, who took four for 23 in thirteen overs.

Thomson was a fast-medium right-arm bowler who could move the ball sharply and most disconcertingly. He had a particular penchant for bowling against Warwickshire and had taken all ten Warwickshire wickets for 49 runs at Worthing early in the season. Sussex still laboured in mid-table, but Thomson's 116 wickets won him a place in the party to tour South Africa. He played in all five Tests in the Republic, but he never appeared for England again.

Warwickshire's journey to the Gillette Cup Final was not without incident. The semi-final, against Lancashire at Old Trafford, was an unhappy affair and had very sad consequences. Warwickshire batted first, and Bob Barber, the left-hander and former Lancashire captain who had left the Red Rose county disillusioned and disgruntled, hit 72, Mike Smith made 58 and they were the main contributors in a formidable total of 294 for seven in what was now the limited sixty overs.

In reply the home side began well, with Green and Worsley hitting 67 off the first twelve overs. Thereafter things went wrong. Mike Smith took two good catches on the leg side to dismiss Entwistle and Grieves, and he then set his field deep, with fielders on the boundary as his bowlers maintained accuracy. The Lancashire batsmen showed their frustration and displeasure at these tactics. Marner and Clayton, in particular, made no attempt to score the necessary runs and offered straight-bat defence to practically every ball. Lancashire crawled to 209 for seven, Warwickshire won by 85 runs and the match ended with the crowd booing the players off the field.

Smith's defence was that he was breaking no rules and that Dexter had won the trophy the previous year by adopting similar tactics. Indeed, it was to be nearly twenty years before legislation was brought in which restricted field placings, and only then were the new rulings made because of precedents set in Australia.

The reaction to Lancashire's performance was more immediate. The committee asked for a survey from team manager Cyril Washbrook, which was to make special reference to the behaviour of several players, following complaints from other counties, with special regard to the way

188

in which Lancashire had batted in the Gillette Cup semi-final. As a result of Washbrook's inquiry, Ken Grieves was sacked as captain and returned to the Lancashire League. Dyson was not re-engaged as he was considered no longer to be of county standard, and Marner and Clayton were dismissed 'on the grounds that their retention was not in the best interests of the playing staff of the club'.

Marner, it will be remembered, was the first Gillette Cup hero, the first cricketer to be named Man of the Match. He joined Leicestershire, while wicket-keeper Clayton joined Somerset.

Lancashire were now in search of a captain and, during the winter, advertised the post in *The Times*, a most unusual step. It was believed that Warwickshire were willing to release A.C. Smith and that he would take over at Old Trafford. This did not transpire and, eventually, Lancashire fell back on the faithful Brian Statham, who did much to restore calm and encourage some young cricketers. It was a turbulent period for Lancashire, who had engaged Sonny Ramadhin for two seasons, only to find that the old magic had left him.

While Lancashire licked their wounds Mike Smith, Bob Barber, Tom Cartwright and David Brown of Warwickshire were among those to set sail for South Africa.

Test cricket was under scrutiny and faced crisis. Attendances at the England–Australia matches were very much down on the 1963 series with the West Indies, and less income had been generated. Although it was not voiced loudly abroad, matches which involved South Africa could not officially be recognised as Tests since South Africa had left the British Commonwealth in 1961 and become a republic.

The answer to the first problem would take some years to solve; the second found an immediate remedy. Meeting at Lord's in July 1965, the Imperial Cricket Conference, founded in 1909 and restricting membership to Test-playing countries within the Commonwealth, changed its name to the International Cricket Conference. This allowed the organisation to embrace South Africa and to offer associate membership to the United States, Fiji and Ceylon. The change could be seen, initially, as being born out of expediency, but ultimately it was to have an advantageous effect on the game by encouraging cricket in such countries as Denmark and Holland.

So Mike Smith and his party were able to play what could be recognised as official Test matches when they flew to South Africa in October 1964. The days of the team boarding a train at Waterloo to be taken to a ship at Tilbury or Southampton were gone, and Smith's men flew out almost unnoticed on election day. It was not a strong side, but it was an interesting one.

The selection followed a strange process. We have spoken of Dexter's political campaign, and the captaincy, presumably, should have passed to Cowdrey, but he announced that he was unavailable. When the majority of the team had been selected Cowdrey, at the eleventh hour, made himself available, but it was decided that there was now no room for him unless Dexter beat the Shadow Chancellor in the Cardiff constituency. As Rex Alston commented before the party flew out, 'A team not containing Cowdrey, Graveney, Russell and Stewart cannot be representative of England's present strength.'

Graveney's artistry and charm was still ignored, and it was three years since he had played in a home Test. 'As to Russell, he has been the best opening batsman and the most prolific scorer in county cricket this season, and Stewart has not been far behind him.'

Edrich, too, had been overlooked. Boycott and Barber were the only established openers in the party, while Barrington, Parfitt and a young batsman who had excelled at Cambridge and done well for Middlesex, Mike Brearley, were to supplement the batting of Smith and Dexter.

Brearley was seen as a gamble for the future with 'many of the attributes of a future England opener and possible captain'. MCC stated he was 'an authentic opening batsman', but none could understand how he could be chosen ahead of Eric Russell, Stewart or Cowdrey. It was hinted that Cowdrey would have been selected at the last if he had agreed to go as an opener, but his relationship with the selectors had become rather strained.

Murray was reinstated as wicket-keeper, although he was to play number two to Parks. Cartwright and Titmus were all-rounders, and Allen and Hobbs, a young Essex leg-spinner who had impressed on MCC's tour of East Africa the previous winter, completed the spin contingent. The doubts concerned the pace men.

Nicholson of Yorkshire, originally chosen, was forced to miss the tour with a back injury. He was never to get another opportunity. Thomson of Sussex replaced him. In spite of his 300 Test wickets, Trueman's star was fading, and it was not felt that he could sustain his form over a long tour. Price and Brown were the other pace bowlers chosen. Neither was particularly fast and both were quite limited in experience.

Few people gave this rather strangely assorted party any chance against a South African side which included the Pollock brothers, McLean, Barlow, Goddard and Bland. The critics were proved wrong. MCC won ten of the seventeen first-class matches they played, drew the other seven, and took the Test series 1–0.

There were disappointments. Brearley could find no sort of form, and he, Brown and Hobbs did not appear in the Tests. To counter this, Smith's captaincy and man-management were again highly praised, and the tour passed off serenely. Not only did England win the first Test, but they held the upper hand in three of the remaining four. They only wobbled at Johannesburg in the fourth Test after Smith had won the toss and put South Africa in to bat.

At Kingsmead, Durban, England were 279 for five when Parks joined Barrington early on the second morning. The pair shared an unbroken partnership of 206, and both made centuries. It was Parks's second and final Test hundred while Barrington's 148 not out was his eleventh. Ten of his Test hundreds had been made overseas, and he had become the first man to score a Test century in all seven Test-playing countries.

The spinners twice bowled out South Africa, for 155 and 226, and England won by an innings shortly after lunch on the fourth day. It was an important win, for England had gone twelve consecutive matches without a victory.

The second and third Tests followed quickly upon each other, separated by the New Year holiday. At Johannesburg, in the second Test, South Africa were again forced to follow on and again Allen and Titmus took the bowling honours. Bob Barber made 97 and shared a second-wicket stand of 136 with Dexter, who then added 191 with Barrington. Dexter's 172 was his ninth and last Test hundred, and it meant that he had scored a Test century against each of the other six Test-playing nations. Rain affected the last day, and Bland's patient hundred brought South Africa a draw.

England indulged in the luxury of fielding an unchanged side for the third Test in succession when the teams moved on to Cape Town, where a dull, uninspiring encounter took place. The pitch was easy-paced, and the batting on both sides was stronger than the bowling. South Africa scored 501 for seven, with Barlow and Pithey making hundreds. Barlow did not endear himself to the English fielders when he stood his ground after Parfitt had appeared to take a perfectly good catch at short-leg. His century was not applauded by England, who later apologised.

In contrast Barrington was given not out when he tickled a leg-side ball from Peter Pollock, but the Surrey man 'walked'. These incidents were all part of a great debate at the time, with the Australian opener Bill Lawry at the centre, as to whether batsmen should 'walk' or wait for the umpire's verdict. Like most cricket controversies it faded without ever being resolved.

Smith scored 121, and England plodded to within 59 of South Africa's score. South Africa were unable to force the pace; England were content to hold what they had. The game ended in stalemate. England kept South Africa in the field for eleven and a half hours, and South Africa responded by batting out their second innings until half an hour before the end of the match. Perhaps the most notable thing in this dreary match was that the two wicket-keepers were the only men not to bowl.

South Africa had their best game of the series in the fourth Test, in which Cartwright came in for Allen. Smith won the toss and after much inspection and debate with manager Donald Carr and senior players he asked South Africa to bat first. Three hours were lost to rain on the first two days, at the end of which South Africa declared on 390 for six.

Parfitt's 122 not out took England to within 6 of South Africa's total. Smith was reprieved when, having allowed the ball to go through to the wicket-keeper, he went to pat down the pitch. Waite had tossed the ball to Van der Merwe, who threw down the wicket and appealed. Umpire Kidson gave Smith out, but Goddard asked that the appeal be withdrawn. It was ironic that in a tour devoid of unpleasantness there should be three 'incidents' concerning umpires.

Barber broke a finger while fielding and took no further part in the match. He returned to England before the rest of the party. Goddard scored his first Test hundred and declared on the last day, setting England a target of 314 at 78 runs an hour. Had Goddard been a little more adventurous, he might well have secured victory for the pitch was beginning to aid the bowlers, but this was not in his character. As it was, England struggled and lost six wickets for 153 runs before the match ended. They owed much to Boycott, who batted resolutely for 76 while those around him fell.

Barber had gone home; Price, Brown and Cartwright were injured. Brearley and Hobbs were not considered, and Murray was brought in to open with Boycott in the final Test, although Parks still kept wicket. Also called into the side was Ken Palmer of Somerset, who was coaching in Johannesburg.

Another draw resulted. Graeme Pollock scored a hundred for South Africa; Boycott 117 for England. The England innings did not end until the fourth day. South Africa led by 67, but there was rain on the last day.

So England won the series, but, in the prevailing climate, statistical success was not all that was needed. As Ron Roberts reported, 'When four drawn Test matches follow hard upon one another, as they did in the last seven weeks of MCC's tour of South Africa, the game has clearly taken a turn for the worse.'

The concern for the future of the game was widespread, and many were asking for the problems to be tackled. The Gillette Cup had shown that grounds could be filled by competitive cricket with a real purpose, but Gordon Ross touched raw nerves when he cast doubt on the future of first-class cricket in an editorial at the beginning of the 1965 season:

> The change in the format and character of life these days has cast a heavy shadow over the possibility of professional three-day county cricket, in its present form, continuing indefinitely. Who has the time these days to take three days off from the office? Who in this affluent society spends his summer holiday in odd days watching county cricket when the sunshine of lands across the seas is now within his purse, or the car in his garage can take him and his wife to the sea in an hour or so? Wives, it might be added, are now a considerable force in exerting their influence on man's affairs.

There were those in authority who were acutely conscious of changing priorities and demands in society and who were subtly trying to bring about reform in a game which by its very nature was resistant to change.

For the first time, if one excepts the triangular tournament of 1912, a twin tour was arranged in 1965, with three Tests against New Zealand followed by three against South Africa. There was also an historic event which passed almost unnoticed. On 1 August Middlesex beat Lord's Taverners by 24 runs in a twelve-a-side game. The proceeds from the game were more than £800, which went to the National Playing Fields Association and to the Middlesex CCC Centenary Youth Trust. The significant thing was that the game was played on a Sunday, at Lord's, the first time the hallowed ground had seen play on that day. And the following season was to see county cricket played on a Sunday for the first time.

Doug Insole had replaced Robins as chairman of selectors, and he had with him May, Bedser and Kenyon. Insole did not follow the Robins pattern of public pronouncement and criticism, and he wanted to give players more chance, a longer period to prove themselves in Test cricket than had been the recent custom. He was also aware that he had taken over in a period of profound change, but he could never have anticipated what was in store for him over the next few years. Insole did not demand brightness before victory as Robins had done, but he was concerned to preserve the spirit of the game, and he was to act in a positive manner that Robins must have envied.

The first action by Insole and his committee was to invite Mike Smith to continue as captain, with both Dexter and Cowdrey playing under

193

him. Trueman was recalled for the first two Tests against New Zealand, but the force was no longer with him, and one of the greatest of fast bowlers and entertainers left the international scene. Few have been blessed with the ability to give so much pleasure. He brought zest and joy to the game which could scarcely afford to lose such a personality. It was Barrington rather than Trueman, however, who stole the headlines in the first Test.

It was played at Edgbaston in cold, miserable weather, and England won by nine wickets. Titmus and Barber bowled well, and Barrington and Cowdrey added 136 for the fourth wicket. Cowdrey made 85 of those runs, batting delightfully until he was hit on the body by a ball from Collinge which trickled on to the stumps.

Barrington, having returned from his triumphant tour of South Africa, had struggled to recapture his best form. At the end of the first day at Edgbaston, he was unbeaten on 61, his best score of the season to date. It had occupied 195 minutes and included only three fours. He reached 85 and remained on that score for more than an hour while twenty overs were bowled. When he finally reached his hundred, after six and a quarter hours, he hit the off-spinner Pollard for 14 in one over, including a six.

Adopting an exaggerated two-eyed stance, Barrington was intent on finding form, and when he was last out for 137 he had been at the crease for 437 minutes. Little more than 20,000 people watched the five days' cricket, and a largely tedious innings such as Barrington had played was no way in which to excite interest in the remaining Tests of the summer. The selectors' response was positive and immediate. Barrington was omitted from the Lord's Test because of the negative methods he had adopted at Edgbaston.

He was replaced by Parfitt, while John Snow, the Sussex fast bowler, came in for Cartwright. As one star rises, another fades. This was Fred Trueman's last Test match.

Snow took four for 80 in his debut match, Cowdrey scored 119 and, in spite of much rain over the last two days, England won by seven wickets with a quarter of an hour to spare.

Before the third Test at Headingley Boycott and Snow suffered injuries which made them unavailable for selection, and Ted Dexter's illustrious career as a batsman came to an abrupt end. Driving to his home in Ealing, he ran out of petrol. Pushing the car to a more convenient position on the road, he lost control, was hit by the car and sustained a broken leg. He virtually retired from cricket at the end of the season, although his Test career was to undergo a brief resurrection three years later.

There is a tide in the affairs of men,
Which, taken at the flood, leads on to fortune

Had Dexter not broken his leg, and had not Boycott been injured, it is doubtful that John Edrich and Ken Barrington would have played against New Zealand. Edrich had scored a century in his first Test against Australia, but he had been overlooked for the tour of South Africa and for the first two Tests against New Zealand. Barrington was still in partial disgrace.

At Headingley, Smith won the toss and England batted. There was pace in the pitch, and Barber cut the fourth ball of the match for four. The Warwickshire all-rounder did not last long, however, edging a ball to the wicket-keeper with the total on 13. Edrich had yet to score when Barrington joined him at five minutes to twelve.

Barrington, determined to make amends for the horror of Edgbaston, raced to 53 out of 89 with fifteen scoring strokes. Edrich became the dominant partner in the afternoon and a straight-driven six off Yuile took him to 93 and past Barrington. In spite of this, Barrington was the first to three figures. His century had come in under three hours, and he had atoned for his first Test negativity. There were two breaks for rain, but at the end of the day England were 366 for one, Edrich 194, Barrington 152.

This was heady stuff, and the scoring did not slacken on the second day. Barrington added only 11 to his overnight score before touching a rising ball to the wicket-keeper. He had hit twenty-six fours and a 'seven'. It was an innings which was to be overshadowed because of Edrich's performance, but it was a brilliant knock with a rich abundance of strokes, including cover drives off the front and back foot, which he had rarely displayed in Test cricket. For most spectators, it was a revelation.

Edrich was on 199 when he lost Barrington, and Cowdrey went cheaply. Parfitt was content to play the supporting role as 109 were added in ninety-seven minutes. Edrich reached 300 when he off-drove Motz for four, and he hit two more boundaries before Smith declared. This was the first triple century by an English batsman since 1938, and it was the highest score by an Englishman in first-class cricket at Leeds. He batted for 532 minutes and hit five sixes and fifty-two fours, the highest number of boundaries in a Test innings. He and Barrington scored 369 in 339 minutes for the second wicket. The bowling was by no means poor, and Edrich's innings was a remarkable achievement by any standards.

The innings came as the climax to an astonishing spell of batting by

Edrich. In exactly a month he had played nine innings, three of them not out, had scored 1,311 runs, average 218.50, and had hit six centuries, including a double and a triple century. His lowest score in the period had been 55 for Surrey against Kent. Edrich's solid defence tended to obscure the fact that he was principally an attacking batsman, excelling in cutting and in driving straight or through the covers.

New Zealand collapsed twice, and England found another hero in Fred Titmus who, on the fourth evening, took the wickets of Yuile, Taylor, Motz and Collinge in one over for no runs. The wickets came on the first, third, fourth and sixth balls of his twenty-first over.

Titmus's performance was vital, for the game went into the fifth day. It was over within sixteen minutes, but as the players left the field it began to pour with rain, and the ground was waterlogged within minutes.

John Edrich and Ken Barrington at Headingley
England v New Zealand at Headingley
8, 9, 10, 12 and 13 July 1965

England   First Innings
R.W. Barber c Ward b Taylor   13
J.H. Edrich not out   310
K.F. Barrington c Ward b Motz   163
M.C. Cowdrey b Taylor   13
P.H. Parfitt b Collinge   32
M.J.K. Smith (capt) not out   2
†J.M. Parks
R. Illingworth
F.J. Titmus
F.E. Rumsey
J.D.F. Larter
   Extras (b 4, lb 8, nb 1)   13

   Total for 4 wickets, dec.   546

BOWLING	Overs	Mdns	Runs	Wkts
Motz	41	8	140	1
Taylor	40	8	140	2
Collinge	32	7	87	1
Yuile	17	5	80	–
Morgan	6	–	28	–
Pollard	11	2	46	–
Congdon	4	–	12	–

fall of wickets
1–13, 2–382, 3–407, 4–516

New Zealand First Innings		Second Innings	
G.T. Dowling c Parks b Larter	5	b Rumsey	41
B.E. Congdon c Parks b Rumsey ..	13	b Rumsey	1
B.W. Sinclair c Smith b Larter	13	lbw b Larter	29
J.R. Reid (capt) lbw b Illingworth .	54	c Barrington b Rumsey .	5
R.W. Morgan b Illingworth	1	(6) b Titmus	21
V. Pollard run out	33	(5) c Cowdrey b Larter .	53
B.W. Yuile b Larter	46	c Cowdrey b Titmus ...	12
B.R. Taylor c Parks b Illingworth ..	9	c and b Titmus	0
R.C. Motz c Barber b Illingworth ..	3	c Barrington b Titmus ..	0
†J.T. Ward not out	0	(11) not out	2
R.O. Collinge b Larter	8	(10) b Titmus	0
Extras (b 5, lb 1, w 2)	8	(nb 2)	2
Total	193	166	

BOWLING	Overs	Mdns	Runs	Wkts	Overs	Mdns	Runs	Wkts
Rumsey	24	6	59	1	15	5	49	3
Larter	28.1	6	66	4	22	10	54	2
Illingworth	28	14	42	4	7	–	28	–
Titmus	6	2	16	–	26	17	19	5
Barber	2	–	2	–	14	7	14	–

fall of wickets
1–15, 2–19, 3–53, 4–61, 5–100, 6–153, 7–165, 8–173, 9–181
1–4, 2–67, 3–75, 4–86, 5–111, 6–158, 7–158, 8–158, 9–158
umpires – J.F. Crapp and C.S. Elliott
England won by an innings and 187 runs

England's three victories in three Tests could not hide the fact that the series was poorly attended and the tour financially disastrous. An attractive South African side drew bigger crowds and gained a decent profit in spite of growing political opposition. In spite of the formation of the *International* Cricket Conference, the South Africans were still outsiders, and the Tests as yet 'unofficial', although the conspiracy of silence on this matter was maintained.

Two of the Tests were drawn, while South Africa won at Trent Bridge thanks to the Pollock brothers. The series saw the return of Eric Russell, the arrival of David Brown and Ken Higgs, and the farewell of Brian Statham, who was recalled for the last Test. He took five for 40 and two for 105, but he stated that he was not available to tour Australia and so ended the Test career of one of the most loyal and honest of fast bowlers. In seventy Tests he had taken 252 wickets.

A briefer Test career ended in 1965 when Fred Rumsey played in the last of his four Tests that summer, having taken a total of fifteen wickets for 362 runs. He enjoyed a very good season for Somerset, but he was not wanted on the voyage to Australia. He continued to give the game good service, and in later years he was to become famous for organising winter tours. Thousands were to benefit from an organisation which enabled them to watch England play abroad.

Like Rumsey, Tom Graveney was left out of the party to travel to the southern hemisphere, although again he was fourth in the national averages and played a prominent part in Worcestershire's retention of the County Championship. They won with a victory over Sussex at Hove in the last match of the season, heading Northamptonshire by a mere four points. In a miserable summer runs were not easy to come by, but, in his first full season, Basil D'Oliveira scored 1,691 runs and took thirty-eight wickets. All-rounders were becoming more and more scarce, and the only cricketer to achieve the 'double' in 1965 was Barry Knight, who was picked to go to Australia.

Northamptonshire's second place in the Championship was the highest point in their history. The man most to catch the eye was a strongly built, aggressive opening batsman from Durham, Colin Milburn.

Sussex's reign in the Gillette Cup came to an end when they were beaten by Middlesex in the quarter-final at Lord's. Five Minor Counties were now engaged in the competition, but they were all eliminated in the first round. In the final, Yorkshire crushed Surrey.

The match was dominated by Geoff Boycott, who hit three sixes and fifteen fours in his 146. He had been under pressure following Barrington's censure for slow scoring, and he had been omitted from the England side for the final Test against South Africa. In the Gillette Cup Final, Boycott played what many still consider to be the best innings of his career. It was rich in personality, characterised by shots of power and beauty, the fusion of consummate technical ability and personal expression.

Boycott was one of four opening batsmen to be in the party to tour Australia, and the sixteen presented few surprises. Allen was preferred to Illingworth, and the pace quartet was Brown, Higgs, Jones and Larter, which did not look a potent force. It was still hoped that Larter could become a Tyson, and Jeff Jones was something of a secret weapon.

The real doubt concerned M.J.K. Smith who, on his batting performances, had not warranted a place in the side. It was asserted that he was needed for his leadership on and off the field, yet the MCC took the unprecedented step of appointing their secretary, S.C. Griffith, as manager and granted him the authority to override the captain in matters of tactics if he thought it necessary.

The series was drawn so that Australia retained the Ashes, but England claimed the moral high ground in the manner of experienced politicians. 'They did more for cricket,' asserted Norman Preston, 'than the majority of International touring sides in recent years. Australia achieved their objective. They retained the Ashes which they have held since 1959, but who really took the honours? Surely, MCC.'

The claim was based on the MCC Committee's demand that each match be approached boldly in an effort to enhance the image of international cricket, which had become tarnished. Certainly, the approach to all matches in the early part of the tour was positive, although MCC were not blessed with the best of luck. Illness kept Cowdrey out of the first Test, and Russell, who had batted with elegant sureness, damaged a thumb on the eve of the Test. He was passed fit to play at Brisbane but split the webbing of his right hand while fielding and batted number eleven. One of the unluckiest of cricketers, he did not play again in the series, although he finished high in the batting averages for the tour.

With only 111 minutes' play possible on the first day and none at all on the second, the first Test was always destined to be drawn. It began with one of the inevitable controversies that were attending Test cricket as Lawry survived a unanimous appeal for a catch at the wicket off the seventh ball of the innings. He went on to score 166, and Walters made 155. England had to follow on, but they were never in danger of defeat.

Cowdrey was back for the second Test, but Brown and Higgs were ill and injured. This meant that England had a new opening attack of Jones and Knight. They both bowled well, and Australia were out for 358.

Boycott and Barber gave England a flying start with 98 in seventy-seven minutes, and Edrich and Cowdrey hit centuries. Only Knight and Allen failed, and England took a first-innings lead of exactly 200, but the later runs had not come quickly enough. The England innings lasted seventy minutes into the fourth day.

Australia lost three wickets for 45 runs in eighty minutes on the last morning to slip to 176 for four, and had Parks not missed a simple stumping chance offered by Burge off Barber, England might well have won. Burge, 34 at the time, went on to make 120, and the match was drawn.

England went to Sydney in high spirits and played some sizzling cricket. Smith won the toss, England batted, and Boycott and Barber scored 234 in 242 minutes. Barber's innings was magnificent. He hit 185 off 255 balls in 296 minutes. He flayed the bowling to all parts of the field and hit nineteen fours. He was second out, at 303, and his aggression took England to a commanding position on the opening day. He was hailed as 'the most exciting player in the world', but this great performance was to be the highest score of his career and his only century in Test cricket.

His dismissal brought about a collapse. Hawke had taken the second new ball, and four wickets fell for 14 runs. England closed on 328 for five and lost nightwatchman Brown without addition the next morning. Edrich stood firm, hit his second Test hundred in successive innings and, with the help of a wagging tail, took England to 488.

Australia ended the second day on 113 for four, but the next day Brown took three wickets in one over with the second new ball and Australia were forced to follow on. In their second innings they collapsed to the combined off-spin of Allen and Titmus, and England won by an innings and 93 runs.

This was England's first victory over Australia for eleven matches and, naturally, was rapturously received. It helped to quell the criticism which had been growing regarding Smith's captaincy and place in the side. He was not scoring runs in Test cricket, and he did not strike the public figure that Dexter had done or command the public respect and affection that belonged to Cowdrey. His strength, his quiet efficiency and rapport with his side, was not a quality that attracted a glare of publicity.

Unfortunately, England's time of triumph was short-lived. The teams moved on to Adelaide where Australia out-batted, out-bowled and out-fielded England. England had been conclusively victorious in Sydney, but now they had to face the unpalatable truth that, in Frank Tyson's words, 'the Australian triumph in Adelaide is more significant than the English victory in the third Test since the former was achieved on an excellent batting surface whereas the Sydney wicket was the ally of the England off-spinners.'

It was not a good toss to win in Adelaide, for the weather was humid and the pitch a little green at the start, and England lost nine wickets on the opening day. They were all out for 241, with McKenzie taking six for 48. By the end of the second day Australia were 333 for three.

Simpson and Lawry had taken Australia into the lead without being separated, and their opening stand was worth 244 in 255 minutes. Lawry made 119, but Simpson batted into the third day, scored 225 and led his side to a total of 516. England's one consolation was that Jeff Jones captured six for 118.

Boycott, Barber and Edrich were out before the end of the third day and, in spite of 102 from Barrington, England were beaten on the fourth. Hawke did most damage this time with five for 54.

Barrington hit another century, 115, at Melbourne, and Smith, out for nought, declared at 485 for nine. Australia lost two wickets cheaply, but Lawry and Cowper then added 212 in five and a half hours. The England scoring rate had dwindled to a crawl towards the end of their innings, and it was now matched by the over-rate as they realised the most that they could hope for was a draw. Lawry was caught off Jones for 108. Cowper went on to record the longest first-class innings in Australia.

When he was finally bowled by Knight he had batted for 727 minutes and scored 307, Australia's only triple hundred in a home Test. He hit twenty fours.

No play was possible on the fourth day, by which time, in any case, the match was dead. Australia had retained the Ashes, and even if England claimed the moral high ground, the truth was that cricket had suffered yet again.

There was little comfort to be gained from the New Zealand part of the tour. The three Tests were drawn, marginally in favour of the home side, and the weather, like much of the cricket, was drear.

Wisden reflected gloomily that cricket seemed to be flourishing everywhere except in England, and that the standard of English first-class cricket had never been lower.

The gloom was to continue for much of the 1966 season. The Clark Report was issued, and most of it was rejected by the counties. They refused to accept a sixteen-match three-day County Championship to be played alongside a sixteen-match one-day County Championship, and although it was felt that twenty overs an hour was desirable, it was believed that such an over-rate could not be brought about by legislation. There was concern over pitches, and some grounds were marked down as being poor in this respect. Some of the recommendations were restating the issues over which battles had already been fought.

In spite of the constant plea for brighter cricket and positive results, 'freak' declarations were discouraged, as were attempts to bring about results through offering runs with 'friendly' bowling.

In 1966 there was play on Sunday in the County Championship for the first time and, in the first twelve matches played by each county, on a home and away basis, the first innings was restricted to sixty-five overs. This was not an experiment beloved by many followers of the game.

One of the interesting recommendations of the Clark Report was that the period of qualification for overseas-born cricketers should be reduced to twelve months, and that each county should be allowed to register one or two such cricketers. There was an avid search for something that would revitalise the game, to alleviate what some saw as the monotony and grind of six-days-a-week cricket. The Gillette Cup had made a great impact, but more was needed to stimulate further public interest.

The Gillette Cup had undergone a subtle change in that the restriction on each bowler had been reduced to twelve overs. Warwickshire beat Worcestershire in a low-scoring but tense final by five wickets. Worcestershire had enjoyed another excellent season, but finished runners-up in the Championship as well as the Gillette Cup.

Under Close, for whom this was to be a memorable season, Yorkshire regained the Championship. Their batting was consistent and their bowling adequate. Nicholson and Trueman both took a hundred Championship wickets, although neither of them could claim to be as potent as he had been in his prime. Illingworth and Don Wilson had fine seasons, and Close augmented the attack admirably while continuing to be an inspiration in the field.

Most counties found difficulties in adapting to Sunday play. Matches were not allowed to start before one o'clock and play had to end by 7.30. There was a half-hour interval for tea. Brought up on three two-hour sessions, cricketers seemed unable to accommodate the new timings on the second day of a match, and the game suffered accordingly.

There was further suffering for England in 1966. An immensely powerful West Indian side under Gary Sobers proved too strong in every department. Jones and Brown could not maintain the form that they had shown in Australia and finally gave way to Snow and Higgs, while each of the first three Tests welcomed a new player to the England ranks, Milburn, D'Oliveira and Underwood. After an absence of more than three years, and at the age of thirty-nine, Graveney was recalled to the England colours. Toil and travel took their toll of Titmus, and Illingworth replaced him after the fourth Test. The summer was also to see England led by three different captains for the first time in a single series.

It all began bleakly at Old Trafford where Hunte and Sobers hit centuries in a West Indian innings of 484. On his Test debut Milburn pushed the ball straight to Gibbs at cover and went for a single. Russell sent him back, but Gibbs had time to sprint in and break the wicket. England never recovered, and on the third morning they followed on. Milburn compensated for his first-innings duck with 94, but the West

Indies won by an innings inside three days. England were humiliated.

Boycott and Graveney returned at Lord's, and Basil D'Oliveira, twelfth man at Manchester, made his Test match debut. More sensational than the recall of the veteran Graveney was the dropping of Mike Smith.

However popular with his men, however good an ambassador abroad, Smith had failed to produce a winning side, and his own form had slumped. Someone had to pay for the humiliation of Old Trafford, and Smith's was the head to roll. It could not have been an easy decision for Insole and his fellow selectors, but desperate times need desperate measures. There was to be even greater desperation before the series was over.

Cowdrey took over the captaincy which many thought should have been his long since, and England bowled out the West Indies for 269 after a fractured first day. Milburn was leg-before to Hall for 6, but Graveney and Boycott added 115. Graveney was finally caught behind for 96, Parks made 91, and England took a first-innings lead of 86. The West Indies were only 10 runs ahead when their fifth second-innings wicket fell on the fourth day.

Cowdrey was later criticised for not pressurising Sobers and Holford more at the start of their innings; this was after the pair had shared an unbroken stand of 274, a record. Sobers made 163 not out, and his cousin Holford 105. Sobers's declaration left England 240 minutes in which to score 284 runs.

They slipped to 67 for four before Milburn and Graveney added 130 and saved the day. Milburn belted his way to 126. It was a flawed but spectacular innings. He lived dangerously. The public loved it. The purists were less convinced.

The draw at Lord's was seen as something of a missed opportunity, but there was optimism for the third Test, at Trent Bridge. That optimism suffered a shock prior to the game when it was announced that Barrington had been omitted. He was physically and mentally exhausted by six years of continuous international cricket during which, for much of the time, he and Cowdrey had carried the England batting. His batting for Surrey during the current season had returned to intro-spection, and it was obvious that he was suffering a breakdown in health. He took a rest from cricket for a few weeks and did not play in the rest of the series.

Initially, all went well at Trent Bridge. Higgs and Snow dominated the first day and bowled the West Indies out for 235. England lost Boycott, Milburn and Russell for 13, but Graveney, 109, and Cowdrey, 96, added 169. D'Oliveira scored 76, and England took a first-innings lead of 90.

D'Oliveira dismissed Hunte and Lashley before the arrears were cleared, and Kanhai was out on the fourth morning with the score on 175, having added 110 with Butcher. Butcher had been jeered for his stonewalling on the Saturday, but on the Monday he cut loose. Nurse made 53 in a stand of 107, Sobers 94 out of 173. Butcher finished unbeaten on 209, and Sobers asked England to make 393 in 389 minutes. They ended the fourth day with 30 on the board.

Only 2 runs had been scored on the Tuesday morning when Milburn mishooked Hall to mid-on. This was the first of five wickets to fall before lunch. Boycott displayed his technically superb defence and kept the enemy at bay for two and a half hours while he made 71. D'Oliveira also batted well, but the game was over at 4.14. The West Indies won by 139 runs.

There were unhappy and unsavoury features in the match. England disintegrated in the field on the fourth day, and Griffith was liberal in his use of the bouncer, one of which struck Underwood, the debutant number eleven, in the face.

England brought in Barber for the Headingley Test, where Sobers won the toss for the fourth time in succession. The West Indies lost four wickets for 154 runs before Nurse and Sobers put on 265 in 240 minutes; Nurse hit 137, Sobers 174. This was annihilation. Cowdrey rang his bowling changes, but he seemed strangely reluctant to bring the leg-spin of Barber into the attack. Cowdrey was unfortunate in that two edges by Nurse cannoned into his chest and dropped to the floor before this very best of slip fielders could grab them. The fates did not treat him kindly.

Sobers declared at 500 for nine. England made 240 and 205, and the game was over shortly after three o'clock on the fourth day. When he went to leave the ground Cowdrey discovered that the tyres of his car had been let down. Such was the mood of the moment.

The selectors made five changes for the Oval Test. They had intended to make six, but Price, the Middlesex pace bowler, was unfit, and Snow retained his place.

Among those to be axed was Colin Cowdrey, who had given so much to English cricket, remained among the top half-dozen batsmen in the world with more than 6,000 runs and 100 Test catches to his credit, but he had failed to turn the tide of defeat as leader. His place went to Brian Close, a Yorkshire professional of the old school, tough and uncompromising, successful as a county captain. He was very much the 'people's choice', or at least the choice of the popular press, and the first non-Oxbridge man to lead England since Len Hutton.

Out went Milburn, Titmus, Underwood and Parks, and in came Amiss for his first Test, John Edrich, Illingworth and, belatedly, Murray.

Close's rival to take over as captain was probably Tony Lock, who had moved from Surrey to Leicestershire where he led the side with considerable vigour, but Close was a pugnacious extrovert who had a good track record. He did not start well because he lost the toss, but he was well served by his bowlers, who tumbled out the West Indies on the first day. He handled his attack well and was quick to introduce the leg-spin of Barber, which pleased the critics.

The new captain was an inspirational fielder at short-leg, and Murray's neat efficiency lifted the out-cricket as a whole. Close was fortunate to have a better fielding side at his disposal than Cowdrey had had at Headingley.

The enthusiasm at dismissing the West Indies was tempered some-what when Hall bowled Boycott, and England were 20 for one. In glorious weather England's troubles worsened on the Friday in front of a capacity crowd. Sobers dismissed both Barber and Edrich, and Amiss and D'Oliveira fell to Hall so that five wickets were down before lunch. The pattern of the game looked familiar.

Close was out when he sleepily left his crease after touching the ball to Sobers at short-leg, and when Illingworth fell to Griffith England were 166 for seven.

Murray edged the first ball he received from Griffith into his pads. It was practically the last false stroke he made. At the other end, Graveney had stood firm among the wreckage and now he was liberated to play the full range of his shots. Here were two of the most exquisite off-drivers in the game at the crease and in form together. It was a regal sight.

By the end of the day, the two men, who had spent so much time in exile from Test cricket while lesser mortals walked the stage, had taken England to 330, Graveney 132, Murray 81. Nor were they separated early on the Saturday. When Graveney was finally run out by Gibbs he had batted six hours for his 165, and he and Murray had added a record 217 in 235 minutes. Graveney hit nineteen fours.

Murray fell soon after, having batted four and a half hours and hit thirteen fours. His 112 was his only Test century, but it was his second in the season against the West Indies, for he had hit a delightful unbeaten 100 against them for MCC in May.

The West Indies must have believed that their troubles were now at an end when Snow joined Higgs. The last pair believed otherwise. Both scored maiden fifties in first-class cricket and put on 128 in just over two hours. It was entertaining for the crowd, but it never became farcical or rustic.

England led by 259 runs, and Snow and Murray continued their joyous celebrations by combining to dismiss both openers cheaply. D'Oliveira bowled Kanhai, and Butcher fell after an aggressive burst of batting. The West Indies closed on 135 for four.

Holford ran himself out early on the Monday, going for a third run as Illingworth was whipping the ball into Murray from third man. Decisively, Sobers, who had scored 722 runs and taken twenty wickets in the series, was out first ball. He attempted to hook Snow, edged the ball into his 'box' and lobbed a simple catch to Close. Hendriks went quickly, and when Nurse was eighth out, caught at square-leg, the West Indies were beaten. The match ended when Barber caught and bowled Gibbs a quarter of an hour after lunch.

The Turning Point
England v West Indies at The Oval
18, 19, 20 and 22 August 1966

West Indies First Innings		Second Innings	
C.C. Hunte b Higgs	1	c Murray b Snow	7
E.D.A. St J. McMorris b Snow	14	c Murray b Snow	1
R.B. Kanhai c Graveney b Illingworth	104	b D'Oliveira	15
B.F. Butcher c Illingworth b Close	12	c Barber b Illingworth	60
S.M. Nurse c Graveney b D'Oliveira	0	c Edrich b Barber	70
G. St A. Sobers (capt) c Graveney b Barber	81	(7) c Close b Snow	0
D.A.J. Holford c D'Oliveira b Illingworth	5	(6) run out	7
†J.E. Hendriks b Barber	0	b Higgs	0
C.C. Griffith c Higgs b Barber	4	not out	29
W.W. Hall not out	30	c D'Oliveira b Illingworth	17
L.R. Gibbs c Murray b Snow	12	c and b Barber	3
Extras (b 1, lb 3, nb 1)	5	(b 1, lb 14, nb 1)	16
Total	268		.225

BOWLING	Overs	Mdns	Runs	Wkts	Overs	Mdns	Runs	Wkts
Snow	20.5	1	66	2	13	5	40	3
Higgs	17	4	52	1	15	6	18	1
D'Oliveira	21	7	35	1	17	4	44	1
Close	9	2	21	1	3	1	7	–
Barber	15	3	49	3	22.1	2	78	2
Illingworth	15	7	40	2	15	9	22	2

fall of wickets
1–1, 2–56, 3–73, 4–74, 5–196, 6–218, 7-218, 8–223, 9–223
1–5, 2–12, 3–50, 4–107, 5–137, 6–137, 7–142, 8–168, 9–204

England	First Innings	
G. Boycott b Hall	4	
R.W. Barber c Nurse b Sobers	36	
J.H. Edrich c Hendriks b Sobers ...	35	
T.W. Graveney run out	165	
D.L. Amiss lbw b Hall	17	
B.L. D'Oliveira b Hall	4	
D.B. Close (capt) run out	4	
R. Illingworth c Hendriks b Griffith	3	
†J.T. Murray lbw b Sobers	112	
K. Higgs c and b Holford	63	
J.A. Snow not out	59	
Extras (b 8, lb 14, nb 3)	25	
Total	527	

BOWLING	Overs	Mdns	Runs	Wkts
Hall	31	8	85	3
Griffith	32	7	78	1
Sobers	54	23	104	3
Holford	25.5	1	79	1
Gibbs	44	16	115	–
Hunte	13	2	41	–

fall of wickets
1–6, 2–72, 3–85, 4–126, 5–130, 6–150, 7–166, 8–383, 9–399
umpires – J.S. Buller and C.S. Elliott
England won by an innings and 34 runs

Much praise was lavished on Close, for it seemed that English cricket had been restored. His enthusiasm and commitment had done much to bring about the victory, although as a player his contribution had been minimal. The victory had been achieved without the help of Cowdrey, Barrington and Dexter, all of whom, it was hoped, would play again. Optimism ran high.

Doubts, however, were expressed concerning Boycott as a Test batsman. Peter West, the TV commentator, was one of those who observed that the Yorkshireman was playing with his bat too far away from his body. Boycott responded by hitting 246 not out in the first Test against India in the following season, 1967. Hobbs, the leg-spinner, made his debut and D'Oliveira scored his maiden Test hundred. Barrington returned and shared a second-wicket stand of 139 with Boycott. The Surrey man made 93 of the runs. Boycott's 246 came off 555 balls in 573 minutes. He hit a six and 29 fours off an attack that was depleted from the first afternoon. It took him 341 minutes, 316 balls, to reach his first hundred, and he suffered the same fate that Barrington had endured. He was dropped from the next Test for slow play.

England won the first Test by six wickets. They won the second by an innings with Graveney getting 151 and Murray equalling the Test record of six catches in an innings.

The trio of wins over India was completed, and Pakistan were beaten twice with the first Test drawn. Barrington scored centuries in all three Tests against Pakistan, and the series saw the debuts of fast bowler Geoff Arnold and wicket-keeper Alan Knott.

The first Test of the series also saw the end of the international careers of the Middlesex pair Russell and Murray. Russell played three magnificent cover drives to the boundary and was then bowled by a beautifully flighted leg-break from Intikhab for 43. He fell for 12 in the second innings and, graceful and prolific as he was, the competition of Boycott, Milburn, Edrich, Barber and Amiss was growing. Murray lost form after his record against India, and the claims of young Knott were very pressing. When the side to go to the Caribbean was chosen the selectors reverted to Parks as first choice.

Close had now led England to victory six times in seven Tests. No England captain can claim a better record over such a period, but he was never to captain England again.

Under Close's leadership, Yorkshire retained the County Championship. They finished ten points ahead of Kent, who were inspiringly led by Cowdrey. Kent's rise was due in no small measure to the continued consistency of their captain as a batsman, to the reliability of Denness and Luckhurst as an opening pair, to the all-round cricket of the West Indian John Shepherd, and to the bowling of Underwood and Graham. Norman Graham was an opening bowler rich in character, and both he and Underwood, quickly becoming one of the most feared bowlers in England, captured more than a hundred Championship wickets at under 14 runs apiece. Kent had a marvellous season and won the Gillette Cup, beating Somerset in a thrilling final.

The County Championship had its good and bad moments. One of the worst was when Middlesex played Hampshire at Lord's. This was a match in which there was Sunday play, to which the cricketers were still finding adjustment difficult. Only twelve minutes were lost to rain over the three days, but the match still ended without either side even being able to take first-innings points: Hampshire 421 for seven declared; Middlesex 371 for seven. Condemnation was universal.

As it was, too, for Close and Yorkshire whose Championship, the sixth in nine years, was tarnished by events at Edgbaston on 18 August.

The captaincy of Close and, in his absence, Trueman had been imaginative throughout the season and was a major reason for the county's success. Neither had a good match against Warwickshire, although over the first two days the game itself was exciting. Yorkshire made 238 and Warwickshire were level with nine wickets down. Brown and Allan scored 4 to give them a narrow lead and the first-innings points. With Cook, a left-arm medium-pacer who played only nine games for Warwickshire over a period of six years, and Cartwright taking four wickets each, Yorkshire were bowled out for 145 in their second innings. This meant that Warwickshire had 102 minutes in which to score 142 to win.

Amiss and Jameson hit well to keep the home side up with the clock, but Yorkshire bowled only twenty-four overs in the 102 minutes, and the over-rate got slower as deliberate time-wasting tactics were adopted. At one point the Yorkshire players left the field when light rain fell. The umpires and the two Warwickshire batsmen stayed in the middle. In the last quarter of an hour, Yorkshire bowled just two overs. One of them was bowled by Trueman, who sent down three bouncers and conceded two no-balls, so lengthening the over. In the end Warwickshire fell 9 runs short of their target with five wickets standing. Yorkshire earned two points for a draw, but the game ended in acrimony.

Warwickshire lodged an official complaint against Yorkshire's tactics, and the *Cricketer* described the events at Edgbaston and the turmoil that followed as 'one of the unhappiest ten days in the game's history'. An executive committee of former county captains – Brian Sellers, leader of Yorkshire's great side of the 1930s among them – investigated the umpires' report on the match and decided unanimously that: 'Yorkshire had used delaying tactics during the second Warwickshire innings and that these tactics constituted unfair play and were against the best interests of the game.'

Close was held entirely responsible for what had happened. He never suggested otherwise and did not regret or apologise for his actions, and he was severely censured. However, he was to suffer more than a censure.

He had already been named as captain of the MCC side to go to the West Indies, but, following the Edgbaston incident and the censure, MCC refused to sanction his appointment. It was apparent that the tour of the Caribbean would, as ever, be a difficult one with political tensions and crowd disturbances constant threats. Close's tough and uncompromising approach threatened danger in such an atmosphere. This was something that neither MCC nor, it was hinted, the British government could face.

Insole was in an intolerable position. He and his selectors had worked hard and successfully at building a side and Close, their chosen leader, was at the heart of their plans. Now those plans were to be put in jeopardy.

Not only did Insole vote to retain Close, but it was later revealed that when the vote was lost he had turned to Mike Smith in the hope that he might lead England through troubled waters. Smith, however, had just announced that he was retiring from first-class cricket. At Lord's on 30 August 1967 Insole, never one to shirk responsibility or confrontation, and Griffith, the MCC secretary, faced the press and announced that Colin Cowdrey had been invited to captain England on the forthcoming tour of the Caribbean. Strained and under pressure, Insole also let slip that the decision to replace Close was taken by the smallest possible margin and that he had voted in favour of Close.

Cowdrey became captain again knowing that he was third choice and did not have the backing of the chairman of selectors. He was also subjected to a vindictive attack in sections of the press who would raise the issue of gentleman and player and the eternal civil war of North versus South. There was unanimity on one thing. Under Cowdrey, England had no chance whatsoever against the West Indies.

One of the ironies of the situation which led to the dismissal of Close was that Yorkshire were condemned for *only* bowling fifteen overs an hour, a rate which years later would be welcomed. It was accepted in 1967 that the optimum over-rate was twenty overs an hour, and Close's tactics brought about this being written into the laws concerning the last hour of the game.

What had not been anticipated when MCC arrived in the Caribbean was that the fast bowling of Hall and Griffith was very much in decline and that the pair were far from being the force that had once caused England batsmen to tremble. Indeed, the surprise of the series was that Snow, maturing into a very fine fast bowler, Brown and Jones were by far the more effective of the two pace attacks. Snow finished the series with twenty-seven wickets at 18.66 runs each. Hall and Griffith took only nineteen between them.

The side took some time to settle when they reached the Caribbean, which was not surprising as they flew from an English winter and were asked to play in the heat of Barbados three days after landing. Cowdrey and Boycott were quickly into their stride, but few could have expected England's dominance in the first Test. Boycott made 68, Cowdrey 72, Barrington 143 and Graveney 118. Barrington reached his fourth century in consecutive Tests with a six. It was his twentieth, and last, century for England.

England made 568 and, in spite of Clive Lloyd's century, the West Indies followed on 205 runs in arrears, but there was only one day remaining. By mid-afternoon, the West Indies were 164 for two. Hobbs then caught and bowled Kanhai, and Lloyd and Holford went quickly. In the last over before tea, David Brown sent back Butcher, David Murray and Griffith. Six wickets had fallen in half an hour for 16 runs. Hall and Sobers were not to be moved, and they batted out the last session to take the West Indies to 243 for eight and draw the match.

England felt, justifiably, that they should have won this game, and they had even more cause to believe that they should have won the second Test. They lost only two wickets on the opening day when Edrich, 96, and Cowdrey added 129 runs for the second wicket. Cowdrey was out for 101 on the second day and England reached 376. They captured the wickets of both openers before the close and next day, Snow, bowling at a lively pace, routed the West Indians. They were all out in under forty-nine overs, following on for the second time in consecutive Tests and 233 runs in arrears. Snow had taken seven for 49, dismissing Sobers first ball, always a boost to the side.

By mid-afternoon on the fourth day England were winning comfortably. When Parks took a diving catch to dismiss Butcher off the bowling of D'Oliveira the West Indies were 204 for five, still needing 29 runs to avoid an innings defeat. At this point there was a riot: bottles were thrown and play was suspended for seventy-five minutes. It was agreed to compensate for this loss by playing seventy-five minutes on a sixth day. This was not a good idea. Nor was it a good idea to restart play, for the English players, visibly shaken, had lost their impetus. Sobers, who had been badly dropped when 7, batted with customary sublimity to score 113 not out and declared with forty-two minutes of the fifth day remaining. England needed 159 to win on a pitch that was disintegrating badly. In a frenetic atmosphere they lost four for 19, with the umpires, having seemingly lost control, giving strange decisions. Four more wickets went down in the extra-time sixth day, but the match was drawn.

Vice-captain Titmus led the team in Antigua before they moved on to Barbados for the third Test. It was here that he was involved in a boating accident. He lost four toes when his left foot was caught in the screw of a small boat, placed in the middle of the craft and unguarded. This was traumatic not only for Titmus but for the whole party. The Middlesex off-spinner received excellent medical attention in Barbados but was forced to return to England for further treatment. Contrary to all expectations, he was back playing first-class cricket a few months later and was to return to the England side six years later.

Lock was flown from Australia to Barbados to replace Titmus. He had captained Leicestershire in a dynamic manner, and in Australia he had led Western Australia to the top of the Sheffield Shield. Initially, however, it was Pat Pocock who came in for his Test debut as replacement for his fellow off-spinner.

On a rain-interrupted first day the West Indies scored 86 for two from 51.1 overs. Snow took five wickets, but the innings did not end until the third day. Facing a total of 349, England began with Edrich, 146, and Boycott, 90, hitting 172 for the first wicket. The England innings did not end until the last morning, by which time they led by exactly 100 runs. Lloyd made his second century of the series, and the match was drawn with England again the dominant side.

Having had the upper hand in three matches, England suffered something of a reverse in the fourth. Sobers won the toss in Port of Spain, Nurse and Kanhai hit centuries and shared a third-wicket stand of 273; the West Indies made 526 for seven declared. There had been much criticism as to the low standard of wicket-keeping in the first three Tests, and England brought in Knott for the fourth Test. He was to make the England wicket-keeping job his own for more than a decade. In this match he hit 69 not out which, following Cowdrey's 148 and Boycott's 62, helped England to reach 404.

The England innings was not over until near the end of the fourth day, and Sobers declared on the last day to leave a target of 215 in 165 minutes. He had a reputation for being something of a gambler, and he was later severely criticised by many in the Caribbean for the chance he took on this occasion, particularly as Griffith was out of action with a thigh injury. As E.M. Wellings reported in support of Sobers, however, 'At the time none believed that England could score at 78 an hour over such a lengthy period, though they might perish in the attempt.'

They did not perish. Boycott and Edrich scored 55 in nineteen overs before Edrich fell to the leg-spinner Rodriguez. There was a period of calm, but after tea Cowdrey cut loose, and Boycott supplied the assurance and solidity that was necessary. He frequently took singles to give his captain the strike, and 100 runs came in eighteen overs. Cowdrey seemed to find the gaps with ease, and by the time he lifted Gibbs into Sobers's hands at mid-wicket, he had made 71 in seventy-six minutes out of a partnership of 118. England now had 42 runs to make in thirty-three minutes. When Graveney was bowled by Gibbs 33 were needed in twenty-seven minutes. Sobers had kept the game open, but at last he was forced to try to close it down. It was too late. Boycott and D'Oliveira teased the field with quick singles, and when D'Oliveira turned Gibbs to square-leg England had won by seven wickets with three minutes, one over, to spare.

This totally unexpected victory brought different reactions for the two captains. Cowdrey was booed for playing two match-winning innings and winning; Sobers was stoned by youths when entering his hotel in Georgetown the next afternoon. The erstwhile hero had committed the ultimate crime of losing.

For no logical reason, the last game of the series had been extended to six days, and on the first of them the West Indies, having lost their first three wickets for 72, reached 243 for three. Kanhai and Sobers scored centuries and added 250 for the fourth wicket; the West Indies were all out for 414 on the second day.

Edrich went for nought, but Boycott and Cowdrey, the lions of England's batting throughout the tour, put on 172 for the second wicket. Boycott hit 116 while Cowdrey struggled but stayed to score 59. They were both out at the same total, and England lost seven wickets for 74 runs. With the score at 259, Pocock, playing his second Test match, joined Lock, playing in his second Test of the series but the forty-ninth and last of his career. It took Pocock eighty-two minutes to get off the mark, but he and Lock took the England innings into the fifth day.

Their ninth-wicket stand was eventually worth 109 runs, and Lock's 89 was the highest score of his career. They had helped reduce the West Indies' first-innings lead to 43. By lunch that had been increased by another 72 without loss, but Snow produced a wonderful spell after the break in which he sent back Nurse, Lloyd and Camacho in the space of seven deliveries. He was to finish the innings with six for 60 to go with his four for 82 in the first innings.

Sobers added 95 not out to his first-innings 152 as the West Indies were bowled out for 264. This left England the last day in which to score 308 to win. The possibility of an England win seemed remote, but so, too, did any likelihood of an England defeat.

Boycott and Edrich negotiated the new ball without any problems, but the advent of Gibbs and Sobers bowling spin brought about a dramatic change. Baffled by Sobers's googly, Edrich was caught at backward short-leg. Four wickets then fell to Gibbs in a four-over spell which cost 4 runs, and England were 41 for five.

This brought together the Kent pair of Knott and Cowdrey, who must have been bitterly disappointed to see all the hard work and success of the last few months seemingly about to be thrown away on the last afternoon of the tour. The pair frustrated the West Indian spinners for two and three-quarter hours. They used their pads effectively and, rushing through their overs, the West Indian bowlers erred in line and length. Knott and Cowdrey had added 127 when, with seventy minutes remaining, the England captain misjudged the line of a ball from Gibbs and was leg-before.

Knott offered two chances which were not accepted, but the strength of the man was that he remained completely unruffled. Snow joined him in a stand which produced 30 in thirty-five minutes. Lock lasted eight minutes, Pocock ten. When Jeff Jones came to the wicket there was time for thirteen balls to be bowled. He survived the final delivery of a Gibbs over, and Knott played out the penultimate over, bowled by Sobers, but was unable to take the single which would have given him the strike for the last over. Jones faced Gibbs's last over of the match with nine men crowded round the bat. He played forward and kept the West Indies at bay. England, 206 for nine, had drawn the match and won the series. Knott was unbeaten on 73. Cowdrey had made 82, Boycott 30, and no other batsman had reached double figures.

The next day Cowdrey and his men flew back to England as heroes. They had received little respect when they had departed; now they were looked upon with awe and Cowdrey had once again proved himself as cricketer, as a man and as captain, although most people would have thought that he had long since proved himself all three.

The MCC party returned to a very different County Championship from the one they had left in September, although the outcome was the same – Yorkshire first for the third year in succession, Kent second for the second year in succession. The difference was in some of the personnel.

In 1968 county cricket took the revolutionary step of opening the door to overseas players through allowing immediate registration. Overseas cricketers had been eligible to play for English counties for some years but only after a period of qualification. Most famous among those to arrive in the mid-sixties were Keith Boyce of Essex, John Shepherd of Kent, and Basil D'Oliveira of Worcestershire and England.

D'Oliveira had come to England in 1960. Barred from playing first-class cricket in the country of his birth, South Africa, because of his colour and the apartheid laws of his country, he sought a cricket career in England. He played for Middleton in the Central Lancashire League for three years, and he was then invited to join Worcestershire. First he had to fulfil the necessary residential qualification, even though no county was contesting Worcestershire's right to play him. At the age of thirty-three D'Oliveira found this frustrating, but nothing could be done, and he spent a year with Kidderminster in the Birmingham League and appeared in non-Championship games for Worcestershire before being qualified in 1965. A year later he was in the England side. By 1968 he had Glenn Turner, Ron Headley and Vanburn Holder as colleagues in the Worcestershire side.

Warwickshire had Lance Gibbs, and Rohan Kanhai had joined 'Billy' Ibadulla in the Warwickshire team. Greg Chappell was playing alongside fellow Australian Bill Alley at Somerset. Lee Irvine, the South African, had joined West Indian Keith Boyce at Essex, and the Championship was graced by Majid Khan (Glamorgan), Mike Procter (Gloucestershire), Barry Richards (Hampshire), Asif Iqbal (Kent), Mushtaq Mohammad (Northamptonshire) and Younis Ahmed (Surrey). Farokh Engineer, the dashing Indian wicket-keeper, was at Lancashire and soon to be joined by Clive Lloyd, while Nottinghamshire had landed the prize catch, Gary Sobers.

Not all counties recognised the immediate benefit of employing an overseas cricketer; not all could afford one. Not all chose wisely, and it was to be many years before Yorkshire broke tradition and engaged a 'foreigner'.

Somerset had long since realised the benefits that could come with an overseas cricketer. Bill Alley, seduced from the Lancashire League by Ben Brocklehurst, had joined them in 1957 and had scored more than 3,000 runs for them in 1961. He was still scoring runs for them in his last season eight years later when he was fifty.

At Trent Bridge, Sobers did not disappoint. Nottinghamshire had been struggling at or near the bottom of the table for several seasons. They were revitalised under Sobers. They climbed to fourth in the Championship, and Sobers himself hit the fastest century of the season, against Kent at Dover. His most famous feat, however, was to hit six sixes in an over from Malcolm Nash of Glamorgan, at Swansea.

There was nothing bludgeoning or brutal about Sobers. His power came from harmony of movement. Nash recalls:

I was very young and very green. I was learning the hard job of becoming a professional cricketer, and this was just another day in the life of a county cricketer. It did not leave me scarred, or very unhappy. It was totally unexpected and I have learned a lot since then. The most important thing that I learned was to master one art before you start

215

messing about with another. At that time I was experimenting with spin bowling before I had learned how to become a swing bowler.

It is not too exaggerated a claim to say that the introduction of overseas cricketers saved the County Championship from a slow and painful death. Salvation, too, came with the introduction of a points system which dispensed with rewarding a first-innings lead and concentrated on winning and the bonus of points for positive cricket in the first eighty-five overs.

The interest of the public was reawakened by the opportunity to see in action on a regular basis such men as Sobers, Richards and Procter. They excited and frequently lifted their colleagues, although they could be intimidating. Tony Brown, who preceded Mike Procter as captain of Gloucestershire, observed that the South African all-rounder was so good at taking wickets, hitting runs or holding catches that he found it difficult to understand why others were not doing the same, and some of the younger players were a bit overawed.

But for the foresight of Gloucestershire, Hampshire and Essex, the British public might never have seen Procter, Barry Richards or Irvine, for a generation of South African cricketers was soon to be forced from the international arena.

Returning from the Caribbean, the victorious England side were faced by Bill Lawry's Australians. The visitors took the first Test in Manchester by 159 runs. In a perversely English way, Pocock and D'Oliveira, the most successful bowler and the most successful batsman at Old Trafford, were dropped for the Lord's Test, in which England were denied victory by the weather after bowling Australia out for 78.

At Edgbaston Colin Cowdrey became the first man to appear in 100 Test matches, and he celebrated by scoring 104. No play had been possible on the first day, and again England's hopes of victory were dashed by the weather.

Cowdrey was unable to play at Headingley because of injury, and Graveney, now forty-one, captained England for the only time. He had two debutants in his eleven, Roger Prideaux, the Northamptonshire opener, and Keith Fletcher, the highly talented young Essex batsman.

Prideaux scored 64 and shared an opening stand of 123 with Edrich. Number three in the England side was Dexter. He had reappeared in two Championship matches for Sussex and hit 203 against Kent at Hastings. On the strength of this he was chosen for the last two Tests against Australia but failed to reproduce his old form and did not play Test cricket again.

His recall had much to do with injuries suffered by Milburn, Boycott and Cowdrey. Graveney, too, was doubtful at Headingley with a hand injury, and Sharpe was at the wicket at Westcliff ready to open for Yorkshire against Essex when the call came for him to make haste to Leeds. England now had fourteen players, and Cowdrey, unfit, Sharpe and Knight were the three to be omitted. For Fletcher, there could not have been a worse debut scenario. An exceptionally fine fielder close to the wicket, he was placed at first slip where he failed to hold three very difficult chances. Jeered by the Yorkshire crowd who wanted the local hero, 'Sharpie', a specialist slip fielder, Fletcher was caught behind for nought, and although he battled well in the second innings and was unbeaten as England drew the match, he was marked. He was to have an outstanding career with Essex and eventually scored more than 3,000 runs for England, but those close to him say that he was scarred by the early treatment he received at the hands of press and public, and he became more introspective. He was not in the side for the fifth Test at The Oval.

This was a remarkable game in many ways. On inspecting the Oval pitch, Cowdrey came to the conclusion that it would best be used by the medium-pace bowlers, and he sought to strengthen his team accordingly. The key man he wanted was Tom Cartwright, but he was injured, as was Barry Knight, and so D'Oliveira, who had not played for England since the first Test, was called to The Oval. The general reason given for his omission was that, although he was still scoring runs, he was no longer the effective bowler he had once been. As he took sixty-one wickets in the season and finished ninth in the national averages with a record almost identical to that of Cartwright, this excuse failed to persuade many people.

On the morning of the Oval Test, Prideaux was forced to withdraw through illness, and D'Oliveira was a late replacement. Graveney and Edrich added 125 after three wickets had gone for 113, and D'Oliveira then joined Edrich in a stand which went into the second day. The pair put on 121 before Ian Chappell bowled Edrich for 164.

D'Oliveira continued to punish the bowling. He was not afraid to hit the ball over as well as through the field as England pressed for quick runs. He drove magnificently, and he hooked and cut with delight. When he was finally caught off Mallett he had made 158, and England reached 494. It was not just the amount of runs that D'Oliveira scored that caught the imagination, but the manner in which they came, for his was the fastest century of the series.

Lawry batted all through the Saturday, scoring 116 runs to add to the 19 he had scored on the Friday evening, but he was out on the Monday without scoring another run. Australia made 324, and England went for quick runs. They were bowled out for 181, but the runs came in three hours, and Australia were left the task of scoring 352 to win at a rate of 54 runs an hour.

They ended the fourth day on 13 for two, and England's success continued when they captured three wickets on the final morning. Three minutes before lunch, with Australia 86 for five, a freak storm broke. In half an hour the ground was under water, but shortly after two o'clock the sun began to shine again. With Cowdrey fretting and viewing his reflection in a mini-lake, the ground staff got to work. They were aided by volunteers from the crowd, and a remarkable transformation was brought about. At 4.45, the game recommenced.

Only seventy-five minutes remained, and the pitch was deadened. Cowdrey switched his bowlers and the fielders crouched around the bat. With thirty-five minutes left Cowdrey turned to D'Oliveira who, with the last ball of his second over from the Pavilion end, brought a ball in sharply from outside off stump to bowl Jarman. The breakthrough achieved, Cowdrey immediately replaced D'Oliveira with Underwood, who took the last four wickets in twenty-seven balls for 6 runs. England won by 226 runs with five minutes to spare.

If Australia had retained the Ashes, England had drawn the series in glorious fashion. Underwood had taken seven for 50, but he was one of many heroes, not the least of whom was Basil D'Oliveira.

The victory came on Tuesday, 27 August 1968, and that evening the selectors chose the party to tour South Africa. It was announced the following day, and it did not include D'Oliveira. Doug Insole offered the explanation that the selectors regarded him as a batsman rather than as an all-rounder for an overseas tour and that, put against the seven batsmen that they had chosen, they had reluctantly omitted him along with Colin Milburn.

To the public at large D'Oliveira's omission following his performance at The Oval caused consternation. It was immediately assumed that the reasons for it were that MCC were bowing to South Africa's racial policies. The Cape Coloured D'Oliveira was moved to the centre of a political cause. There were angry exchanges, resignations from MCC and a special meeting called with David Sheppard as chief spokesman for the 'rebels'.

The whole affair was not entirely unexpected. MCC had written to Dr Vorster, the South African Prime Minister, in January, asking for his government's reaction if D'Oliveira were to be included in the MCC party to tour the Republic. No written reply was received, but there were also enquiries made by the President of MCC, Sir Alec Douglas-Home, when he visited South Africa. Sir Alec advised MCC that the strongest possible side should be picked, but he also clarified the point that nothing would shake South Africa's apartheid policy.

Minister of Sport Denis Howell assured the House of Commons that MCC had informed him that the party to tour South Africa would be chosen on merit and that should any member of the chosen party be rejected by the host country, the tour would not take place.

It was against this background that the fifteen names were announced on 28 August. Insole bore the brunt of criticism for the omission of D'Oliveira, but press and public also turned their fury on MCC, as an archaic ruling body in an age of enlightenment.

The attention then passed to Tom Cartwright, whose injury had allowed D'Oliveira his place at The Oval. He had been unfit to play for Warwickshire in the Gillette Cup Final, which the Midlands county won in style, but the selectors had been told that he would be able to tour. On 14 September Cartwright played in a fifty-over match for Warwickshire against a Gillette Invitation XI. The match was ruined by rain, but not before Cartwright had bowled his ten overs and had accounted for the England skipper. All now seemed well, but Cartwright broke down again and on 16 September the selectors held an emergency meeting. With Knight and Illingworth both unavailable, England had one obvious replacement as an all-rounder: D'Oliveira. After a meeting lasting ten minutes, the Worcestershire player, born in South Africa, was named as Cartwright's replacement.

The next day Prime Minister Vorster announced that South Africa was not prepared to receive a team forced upon the country by people with political aims. The tour was off.

To compensate for the loss of the tour to South Africa, MCC planned to send the side to India and Pakistan, but financial problems caused the abandonment of the Indian leg of the tour. Why the Pakistan leg of the tour was not abandoned, too, will ever remain a mystery. The country was in political upheaval with riots and chaos everywhere.

The first Test in Lahore was frequently interrupted by pitch invasions and ended in a draw after Cowdrey had scored his twenty-second, and last, hundred for England. The second match at Dacca was riot-free but was played on a dreadful pitch and was drawn, with D'Oliveira scoring a fine hundred.

Milburn flew from Perth, where he had been playing for Western Australia, to augment MCC and reached a hundred off 163 balls in the third Test in Karachi. He made 139 and shared a second-wicket stand of 156 with Graveney. Graveney's 105 was his eleventh and last century for England.

On the third day England were 502 for seven with Alan Knott 4 runs short of a maiden Test century. A mob several hundred strong broke down the gates and, carrying political banners, swarmed across the outfield. The Test and the tour were over.

The sad sixties had reached their nadir.

6

Evolution and Revolution, 1969–77

English cricket entered a new phase in 1969. On the administrative side the Test and County Cricket Board now managed affairs, although as S.C. Griffith was secretary of both MCC and the TCCB, many found it hard to discover what changes had actually taken place, for the personnel appeared to be the same. One of the first decrees made by the TCCB was to confirm that South Africa's visit to Britain in 1970 would take place, and this was supported by MCC. The question as to whether Rhodesians would be welcomed as part of the side was left in abeyance. Since Ian Smith had made a unilateral declaration of independence in Rhodesia the whole relationship between Britain and the former colony had been more than strained by the imposition of sanctions.

In giving their confirmation of the South African tour in 1970, the TCCB were shutting their eyes as to what was happening on the Springboks' rugby tour of Britain where political protest was becoming increasingly more violent and causing disruption. They could also be accused of being insensitive to the fact that Learie Constantine, the dynamic West Indian all-rounder, had been appointed Britain's first black peer.

As ever, first-class cricket was slow to react to what was happening in the world. At a time when man was first walking on the moon and discovering that it was neither blue nor made of cream cheese, cricket was steadily losing money, struggling to reconcile traditions to the reality of economic necessities. One could take Essex as an example of the problems with which counties were having to contend.

Essex had been faced with extinction in 1965 and 1966 when the balance sheet recorded substantial losses. Maintaining the spirit and ideal of a *county* club, Essex had continued to stage festivals at Leyton, Westcliff, Colchester, Clacton, Ilford, Brentwood, Southend and Romford. They had been the first county to play Championship cricket on a Sunday when they played Somerset at Ilford in 1966. In spite of this effort to make first-class cricket more accessible to the public, and other innovations and enthusiasms, Essex lost money. Only the festivals at Southend and Romford, where the pitch was criticised, showed a profit. There were losses at all the other grounds, and, overall, the county club was losing more than £7,000 a year, which was unsustainable.

Trevor Bailey retired as captain in 1966, and Brian Taylor was appointed to succeed him. Few captains can have taken over in more difficult circumstances. He was thirty-five years old and immediately lost the services of his best player, Barry Knight: the England all-rounder had anticipated that he would be offered the captaincy. When he was not he stated that he would not play for Essex again, and he joined Leicestershire. Essex did not want to lose him, and Knight had to spend a twelve-month period of qualification for his new county.

Essex were to overcome his loss as they were to overcome more pressing problems. Bailey had left them with one great legacy. On a visit to the Caribbean he had discovered Keith Boyce and brought him to England to qualify for Essex. A fast bowler and a spectacularly aggressive batsman, Boyce became an instant favourite with the crowd, and he was to prove to be a marvellous investment as the one-day game developed. But the immediate Essex priority was survival.

The 'economies' subcommittee applied ruthless measures. A system of redemption of Green Shield stamps was instigated, and there was an abundance of fund-raising activities conducted free of charge by loyal members of the club. The staff was cut back, and second-eleven cricket was reduced to a minimum. The most stringent economy was that Brian Taylor was told he must operate with a staff of twelve, including himself. This was one of the most severe measures ever inflicted upon a county club, but it brought dividends.

Essex had recognised the implications and the gains that were to be made from engaging overseas players, but they were governed by financial restrictions. They had engaged Lee Irvine, a little-known batsman from Natal, as their first overseas cricketer rather than recruiting an established Test player. It was the first of several shrewd overseas acquisitions. Within two years of joining Essex Irvine was to become a Test cricketer, playing against Australia in 1969–70.

Hobbs and Fletcher, soon to be an England regular, were already Test players, and John Lever was to win his first cap in the 1970s. Lever was to point to those days in 1969 as being vital to his development as a bowler: 'I learned to bowl because I had to bowl. There was nobody to take my place.'

The tight comradeship helped Essex to rise to sixth in the

Championship, but the initial impetus for their revival, on the playing field and on the balance sheet, came from the John Player League.

There had been agitation for some years for a one-day championship to run alongside the County Championship, just as there had been a concerted move towards Sunday cricket, but there had been a lack of vision as to how these ideas could be realised. Championship matches had been played with Sunday as the second day, and while these games had drawn more spectators they had proved far from satisfactory. Cricketers had seemed incapable of adapting to the one o'clock to seven o'clock playing hours.

In 1969 the Sunday League was introduced. The seventeen counties were to play each other once,, and the matches were to be forty overs per innings. The league was to be sponsored by John Player, the tobacco company. It is no secret that the players regarded this Sunday venture with some scepticism, but Stuart Turner, the Essex all-rounder and the first man to take 300 wickets and score 3,000 runs in the competition, was to say later, 'We won a couple of matches, and we suddenly thought we could do well in this league, and it became important to us because crowds of people turned up to watch.' Moreover, cricketers who had been barely recognisable were to become familiar faces to millions who watched the Sunday League matches on television.

But there were hazards attendant on the Sunday League and prices to be paid. Colin Cowdrey was the first to pay a very high price. Kent began with a comfortable win over Hampshire and followed this by trouncing Somerset by nine wickets at Bath. It became three Sunday League wins in a row when Sussex were beaten at Folkestone, and Kent went top of the league when they gained a five-run victory over Glamorgan at Maidstone. Kent had been boosted by a fourth-wicket stand of 45 in ten overs between Knott and Cowdrey, and shortly after Knott was out, with the score at 108 for four in the thirty-second over, Cowdrey tore an Achilles tendon and had to retire hurt.

The injury was serious enough to keep Cowdrey out of cricket until the last match of the season. With Insole and May unavailable, the TCCB's first selection panel was chaired by Alec Bedser, who was aided by Don Kenyon, A.C. Smith and W.H.H. Sutcliffe. The committee's first action was to reappoint Cowdrey as England captain, but now they were faced with a dilemma. The previous contenders for the England captaincy had disappeared, and a look at the county captains of the time suggests that the selectors had five men to choose from – Tony Lewis, Illingworth, Stewart, Graveney and Close.

Close's success as a captain was undeniable. In 1969 he led Yorkshire to triumph in the Gillette Cup Final, even though they were without

Boycott, who was injured. The victory was achieved in spite of the fact that Trueman had retired and Illingworth had moved to Leicestershire. One of the features of the final was Close's tactical brilliance, and he made a significant personal contribution, but he remained *persona non grata*. His sin at Edgbaston in 1967 was never to be forgiven.

Graveney had led England once in an emergency and had succeeded Kenyon as captain of Worcestershire, but he was now forty-two, and he had never been totally in accord with authority. He was chosen for the first Test and scored 75. He had been granted a benefit in 1969 and had agreed to play in a match at Luton on the Sunday, the rest day, of that Old Trafford Test. He asked Alec Bedser's permission to play in the match, which was for his benefit. Rightly, Bedser, mindful of Cowdrey's injury and believing that being paid to play for England was sufficient, refused. Graveney disobeyed Bedser and played at Luton. It should be said that Graveney was paid £1,000 for appearing at Luton, which was more than double his remuneration for playing five days' Test cricket. The outcome was that, two days after the Test, the TCCB found Graveney guilty of 'a serious breach of discipline' and told the selectors that he must not be considered for the next three Tests. He never played for England again.

Stewart had fallen out of favour with the selectors, although he was reviving Surrey's fortunes, scoring heavily and fielding brilliantly.

Tony Lewis had won his blue in all three years at Cambridge and had been a much respected captain in his final year. He had first played for Glamorgan when he was seventeen and had become captain in 1967. He had fashioned a most attractive side and he led them to a resounding Championship success in 1969. It was only the second time that they had won the title, and they owed much to left-handed opener Alan Jones, the Pakistani Majid Khan, the tireless bowling of Don Shepherd and Malcolm Nash and, not least, to Lewis's firm and gentle captaincy allied to his stylish batting and outstanding fielding. Many had been pressing his claims for a place in the England side for several seasons, and with the retirement of Barrington it seemed that the selectors might turn to him, but they turned instead to Sharpe, Hampshire, Fletcher, Parfitt and Denness. It was to be three years before the selectors gave Lewis his chance as batsman and captain, but by then it was too late.

And so the mantle of captaincy to face the West Indies and New Zealand in 1969 fell on Raymond Illingworth. He had re-established himself in the England side since Titmus's accident and, unable to come to terms with Yorkshire, he had moved to Leicestershire as captain. With the Australian McKenzie also in the side, Leicestershire began the season in storming fashion, and they were second in the Championship at the end of May. With the first Test due to start on 12 June, Illingworth was heavily supported by the press. They saw him as a natural heir to Hutton and Close, and, in some cases, as an amalgam of both. He was in pole position and was duly named as England captain.

He was later to describe Brearley rather ungraciously and irritably as being England's luckiest captain, but he could reflect on his own good fortune. He took over at a time when West Indian cricket was in a sort of limbo. Hall and Griffith had gone, and Holder and Shillingford hardly equalled them in pace and fire. Clive Lloyd's great days were ahead of him. Kanhai was absent and Sobers had knee problems. England won two and drew one of the three Tests.

England hit four centuries in the series, and they all came from Yorkshiremen: Boycott, Hampshire and Illingworth himself. As in the Caribbean, the new-ball bowling of Snow and Brown was far superior to that of their West Indian counterparts.

Against New Zealand, Brown was replaced by Alan Ward of Derbyshire and Surrey's Geoff Arnold, but the result was the same, two wins and a draw. The bowling star of this series was Derek Underwood who, in three Tests, took twenty-four wickets at just over 9 runs each. The batting star was John Edrich, who hit 115 at Lord's and followed this with 155 in the drawn game at Trent Bridge. Sharpe hit 111, his only Test century, and the pair added 249 for the second wicket.

Six Tests, four wins and two draws. Illingworth had passed his first examination with honours. All, it would seem, was well. But that was far from being the case.

On 23 May, two days before Cowdrey's injury at Maidstone, Northamptonshire had beaten the West Indian tourists, but on the evening of their victory came tragedy. Colin Milburn was involved in a car accident in which he lost his left eye. He was to fight his way back to reappear four years later, but his comeback was brief and he never played for England again. His last Test-match innings had been the century in Pakistan, and it is sad to recall that this burly entertainer played in only nine Tests.

In one season Graveney and Milburn were lost to Test cricket, and there were those who were not happy with Illingworth's leadership. Jim Swanton in the *Cricketer* was one who condemned Illingworth as a master of the dour and dreary. There was a cry for brighter batting and quicker over-rates. Certainly, Hampshire and Boycott had tested spectators' patience during the summer, but then Glenn Turner had carried his bat through the second innings of the Lord's Test for 43 out of 131. He was at the crease for 253 minutes and faced 226 balls. It took him many years to throw off the nickname of the 'strokeless wonder'.

225

There was, too, the nagging question of the visit of the South Africans to England in 1970. In 1969 Wilfred Isaacs's South African side toured England in June, July and August, playing four first-class matches and several minor ones. At Oxford the pitch was vandalised, but still cricket administrators refused to accept that the game was irretrievably caught in a web of politics.

In September 1969 the programme for South Africa's tour of England was published. There was already concern as to what demonstrations would confront the Springbok rugby players who were beginning a tour in November. Demonstrations against Wilfred Isaacs's side had been limited, but they had grown in intensity. One of those to join in the action was a nineteen-year-old first-year engineering student at Imperial College named Peter Hain. Hain, now a Labour MP but then a Young Liberal, was South African from a liberal Pretoria family. His anti-apartheid feelings and policies were based firmly on his own youthful experiences in the Republic. In September, shortly after the tour fixtures were announced, he launched the Stop the Seventy Tour Committee, based on a platform of non-violent protest. He drew much support.

The rugby tour highlighted major problems, namely the cost of polic-ing matches and the injuries and arrests that inevitably followed such policing. It was soon apparent that the cost of policing just one three-day match between a county and the South Africans would more than wipe out any profit made from the tour.

David Sheppard, by now the Bishop of Woolwich, was one of the leading non-violent opponents to the tour and was supported by eminent Conservative and Labour MPs. More than a hundred Liberal and Labour MPs signed a letter to MCC stating their objections to the tour and their intentions of joining peaceful protests should the tour go ahead. In spite of all these public declarations, the TCCB reiterated in December that the tour would go ahead.

The TCCB had emphasised their aversion to racial discrimination, and Jack Cheetham, President of the South African Cricket Association, announced that the South African side would be chosen on merit, irre-spective of colour. This assertion was greeted by black leaders in South Africa as empty words. When the team under Ali Bacher was announced it consisted of fourteen white cricketers. By then MCC's tour of East Africa scheduled for early 1970 had been cancelled, with Uganda accus-ing MCC of double standards.

The Professional Cricketers' Association, barely three years old and once cruelly described as the 'only trade union in which the members are more right-wing than the bosses', voted heavily in favour of the tour going ahead, and it was clear that most MCC members shared the same view. But the pace of events was quickening uncontrollably. A dozen county grounds were attacked in a co-ordinated campaign. A delegation from the House of Lords met James Callaghan and Denis Howell at the Home Office. In a television interview, Prime Minister Harold Wilson declared that MCC had made a very ill-judged decision in inviting the South Africans. A fund was set up to raise money to police the tour. Battle lines were clearly drawn. Friends were divided.

Those likely to play against the South Africans in representative matches were informed by the TCCB that they would be insured. There was a debate in the House of Commons concerning the tour; the opposition grew stronger and stronger, and more and more it came from respected and fair-minded people in high positions.

On the day that the fund was set up to save the tour the Supreme Council of Sport in Africa threatened the withdrawal of thirteen African countries from the Commonwealth Games which were to be held in Edinburgh in July. The fund itself failed to gain the support that its organisers had anticipated. Then came the momentous news that, at a meeting in Amsterdam, South Africa had become the first nation ever to be expelled from the Olympic movement.

Further opposition to the tour came from the Royal Commonwealth Society, the Archbishop of Canterbury, the Chief Rabbi and, by implication when it was announced that the Queen would not attend the Lord's Test, the Palace. There were anxieties expressed by the Race Relations Board, the Inner London Teachers' Association and by people who lived close to Lord's.

In spite of all these objections and misgivings, the Cricket Council decided on 18 May that the tour should proceed as arranged, but that no further Test tours between England and South Africa would take place until cricket in the Republic was played and teams were selected on a multiracial basis. Brave as this decision was seen in some quarters, it was totally unrealistic, for the tour was already under a state of siege before it had begun.

On 21 May James Callaghan asked representatives of the Cricket Council to meet him at the Home Office, where he requested that the tour be cancelled 'on the grounds of broad public policy'. A letter to the chairman of the Cricket Council from the Home Secretary was, in effect, a government directive and, on 22 May, a statement was made on behalf of the Cricket Council which read:

At a meeting held this afternoon at Lord's, the Cricket Council considered the formal request from Her Majesty's Government to withdraw the invitation to the South African touring team this summer.

With deep regret the Council were of the opinion that they had no alternative but to accede to this request and they were informing the South African Cricket Association accordingly.

The issue was settled, and it was to be a quarter of a century before England and South Africa met again on the cricket field. Wounds were to run deep for many years and there are scars that are yet to heal.

Among the walking wounded there was great sympathy for Billy Griffith, the MCC secretary, who had worked tirelessly and, in particular, for Maurice Allom whose period of office as President of MCC coincided with the crisis. He was constantly needed for meetings, and the year to which he had so looked forward, the crowning of a dedicated career, was spoiled.

The bitter disappointment for Allom was that his term as president would be marred by the fact that there would be no touring team to entertain. In the absence of the South Africans a series was arranged between England and the Rest of the World, a side which included great players like Sobers, Kanhai, Barry Richards, Lloyd and the Pollocks, but very few people came to see the matches. They lacked the feeling of authenticity.

Amid all the political turmoil the introduction of a new leg-before-wicket law became obscured, as did a proposal by Ben Brocklehurst for a World Cup competition.

Brocklehurst had captained Somerset and, as a businessman, he had saved the *Cricketer* from extinction. He had increased the circulation and, eventually, he bought out the rival publication, *Playfair Cricket Monthly*. Behind the scenes he was a man who did much to further the interests of the game as a whole.

In November 1969, through the *Cricketer*, Brocklehurst had suggested to Lord's that a World Cup should be set up in 1972 as a means of giving a boost to cricket as a whole and of bringing much needed revenue to the game. The initial idea was that the competition would involve all Test-playing nations and would be played on a limited-over basis of one-day matches in leagues. The matches would be played over a period of ten days at Lord's and Headingley.

With the South African problem dominating and the authorities concerned about changes in the first-class programme, an alternative scheme was put forward. This would involve England, Australia, the West Indies and the Rest of the World, and would take a minimum amount of time out of the first-class programme while still establishing the merits of the competition.

Brocklehurst presented full financial details and suggested to 'Gubby'

Allen, the MCC treasurer, that cricket could benefit to the tune of £60,000. Allen and Billy Griffith accepted the idea in principle, but made no firm commitment. Ben Brocklehurst researched the background thoroughly, contacting likely sponsors and examining likely obstacles. Full details were passed to the TCCB with the request that it would now be wise for two directors of the *Cricketer* to discuss the project with two members of the TCCB so that the plans could be fully outlined.

For some incomprehensible reason, this meeting was not allowed. Instead, Ben Brocklehurst received a letter, dated 22 July and signed by Griffith, which stated that the TCCB Public Relations and Promotion subcommittee had now had time to examine the proposal and that although they were generally enthusiastic as to its concept, they had certain reservations.

They were doubtful that the public would show sufficient interest in the competition following a major Test series between England and Australia, and they strongly doubted that there would be any interest in a match between Australia and the West Indies played in this country. They added:

> The structure of cricket could possibly be changed by 1972, but under the present system it would seem that the end of the season well into September, allied with the start of the football season early in August and the possibility of a clash with the Olympic Games, could well work against the viability of your enterprise in 1972.

The subcommittee also felt that Ben Brocklehurst was being too optimistic in his estimate of television interest and receipts, and they were rather contemptuous of the idea that he would be able to raise £50,000 in sponsorship.

Brocklehurst had structured his financial planning on the accounts of the Australian tour to England in 1968, and he had contacted a host of organisations to test support. His reply to the TCCB was that he would do more research and come back to them, but time was now pressing, for the idea would have to be approved at the TCCB's meeting in November/December if there were to be a competition in 1972.

He met and discussed plans with Colonel Heald, the public affairs manager of W.D. & H.O. Wills, the tobacco company. There was an enthusiastic response, and the possibilities of including Pakistan, India and New Zealand and of holding the competition biennially in different parts of the world were considered. Wills confirmed that they would be prepared to sponsor the first tournament and would wish to have an option on any subsequent series.

229

From a position of strength, with answers to all the doubts expressed by the TCCB subcommittee, Brocklehurst was able to write to Griffith on 14 October 1970 giving confirmation of Wills's sponsorship and providing data which proved the viability of the competition. Not least of his arguments was that 'A World Cup based on the principles already outlined will surely complement Gillette Cup and John Player League cricket, which is amply proved to be capable of bringing back the crowds and the revenue.'

The suggestion that representatives of the *Cricketer*, the TCCB and the sponsor should meet was once more ignored, but greater surprises were in store for Ben Brocklehurst. He was astonished by the reply he received from the TCCB. Having met all their requirements, he was now told, 'While not slow to recommend sponsorship in the normal way we do not feel that such a prestigious event should be subject to commercial sponsorship in a direct sense.' Where earlier doubts had been expressed as to public interest in a match between Australia and the West Indies in England, the TCCB now demanded that 'any concept of the dimension of a World Cup should be all-embracing'. The subcommittee would make investigations at international level, although it transpired that those investigations could not be made until eight months later.

Meanwhile, Brocklehurst himself made a direct approach to leading members of the Australian Board of Control who, within half an hour, welcomed the idea if the TCCB could fit it into the 1972 tour schedule. They were unanimous in welcoming the project, particularly as all expenses were to be covered by sponsorship.

On 3 February 1971 Brocklehurst arranged that Colonel Heald and Billy Griffith should meet, for Wills would be willing to cover what sums the TCCB wanted to stage the competition. Griffith explained that it was now too late to set it up for 1972 and asked that it should be reserved for 1973.

In May 1971 information regarding the competition and the sponsor was leaked to the press by the TCCB and was fully explored by Frank Keating in the *Guardian*. A few days later Griffith was quoted in the *Daily Express* as saying, 'Financial viability would be a number one requirement and as I see it that would mean an international sponsor prepared to put up £100,000 or more.'

Donald Carr, Assistant Secretary of MCC at the time, hinted surprise that Brocklehurst was ever given encouragement to research the project, the suggestion being that officials and committee were rather loath to take on ideas from outside. Rulers in any field tend to preserve their own position rather jealously.

Most astonishing, of course, is that these agonising transactions were taking place at a time when, in 1970, the counties lost £156,000 between them. Of the seventeen counties, only Leicestershire, with £724, and Worcestershire, with £1,351, made a profit. Leicestershire's profit came because of local donations of £27,000 while Worcestershire received a supporters' club gift of £10,000. And this at a time when Brocklehurst's negotiated sponsorship of £50,000 from Wills was rejected because those in power felt that 'cricket should stand on its own two feet'.

The World Cup was not to come into operation until 1975, and the final, *between Australia and the West Indies*, was a sell-out.

The frustration for Brocklehurst was that he was never allowed to talk to the people with whom he was trying to deal. Any bitterness at the way in which he was treated has long since evaporated, and he has continued to serve the game nobly. He has, perhaps, one regret: 'Most of us want to support the establishment but the methods they employ are difficult to follow, and so far the *Cricketer* has been given no acknowledgement for the idea which was theirs.'

In turning to the Gillette Cup and John Player League for evidence in support of his World Cup proposals, Ben Brocklehurst was showing good sense, for the advent of the limited-overs game had given English cricket a much needed boost. It had rejuvenated many cricketers, made fresh demands, placed an emphasis on fielding and, for much of the time, was played in front of large and enthusiastic crowds who tended to lift the participants. There were cricketers who, for the first time, felt capable, contributory and appreciated. There were, most importantly, three trophies to play for when for years there had been one, and that was often monopolised by two or three counties. There were sides who, by the nature of their resources, would now concentrate their efforts on the one-day game. Foremost among them in the 1970s was Lancashire.

They won the John Player League in the first two years of its existence, 1969 and 1970, and they took the Gillette Cup three years running, 1970, 1971 and 1972, and won that trophy again in 1975. These triumphs came about after a period of considerable difficulties.

We have already touched upon the events which led to the departure of Marner and Clayton, the sacking of Grieves and the decision of Barber to move to Warwickshire. It was apparent that much was wrong throughout the club, and the first place where health needed to be restored was in the boardroom.

A saviour arrived in the shape of Cedric Rhoades. A fierce critic of the administration, he won a place on the committee and soon became chairman. He helped to save the club financially, and his burning ambition was to bring back glory days to Lancashire cricket. He drew up new terms of agreement for the players which gave added pride and incentive in playing for the county, and he was quick to understand the benefits of the immediate registration of overseas cricketers. Thwarted in his attempt to sign Sobers, he turned his attention to Farokh Engineer, the charismatic Indian wicket-keeper, and, with a stroke of genius, added Clive Lloyd to the side in 1969 via residential qualification.

The years of turbulence had brought changes in captaincy and an atmosphere of acrimony. Brian Statham had become captain in 1965 and held the position for three years. He was neither a great tactician nor a great leader, but he provided a necessary period of stability and encouragement. When he stood down at the end of the 1967 season he was succeeded by Jack Bond.

The appointment of Bond took everyone by surprise, except for those closest to the club. He had made his Lancashire debut in 1955, and it took him six years to establish a regular place in the side. Following a broken wrist, he spent much time in the second eleven, frequently captaining the side impressively. Rhoades and his committee saw in Bond the qualities that could bring about on the field the revolution that they had precipitated in the boardroom. Bond was the first of a new breed of cricketer, the first man to win fame and fortune on the strength of what he achieved in limited-overs cricket. He was a significant figure in that in the first half of the 1970s he brought about changes in attitudes which were in themselves revolutionary.

Bond was an original thinker where the one-day game was concerned. He selected teams for an occasion and changed batting orders as befitted the situation. He dismissed the obsession with pace bowling and deep-set fields, and he concentrated on accuracy.

Within eighteen months of taking over, he had lost Statham, Higgs and Pullar, but he brought to the fore David Lloyd, Barry Wood, Ken Shuttleworth and Jack Simmons. His approaches to the team and to the game were refreshingly realistic. He admitted the weaknesses of his side, forced individuals to face their limitations and demanded a reassessment of attitudes to the game. He stressed the importance of fielding and made it clear from the outset that he would tolerate no one in the side who was not totally committed to raising the standard of fielding to the highest level. To see Bond and Lancashire in the field became one of the joys of cricket. He insisted on physical fitness and set his men examples which they must have found daunting. He emphasised accuracy in bowling and care in field placings. He asked for a zestful approach in batting which increased the scoring rate. He drove away the apathy from Lancashire cricket, and as he cured the county of the canker that had troubled it, so the people flocked back to watch.

The margin of victory in the first John Player League in 1969, one point, was unflattering for the title had been won with three matches remaining. When the title was retained the following year the deciding match came against Yorkshire at Old Trafford on 30 August. For the first time since the Australians' visit in 1948, the gates at Old Trafford were closed on a capacity crowd of 33,000. Lancashire won by seven wickets with twenty-five balls to spare, and the crowd stayed on the ground in celebration for more than an hour after the end of play. A week later Lancashire won the Gillette Cup.

Wherever Lancashire went under Bond, huge crowds turned out to watch them. They were entertainers, but they had earned the greatest of honours: they were the side everyone wanted to beat. They surrendered their John Player League title in 1971, finishing four points behind Worcestershire and Essex, but they retained the Gillette Cup after some pulsating matches.

The quarter-final against Essex at Chelmsford attracted 8,000 people, a number never seen on that ground before, and Lancashire won by 12 runs as exchanges became passionate on and off the field. But this game was as nothing compared to the semi-final against Gloucestershire at Old Trafford, arguably the first one-day match to pass into cricketing folklore.

Again the gates were closed and thousands shut outside before play started. The match was interrupted by rain, and it lasted from 11.00 a.m. until 8.50 p.m. Gloucestershire batted first and began with a stand of 57. Nicholls played well for 53, and Procter gave the innings impetus with 65 which included a six and nine fours. He was the victim of an astonishing leg-side catch by Engineer, and with Simmons maintaining a relentlessly accurate leg-stump attack, Gloucestershire were restricted to 229 for six.

Lancashire began solidly, and Wood, Pilling and Clive Lloyd then increased the tempo. Lloyd took 16 off five balls from Procter before Wood was run out off the last ball of the over when attempting a quick single. The off-breaks of John Mortimore restricted the scoring and brought about the end of Lloyd, who was beaten in the flight as he advanced down the pitch. Engineer hit his own wicket, and suddenly Lancashire were 163 for six, 67 runs short of their target, with fourteen overs remaining and just four wickets standing.

The light was fading fast, and Bond was asked if he wanted to go off, but he reasoned that if the game were halted, the Gloucestershire bowlers would be refreshed in the morning. He might also have reckoned that it is probably easier to bat in the dark than it is to field. In deepening gloom he and Simmons added 40, but when the burly off-spinner was out Lancashire still needed 27 from five overs.

David Hughes now joined Bond. He was essentially a young left-arm spinner with limited batting achievement and experience. In an attempt to acclimatise himself to the light on the field he had sat in a dark corner of the dressing room awaiting his turn. Legend has it that, on arriving at the wicket, his captain said to him, 'Don't go daft. Take things as they come.' Hughes had replied, 'If I can see them, skipper, I think I can hit them.'

John Mortimore began his eleventh over still refusing to adopt the tactic of later one-day off-spinners: spearing the ball in flat at the middle and leg stumps. He tossed the ball up and relied on his mastery of flight and considerable powers of spin to beat the batsman. Hughes, quick on his feet, moved down the pitch and hit the first ball of the over beyond extra-cover for four. The next ball was hit high over long-on for six while the third was slashed into the off-side field for two. The fourth ball was hit wide of mid-on for another two, and the fifth ball of the over was driven majestically through the covers for four. Hughes swung the last ball of the over high over mid-on for a six, and the scores were level. The over had produced 24 runs.

Bond nudged the fifth ball of the next over past gully for the winning run, and the crowd surged on to the pitch. This was a famous victory and was witnessed not only by a capacity crowd but by millions on television, which was making more and more people acquainted with the game.

One must feel sympathy for Gloucestershire. Tony Brown, their captain, recalls:

The only time you could actually see the ball was when it got hit up into the sky. When David Hughes hit the ball along the ground you couldn't see it. I remember he hit one out to extra-cover, and I was at long-off on the pavilion side. Mike Bissex shouted, 'Where is it? Where is it?' and Roger Knight said, 'It's all right. It's coming towards me.' That was the sort of thing. You couldn't see it. He hit one over the top of me, and I saw it as a black pea in the sky against this dark blue, and it just went straight over my head.

Lancashire beat Kent in dramatic fashion in the final and won the Gillette Cup for the third year in succession in 1972, after which Bond announced his retirement. He had been the first man to recognise the extra dimensions provided by the one-day game, and he had the intelligence and tactical sense to exploit them. He loved the weekly audience of thousands of people in the ground and often the millions watching on television, and it was said that he hated Mondays more than anything else in cricket. He loathed leading his side out on to the field backed by rows of empty seats where the previous day there had been men, women and children bubbling with excitement.

Lancashire would surrender their crown as kings of one-day cricket to Kent before the end of the decade, but first Kent fulfilled Cowdrey's ambition of winning the County Championship. They had not taken the title since 1913, and Cowdrey had stated that 1970 was to be his penultimate season as captain. At the end of June, Kent were bottom of the table, but they were unbeaten in their last thirteen matches and finished seventeen points ahead of Glamorgan, the winners in 1969.

With several players, including Cowdrey, often on international duty, they relied heavily on reserve strength and were well served. Denness and Luckhurst were a most reliable opening pair, and Denness's captaincy when Cowdrey was absent won high praise. Shepherd, asked to do much work, took eighty-four Championship wickets, and Underwood again topped the bowling averages. There was some fine all-round cricket from Johnson, and the batting of Asif Iqbal always brought excitement. He became a great favourite with the Kent supporters.

It was a lean season for records with only three batsmen – Turner, Boycott and Bolus – reaching 2,000 runs, and only four bowlers – Don Shepherd, Gifford, Hobbs and Titmus – taking 100 wickets. The restricted programme (sides now played only twenty-four Championship matches) was beginning to take its toll.

With ten centuries and 2,379 runs, Glenn Turner was the outstanding batsman of the season. His progress from the dour New Zealand Test player of the previous season was remarkable, and *Wisden* was not alone in suggesting that he had an aura of greatness about him. At twenty-three he had youth on his side, and he was to give Worcestershire substance over the next few seasons; for many of the stalwarts had gone, and 1970 was Tom Graveney's last season, although he still managed to finish second to Sobers in the national averages.

Cowdrey was not happy about his own fitness and form in the early part of the season, but he gradually returned to his best and played in the last four of the England–Rest of the World matches. By then, however, Illingworth had further established his position and was playing well. After the third match at Edgbaston, Illingworth was named as captain of the party to tour Australia in the winter. Cowdrey was deeply hurt. He was about to realise his ambition of leading Kent to the Championship, but the burning passion to lead England to victory in Australia was denied him. He was asked to be vice-captain of the side, but the latest rejection he had suffered was probably one too many. He hesitated for some weeks before agreeing to serve under Illingworth, and he was never happy on the tour, particularly as the mood and style of Illingworth's leadership was not in keeping with Cowdrey's own idea of captaincy.

Ironically, where once the press had been supportive of Close and hostile to Cowdrey's appointment to take the side to the Caribbean, they were now very much on the side of Cowdrey. There was much rancour, and the choice of Illingworth was bitterly opposed in many quarters. The antagonism was not restricted to the English press. E.M. Wellings observed, 'The attitude of numerous Australians has never in my experience been so hostile to an England captain in advance of the tour.'

Some of the criticism centred on the selection of the tour party, and Illingworth was accused of something akin to nepotism and of perpetuating the North–South civil war when the Yorkshire slow left-arm spinner Don Wilson was named ahead of the highly successful Essex leg-spinner Robin Hobbs. The choice, too, of Peter Lever and Ken Shuttleworth, the Lancashire bowlers, drew much criticism, but this intense hostility towards the captain served only to draw the party closer together behind him.

Rarely has a side faced such a gruelling schedule. The philosophy of profit and greed which was to permeate the 1980s was already taking shape. For the first time, six Tests were arranged for the tour, and these were to be followed by two Tests in New Zealand. Nor did it end there, as E.M. Wellings reported in *Wisden*:

> Illingworth was put in an unfortunate position when the manager, Mr D.G. Clark, supported by two visiting MCC officials, Sir Cyril Hawker (President) and Mr G.O. Allen, agreed with the Australian officials to change the tour programme during the rain-ruined third Test at Melbourne and play an extra Test. It meant a very heavy programme of big matches, four Tests in quick succession with only four-day fixtures separating them. The rearrangement gave Australia gates amounting in value to £70,000. English cricket received no share of the extra revenue.

The early signs on the tour were not promising. One defeat and no first-class victory was the prelude to the first Test. On top of that, Alan Ward, a bowler of genuine pace who had been seen as the joint spearhead of the England attack with John Snow, broke down and returned home. He was replaced by a young and somewhat raw Surrey fast bowler, Bob Willis.

Ward's absence from the first Test brought a debut for Shuttleworth. He took five for 47 in Australia's second innings, but his Test career was to encompass only five matches.

England surprised everyone in the first Test by not losing. Stackpole hit a double century and shared a third-wicket stand of 209 with Walters, who made 112. But Australia lost their last seven wickets for 15 runs in forty-five minutes and were out for 433. Snow took six for 114.

Consistent batting allowed England to reach 464. Luckhurst hit 74 on his Test debut, and Cowdrey became the holder of the record for the most runs to be scored in Test cricket. The England innings did not end until the fourth day, and the match was drawn.

Australia were in a transitional phase. They had been totally outplayed by South Africa a year earlier, losing all four Tests in the Republic in the last series before South Africa's excommunication. The series against Illingworth's side witnessed the Test debuts of Rodney Marsh, Greg Chappell and Dennis Lillee. Chappell scored a century in his first Test and shared a sixth-wicket stand of 219 with Redpath as Australia reached 440 in reply to England's 397. The England innings had been founded on an opening partnership of 171 between Boycott and Luckhurst, who hit 131 in this his second Test match although handicapped by a damaged thumb. When England batted a second time John Edrich, accommodating and happy to bat lower in the order, scored 115 not out, and Illingworth declared, setting Australia a target of 245 in 145 minutes. With Lawry scoring 6 in the first sixty-eight minutes, inevitably the match was drawn.

Illingworth was winning few friends in Australia, but it was Lawry who was now coming under most pressure. A solid, eminently reliable left-handed opening batsman, he possessed immense powers of concentration, but as a captain he had become negative and unimaginative.

The Melbourne Test was abandoned after three days of continuous rain and the extra Test was forced into the touring programme as compensation. As the weather brightened, though, it was agreed that a forty-over match would be played on what would have been the final day of the Test, 5 January 1971. This hastily concocted idea was to have revolutionary, far-reaching consequences and was to shape the future of international cricket in a profound way.

The unprecedented decision to call off a Test with two days remaining and the cavalier way in which an extra Test was arranged brought down justifiable wrath on the heads of Hawker, Allen, Clark, Bradman and the rest, but there have always been those in cricketing authorities who believed they were answerable to no one. But these eminent men

237

did not envisage what they were unleashing when they sanctioned the forty-over game.

England were bowled out in 39.4 overs for 190, of which John Edrich made 82. Australia won by five wickets with forty-two balls to spare. Eight-ball overs were bowled, as was customary in Australia at that time. Ian Chappell scored 60, and nine of the fourteen wickets to fall were captured by spinners. These facts mattered little when set against the most significant aspect of the match: 46,000 had paid to watch it. The one-day international was born. From 1972 onwards a limited-overs series was to be a feature of every English season. Within fifteen years the one-day international was to become the most popular form of cricket in Australia and on the Indian subcontinent, and millions flocked to see the matches. By 1995–96 one-day internationals were outnumbering Test matches by four to one. A year later the ratio was five to one.

These events lay in the future. The present was England's journey to Sydney for the fourth Test. Cowdrey, out of form and out of sorts with himself and the tour, stood down while Willis made his Test debut at the expense of Shuttleworth. Illingworth won the toss, and Boycott and Luckhurst began well with a stand of 116. England passed 200 for the loss of only two wickets, but Mallett came back after tea to dismiss Fletcher, D'Oliveira and Knott in the space of thirty-nine balls as the score slipped to 219 for six. Illingworth, too, was out before the close, which came with England on 267 for seven.

Snow, Peter Lever and Willis regained the initiative on the second day. England seized an early advantage when both openers, Ian Chappell and Lawry, were out with the score on 38, but by the end of the day the match was evenly balanced again with Australia 189 for four.

The third day began triumphantly for England, as D'Oliveira induced Redpath to offer a catch to Fletcher off the first ball. Illingworth now crowded the bat as Underwood attacked, adopting the ancient maxim that if a batsman thinks the ball is turning, it is turning. Australia succumbed. The last five wickets fell for 47 runs, and England had snatched a lead of 96. By the end of the day this had been extended to 274, and England still had seven wickets in hand. This was a fine achievement, for Luckhurst, Edrich and Fletcher had gone for 48.

D'Oliveira was out for 56 just 3 runs into the fourth morning, but Illingworth batted briskly in a stand worth 95, and Boycott, who played a masterly innings after running out Edrich, finished unbeaten on 142. He judged his knock perfectly, breaking the heart of the Australian bowling, and batting to a rate which allowed Illingworth to set a target of 416. More significantly he gave the England bowlers more than nine hours in which to bowl out the opposition.

If Boycott was England's man of the series with the bat – he averaged 93.85 and scored 657 runs in five Tests – then Snow was undoubtedly the best bowler, with thirty-one wickets to his credit. The second innings of the fourth Test at Sydney was his finest hour. He tore into the Australian batting and immediately had Ian Chappell caught by D'Oliveira. Redpath soon followed, and Snow wrecked the younger Chappell's stumps. Lever had Walters caught behind, and the Australian innings was in ruins at 21 for four. Lawry and Stackpole steered their side to 64 by the close, but few had any doubts about the outcome of the match.

Any hopes the Australians may have had were extinguished first thing on the last morning. Lever flung himself to his left to catch Stackpole at third slip, and Willis took another fine slip catch to account for Marsh. On both occasions, John Snow was the bowler. Mallett offered defiance before Willis had him caught behind to claim the first of his 325 Test wickets. McKenzie, playing his last Test match, was struck in the face by a ball from Snow and forced to retire, and the Sussex pace bowler dismissed both Gleeson and Connolly with the score on 116 to give England victory by 299 runs.

Lawry had battled courageously throughout the Australian innings and finished unbeaten on 60. Only one other batsman, Stackpole, 30, scored more than 6. Snow finished with seven for 40 and was the man of the moment.

The fifth Test was the rescheduled extra match and was played at Melbourne. The wicket was perfect, and, from the outset, the match was destined to be drawn. Ian Chappell hit a century on the first day when Australia made 260 for one. Lawry declared at 493 for nine, leaving Rodney Marsh (whose wicket-keeping in his debut series was poor) unbeaten only 8 short of a maiden Test century. England responded with centuries from Luckhurst and D'Oliveira, but both were later injured. It was probably for this reason that England, who finished 101 runs short of Australia on the first innings, declined to attempt a target of 271 in four hours. Boycott and Edrich took them to 161 without being parted.

The knives were being sharpened for Lawry, who was censured for setting England such an easy target at Melbourne. England may have declined the challenge, but the press accused Lawry of nearly throwing away the rubber. The sixth Test at Adelaide was to mark the end of his Test career, although it was Illingworth who drew the most criticism in this game. Edrich made 130, Fletcher 80, and England reached 470. With Peter Lever to the fore, Australia were bowled out for 235, but Illingworth did not enforce the follow-on. It was his failure to do so which brought condemnation.

When England batted a second time Boycott hit his second century of the series. Illingworth's declaration left Australia 500 minutes in which to score 469 runs to win. Stackpole and Ian Chappell hit centuries and added 202 for the second wicket, but Australia finished on 328 for three.

And so to Sydney again with England one up in the series and needing only a draw to regain the Ashes. This seventh Test in the series was scheduled for six days; the rubber was the longest in Test history.

Australia caused a sensation by dropping Bill Lawry. It had been expected that Ian Chappell would replace him as captain, but it was believed that Lawry would retain his place in the side. He was replaced by Ken Eastwood, a solid left-hander, two years older than Lawry but of limited experience. It was to be Eastwood's only Test. Boycott was unfit to play for England, but Luckhurst had recovered from his broken finger and returned to open with Edrich. Chappell won the toss and asked England to bat, a decision which seemed fully justified by the end of the second day.

England struggled from the start, and their plight would have been sorry indeed but for a fighting 42 by Illingworth after five front-line batsmen had gone for 98. Spinners O'Keefe and Jenner exploited the conditions well, and England were out for 184. Snow and Lever quickly struck back for England, removing both openers for 13 before the close.

In the first encounter at Sydney there had been some bad crowd behaviour and pitch invasions, but they did not have the menace that some saw in the crowd reactions on the second day of the seventh Test.

Underwood, Willis and the sheer persistence of Illingworth's attacking cricket had brought England back into the match. With the score on 195 for seven, Jenner ducked into a short-pitched ball from Snow and was struck on the head. He was forced to retire hurt although he returned at 235 for eight. Umpire Rowan warned Snow for what he interpreted as the persistent use of the bouncer; in fairness, Snow had not overused this delivery although he had maintained aggression at all times. Illingworth reacted angrily to Rowan's warning of Snow and waved his finger at the umpire while engaged in an altercation. It was one of the most blatant examples of arguing with an umpire that had been seen on a cricket field.

The ball which struck Jenner was the last of an over, and as Snow took his position at long-leg he was met by a storm of booing, and some beer cans were thrown. Illingworth indicated that he would change the positions of Snow and Willis in the field, but Snow brushed the suggestion aside. The beer cans were cleared and he took up his position on the boundary fence where a drunken spectator almost immediately grabbed him by the shirt. Willis came to intervene, but Illingworth was now taking the unprecedented step of leading his side off the field.

In circumstances far worse than this mild storm at Sydney Hutton and Cowdrey had stood their ground, and Illingworth's action, in the opinion of many, sullied the game and whatever else he achieved on the tour. There are still those in cricket who have never forgiven him for what he did. E.W. Swanton referred to the incident as England's 'Day of Shame'.

The batsmen stayed in the middle while umpires Rowan and Brooks went to the England dressing room and informed Illingworth that the field was perfectly fit for play and that unless the England side returned to continue the match immediately, it would be taken that they had conceded it. Play then continued for another forty-five minutes, and Australia reached 235 for seven.

Willis took two of the three wickets that fell on the third morning as Australia gained a first-innings lead of 80. Edrich and Luckhurst wiped out this advantage in their opening partnership. The fall of four wickets for 71 runs saw the initiative move back to Australia, but at this point the veterans, D'Oliveira and Illingworth, stood firm. By the close they had taken the score to 229.

Illingworth added only 4 to his overnight score before falling leg-before to Lillee, and D'Oliveira added 10 before being taken at slip off the same bowler. Knott, Snow and Lever made useful contributions, and England's total mounted to 302. Australia required 223 to win and had more than two days in which to get the runs.

England could not have had a happier beginning. With his sixth ball, Snow wrecked Eastwood's stumps. The joy was short-lived. In the fifth over of the innings, Stackpole hooked Lever to long-leg. In attempting to take the catch, Snow crashed into the fencing and fractured and dislocated the little finger of his right hand. He had bowled two overs, taken one for 7, and now he was out of the match.

The wicket was placid and England were without their main strike bowler. During his period of captaincy Illingworth was frequently accused of under-bowling himself, of being reluctant to take on a responsibility which was his. Such a criticism could not be levelled at him now. Lever accounted for Ian Chappell, caught behind, and Stackpole was fortunate not to suffer the same fate. It was Stackpole who represented the danger to England, hitting two sixes and six fours and offering belligerence. Crucially, he was deceived and bowled by Illingworth, who also dismissed the in-form Redpath. Willis had Walters out cheaply, and Australia were 96 for five. England had overcome the loss of Snow in the best possible manner.

Greg Chappell and Marsh took the score to 123 before the close, but the odds were still slightly in favour of England.

Underwood had not been at his best on the fourth day, but on the fifth morning he struck early, bowling Marsh with only 8 added to the overnight score. Greg Chappell remained as Australia's last hope, and when Illingworth drew him forward and had him stumped by Knott England were close to victory. It came at 12.36 when Underwood had Jenner caught by Fletcher. England had recaptured the Ashes after an absence of twelve years.

England Regain the Ashes and Illingworth Leads a Walk-off
Australia v England at Sydney Cricket Ground
12, 13, 14, 16 and 17 February 1971

England First Innings		Second Innings	
J.H. Edrich c G. Chappell b Dell . . .	30	c I. Chappell b O'Keefe .	57
B.W. Luckhurst c Redpath b Walters	0	c Lillee b O'Keefe	59
K.W.R. Fletcher c Stackpole b O'Keefe	33	c Stackpole b Eastwood .	20
J.H. Hampshire c Marsh b Lillee . .	10	c I. Chappell b O'Keefe .	24
B.L. D'Oliveira b Dell	1	c I. Chappell b Lillee . . .	47
R. Illingworth (capt) b Jenner	42	lbw b Lillee	29
†A.P.E. Knott c Stackpole b O'Keefe	27	b Dell	15
J.A. Snow b Jenner	7	c Stackpole b Dell	20
P. Lever c Jenner b O'Keefe	4	c Redpath b Jenner	17
D.L. Underwood not out	8	c Marsh b Dell	0
R.G.D. Willis b Jenner	11	not out	2
Extras (b 4, lb 4, w 1, nb 2)	11	(b 3, lb 3, nb 6)	12
Total	184	. . . .	302

BOWLING	Overs	Mdns	Runs	Wkts	Overs	Mdns	Runs	Wkts
Lillee	13	5	32	1	14	–	43	2
Dell	16	8	32	2	26.7	3	65	3
Walters	4	–	10	1	5	–	18	–
G.S. Chappell	3	–	9	–	–	–	–	–
Jenner	16	3	42	3	21	5	39	1
O'Keefe	24	8	48	3	26	8	96	3
Eastwood	–	–	–	–	5	–	21	1
Stackpole	–	–	–	–	3	1	8	–

fall of wickets
1–5, 2–60, 3–68, 4–69, 5–98, 6–145, 7–156, 8–165, 9–165
1–94, 2–130, 3–158, 4–165, 5–234, 6–251, 7–276, 8–298, 9–299

Australia   First Innings   Second Innings

K.H. Eastwood c Knott b Lever ...	5	b Snow 0
K.R. Stackpole b Snow	6	b Illingworth 67
†R.W. Marsh c Willis b Lever	4	(7) b Underwood 16
I.M. Chappell (capt) b Willis	25	(3) c Knott b Lever 6
I.R. Redpath c and b Underwood .	59	(4) c Hampshire
		b Illingworth 14
K.D. Walters st Knott b Underwood	42	(5) c D'Oliveira b Willis . 1
G.S. Chappell b Willis	65	(6) st Knott b Illingworth 30
K.J. O'Keefe c Knott b Illingworth .	3	c sub (Shuttleworth)
		b D'Oliveira 12
T.J. Jenner b Lever	30	c Fletcher b Underwood 4
D.K. Lillee c Knott b Willis	6	c Hampshire b D'Oliveira 0
A.R. Dell not out	3	not out 3
Extras (lb 5, w 1, nb 10)	16	(b 2, nb 5) 7
Total	264	160

BOWLING	Overs	Mdns	Runs	Wkts	Overs	Mdns	Runs	Wkts
Snow	18	2	68	1	2	1	7	1
Lever	14.6	3	43	3	12	2	23	1
D'Oliveira	12	2	24	–	5	1	15	2
Willis	12	1	58	3	9	1	32	1
Underwood	16	3	39	2	13.6	5	28	2
Illingworth	11	3	16	1	20	7	39	3
Fletcher	–	–	–	–	1	–	9	–

fall of wickets
1–11, 2–13, 3–32, 4–66, 5–147, 6–162, 7–178, 8–235, 9–239
1–0, 2–22, 3–71, 4–82, 5–96, 6–131, 7–142, 8–154, 9–154
umpires – T.F. Brooks and L.P. Rowan
England won by 62 runs

When one considers that England were without the leading batsman, Boycott, now back in England with his left arm in plaster, and that their most successful bowler, Snow, was denied them at a crucial stage of the match, the achievement reached heroic proportions. It was the first time since 1888 that Australia had failed to win a Test in a home series, yet, inescapably, England's victory was tarnished.

When given run out at Adelaide, Boycott had flung his bat to the ground. Snow had been given to menacing histrionics, and, of course, Illingworth had remonstrated angrily with an umpire and led a walk-off. That Illingworth had led the side under extreme pressure, not the least of which was that he was an unpopular choice for the captaincy, and that England had not had one leg-before-wicket appeal upheld in the entire series were among reasons that could be offered for the outbreaks of unacceptable behaviour, but there was nothing that could excuse them.

Rex Alston was not alone in his opinion when he observed:

One wonders at what cost this victory was won. It is difficult for us at home, dependent on the views of journalists and commentators on the spot, to form a fair judgement on the behind-the-scenes tensions, but clearly the English team were not the best ambassadors for sport as we used to know it. The behaviour at times of the captain and his leading batsman and bowler, Boycott and Snow, left a nasty taste in the mouth, and the TCCB have some difficult decisions to make before the next tour.

The hard, professional approach was not to the liking of many, and in displaying open dissent at an umpire's decision cricketers had exacerbated a canker which could infect the very fabric of the game.

If the TCCB heeded advice and turned to another captain, who could they choose? Cowdrey had ruled himself out by form and attitude in Australia, and he had already stated that 1971 was to be his last as captain of Kent. He played in the second Test in New Zealand, and the general feeling was that this would be the end of his international career. The one-day international at Melbourne was, indeed, his single appearance in that form of cricket, but there was to be an epilogue for Cowdrey's great Test career.

England won one and drew one of the two Tests in New Zealand. The first saw D'Oliveira score the last of his five Test hundreds, Underwood take twelve for 97 and Bob Taylor make his Test debut. Taylor, a man of great warmth and charm, had proved himself the ideal tourist. He was an immaculate wicket-keeper, as good as any in the world, but it was his penance to be playing at the same time as Alan Knott. It was the latter who took the honours in the Test at Auckland where he hit 101 and 96. This Test was played over four days without a break and, interestingly, New Zealand were unable to include Murray and Pollard in their side, for both men refused to play cricket on a Sunday.

Even while Illingworth and his men were regaining the Ashes in Australia, the issue of captaincy was haunting English cricket. There had been rumours of disquiet at Yorkshire, but there had been little dissent when Illingworth moved to Leicestershire. There was unhappiness at Binks's decision to retire and unease at the doubts attending the action

244

of off-spinner Cope, but the bombshell came at the end of the 1970 season. The announcement issued by Yorkshire took all by surprise:

> After long and careful consideration your Committee decided not to re-appoint D.B. Close as first-team captain for 1971 and in view of this decision it was also decided that he should no longer be a playing member of the team.

Close had led the county to four Championships and two Gillette Cup triumphs, and he had helped restructure the side after departures and retirements. For all his public image as being somewhat irresponsible and a personal underachiever as batsman and bowler, Close was recognised as an inspiring captain, brilliant at bringing the best out of others, an outstanding tactician and a cricketer with an encyclopedic knowledge of the strengths and weaknesses of opponents. His team respected him, were mostly in awe of him and ever loyal to him. His dismissal caused an uproar. The civil strife in Yorkshire became national news, and it took many years and much more bloodshed before there was even a suggestion that wounds were healing.

The main reason offered for sacking Close was his outspoken dislike of one-day cricket, particularly the Sunday League. He was not alone in his unease at the proliferation of this form of cricket. Russell and Parfitt were to retire from Middlesex at the end of the 1972 season. Russell still had a year of his contract to run, but Brearley had been appointed captain of Middlesex in 1971 and had instigated a period of change. Russell believes that it was important for Brearley to break the dominance that the 'gang of four' – himself, Parfitt, Murray and Titmus – had on the side if he were to achieve anything. At his own suggestion Russell was left out of the Sunday League side in order to give the promising Clive Radley more experience and a chance to develop. Russell felt that the Sunday League was a waste of time, and he was of a generation that did not relish taking the path that they saw cricket following. He had twice been the first batsman to reach a thousand runs in the season; once he had given Brearley a head start and beaten him to become the first man to 2,000 runs. In his last season, 1972, he failed to reach a thousand runs for the first time in fourteen years. He has admitted that his mind was on other things. Like many cricketers nearing retirement, he was concerned about the future. He had invested his benefit money in a property development business and this was claiming more of his attention. In the early 1970s many professional cricketers still viewed the ends of their careers with apprehension and uncertainty.

Close was forty years old and had been sacked by the county that was his life. He was deeply upset, but he was also fortunate. He was asked to play for Somerset. He topped his new county's Championship batting averages in 1971, and he was appointed captain the following year. He led them with distinction until 1977, and he still made appearances in first-class cricket until he was fifty-three.

While Close thrived at Somerset, helping to bring on young players like Ian Botham, Yorkshire floundered. Boycott was appointed captain ahead of the more senior Phil Sharpe, who was not even named as vice-captain, that job going to Don Wilson. When the season began Boycott was still recovering from his broken left arm. Yorkshire finished thirteenth in the County championship, fourteenth in the John Player League and made an early exit from the Gillette Cup. It was described as the worst season in the county's history and they lost £8,000. Only Boycott and Richard Hutton could draw comfort from the season as players.

Hutton was one of two cricketers to make their England debuts during the season, the other being John Jameson. Hutton, son of the great Len, was a fast medium-pace right-arm bowler and hard-hitting batsman. He had won his blue in all three years at Cambridge and had proved himself to be a fine cricketer in his own right, overcoming the burden of a famous father. He was strong and positive, and he demonstrated his talents in two matches against Pakistan and three against India. He looked set for a long run in the England side, but the following season saw the arrival of Tony Greig.

Illingworth retained the England captaincy for 1971, but he did not enjoy the most successful of summers. In the first Test against Pakistan at Edgbaston, Zaheer Abbas hit 274, Mushtaq Mohammad 100 and Asif Iqbal 104 not out. Pakistan scored 608 for seven declared and England were forced to follow on in spite of Knott's century. They were saved from defeat by Luckhurst's second-innings hundred and, more specifically, by rain on the last day.

Cowdrey was chosen for this Test, but it was the last he was to play in England. Why did he not captain England more? The question has run throughout much of this narrative. Some who played under him suggest that he was not a 'players' man' in the sense that M.J.K. Smith was, nor a dominant leader in the mould of Peter May or even Ray Illingworth, but few cricketers have served their country better.

Boycott was back for the Lord's Test and scored a century in a match ruined by rain. In the Headingley match he hit another century, his third in successive Test innings, and England won by 25 runs. Pakistan should have been mortified to lose. They needed 231 in 385 minutes and reached 184 for five. They passed 200 with seven wickets down, and then lost three wickets in four balls to Peter Lever to be all out for 205.

The first Test against India, at Lord's, saw a resurgence of unacceptable behaviour by an England cricketer. This was the year when India could boast the triple spin threat of Bedi, Venkataraghavan and Chandrasekhar, and they took seventeen wickets between them in the Lord's Test. India led by 9 runs on the first innings and then bowled England out for 191. Needing 183 to win, India went for quick runs, for the sky was darkening and the weather threatening. Gavaskar pushed a quick single off Snow, and the bowler barged him as he ran. Snow was banned from one Test as a disciplinary measure. Rain prevented any play after tea when India were 38 runs short of their target with two wickets standing.

Centuries by Illingworth and Luckhurst gave England the better of the drawn second Test at Old Trafford, which extended England's unbeaten run to twenty-six matches. There was no play on the last day when England might have won, but they were handicapped by an injury to Norman Gifford, who broke a thumb fielding and was unable to bowl in the match.

Underwood was brought back for the final Test at The Oval, which was again dominated by spin. Ray Illingworth tasted defeat for the first time as England's captain, and India beat England for the first time in twenty-two Test matches in England. They needed 173 to win and got the runs for the loss of six wickets midway through the fifth afternoon.

Engineer played a major part in the victory, and Bedi, Venkataraghavan and Gavaskar were all to follow him into county cricket. The excitement and glamour of the overseas players were beginning to be questioned in some quarters, where they were seen as threats to the English game by restricting the development of young cricketers. By 1971 Northamptonshire had Mushtaq Mohammad and Sarfraz Nawaz in their ranks. Sarfraz did not play the following year, but by then they had Bedi. Gordon Greenidge had now joined Roy Marshall and Barry Richards at Hampshire, and although Marshall was soon to retire, Richards and Greenidge, of South Africa and the West Indies, were to form one of the most attacking and successful opening partnerships the game has seen.

In the same year Gloucestershire had Zaheer Abbas and Sadiq Mohammad playing alongside Mike Procter, and Julien and Fredericks were among others to grace the county scene. Intikhab Alam had captained Pakistan against England and returned to Surrey in July 1971 to help in the final stages of their campaign to win the Championship for the first time since the days of May and Surridge.

Surrey did not clinch the title until the final match of the season when they met Hampshire at Southampton. Edrich and Stewart scored 109 for the first wicket, but Surrey were bowled out for 269. This meant that they had gained four batting points, for the system in operation since 1968 allowed a point for every 25 runs over 150 scored in the first eighty-five overs of the first innings. The four batting points took Surrey to within two points of the title. A point was awarded for every two wickets and tension was high, for, with Marshall in majestic form, it was not until the fifty-eighth over that Surrey captured the all-important fourth wicket, Intikhab having Gilliat caught behind.

Bottles of champagne were brought out, and Stewart and his men celebrated on the pitch, which could be one reason why Surrey lost the match. Surrey won the Championship with 255 points, which was the same number as Warwickshire achieved, but Surrey took the title with eleven wins to the Midlands county's nine.

Warwickshire realised their ambition by winning the title in 1972. This success was brought about by the energy and foresight of two men: Derrick Robins, a wealthy man totally dedicated to the game, and Cyril Goodway, a shrewd and outstanding chairman.

Robins set his heart on Warwickshire winning the Championship and put his weight and money behind the project. He was helped by the rule which allowed for the immediate registration of an overseas player, but Lance Gibbs, a Test player of long standing and a very great off-spinner, had begun a residential qualification in 1967 and was able to appear in the Championship in 1968. He was joined in the side that year by Rohan Kanhai, his West Indian team-mate.

Kanhai had played league cricket in Scotland and Lancashire, and Warwickshire had been interested in him for some time. Initially, however, they had made approaches to Eddie Barlow, the South African all-rounder, but he had refused all inducements to come to play in England. It was then, on the recommendation of A.C. Smith and David Brown, that Warwickshire turned to Kanhai and signed him on a three-year contract. He was subsequently to play for them until 1977.

Warwickshire were not finished yet, because on 1 December 1970 they brought to the notice of the registration subcommittee that Kanhai had a home in Blackpool and had been living in England for more than five years. The committee accepted Warwickshire's point that Kanhai was resident and that the county was entitled to register another overseas cricketer. On Kanhai's advice, Warwickshire considered Alvin Kallicharran. Derrick Robins had seen Kallicharran (who would make a century on his Test debut against New Zealand in April 1972) and supported Kanhai's recommendation. A.C. Smith flew to the Caribbean and signed Kallicharran on a three-year contract in the face of strong

248

opposition from other counties vying for his signature.

Warwickshire had no difficulty in obtaining a work permit for Kallicharran, although Middlesex, in contrast, were having extreme difficulty in obtaining a permit for Larry Gomes, a virtually unknown West Indian. Eminence and the length of contract offered were important factors.

Yet a fourth West Indian was added to the staff at Edgbaston in 1972, wicket-keeper Deryck Murray. Murray had been up at Cambridge in 1965 and 1966 and, under existing regulations, was allowed to play for Nottinghamshire during the vacation. Far more successful on the cricket field than in the examination room, Murray moved to the University of Nottingham. An extension to his registration was granted, and it was also allowed that his period of residence be considered as having started in January 1964. In 1972 he was given special and immediate registration to join Warwickshire on the grounds that since he had been a registered county cricketer before 1971, his recruitment by the Midlands county did not unbalance their quota of overseas players. It should be remembered that Ibadulla, the Pakistani Test cricketer, was also on the Warwickshire staff and played in five Championship matches in 1972.

Another newcomer to the Warwickshire staff was Bob Willis. He was a Test cricketer and had helped Surrey win the Championship in 1971, but Micky Stewart still refused to award him his county cap. Hurt, Willis left Surrey to join Warwickshire, although his registration was contested, and he was not permitted to play for his new county until July. He began uncertainly, but, in the last home match, he took eight Derbyshire first-innings wickets for 44, wrapping up the innings with a hat-trick.

There were many who argued that Warwickshire had 'bought' the title, but the acquisition of a noted overseas cricketer was no guarantee of success. The euphoria that had attended Sobers's first season with Nottinghamshire was fading fast. He stood down as captain after the 1971 season, but was reappointed when Nottinghamshire summarily dismissed Bolus the following season. Bolus was immediately appointed captain of Derbyshire, his third county. In 1974, Sobers's last season, Bond joined Nottinghamshire as captain in the hope that he would repeat the triumphs he had achieved at Old Trafford. The move turned out to be a disaster for county and player.

The departure of Sobers brought no glowing epitaph from *Wisden*:

His last season with the club was on a par with his others. There were magical moments: the outstanding memory being his century in eighty-three minutes against Derbyshire at Ilkeston which in the outcome turned out to be the fastest of the season and won him the

249

Lawrence Trophy, as well as the National Sporting Club's prize.

It remained a strange fact that in the County Championship Sobers never did himself justice. Playing Test cricket he was always able to raise his performance but, regrettably for Nottinghamshire, members saw too few glimpses of the great all-rounder.

The truth was, as Warwickshire had realised and as Graham Gooch was to say at the end of the decade after savaging the Midlands county's South African bowler Anton Ferreira, 'There is no point in signing an overseas player unless he's going to win you something.'

There were counties in the 1970s who were failing to grasp the impact that a front-line overseas cricketer could have, irrespective of the fact that even the greatest cannot guarantee success. What troubled some critics was that experience in the County Championship was helping to turn other nations' players into Test cricketers. We were aiding the 'enemy'. Greg Chappell, for example, honed his skills with Somerset. Essex gave two years' employment to Lee Irvine, who arrived as an unknown and departed as a very successful batsman for South Africa. He was followed by Bruce Francis, an opening batsman from New South Wales, who played two seasons in county cricket and immediately won a place in the Australian side on the 1972 tour.

While the argument that England was helping to develop other country's cricketers had substance, it failed to take into account the positive factor that many of those cricketers were enriching the county game. They set standards, and they offered young players a challenge which they might not otherwise have met. Most important, and so often ignored or disregarded by authority, they gave immense pleasure to the paying customer. In his prize-winning history of Warwickshire cricket Leslie Duckworth paid the following tribute to Rohan Kanhai:

> I shall always feel a personal debt of gratitude to Warwickshire for engaging him, not so much because of the runs he has scored for them, though they have been entertaining enough in all conscience, but because I was able to see again in him what batsmen were like in the days when they still believed it was their main function in life to hit the ball hard – plus, of course, the personal panache he brought to the game. Sometimes he would let quite hittable balls pass him for no apparent reason, but then the tiger that always lurked beneath that seemingly benign exterior would stir and pounce and you would see a cut of blinding brilliance, or a drive that would make you instinctively draw your hand away from even the thought that you might be called upon to stop it. He was sometimes a man of moods – aren't we

all? – but he let the younger generation of Warwickshire players and spectators see what real batsmanship could be, and I knew that I had not dreamed there were really such batsmen once. For that I shall be eternally grateful.

Duckworth's tribute to Kanhai is a necessary corrective to those criticisms which see only harm in the importation of players.

Kanhai scored 1,437 Championship runs in 1972, Warwickshire's title year, and the runs came in twenty matches, for a reduction in the number of Championship games had been made in order to accommodate the new competition introduced in 1972, the Benson and Hedges Cup.

As a fifty-five-over tournament, it was more acceptable than the Sunday League to players who had been reared on the three-day game. The competition had its teething troubles. In the first place the four qualifying leagues were structured on a geographical basis which meant that they were unequal in strength. Second, three days were allocated to each game, and this brought several periods of inactivity in the early part of the season.

The first year of the cup saw three points awarded for a win and one bonus point given for bowling out the opposition, a reward which perhaps should have been given an extended run. Only Leicestershire qualified for the quarter-finals with a 100 per cent record, and they also bowled out the opposing county in each of their four matches. They had overwhelming victories against Lancashire and Warwickshire in the quarter- finals and semi-finals and huge crowds flocked to Grace Road on each occasion.

The final at Lord's drew a crowd of 18,000 which, considering that there had been heavy rain in the early morning, was good. Leicestershire's opponents were Yorkshire, who had a better season than their previous one but were still well short of former glory. Once again they played a final without Boycott, and Sharpe led the side. They were restricted to 136 for nine from the fifty-five overs, which was never going to be adequate, and Leicestershire won by five wickets with 8.1 overs to spare.

It was not a great match, but for Leicestershire it was the greatest of occasions. They had attained first-class status in 1895 and had never looked likely to win the Championship, but now they had claimed a major trophy for the first time. Cricket had received a further boost: each season there were now four competitions to excite players and public.

Leicestershire's success was another triumph for Illingworth, who led them to within one point of winning the John Player League as well. He

251

appeared in only Championship matches, for he had retained the England captaincy. Under him, England would retain the Ashes.

England won the first Test, but Australia levelled the series at Lord's when Massie took sixteen wickets on his Test debut. This was more than half the wickets he was to take in the whole of his Test career.

The third Test at Trent Bridge was drawn, and England were assured of keeping the Ashes when they won convincingly at Headingley. The England hero in this match was Underwood, who had match figures of ten for 82 with the help of a pitch that took spin from the first day. A freak storm had flooded the pitch the weekend before the match, and it had been artificially dried. It was bare and damp. The spinners were thoroughly happy, and the match was over in three days.

The rubber was squared when Australia won a six-day encounter at The Oval. Statistically, the series belonged to Australia. Their batsmen hit five centuries; England's did not manage one. Lillee took thirty-one wickets in five Tests; Massie twenty-three in four. Snow's twenty-four wickets in five Tests was England's best offering.

M.J.K. Smith, who had come out of retirement, appeared in three Tests, but with little success, and Edrich had a dismal series. England introduced two new Test players in the series: Barry Wood, who played at The Oval, and Tony Greig, who appeared in all five matches.

Greig had played for England against the Rest of the World in 1970, but, in spite of efforts by some publications, these matches were never recognised as Tests. He scored more runs than any other English batsman against Australia in the series and took ten wickets. He also played in all three matches in the first Prudential Trophy, which was played in late August after the Test series. Dennis Amiss, whose batting developed strongly during the season, became the first man to hit a century in a one-day international, while Greig's batting in the final match helped England to the trophy. Two wickets fell with the score on 172 so that England were 8 runs short of victory with just two wickets standing. Greig took matters into his own hands and hit Massie for two boundaries to win the match.

There were two interesting features about these matches. The first was that England selected Bob Woolmer as an all-rounder, and he batted at number nine. His Test debut was still three years away. Second, with Illingworth injured during the Oval Test, Bedser and his co-selectors recalled Brian Close to captain England in the one-day series.

The irony in this appointment was that one of the excuses Yorkshire offered for sacking Close was his outspoken criticism of limited-overs cricket, yet, as captain of Somerset, it was in this brand of cricket that he was most successful. He had a new lease of life in the West Country. He was deeply respected by young cricketers, who, as in Yorkshire, were in awe of him, and they quaked at the dressing down they were given for lapses of technique or concentration. Ian Botham was to say of him, 'He gave me the killer instinct.' Praise indeed.

Illingworth was unable to lead the side to India and Pakistan, but this time the selectors did not turn to Close to replace him. They chose instead Tony Lewis, the Glamorgan skipper, who had not appeared in Test cricket before. Certainly, there had been those who had pressed his case for inclusion in the England side on merit as a batsman, but when the call finally came it was arguably a little too late. In spite of this, Lewis acquitted himself admirably. He was possibly the most popular touring captain to the Indian subcontinent. He was enterprising and well liked by his players, and, as an ambassador for his side and for the game, he won acclaim in India which still shows no signs of diminishing.

Lewis led an England side that was in transition. D'Oliveira's Test career was at an end, and Boycott, Edrich and Snow were not members of the party. Mike Denness was a rather surprising appointment as vice-captain, although he had been impressive as captain of Kent. The team itself felt ill-prepared for the first Test, which began in Delhi little more than a fortnight after their arrival in India and finished on Christmas Day.

On a grassless wicket India were bowled out for 173. A wonderful burst from Geoff Arnold reduced the home side to 59 for five, and Abid Ali was alone in offering any resistance. Arnold finished with six for 45, and there were two wickets each for Cottam and Greig.

Barry Wood and Dennis Amiss scored 61 for England's first wicket, but an outstanding spell of bowling by Chandrasekhar destroyed the tourists' first innings. He sent back Wood, Fletcher and Lewis inside eight deliveries, finishing with eight for 79, and only Tony Greig's defiantly aggressive unbeaten 68 took England to a first-innings lead of 27.

India seemed to have taken a grip on the match when Solkar and Engineer shared a sixth-wicket stand of 103, but their last five wickets fell for 27 runs, and England needed 207 to win. Amiss and Fletcher were out with only 20 scored, and Denness left at 76. Wood and Lewis took England to 106 for three at the end of the fourth day, and Wood was out with 1 run added on the final morning. Greig now joined Lewis, and they shared an unbroken stand of 101 which took England to victory shortly after lunch on Christmas Day. Lewis followed his debut duck with 70, and Greig brought his total of runs for the match to 108 without being dismissed. It was a marvellous start for England and for Tony Lewis.

Arnold, who had bowled so well in Delhi, was taken ill on the eve of the Calcutta Test and was replaced by Chris Old, who was retained for the rest of the series, replacing Cottam. Greig had another fine match, but India won by 28 runs and levelled the series.

They took a 2–1 lead when they won by four wickets in Madras, and the last two Tests were drawn to give them the rubber. Roope and Birkenshaw made their debuts at Kanpur, where Lewis hit 125 in 267 minutes. It was the first century hit by an England batsman for ten Tests, and it was an innings of serenity and power. He came to the crease at a time when the Indian spinners threatened to dominate, and he played Bedi in superb fashion, moving down the pitch and hitting the great left-arm bowler over the heads of the fielders. This was classical batting, as intelligent in thought as it was beautiful in execution.

Fletcher and Greig emulated the skipper in the final Test, hitting maiden Test hundreds and sharing a fifth-wicket stand of 254 after four wickets had gone for 79. The match was drawn after England had been set the unlikely target of 213 in ninety minutes.

The three Tests in Pakistan were drawn, and batsmen thrived. Dennis Amiss hit 112 and 16 in the first Test, 158 and nought in the second, and 99 and 21 not out in the third. He was to follow this with 138 not out in England's second innings of the first Test against New Zealand in 1973. He had taken some time to establish himself, but here was a very fine batsman.

Those who saw him when he first arrived at Edgbaston as a boy say that he arrived as the complete technician. It is doubtful whether any English batsman since the Second World War has had a better technique. There was a harmony in the movement of feet, hands and head which, in itself, gave great aesthetic pleasure. He was the perfect model for any young player, and there was a calm and dedication about him which brought a personal expression to his batting.

If Amiss was ultimately a success on the tour, there were two among the sixteen-strong party who were unqualified successes almost from the outset: Keith Fletcher and Tony Greig. They showed a consistency which none of their colleagues could approach. For Fletcher, 'the incubation period in Test cricket had lasted a long time' (this first Test century came in his twentieth game for England), but on this tour his batting was mightily impressive. As Clive Taylor reported in his review of the tour:

He had been sent on the tour in what was publicly described by the selectors as 'a last chance', and he proved himself the best of the

England batsmen. Technically, he had always been good, but now he showed authority as well. He scored his first hundred in Test cricket in Bombay, yet the innings that did him greatest credit was one of 97 not out on a turning wicket at Madras. It is difficult to imagine that any of the world's current players could have batted better on it.

Greig was a very different character. On the surface at least he was so supremely self-confident that it would have been a surprise had he not been a success. He responded with passion and courage to any crisis and worked out his own solutions to the problems that the Indian spinners posed. His bowling was extraordinarily effective, and his catching could be inspirational. Newly appointed captain of Sussex, he was already being spoken of as a future England leader. There were those who were critical of his aggressive histrionics, but he was a showman, and the crowd responded to him with delight.

Had Tony Lewis equalled Greig's performances on the field, his success as a diplomat off it would have won him the captaincy of England for the 1973 season, for Bedser supported his candidature. As it was, Illingworth resumed the leadership and Lewis served him in the first Test against New Zealand. He scored 2 twice and missed the rest of the season with injury, handing over the Glamorgan captaincy to Majid Khan.

England faced stiffer opposition than anticipated from New Zealand, and there was a growing realisation that the six Test-playing nations were drawing closer and closer together in strength. The New Zealanders arrived at Trent Bridge for the first Test unbeaten. Not only that, but Glenn Turner had become the first batsman in thirty-five years to score a thousand runs before the end of May; this was to be one of their problems. Turner had reached his peak too soon, and his single score above 11 in five Test innings was 81 in the second innings of the third and final Test.

The first Test was a match in which four innings took on heroic proportions. Illingworth won the toss and England were bowled out before lunch on the second day for 250. Before the end of the day, England were batting again. Snow, Arnold and Greig had rushed out New Zealand in under forty-two overs for 97, of which 20 were extras. The start of the innings had given no indication of what was to come, for Snow in particular was wayward. It was Greig who brought about the transformation, dismissing both openers and finishing with four for 33.

255

England's second innings began disastrously. Boycott, Roope, Lewis and Fletcher were back in the pavilion with only 24 runs on the board. Greig counter-attacked with an innings in which he used his long reach to good effect and in which he was ever willing to hit the ball hard. He scored 139 in a partnership with Amiss which was worth 210. His hundred came off 178 balls, and when he was finally out he had hit sixteen fours and given regal entertainment. Amiss now abandoned his purely supportive role and moved on to the attack; when Illingworth declared he was unbeaten on 138.

New Zealand were left the task of scoring 479 to win the match, a total which had never been approached in the fourth innings of a Test. They lost their openers, Turner and Parker, both Worcestershire players, at 16 and finished the third day on 56 for two. Hastings went first thing on the Monday morning, and Burgess was dismissed at 130. Only one more wicket fell during the day when Congdon was bowled by Arnold for 176. He had hit eighteen fours and batted quite magnificently before falling little over a quarter an hour before the close, beaten, one felt, by exhaustion.

New Zealand closed on 317 for five, and on the last morning Pollard and Wadsworth continued to defy the England bowlers in the hope of taking their side to an astonishing victory. Shortly before lunch, however, Wadsworth was caught at slip by Roope off Arnold.

Pollard, who was leg-before to Greig for 116, and Wadsworth, 46, had added 95, but once they were parted New Zealand faced defeat. The last five wickets fell for 38 runs, which was also the margin of England's victory.

In mentioning Roope one should record that the Surrey player won twenty-one Test caps for England, had a highest score of 77, but averaged over 30. He was consistent, reliable and, above all, the finest slip fielder of his generation. Tim Lamb was to pay him the compliment of saying that he wished that all his career he had bowled with Roope at first slip.

Old for Lewis was England's change for the second Test, in which New Zealand again came close to victory. Bowled out for 253, England saw New Zealand bat for two and a half days to score 551 for nine; at the time this was their highest score in Test cricket. Congdon, Pollard and Burgess all hit centuries after the openers, Turner and Parker, had gone for 10.

England needed to score 298 to make New Zealand bat again, and they faced a grim struggle for survival. Boycott, Amiss and Roope battled manfully, but England lost four front-line batsmen before the arrears were wiped off. The heroism came from Keith Fletcher, who never concentrated solely on defence. He realised that runs were as important as survival and batted accordingly. Illingworth stayed for two hours, but he fell to Howarth, the first of four wickets to go down for 33 runs. At 368 for eight, England's position was perilous. Arnold joined Fletcher, and the pair added 92 in eighty-seven minutes and saved the game. Fletcher batted with complete authority and took 16 in one over from Pollard. When he was caught on the boundary five minutes from the close he had batted for 379 minutes and hit two sixes and twenty-one fours in his 178.

This was one of the great Test innings, yet it was watched by a small last-day crowd and, in BBC Television's review of the season, it scarcely got a mention. The fates were less than kind to the Essex man, who was soon to take over the captaincy of his county.

He was England's batsman of the summer. He scored 81 in the third Test at Headingley and shared a third-wicket stand of 119 with Boycott, who scored a century. England won by an innings and 1 run to take the series by two matches to nil, a far from fair reflection of New Zealand's performance in the rubber.

The second half of the season saw a visit from the West Indies, who were now led by Rohan Kanhai. The West Indies used thirteen players in the three Tests, and only two of those, Inshan Ali and Foster, were not attached to English counties.

The West Indies had not been enjoying the best of times. They had recently lost at home to Australia, who were emerging as a strong side, and they had not tasted victory in twenty Test matches. That miserable run ended at The Oval, which, against tradition, was the venue of the first Test. Clive Lloyd hit a century, and Keith Boyce, one of several overseas cricketers whom Essex helped turn into a Test player, had match figures of 11 for 147. The West Indies won by 158 runs, but there was consolation for England in that Frank Hayes, making his Test debut, made 106 not out. He had been blooded in the one-day series against New Zealand, a series blighted by rain with England winning the only match to be completed.

Much was expected of Hayes. Fair-haired, stylish with a natural flair for the game, he had begun his Championship career for Lancashire with two innings in the 90s. Three years later, 1973, he played magnificently for The Rest against Tony Lewis's MCC Tour XI in the Test trial at Hove. His two innings of great charm earned him his place in the one-day series against New Zealand and in the Test series against the West Indies. He was considered to be the most exciting batsman in England, but nothing ever went quite right for him after that first Test hundred. He considered Illingworth the best captain he ever played under, but Illingworth's reign was nearing its end. His own period as captain of Lancashire was neither happy nor successful, and he was not a lucky cricketer. He played all of his nine Tests against the West Indies at a time when they were again becoming a major force in world cricket, and, nervous by nature, he never had a chance to establish himself gradually in the England side. An intelligent man, courteous and sensitive, he was destined to become England's lost hero.

The second Test at Edgbaston was drawn; it was a sad match. Roy Fredericks scored 150 as the West Indies made 327. Geoff Boycott twice retired hurt in his innings of 56 not out, having first been hit in the ribs and then on the arm. Early in his innings, however, Boycott survived a confident appeal for a catch at the wicket off Boyce. Kanhai and his side were incensed when umpire Fagg turned down the appeal, and Kanhai made his feelings plain for some time. The West Indian anger was probably fuelled by the fact that Boycott had gained something of a reputation for surviving situations in which lesser-known cricketers would not have been so fortunate. One county bowler ruefully remarked after a leg-before appeal against Boycott had been rejected, 'If it had been the bloke batting the other end, the finger would have gone up.'

When play began on the third day Alan Oakman, a former first-class umpire, was walking to the middle with 'Dickie' Bird, then a novice umpiring his second Test. It transpired that Fagg was angered by Kanhai's constant signs of dissent and was withdrawing from the match unless he received an apology. He resumed after the first over following talks with Alec Bedser and Esmond Kentish, the West Indian manager. Mr Kentish stated that the West Indies team were 'fully satisfied with Mr Fagg's umpiring'. It was a sad interlude, and symptomatic of changing attitudes.

The third Test at Lord's was marred by a malaise of a different kind. On the Saturday afternoon there was a harsh intrusion from the increasingly violent world of politics. The game was held up for an hour and a half when a telephone message claimed that a bomb had been placed at the ground. Hoax calls were common at the time, when IRA activity was intense. The stands were cleared. Some people were moved outside the ground; others sat on the playing area itself. A police search found nothing, and the game restarted.

The stoppage provided England with their only respite of the match. Over the first two days Kanhai and Sobers hit majestic hundreds, and Bernard Julien pounded a tiring attack for 121. Kanhai declared at 652 for nine, and the West Indies won by an innings. Fletcher, with innings

258

of 68 and 86 not out, and Greig, 44, were the only English batsmen to pass 40.

Five England bowlers conceded more than 100 runs. Willis's four for 118 was a worthy effort on a placid pitch. Tony Greig displayed his unique capacity for engaging the crowd by raising his arms in acclaim when the bowling figures were read out over the public address system. He had the ability to lighten even the gloomiest periods, and he made supporters feel England were winning even when they were being trounced. He took three for 180 in thirty-three overs.

The defeat by an innings and 226 runs marked the end of Illingworth's career as England captain and as a Test player. He had led his country in thirty-six Tests, and regained and held the Ashes. Yet, strangely, he never suggested permanence. It was as if he had been appointed to office grudgingly.

Illingworth was forty-one when he was relieved of his post, but the selectors had no ready-made successor. Lewis would have been the ideal person to have taken over, but injury had restricted him to three Championship matches for Glamorgan, and his form was poor. So Bedser and his committee turned to the man who had been Lewis's understudy on the diplomatically successful tour of India and Pakistan, Mike Denness.

He had enjoyed a wonderful season as captain of Kent. Believing that the players at his disposal were best suited to the limited-overs game, he had fashioned his approach accordingly and Kent had won both the John Player League and the Benson and Hedges Cup. They had also finished fourth in the Championship, and Denness himself had scored freely, hitting four centuries and finishing high in the averages. On the debit side was the fact that he had not been selected for any of the Tests against New Zealand or the West Indies, so that the selectors were naming as captain a batsman whom they had not considered good enough to be in the side.

Denness first led England in the two one-day internationals against the West Indies, which were played in early September. England won the first match by one wicket with three balls to spare. Denness hit 66 and was named Man of the Match. The West Indies won the second game by eight wickets.

This short Prudential Trophy series had some interesting features. Sobers was caught behind off Old for nought in the first match, and this was the one and only limited-overs international in which the great all-rounder appeared. In trying to restructure in advance of the tour to the Caribbean, the England selectors made several changes. Bob Taylor kept wicket, and Mike Hendrick, the Derbyshire fast medium-pace bowler, was introduced to international cricket. So, too, was M.J. Smith, the Middlesex opening batsman. He had been called to join the party for the third Test but had not played. He was then selected to open in both the one-day matches against the West Indies, but he was not named in the tour squad, nor did he ever play Test cricket.

Mike Smith had batted well throughout the season, although Middlesex finished low in the Championship, which was won in emphatic style by Hampshire. The South Coast county won ten and drew ten of their twenty matches. They did not supply a single player to the England side, but they had the best and most exciting opening pair in the country in Barry Richards and Gordon Greenidge.

Those who played on the county circuit in the 1970s are unanimous in their opinion that Barry Richards was the greatest batsman they ever saw. Tall and fair, Richards had the casual air of one to whom batting came easy. The excommunication of South Africa from international cricket meant that his Test career was limited to four matches, in which he scored 508 runs, and he spent the rest of his career playing in Australia and England. He scored over 28,000 runs and hit eighty centuries, yet the feeling was that he could have broken all the records had the challenge been greater and had he found the task more demanding.

Gordon Greenidge was to punish England bowlers for many years. He was an explosive batsman, capable of destroying any attack. He and Desmond Haynes were to form one of the greatest of Test-match opening partnerships, although ironically, Greenidge, who was brought to England at the age of twelve, was eligible to play for England had he so wished.

With David Turner, a left-handed batsman and fine fielder, in support, the Hampshire batting was known to be strong, but it was generally thought that their bowling was weak. Astutely handled by Gilliat, it proved more than adequate in taking Hampshire to the Championship for the second time. Herman, once of Middlesex, and Mike Taylor, unwisely jettisoned by Nottinghamshire at the same time as Bolus, were medium-pacers who, with Mottram (playing his first full season), used the new ball to excellent effect. The veteran Peter Sainsbury, the sole survivor from Ingleby-Mackenzie's Championship-winning side, and David O'Sullivan were successful spinners.

O'Sullivan was a New Zealand Test cricketer who, like Sainsbury, bowled slow left-arm. He contributed much to Hampshire's triumph, but he was released at the end of the season. The regulations stated that each county was allowed only two overseas players. This did not affect Greenidge, who was qualified by residence, but Hampshire wanted to sign a young fast bowler from Antigua named Andy Roberts, and O'Sullivan had to go. In some quarters doubts had been expressed concerning the legality of O'Sullivan's action, and this may have persuaded Hampshire to release him, but it is more likely that they realised they were exchanging a good bowler for a great one.

If Hampshire owed a great deal to their overseas opening batsmen, Gloucestershire were indebted to three imported cricketers for their success in the Gillette Cup. They had a hard path to the final, and the Men of the Match in the first three rounds were Roger Knight (now secretary of MCC), David Shepherd (now one of the world's finest umpires) and Knight again as Glamorgan, Surrey and Essex were beaten.

These victories were close, but they could not compare with the semi-final, in which Gloucestershire beat Worcestershire at New Road before the biggest crowd seen on the ground since the visit of Bradman's Australians in 1948. Worcestershire had a grip on the game when they dismissed Nicholls and Knight with 32 scored, but then they dropped Procter off the first ball he received from Brain and put him down again when he had made 18. He went on to make 101 in 165 minutes to take his side to 243 for eight.

Headley and Turner, both of whom had played against England during the season, scored 123 for Worcestershire's first wicket. Turner made 109, but the scoring rate fell a little below what was required. With 41 needed from six overs and six wickets standing, Procter produced a spell that won the match, taking three wickets, including that of Turner, and Gloucestershire scraped home by 5 runs.

In the final against Sussex they recovered from the loss of Sadiq Mohammad, Roger Knight and Zaheer Abbas for 27 runs to reach 248 for eight. Procter revived them with an innings of 94, but, at 106 for five, Gloucestershire were far from happy. When Procter departed skipper Tony Brown took charge and hit 46 out of the 68 runs scored over the last eight overs. He finished unbeaten on 77 and a tight spell of bowling brought him the individual award as his side won by 40 runs. The victory constituted their first triumph in a major competition in modern times.

The limited-overs competitions had captured the public imagination and given cricketers added incentive, but there was concern as to crowd behaviour at these matches in particular, and in general. The behaviour of the crowds during the England–West Indies series had given cause for concern, and it was apparent that not only were public manners in decline, but that one-day cricket was beginning to attract a new kind of supporter. These problems would not diminish in the next few years; but the immediate concern was to choose a side to go to the Caribbean under Denness.

The generally held view was that a weakness in batting was England's main problem, yet Boycott was long since established and Amiss, Fletcher and Greig had all proved themselves. Knott was a wonderful player to have at number seven or eight, and the selectors obviously felt confident enough of the batting to ignore the claims of John Edrich, now captain of Surrey. On departure the party under Denness was considered to be without any hope of success.

Only two first-class matches were played before the first Test and both were drawn. The England players were disappointed not to win the first, for Boycott had hit 261 not out and Amiss 109. The pair put on 252 for the first wicket. Arnold took five wickets in the first innings and Willis four in the second, but the tourists were thwarted by a last-wicket stand. Greig, vice-captain of the side, hit 70 and 100 not out against Trinidad, but this match, too, was a disappointment.

All that the pessimists had predicted came true when the West Indies won the first Test comfortably by seven wickets. With Boycott, 93, and Amiss, 174, scoring 209 for the first wicket when England batted a second time, it seemed that the game could be saved, but the last nine wickets went down for 64 runs.

In spite of the supreme efforts made by Amiss and Boycott, the lasting memory of this Test at Port of Spain was an incident that took place at the end of the second day when the West Indies' score was 274 for six with Kallicharran unbeaten on 142. Julien played the ball to Greig at silly point and turned to walk to the pavilion as Knott pulled up the stumps. Seeing Kallicharran out of his ground, Greig threw down the stumps at the bowler's end and appealed. Umpire Sang Hue correctly gave Kallicharran 'run out', for the ball was not dead. Greig's action was spontaneous and certainly without evil intent. It was within the letter of the law, although some may argue it was not within the spirit of the game.

The crowd reacted angrily, and the England side were besieged in their dressing room for two hours while representatives of the West Indian Board and of the touring party debated the issue: the appeal was withdrawn and Kallicharran continued his innings. The West Indian Board said that this was 'in the interests of cricket generally and this tour in particular'. The laws of the game had been bent in order to avoid crowd violence in the coming weeks of the tour.

Pocock took five for 110 in the first innings of the first Test, but this was the only glimmer of light for the England bowlers. In the second Test he had none for 152 as the West Indies made 583 for nine declared to take a first-innings lead of 230. At 271 for seven, England faced defeat, but then came the great escape. Dennis Amiss batted for 570 minutes, faced 563 balls and hit a six and forty fours in his innings of 262 not out, the highest of his career. This innings brought Amiss's aggregate of Test runs within a twelve-month period to 1,356, and he was to continue to flourish without ever quite receiving the plaudits that were his due.

Pocock gave Amiss noble support for eighty-three minutes, and Willis batted out the last fifty-three minutes so that the game was saved.

The third Test followed a pattern similar to the second. The West Indies introduced their new fast bowler, Andy Roberts, already signed by Hampshire, and the first Antiguan to play Test cricket. He had a quiet debut, but Rowe, who had hit 120 in the second Test, enjoyed a personal triumph. Put in to bat, England had made 395, thanks mainly to a sixth-wicket stand of 163 between Knott and Greig. Greig hit 148 and followed it by taking six for 164 as the West Indies reached 596 for eight; Lawrence Rowe scored 302.

In the opinion of those who saw Rowe in his formative years in Jamaica, he was a better batsman than Sobers or Viv Richards, but he was destined never to show the world his true greatness and has become something of a forgotten figure. Injury had caused him to miss the series against England in 1973 and injury was to plague him at regular inter-vals thereafter. Derbyshire achieved a coup comparable to the one Nottinghamshire had achieved in signing Sobers when they acquired Rowe for 1974, but he disappointed over two seasons and badly injured an ankle. That was to be typical of his career.

In Bridgetown, however, he savaged England, hitting a six and thirty-six fours in his 430-ball innings. England went into the last day on 72 for four and again lost five wickets before clearing the arrears. This time they were saved by Keith Fletcher, who batted throughout the last day and finished unbeaten on 129. Knott again helped in the salvation with 67 in a sixth-wicket stand of 142.

The fourth Test was ruined by rain, although not before Amiss and Greig had scored hundreds. And so to the last Test, in Port-of-Spain, to which six days had been allocated. This was an historic match in that it marked the end of the Test careers of two great cricketers, Sobers and Kanhai.

The pitch offered some help to the spinners from the start, but it was never a vicious surface. Denness won the toss and England batted. There was a mistake in the field by the West Indies early on which, arguably, cost them the match. Boycott had scored 9 and was stranded in mid-pitch. Kanhai had run from a fielding position close to the wicket to fine-leg to retrieve the ball, but his throw to the bowler's end was wild, and Boycott escaped. By the end of the day he was on 97, and England were 198 for four.

Apart from this lapse on the part of their captain the West Indies' fielding was excellent, and batting was never easy because of the uneven bounce. The left-arm wrist spinner Inshan Ali was particularly testing. Boycott was not at his best, but no man ever showed more determination and application, more reluctance to surrender his wicket. He was caught wide down the leg side, one-handed, early on the second day, for 99. Boycott's dismissal heralded a collapse, the last six wickets falling in ninety minutes for 63 runs.

Fredericks and Rowe, as they had done throughout the series, gave the West Indies a fine start. They both displayed excellent technique in difficult conditions, and although Fredericks and Kallicharran fell to Pocock, the West Indies ended the day in a position of strength, 174 for two.

At Kingston in the second Test Tony Greig had tried to develop his off-cutters. On the third day at Port of Spain he seemed to have perfected them. At lunch the West Indies were 208 for two, Rowe 90, Lloyd 40. The score had advanced to 224 when Greig had Lloyd caught behind. Sobers, Kanhai and Murray quickly followed. In the space of twenty balls, Greig had taken four wickets for 6 runs.

The West Indies had only just edged into the lead when Rowe hit a full toss into the hands of Boycott. The last three wickets fell for 5 runs, and what had threatened to be an unassailable lead had been restricted to 38. In *Wisden* Clive Taylor described Greig's performance as 'a spell of bowling that will rank among the best in Test history'. On the third day he had taken eight for 33 in 19.1 overs.

In spite of Greig's effort England remained in difficulties, losing Amiss and Denness for 44. Fletcher steadied the innings as he and Boycott, more impressive and even more determined than in his first knock, added 101. Fletcher was finally bowled by Julien, and England ended the fourth day on 158 for three.

The play was frequently interrupted by brief showers so that a variety of doubts clouded the final outcome. It looked like a West Indian victory when, on the fifth day, the dismissal of Pocock, the nightwatchman, was the first of three wickets to go down for 7 runs. Boycott completed his outstanding hundred and had batted for nearly seven hours when he played forward to Gibbs and was bowled. He stayed at the crease, unaware of what had happened, although a bail lay on the ground. Umpire Sang Hue, at Gibbs's end, consulted with the square-leg umpire before ruling Boycott out, for the ball had turned so far that Sang Hue's view had been obscured by Boycott's front pad.

Thankfully for England, Knott again showed resolution and considerable technical ability. When he was leg-before to Sobers for 44 he had ensured that the West Indies faced a challenging target, 226.

They closed on the penultimate day at 30 for nought, and England knew that they must break the formidable Fredericks and Rowe partnership as quickly as possible if they were to have any chance of winning the match.

Greig had opened the attack bowling his off-breaks, and spin was to dominate the final day. Tension was high, but at first the West Indies seemed untroubled. At 63 Rowe played back to Birkenshaw in a casual manner and was leg-before. Two balls later Kallicharran, a powerfully aggressive force in the early part of the series, was caught at slip off bat and pad to collect a 'pair'. Fredericks had looked totally unaffected by the tension and was batting with calm authority when he turned a ball from Birkenshaw past Boycott at square-leg and took a comfortable single. Surprisingly, he pivoted for a second run. Lloyd hesitated until Fredericks was halfway up the pitch and then ran past him, leaving the opener stranded by several yards. In nine balls the West Indies had lost three major wickets for 2 runs.

The West Indian batsmen were less able to cope with the stress of the situation than England, and Lloyd and Kanhai fell to Greig, who once more seized the moment. There remained the problem of Sobers, who displayed all the pedigree of his ninety-three Test matches in an innings which mocked the dithering and uncertainty of his colleagues. He and Murray, who also displayed an excellent temperament, added 50 before Sobers went forward to Underwood, played over the ball and was bowled. Underwood had not had a good tour, but with this vital wicket he had earned his place in the team. Almost immediately, Julien fell to Pocock, and when Murray drove at Greig to be caught at slip the West Indies were 166 for eight.

The battle was far from over. Boyce was a forceful batsman, as many of Essex's opponents had discovered, and Inshan Ali showed remarkable composure, helping to add 31 in an hour. After much consultation with Greig and Fletcher, Denness decided to take the new ball. Inshan Ali went for a big hit and was caught at deep mid-off at a time when he needed only to push for singles. Arnold bowled Gibbs, Boyce was left stranded, and England had won by 26 runs, a remarkable victory which levelled the series.

Greig's Match

West Indies v England at Queen's Park Oval, Port of Spain, Trinidad
30, 31 March, 2, 3, 4 and 5 April 1974

England First Innings		Second Innings	
G. Boycott c Murray b Julien	99	b Gibbs 112	
D.L. Amiss c M Kanhai b Sobers ..	44	b Lloyd	16
M.H. Denness (capt) c Fredericks b Ali	13	run out	4
K.W.R. Fletcher c Kanhai b Gibbs .	6	b Julien	45
A.W. Greig lbw b Gibbs	19	(6) c Fredericks b Julien .	1
F.C. Hayes c Rowe b Ali	24	(7) lbw b Julien	0
†A.P.E. Knott not out	33	(8) lbw b Sobers	44
J. Birkenshaw c Lloyd b Julien	8	(9) c Gibbs b Ali	7
G.G. Arnold run out	6	(10) b Sobers	13
P.I. Pocock c Lloyd b Ali	0	(5) c Kallicharran b Boyce	5
D.L. Underwood b Gibbs	4	not out	1
Extras (b 2, lb 3, nb 6)	11	(lb 4, nb 11)	15
Total	267	263	

BOWLING	Overs	Mdns	Runs	Wkts	Overs	Mdns	Runs	Wkts
Boyce	10	3	14	–	12	3	40	1
Julien	21	8	35	2	22	7	31	3
Sobers	31	16	44	1	24.2	9	36	2
Inshan Ali	35	12	86	3	34	12	51	1
Gibbs	34.3	10	70	3	50	15	85	1
Lloyd	4	2	7	–	7	4	5	1

fall of wickets
1–83, 2–144, 3–133, 4-165, 5–204, 6–212, 7–244, 8–257, 9–260
1–39, 2–44, 3–145, 4–169, 5–174, 6–176, 7–213, 8–226, 9–258

West Indies First Innings		Second Innings	
R.C. Fredericks c Fletcher b Pocock	67	run out	36
L.G. Rowe c Boycott b Greig	123	lbw b Birkenshaw	25
A.I. Kallicharran c and b Pocock ..	0	c Fletcher b Greig	0
C.H. Lloyd c Knott b Greig	52	c and b Greig	13
G. St A. Sobers c Birkenshaw b Greig	0	(6) b Underwood	20
R.B. Kanhai (capt) c and b Greig ..	2	(5) c Fletcher b Greig ...	7
†D.L. Murray c Pocock b Greig ...	2	c Fletcher b Greig	33
B.D. Julien c Birkenshaw b Greig ..	17	c Denness b Pocock	2
K.D. Boyce c Pocock b Greig	19	not out	34
Inshan Ali lbw b Greig	5	c Underwood b Greig ..	15
L.R. Gibbs not out	0	b Arnold	1

Extras (b 11, lb 4, nb 3) 18   (b 9, lb 2, nb 2) 13

Total 305 199

BOWLING	Overs	Mdns	Runs	Wkts	Overs	Mdns	Runs	Wkts
Arnold	8	–	27	–	5.3	1	13	1
Greig	36.1	10	86	8	33	7	70	5
Pocock	31	7	86	2	25	7	60	1
Underwood	34	12	57	–	15	7	19	1
Birkenshaw	8	1	31	–	10	1	24	1

fall of wickets
1–110, 2–122, 3–224, 4–224, 5–226, 6–232, 7–270, 8–300, 9–300
1–63, 2–64, 3–65, 4–84, 5–85, 6–135, 7–138, 8–166, 9–197
umpires – S. Ishmael and D. Sang Hue
England won by 26 runs

John Woodcock, cricket correspondent of *The Times*, was unequivocal in his choice of Man of the Series:

> With another titanic display Tony Greig made the victory possible. His 13 wickets in the match for 156 runs, coming after all that he had done at Bridgetown and Georgetown, made him the man of the series, above even Amiss and Rowe. It is hard to think that anyone has ever had a much greater all-round influence on three successive Test matches than Greig.

Praise for England's win was grudging, for they had been outplayed for most of the series, the West Indies were unquestionably the stronger and better side, and it seemed a travesty of justice that England had escaped with a drawn series. There are qualities that are greater than flair and technical ability, however: determination and resilience, and England had shown them in abundance. The two great escapes were, in themselves, astonishing performances and deserved the highest praise. John Woodcock was right when he summed up the Caribbean expedition by saying, 'In some ways the tour had created more problems than it had solved – but it had proved again that England's cricketers never know when they are beaten.'

What were these problems that had been created?

In the first instance there was the question of captaincy. The selectors had done Denness no favours by thrusting him into the job of leading a side on a difficult tour without playing him in one home Test the previous summer. He started from the handicap of being labelled a batsman short of Test class, and he did little in the series to convince people that

267

the description was unfair. He had led the side admirably in the final Test, but his lack of awareness and organisation had been painfully apparent before then.

In contrast Greig, his lieutenant, had flourished. Greig anticipated Ian Botham in the way he played his cricket: whatever he did demanded a response. He was capable of enraging a crowd, but he could quickly turn that rage to laughter. He had the ability to charm, and he gave his all to every aspect of the game and to England. He outlived the diplomatic catastrophe of his action in the first Test to become a favourite and the undisputed hero of the tour.

Greig's triumphs underlined England's second unsolved problem. Who but he was capable of bowling out a Test side as strong (and as packed with left-handers) as the West Indies? In the Test series Greig had taken twenty-four wickets at 22.62 runs each. Second to him was Jack Birkenshaw, a useful and thoughtful cricketer, whose two wickets cost him 48 runs each and whose Test career ended with this series. No other bowler had an average under 50; none took more than nine wickets.

For the batting, Amiss had done spectacularly well, Fletcher had battled bravely and Boycott had succeeded through sheer application after an uncertain start, but these were mature players. The young batsmen, Hayes and Jameson, had been bitterly disappointing.

In 1974 there were other concerns regarding the game in general. Worldwide, there were hints that sledging had become endemic and that it occasionally had racial overtones.

For players and counties, there was the increasing problem that the growth in the number of international fixtures was making greater and greater demands. Six Test matches and four one-day internationals meant that Tony Greig missed eleven of the twenty Championship games played by Sussex in 1974, and other counties were similarly handicapped.

Preceding the heavy international programme, there was a Test trial, an exercise which had long since ceased to have meaning. This match was played at Worcester at the end of May and saw Boycott hit a century in each innings and John Edrich hit 106 and 95. Tony Lewis captained The Rest, but his form fell away during the season and he announced his retirement in July.

The County Championship was reconstructed yet again with the two first innings limited to 200 overs. Should the side batting first be bowled out inside 100 overs, then the unused overs could be added to the innings of the side batting second. Bonus points were now restricted to four batting and four bowling points, and play in each match was extended by one hour by making the starting time on the first two days 11.00 a.m.

The Championship was won, somewhat fortuitously, by Worcestershire. The reigning champions, Hampshire, led the table for most of the season, but, hit by bad weather, they failed to win a game after the first week in August. Their final match was abandoned without a ball being bowled while Worcestershire, at Chelmsford, had sufficient time to bowl out Essex for 84 and so gain four bonus points which gave them the title by a margin of two points. Norman Gifford, the captain, took seven for 15 against Essex, but Worcestershire's principal strength was in their overseas quartet, Turner, Headley, the New Zealander Parker and Holder.

Holder was one of three overseas bowlers to finish in the top four of the national averages; the two bowlers to claim a hundred wickets were Andy Roberts, top with 119 wickets at 13.62 runs each, and Bishan Bedi. The top three places in the batting averages were all filled by overseas players: Clive Lloyd, Barry Richards and Glenn Turner.

Kent maintained their one-day success by beating Lancashire in the Gillette Cup Final when the match was decided on the Monday, and Leicestershire had another success, winning the John Player League. Ray Illingworth continued to be a source of inspiration, and another Yorkshire exile, Brian Close, brought Somerset to within two points of their first ever honour. They were thwarted when their last Sunday League game, against Leicestershire, was abandoned because of rain. Interestingly, Close, having voiced his disapproval of limited-overs cricket, particularly the forty-over variety, won a special award for establishing a new league record by hitting nineteen sixes in the season.

Leicestershire came close to winning two trophies, for they were beaten by 27 runs by Surrey in the Benson and Hedges Cup Final in spite of a hat-trick from Ken Higgs, once of Lancashire. Illingworth had demonstrated the changing philosophy of the one-day game by preferring a young medium-pacer, Booth, to the Test off-spinner Birkenshaw. The Gold Award in the final went to the Surrey captain, John Edrich, who was back in the England side.

He and Fletcher hit centuries in the first Test against India, a Test which England won and in which Mike Hendrick made his debut. And so to Lord's, where Amiss, Denness and Greig made centuries and Edrich hit 96 in England's total of 629. This time there was victory by an innings, as there was at Edgbaston where David Lloyd, playing in his second Test match, hit 214 not out. He and Denness, 100, put on 211 for the second wicket, and England lost only two wickets in the whole match. Tony Greig finished sixth in the Test batting averages against

India, and he averaged 79.50.

Pakistan offered a sterner challenge and all three Tests were drawn, although England would certainly have won the first two if rain had not prevented any play on the final days. At Lord's, on a damp pitch (rain had seeped under the covers), Underwood took five for 20 and eight for 51. In the second innings he had a spell of six for 2 in fifty-one balls. England needed 60 on the last day with all their wickets intact, but no play was possible.

Pakistan did best at The Oval where Zaheer Abbas scored 240 of their 600 for seven declared, but England made 545, with Amiss and Fletcher getting hundreds.

In spite of England's successful summer, there was a frustration with Test cricket as one match followed another in an interminable pattern. The public was less than enamoured by twin tours, and, with the weather poor, the amount distributed to counties from Test receipts dropped by £135,000. Several counties faced acute financial problems, and Middlesex even talked of bankruptcy.

There were good days for the counties – Kanhai and Jameson scored 465 in 100 overs for Warwickshire's second-wicket against Gloucestershire at Edgbaston in July – but there was also a feeling that first-class cricket was growing further away from its roots. County games were no longer staged at places like Clacton, Frome or Hinckley as attempts were made to cut costs, and the days had gone when a county would turn to a leading club player to join the side in August. These changes were almost imperceptible at a time when the main talking point was Geoff Boycott.

His reign as Yorkshire captain was not going well, and the White Rose county struggled from season to season. He retained aspirations of becoming captain of England, although when he informed Alec Bedser of his willingness to lead the side, it had been implied to him that his name was not even under consideration. He enjoyed a record benefit in excess of £20,000 in 1974 and played in the first Test against India, scoring 10 and 6. He asked not to be considered thereafter, and there were rumours that he was unwilling to play under Denness, whom he considered a lesser cricketer than himself. Boycott remained the leading English batsman in the country, and when the party of sixteen to tour Australia under Denness's captaincy was announced it was no surprise that Yorkshire's opening batsman was high on the list.

There were some surprises, though: Tony Greig was in the party but had been replaced as vice-captain by John Edrich. No reason was given for this, but the general view was that Greig was too independent a voice, a controversial character who was prone to publicise his own opinions. It was believed that Snow had suffered exclusion from the party for similar reasons.

The choice of Peter Lever ahead of Snow was scarcely justifiable, either on quality or on current form. One cynical reason given by some on the county circuit for Lever's inclusion was that he had bowled well on television. He had not played in any of the Tests against India or Pakistan. The pace attack in those matches was in the hands of Willis, Hendrick, Old and Arnold, all of whom were in the side to tour Australia, even though Arnold had been suspended for two county matches for showing dissent in a Sunday League game when the umpire gave a leg-side wide against him.

The spin attack was limited to the expertise of Underwood and Titmus, recalled to the England side for the first time since his boating accident in Barbados almost seven years earlier.

Nearly a month after the team was announced Boycott withdrew from the party on the grounds that he was still suffering from the pressures and tensions of international cricket and felt unable to stand up to the rigours of an Australian tour. Others offered less charitable excuses on his behalf. Ray Illingworth, in one of those unfortunate public outbursts that were to mar his period as chairman of selectors twenty years later, was quoted in the *Sun* as criticising Denness: 'In the West Indies he handled the England side very badly. It was more like Fred Karno's army, and Denness was at fault. I don't blame Geoff for not fancying being a part of a repeat performance this winter.'

Illingworth's voice was a lone one. *Wisden* felt that it was about time that Boycott came to terms with himself, and Fred Titmus described Boycott's withdrawal as unforgivable, commenting that many cricketers would have paid their own fare to Australia for the honour of wearing an England sweater.

Brian Luckhurst was drafted in as Boycott's replacement. The Yorkshireman's self-imposed exile was to last three years and embrace thirty Test matches, but he was to survive this and other wayward antics for which lesser men would have suffered permanent ostracism. Boycott has ever been a survivor.

For England, the 1974–75 tour of Australia was a total disaster. Initially they were taken completely by surprise by the attack with which they were confronted. Dennis Lillee had suffered a back injury when playing against the West Indies and had spent some time with his back in plaster. There were some doubts as to whether he would be able to play again, and all were convinced that he would never be able to generate the pace with which he had formerly troubled such English batsmen as

271

Edrich. Although good reports abounded regarding the medium-pacer Max Walker, Australia appeared to lack both a replacement for Lillee and any bowler of quality to share the new ball with him.

It was soon apparent from the early Sheffield Shield matches that Lillee was fit and was bowling quickly. Selected to open the bowling with him in the first Test was Jeff Thomson, who had moved to Queensland from New South Wales because he had been unable to hold a regular place in the latter state side. He had, in fact, played in a Test match against Pakistan two years earlier when he bowled nineteen overs and had taken nought for 110.

Lillee and Thomson attacked psychologically as well as physically, and they both went into print asserting that they used the bouncer in an effort to hit batsmen and so intimidate them. There was nothing unusual in a war of words, but Australia had the artillery with which to back up the statements. Thomson was lethal. The pitch at Brisbane offered uneven bounce – it had been prepared by the Lord Mayor – and Thomson, who bowled with a slinging action that was perfectly legal, was able to make the ball rear off a length even on a good surface. His pace devastated England, who lost four wickets in the first two hours of their innings after bowling Australia out for 309. That England came to within 44 of the home side's total was due almost entirely to Tony Greig, who hit a memorable, if eccentric, 110. He was wild on occasions, hit some wonderful shots through the covers, and attempted to provoke an unsettled Lillee and the other Australian bowlers by shadow-boxing under bouncers. Amiss and Edrich both sustained injuries. Edrich had a bone broken in his right hand in the over before he was out, and Amiss suffered a broken thumb. In the second innings they both became victims of Thomson's explosive deliveries, and the Queensland pace man had six for 46, finishing with nine for 105 in the match.

Australia were alight; England were nearly in shreds. No blame could be put on Denness, who had fielded magnificently and who had handled his bowling attack well, although, on occasions, it seemed that there was more than one captain on the field. Denness's problem was simply that Ian Chappell had so much more power at his disposal.

England were already in need of repairs. The injuries to Edrich and Amiss had reduced the number of specialist batsmen to four (plus the all-rounder Greig) and, in one Test match, Lillee and Thomson had sent shivers through the England camp, emphatically changing the psychological balance of the series. England's response was to call for reinforcement, in the form of Colin Cowdrey.

Cowdrey was forty-two years old and had not played Test cricket for nearly four years. As E.W. Swanton reported, the Australians 'were mystified that Cowdrey should want to come under fire again at his time of life'. It was not a step that they themselves would have taken.

In responding to the SOS, Cowdrey was equalling a record in that this was his sixth tour of Australia. Within four days of arriving he was playing in the second Test at Perth. He performed heroically, ducking the barrage of bouncers, calming the pace men and hitting 22 and 41, but England lost by nine wickets. Thomson claimed another seven wickets to add to the nine he had in the first Test. This time he hit Luckhurst on the hand, and the Kent man batted number seven in the second innings with Cowdrey opening.

It was not just the pace of Lillee and Thomson that routed England but the magnificent way that they were supported in the field. The catching in the slip and gully area was outstanding, and, at Perth, Greg Chappell established a Test record by holding seven catches.

The Australian first innings owed much to Walters and Edwards, who added 170 for the fifth wicket. Walters scored a hundred between tea and the close of play on the second day. He reached his century by hooking the last ball of the day flat over square-leg for six. The unlucky bowler was Bob Willis, who had a good series in spite of suffering knee problems which kept him out of the sixth Test and the matches in New Zealand. It was his sight of Lillee and Thomson on this tour that made him vow that England should have a fast bowler who could fight fire with fire, and his day was to come.

At Melbourne he showed his growing stature by taking five for 61 and bowling England to a 1-run first-innings lead. At twenty-five he was the youngest man in the party.

The Melbourne Test ended dramatically. Amiss made a superb 90 in the second innings and put on 115 for the first wicket with David Lloyd. This should have put England in a strong position, but of the later batsmen only Greig, 60, came to terms with Thomson, Lillee and Mallett, and Australia had more than a day in which to score 246 to win. They began the last day with 4 runs on the board, but lost Edwards and Ian Chappell for the addition of 1. Nevertheless, they seemed to be cruising to victory when they required 55 from the last fifteen mandatory overs with four wickets standing. Greig bowled splendidly, and he dismissed Marsh and Lillee to leave Australia on 235 for eight. He bowled the thirteenth over of the fifteen and conceded only two singles. Underwood followed this with a maiden, and Australia, perhaps afraid of losing, finished 8 runs short of their target, even though Hendrick had broken down in the third over of the match and did not bowl at all in the second innings.

Luckhurst and Fletcher, who had suffered more than most at the

273

hands of the pace men, had been omitted from the Melbourne Test, but Fletcher was recalled for the fourth Test when Denness took the brave and unexpected step of dropping himself. John Edrich led the side, but he could not stop Australia recapturing the Ashes. He made 50 in the first innings and was forced to retire in the second after being hit in the ribs first ball by Lillee. He returned after a visit to hospital which revealed two fractures, and battled two and a half hours for 33 not out in an attempt to save the game. Willis and Arnold gave staunch support, but Australia won by 171 runs.

Most of England's runs in the series came from Greig and Knott, numbers six and seven in the order, but Knott's century at Adelaide could not prevent Australia's fourth win in five Tests. Thomson injured himself playing tennis during the rest day and could not bowl in the second innings, but his thirty-three wickets in nine innings emphasised his effect on the outcome of the series.

He was unable to play in the final Test, while Lillee bruised his right foot and only bowled six overs, by which time he had dismissed Amiss to claim his twenty-fifth wicket of the series. Untroubled by the pair who had tormented them, England scored 529, having earlier bowled out Australia for 152. Peter Lever had taken six for 38.

Max Walker had eight wickets in England's innings, but the stars were Fletcher, 146, and Denness, 188, who added 192 for the fourth wicket. England won by an innings.

This was Colin Cowdrey's 114th and last Test, and when he left the international scene he had scored more runs than any other English batsman and established a world record with 120 catches. He had faced some bitter disappointments, but he had 'done the state some service'.

Like Cowdrey, Titmus and David Lloyd ended their Test careers on the tour of Australia. Bruised and battered, Lloyd returned to England, and Barry Wood flew to New Zealand to replace him.

The New Zealand leg of the tour provided the ultimate ironies. In the first Test at Auckland Denness and Fletcher followed their partnership in the final Test in Australia with a fourth-wicket stand of 266. Both men had looked unhappy against the pace of Lillee and Thomson, but against a slighter New Zealand attack Denness hit a sparkling 181 and Fletcher an equally scintillating 216. Barry Wood, having arrived three days earlier after a 63-hour flight, was out first ball.

Greig continued his mastery with ten wickets in a match which ended little over three-quarters of an hour into the final day's play. New Zealand faced an innings defeat at 140 for nine, but Geoff Howarth and Ewen Chatfield, both playing in their first Test match, delayed the inevitable with a stand of 44. In an attempt to dislodge Chatfield, Peter

Lever bowled a bouncer which the number eleven deflected into his left temple. He collapsed, and for a few seconds his heart stopped beating. The England physiotherapist Bernard Thomas acted quickly, applying heart massage and mouth-to-mouth resuscitation. Thomas's expertise saved Chatfield's life, and the New Zealander, who had sustained a hairline fracture of the skull, was back in Test cricket two years later.

The tempestuous pace of Lillee and Thomson had broken bones and caused discomfort, but the gentler pace of Peter Lever had brought a batsman close to death. The speed, aggression and liberal use of the bouncer by the Australian and West Indian fast bowlers in particular had become more dangerous and more threatening to the game as a whole than had been the leg theory, or 'bodyline', of Larwood and Voce in the early 1930s, yet now there was no flurry of diplomatic activity, nor did authority seem capable of exerting control.

Certainly, the Australians lost friends when they beat Sri Lanka, not then a Test-playing country, in a World Cup match at The Oval in June 1975. Facing a massive target of 329 in sixty overs, Sri Lanka batted bravely and made 276 for four, cutting and hooking a relentless battery of short-pitched bowling. Mendis was struck on the head by a ball from Thomson, and Wettimuny deflected a rising ball into his body. Batting with a runner, he was hit on the instep and as he staggered in pain Thomson attempted to run him out. Both batsmen were taken to hospital.

This was a lone blight on an inaugural competition which was highly successful. Sponsored by Prudential Assurance Company to the extent of £100,000, the first World Cup doubled that sum in gate receipts. Some 158,000 people watched the fifteen matches which were played between 7 and 21 June. If only Ben Brocklehurst's original idea had been taken up, cricket might not have been struggling for six years for economic survival.

The opening match at Lord's drew a crowd of 20,000, and with Amiss scoring a century England reached 334 for four in their sixty overs. In response India, who had omitted Bedi, gave a disgraceful batting display, making 132 for three in their sixty overs with Gavaskar batting throughout the innings for 36. He was severely censured and later offered an apology.

On the same day at Headingley the doubts that were expressed to Brocklehurst as to whether the British public would be interested in a match between two visiting nations were firmly answered when the gates were closed for the first time in nine years. The match was between Australia and Pakistan.

England met Australia in the semi-final at Headingley ten days later and, incomprehensibly, on the same strip that had been used for the Australia–Pakistan game. Worn and watered, it provided an ideal surface for swing bowling in a heavy atmosphere. Gary Gilmour, left-arm fast-medium, was in his element and bowled an uninterrupted spell of twelve overs in which he took six for 14. England were out for 93, but Old and Snow, back in favour temporarily, helped reduce Australia to 39 for six before Gilmour joined Edwards to win the match.

A crowd of 26,000 paid £66,950 to see the West Indies beat Australia by 17 runs in a glorious Lord's final which lasted from 11.00 a.m. until 8.43 p.m.

The World Cup brought about a great change in the thinking regarding limited-overs international cricket. The matches began to proliferate and, given further impetus by the activities of a media tycoon, they would eventually outnumber Test matches by four to one.

For the time being, however, England's fate was concerned again with an Ashes series. The casualties following the traumas in Australia were primarily selectors. Wheatley and Bond were not able to continue in their positions, and Brian Taylor failed to gain re-election. Sir Leonard Hutton, Ken Barrington and the umpire Charlie Elliott joined Alec Bedser, who remained as chairman.

Bedser was to have a long reign which transcended several cricketing crises, but he tended to do his job and not make public pronouncements or displays. There was no panic purge after the rout in Australia. There were two players in the side for the first of the four Tests who had not been on the Australian tour, and one of them was John Snow, hero of many a battle. The other was Graham Gooch.

Gooch had first appeared for Essex in a Sunday League game in 1973 when he had neither batted nor bowled. When he first played for England he was a fortnight short of his twenty-second birthday and had barely one full first-class season behind him. The century he scored for Essex against Kent at Colchester at the beginning of June was the second of his career. His Test debut turned out to be a disaster, but the selectors should have been commended for the vision that they displayed in recognising a remarkable talent.

It was a year in which other talents began to blossom. *Wisden* said of the nineteen-year-old Ian Botham of Somerset that he 'continued his development as a useful seam bowler of increasing pace, while his brilliant fielding and batting laden with potential make him a great asset'. Leicestershire, who had the best season in their history, winning the Championship for the first time and taking the Benson and Hedges Cup for the second time in four years, included an exciting prospect in their

276

ranks for three matches, David Gower. He also appeared in the John Player League, which was won by Hampshire, and advanced his cause against some unsuspecting counties.

Stuart Turner recalled playing against him for Essex at Grace Road at a time when the Home County were very much in with a chance of winning the Sunday League. They captured the first five Leicestershire wickets for 81 runs, and, as Turner said, 'We weren't worried about getting the fair-headed left-hander out. He was a youngster, and we never thought he would score quickly. It was better to leave him in.' Gower got 57 not out, and Leicestershire won by 56 runs.

There was no such happy result for Gooch at Edgbaston. There was a crucial decision made on the first day for which Denness took all the blame. He won the toss and invited Australia to bat first. It is hard to think that Denness made this decision without discussing it with Bedser, other selectors or senior players. As John Woodcock wrote:

> Denness's decision to put Australia in to bat, on an overcast Edgbaston morning, is assured of a permanent place among the game's great disasters. At the time it seemed a not unreasonable chance to take; but the ball never moved about, at the start of the match, as Denness and his bowlers had hoped it would, and no sooner had England started their own first innings, on the second afternoon, than a heavy storm committed them to batting on a pitch that was wet on top and hard underneath. By the close of that day England, at 83 for 7, were doomed to follow on, which they duly did, 258 runs behind.

Australia won by an innings and 85 runs just after three o'clock on the fourth afternoon. Gooch lasted three balls in the first innings and seven in the second. He was caught behind off Walker in the first innings, and off Thomson in the second. One of the great careers of modern Test cricket had begun with a 'pair'.

It was later said that Denness's decision when he won the toss was entirely his own, that Hutton had believed the pitch was full of runs and that Bedser had stood aside and offered neither advice nor influence. Denness was doomed. His scores of 3 and 8 and his inability to cope with Lillee, Thomson and Walker, allied to his 'great disaster', put him in an untenable position. He offered to stand down, and Tony Greig became England's captain.

Greig, it will be remembered, had been deposed as vice-captain for the tour of Australia, and John Edrich had led England when Denness decided to drop himself from the Sydney Test. Edrich led a Surrey side which recovered well after a poor start to the season while Greig's

Sussex finished bottom of the Championship. Edrich had come to captaincy through seniority and consistent application. Greig's ascent to leadership was a product of his flair. From the time when he had toured India and Pakistan with Tony Lewis's side he had displayed the mark of a man destined to captain England. He had the bonus of being the people's choice.

Fair-haired, six feet seven inches tall, he was a dominant figure in every respect. A dashing cricketer, desperately eager to succeed and always in a hurry, he exuded confidence and relished a fight. Handsome and brave, he had a personality that could charm and he possessed the power to entertain. He had developed a style of batting that saw him lift the bat above stump height as the bowler approached, and he was constantly looking to drive, which he did often with might and glory. His career was dotted with controversy because he was as multi-faceted as he was multi-talented and, from time to time, there were demons below the surface; although not all were of his own making. We view our public figures with little thought to the man or woman behind the accepted image, and if they show human frailty, we are quick to turn upon them for not fulfilling our dreams or our ideals.

In truth the public knew little of Tony Greig, and they certainly could not fully comprehend such news items as that of April 1975, which told how he 'suffered severe facial abrasions when he collapsed at Heathrow Airport upon his return from South Africa, where he had played for Derrick Robins' XI at the end of their tour. He was treated at Hillingdon Hospital and kept overnight for observation at the Royal Sussex County Hospital, but returned home the following day, saying he felt fully recovered after some exhausting travel.' It was to be another three years, after the storm broke, that the public would learn that Greig suffered from a form of epilepsy.

He was to endure the criticism from some quarters that he should not captain England because he was South African. That he was born and educated in South Africa and had learned his cricket there was indisputable, but the implication that he should not represent England irked his father in particular. 'Sandy' Greig had been a flight commander with Bomber Command, had flown two arduous tours and completed more missions than the RAF considered either desirable or possible. He had won the DSO and DFC, and, towards the end of the Second World War, he was posted to the Empire Air Navigation School in South Africa where his expertise could be used as an instructor and where he would be prevented from undertaking any more missions. Fate had decreed that he should marry and settle in South Africa, but he still had the right to feel that his sons were eligible to play for

278

England, even though he was a Scotsman.

The whole question of qualification was, to say the least, somewhat bizarre. In May 1966 it was reported that Tony Greig, along with Basharat Hassan of Nottinghamshire, had begun his twenty-four month residential qualification period. At the beginning of the following year Greig appealed against the imposition of the two-year term on the grounds that an amendment had been brought in which allowed crick-eters in his position to serve a one-year period of qualification. His appeal was upheld and he made his Championship debut a few months later.

This was not the end of the matter. In April 1968 the registration committee was asked to reconsider Greig's status and to approve the Sussex claim that he was English-born. The evidence in support of Greig was that his father had a family business in the United Kingdom which he visited at regular intervals and that Greig himself was now the holder of a British passport and was permanently resident in the United Kingdom. The appeal was rejected. The committee agreed unanimously that Greig could not be considered an English-born cricketer until he had resided permanently in the country for the required period of five years.

In October 1973 the committee was again asked to reconsider Greig's position. Again they ruled that under the existing regulations Greig was an overseas player. At that time he had already represented England in nineteen Tests.

This, then, was the background to the new England captain. Bedser was to offer the opinion that he thought that Greig was the best captain England had during his period of chairmanship. Hutton, whose time as a selector was brief, felt that Greig was a little too sure of himself. Sir Leonard did not recognise that this was one of Greig's strengths. He knew who he wanted in his team, and although he tended to captain emotionally – you either attacked or defended – he was an inspiring leader and his own contribution with bat and ball breathed new life into English cricket.

He succeeded in drawing the three remaining matches of the Ashes series. Each game was touched by heroism and strange incidents, and there were three new faces in the England team.

At Lord's Gooch was retained, and David Steele and Bob Woolmer were introduced. Steele was a grey-haired, bespectacled right-handed batsman from Northamptonshire. He was thirty-four and was a solid, gritty player who bowled slow left-arm to augment his batting. He was always considered an average county cricketer, but he seized the oppor-tunities offered by a short Test career to the extent of becoming a

279

television sports personality of the year. Woolmer was chosen primarily as a medium-pace bowler who was a very dependable late middle-order batsman.

Wood, Edrich, Amiss and Gooch were all out for single figures, and Greig strode to the wicket to join Steele with England 49 for four, and the match only seventy-five minutes old. Greig gave a pulsating display, hitting 96 in two and a half hours. Steele, playing forward at every opportunity, hit 50. Woolmer and Knott did well, and England scored 315. They then reduced Australia to 81 for seven before Lillee joined Edwards, who made 99, and hit the highest score of his career, 73 not out. England led by 47 and soon moved into a strong position. Wood and Edrich put on 111 for the first wicket, Edrich and Steele added 104 for the second. Edrich made 175 off 420 balls, the last of his twelve Test hundreds, and Greig's declaration left Australia a target of 484 in 500 minutes. They finished on 329 for three.

The match became famous as it was the first time a streaker appeared on the field at Lord's. It was a match that had more significance in restoring the faith of England supporters. In the *Cricketer*, John Woodcock wrote:

> For the first three days the gates were closed. I don't remember a Test match in which an English crowd identified itself more enthusiastically with England's fortunes. After the winter's privations, every run was cheered, every wicket too.

After Lord's, Gooch's Test career was put on hold for three years. John Hampshire, for the last time, and Fletcher returned, and a first cap was given to Phil Edmonds, the left-arm Middlesex spinner and former Cambridge University captain, who was a fine fielder and a very useful batsman. In his first twelve overs in Test cricket, he took five wickets for 17 runs. England led by 153 on the first innings, and Steele made 92 as they scored 291 in their second. Australia ended the fourth day on 220 for three, and the game was interestingly poised, but when the players arrived at Headingley the following morning they found that the ground had been vandalised. The Football Ground End of the pitch had been mutilated with oil and knives, and no play was possible.

Throughout London at that time, one was confronted by a statement painted in large white letters on walls, bridges and buildings proclaiming that George Davis was innocent and that we should ask O'Mahoney. Davis was serving a seventeen-year prison sentence, and the campaign of sign-writing was part of a protest demanding his release. These campaigners vandalised the pitch at Leeds, apologising for their action

280

but claiming that they needed to bring their plea for justice to a wider audience.

Davis was released from prison in May 1976, after serving one year of his seventeen-year sentence. Sixteen months later, he was arrested after a bank raid, and in 1978 he was given fifteen years for robbery. He could argue that he had made his mark on Test cricket.

The final Test of the series, at The Oval, was the last in England to be allotted six days. It was drawn after England had staged a fightback of heroic proportions. Bowled out for 191 on the fourth morning, they followed on 341 runs in arrears. The England batsmen displayed great tenacity and batted into the sixth day. Edrich scored 96, Steele 66, Roope 77, which was his highest Test innings, and Knott 64. The main saviour was Bob Woolmer, who showed immense powers of concentration in taking 394 minutes to reach his first Test century. He was last out, having made 149 out of England's 538. Australia had eighty-five minutes in which to score 198. They were 40 for two, and the extra half-hour was not claimed.

A season which had begun in gloom had ended with England in a far happier state of mind. The sun had shone, big profits had been made, although many counties still remained in financial difficulties, and Greig had lifted English cricket from the depths. On the domestic front Leicestershire had surprised Hampshire, a powerful batting side and winners of the Sunday League, in the semi-final of the Benson and Hedges Cup and had gone on to win the trophy for the second time. They beat Middlesex in the final, and Middlesex had the unhappy experience of losing the Gillette Cup Final as well. There they were conquered by Lancashire, who won the cup for the fourth time in seven years.

Disappointed as they must have been, Middlesex could take comfort in the resurgence of their cricket under the leadership of Mike Brearley.

Brearley had been appointed captain of the county in 1971. There was opposition to his appointment because many felt that Parfitt was being badly treated and that Brearley was not a good enough cricketer. This may seem a strange assessment of one who had come from Cambridge where he had captained the side for two years with a record aggregate for a university career. He had toured South Africa with MCC and had led an MCC under-25 team in Pakistan, 1966–67, scoring 312 not out against North Zone at Peshawar.

An outstanding scholar, he missed the seasons of 1966 and 1967 when he was pursuing further academic studies, and for the three seasons 1968 to 1970 he played only in the holiday period. He had been approached by both Warwickshire and Worcestershire with a view to

281

captaincy, but the Middlesex committee, particularly Mike Murray and Charles Robins, recognised his value to their county and persuaded him to remain at Lord's. He agreed to give up his job in Newcastle where he was teaching philosophy and to play cricket full time.

In his own words, 'It was the idea of captaincy that led me back to Middlesex. I like to be bossy. I hate to get bored. I want to be doing something all the time, and the tactics of the game fascinated me. I liked the idea of the inter-relation with people, and, above all, I like trying to get the best out of people.'

A lesser man would not have succeeded in the task with which Brearley was entrusted. When he took over the captaincy he had not scored a Championship century, nor scored a thousand runs in a season for Middlesex. It took him until 1973 to do either, but he began to bridge the gap between the experienced and less experienced in the Middlesex side and to establish an equality of structure which lifted morale and heightened performance. To lead Middlesex to two finals in 1975, John Murray's last season, was the first sign of what he was accomplishing. Greater things lay ahead.

One of Brearley's priorities with Middlesex was to obtain the services of a mature and proven overseas cricketer. While Venkataraghavan, Majid Khan, Asif Iqbal and Bishan Bedi graced the county circuit, and such talents as Clive Rice, Ken McEwan and Viv Richards had burst upon the scene, Middlesex were employing Larry Gomes, a shy, nervous teenager of great charm but little experience. He was a player of considerable potential, who was to play Test cricket in 1976, but with Middlesex he was learning his trade. What the county needed was a Sarfraz Nawaz, the Pakistani pace bowler operating with Northamptonshire, a bowler who could take 100 wickets in a season.

Middlesex found such a player when the West Indies came to England in 1976, although Wayne Daniel was never quite to emulate Sarfraz in taking 100 wickets in a season. But neither Daniel nor Gomes was in the Middlesex side that carried off the Championship in 1976. When one considers the significant part overseas cricketers had played in the successes of such counties as Lancashire, Hampshire, Kent and Leicestershire, Middlesex's achievement under Brearley was most praiseworthy.

There was a four-pronged bowling attack in Selvey, Allan Jones, Edmonds and Titmus, while Radley, Barlow and Brearley gave the batting backbone and consistency. Allan Jones was a fiery fast bowler who had been acquired from Somerset. He played for four counties and had his brushes with authority. When he retired he became a respected umpire, poacher turned gamekeeper. Brearley and Selvey found their

Cowdrey and Sobers toss up at
Lord's, 1966. Cowdrey was
deposed as captain by the end of the
series.

Close, captain in the final Test, 1966,
celebrates England's victory with
Gary Sobers.

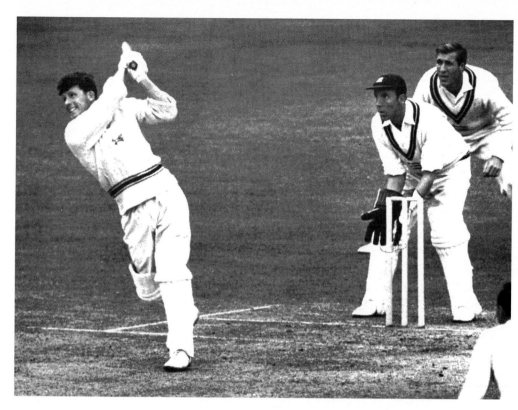

Middlesex v Leicestershire, Lord's, 1966. Booth hits out while Murray and Parfitt, Middlesex's England players, look on. Murray, an immaculate wicket-keeper, scored a century for England against West Indies in 1966, while Parfitt, a brilliant fielder, had scored a host of runs against Pakistan four years earlier.

Parfitt is bowled by Oakman of Sussex. The wicket-keeper is the England player Jim parks.

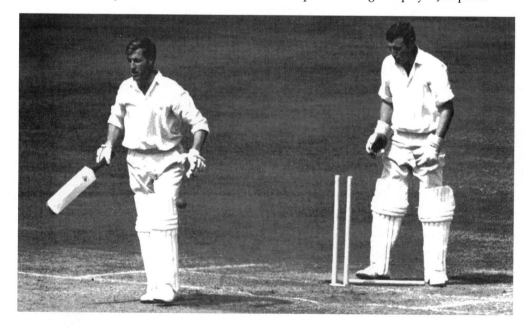

Alan Knott, Kent and England, square cuts a ball for four.

Basil D'Oliveira, a man of dignity at the centre of controversy. Arnold Long of Surrey is the wicket-keeper.

Eric Russell, Middlesex's stylish opening batsman who was never quite able to establish a permanent place in the England side and was desperately unlucky with injury. Here he is caught behind.

In 1968, counties were allowed to contract an overseas player. Essex turned to the hard-hitting Lee Irvine, a South African, who later broke the news of the Packer rebellion.

Bill Lawry, the Australian captain, and Ray Illingworth, the England captain, share a drink after England's victory at Sydney, January, 1961. England won the series.

One of the best of county cricketers never to win a full England cap, Glamorgan's Alan Jones.

Richard Hutton, son
of Sir Leonard, has
Engineer caught by
Illingworth,
England v India,
1961.

Hutton strikes again
as Viswanath is
caught behind by
Knott. Amiss is at
slip.

Another victim for Knott. John Snow is the bowler.

Mike Procter in action. Such was the South African all-rounder's contribution to Gloucestershire cricket that the county was dubbed 'Proctershire'.

David Steele, a passing hero.

Mike Denness, a brave but torrid time as England's captain. He brought many honours to Kent.

Mike Brearley, the England captain, and Derek Underwood celebrate England's victory over Australia at Old Trafford, July 1977. Underwood took six for 66 in Australia's second innings.

way into the England side against the West Indies, and Barlow made his Test debut on the tour of India. Radley was to become an England cricketer within the next two years.

Kent's total assurance and strength in depth took them to their third John Player League title and to their second Benson and Hedges Cup triumph in 1976. They were often weakened by Test calls, but they had mastered the art of the one-day game. They had several players who could 'do a bit of everything', a vital quality, and they had been quick to realise, like Bond at Lancashire, that excellence in fielding was paramount. Men like Ealham and Johnson, who held four catches in the Benson and Hedges Cup Final, were outstanding in this area of the game.

If Middlesex, in winning the Championship, owed nothing to overseas cricketers, Northamptonshire, who finished second to them and who won the Gillette Cup, owed much. For so long the Cinderellas of cricket – they went four years without a Championship victory in the 1930s – Northamptonshire beat Lancashire by four wickets with five balls to spare in the Gillette final. They were captained by Mushtaq Mohammad, and Sarfraz Nawaz and Bishan Bedi were also members of the victorious side. Bedi had a most disconcerting manner in county cricket. As one opponent said, 'You hit him for six, and he would stand there smiling at you and applauding you. And you felt that he had something up his sleeve, that he had wanted you to hit him and that now he was going to get you out.'

The Man of the Match in the Gillette final was Peter Willey. He was one of twenty-one players to appear for England in the 1976 series against the West Indies. Greig was appointed captain for all five Tests, and he had great influence on who was selected. Brearley opened in the first two Tests, and England had a different first pair in each match. The most interesting pairing came at Old Trafford, where Edrich and Close were the openers. They had a combined age of eighty-four.

Greig had insisted that Close be recalled to the side at the age of forty-five because of his ability to stand up to the West Indian pace men, and his average of 33.20, second in the England averages, from three Tests vindicated his selection, but this really did mark the end of the road for the old warrior.

The might with which England was confronted was exceptional. Viv Richards hit double centuries at Trent Bridge and The Oval, and, although he missed the Lord's Test, he scored 829 runs in four matches.

The bowling, too, was frightening at times: Holding and Roberts were too quick for most of the English batsmen. Holding missed the first Test, but he finished with twenty-eight wickets at under 13 runs each. At The Oval, where the West Indies scored 687 for eight, he gave one of the most magnificent displays of fast bowling seen in this country, taking eight for 92 and six for 57 as England made 435 and 203. Dennis Amiss, in his only Test of the summer, scored 203, looking 'the only class batsman in the side' and playing 'nobly for five hours twenty minutes'.

Greig and Knott had hit centuries at Headingley, and Steele at Trent Bridge, but, having drawn the first two Tests, England were beaten at Old Trafford and Headingley as well as The Oval. Greig had heralded the series by declaiming that if one got the West Indies down then they would grovel, and he intended to 'make the West Indians grovel'. The general feeling was that this challenge was good publicity but that it roused the West Indies to new heights. At Old Trafford England were bowled out for 71, and when they began their second innings on the Saturday evening, needing 552 to win, they were subjected to an unrelenting barrage of bouncers. Edrich and Close withstood them so that the bowling was as unsuccessful as it was unsavoury. Umpire Alley at last warned Holding for intimidatory bowling, and Clive Lloyd admitted that his 'fellows got carried away', but the problem remained.

Among those who played in the series, Steele, Snow, Hayes, brought back at Manchester, Edrich and Balderstone never played Test cricket again as the selectors searched for fresh faces and new blood. They introduced four players to international cricket during the Prudential Trophy series, which the West Indies won 3–0: Barlow, Botham, John Lever and Randall.

Randall, Barlow and Lever were in the party that toured India in 1976–77, while Botham, along with Gatting of Middlesex and Athey and Stevenson of Yorkshire, went to Australia on a Whitbread Scholarship.

The selection of the side to tour India drew criticism. Fred Trueman, on the radio, was incensed that David Steele had been omitted, arguing that he had been chosen to face the fire of Australia and the West Indies and was not allowed the respite of a 'softer' series against India. There was also concern, and not for the last time, that Roger Tolchard, the Leicestershire wicket-keeper, was chosen ahead of Bob Taylor. The argument offered in favour of Tolchard was that he could be used as a batsman if required. This, indeed, was what happened. He appeared in four Tests while Knott remained as keeper.

For Greig and for England, the tour was an overwhelming success. They won the first three Tests, an achievement unprecedented by any side in India, to claim a rubber on Indian soil for the first time since the war. Dicky Rutnagur saw many reasons for the triumph. He wrote:

England's superiority came from dedication to the task on hand, zest, determination, a thoughtful approach and a bond of brotherhood between the players. They were inspired by their flamboyant and articulate captain, Tony Greig, and team management, under Ken Barrington, must also take credit for the discipline that prevailed. Greig's charisma enabled him to extract maximum effort from his players. In planning and matters of strategy, he was fortunate to have such shrewd and experienced aides as Barrington, Brearley, Fletcher and Knott. Their contribution to tactics was conspicuous.

Amiss hit 179 in the first Test, reaching his century with a six, and Greig scored a slow 103 in the second, but the real strength of the England side was in the bowling, where the pace men surpassed all expectations. Lever had a sensational debut, taking seven for 46 and three for 24 at Delhi in the first match. He was charged with using Vaseline on the ball, an accusation which proved groundless, and he met his challenge with such dignity and calm as to set a tone for the tour.

England's ten-wicket victory in the second Test in Calcutta owed a great deal to Bob Willis, who had returned to the fray of international cricket after long battles against injury. He had done well in two Tests with the West Indies, and he claimed seven wickets in Calcutta and eight in Bangalore, where England were beaten.

Old and Greig, who bowled mainly off-breaks, gave able support, but the most successful bowler on either side was Derek Underwood. Unfairly criticised as a good bowler only when the wicket gave him assistance, an umbrella that England captains took around with them in case of rain, Underwood proved his worth on the hard pitches of India and took twenty-nine Test wickets at 17.55 runs each, a feat unequalled by an England bowler in India.

Underwood's flat-footed, rather plodding approach to the stumps was far from beautiful, but the fluidity of his action as the left-arm came over was a joy. He was hard to categorise. He was a left-arm spinner, but his pace varied from slow-medium to comparatively brisk, and variations of pace, amount of turn and, above all, relentless accuracy were his strengths. He relied less on trajectory than did most spinners, but he frustrated batsmen into sterility, and he was one of the most potent destructive forces of his age. 'Deadly Derek' was his most suitable epithet.

It was during the Centenary Test at Melbourne that Underwood took his 250th Test wicket. This Test was the brainchild of Hans Ebeling, a former Australian Test player, and celebrated a hundred years of Test cricket, the first Test match having been played at Melbourne in 1877.

285

There was a memorable gathering of international cricketers, and there were personal triumphs for Rodney Marsh, Chris Old, Dennis Lillee and Derek Randall.

Randall had appeared in four Tests in India without making his mark, but, in the Melbourne celebration, when England were set 463 to win, he hit 174 off 353 balls in 446 minutes with twenty-one fours. He and Amiss added 166 for the fourth wicket.

Randall's performance was joyfully received. Australia won by 45 runs, which was exactly the margin by which they had won the first Test 100 years earlier. Her Majesty Queen Elizabeth II and the Duke of Edinburgh were introduced to the teams on the final day. Everybody was happy.

And then the bombshell landed.

7

Packer and After: The Age of Brearley and Botham, 1977–82

The first hints that a bombshell was about to explode came from South Africa. At a dinner in Johannesburg, Lee Irvine received a presentation to mark his retirement from cricket and in his acceptance speech he named Eddie Barlow, Graeme Pollock, Mike Procter and Barry Richards as having signed lucrative contracts to play in an eight-week series of matches throughout the world. The *Sunday Times* of Johannesburg had already given an indication that something was afoot.

A fortnight later, on 1 May 1977, the *Bulletin*, an Australian newspaper founded in 1880 and owned by Australian Consolidated Press, whose chairman was Kerry Packer, announced that a huge sporting deal which involved thirty-five of the world's top cricketers had been completed. The contract committed these cricketers to play specially arranged five-day and one-day international matches and three-day round-robin tournaments. The deal had been put together by a sports and television company – the proprietors of Australian TV's Channel Nine – whose chairman was, again, Kerry Packer.

Of the thirty-five cricketers initially signed, eighteen were Australian and seventeen were from overseas. The overseas signings included Tony Greig, who was to captain one side, John Snow, Alan Knott and Derek Underwood. Boycott had declined to sign, and Richie Benaud and his sports consultancy company had agreed to help in the management of the series.

It transpired that many of the signings had taken place during the New Zealand–Australia series in February and March 1977 and during the Centenary Test, and that Tony Greig had been a leading protagonist in helping Packer to recruit players for what was immediately dubbed a 'circus'.

The Cricket Council's reaction was also immediate. An emergency meeting was held and the chairman, Freddie Brown, issued a statement to the effect that Greig was not to be considered as England's captain for the forthcoming series against Australia. The Council's reason was that Greig's action had 'inevitably impaired the trust which existed between the cricket authorities and the captain of the England side'. Brown added, 'The captaincy of the England team involves close liaison with the selectors in the management, selection and development of England players for the future and clearly Greig is unlikely to be able to do this as his stated intention is to be contracted elsewhere during the next three winters.'

By taking such prompt action, the Cricket Council had accepted the responsibility of sacking Greig themselves and had not left it to the selectors. The selectors' position was also made easier when they were told that sides for the three-match Prudential Trophy, which would precede the Test series, and for the first three Tests should be chosen on merit. This clearly meant that Knott, Greig and Underwood could be selected.

Kerry Packer arrived in England and held a press conference at which he stated, 'It is not a pirate series but a Super-Test series. I have sent telegrams to all the cricketing bodies but they don't reply. I am willing to compromise but time is running out.'

The strongest weapon in his artillery was the assertion that nobody had bothered to pay the players what they were worth and that one only had to look at what tennis players and golfers were earning.

The explosion had taken the cricketing public by surprise, but the reasons for Kerry Packer's detonation soon became clear. He was bitterly disappointed that an offer his television company, Channel Nine, had made to the Australian Board of Control for rights to screen conventional Test cricket had not been given the consideration it deserved.

The Australian Cricket Board had emphasised its 'special relationship' with the Australian Broadcasting Company. Now, three years on, things were to be very different, and it was on this point that Packer and the International Cricket Conference could not agree. Peace was impossible because Packer demanded exclusive television rights from the Australian Board of Control from 1981 onwards. The International Cricket Conference could not impose such a restriction on one of their members. The battle continued.

Packer increased the number of cricketers under contract to him to fifty-one, and Dennis Amiss and, later, Bob Woolmer joined World Series Cricket.

The International Cricket Conference responded by decreeing that any cricketer who appeared in a match previously disapproved by their body would no longer be eligible to play Test cricket until application had been made to them by the governing body of his country and permission granted. Matches arranged by Packer and Benaud and their companies were, of course, disapproved.

In August the TCCB embraced the ICC's ruling in a new sub-rule, and added:

> No county shall be entitled to play in any competitive county cricket match, any cricketer who is and remains precluded from playing in a Test match on the above grounds before the expiration of a period of two years immediately following the date of the last day of the last match previously disapproved by the ICC in which he has played or made himself available to play.

Kerry Packer had already announced that he was taking out an injunction and asking for damages in the High Court against the ICC and TCCB, and the TCCB gave an undertaking that no Packer player would be banned until the court hearing. That hearing began in late September 1977 and lasted for thirty-one days. The judgment was 221 foolscap pages long and took five and a half hours to deliver.

Mr Justice Slade found in favour of the plaintiffs: Greig, Snow and Procter. He declared that the changes to the rules brought about by the ICC and the TCCB were void for they constituted a restraint of trade. The judgment made special reference to Tony Greig in that when he signed his contract with World Series Cricket and helped in the recruitment of others he was still generally regarded as captain of England and could confidently have looked forward to being reappointed, but neither he nor any of the other England cricketers had been offered any kind of legal commitment with the Cricket Council, nor had they been given any guarantee of employment by the TCCB.

The costs to the TCCB were estimated at a ruinous quarter of a million pounds, although, as the ICC were co-defendants, it was presumed that they would share part of those costs. Packer himself had helped the TCCB by paying £150,000 for the television rights for his Channel Nine to cover the 1977 series, and then came the news that Cornhill Insurance were to sponsor Test matches in England from 1978 onwards. The TCCB had already agreed for Schweppes to sponsor the County Championship in 1977 so that as England prepared to enter the 1980s each sector of competitive cricket had its sponsor. Packer's victory had brought about radical changes, and nothing was ever to be quite the same again.

The names of Packer and Greig were generally vilified. They were seen as the demon kings in a pantomime which had no happy ending. Greig, Knott, Woolmer and the rest were regarded in many quarters as being 'disloyal'. Packer admitted that he had put Greig in a most difficult position by swearing him to secrecy while negotiations were going on, but, as he explained, 'I don't know of any business in the world which is done on the basis of people going to their opposition and telling them that they're about to do a deal and giving them the opportunity to stop them.'

As the heat of battle diminished, sounder judgements prevailed. Ian Wooldridge in the *Daily Mail* suggested that the only surprise was that such a revolution had not taken place before. Michael Melford in the *Daily Telegraph* congratulated Kerry Packer on creating harmony among the world's cricket administrators while Jeff Stollmeyer, President of the West Indies Board, sensitively commented, 'I don't see how anyone can condemn the players. After all, their careers are not all that permanent.'

The establishment flung up their arms in horror at the action of Greig and his men, but they were people who mostly enjoyed lucrative lives from business and commercial interests. All that the Packer men were doing was following the normal human pattern of moving from a job that offered them x pounds a year to a job that offered them double x pounds a year, but, as cricketers, like teachers or social workers or nurses, they were supposed to find satisfaction and a sense of vocation in their work and not worry about money.

Greig continued to captain Sussex in 1977, but Arnold Long took over the following year, and in July 1978 Greig requested that he be released from his contract. In *Wisden* Jack Arlidge had more than a hint of sadness in his epitaph:

> The controversial career, which had started back in 1966, was over. It was not until late September, however, that the secret of Greig being an epileptic, which a few of us had known from an early match with the Second XI, was revealed. His association with Packer proved a great blow to the club and the game, but we can still admire the spirit and will-power which enabled him to become so fine a player despite such a handicap.

Greig's fate was similar to that suffered by Oscar Wilde in a different context nearly a hundred years earlier. People still went to see his plays, but they did not mention his name any more. Greig could be consoled by the fact that in the years to come it would be difficult to find a county cricketer who did not hold him in esteem, believing that, by his actions,

290

he had improved the lot of the profession as a whole.

It was against the background of the Packer Affair that the 1977 season was played. Dennis Lillee had stated that he was unavailable to tour England with the Australians, and it was later assumed that he was saving his energies for World Series Cricket the following winter. John Murray replaced Len Hutton on the selection committee, and it was announced that, in future, it was to be the chairman of selectors, not the captain, who was to have the casting vote on the committee.

The first task of the committee was to appoint a captain in succession to Greig; they turned to Brearley, who had been vice-captain on the tour of India and in Australia. Initially, his appointment was for the three one-day internationals and the first two Test matches, although the appointment for the Tests came only after he had hit 78 and shared an opening stand of 161 with Amiss in the third Prudential match at The Oval. This game, which ended in heavy rain with pools of water on the pitch at 8.15 p.m., was the only one in which Australia were victorious. The play continued in pouring rain because the players were reluctant to come back on Jubilee Day, 7 June.

Brearley was to make a considerable mark on the season. He led Middlesex to victory in the Gillette Cup, beating Glamorgan in the final with relative ease. Middlesex also shared the Championship with Kent, who did remarkably well considering that Colin Cowdrey and Brian Luckhurst had retired and Denness had left the county under rather strained circumstances and signed a three-year contract with Essex.

Brearley caused a stir in the fashion world when he went out to bat for Middlesex against MCC at the start of the season wearing protective headgear with flaps at the sides to safeguard the temples. It was a style that was to catch on.

Brearley was to win his highest praise in the Ashes series. He had much enjoyed being part of the happy, victorious side in India, and he was adamant in selection that the spirit of this side should be maintained and that no discrimination should be made against the Packer players. The twelve who appeared in the first two Tests had all seen duty in India, although Geoff Miller, the Derbyshire off-spinner, had not appeared in a Test match during the tour. The mould was broken in the third Test, for Geoff Boycott had announced he was prepared to return to the international arena.

Boycott had turned down a lucrative offer from Packer on the excuse that it would interfere with his cricket for Yorkshire. In spite of his allegiance to his native county, Boycott was having a far from happy time as Yorkshire's captain. Among batsmen he remained supreme, but, at the end of the season, Don Brennan, the former Yorkshire and England

291

wicket-keeper and a member of the county selection committee, waged a public campaign to have Boycott replaced as skipper. Other members of the committee supported Brennan, but public opinion was firmly behind their favourite son, and he was re-elected captain. There was some compromise with Brennan, who resigned from the committee on the issue, in that an element of responsibility was taken from Boycott by the announcement that Ray Illingworth was to become the Yorkshire team manager in April 1979.

Illingworth's decade as Leicestershire captain ended in 1978 when he celebrated his forty-sixth birthday. The Midlands county had enjoyed glory under Illingworth that they had not known before. They won the John Player League in 1977 for the second time to add to the Championship and two Benson and Hedges Cup triumphs that they had won under the Yorkshireman.

When Illingworth arrived back at Yorkshire in 1979, however, Boycott was no longer captain. He had been ousted and replaced by John Hampshire, and civil war was rampant.

By the time Boycott was brought back into the Test side, England were one up in the series against Australia. The first match had been played at Lord's as part of the Queen's Jubilee celebrations. Needing 226 to win, Australia had finished on 114 for six and the match was drawn. This was gratifying to England, who had trailed by 80 runs on the first innings in spite of Bob Willis taking seven for 78. Bob Woolmer had hit 120 and Tony Greig 91 to put England back in contention.

Woolmer hit 137 in the second Test at Old Trafford. Randall and Greig scored well, Underwood took six second-innings wickets, and England won by nine wickets. This was to be Underwood's last five-wicket haul in a Test match, just as it was to be Bob Woolmer's final Test hundred.

Woolmer had started as a late-order free-hitting batsman and medium-pace bowler, but as he climbed to number three in the England order his emphasis was on solid defence and unlimited concentration. It was as if there had been a personality change brought about by Test cricket. He was to return to the England side in the post-Packer era, but by then his momentum had been lost. His destiny was to become an outstanding coach with Warwickshire and South Africa.

England made three changes for the third Test, Boycott and Hendrick came in for Amiss and John Lever while Ian Botham made his Test match debut at the expense of Chris Old who, a week later, was to hit a century in thirty-seven minutes for Yorkshire against Warwickshire at Edgbaston, the second-fastest hundred then recorded.

It was apparent by the time Australia arrived at Trent Bridge for the third Test that this was a side that lacked sparkle. In comparison to previous Australian teams they were without drive and colour – it seemed that the involvement with World Series Cricket had more than taken its toll. They also experienced wretched weather.

At Trent Bridge they won the toss and batted first. They lunched at 101 for one, but on the resumption McCosker was well caught at first slip by Brearley off Hendrick without addition. Greg Chappell and David Hookes looked safe enough and drinks were taken after an hour with the score at 131.

Botham had bowled an innocuous first spell, but when brought back after the break he dismissed Chappell with his first delivery, the first wicket in a spell of four for 13 in thirty-four balls. With Willis accounting for Hookes and Greig for Robinson, Australia crashed to 155 for eight. There was a recovery, but Botham finished with five for 74 on his Test debut and Australia were bowled out for 243 on the opening day.

At the end of the second day England were 1 run short of Australia's total with five wickets standing: Boycott was on 88, and Knott 87. England had been in a precarious position, having lost five wickets for 82 runs, and Boycott had run out the local hero, Derek Randall, for 13. The Boycott–Knott partnership was vital. It realised 215 runs, and both batsmen scored centuries. Boycott celebrated his return from self-imposed exile with 107, the ninety-eighth century of his career, and Knott's 135 remains the highest score by an England wicket-keeper against Australia; he also became the first keeper to reach 4,000 runs in Test cricket. Botham, dropped first ball, made 25. John Woodcock wrote, 'He won't always have it so good.' For once the sage of Longparish was wrong.

England took a first-innings lead of 121 and, in spite of McCosker's century, they bowled out Australia for 309. Willis, an increasingly potent force, took five wickets. Brearley and Boycott began England's quest for victory with a stand of 154, and the match was won at a quarter to five on the last afternoon by seven wickets. Boycott was unbeaten on 80, and England went to Headingley two up in the series.

Four days after the Test, Boycott scored 104 against Warwickshire at Edgbaston in Rohan Kanhai's benefit match. Then he returned to Headingley to take his place in an England side which showed one change, Roope for Miller, from the side that won at Trent Bridge.

England won the toss but had the unhappiest of beginnings when Brearley was caught behind off the third ball of the match. The rest of the day was celebration, and at the end of it England were 252 for four with Boycott unbeaten on 110. With a sense of theatre not usually associated with him, Boycott had chosen the occasion to complete his 100th hundred, the first batsman to accomplish the feat in a Test

match. Boycott had extended the drama by scoring it on his home
ground.

Boycott's 100th Hundred – England Regain the Ashes
England v Australia at Headingley
11, 12, 13 and 15 August 1977

England First Innings
J.M. Brearley (capt) c Marsh
  b Thompson 0
G. Boycott c Chappell b Pascoe ... 191
R.A. Woolmer c Chappell b Thomson 37
D.W. Randall lbw b Pascoe 20
A.W. Greig b Thomson 43
G.R.J. Roope c Walters b Thomson . 34
†A.P.E. Knott lbw b Bright 57
I.T. Botham b Bright 0
D.L. Underwood c Bright b Pascoe 6
M. Hendrick c Robinson b Pascoe . 4
R.G.D. Willis not out 5
  Extras (b 5, lb 9, w 3, nb 22) 39

  Total 436

BOWLING	Overs	Mdns	Runs	Wkts
Thomson	34	7	113	4
Walker	48	21	97	–
Pascoe	34.4	10	91	4
Walters	3	1	5	–
Bright	26	9	66	2
Chappell	10	2	25	–

fall of wickets
1–0, 2–82, 3–105, 4–201, 5–275, 6–398, 7–398, 8–412, 9–422

Australia First Innings   Second Innings
R.B. McCosker run out 27   c Knott b Greig 12
I.C. Davis lbw b Hendrick 0   c Knott b Greig 19
G.S. Chappell (capt) c Brearley
  b Hendrick 4   c Greig b Willis 36
D.W. Hookes lbw b Botham 24   lbw b Hendrick 21
K.D. Walters c Hendrick b Botham 4   lbw b Woolmer 15
R.D. Robinson c Greig b Hendrick . 20   b Hendrick 20

†R.W. Marsh c Knott b Botham ...	2	c Randall b Hendrick 63
R.J. Bright not out	9	c Greig b Hendrick 5
M.H.N. Walker c Knott b Botham .	7	b Willis 30
J.R. Thomson b Botham	0	b Willis 0
L.S. Pascoe b Hendrick	0	not out 0
Extras (lb 3, w 1, nb 2)	6	(b 1, lb 4, w 4, nb 18) ... 27
Total 103		248

BOWLING	Overs	Mdns	Runs	Wkts	Overs	Mdns	Runs	Wkts
Willis	5	–	35	–	14	7	32	3
Hendrick	15.3	2	41	4	22.5	6	54	4
Botham	11	3	21	5	17	3	47	–
Greig	–	–	–	–	20	7	64	2
Woolmer	–	–	–	–	8	4	8	1
Underwood	–	–	–	–	8	3	16	–

fall of wickets
1–8, 2–26, 3–52, 4–57, 5–66, 6–77, 7–87, 8–100, 9–100
1–31, 2–35, 3–63, 4–97, 5–130, 6–167, 7–179, 8–244, 9–245
umpires – W.E. Alley and W.L. Budd
England won by an innings and 85 runs

The game was virtually settled on the second day. Boycott took his score to 191, and England made 436. By the close Australia were 67 for five and totally demoralised. Hendrick took a wicket with his second ball and another with the first ball of his third over. Randall brilliantly ran out McCosker, and the demon Botham set to work again.

On the Saturday morning Hendrick and Botham continued to swing the ball, and Australia were out for 103 (Botham five for 21). They followed on and Chappell displayed his fine technique against the moving ball. Most of the final session was lost to bad light, and Australia closed on 120 for four.

The Monday was damp and play could not start until two o'clock. Chappell added 7 before pushing forward to Willis and giving a catch to second slip. Botham was injured and unable to bowl, and Marsh hit fiercely in an eighth-wicket stand with Walker.

Willis wrecked Walker's stumps and then Thomson's, which brought him 100 wickets in twenty-eight Tests. At 4.39 Marsh drove at Hendrick and skied to Randall at cover, who took the catch and did a somersault in jubilation. England had regained the Ashes.

The match at The Oval was drawn, and Tony Greig's Test career ended with a duck. He had played fifty-eight consecutive matches and had been England's finest all-rounder since Trevor Bailey. Fortunately for England, one of the greatest all-rounders the game has known was already in the side. For the time being, at least, in spite or because of Packer, things in the England camp looked rosy.

On the home front there were disturbing signs. The TCCB had decided to introduce fines for slow over-rates, a worthy gesture but a creator of farce in many instances. More worrying was the behaviour of some spectators.

The one-day game had attracted people who were not versed in the traditions of the game, and there were signs in some quarters that a Sunday League match was being treated as an occasion on which it was possible to drink all afternoon. There was an attendant rowdiness and barracking; not that cricket alone was guilty. We were passing into an age where catcalls and jeers accompanied the taking of a place kick in rugby, a moment which, for a century, had been accorded the courtesy of silence.

Mike Procter led Gloucestershire to victory in the Benson and Hedges Cup. There was a dramatic semi-final at Southampton in which Procter ripped out the heart of the Hampshire batting with four wickets in five balls. Bowling at his fastest, he knocked over Greenidge's stumps with the fifth ball of his third over. With the first three balls of his fourth over he trapped Richards and Jesty leg-before and bowled Rice. David Turner and Nigel Cowley added 109, but Hampshire were out for 173, 7 runs short of Gloucestershire's total.

In the final at Lord's Gloucestershire took on Kent, the holders, and won a resounding victory by 64 runs. Andy Stovold batted at the top of his form and made 71. He also held three catches behind the stumps and took the Gold Award. Zaheer made a sparkling 70, and Gloucestershire reached 237 in their fifty-five overs. Kent had caused surprise in their selection, preferring the inexperienced Clinton to Chris Cowdrey, who had made a century in the quarter-final, and Johnson. Clinton was bowled by Brain without scoring, and Rowe also went for nought. Kent were never in the hunt.

Trouble started towards the end of the match when spectators began to run on the pitch in premature celebration. When the presentations were made in front of the pavilion police were forced to hold back fans. There were scuffles. Helmets went flying, and police and spectators were injured. Jack Bailey, Secretary of MCC, condemned the behaviour of Gloucestershire fans, calling it disgraceful and fearing a future when the crowd would have to be fenced off from the playing area.

The success of England, and Brearley's personal triumph in leading Middlesex to a share of the Championship and victory in the Gillette

Cup, drove away thoughts of the unpleasantness created at the end of the Benson and Hedges Cup Final. Jubilee year had been Brearley's year, and now he took the England side off to Pakistan and New Zealand. There were new faces in the side in Cope, the Yorkshire off-spinner, Rose, the Somerset left-hander, and Gatting, a batsman of great potential. His Middlesex colleague Clive Radley joined the side later.

The three Tests in Pakistan were drawn and were characterised inevitably by crowd disturbances and by the tedious cricket that the pitches produced. Botham did not figure in this series, which was something of a surprise.

On the eve of the third Test, England played a Sind XI in a thirty-five-over match that was intended to be a gentle warm-up. It turned out to be a disaster for Mike Brearley, who had his left arm broken by a ball from Sikander Bakht, the only ball all day to rear off a length, and he flew back to England the same night. Boycott took over the captaincy and in his second match as England's skipper, the first Test in New Zealand, he had the indignity of leading his country to their first defeat at the hands of the Kiwis. England were bowled out for 64 in their second innings with Richard Hadlee taking six for 26.

Hadlee was to join Nottinghamshire a few months later, a move that brought considerable reward to player and county. Essex had attempted to sign him on an eight-week contract when Boyce was injured, but the TCCB had rejected the proposal. So, too, in spirit had Richard's wife Karen. The offer from Essex officials had come by telephone at three in the morning, and Karen had suggested quite forcefully that Richard could play for whoever he liked except for a county that did not know the time in New Zealand.

Clive Rice, all-rounder of the year in 1977, had been appointed captain of Nottinghamshire for 1978. On his return from his native South Africa he announced that he had signed to play for Kerry Packer's organisation and he was instantly dismissed by Nottinghamshire. Rice sought action in the High Court, but the county club had second thoughts and reinstated him to the team, but not the captaincy. In the meantime they had signed Hadlee as his replacement, and they now found themselves with two of the world's most prominent all-rounders on their staff.

Smedley, who had been deposed, was made captain again. In July 1979 Smedley was again relieved of his duties and Rice appointed. The latter was to prove to be one of the best county captains English cricket has known, although, perhaps, he lived in the shadow of his friend and

297

colleague Richard Hadlee, a more flamboyant character, and seldom received the praise he deserved.

It was England's young all-rounder Ian Botham who took all the applause in the second Test in New Zealand. He scored his first Test century, 103. He also took five for 73 and three for 38 and so became only the second England player after Greig to score a hundred and take five wickets in an innings in the same Test. England won by 174 runs.

Botham took five wickets in an innings again in the third Test, which was drawn. This was only Botham's fifth Test match, but he already had twenty-seven wickets to his credit. It was Clive Radley's second Test, and he made a masterly 158.

A record of one win and one loss in six Tests was hardly a suggestion that the tour was a triumph, yet pieces of the jigsaw puzzle were beginning to fit into place. The talent of Botham had been confirmed, as had the growing strength and pace of Willis and the all-round qualities of Edmonds. There were still doubts about the batting, but Radley had laid an immediate claim for a place. There was also the bonus that in Bob Taylor, who kept immaculately in Pakistan and New Zealand, England had not only a most capable successor to Knott but a keeper as good as any in the world.

The choice of the second wicket-keeper on the tour – Paul Downton, understudy to Alan Knott at Kent and with only a handful of first-class games to his credit – was much resented and seemed an insult to men like Smith of Essex, Taylor of Somerset and Bairstow of Yorkshire who were keeping regularly and well, particularly the first two.

Pakistan and New Zealand, having entertained England, followed them home for a twin tour. Pakistan, stripped of many of their leading players by World Series Cricket, were an inexperienced side. They were overwhelmed in the two one-day internationals, in which Clive Radley confirmed his quality and temperament for international cricket and David Gower made his England debut. In the second match at The Oval, Gower scored 114 not out and reached his hundred off 116 balls. Boycott led England in the first match but damaged a thumb and could play neither in the second game nor in the first Test. Bob Willis captained England in the Prudential Trophy game at The Oval, but Brearley was fit to return for the Test.

This match set the pattern for the summer: England won by an innings. Chris Old took four wickets in five balls in Pakistan's first innings and finished with seven for 50. Radley and Botham scored hundreds, and Gower pulled the first ball he received in Test cricket for four, before going on to make 58.

The England batting line-up was described as being remarkably inexperienced, and it boasted even fewer caps in the second Test when Gooch was recalled to the colours in place of Barry Wood. He took his second chance in Test cricket with a knock of 54, but Botham dominated the match. He hit 108, his hundred coming off 104 balls. England scored at 4 runs an over, making 364, and bowled out Pakistan for 105. Willis took five for 47 and Edmonds four for 6. When Pakistan followed on Botham established a record with eight wickets for 34 runs. In his final spell he took six for 8 in fifty-three deliveries, and England won by an innings. The third Test was ruined by rain and ended in a draw.

New Zealand were then swept aside by three Tests to nil. At The Oval Gower hit a maiden Test century, and Gooch scored 91 not out as England won by seven wickets. Boycott returned with 131 at Trent Bridge and opened the innings with Gooch. The pair put on 111, and Brearley, who dropped to number five, made 50. It was only the second time in the summer's Tests that he had passed 20. Botham took six for 34 and three for 59, and England won by an innings.

Victory at Lord's in the third Test came by seven wickets, and Botham had match figures of eleven for 140. In thirteen Tests under Brearley, England had now won eight and drawn five. These were heady days. England were being hailed as world champions, for their record under Brearley in one-day internationals stood at 7–2 in their favour.

Botham was being celebrated as the greatest all-rounder since W.G. Grace. He had appeared in only eleven Test matches, but he already had sixty-four wickets and three centuries to his credit. He was one of four bowlers to take 100 wickets in first-class cricket during the season, the others being Underwood, John Lever and Selvey, and he was exciting a popular interest in the game.

Young batsmen were emerging, too, with Gower and Gooch selected for Australia with Brearley's side, and Tavaré, Larkins and Gatting earning Whitbread Scholarships. The real problem concerned Brearley himself. He scored only 144 runs in eight Test innings during the summer, averaging 20.57. His critics were legion, and there was open hostility to him in the North where Boycott was championed as England's captain. Brearley was even booed on some Northern grounds where the battle was seen not simply as North against South, great player against average county player, but as a contest between the privileged academic gentleman and the working-class lad. Ironically, Brearley's political sympathies were more traditionally working-class than those of many whom he led. Bedser and his selectors rightly stuck by Brearley, whose men were 100 per cent behind him, and Boycott ended the season being sacked as captain of Yorkshire.

Kent, who had shared the Championship with Middlesex in 1977, won the title outright in 1978. Essex were second, their highest ever position, surpassing their third place of eighty-one years before. Kent, with Knott, Woolmer and Underwood in their side all season, also won the Benson and Hedges Cup, beating Derbyshire, captained by Eddie Barlow, the South African, in the final.

The Gillette Cup produced the most exciting match of the 1978 season when Somerset beat Essex in the semi-final at Taunton. Viv Richards hit 110, and Somerset made 287 for six. The last over arrived with Essex needing 12 runs to win and with two wickets standing. Smith hit a single and East edged a four before being bowled. Dredge delivered a no-ball and, in the tension and excitement that ensued, 3 runs were scored with the help of an overthrow. When the last ball arrived Lever needed to score 3. He hit cleanly, but Smith was narrowly run out by Rose as he went for the third run. The scores were level, and Somerset won by having lost fewer wickets.

In the final Somerset failed to produce their true form in spite of Botham's 80, and Sussex, led by wicket-keeper Arnold Long, won with ease. This was a fine achievement by Sussex, who had experienced a traumatic season with the departure of Tony Greig.

Hampshire experienced an even more traumatic year when Barry Richards and Andy Roberts walked out in mid-season, yet they went on to win the John Player League. Three sides (Somerset and Leicestershire were the others) finished level on points, but Hampshire, who played their last five games without Richards and Roberts, had the superior run-rate. Somerset had lost the Gillette Cup on the Saturday, and on the Sunday their agony was complete. Needing only to defeat Essex at Taunton to take the John Player League, they were beaten by 2 runs in front of a capacity crowd who paid record receipts.

Botham had the consolation of a winter in Australia in defence of the Ashes. The selection procedure brought two casualties: Boycott was replaced as vice-captain by Bob Willis, a good team man, and John Murray resigned as a selector. Murray's version of events was that the party was chosen with Bairstow as understudy to Taylor, but Brearley had insisted that he wanted every member of the squad to be competing for Test places. He lobbied for Roger Tolchard, who could be used as a batsman, as on his previous tour, and a wicket-keeper. Murray felt that if his advice was not acceptable when it came to choosing wicket-keepers, then there was little point in him remaining on the committee. Ironically, Tolchard suffered a facial injury on the tour and Bairstow was flown out to replace him.

There was little doubt that Brearley's side would retain the Ashes. The rapidly maturing Botham, the newly arrived Gower, plus Willis,

300

Boycott, Taylor and Emburey, an off-spinner who had made his debut in the last Test against New Zealand, were the nucleus of a team that offered far more strength than an Australian side decimated by the Packer revolution. Hughes and Yallop were useful batsmen, but nowhere near the Chappell class; however, a fast bowler, Rodney Hogg, emerged and proved to be a bowler of quality. He set a record with forty-one wickets in the six Tests. In the third Test a left-handed batsman, Allan Border, made his debut and immediately excited the interest of World Series Cricket.

It was a generally low-scoring series, and Gower and Randall were England's only century-makers. The bowlers thrived: Botham and Miller each captured twenty-three wickets; Miller, at 15.04, topped the England averages while Botham, at 24.65, was fifth and bottom. John Lever played in one Test and had figures of five for 48.

The series was one-sided. England won the first, second, fourth, fifth and sixth Tests by big margins and lost the third by 103 runs. Brearley became the second England captain after Hutton to recapture and then defend the Ashes successfully, and was the first captain to gain five Test victories in Australia.

Brearley and his men had done all that could have been asked of them, but the opposition of the 'circus' detracted from their achievements. In *Wisden* Alex Bannister reviewed the situation and the pressure on the Australian authorities:

> The competition from World Series Cricket put heavy demands on the Australian authorities, and the game at large suffered from an over-heavy programme and too much exposure on television. The well-oiled and professional WSC publicity machine often distracted attention from the Ashes series, and the public grew tired of supporting a losing team. An original error was perhaps made in playing two Tests on the over-worked ground at Sydney, where Packer was strongly established. A brave effort was made to stimulate interest with skydivers arriving with the match ball, or the coin, marching displays and athletic events during the intervals. But the essential factor of a winning Australian team was missing and attendances dropped to alarming levels by the final Test.

The razzmatazz of parachutists and marching bands had little to do with cricket or the dignity of the game and it certainly did not hide the fact that many of the best players in the world were operating with Kerry Packer. Some countries had already found this an intolerable situation and broke ranks by selecting Packer players for Test cricket.

301

Following the humiliation in England, Pakistan selected the WSC players for the series against India and Australia, while the West Indies were unable to contemplate defeat in India and recalled Lloyd and the rest for the Prudential World Cup in England.

This second World Cup, in 1979, was highly successful. Sri Lanka enhanced their claim for Test status by beating India, and England reached the final with a 9-run victory over New Zealand in the semi-final. The West Indies beat Pakistan in the other semi-final.

It was felt at the time that England had made serious errors in selection. Gatting was named in the party of fourteen, but he was a raw recruit and lacked experience. He played no part in the tournament and when Willis was declared unfit for the final, England had no replacement. John Lever had not been chosen, and Brearley had to find twelve overs from Boycott, Gooch and Larkins. They cost 86 runs.

Although Gooch and Larkins were in the side, Brearley decided that he would be Boycott's opening partner. This decision could have cost England a chance of winning the World Cup, although the West Indies would probably have triumphed whatever the circumstances.

Brearley's decision to ask the West Indies to bat first when he won the toss was justified as Botham, Old and Hendrick obtained early movement. Greenidge was run out by Randall's intelligent underarm throw to the bowler's end, and with Haynes, Kallicharran and Lloyd all failing, the West Indies were 99 for four after thirty overs. England were definitely on top.

The next twenty-one overs changed the complexion of the game. In that time Viv Richards and Collis King added 139. The stand occupied seventy-seven minutes and was dominated by King, whose chances and success as an all-rounder in Test cricket were limited and who had failed to find form as Glamorgan's overseas player. In a display of awesome power King drove, hooked and pulled, hitting three sixes and ten fours in his 86. It was breathtaking, and it took the pressure off Richards, who was first subdued by Edmonds and then negotiated a difficult period.

Richards reached his hundred in the fifty-second over; the West Indies now lost four wickets for 48 runs in the last eight overs, but Richards remained unbeaten. The last ball of the innings was bowled by Hendrick, who attempted to bowl a yorker on off stump. Anticipating the delivery, Richards got into position and pulled the ball into the Mound Stand for six. It was the third six in his innings of 138, which also included eleven fours.

Needing 287 to win, England were given a sound start by Boycott and

Brearley, but there was the rub. It took Boycott seventeen overs to reach double figures, and when Brearley was caught off Holding the score was 129 from thirty-eight overs. The asking rate was now more than 7 an over, and the later exciting stroke-makers – Randall, Gooch, Gower, Botham and Larkins – were sacrificed in chasing the impossible against so strong a West Indian attack. Joel Garner finished the match by taking five wickets for 4 runs in eleven balls.

It was a disappointment, but nineteen days later England began the first of four Test matches against India. They won by an innings and 83 runs. Boycott hit 155, and Gower 200 not out, the first double century of his career.

The remaining three Tests were drawn, but they were significant. In the second innings at Lord's Botham had Gavaskar caught at slip. It gave him 100 wickets in Test cricket only two years and nine days after his debut, which was, at the time, a record.

In the next Test at Headingley, which was ruined by rain, Botham hit 137. England finished the first day on 80 for four with Botham on 9. There was no play for two days, but on the fourth morning he scored 99 before lunch.

At The Oval he completed a thousand runs in Test cricket, so achieving the 'double' in twenty-one Tests, another record. Bairstow and Alan Butcher, the Surrey left-hander, made their debuts in this match: for Butcher it was his only Test. The hero of the hour was Gavaskar, who hit 221 while India, needing 438 to win, scored 429 for eight in a wonderful attempt at victory. They were thwarted at the last by the accuracy of Botham and Willey.

Botham had other joys in 1979. His county, Somerset, and Essex began the season as the only counties never to have won a major honour, although both had come close in 1978. Remarkably, in 1979 these two Cinderella counties shared the four titles, and Essex in particular entered a period in which they were to become the dominant team for the next decade.

Somerset's desperate desire to win something cost them dearly at first. On 24 May they met Worcestershire at New Road in their final zonal match in Group A of the Benson and Hedges Cup. Having already completed their programme, Gloucestershire were out of the reckoning. Somerset had won three matches and Worcestershire and Glamorgan had won two. Glamorgan's last fixture was against Minor Counties (South), a game they were expected to win with ease, so if Somerset lost to Worcestershire, three counties would finish on nine points, and the two qualifying places for the quarter-finals would be decided on bowlers' striking rates, where Somerset had an advantage.

303

Batting first against Worcestershire, Somerset opened with skipper Brian Rose and Peter Denning. The West Indian pace man Vanburn Holder opened the attack for Worcestershire. After one over in which the only run scored was a no-ball, Rose declared the Somerset innings closed. Following the customary between-innings interval, Worcestershire began their reply: it lasted for ten balls, and Glenn Turner scored two singles which gave his side victory by ten wickets.

The whole match had lasted less than twenty minutes, and although Somerset had deliberately forfeited the game, they had preserved their superior striking rate and qualified for the quarter-finals. As it transpired, Glamorgan's game was ruined by rain, and Somerset would have qualified anyway.

Worcestershire were incensed, as were the hundred or so spectators who had braved cold and damp conditions to see the game and who now had their entrance money returned. Most people connected with cricket condemned Rose's action, but one cannot believe that Rose took the course he did without discussing the matter with others, including members of the county committee. The point was that Rose had violated the spirit of the game, but he had broken no rules.

This was the defence that Somerset offered when the matter was debated at a special meeting of the TCCB at Lord's a week later. In the debate only Derbyshire supported Somerset on the grounds that they had contravened no rule. By seventeen to one, Somerset were disqualified from the Benson and Hedges Cup for bringing the game into disrepute, and the rules were amended to prevent a declaration. However, when the Somerset Yearbook was published the following spring it made no mention of the Benson and Hedges Cup.

There was consolation for Somerset. They made a complete reversal of the events of the previous season. On Saturday, 8 September 1979, against Northamptonshire before a packed house at Lord's, Richards, who came to the wicket in the seventh over with the score on 34 for one, batted until the sixtieth over of the innings and hit 117, a masterful knock which included eleven boundaries and not the semblance of a chance. Botham and Garner hit lustily in the closing stages, and Somerset reached 269 for eight.

Handicapped by the fact that skipper Jim Watts had broken a bone in his hand while fielding and would be unable to bat, Northamptonshire were struggling from the first over when Garner had Larkins leg-before. He dismissed Richard Williams with the score on 13, but a brave partnership between Geoff Cook and Allan Lamb realised 113 in thirteen overs. Cook was run out by Roebuck, and when Lamb was stumped off Richards for a belligerent 78, Northamptonshire were doomed.

304

Joel Garner, the 'Big Bird', finished with six for 29 in 10.3 overs, and Somerset took the Gillette Cup by a margin of 45 runs. It was their first major trophy.

Next day came their second. They went to Trent Bridge and, before the biggest Sunday crowd of the season, they beat Nottinghamshire by 56 runs to take the John Player League.

A fortnight earlier Essex had claimed the second of their titles. They had qualified for the quarter-finals of the Benson and Hedges Cup level on points in their group with Surrey, who had beaten them by 7 runs at The Oval. The quarter-final against Warwickshire featured a memorable innings by Gooch. He had lost his opening partner, Lilley, on 2, and it had taken him eight overs to open his score. After ten overs, with Willis bowling at his best (his first six overs cost 1 run), Essex were 19 for one.

McEwan helped Gooch to add 105, and once Gooch was in his stride he flayed the Warwickshire bowling to all parts of the field. Even with a ring of fielders shielding the boundary, he found the fence nineteen times and once he lifted a massive six into the Chelmsford car park. Willis trapped him leg-before to the second ball of the final over, but by then he had made 138, and Essex's 271 for five was too much for Warwickshire.

It was after this match that Gooch made his remark that there was little point in signing an overseas player if he was not going to win you something. He was referring in particular to Ferreira, the South African medium-pacer whom Warwickshire had signed and whose eleven overs cost 72 runs for the wicket of Lilley.

In the semi-final Essex came back from the dead to beat Yorkshire. Boycott was unfit, but Lumb and Hampshire scored 107 for the first wicket while the former skipper offered criticism from the commentary box. Hampshire fell to a running catch on the boundary by Turner, and Yorkshire fell apart, mustering a disappointing 173 for nine. Lilley again went cheaply, and Essex lost wickets every time they looked like taking control of the game. Victory eventually came off the last ball of the fifty-fourth over when Neil Smith, the wicket-keeper whom Yorkshire had rejected, stroked Cooper to the cover boundary.

The final, on a glorious summer day in July, produced a great match. Essex's opponents were Surrey, the only side to have beaten them, but Lord's seemed to belong to Essex. Certainly, the neutrals had moved their support to Essex, who were to win their first trophy after 103 years as a county cricket club. Mike Denness, twenty-eight times an England player, said that he had never before in his entire career been greeted by a roar like the one that welcomed him and Gooch as they came down the pavilion steps to begin the Essex innings. The pair scored 48 for the first wicket, and then Ken McEwan joined Gooch, and we saw champagne cricket. At lunch Essex were 166 for one from thirty-seven overs.

Only 6 runs had been added after lunch when McEwan sliced Hugh Wilson to Jack Richards behind the stumps. McEwan's 72 had come off ninety-nine balls, and he and Gooch had added 124, which was a record for the final. Fletcher played a delightful cameo innings of 34 off thirty balls, and Gooch moved to the first century recorded in a Benson and Hedges final. He was out in the fifty-third over for 120, which included three sixes and eleven fours. Here, indeed, was power and glory. Essex's total of 290 for six remains the highest score made in a final of the Benson and Hedges Cup.

In spite of the early loss of Butcher, of whom much had been expected, and of the hard-hitting Monte Lynch, Surrey made a splendid bid for victory and, at one time, Roger Knight and Geoff Howarth were rivalling Gooch and McEwan with their scoring rate. The task proved too great, however, and Essex won by 35 runs.

It was a highly emotional occasion, and it emphasised how important the Benson and Hedges Cup and the Gillette Cup had become. Cricketers who knew that they would never play for England still dreamed of appearing in a national final and playing in front of a packed house at Lord's. Such dreams have increased with the years.

Essex were already well ahead in the County Championship by the time they won the Benson and Hedges Cup, and they never slackened their grip on the title. They were confirmed as champions when they beat Northamptonshire at Northampton by seven wickets on 21 August. The fact that they finished seventy-seven points in front of Worcestershire would suggest that the title was theirs long before then.

The strength of Essex lay in their wonderful team spirit and the sheer joy that they had in playing the game. The nucleus of the team had come together in a period of adversity, when financial crisis brought the club close to extinction and when they operated with a staff of twelve players.

They had also shared bitter disappointments. Three times they had finished level on points at the top of the John Player League; three times they had been deprived of the title by mathematical calculations.

There had been some wise acquisitions. Neil Smith had come from Yorkshire to succeed Brian Taylor and, for a brief period, he was as good as any keeper in the land. Brian Hardie had been brought down from Scotland to give substance to the batting. Wrongly considered a stonewaller because of one rearguard innings, he was, in fact, a power-ful hitter of the ball. In the mid-1970s Mike Brearley had recognised Essex as a formidable side only lacking strength at number five. Hardie provided that strength, although he frequently opened the innings.

Denness brought the experience of winning, and Fletcher had matured into one of the most able captains the county game has seen. He read the game with acute perception. He knew the strengths and weaknesses of others, and his judgements were shrewd. Behind him was a fine Test record for which he had been given scant recognition, and the criticism he had received had tended to drive him closer to his team and to Essex. Within the next few years he was to receive accolades which were long overdue.

Gooch, Fletcher's designated lieutenant, was rapidly growing into one of the most powerful batsmen in the world, although his first Test century was still a year away, and in 1979 his record could not compare with that of Ken McEwan.

When one reflects on cricket in England in the late 1970s and early 1980s the image of Ken McEwan batting with regal splendour constantly recurs. Here was a beauty of style that will remain a joy for ever. He had come to England from South Africa in 1972 and had played for Sussex's second eleven, but Sussex felt that they had no room for him as an overseas player and, in 1974, he joined Essex. For the next decade this charming and dignified man graced the cricket grounds of England, shared in the winning of every trophy county cricket had to offer and scored with a consistency and abundance that only Barry Richards of other South African batsmen could rival.

Shy and modest, descended from Scottish immigrants, McEwan refused to follow such cricketers as Allan Lamb and Tony Greig into the England side. 'I just wouldn't feel right walking down the steps at Lord's with three lions on my sweater,' he said.

Eventually, he left Essex to return to South Africa and farm, although there was much cricket left in him and many records within his reach. It was just that he was tired of driving up and down the motorways of England with no hope of Test cricket at the end of the journeys.

By 1984 Robin Marlar in the *Sunday Times* considered McEwan as second only to Gooch among players in England, for he treated 'batting like the ancients, awaiting strike in a sideways-on stance, and almost still'. McEwan rarely, if ever, complained, but that his best years should coincide with South Africa's period of excommunication was a tragedy for Test cricket and for the game as a whole.

With the loss of Keith Boyce through injury, Essex turned to another West Indian pace bowler, Norbert Phillip. He was never in the top rank, but he was quick, and he provided the perfect foil for John Lever, left-arm fast-medium, always fit, a splendid team man, and one of the two bowlers to take more than a hundred wickets in 1979. Bob Willis said of

Lever that the England side was always better for having him in the eleven.

To back them in both batting and bowling were such men as Stuart Turner and Keith Pont. Turner was the epitome of all that was good in county cricket. He performed above his natural ability, always gave 100 per cent, was constantly bristling with endeavour and was one of those 'bread and butter' cricketers upon whom all successful sides are built.

Between 1979 and 1986 this team, with gradual additions and amendments, like the arrival of Foster and Pringle, was to win the Championship four times, the Sunday League three times and the NatWest Trophy and Benson and Hedges Cup.

Elsewhere, cricket was moving rapidly and changing complexion even faster. In Australia peace was declared and the marriage was announced of the Australian Cricket Board and World Series Cricket. Kerry Packer had won his bride and the dowry that came with her. In celebration the Australian Board implored England to send a team to Australia in 1979–80 to play three Tests and a series of one-day internationals in a triangular tournament involving the West Indies.

England agreed, somewhat reluctantly. Australia recalled their Packer players to the fold; England called on Underwood. The finger of scorn was pointed at Brearley as critics observed that the first time he was confronted by the full-strength Australian side under Greg Chappell, and with brother Ian back in the side, he was trounced by three Tests to nil. Matters were not quite as simple as that.

Cricket had become subservient to the demands of television. The whole package was the germ of a disease which was to spread throughout the world in the next decade. The sickness dictated that Test cricket, limited-overs internationals and television coverage were all that mattered in the game. It brought with it coloured clothing, white balls and floodlit cricket, and an element of theatrical dissent which was to become a canker.

Never can England have begun a tour in such an atmosphere of rancour. The party was already in Australia before playing conditions for the tour had been agreed, but the negotiating skills of Alec Bedser and Mike Brearley brought about a satisfactory solution to this problem. On top of this, Ray Steele, the Australian official, had made derogatory remarks about 'whingeing Poms', and the Australian Board was resentful that it had had to increase its guarantee to England players to woo them into making the trip. Another argument broke out as to who should pay for England to have practice under floodlights. The Australian Board insisted that the TCCB should foot the bill, but they later relented and agreed to pay for the electricity.

The return of the WSC players to the domestic scene in Australia was marked by the fact that six of them were reported by umpires for swearing in Sheffield Shield matches. Ian Chappell threw away his bat in disgust after brushing with an umpire in the match between South Australia and the England tourists, but he received only a suspended sentence. He had already served a three-week suspension for swearing in the match between South Australia and Tasmania, and missed the first Test against the West Indies.

The crowd at the first Test between England and Australia at Perth witnessed Dennis Lillee arriving at the crease wielding an aluminium bat. Brearley, the umpires and Greg Chappell, the Australian captain, objected to him using the bat, but it took ten minutes to persuade him to change it for a conventional model. During this time he threw something of a tantrum, but the Australian authorities showed their weakness in handling the whole incident. They had paid a heavy price for making peace with Kerry Packer, and one of their publicised concessions was that they would listen to and consider what the players wanted. Priorities became sadly distorted.

It is hardly likely that the players wanted the excessive and cluttered international programme that was devised. The emphasis on internationals meant that Kim Hughes, captain of Western Australia, was not available to play for his state in a single first-class match.

Ray Steele's inflammatory comments were tactfully handled by Alec Bedser, but nothing could be done to quell the loutish behaviour of some of the spectators and some of the Australian players. The divide between WSC players and those who had stood outside the organisation was apparent. Brearley was taunted by Lillee and booed wherever he went. His crime was obvious. He had received a university education and had led England to convincing victories over Australia in two successive Ashes series. In a day–night one-day international at Sydney the England fielders were pelted with missiles.

England did what Australia fully expected them to do: they lost all three Tests. The Ashes were not at stake, but Australian pride was restored even if the game was sullied.

England gave first Test caps to Dilley and Larkins. Botham took eleven wickets in the first Test, while Boycott carried his bat through the second innings for 99. Gower was left unbeaten on 98 in the second Test. At Melbourne Botham hit a century and Gooch ran himself out on 99. The party must have been much relieved to fly to Bombay to play India in a Test which celebrated the Golden Jubilee of the formation of the Indian Board of Control.

England won the match by ten wickets inside four days. Ian Botham became the first cricketer to score a century and to take ten or more wickets in the same Test match. He batted 206 minutes and hit seventeen fours in his 114. Coupled with this he took six for 58 and seven for 48. Graham Stevenson, the Yorkshire medium-pace bowler, made his Test debut, and Bob Taylor established a world Test record with ten catches in the match, seven of them in the first innings.

This was meant to be Mike Brearley's last match as a Test cricketer. The tour of Australia had come as an emergency epilogue. Readily available for his county, Brearley celebrated by leading Middlesex to the County Championship and to the Gillette Cup in 1980.

He had the advantage of a finely balanced, quality attack. Believing that Wayne Daniel would be selected for the West Indian touring party, Middlesex signed Vincent van der Bijl, a gentle giant from South Africa who bowled relentlessly accurate fast-medium with a grudging action which suggested that he was reluctant to let the ball go. Let it go he did, for he finished second in the first-class bowling averages with eighty-five wickets. Daniel was not chosen by the West Indies, and Middlesex suddenly found themselves with the most fearsome attack in the Championship.

To support this pair were Selvey and the up-and-coming Simon Hughes, while the spin duo of Emburey and Edmonds was the best in the country. Ever ready to step in when required was the veteran Fred Titmus.

Brearley not only led the side with his customary flair and intelligence, but, whatever his failings at Test level, he batted with confidence and consistency. He was most ably served by Clive Radley, blond and chunky, who judged the length of each ball expertly before steering it through the field and scurrying for his runs. He was a brilliant fielder and a constantly busy cricketer, a true professional, rightly respected and admired.

Like Radley, Graham Barlow was a brilliant fielder who patrolled the covers with the stealth and anticipation of a cat. He was just short of true Test class, but his left-handed batting was rugged, dependable and aggressive. He struggled with a back injury, and he played with success for as long as he did through sheer determination. He was totally adaptable, a wonderful servant to the club.

So, too, was Mike Gatting, who would come to the wicket swinging his bat, take his guard and offer the bowler no sight of his stumps with his stocky figure. His whole posture said 'they shall not pass', but he was no purely defensive rock. He was a pugnacious batsman, capable of destroying any attack in the country. He was slow to realise his potential

310

in Test cricket, but he was a dominant force in the county game, honest, open and brave, a fighter for his cause. He was to succeed Brearley as captain of Middlesex in 1983, and his record as captain was in no way inferior to Brearley's, although the style may have been different. Gatting was the tough, hardened professional, scarred in battle and honoured for those scars.

Giving more substance to the batting, often as an opener, was wicket-keeper Paul Downton, imported from Kent. His arrival caused Ian Gould to depart to Sussex, where he found glory. Highly regarded by John Murray, Downton never quite captured the imagination of the public, but he was a very effective and reliable keeper and a batsman good enough to score more than 8,000 runs in first-class cricket.

One could never call Roland Butcher reliable, but here was a batsman of immense flair. In the Gillette Cup Final, when Middlesex were behind the required run rate, he hit three sixes and five fours and finished with 50 not out to bring victory over Surrey by seven wickets with 6.1 overs to spare. Brearley was unbeaten on 96, but Butcher's innings earned him the Man of the Match award from adjudicator Ian Botham.

Born in Barbados, he batted with Caribbean zest. He was never consistent, but, two or three times a season, he was capable of winning a match off his own bat. England picked him for a Prudential Trophy match late in the 1980 season and he hit 50 off thirty-five balls. He was selected to go to the Caribbean with Botham's side where he played in three Test matches but not with great success.

Middlesex shared top-billing with Essex in the late 1970s and early 1980s. One of the secrets of their success was that both counties were able to bring about gradual changes to their personnel while never lapsing in standard.

In 1980 the Essex cupboard was bare. They were beaten in the final of the Benson and Hedges Cup, which was held over until the Monday because of rain. Northamptonshire took the trophy, winning by 6 runs. The Gold Award was won by Allan Lamb for his innings of 72.

South African-born Lamb had an outstanding season, finishing top of the national batting averages. Two other South Africans, Kepler Wessels of Sussex and Peter Kirsten of Derbyshire, were third and fourth. Glenn Turner, Javed Miandad, Clive Rice, Viv Richards and the New Zealand left-hander John Wright all followed close behind. The two bowlers to take a hundred wickets were Dilip Doshi of Warwickshire and Robin Jackman, the Surrey medium-pacer, who was impressive.

Doshi, the Indian slow left-armer, was a member of the Warwickshire side under Bob Willis which won the John Player League, some comfort for a couple of years of poor form in the Championship.

Cups eluded Somerset, who were hard hit by Test calls. Richards and Garner were with the West Indian side although Richards did appear in four games at the end of the season and hit 170 against Gloucestershire. Gavaskar was recruited to replace him and played some of those exquisite innings which marked his illustrious career, but he was never quite attuned to county cricket. Botham missed half of Somerset's matches in 1980, for he was appointed captain of England.

Bob Willis had been vice-captain to Brearley on the tour of Australia and in the Jubilee Test in India, and when Botham had been co-opted on to the selection committee during the tour Bedser had insisted that nothing of significance should be read into the move.

Brearley had left no obvious successor. Deposed at Yorkshire, where his relationship with manager Ray Illingworth was said to be becoming strained, Boycott's quirks of behaviour had made him increasingly unacceptable as an England captain. Willis, the faithful sergeant-major, had enough on his mind as spearhead of the England attack, and within the side there were no other obvious candidates. Roger Knight, captain of a Surrey side managed by Micky Stewart, was a good leader with the right pedigree and was much respected, but he was short of Test quality and did not possess the dynamic self-confidence of Brearley, which had enabled the Middlesex man to transcend his own playing limitations. Had he still held a place in the England eleven, Keith Fletcher, in the middle of a stunning period of success as captain of Essex, would have been an automatic choice, but his Test career was three years in the past, or so it was believed.

The debate raged, and there was more than one critic who said that he could not see what all the fuss was about and that the twenty-four-year-old Botham was the man for the job, even though he had never captained a county side. Eighteen months later those same voices were saying that he should never have been captain.

Botham made two mistakes. First, he had become too great a hero, too great a performer, and therefore was ripe to be knocked down and put in his place. Second, he captained England against the West Indies at their strongest, a mistake Brearley never made!

Nevertheless, the first Test at Trent Bridge was the only one in which England were beaten during the damp summer of 1980; and they only lost by two wickets. Chris Tavaré won his first England cap in this match, which was England's first defeat in a home Test since Cornhill Insurance had begun their sponsorship.

At Lord's Gooch hit his first Test century. It was an exciting affair, full of powerful shots which brought him 123 out of 165 in 211 minutes. He hit a six and seventeen fours and faced 162 balls. The rest of the England batting collapsed, and with Haynes, 184, and Richards, 145, scoring 223 for the West Indies' second wicket, rain came as something of a relief for the home country. The West Indies also had the better of the third Test, but England held the upper hand in the fourth at The Oval where Peter Willey hit an unbeaten 100. The match at Headingley lost the first and third days to rain.

There was a sixth Test to end the summer, the Centenary Test between England and Australia at Lord's. It was a ghastly match. If it were to celebrate a hundred years of Test cricket in England, then it should have been played at The Oval, where the first Test in England was staged. Several of the players gave the impression that they were not too keen to play, and, on the Saturday, with the sun shining, the umpires made several pitch inspections before allowing play to resume. Their reasons were not the pitch itself but old pitches close to that on which the match was being played. When Bird and Constant returned to the pavilion after their fifth inspection, Constant was assaulted in front of the Long Room by some angry MCC members. The announcement that play would continue until eight o'clock to compensate for time lost was greeted with derisory laughter, for it was obvious to all that, in a fading August, the light would have gone by shortly after seven.

What comforts there were from the match, and it is hard to recall any, were centuries for Australia from Wood and Hughes (an attractive one) and Boycott's second-innings century for England which took him past 7,000 runs in Test cricket. The match was drawn.

Botham had a wretched game. He failed to score and bowled mostly slow-medium off-breaks, or what appeared to be off-breaks, to a circle of fielders who were positioned mainly in no man's land. His generally poor performances against the West Indies had already given indication that captaincy was affecting the great man adversely.

It was difficult to assess what England had gained from the summer – a confident and maturing Gooch, the promise of Dilley and debuts for Tavaré and Athey, but little else of consequence.

Although the series against the West Indies had, for the most part, been conducted cordially, these were becoming troubled times. The hostility, sledging and dissent that England had experienced in Australia were not confined to that country. In a Test match in New Zealand Michael Holding had angrily and disgracefully kicked over the stumps when an appeal for a catch at the wicket had been rejected. To counter the bouncer, helmets had become the norm. Young players entering county cricket were surprised at the amount of verbal abuse that they witnessed, and as the *Evening News*, once a great supporter of cricket, died, television and the press maintained a constant search for conflict and controversy. As was to become apparent in the riots in Brixton and Toxteth in 1981, the United Kingdom was not at ease with itself.

The revolution caused by World Series Cricket had influences that were both good and bad, and it soon became obvious that one of its less than healthy effects was to bring about a proliferation in international cricket. Authorities throughout the world greedily and short-sightedly grabbed at what could be earned from Tests and one-day internationals, and the television rights, with scarcely a moment's consideration for their domestic competitions.

Close to extinction in the mid-1960s, the County Championship, now sponsored by Schweppes (and later by Britannic Assurance), had seen an improvement in its health. From 1981 onwards the TCCB decreed that pitches should be fully covered for all Championship matches, thereby denying future generations one of the greatest delights the game had to offer, a quality batsman contending with a good spin bowler on a sticky wicket. The experiment of covered pitches had first been tried in 1959, but it had been quickly abandoned. Now it was introduced to try to make county cricket as much like Test cricket as possible. This was not to be the last sacrifice demanded of the domestic first-class game.

Before this decree on pitches could come into operation the selectors had to choose a team to go to the Caribbean. There were three aspects of the chosen party which caused concern. As manager, A.C. Smith was given powers which were generally in excess of those accorded to previous tour managers. In this the TCCB were following a pattern which had been established at Surrey and Yorkshire, two counties who had cricket managers. What disturbed observers of the game was the haze as to where the captain's duties ended and the manager's began. Did the manager become captain during the lunch and tea intervals? There was criticism that Botham was being put in an ambiguous position on his first tour as captain, a tour which seemed difficult enough even before it began.

The choice of wicket-keepers also brought criticism. Following his ten catches and the establishment of a Test record, Bob Taylor was dropped in favour of Alan Knott. When Knott announced that he was no longer prepared to tour, Bairstow and Downton became the keepers to get the vote, even though Taylor was in top form and batting better than ever.

No left-arm bowler found a place in the party, and Robin Jackman, taker of 121 wickets at 15.40 runs each in 1980, was ignored. It was this omission – Stevenson was preferred – which triggered anger on the county circuit. Gloucestershire players, interviewed on television, commented, 'If he is not chosen, what chance is there for the rest of us?'

314

If the County Championship was where a cricketer had to prove himself, what more did Jackman have to do?

While one can understand the selectors' reluctance to send a reliable medium-pacer to the Caribbean, it would not have been difficult to afford him a place. It transpired that Jackman was soon to join the party; Willis broke down in Trinidad and did not appear in a first-class match. Jackman was called in as replacement.

The first Test at Port of Spain was a disaster. The start was delayed because the pitch had been vandalised by those protesting against the omission of Deryck Murray, the captain of Trinidad. Botham damaged a finger and had to retire for repairs, leaving Miller to take charge. Botham was also hit for a record 24 runs in one over by Roberts, and England lost by an innings.

The second Test did not take place. The team had been in Guyana for two days when they were joined by Jackman. Like Bairstow, who had captained Griqualand West, and other England players, Jackman had spent winters playing in South Africa. It was suggested that, in Jackman's case, this contravened the Gleneagles Declaration, an agreement outlawing sporting participation with South Africa as long as apartheid remained a policy of that country. The British High Commissioner in Georgetown was informed by the Minister of Foreign Affairs of Guyana that Jackman's visitor's permit was to be withdrawn and that he must leave the country. The Cricket Council's response was that as it was no longer possible for England to select their side without restrictions being imposed upon it, they would not play the second Test. For a while, the whole tour was in the balance, but the representatives of the other islands where England were due to play met and agreed that the tour should continue.

England did play a one-day international in Guyana, but even that took place in an atmosphere of uncertainty as to the Jackman affair. The Surrey bowler made his Test debut in Barbados and took the wicket of Gordon Greenidge with his fifth ball. By now England had also lost Brian Rose with eye trouble; the Test in Trinidad was to be the last of his nine appearances for England.

With Richards scoring 182 not out, the West Indies won the Bridgetown Test by 298 runs, but the whole game was overshadowed by the sudden death of Ken Barrington. Assistant manager on the tour, the former Surrey and England batsman died of a heart attack on the second evening of the match.

The England players were shattered, and much of the next three days was played in something of a mist. He had helped many of those in the party, and his advice in the nets and on technical matters was much

315

sought. He was well loved by the players, and batsmen, Gooch in particular, owed him a great deal. Gooch's 116 in the second innings, as he has
said himself, was something of a monument to Barrington.

The remaining two Tests were drawn, with Boycott, Willey, Gooch
and Gower all scoring centuries, but the West Indies had the best of both
encounters.

Few captains have had more to contend with than Botham had on this
tour, and, although he remained cheerful, his form suffered. He took
fifteen wickets in the series, which was a creditable performance for an
attack which, never strong, was weakened by injury, but his highest
score in the Tests was 26, and on the whole tour only 40. Botham was an
instinctive cricketer, a joyful one, and, as such, was not best served by
the restrictions of captaincy.

At the beginning of the 1981 season Botham remained in charge with no
obvious challenger on the horizon, but, like Dexter, the personal zest
that characterised him as a cricketer never became apparent in his
captaincy when, surprisingly, he trod so warily.

Thomson was not in the Australian party challenging for the Ashes,
but a new torment threatened England in the form of Terry Alderman,
who took nine wickets on his Test debut as Australia won by four wickets. The England performance was lacklustre. Downton, preferred to
Taylor on the grounds of his batting ability, had a poor match behind the
stumps, and Botham took much criticism for the ineptitude of the
England performance.

Emburey for Hendrick and Taylor for Downton were the only
changes England made for the Lord's Test, where Boycott won his
hundredth cap. It also proved to be Woolmer's last appearance for
England; he was not the player he had been in his days with World
Series Cricket.

The match was drawn, but it offered no comfort to those who loved
the game. Forced on to the defensive because of his lack of success – he
had led England in twelve Tests of which eight had been drawn and four
lost – Botham's captaincy took on an almost loutish manner. On the
Saturday at Lord's when the public-address system announced that
McEnroe had ended Borg's reign at Wimbledon, there was an atmosphere of gloom, for it seemed that sport had succumbed to the yob
dominance that was now sweeping society as a whole.

Botham, leg-before to Lawson for nought in the first innings, was
bowled by Bright, a left-arm spinner of moderate accomplishment, for
nought in the second. He left the field angrily, seemingly blaming the
world in general and critics in particular for his misfortunes. At the end

of the match he resigned the captaincy.

One of the depressing aspects of England under Botham was the tendency to play as individuals rather than as a team. At Lord's, for example, Boycott batted four hours for 60 in the second innings when it was essential that England pressed for quick runs, but the days when selectors demanded brighter cricket rather than victory had gone. England had just equalled their longest sequence without a win.

The third Test match at Headingley was only nine days away, and England needed a captain. The selectors asked Mike Brearley to return to Test cricket and attempt to save the situation. He agreed. He had been in good form for Middlesex, and the challenge excited him. As expected, Woolmer was omitted to accommodate Brearley, and Old replaced Emburey. This left Willey as England's only spin option, a decision which was strongly criticised.

Kim Hughes won the toss, and Australia batted. Fifty minutes were lost to the weather on the opening day, at the end of which Australia were 203 for three. Dyson made a positive century, and Hughes looked in fine form, but the encouraging aspect of the game from England's point of view was the form of Botham. He seemed to run in with all his old vigour, and he had Wood leg-before with his fifth ball. Sadly, the fielding and the rest of the attack were less impressive. Dilley was particularly wayward. When he bowled Dyson the Kent pace man gesticulated his contempt for the crowd. It was an action both immature and disgraceful, but symptomatic of falling standards of behaviour.

Dilley bowled nightwatchman Bright early on the second day, which followed a rather pedestrian course. It was enlivened after tea by Botham, who produced a spell of five for 35, which confirmed the impression that he was a much better player without the burden of captaincy.

Hughes's declaration left England two rather wild overs on the Friday evening from which they scored 7. Gooch was out to the first ball he received on the Saturday morning, playing across the line to Alderman. Brearley was caught behind, as was Gower, who had been dropped at slip the ball before. Boycott's leg stump was knocked back by Lawson. Gatting was leg-before pushing half forward, having been dropped at slip off a simple chance. Willey was yorked, and Taylor gave Marsh catching practice. Botham offered a belligerent counter-attack until he received a vicious lifter from Lillee which gave Marsh the record number of victims in Test cricket.

When Dilley lobbed a simple return catch to Lillee, England followed on 227 runs in arrears. Gooch was caught at slip off Lillee's third ball. Brearley made 14, and England came off for bad light. By six o'clock the

317

sun had broken through, and the light was better than it had been all day, but play did not resume. The rules had defied interpretation, and the paying customers were angry. The game had become alienated from its supporters, and those in authority remained arrogant and aloof. The England team itself had never been lower in public esteem. The odds being offered on an England victory were 500 to 1, which did not seem generous.

Monday suggested that it would be a day of formality. The Australian bowlers maintained a fuller length and a straighter line than the England bowlers had done. Brearley and Gower were caught at slip, and Gatting was leg-before. Peter Willey, with his two-eyed legs-splayed stance, offered a resistance that was as determined as he was refreshingly outspoken, before slicing an attempted cut into the hands of Dyson. Boycott was leg-before, although he did not seem to relish the decision. Taylor quickly followed the Yorkshireman and, by mid-afternoon, England were 135 for seven, still 92 runs short of avoiding an innings defeat. Several journalists and players had checked out of their hotels, which seemed a wise course of action.

By tea Botham and Dilley had advanced the score to 176. Botham had done what he always did best, batted with natural aggression and total lack of inhibition. Between tea and six o'clock he scored 106 of the 175 runs scored in twenty-seven overs. He moved down the pitch and hit Alderman high for six. Fours were crashed to all parts of the field, including, occasionally, over the heads of the slips, yet even these were not blemishes. When Lillee tried the bouncer Botham hooked it ruthlessly to the boundary. He reached his century off eighty-seven balls. Some suggested comparisons with Gilbert Jessop, but Jessop was not in this class. He hit only one Test century and averaged just over 21 in Test cricket. Botham needed no comparisons. He stood and smote majestically in his own right. This was an innings of immense magnitude. This was greatness.

In eighty minutes Botham and Dilley added 117. The left-handed Dilley drove through the covers with style and power. Often he did not move his feet, but his reach was fine and his heart was brave. He hit nine fours in his 56, and he helped make certain that Australia would have to bat again.

Bright was grossly underbowled. He was not a spinner of real Test class, but he would have offered contrast when Botham and Dilley were slaughtering the pace men. Old kept the momentum alive, helping Botham to add 67 in fifty-five minutes before being yorked by Lawson.

When Willis joined Botham the England lead was still under 100, but Willis did all that he had to do. He survived the balls that were bowled to him while Botham drove fours and took singles off the last ball of the over. The day ended with England on 351 for nine, Botham 145, Willis 1.

Botham had hit nineteen fours in reaching his century, and a searing cover drive on the last morning brought him his twenty-seventh boundary, in addition to the six off Alderman. Willis took a single and then edged Alderman low to second slip. Australia needed 130 to win.

With the acumen of the psychologist, Brearley gave the new ball to Botham and Dilley. Two deliveries from Botham, one a no-ball, produced 8 runs, and Australia were on their way, but, in the third over of the innings, Wood drove at Botham and was caught behind. This seemed of little import as Dyson, batting with the confidence of a first-innings century, and Trevor Chappell took the score past 50.

Dilley had conceded 11 runs in two overs, and Brearley brought on Willis to bowl five overs into the breeze up the hill. Willey replaced Willis, who was switched to the Kirkstall Lane end with the score on 48 for one.

Injury and limited success in the county game had caused doubts as to Willis's future. He was not originally selected for this Test on the grounds of fitness, but he had phoned the selectors and assured them that he was able to play. What he produced at Leeds on 21 July 1981 will ever remain as one of the greatest exhibitions of bowling that the game has known.

He bowled very fast, just short of a length and on a straighter line than he had adopted in the first innings. A violent lifter caught Chappell deflecting the ball off his glove from in front of his face and into the wicket-keeper's gloves. In the last over before lunch Hughes edged a fierce delivery low and to the left of Botham at third slip. The catch was taken with a breathtaking sureness. Yallop was held by Gatting at short-leg off bat and pad, and Willis had taken three wickets in eleven balls. Australia lunched at 58 for four.

Old had taken over from Willey shortly before lunch and was bowling accurately into the breeze. Border played back to him, misjudged the bounce and edged the ball into his stumps. Dyson, still batting confidently, had hooked Willis for four but, attempting to repeat the shot in the same bowler's next over, he gloved the ball down the leg side to Taylor.

Typically, Marsh was pugnacious. He swung terrifyingly at Willis, and Dilley at fine-leg took a superbly judged catch. Had he not held the ball, it would have gone for six. Lawson hung out his bat, and Taylor took the 1,271st catch of his career, so passing John Murray's record for first-class cricket.

Australia were now 75 for eight, and one even dared to contemplate the unthinkable, an England victory. This thought receded when Bright

319

clouted two leg-side fours in one over from Old, and Lillee twice hit Willis through the off side to the boundary. In four overs 35 runs were added. Brearley maintained calm and firm control. Willis, intelligently, bowled a fuller length, and Lillee scooped the ball towards mid-on where Gatting, running in, held a good catch as he fell forward.

Alderman came to the wicket with 20 runs needed, and Brearley brought on Botham for the *coup de grâce*. The tension was now at its highest, and twice in three balls Old put down Alderman at slip. It did not matter. Willis ended all uncertainty when he knocked Bright's middle stump out of the ground. England had won by 18 runs. It was the first time for eighty-seven years that a Test side had won after being asked to follow on.

The Great Escape – Botham and Willis
England v Australia at Headingley
16, 17, 18, 20 and 21 July 1981

Australia First Innings		Second Innings	
J. Dyson b Dilley	102	c Taylor b Willis	34
G.M. Wood lbw b Botham	34	c Taylor b Botham	10
T.M. Chappell c Taylor b Willey	27	c Taylor b Willis	8
K.J. Hughes (capt) c and b Botham	89	c Botham b Willis	0
R.J. Bright b Dilley	7	(8) b Willis	19
G.N. Yallop c Taylor b Botham	58	(5) c Gatting b Willis	0
A.R. Border lbw b Botham	8	(6) b Old	0
†R.W. Marsh b Botham	28	(7) c Dilley b Willis	4
G.F. Lawson c Taylor b Botham	13	c Taylor b Willis	1
D.K. Lillee not out	3	c Gatting b Willis	17
T.M. Alderman not out	0	not out	0
Extras (b 4, lb 13, w 3, nb 12)	32	(lb 3, w 1, nb 14)	18
Total for 9 wickets, dec.	401		111

BOWLING	Overs	Mdns	Runs	Wkts	Overs	Mdns	Runs	Wkts
Willis	30	8	72	–	15.1	3	43	8
Old	43	14	91	–	9	1	21	1
Dilley	27	4	78	2	2	–	11	–
Botham	39.2	11	95	6	7	3	14	1
Willey	13	2	31	1	3	1	4	–
Boycott	3	2	2	–	–	–	–	–

fall of wickets
1–55, 2–149, 3–196, 4–220, 5–332, 6–354, 7–357, 8–396, 9–401
1–13, 2–56, 3–58, 4–58, 5–65, 6–68, 7–74, 8–75, 9–110

England First Innings		Second Innings	
G.A. Gooch lbw b Alderman	2	c Alderman b Lillee	0
G. Boycott b Lawson	12	lbw b Alderman	46
J.M. Brearley (capt) c Marsh b Alderman	10	c Alderman b Lillee	14
D.I. Gower c Marsh b Lawson	24	c Border b Alderman ...	9
M.W. Gatting lbw b Lillee	15	lbw b Alderman	1
P. Willey b Lawson	8	c Dyson b Lillee	33
I.T. Botham c Marsh b Lillee	50	not out	149
†R.W. Taylor c Marsh b Lillee	5	c Bright b Alderman ...	1
G.R. Dilley c and b Lillee	13	b Alderman	56
C.M. Old c Border b Alderman ...	0	b Lawson	29
R.G.D. Willis not out	1	c Border b Alderman ...	2
Extras (b 6, lb 11, w 6, nb 11)	34	(b 5, lb 3, w 3, nb 5)	16
Total	174	356	

BOWLING	Overs	Mdns	Runs	Wkts	Overs	Mdns	Runs	Wkts
Lillee	18.5	7	49	4	25	6	94	3
Alderman	19	4	59	3	35.3	6	135	6
Lawson	13	3	32	3	23	4	96	1
Bright	–	–	–	–	4	–	15	–

fall of wickets
1–12, 2–40, 3–42, 4–84, 5–87, 6–112, 7–148, 8–166, 9–167
1–0, 2–18, 3–37, 4–41, 5–105, 6–133, 7–135, 8–252, 9–319
umpires – D.G.L Evans and B.J. Meyer
England won by 18 runs

Within forty-eight hours the prestige of English cricket had been restored. Brearley had raised the side in the field, and Botham, Man of the Match, was reinstated as the greatest all-rounder since W.G. Grace. And what of Bob Willis?

Before the match began many people considered him to be no longer a bowler of international quality. He had responded by taking eight for 43 to win a match that was all but lost. He bowled like a man possessed. There was fire in his eyes and in his heart. This was a bowling performance that transcended interpretation by statistics, for it was accomplished through passion and extraordinary human endeavour. As he knocked over Bright's wicket he wheeled away to the pavilion, face almost drawn with accumulated passion, his arms held out in expression of the exhilaration within him. 'Botham rekindles the Ashes', blared the headlines. Willis had fanned the flames.

321

This was the first series in England in which there was play on Sunday, although not at Lord's or Headingley. At Edgbaston, the venue of the fourth Test, the game ended on the Sunday. England made one change with Emburey replacing Dilley. Brearley moved up to open, with Gooch dropping down to number four. Gooch had a most disappointing series and was left out of the side for the last Test at The Oval.

The Edgbaston match was remarkable in that it was the first Test since the war in which no batsman reached 50. Australia led by 69 runs on the first innings and bowled England out for 219 on the Saturday. This meant that they needed just 151 runs to win. Wood was leg-before to Old on the third evening, and when play began at noon on the Sunday Australia were 142 runs short of victory with nine wickets standing.

The day was hot and the crowd was large and noisy. In the sixth over of the day, Willis had Dyson leg-before when he played back. Hughes hooked Willis to Emburey on the square-leg boundary 10 runs later. Australia were 29 for three, and the phantom of Headingley was looming.

Border and Yallop set about restoration and attempted to dampen Willis's fire. They both had escapes and, at lunch, Australia were 62 for three. Emburey, who had made an invaluable unbeaten 37 and shared an eighth-wicket stand of 50 with Old on the Saturday, broke the partnership when he had Yallop taken at silly point. The crucial wicket came 18 runs later when Emburey caused a ball to jump at Border, who gave a simple catch to short-leg. Australia were 105 for five, and victory was tantalisingly close.

Marsh cut his first ball for four, and he was at the crease with Kent, who had scored 46 in the first innings and was making his Test debut, when Brearley called up Botham to take over from Willis at the City End. Brearley had already asked Willey to warm up but had changed his mind and turned to Botham, who was reluctant to bowl. He had lacked pace and rhythm in the first innings. Now he pounded in with all his old ferocity. Marsh swung wildly and had his stumps scattered. Next ball Bright was totally beaten by a delivery that was fast and low. Australia were 114 for seven, and the ghost walked.

The crowd bayed for blood every time that Botham ran in. As Richie Benaud so aptly commented as the roar grew, 'The score at the moment is Lions one, Christians nil.'

Incomprehensibly, Lillee chased a wide delivery and Taylor took the catch at the second attempt. Kent, the last authentic batsman, drove desperately and was bowled off his pads. Alderman was beaten by two deliveries and bowled by the third. In twenty-eight balls Ian Botham had taken five wickets for 1 run. The last six Australian wickets had gone down in forty-seven minutes for 16 runs. Lightning had struck twice. England had won by 29 runs.

Australia went to Old Trafford 2–1 down in a series which, in truth, they should have been winning 3–0. England clinched the Ashes in Manchester, winning their third rubber against Australia under Mike Brearley's captaincy. There was no close finish this time. England led by 101 on the first innings, and Willis took three wickets in an over. Earlier he and Allott, making his Test debut, had added 56 for England's last wicket. Allott hit his maiden first-class fifty.

Tavaré, recalled to the side in place of Willey, scored 78 in 423 minutes, the slowest fifty in English first-class cricket at that time. In contrast Botham hit 118 off 102 balls in 123 minutes. His century came off only eighty-six balls, and his six sixes in a Test innings was a record.

At the insistence of Brearley, England had recalled Knott in place of Taylor to strengthen the batting. This was his penultimate Test; he made 13 and 59. It was typical that he should be at the crease when the last Test, at The Oval, was drawn. He was unbeaten on 70. A record of 4,389 runs, including five centuries, and 269 dismissals in ninety-five Tests tells its own story, but it only indicates a fraction of his value to his side where he was a constant source of inspiration. Eccentric in his food fads and his rituals he may have been, but he had an inner strength and dedication that very few have ever been able to match. He fashioned his own batting technique with pushes and dabs that frustrated the bowler because he seemed to anticipate every delivery. To the end of his career in 1985, he remained in the opinion of the majority the best wicket-keeper in the world. His colleague and friend Derek Underwood expressed the view that Kent should pay for a taxi to bring him to every match, just on Sundays if he wished, so valuable was he to the side, so great a difference would his presence make. He was never extrovertly spectacular, but he pulled off some extraordinarily spectacular dismissals. He pleased all schools of thought because he was a fine batsman and a supreme wicket-keeper. His departure left a void that was never to be filled to the satisfaction of all.

The Oval Test finally marked the end of Brearley's Test career, too. No captain had ever ended his Test career with such a dramatic series victory. His strengths and weaknesses have been paraded in these pages, and yet perhaps his greatest strength of all was that it did not really matter to him. He never believed that cricket was the most important thing in the world.

England owed most for the victory in the Ashes series to Botham, whose ten wickets at The Oval gave him thirty-four for the rubber. He was a cricketer reborn and, more than that, he imbued others with a love of the game, and drew young people to watch cricket. It became fashionable within the next few years to conduct character assassinations of Botham, referring to allegations about his private life, his weight and the public image he often presented, but the simple truth came in words like those of a young woman undergraduate at Oxford: 'I'd never been interested in cricket until my father took me to see Ian Botham in 1981. I've tried never to miss a match since.'

The greatness and the magnetism were undenied, but that he was not a captain was also apparent. So, once again, who would succeed Brearley?

In the Benson and Hedges Cup Somerset roared to victory over Surrey, but their might, apart from Botham, lay in the two West Indians Joel Garner and Viv Richards. The first took five for 14 in the final, the second, the most spectacular batsman in the game, hit 132 not out in forty-two overs.

The 1981 Championship saw a wonderful struggle between Nottinghamshire and Sussex which was eventually decided, with a little fortune, in favour of the former. Sussex were well led by John Barclay, who was to do much for young people and for the game as a whole, but who was never close to international class. Ian Greig, the younger brother of the former England captain, had a fine all-round season and was to win two Test caps in 1982, while Paul Parker was in the England side against Australia at The Oval. The Sri Lankan-born Gehan Mendis was an excellent opening batsman, but the real strength of the side was to be found in Imran Khan, the Pakistani all-rounder, and Garth le Roux, a South African pace bowler.

Nottinghamshire were indebted to the England selectors for not calling on the ebullient Derek Randall and had excellent service from off-spinner Eddie Hemmings, formerly with Warwickshire. Again, though, the main strength was in two overseas cricketers. Richard Hadlee took 105 wickets and topped the national averages; he also scored over 700 runs. Clive Rice scored nearly 1,500 runs and took sixty-five wickets; he also proved to be one of the most astute captains the first-class game in England has known.

The sixty-over knockout competition, now sponsored for the first time by the NatWest Bank, was won in thrilling manner by Derbyshire. Chasing Northamptonshire's 235 for nine, they lost six wickets and levelled the scores when Miller and Tunnicliffe ran a leg-bye off the last ball of the match. Their main thrust in batting had come from a second-wicket stand of 121 between the New Zealander John Wright, an outstanding player off the back foot, and the South African Peter

Kirsten. Derbyshire were captained by Barry Wood, the former Lancashire and England player, now forty-one.

The John Player League had gone to Keith Fletcher's Essex who, as already discussed, were recognised as one of the two most prominent county sides of the time. It was to Fletcher that the selectors turned when they chose the man to captain the side to India. He was thirty-seven and had been out of the England side for five years.

In the prevailing atmosphere the appointment of Fletcher was welcomed. It was seen as a just reward for a man with a good Test record who had fought hard to overcome early prejudices and who had proved himself to be a most sagacious captain at county level with a fine tactical awareness. Similar approval was to greet his appointment as England manager/coach on a five-year contract in 1992. That appointment, too, was to end in grief.

There were problems about the tour of India before it began. The clash between Illingworth and Boycott at Yorkshire had resulted in the manager temporarily suspending Boycott for his public criticism of his omission from the Sunday League side. The White Rose county was in a state of open civil war.

Boycott was at the centre of another controversy. When the party to tour India was announced the Indian government reacted by stating that the presence in the side of Boycott and Geoff Cook, the Northamptonshire captain, was unacceptable as both had recently played cricket in South Africa. There was a flurry of diplomatic activity, further complicated because Boycott was holidaying in Hong Kong. The greatest fear on the part of cricket administrators was that if the tour were cancelled, the cricket world would divide into two sections, black and white. The South African question was becoming more and more sensitive each day. The West Indies had cancelled a series against New Zealand because that country had played South Africa at rugby.

The Boycott–Cook problem was resolved by the two players making a statement which announced their repugnance for apartheid. This statement was accepted by Mrs Gandhi and her government, and the tour went ahead.

There were few other problems at the start of the tour, but Fletcher proved to be an inflexible captain. Scarred by his own experiences against Lillee and Thomson and being himself a master of spin, he believed that pace would defeat India. On Indian pitches this was poor judgement. England lost the first Test and thereafter draw followed draw with slow pitches and abysmal over-rates. A few months later it was decreed that ninety-six overs a day should be bowled in Test

325

matches. (In 1987 the ICC would demand a rate of fifteen overs an hour.) Barely thirteen overs an hour were managed between India and England, and the England players did not enjoy the series.

Botham completed the double of 2,000 Test runs and 200 Test wickets, but, having taken nine wickets in the first Test, he was as blunted as anyone in the games that followed.

Boycott and Tavaré scored centuries in the third Test in Delhi, and Fletcher declared at 476 for nine, but India still led on the first innings. At Eden Gardens, Calcutta, Boycott scored 18 and 6, which gave him two world records, 193 Test innings and 8,114 Test runs. He had passed Sobers's record aggregate during his 105 at Delhi, then batted with a degree of levity at Calcutta, where he was substituted because he felt unwell – and had gone off to play golf. A few days later, a fortnight after breaking the world record, he was flying back to England because of physical and mental tiredness. A month later he was opening the batting for the rebel England XI in South Africa.

Boycott had set up a record, left a note, and walked out of Test cricket. His career as a cricketer, a captain, a committee member and even as a commentator was constantly shrouded in controversy. He was not a natural-born batsman. He did not possess the innate flair of a Compton or a Gower. He did not have the easy command of technique and the range of shots with which Hutton was gifted. Yet the respected umpire 'Dickie' Bird would not be alone in saying that if he had to choose a man to bat for his life, it would be Geoff Boycott. Boycott dedicated himself to the game. He worked tirelessly to eradicate faults from his batting, to eschew any hint of danger. This self-centred approach won him few friends among fellow players, and he always aroused conflicting passions.

Never was this more apparent than in Yorkshire itself where, following the triumphs of the sides under Sellers, Yardley, Burnett and Close, there was a drought in team success. Bereft of eleven heroes, many concentrated all their passions on one, Geoff Boycott, but perhaps this was a role for which this dedicated opening batsman was miscast. By his prowess and his very nature, he drew attention to himself and to his deeds, but he was never quite able to cope with that attention. He needed its recognition just as he needed the assurance of the wealth he accumulated, but his enigma was that he was a solitary figure and only at home in his own world at the crease.

With Boycott departed, England had two more Tests in India. Gooch scored a century in one, and Botham in the other. Then the team went to Sri Lanka to welcome that country to Test cricket with a match in Colombo. Geoff Cook made his debut, and England won, although with

326

some anguish. Sri Lanka were 152 for three at the end of the third day but lost their last seven wickets for 8 runs in sixty-eight balls on the fourth morning. Emburey had a spell of five for 5 and finished with six for 33. Reports suggested that, rather than Fletcher, it was Willis who roused England from their slumbers.

Victory came by seven wickets, but by that time another bombshell was about to explode in the world of cricket.

8

Fall from Grace, 1982–88

Rumours concerning the Packer revolution had circulated long before the news officially broke. In contrast the rebel tour of South Africa in the spring of 1982 took people by surprise. On 27 February, just six days after the conclusion of the inaugural Test in Sri Lanka, a group of England cricketers flew from London to South Africa to play a series of matches. They had taken every precaution to keep their plans secret, but when the news of the venture became known the TCCB made every effort to persuade them not to play in the Republic. The pleas and warnings went unheeded by the cricketers concerned, five of whom – Gooch, Boycott, Lever, Emburey and Underwood – had been members of Fletcher's side in India. Another five – Humpage, Old, Woolmer, Sidebottom and Les Taylor – were already in South Africa where they were involved in various coaching and playing engagements. A third group of five – Knott, Hendrick, Willey, Amiss and Larkins – had spent most of the winter in England and flew to South Africa with the others.

On 9 March, their warnings having been ignored, the TCCB had no option but to impose a ban on the cricketers concerned: Gooch and company were barred from international cricket for three years. The TCCB justified their action by saying that they had a duty 'to protect our legitimate and important objective towards achieving multiracial cricket'.

Attitudes towards the South African problem by the cricket establishment remained ambivalent. Some in England had many friends on 'the other side', and the cricketers from the Veldt had always been warm, friendly, generous and courteous people whose manners and cricketing traditions were understood and admired. In undertaking the tour, sponsored by South African Breweries, the English cricketers had broken no TCCB rules, but the most that could be said in their favour was that they

328

had been politically naive. Had they been soccer players, the ban imposed by FIFA would have been for life and would have taken immediate effect with no chance of appeal.

Had the TCCB not acted, the forthcoming tours of England by India and Pakistan would have been in jeopardy, for the United Kingdom's attitude towards the boycott of South Africa was being considered with increasing scepticism in many quarters.

It is hard to have sympathy for the rebel band. The whole plan had been plotted during the tour of India, and the principal conspirators were Gooch and Boycott. The latter, as we have seen, achieved personal landmarks and then walked out. Gooch was hatching his plot behind the back of his county captain, colleague and friend.

The group offered several excuses for their action, the most notable of which was that nobody had ever given them any assurance that they would continue to be picked for England, but then they were living in a society where the notion of a job for life in banking, education or any other profession had recently passed into history. This was a period of conflict. The year was to be dominated by the Falklands War, and South Africa itself was to suffer increasing outbreaks of urban terrorism.

Perhaps one of the most ludicrous reasons offered for joining the tour was that ascribed to Les Taylor, the Leicestershire pace bowler, who was quoted as saying that he joined the party since he saw no prospect of playing for England because of his mining background. That the cricket establishment remained class-conscious was true, but they have never shunned a fast bowler from the mines.

Few of us ever like to admit that our actions are dictated by finance, but Gooch, elected captain by his fellows, and the others received between £10,000 and £40,000 for their three weeks' work. To many eyes that would seem reason enough for going. Cricketers are notoriously concerned about the uncertainty of their futures, and it cannot be easy to refuse a temptation that would allow you to pay off your house mortgage by playing cricket in a beautiful country for a few weeks, whatever the political system.

There were those who refused, Ian Botham and Geoff Cook among them. Botham said he would never be able to look his friend Viv Richards in the eyes again if he accepted the offer, and he jokingly added that he did not think the South Africans could afford him anyway.

The tour was not the success that the South African authorities had anticipated, but Gooch and his men survived well. Despite the three-year ban several were to return to Test cricket, to enjoy bumper benefits and to find their way on to the honours list.

The mercenary path taken by Gooch and the others was not a solitary

329

one, for the nation had moved into an age where profit had become the only motive; indeed it had become something of a god.

For some years the disease had gripped soccer in a variety of forms. There had been a time when a boy or girl born in Ipswich or Swindon would never have contemplated supporting sides other than Ipswich Town or Swindon Town. Now, a boy born and bred in the East End of London would claim that his allegiance was to Liverpool, Manchester United or Leeds United, as long as they were winning. Television had brought big, wealthy clubs closer and distanced people from their local communities.

Cricket was following a similar pattern, not so much in people changing allegiances, but in their being wedded to success. Once men had gone to watch their counties and to see Hammond, Hutton, Compton or Trueman. The Championship was monopolised by a select group, but that did not matter, for the game was enjoyed and the sight of the great entertainers was enough for the public. Now winning had become all-important, so that Kent committee members could say in the early 1980s, 'We are in a transitional period, and we know that we are not going to win anything this season. We know also that that will cost us two thousand members at the end of the year.'

Sussex supporters had let down the tyres on the Essex mini-bus after their county had been beaten in a NatWest Cup quarter-final; Doug Insole, the Essex chairman, railed at Essex followers when there was unruly behaviour in a Sunday League game. Some behaviour on the pitch was becoming questionable, and sledging was still rampant in international cricket.

It was against this background that Peter May became chairman of selectors in 1982 with a special requirement that he should restore more discipline and order into the game. Alec Bedser continued on the committee. In his twelve years as chairman, he had received no payment other than travel expenses, and this at a time when sponsorship was pouring money into the game, and a county like Essex, organised as a streamlined business under the stewardship of Peter Edwards, could claim that all its first-team players had sponsored cars, and that the senior administrators and many second-team players had them, too. Aware of these anomalies, Bedser, on his retirement from the chair, recommended that May should receive a salary of at least £1,700 a year, which, for the responsibility being undertaken, was hardly excessive. May himself could certainly not contemplate giving up his position with Wills, Faber and Dumas, and the time he allocated to his duties as a selector were, of necessity, limited.

May's principal problem was, of course, that he and his committee

330

would have to choose sides that did not include some of the best players in the land. His first step was to dismiss Fletcher from the captaincy
with, it was reported, an uncharacteristic lack of grace. May could not
have been impressed with Fletcher's seeming lack of awareness as to
what was going on among those he was supposed to be leading, nor
would May have been happy with Fletcher's reaction to an umpiring
decision when he knocked back his off stump. Fletcher was a shrewd
tactician, but he had been outmanoeuvred in India. It was not a good
year for him. Even with players like Gooch and Lever available all
summer, Essex won nothing. The arch-enemy Middlesex regained the
County Championship in Brearley's last year of captaincy. Another
south-eastern county, Surrey, crushed Warwickshire in the NatWest
Trophy while Somerset gained an equally emphatic victory over
Nottinghamshire in retaining the Benson and Hedges Cup. Sussex won
the John Player League for the first time.

What comfort could May and his selectors find in all this? Brearley
was on the point of retirement. Somerset still owed much to Garner and
Richards. The two most feared bowlers in the country, Marshall, the only
one to take 100 wickets, and Sylvester Clarke of Surrey were both West
Indians. Top of the batting averages by a big margin was Glenn Turner,
Worcestershire's New Zealander, who reached his hundredth hundred
by hitting 311 not out in a day against Warwickshire. Second, third and
fourth places in the averages went to Zaheer Abbas, Alvin Kallicharran
and Peter Kirsten.

May was open about his dislike of the way in which counties clus-
tered to engage overseas players. Like several others, he had been
angered when Middlesex rushed to sign Jeff Thomson as soon as they
learned that he had not been selected in the Australian side to tour
England in 1981. In the event Thomson played only half a season,
returning to Australia after an operation for appendicitis.

Few chairmen could have started their terms of office with the dice
loaded so heavily against them, but May knew the qualities he wanted.
Bob Willis, who had resisted the tempting offers from both Packer and
the South African Breweries, was the epitome of all that was loyal and
good. He had rallied England in Sri Lanka and, having served periods
as vice-captain, he now took over the leadership of his country for the
1982 three-Test home series against India. He won the first Test and drew
the next two, and his captaincy was extended to include the three Tests
against Pakistan.

Randall and Edmonds were recalled to the colours, and there were
first caps for Allan Lamb and Derek Pringle. Pringle had blossomed into
a fine all-rounder and captain at Cambridge, where he was in his third

331

year. The Varsity Match was no longer the great event it had been in May's time and in a domestic season crowded with Tests and one-day internationals it was scheduled to coincide with the second Test against India at Old Trafford. To the consternation of traditionalists, Pringle opted to play for England rather than leading his university, but his decision was made with the full backing and encouragement of his fellow undergraduates.

Lamb had qualified for England by residence and now held a British passport. He was the son of British parents, but he was South African by birth, which was unmistakable when he spoke. There was an irony, though, in that here was a South African playing for England while Englishmen who had played in South Africa were barred.

Randall celebrated his return with 126 and Willis marked his first Test as captain with nine wickets. Willis was less successful in the second Test when Patil hit him for six boundaries in one over of seven balls (the third delivery was a no-ball). Botham hit his tenth Test century in this match and shared a sixth-wicket stand of 169 with Geoff Miller, who made 98.

The might of Botham continued. At The Oval he reached a double century off 220 balls in 268 minutes. It was, in terms of balls received, the fastest double century recorded in Test cricket. He was out for 208 when he attempted to reverse-sweep the slow left-arm spin of Doshi. The reverse-sweep had become an ugly addition to the batsman's vocabulary. It was pioneered in the one-day game, and there was an air of audacity about it which appealed to Botham. In its defence it could be said that several batsmen scored many runs with the shot. Botham hit four sixes and nineteen fours; with Lamb, who hit a maiden Test hundred, he added 176 for the fourth wicket.

Lamb was now established in the side and Gatting was restored for the series against Pakistan. At Edgbaston, England introduced Ian Greig and Eddie Hemmings while Derek Randall moved up the order to open the innings instead of Geoff Cook. This was not the first time that Randall was asked to play this role, but it was not one for which he was suited, though he scored a hundred against Pakistan in this match. He was a great crowd pleaser, mostly because he so patently enjoyed the game. If he could be criticised for his constant movement at the crease, he compensated for this with exuberant brilliance in the field. He chased, picked up and threw with consistent energy and enthusiasm. He lit up England's out-cricket, and his joy was infectious.

Ian Greig took four wickets on his debut, but the lasting memory from this game was Bob Willis's second-innings bowling, when he launched a very fast attack on Zaheer Abbas. He bowled to what had been thought of as one of that fine batsman's strengths, a line outside off stump

332

encouraging the drive. It appeared that he brought in another slip after every delivery, and Zaheer succumbed, caught behind for 4.

Willis withdrew from the second Test at Lord's because of a stiff neck, and Gower captained England for the first time. The shape of things to come. It was not a happy experience for Gower. Mohsin Khan scored 200, and Pakistan won by ten wickets. England's problem was that, in Botham, Pringle, Greig and Jackman, they had four bowlers who virtually duplicated each other, and the attack lacked variety.

Vic Marks came in for Hemmings in the last Test as England searched for the best alternative to the unavailable Emburey, and Willis returned. There was also a new opening batsman in Graeme Fowler, and his 86 in the second innings was crucial to England's three-wicket victory.

Having enjoyed the luxury of two series triumphs, Willis had no serious rival as captain for the Ashes series in Australia in 1982–83, but his side never looked strong enough to trouble their hosts, who now had Greg Chappell back in charge and a pace attack that was strong enough to operate successfully without both Alderman and Lillee after the first Test. Alderman was wretchedly unlucky when, on the second afternoon, he brought down a pitch invader with a flying tackle and so badly dislocated his shoulder that he was out for the rest of the season.

The Australians were further strengthened by the fact that Kepler Wessels, the left-handed opening batsman from South Africa who had scored many runs for Sussex, was now eligible to play for them. He scored 162 when he made his debut in the second Test.

In contrast England desperately missed Gooch. They never found a satisfactory opening pair and, worse, Botham did not have a good tour. He had put on weight and suffered a back injury which reduced his effectiveness as a bowler.

Willis bowled well, but he did not find the tasks of leading the side and being the main strike bowler easy to combine. Often on the field he appeared to be leaving decisions to Botham and other senior players, including the vice-captain, Gower.

Gower was one of England's two centurions in the Tests, Randall being the other. Lamb also played with some consistency, but the batting was not strong.

There were three off-spinners in the party. Miller played in all five Tests, Hemmings, who scored 95 in the last Test, played in three and Marks figured only in the one-day World Series matches. None of them was particularly successful.

Pringle was fortunate to be selected for the tour. He was to develop into a Test cricketer, but at this stage he was very raw and prone to accident. He was out of action at one time when he strained his back writing a letter home. He became something of a figure of fun, yet by the end of his career he had become one of the people's favourites.

New to the international scene was Norman Cowans, the twenty-one-year-old Middlesex fast bowler who was born in Jamaica. Cowans had immense potential and took six for 77 in the second innings of the fourth Test, a dramatic affair which England won by 3 runs, but he was constantly plagued by injuries. He moved on to Hampshire in 1994, but his was a career that flattered to deceive.

England's real failure was rooted in the original selection of the party. The omission of Gatting and Edmonds was incomprehensible, as was the overlooking of Trevor Jesty, the Hampshire all-rounder. Jesty had had an outstanding season, but his name was not included in the party when it was announced in early September. Hampshire were playing Warwickshire at Southampton at the time, and Jesty's response was to score his eighth century of the season in the second innings. He hit two sixes and twenty-two fours in his 134 and reached three figures in eighty-two minutes. Willis did not introduce himself into the attack while Jesty was making his main assault on the Warwickshire bowling, and the Hampshire crowd barracked the England captain mercilessly for what they saw as his cowardice and for the non-selection of Jesty.

Jesty was belatedly called up to strengthen the side for the one-day World Series and performed creditably, but even here England struggled. They had lost the Test series by 2–1 with two drawn, and they failed to make the final of the triangular one-day tournament where Australia and New Zealand were the other sides. At Adelaide, Gower hit his third century of the series and England established a record score of 296 for five; only for New Zealand to beat the record three hours later as they won by four wickets with seven balls to spare.

England were learning that the cricket world was no longer as they once knew it. One former England captain who was covering the tour was surprised to find that a national newspaper had sent one reporter to cover the cricket and three to prowl around the hotel to see what scandal or gossip they could discover. There were more surprises in store. England went to New Zealand to play three one-day internationals and lost them all.

This was not a good omen for the third World Cup, in 1983, again to be played in England and sponsored for the last time by Prudential. The competition was much improved on the first two, mainly because it was decided that each country should play the others in their group twice. There was some fine cricket and some major upsets. England beat New Zealand at The Oval and lost to them at Edgbaston, but it was England who went through to the semi-final. New Zealand failed to do what was expected of them and lost to Sri Lanka, so missing their place in the last four.

England were beaten by India in the semi-final, and Kapil Dev's side went on to record a famous victory over the West Indies in the final. Gower and Lamb scored centuries for England during the tournament, and Graeme Fowler passed 50 four times in seven innings, yet May's committee had again made some odd selections and omissions. There was no place for Randall or Jesty, although both were in the squad of fourteen players. At the start of the season May had expressed the opinion that the best wicket-keeper must be chosen and that if a side had not scored enough runs by the time number eight or nine came in, then they were unlikely to win anyway. When it came to the final selection, Ian Gould, the likeable Sussex keeper, was preferred to Bob Taylor.

Taylor returned for the Test series against New Zealand, a four-match rubber which England won 3–1. At The Oval Fowler, Tavaré and Lamb all hit second-innings centuries, and England won by 189 runs in spite of some fine bowling by Richard Hadlee. At Headingley New Zealand won a Test match in England for the first time, but England took the matches at Lord's and Trent Bridge.

At Lord's England introduced three players new to Test cricket, Nick Cook, the Leicestershire slow left-arm bowler, Chris Smith, the Hampshire opening batsman and a South African by birth, and Neil Foster, the Essex fast bowler. Cook celebrated his debut with five for 35 and three for 90. In contrast Smith was leg-before to Richard Hadlee to the first ball he received, while Foster, chosen against the advice of his county who believed that he had not fully recovered from a back operation which had necessitated the insertion of two metal plates, took one wicket.

Cook took another nine wickets in the final Test, but his international career did not maintain this level. Willis enjoyed an excellent series, and Botham hit a century at Trent Bridge, yet there were suspicions that his great powers as an all-rounder were beginning to wane.

Somerset were still a force and took the NatWest Trophy when they beat Kent in front of a capacity crowd at Lord's. They also finished second in the John Player League and enjoyed record membership receipts. These were golden days for the county. It was not just the glory of Botham that people flocked to see, but the fast bowling of Joel Garner and the batting of Viv Richards. Gentle and courteous as a man, 'Big Bird', the six-foot eight-inch Garner, was a fearsome adversary on the pitch. He almost lolloped to the crease, but he brought the ball down from such a height, and made it cut and move as well as lift, that he gave batsmen a multitude of problems.

Viv Richards was considered by the majority of cricket followers to be the best batsman in the world. His batting was characterised by haughtiness, arrogance. He would glare contemptuously at bowlers and smite them with disdain. He had enormous flair, an ability to readjust in mid-shot and to hit so hard that even a miscue would go for four or six. He was a magnetic attraction. In spite of this trio Somerset never managed to win the County Championship.

Essex achieved this feat again in 1983. They had Gooch regularly available, and McEwan was the only batsman in the country to top 2,000 runs. The attack was balanced and potent. John Lever recovered from a serious illness in mid-season to take 106 wickets at little over 16 runs each. He was one of four bowlers (the others were John Emburey, Derek Underwood and Norman Gifford) to take 100 wickets or more. Like Lever, Emburey and Underwood were exiled from international cricket, and Gifford, now with Warwickshire, was forty-three years old. Five of the first six batsmen in the national averages were overseas cricketers. May and his selection committee, needless to say, continued to have problems.

Middlesex ran Essex close for the Championship and beat them by 4 runs in an enthralling Benson and Hedges Cup Final. Essex had seemingly done enough in restricting Middlesex to 196 for eight in their fifty-five overs. Gooch and Hardie savaged Cowans, Daniel and Williams, and Essex were 71 without loss after ten overs. Gooch was taken low down by Downton off Williams at 79, but, even so, with McEwan and Hardie together, Essex were 113 for one from twenty-five overs at tea.

Gatting showed great intelligence in his captaincy. He abandoned the idea that this was a limited-overs game and set attacking fields as if in the early stages of a Championship match. His brave move was successful. Essex fell apart and were bowled out with the first ball of the last over. Cowans had returned from his early traumas to take four wickets.

Trauma is an appropriate word for Yorkshire's cricket. Illingworth, fifty years old, had assumed the captaincy of the county he was managing. He led them to the John Player League, their first trophy in fourteen years. They beat Somerset, who finished level with them on points, by virtue of more away wins. This may have been cause for some celebration, but few supporters saw this title as adequate compensation for this proud county finishing bottom of the County Championship with a victory over Hampshire in June as their only success. The repercussions were as serious as they were inevitable.

Athey refused a new contract and joined Gloucestershire. The committee decided on a youth policy and sacked Boycott. Illingworth was relieved of the captaincy and reverted to a solely managerial role. Bairstow was appointed the new skipper.

It was hard to see how dismissing Boycott would improve the fortunes of the side. He scored 1,941 Championship runs in 1983, but, increasingly, the opinion was being formed in the outside world that he was not popular with his colleagues or recognised as a team man. Within Yorkshire itself there were two distinct camps, and the pro-Boycott campaign forced the committee to reconsider their decision. The first vote had seen eighteen to seven in favour of Boycott being dismissed, and a second vote brought about a comparable result.

Battle lines were drawn, and a new committee came into power with Boycott being elected as member for Wakefield. He was reinstated as a player in January 1984, and by the end of that year Illingworth had been sacked as manager. Yorkshire were narrowly beaten in the semi-final of the Benson and Hedges Cup by Warwickshire, but reaching the last four of this competition was the highlight of their year. They finished four-teenth in the Championship, second to bottom in the John Player League and were humiliated in the first round of the NatWest Trophy by Shropshire. This was only the fourth occasion in the history of the sixty-over competition that a Minor County had beaten a first-class county.

Not surprisingly, there were no Yorkshire players in the party that Bob Willis took to Fiji, New Zealand and Pakistan in the early months of 1984, a party which endured as many indignities as those suffered by Yorkshire. Early on, there were no indications of the problems that were to come. Willis became England's leading wicket-taker when he claimed his 308th Test victim in Wellington, and Randall and Botham shared a sixth-wicket stand of 232 in the same Test. Randall hit 164 and Botham 138. Botham also took five for 59 in the first innings, but Martin Crowe and Jeremy Coney hit centuries for New Zealand, and the match was drawn.

With Foster and Dilley unfit, England called in Tony Pigott to play in the second Test at Christchurch. The Sussex pace bowler was coaching and playing in Wellington and was not a member of the official squad. England included neither Cook nor Marks, the two spinners, in their side, and the attack, according to Bob Willis, performed worse than any other he had seen in his eighty-five Tests. New Zealand made 307 on a pitch on which 150 would have seemed a good score, and England were brushed aside for 82 and 93.

Things were as bad off the field as on, for a Sunday newspaper alleged that England players had been smoking marijuana. A TCCB investigation conducted by the harassed manager A.C. Smith found no evidence to support these allegations.

The team was under stress. Bob Taylor, forty-two years old, was the only wicket-keeper in the side. He took some time to recover from a muscle strain, and Paul Downton was ready to fly from South Africa to replace him, but Taylor's injury mended just as the Middlesex keeper was about to go to New Zealand.

From the second Test at Christchurch until the end of the tour in Pakistan, the itinerary allowed for nothing but Tests and one-day internationals, a programme for disaster. New Zealand had marginally the better of the draw in Auckland and so won their first rubber against England after fifty-four years as a Test cricket country.

There was no respite in Pakistan, where Abdul Qadir's leg-spin won the first Test. This marked the end of the tour for Willis and Botham. Willis returned home with a viral infection, and Botham went back to England to have an exploratory operation on a knee. It was generally believed that his Test career was at an end, but he was to prove people wrong. Gower took over the captaincy and scored 152 in the drawn Test in Faisalabad. He followed this with 173 not out at Lahore. This match, too, ended in a draw, but Pakistan were only 26 runs short of victory with four wickets standing when time was called. Cowans thwarted them by taking five wickets in twenty-two balls, including three in one over, but Pakistan had won a rubber against England for the first time.

Defeats at the hands of both New Zealand and Pakistan left May and his selectors in a sorry plight. They could still not call upon Gooch, Emburey and the rest, and in the summer of 1984 the West Indians were upon them. May could only watch as Gooch became the first player for eight years to exceed 2,500 first-class runs in a season. He established a new Essex record and played a considerable part in his county's triumphs in retaining the Championship and winning the John Player League, the first time any county had achieved such a double.

Gooch was at the height of his powers, and England were in desperate need of a batsman of his quality. He remained unrepentant after his South African venture, even batting in a Western Province cap when he played for Essex against MCC at Lord's. Others to star in the Essex double success were McEwan, the South African, and John Lever, one of two bowlers in the country to take a hundred wickets.

The other was Richard Hadlee, the New Zealand all-rounder, who enjoyed an outstanding season, taking 117 wickets and scoring 1,179 runs to complete an astonishing 'double' in twenty-four matches. Robinson, Randall and Broad all scored heavily in the Nottinghamshire order, while the inspiring captaincy and all-round cricket of Clive Rice nearly brought his side the Championship.

The last round of matches saw Essex travel to Old Trafford where McEwan, whose hundred came in eighty-three minutes, and Prichard set up victory in two days. Nottinghamshire were playing Somerset at Taunton and a win would have given them the title by a margin of two points. Botham, now captain of Somerset, left Nottinghamshire a target of 297 in sixty overs. Rice played a marvellous innings, hitting 98 off 109 balls before being caught by substitute Ollis off Marks. Botham had relied almost entirely upon his spinners, Marks and Booth; when Booth began the last over 14 runs were needed with the last pair together. Mike Bore hit two fours and a two; then, on the fifth ball of the over, he drove straight and high only for Ollis to take the catch on the boundary edge. Essex had won the Championship.

Gooch, McEwan, Lever, Hadlee and Rice were all superb cricketers, and not one of them was available to the England selectors.

The NatWest Trophy had a climax as thrilling as the County Championship. Emburey turned the last ball of the match, bowled by Ellison, to the square-leg boundary to give Middlesex victory over Kent. The Benson and Hedges Cup produced no such excitement as Lancashire beat Warwickshire with ease.

Willis led Warwickshire to the final, but he no longer led England. He was thanked publicly and politely for what he had done during his period of captaincy, but he was replaced by David Gower, who made the same fatal error as Botham – he accepted the captaincy of England when the West Indies were the opposition.

To the surprise of some, Botham reported fit and played in all five Tests, but there was an awesome indication of the shape of things to come in the first Texaco Trophy one-day international. At Old Trafford Viv Richards hit 189 not out, the highest score made in a limited-overs international, off 170 balls with five sixes and twenty-one fours.

England introduced Andy Lloyd to international cricket in this match, and the Warwickshire opener was chosen to play in the first Test. He lost Fowler and Randall, both for nought, and, with his score on 10 and England 20 for two after thirty-three minutes, he had his face damaged by a ball from Malcolm Marshall. He was in hospital for several days, with concern over his eyesight, and he did not play again during the season; nor did he ever play international cricket again.

Lloyd was a more than useful player who captained Warwickshire from 1988 to 1992 and shaped the side that was to win the Championship and all else in the early 1990s. It was he who asked that Dermot Reeve be appointed vice-captain, and one feels that Lloyd has never been given credit for the part he played in the phenomenal success of the Midlands county. His Test career was symbolic of the fact that he

339

was not a lucky cricketer.

Pringle took five wickets in that Edgbaston Test, but Gomes and Richards scored hundreds, and the West Indies won by an innings. At Lord's they had an even more emphatic and sensational victory.

Chris Broad, the left-handed Nottinghamshire opener, made his Test debut, hit 55 and shared a first-wicket partnership of 101 with Fowler, who went on to make 106. Broad had been with Gloucestershire and had left that county because he believed that the selectors never looked in the direction of the Severn. He was a determined cricketer with a sound temperament and capable of dealing with fast bowling, but he was to figure as something of a controversial figure.

Botham became the first English bowler to take eight wickets in an innings against the West Indies in England, and his eight for 103 helped the home side to a first-innings lead of 41. He also completed 4,000 runs in Test cricket; and with Lamb scoring 110, Gower was able to set the West Indies a target of 342.

Gower had been roundly criticised in the press for not declaring on the Monday evening and subjecting the West Indian batsmen to an awkward half-hour. On the Tuesday morning England scored only 13 runs and lost two wickets, but the West Indies had to score at nearly 5 an over to win. Haynes was run out at 57; Greenidge, 214, and Gomes, 92, then shared an unbroken stand of 287 in 236 minutes to bring the West Indies victory with nearly twelve overs to spare. The runs had come at more than 5 an over.

Allan Lamb hit another century in the third Test, at Headingley, and Paul Allott took six for 61, but Gomes, matured from the lad who had been unable to hold a regular place in the Middlesex side, made 104 not out, Marshall took seven for 53, and the West Indies won by eight wickets.

This Test saw the debut of Paul Terry and the end of Bob Willis. It was appropriate that his international career should end on the ground that had witnessed his greatest triumphs. He had an early success when Greenidge was caught at slip by Botham off his bowling, but thereafter he became the victim of a violent batting assault by Michael Holding, who hit five sixes in his 59. Willis conceded 123 runs in eighteen overs, but he had two catches put down off his bowling before Allott held a skier to account for Holding. It was Willis's 325th and last Test wicket. No fast bowler has ever given more of himself to England than Bob Willis. His was not a classic action, but he bowled with all the fire a soul could muster. He fell ill again and retired from first-class cricket at the end of the season.

Even with Holding's dismissal the West Indies were not finished.

Marshall had fractured his thumb in two places while fielding, but he batted one-handed and lasted long enough to give Gomes a chance to complete his century. Then he started bowling and took seven wickets.

At Old Trafford, Lamb scored his third century in successive Tests, but England lost by an innings. In their search for an off-spinner, England brought Pocock back after a long absence, but this game saw Paul Terry's brief Test career come to an end. He had his left arm broken by a ball from Winston Davis. Terry returned to bat one-handed with his left arm in a sling underneath his sweater. Much as one commended his courage, one felt that the cricket was less than savoury.

At The Oval the West Indies completed the 'blackwash' and became the first side to win all five Tests in a series in England. England's only compensation could be in the fact that Botham became the first man to complete the double of 300 wickets and 3,000 Test runs. His 300th victim was Dujon, who was caught at slip by Tavaré.

Agnew and Ellison were both called up for this Test and retained their places for the Test match against Sri Lanka. Lamb scored his fourth Test hundred of the summer, but the Sri Lankans gained the plaudits with their exciting stroke-play and wonderful enthusiasm for the game.

Jonathan Agnew was a bowler of genuine pace. A genial man, he was possibly too friendly a person to become a really hostile fast bowler, and he did not achieve at Test level what could have been expected of him. He also left cricket earlier than might have been expected in order to become cricket correspondent of the BBC, a post for which his warmth and humour made him most suited.

Cricket now seemed to be operating in a world of its own. While there were discussions afoot aimed at reducing the length of time that an over-seas player had to be resident before becoming eligible to represent England, the South African athlete Zola Budd was granted British citizenship within thirteen days of application (albeit to accompanying cries of protest). The manoeuvrings on her behalf were ultimately fruit-less, as she did not bring home the Olympic prizes that had been expected. Another potential star claiming to be British, Graeme Hick, in whom Zimbabwe had invested so much, made a first Championship appearance for Worcestershire at The Oval at the end of the season.

The only violence of which cricket seemed aware was that inflicted upon the England team by Holding, Marshall, Greenidge and Richards, but elsewhere in the country were the running battles attending the miners' strike and, in October, the devastation caused by the IRA bomb-ing of the Grand Hotel at Brighton during the Conservative Party Conference.

Cricket was unable to hide for ever from the tragedies and dilemmas of the modern world. Within a few hours of their arrival in New Delhi in November 1984, David Gower's party learned that the Indian prime Minister Indira Gandhi had been assassinated. The world was stunned, and cricket in India, which was celebrating the golden jubilee of the Ranji Trophy, became of minor importance.

The generosity of the Sri Lankan Cricket Board and of the Sri Lankan President enabled the England party to find sanctuary in that beautiful island for a fortnight, and there was much discussion as to whether the tour should continue. The schedule was rearranged, and three matches were played before the first Test in Bombay at the end of November. On the eve of this Test the England party was entertained by the British High Commissioner to Western India, Percy Norris, and his wife. The following morning, Mr Norris, a passionate cricket-lover, was shot dead as he was being driven to his office.

The majority of the players and the press would have voted to return home immediately, but Tony Brown, the former Gloucestershire captain and now the England manager, remained calm and maintained a sense of perspective. He sought advice from various sources and, having discussed the matter with the TCCB, he accepted the decision that the tour should continue. The two murders, though both political, were unrelated, and it was believed that the England team were in no danger. India itself was in turmoil, but it was hoped that cricket would offer both comfort and a source of unification. It is certain, though, that no Test series has ever had such a sadder beginning. The two teams stood in silence for a minute in the Wankhede Stadium in memory and tribute to Mrs Gandhi and Mr Norris.

The England party was a strange one. Botham had asked not to be considered for the tour. He felt in need of a rest after the continuous conflicts of the past few years. He was replaced by Chris Cowdrey, whose selection caused many raised eyebrows. As an all-rounder Cowdrey, son of the great Colin, was of limited ability for his bowling, medium-pace, was well short of international class. Nor was he more than a good county batsman, but he was a fine fielder and a great enthusiast who had the ability to lift those around him.

Having coped well with the West Indian pace men, Chris Broad was omitted from the party to tour India and his place was taken by his Nottinghamshire opening partner Tim Robinson. Like David Steele some years before, Broad had braved the fire only to be jettisoned when the heat lessened.

Taylor had retired, and the wicket-keeping was now in the hands of Paul Downton and Bruce French. It was the Middlesex man who kept in all five Tests.

In view of what they had endured since they left home it was not surprising that England were beaten in the first Test, but they could take heart from their general performance. Chris Cowdrey took a wicket with his fourth ball in Test cricket, and although England were mesmerised by the leg-spin of Sivaramakrishnan in the first innings, they battled well in the second. The most gratifying innings came from Mike Gatting.

Gatting had been named as vice-captain of the party, but there was a feeling that he was being given a last opportunity to prove himself a batsman of international quality. At Bombay he played his thirty-first Test, and his second innings was his fifty-fourth in Test cricket. At last he revealed that he could do at international level what he did weekly at county level: dominate an attack and play with a certainty and aggression that few could equal. He batted for 310 minutes, hit twenty-one fours and made 136, his first Test century, but he could not save England from defeat.

England fielded an unchanged side in Delhi and appeared to have lost all hope of remaining in contention in the series when Gavaskar won the toss and India batted.

Of the England bowlers, Ellison, Edmonds and Pocock stuck to their task well, and India were restricted to 307. A massively defiant innings of 160 in 508 minutes from Tim Robinson (playing in his second Test) took England to a position of strength and, with some useful contributions from others, particularly Downton, England took a first-innings lead of 111. India fell to the England spinners, and the series was levelled. England's victory by eight wickets ended a sequence of thirteen Tests without a win, and it was apparent that while the visitors were a team united in spirit and purpose, India were not.

Chris Cowdrey later paid tribute to Gower's leadership on this tour. He told his players that they must accept all decisions, however controversial, and that he and Tony Brown would make representations on their behalf, but that they should not allow themselves to show dissent or to be distracted from their task. The tragedies which had taken place in India since their arrival had tended to bind the England party even closer. In contrast there were divisions in the Indian camp over the distribution of prize money. Gavaskar was well below form, and Kapil Dev was dropped for the Calcutta Test after throwing his wicket away in Delhi.

The Calcutta Test was a dire affair. Shastri took 354 balls, seven and a half hours, to score 111, and India batted into the fourth day. All this seemed so perverse. Shastri was by nature a fast scorer. Within a week he was to hit the quickest double century in first-class cricket and to

343

equal Sobers's record of six sixes in an over. The match, too, saw Azharuddin score 110 on his Test debut, but the rest was best forgotten.

Allott had broken down injured, and Agnew had been flown to India to strengthen the side, but it was another quick bowler, Neil Foster, who took the honours in the fourth Test at Madras. He replaced the out-of-form Richard Ellison, while Kapil Dev returned after his one-match 'suspension'. The changes that had come over the two sides within a period of six weeks were remarkable. Excellent team spirit had transformed England from a much criticised and dispirited group of losers into a winning combination. India had descended from the heights of victory in the first Test to a group of individuals seemingly disenchanted by Gavaskar's captaincy and ravaged by rumours of internal dissent.

India had the chance to redeem themselves when Gavaskar won the toss and elected to bat first on a pitch which looked full of runs. In the second over of the match, bowled by Foster, Gavaskar hit two fours. In Foster's next over he hit another boundary and then played across the line and was bowled. Srikkanth drove at the first ball of the next over and was caught behind. India were 17 for two.

The cricket bordered on frenzy. Vengsarkar drove majestically, was missed at slip and then was deceived by a steeply rising ball from Foster which he edged fast and straight to second slip. The score was 45 for three from twelve overs. By lunch it had advanced to 102.

Mohinder Amarnath and Azharuddin threatened to take control in the afternoon session, and Amarnath hit four boundaries in succession off Edmonds. The return of Foster brought an end to the aggression. Amarnath chased a widish delivery and edged to the wicket-keeper. Cowdrey knocked back Azharuddin's middle and leg stumps, and in the next over Foster had Shastri caught behind.

Three wickets had fallen for 12 runs, but Kapil Dev and Kirmani responded with belligerence. The spree ended when Kapil Dev was well caught at long-off, and the last three Indian wickets went down in ten overs, two of them to Foster who had bowled splendidly, taking six for 104. Fowler and Robinson took England to 32 by the close.

Only one wicket fell on the second day, that of Robinson, who pushed forward to a leg-break and was caught behind for 74. There were few other alarms. Fowler reached a sensible hundred, and England closed on 293 for one, totally in command.

Fowler and Gatting both reached double centuries, and their second-wicket partnership was worth 241. Having batted for just over nine hours, Fowler wearily edged a ball to the wicket-keeper while Gatting, who was at the crease for eight hours, was caught on the long-on boundary as he savaged the Indian attack.

Gower declared on the fourth morning an hour before lunch, and Neil Foster immediately shattered the Indian batting with another blistering spell. He had Gavaskar taken at first slip, Vengsarkar well taken low down on the leg side by Downton and Srikkanth caught when hooking impetuously. Between lunch and tea Amarnath and Azharuddin added 101 in thirty-two overs. It looked as if they would take India into the last day, but Amarnath hooked Foster and Cowans took a good catch. Azharuddin reached his second century in his second Test, and India closed at 246 for four.

India's hopes died when the spinners sent back both Azharuddin and Shastri in the first half-hour of the last day. Kapil Dev, Kirmani and Chetan Sharma ensured that India survived well into the afternoon, but the issue was rarely in doubt, and England gained a famous victory by nine wickets.

An Unprecedented Triumph in India
India v England at Chidambaram Stadium, Chepauk, Madras
13, 14, 15, 17 and 18 January 1985

India	First Innings		Second Innings	
S.M. Gavaskar (capt) b Foster		17	c Gatting b Foster	3
K. Srikkanth c Downton b Cowans		0	c Cowdrey b Foster	16
D.B. Vengsarkar c Lamb b Foster . .		17	c Downton b Foster	2
M. Amarnath c Downton b Foster .		78	c Cowans b Foster	95
M. Azharuddin b Cowdrey		48	c Gower b Pocock 105
R.J. Shastri c Downton b Foster . . .		2	c Cowdrey b Edmonds .	33
Kapil Dev c Cowans b Cowdrey . .		53	c Gatting b Cowans	49
†S.M.H. Kirmani not out		30	c Lamb b Edmonds	75
N.S. Yadav b Foster		2	(10)c Downton b Cowans	5
L. Sivaramakrishnan c Cowdrey				
b Foster		13	(9) lbw b Foster	5
C. Sharma c Lamb b Cowans		5	not out	17
Extras (lb 3, nb 4)		7	(b 1, lb 4, nb 2)	7
Total		272	412

BOWLING	Overs	Mdns	Runs	Wkts	Overs	Mdns	Runs	Wkts
Cowans	12.5	3	39	2	15	1	73	2
Foster	23	2	104	6	28	8	59	5
Edmonds	6	1	33	–	41.5	13	119	2
Cowdrey	19	1	65	2	5	–	26	–
Pocock	7	1	28	–	33	8	130	1

fall of wickets
1–17, 2–17, 3–45, 4–155, 5–167, 6–167, 7–241, 8–243, 9–263
1–7, 2–19, 3–22, 4–212, 5–259, 6–259, 7–341, 8–350, 9–361

England	First Innings		Second Innings	
G. Fowler c Kirmani b Kapil Dev . .	201		c Kirmani b Siva	2
R.T. Robinson c Kirmani b Siva . . .	74		not out	21
M.W. Gatting c sub (G. Sharma)				
b Shastri	207		not out	10
A.J. Lamb b Amarnath	62			
P.H. Edmonds lbw b Shastri	36			
N.A. Foster b Amarnath	5			
D.I. Gower (capt) b Kapil Dev	18			
C.S. Cowdrey not out	3			
†P.R. Downton not out	3			
P.I. Pocock				
N.G. Cowans				
Extras (b 7, lb 19, nb 17)	43		(lb 1, w 1)	2
Total for 7 wickets, dec.	652		for 1 wicket	35

BOWLING	Overs	Mdns	Runs	Wkts	Overs	Mdns	Runs	Wkts
Kapil Dev	36	5	131	2	3	–	20	–
Sharma	18	–	95	–	–	–	–	–
Sivarama-krishnan	44	6	145	1	4	–	12	1
Yadav	23	4	76	–	–	–	–	–
Shastri	42	7	143	2	1	–	2	–
Amarnath	12	1	36	2	–	–	–	–

fall of wickets
1–178, 2–419, 3–563, 4–599, 5–604, 6–640, 7–646
umpires – M.Y. Gupte and V.K. Ramaswamy
England won by 9 wickets

The fifth Test (which produced another Azharuddin century) was drawn, and so Gower became the first visiting captain to win a series in India after going behind in the rubber. This was achieved in spite of Azharuddin's three centuries in his first three Tests and in spite of what England had had to bear. England also beat the reigning world champions 4–1 in the limited-overs series. In the limited-overs international competition in Australia which followed (one of many that were beginning to break out like rashes all over the world), England did not fare well, but May, Gower, Tony Brown, Gatting and the rest could be well pleased with the advances that had been made without Gooch and other banned 'stars'. Their exile, though, was virtually complete and they would be available for selection at the start of the 1985 England season.

Those who had not taken the gold and gone to South Africa could have been excused for asking, 'What price loyalty?' As he himself had predicted, Pat Pocock did not play Test cricket again after the tour of India; nor did Graeme Fowler, double centurion in the historic victory in Madras.

A jaunty left-hander who could keep wicket as well as open the innings, Fowler played in the first Texaco Trophy one-day international against Australia, after which his season fell apart. He lost form completely and was omitted not only from the England side but from the Lancashire first eleven. He began to score runs again in 1986, but he was no longer in contention for a Test place. Foster, the hero of Madras with eleven wickets on a pitch which gave no assistance to pace bowling, was not even named in the squad for the first Test at Headingley, and, plagued by injury and illness, he appeared only once in the series. A bout of glandular fever kept him out of the NatWest Trophy final in which Essex met Nottinghamshire.

Put in to bat, Essex had early problems as the ball moved about appreciably, but Gooch and Hardie batted with total conviction. They did not put a run on the board until the fourth over, but the tempo increased and by the time Gooch was bowled by Pick for 91 in the forty-ninth over, the score was 202, a record stand for the competition. Hardie, playing one of the best innings of his career, was run out for 110 and, with 77 runs coming in the last ten overs, Essex reached a formidable 280 for two. Ken McEwan, in his last appearance at Lord's, was unbeaten on 46; 30 of these runs came out of the 56 added with Pringle in the last four overs of the innings.

Robinson and Broad responded mightily for Nottinghamshire, putting on 143 for the first wicket, but then the innings faltered. Robinson, Rice and Hadlee were all out as they tried to force the pace and, with Randall and Martindale together, 37 runs were needed from the last three overs. When Pringle began the last over Nottinghamshire required 18 to win with Randall on strike. Pringle adopted a leg-stump attack, and there were gaps in the field on the off side. Randall stepped outside leg stump and drove to the off for 2. He repeated the shot next ball, but this time he reached the boundary. Another 2 followed, and Nottinghamshire needed 10 off three balls. Randall again crashed the ball to the Tavern boundary, and the fifth ball was driven majestically

347

past long-off for four. Stuart Turner, the fielder, said later that, in the gathering dusk, he had no idea where the ball was going once it left the bat.

Fletcher rearranged his field and calmed his men. Pringle tucked up Randall as he attempted to drive, and Prichard plucked down the catch at mid-wicket to give Essex victory by 1 run.

Randall's Test career had ended with the first match against the West Indies the previous season, but his impish batting had excited a capacity Lord's crowd and brought to a grand finale what was arguably the finest one-day encounter ever seen at 'headquarters'. Clive Rice commented with typical good humour, 'I would have had to apologise to Fletch if we had won. They were beating us for nine-tenths of the game, and Arkle nearly snatched it in the last over.'

The victory meant that Fletcher had become the first captain to win all four major competitions. The following day Essex went to Trent Bridge to play Nottinghamshire in a John Player League match, and Gooch and Hardie gave a repeat record-breaking performance with 239 for the first wicket. Gooch hit 171 off 135 balls with three sixes and eighteen fours. A week later Essex beat Yorkshire at Chelmsford to win the Sunday League for the second year in succession. Earlier in the season they had reached the Benson and Hedges Cup final where they had been beaten convincingly by Leicestershire, who had been strengthened by the arrival of Peter Willey. The all-rounder hit 86 not out, took the Gold Award and won back his place in the England side.

The County Championship, now sponsored by Britannic Assurance, was in doubt until the last round of matches, although Middlesex took the title by a margin of eighteen points by crushing Warwickshire at Edgbaston in the final match. Gatting's leadership was again a significant factor in Middlesex claiming another trophy, the most important one of all, but he was superbly supported by Barlow, Slack, Radley and Butcher, and the bowling remained balanced and highly effective.

Not all counties enjoyed such happy seasons as Middlesex and Essex. In mid-season Sussex announced that they would not be re-engaging Ian Greig. He had not enjoyed a spectacular season, but he was still short of his thirtieth birthday and, in the recent past, had played a vital part in Sussex winning the Sunday League and in making their strongest ever challenge for the Championship. He had also won two England caps. The tedious and inevitable politics that attend first-class cricket in England was suspected, and the Sussex coach Stewart Storey was regarded as being Greig's main adversary. Storey himself was to suffer dismissal a year later.

It was apparent, too, that all was not well at Somerset. Viv Richards topped the national batting averages, and Botham finished fourth. Peter Roebuck, too, scored plentifully, and Garner terrorised most batsmen when respite from his knee injury allowed him to play. Marks took sixty-seven Championship wickets, but he was rather expensive, and Somerset had the indignity of finishing bottom of the County Championship.

At the end of the year Botham resigned the captaincy and accepted a one-year contract instead of the two-year deal he was offered. He cited his many interests outside cricket as being the reason for his resignation of the captaincy, a position that was filled by Roebuck, but there was a sense of unease in Taunton and around the Mendips.

In November Botham walked from John o'Groats to Land's End to raise money for research into leukaemia, yet, in many quarters, there remained a reluctance to give him any credit, let alone praise him, for his good deeds. He was ever to remain a dominant and controversial figure, but England lauds its heroes most when they are dead.

Accompanying Botham for part of his charity walk was the brother of Allan Border, the Australian captain. Border had taken over from Kim Hughes the previous winter. Hughes had publicly and tearfully resigned following what he saw as subversion by members of his team and by some in authority. Both he and Yallop were then surprisingly omitted from the party to tour England and reacted by signing contracts to play in South Africa. Alderman, Rackemann, Hogg and Maguire were among those to accompany them, so that the team that came to England to defend the Ashes was considerably weakened. On top of this, Dick Wellham, Wayne Phillips and Graeme Wood, who had originally intended to join the group in South Africa, changed their minds and found places on the tour of England. The party was divided as well as weakened, and not even Border's firm and intelligent leadership could put the pieces together again. He began the tour with four centuries, but the support he received lacked consistency.

England, in contrast, showed instant forgiveness towards their South African rebels. Gooch, Emburey and Willey were in the side at Headingley, as were Botham and Allott, which meant that the selectors had made five changes from the eleven which had played the final Test in India. Later in the summer first Test caps were to be given to Arnold Sidebottom and Les Taylor, two more who had been on the rebel tour of South Africa. If May and his co-selectors believed that the South African issue was at an end, they were very much mistaken.

Gower led England, but, in spite of his success in India, his position was in doubt at the beginning of the season, for his own form was uncertain. He made 3 and nought in the first two Texaco Trophy matches, and there was deep concern. At Lord's he and Gooch scored 202 in thirty-seven overs for the second wicket, and England won. Gower's 102 was his first century as England's captain, and it was apparent to all that the warmth and wishes of the crowd were with him.

The Test series began with an England victory at Headingley. Tim Robinson hit 175, Botham took three wickets in four balls and England won by five wickets, making rather heavy weather of a simple task. At Lord's, Allan Border played a wonderful innings of 196, and England succumbed to the leg-spin of Bob Holland. Gower hit 166 in the draw at Trent Bridge, while at Old Trafford Gatting made 160, his first Test century in England, but the match was again drawn.

The decisive victory for England came at Edgbaston where Richard Ellison captured ten wickets, including four in fifteen balls in the second innings. Gower put Australia in to bat for the second Test in succession and was indebted to Ellison's six for 77, which helped to restrict the visitors to 335. The innings lasted into the third day, but then Gower hit 215 and shared stands of 331 in 343 minutes for the second wicket with Robinson and 94 for the third with Gatting, who went on to reach his second hundred in successive Test innings. The rate of England's scoring gave the bowlers the chance to bowl out Australia for a second time, and victory by an innings and 118 runs came with just under twelve hours to spare.

The win at Edgbaston was followed by another innings victory at The Oval. England ended the first day on 376 for three. Robinson had fallen early, but Gower hit his third century of the series and shared a second-wicket stand of 351 with Gooch. The latter finished the day unbeaten on 179, and there was speculation that he might beat Sobers's record of 365, but he was caught and bowled by McDermott after adding just 17 to his score on the second morning. Ellison had another good match, taking five for 46 in Australia's second innings.

The emergence of Ellison was but one of several assets with which England were blessed during the summer. Gower, with 732 runs in the six-match rubber, had proved himself to be capable of carrying the cares of captaincy and of retaining his outstanding and exquisite quality as a batsman. Gatting had at last proved himself to be of Test standard, and Gooch had returned in majestic form. Many questioned the value of playing six Tests and of giving four days to some of the county games which involved the Australians, but there was a general air of contentment. The Ashes had been regained, and England seemed strong again.

The state of euphoria was short-lived. In an effort to ease the transition from county to Test cricket, England 'B' tours to Bangladesh, Sri

Lanka and Zimbabwe had been arranged for the winner of 1985–86. Of the team chosen, Mark Nicholas, the captain, Bill Athey, Martyn Moxon, Kim Barnett and Chris Smith had played or coached in South Africa, and the South African connection was unacceptable to the governments of Bangladesh and Zimbabwe. The visits to those countries were cancelled. Sri Lanka allowed the tour to go ahead, but even there cricket was under threat from the activities of the Tamil separatists.

The South African issue would not go away. Bishop Desmond Tutu called for international sanctions against his country, but Margaret Thatcher reiterated her opposition to sanctions, and England was to be viewed with suspicion by other members of the Commonwealth.

Although the demonstrations against Gower's side in the Caribbean in the early months of 1986 were muted and peaceful, there was a constant undercurrent of protest against Gooch and those who had accompanied him on the rebel tour of South Africa. An article by the Deputy Prime Minister of Antigua led to Gooch threatening to return to England before the final Test, and only the persuasive powers of Gower and Donald Carr prevented Gooch from carrying out his threat. This was only one of the incidents which marred the tour.

England's form before the first Test was poor, and in the first one-day international three days before the start of the Test Gatting was hit in the face when he missed an attempted hook at a ball from Malcolm Marshall. He sustained a broken nose, and the injury was so severe that he was forced to return to England for special treatment. Wilf Slack was sent to the Caribbean as replacement, and when Gatting rejoined the party he immediately suffered a broken thumb and played in only the final Test.

Slack, the Middlesex left-handed opener, was one of three England players to make their Test debuts in the series. The others were Greg Thomas, the Glamorgan pace bowler, a surprise selection, and David Smith, the Worcestershire left-hander who had joined the Midlands county from Surrey, returned to The Oval and then moved to Sussex. A fiery character, he played fast bowling well, but he never did himself justice at Test level. The 1986 tour of the Caribbean was not the best on which to become acclimatised to international cricket.

Gower's languid captaincy had been suited to India and to a 'friendly' home series against a weak Australian side. In the West Indies against Richards's four-pronged pace attack, a firmer hand was needed. An air of indolence prevailed, which was interpreted as a lack of commitment. Cricket had moved into an era of whingeing. There were constant complaints about inadequate practice facilities, and there was a tendency to avoid practice rather than to show imagination and make the best of what was available.

Senior players who may have helped and advised the less experienced showed a marked reluctance to do so and Botham, in particular, was severely criticised in this respect. A natural, instinctive cricketer, he was ever a reluctant practiser. Such men of genius are not born for the nets, but an example was needed, and Botham was found wanting. His own performance provided no compensation. He endured the worst Test series of his career. Gooch's performances, too, failed to meet expectations. He could never understand why there was so much antipathy to his South African venture, and his sense of persecution infected the rest of the side.

England's cricketers did not score a first-class century on the tour. Victory over Jamaica was their only first-class win in ten matches. They lost the one-day series by 3–1 and were beaten in all five Tests, so suffering their second 'blackwash' at the hands of the West Indies. Gower's average of 37 placed him top of England's Test averages. Marshall, Garner, Holding and the newcomer Patterson caused havoc, and batsmen such as Robinson, successful against the gentler pace of the Australians and Indians, were found all too vulnerable against real speed.

The closest that England came to victory in the Test series was in the second match, at Port of Spain, where they lost by *only* seven wickets. In the final Test, which the West Indies won by 240 runs, Viv Richards hit 110 not out off fifty-eight balls in eighty-three minutes. The misery did not end there. There were troubles ahead, and the music had to be faced.

England's tour of New Zealand in 1984 had produced allegations that members of the side had smoked marijuana. The *Mail on Sunday* had cited Botham as a guilty party. In response Botham had instigated a libel action. The case was settled out of court in order, according to the editor of the Sunday newspaper concerned, to avoid disastrous consequences for English cricket in general and Botham in particular. Part of the settlement was that Botham should contribute an article to the *Mail on Sunday* in which he admitted that he had, in the past, used marijuana.

The Test and County Cricket Board had been accused of weakness on previous occasions when, confronted by misdemeanours from Willis, Fletcher and Botham himself, they had simply warned the culprits as to their future actions. Having agreed to support the Sports Council in its campaign against drug-taking, the TCCB had no option but to punish Botham, and he was suspended from 29 May until 31 July. He was available for England for only the last of the six Tests played in the summer of 1986.

The whole matter was a deep embarrassment for cricket's governing body, for, following the tour of New Zealand in question, the TCCB had stated that their investigations had found no substance in the allegations made. Those investigations had been conducted by the tour manager, A.C. Smith, now Chief Executive of the TCCB.

Botham remained the Jekyll and Hyde of cricket. It was revealed that his walk from John o'Groats to Land's End had realised £880,000 for the Leukaemia Research Fund. He performed excitingly with the bat before and after his suspension, but his bowling showed signs of decline. He was to leave Somerset at the end of the season, but lack of form was not the reason for his departure.

In late August the Somerset committee decided not to renew the contracts of Viv Richards and Joel Garner, the two West Indians who had played so great a part in the county's one-day successes over the past eight years. It was a brave and bold move prompted by the new limit on the number of overseas players that counties were to be allowed and by the fact that the great New Zealand batsman Martin Crowe, whom Somerset had contracted, was becoming a centre of interest for other counties. Somerset did not wish to lose his registration. He was a good team man who was most encouraging to young players. Garner, troubled by injury, was a great bowler at the end of his career. Richards remained a power in the land, but a decision had to be made.

The reasoning of the Somerset committee was logical in a cricketing sense, but it went against the views of supporters who had a strong sentimental attachment to the two West Indians whom they saw as being at the very heart of Somerset's golden years. Botham threatened to leave if his two friends were not reinstated. The committee's decision now involved a struggle concerning player power.

A Special General Meeting was called in an effort to unseat the committee, but the committee won two motions by majorities of more than a thousand. The trouble had been brewing for some time, but those closest to events knew what was the wisest course and best for the club, and they reacted accordingly. Botham left Somerset and joined Worcestershire. His great days were now behind him.

The season was a watershed in other ways, for in September Geoffrey Boycott was not re-engaged by Yorkshire. This time there was muted protest, but the decision was not reversed. Boycott was forty-five and Yorkshire's last link with the highly successful side of the 1960s. He had scored 29,485 Championship runs, average 58.27, for Yorkshire, but the career of England's greatest post-war opening batsman ended with a whimper rather than a bang.

Times were changing. In 1986 John Player ended its sponsorship of the Sunday League with Hampshire as winners. Refuge Assurance took over for five years, but the competition had run its course, although few were willing to admit it. The BBC retained screening rights but had seemingly lost interest and television coverage had become sparse. Within a few years Sky Television was to add Sunday League cricket to their collection on their channel of perpetual sport.

Gower's captaincy of England also came to an end in 1986. He returned from the Caribbean disaster to face a storm of criticism, much of it directed at him personally. There was a reprieve when he batted well in the second of two Texaco Trophy matches – England and India won one each – but the sword of Damocles was soon to fall. At the beginning of June India, with Kapil Dev back in charge, beat England by five wickets in the first Test at Lord's. Gower paid the price, and Gatting replaced him as captain.

For the second match at Headingley John Lever, thirty-seven years old, was brought back as it was believed that his left-arm medium-fast bowling would be admirably suited to the conditions. He and his Essex colleague Derek Pringle took thirteen wickets between them, but India won by 279 runs. Gower had reported unfit, and Athey replaced him while Bruce French, the Nottinghamshire wicket-keeper, came in for Downton, who had had a poor game at Lord's.

Gatting's period of captaincy had not begun well, but he played a fine innings in the last match of the series, at Edgbaston, which England drew, so ending a run of seven defeats.

Wayne Larkins was originally chosen as Gooch's opening partner at Edgbaston, but he withdrew with a damaged finger, and Kent's Mark Benson came in for his first Test. This was Gooch's third different opening partner in three Tests. Neil Radford, making his international debut and born in Northern Rhodesia, and Foster also came into the England side to bring the number of players that the selectors had called upon for the three Tests against India to nineteen.

Gooch was out to the fourth ball of the match; Athey to the sixteenth without a run scored. Benson and Gower added 61 so that the position was still desperate when Gatting came to the wicket. He could have been out to his first scoring stroke, and he should have been out to his second. He edged a ball from Chetan Sharma between first slip and wicket-keeper at catchable height. Gavaskar and More left it to each other. The chance was gone, and Gatting went on to make 183 not out. How slim is the line between success and failure.

Ultimately, the match ended with India, needing 236 for victory, on 174 for five.

The selectors were in a dilemma. No settled side had been found, and Gatting was quickly named as captain for the imminent series against New Zealand and for the winter tour of Australia. If the decision was hastily taken, it is difficult to see what other options were open to the selectors. The series against India and New Zealand were separated only by the Benson and Hedges Cup Final, in which Gatting led Middlesex to a thrilling victory over Kent. The match ended in pouring rain.

The selectors contemplated bringing back Underwood, but the only shreds of evidence that they could be offered as to his form after the final Test against India were the eleven overs he bowled in the Benson and Hedges Final. Moxon won his place as Gooch's fourth opening partner in four Tests following centuries for Yorkshire in both innings against the Indians. The runs came in the Indians' last county match of their tour when, in jubilant mood, they fielded a weak attack, resting all of their main bowlers.

The series against New Zealand was no more rewarding for England than that against India had been. The first Test was drawn, Gooch and Martin Crowe scoring centuries, and the second, at Trent Bridge, was won by New Zealand by eight wickets. Richard Hadlee took ten wickets and John Bracewell hit 110. England gave a first Test cap to Gladstone Small of Warwickshire.

Ian Botham was back for the Oval Test and celebrated accordingly: he had Edgar caught at slip with his first delivery. The last ball of his second over trapped Jeff Crowe leg-before, and Botham had become the leading wicket-taker in Test cricket. He later accounted for Coney to bring his total of wickets to 357. He then hit 59 off thirty-six balls, including 24 off one over from Stirling. The prodigal son had returned with a vengeance.

There were centuries from Gower and Gatting, but the match was drawn, and New Zealand had won a Test series in England for the first time.

It was hard now to see where the selectors could turn. They had sacked one captain and, if one includes the Texaco Trophy matches, had used twenty-eight players during the 1986 season. A twenty-ninth, Larkins, had been chosen for the match against India at Edgbaston, having appeared in only four first-class matches in the season and played eight innings in which his highest score was 12.

The fixture list had become so congested with international encounters that the opportunities for players to prove themselves at domestic level, and for young cricketers aspiring to top honours to test their skills against those who had already reached the summit, were becoming increasingly limited. In Australia the domestic game had been sacrificed in the quest for more money, and the national side was labouring as a consequence.

That international cricket was the game's major source of revenue was undeniable, but the goose that was laying the golden eggs was threatened by death through excess demand. What once had been a special event was becoming a weekly meeting. There was a danger that cricketers themselves were losing a sense of perspective. Test players derived substantial incomes from interests outside the game, but those incomes were entirely dependent upon commitment to and continued success in the game itself. The extensive television coverage of Tests and one-day internationals afforded some players the opportunity to display wares in which they had a commercial interest. Temptations were great and were not resisted. As the profits grew, cricket became cheapened.

For the most part, the county game remained unsullied. Dennis Amiss hit his hundredth hundred, and Gordon Greenidge and Graeme Hick scored 2,000 first-class runs in the season. Neither, of course, was English, although the following year the period of qualification for an overseas player to become eligible to play for England was reduced from ten to seven years, and Hick's Test career drew closer.

Three bowlers claimed 100 or more wickets, the two West Indians, Marshall for Hampshire and Walsh for Gloucestershire, and the Essex pace bowler Neil Foster, who took 100 wickets in the Championship alone.

Essex had caused a pre-season sensation by registering Allan Border, the Australian captain, as their overseas cricketer. He batted splendidly and topped the county averages, but he was not available in the closing weeks of the season, having had to return to Australia for international duty. Even so, Essex, under Gooch's captaincy, finished strongly and took the Championship by a margin of twenty-eight points from Gloucestershire.

It was a former Gloucestershire player who became the romantic hero of the season. Left-arm spinner John Childs had been released by the western county at the end of 1984 and, at the age of thirty-three, he believed his first-class career was over. To his astonishment, he was offered a one-year contract by the reigning County Champions, Essex. His tally for the 1985 season had been five first-class wickets at 105.60 runs each. Again, he was resigned to returning to his career as a sign-writer, but Essex offered an extension to his contract, insisting that they believed him to be a fine bowler. Their faith was rewarded. In 1986 he took eighty-nine wickets at 16.29 runs apiece and played an integral part in Essex taking the title. In four matches in August he took more wickets than Emburey and Edmonds took all season. It was the Middlesex

356

pair who went to Australia with Gatting's side, however, while Childs, listed as a reserve, was to win two Test caps in 1987.

In contrast Trevor Jesty was to get no reward for his years of endeavour, yet, in 1986, he played what was arguably the most attractive innings of the season. Like Childs, he had changed counties, moving from Hampshire to Surrey in 1985. A year later Surrey reached the semifinal of the NatWest Trophy and met Lancashire at The Oval. Lancashire were bowled out for 229, but they reduced the home side to 173 for seven and seemed well set for victory. Jesty had been batting magnificently, but had to employ a runner after pulling a leg muscle when he had scored 76. Clarke hit fiercely, but when Pocock was bowled Surrey were still 24 short of victory with only Martin Bicknell to partner Jesty.

The former Hampshire player reached a magnificent hundred. He drove with majesty, and every shot rekindled memories of cricket's golden age. When the penultimate over began Surrey needed 7 to win. Jesty hit a two, and, off the fifth ball, he attempted a massive lofted drive. It was, perhaps, his first injudicious stroke, but it looked like the winning hit until Fowler, running round the boundary, held a spectacular catch as he tumbled. Jesty was out for 112, and Lancashire had won by 4 runs.

After the game Fowler commented, 'I had done nothing all day. I was out for nought, but, with seven balls to go, I took the catch that won the match and was a hero.' Sussex beat Lancashire in the final.

At the end of the 1987 season Jesty would move to his third county, Lancashire. Surrey released him because they wanted to encourage younger players. He moved into that legion of cricketers who graced the game, but who failed to find a prominent place in its history. Few who saw that innings at The Oval, however, will forget him.

Neither Childs nor Jesty went to Australia with Gatting's side, and Gooch, too, was absent. The Essex opener dithered for some weeks before informing Peter May that he was unavailable. The reasons were domestic. He had recently become the father of twins, but there was also a prevailing rumour that he was planning another South African venture. There were suggestions that he had presented a list of willing tourists to the South Africans, who had rejected the party on the grounds that it was not strong enough and did not contain enough players of note. It must be emphasised that these were merely rumours, but the South African connection was to continue to haunt Gooch for some time yet.

Gatting's party did include three players who were to make their Test debuts on the tour, Phillip DeFreitas, Jack Richards and, for one match only, James Whitaker of Leicestershire.

Bruce French had been injured in the first Test against New Zealand, but he had recovered in time to play in the remaining two matches of the series. Neat and tidy as he was, he never looked to have a permanent hold on the England wicket-keeping spot, and he gave way to Surrey's Richards for the Ashes series.

Richards was a good keeper and a very capable batsman. He hit 133 in the second Test and took five catches in the first innings of the fourth Test, but he was never an easy man to handle and had the unenviable reputation of being a bad tourist and a poor team man. Had he had a more engaging personality, he would have certainly won more Test caps and enjoyed a more fruitful time with Surrey.

In 1987 that county was to cause a surprise by naming Ian Greig as their captain. Greig had been managing a sports centre in Brisbane since his release by Sussex, but Surrey saw him as the man who could bring about an end to dressing-room dissension at The Oval and help to establish a side which could recapture former glories. At the recommendation of the cricket subcommittee and of Greig, Richards would be released by Surrey at the end of the 1988 season, although he had a year of his contract still to run. He had been England's wicket-keeper as late as August that year, but there was no indication that any other county offered him employment. Greig was to lead Surrey to the end of the 1991 season and returned to Australia in the autumn of 1992. He maintained belief in young players even when they were failing and kept faith with men like Graham Thorpe when others might have weakened under criticism. He brought Waqar Younis to The Oval, but, in keeping with most men who choose the hard and honest path rather than the easy and popular one, he received little thanks and scant reward for his efforts.

In the 1986–87 tour of Australia, Richards kept wicket in all five Tests, but, ironically, was replaced by French in the closing stages of the one-day competition. DeFreitas made his Test debut alongside Richards, and had a most promising first tour. Botham hit 138 in the first Test, but he never quite reached his former heights. Dilley and Small formed a successful opening attack, and Emburey, vice-captain on the tour, and Edmonds were a formidable spin duet. The batting was solid and dependable with Chris Broad outstanding.

The left-handed Nottinghamshire opening batsman had been out of the England side since his promising displays against the West Indies and Sri Lanka in 1984. In Australia he steered England to victory by seven wickets in the first Test and, in the second match in Perth he hit 162, sharing a first-wicket stand of 223 with Bill Athey. Gower and

358

Richards also scored hundreds as England made 592 for eight declared, but the match was drawn.

At Adelaide Broad made 116 and Gatting 100. The pair shared a second-wicket stand of 161, but a benign pitch doomed the match to be drawn.

At Melbourne England won by an innings and 14 runs and retained the Ashes. Ian Botham produced his best bowling performance of the series, taking five wickets in a Test innings for the twenty-seventh time, but the main honours again went to Broad. He hit 112 and so followed Hobbs, Hammond and Sutcliffe in scoring three centuries in a series in Australia. Perhaps Broad does not merit a permanent place in such illustrious company, but he served England well. He was immensely solid, played pace well and bravely, was not afraid to hit the ball and exuded strength and self-confidence.

Australia won the final Test, but England had already won the series. To add to the triumph, they took the special one-day tournament held in Perth as part of the celebrations for Australia's America's Cup triumph and the Benson and Hedges World Series which involved Australia and the West Indies. Under Emburey, England won the Sharjah Cup in the Middle East in April. Rarely had there been so successful a winter for English cricket.

One must accept that, inevitably, the power and success of one side is allied to the weakness of the other. Australia struggled with a substandard attack and with batsmen like Dean Jones, Geoff Marsh and Steve Waugh just beginning to find their feet in Test cricket. This should not detract from England's achievements. Gatting's captaincy was happy and positive. Team spirit was excellent; for this much credit must be given to the manager, Peter Lush, and to his assistant Micky Stewart.

Lush had had a career in advertising and public relations before becoming public relations and marketing manager of the Test and County Cricket Board in 1974. He held that position until 1987, and during his time in office did work of tremendous value to the game, operating for many years from what appeared to be akin to a broom cupboard on the first floor of the pavilion at Lord's. He marketed cricket and negotiated sponsorship with tact and good humour, well aware of the traditions and sensitivities of the game he was representing but also appreciating its need for money. It was generally believed that he would become Chief Executive of the TCCB, but the post went to A.C. Smith, whose background in the game was more extensive and who, therefore, was subject to no suspicions from the game's establishment. Peter Lush set up his own company which still dealt with cricket on a consultancy basis.

He had managed the 'B' team in Sri Lanka in 1986 and was to be associated with the management of England sides until 1991, but the good times really ended with the 1986–87 tour. Nothing after that was so easy or so joyful.

From the start of the 1987 season it all seemed to go wrong for England. Gooch could find no sort of form and did not appear in a Test match, although he made a century in the MCC Bicentenary game at Lord's in August. This was a celebratory match which provided an oasis of fun and calm in a desert of rancour. It gave a hint of what Test cricket was like before it became virtually open warfare. The series that year between England and Pakistan was very close to open warfare.

The tourists were angered at the outset when they felt that they were thrown to the press as soon as they arrived in England. In the first Texaco Trophy at The Oval there was an altercation between Botham and Javed Miandad, and there were accusations of cheating against the Pakistanis. The Pakistan team and management objected to David Constant and Ken Palmer being on the panel of Test umpires, but the TCCB refused to replace them. Both stood in two Test matches.

The first two Tests were ruined by rain. At Old Trafford, where Tim Robinson returned with a century and Neil Fairbrother made his Test debut, Pakistan bowled only eleven overs in an hour when Imran was off the field and Javed was leading the side. This brought criticism from Micky Stewart, the newly appointed England team manager, which drew a response from Haseeb Ahsan, the Pakistani team manager. Haseeb, a man of great charm, was to be involved in several verbal battles throughout the tour, and those who believed that the war came to an end when the Pakistanis returned home in September were very much mistaken.

For the third Test at Headingley England brought in David Capel, the Northamptonshire all-rounder. He hit 53 as England were bowled out for 136, but, primarily, England were looking to his bowling rather than his batting and, in that area, he failed. Neil Foster took eight for 107, but Pakistan won by innings and 18 runs, with Imran Khan's seven for 40 bringing about the second-innings collapse.

This victory gave Pakistan the series, for the matches at Edgbaston and The Oval were drawn. England came close at Edgbaston. Needing 124 from eighteen overs, they finished on 109 for seven, thwarted by Imran and his new all-rounder protégé Wasim Akram. At The Oval Javed hit 260, Salim Malik and Imran scored centuries, and Pakistan made 708. Ian Botham established another, this time unwanted, record by conceding 217 runs in his fifty-two overs, which brought three wickets.

Acrimony was not restricted to the series between England and

Pakistan. Some MCC members saw the TCCB's activities as an encroachment on their rights at Lord's, and there was concern over the revolution that the president, Colin Cowdrey, was bringing about. The treasurer, D.G. Clark, had resigned, and the controversial secretary, Jack Bailey, was forced into early retirement. A Special General Meeting was called, and Cowdrey and the committee, rightfully, received backing for their actions, but the whole affair reflected the fact that the mood of the game and its administrators was changing and that people neither fully comprehended nor welcomed what was happening.

In spite of this domestic cricket continued to give joy to the faithful. Yorkshire, having not renewed Boycott's contract and appointed Phil Carrick captain in place of David Bairstow, won the Benson and Hedges Cup for the first time. With Capel making 97, Northamptonshire scored 244 for seven in their fifty-five overs. Yorkshire reached the last over at 240 for six. The first four balls yielded 3 runs. Then Sidebottom pushed a single; if Bailey's underarm throw had hit the stumps, Yorkshire would have needed to score from the last ball. As it was, with the scores level, Love, Gold Award winner, blocked the last delivery and Yorkshire won by virtue of losing fewer wickets.

With their new acquisitions, Botham and Dilley, Worcestershire took the Sunday League, but the team of the season was Nottinghamshire, who finished second in the Refuge Assurance League and won both the County Championship and the NatWest Trophy. This was a fitting climax for two great cricketers, Clive Rice and Richard Hadlee, whose careers in county cricket ended in 1987.

In 1985 Hadlee had achieved a remarkable 'double'. Even more remarkably, he came close to repeating the feat in 1987 with 1,111 runs, average 52.90, sixth in the national averages, and 97 wickets at 12.64 runs each, clearly top of the bowling averages. Ted Dexter was to remark that he could generate pace and movement even on the most benign of pitches, and his 431 Test wickets for New Zealand is testimony to this.

If Clive Rice's figures are less spectacular, his contribution to Nottinghamshire cricket was in no way inferior to Hadlee's, and he will always rank as one of the outstanding cricketers of the 1980s and one of the finest captains. That his career coincided with South Africa's exile from the mainstream of the game was a tragedy for him and for cricket.

Rice, his retirement from county cricket imminent, had been replaced as captain of Nottinghamshire by Tim Robinson, but as the 1987 season progressed, Rice was reinstated. Success beckoned, opportunities were being missed, and Rice's acumen and leadership qualities were needed. Never were they more apparent than in the final of the NatWest Trophy.

Overnight rain, a delayed start and more rain meant that the match had to be reduced to fifty overs and had to be finished on the Monday. Northamptonshire, beaten finalists in the Benson and Hedges Cup, made 228 for three in their fifty overs and enjoyed the best of the conditions. With Winston Davis bowling out of the darkness of the pavilion, Nottinghamshire lost their first four wickets for 38 runs, and when play ended at 7.10 on the Saturday evening, the score was 57 for four from twenty-one overs with Rice on 20.

Birch was dismissed with the score on 84 in the twenty-ninth over, but Rice first calmed all nerves and then gradually increased the run-rate to give a glimpse of an unexpected victory. He was caught at mid-on for 63 in the forty-first over after he and Hadlee had added 62 in twelve overs, and he had prised loose Northamptonshire's grip on the game.

Fifteen runs came from the forty-fourth over, but Hadlee could have been caught three times off the luckless Williams. French batted with intelligence and excitement, and a target of 51 from five overs came down to 8 runs from the last, which was to be bowled by Capel. French was run out off the first ball, but Hadlee claimed the strike. He hit high and straight for six and pulled the next ball to the Tavern boundary for the winning runs. He finished unbeaten on 70.

The whole match epitomised what Rice and Hadlee had done for Nottinghamshire cricket and what joys the domestic game still offered, yet Rice left England troubled at the state of cricket generally. He was saddened and perplexed by the lack of commitment shown by many players and instanced an occasion when he saw only two Warwickshire cricketers who thought they were in need of practice. One was Andy Moles, then a young man fighting to establish himself in the game; the other was Alvin Kallicharran, veteran of sixty-six Test matches.

Anne Bickerstaff echoed Rice's concern when she moved from administration in the theatre to administration at The Oval. She left a profession in which ambition and the passion to succeed even in the humblest of roles was paramount, only to discover young men who lacked all drive and were content to jog along in second-eleven cricket on the chance that something might turn up.

The blame for cricket's failings, of course, was not accepted by players themselves or by those who ran the game. The faults, they insisted, lay elsewhere. There was too much travel, too much cricket and the schools were not providing the cricketers.

Travel had become considerably easier and less demanding than it had been in the inter-war years. George Rainey Brown, now in his nineties, recalls that, playing for Essex in 1932, he had to travel from Leyton to Weston-super-Mare and from there to Scarborough. Having played Yorkshire, the team had to return to the West Country to meet

Gloucestershire at Cheltenham. All the journeys were made by train. The six dominant counties, of which Essex was not one, arranged their fixtures first, and the poorer counties took what crumbs were offered them. By the 1980s sponsored cars were the fashion, and fixtures were more carefully ordered.

Even if a player appeared in every first-class and one-day match, he would never play as many innings or bowl as many overs as a cricketer of the 1930s, who had only first-class matches to contend with, many more of them. Only Eddie Hemmings, the Nottinghamshire off-spinner, sent down anywhere near the number of deliveries that his predecessors had bowled.

The blame set against the schools had more substance but little reasoning. Generations of professional cricketers had once taken up places as groundsmen and coaches in public schools when they retired, but few, if any, now could prepare a pitch, and it had become more fashionable to seek jobs in the city or with public relations organisations. The number looking for a position in the media increased yearly, and many created niches while they were still earning livings as professional cricketers.

In the decade after the Second World War young men entering teaching were enthusiastic about running cricket and football teams and producing school plays. By the end of the 1970s such enthusiasms were seen as professional suicide, for computer courses and a knowledge of the ever-changing educational jargon were essential to advancement, rather than an umpire's coat or a track suit. The devaluation of school sport was compounded by Margaret Thatcher's decision to sell off school playing fields. Not only did this severely limit playing areas, it showed quite clearly the importance that the government placed on school sport. The only hope lay in the work done by clubs in encouraging youngsters, and, invariably, that work was carried out by third-team players, men of limited ability who prepared pitches, arranged fixtures, rarely batted or bowled, but who gave their hearts and time to the game. The debt that cricket owes to them for its survival is incalculable.

England's next mission was the World Cup in India and Pakistan. There was scepticism as to how the tournament would be staged. The previous three World Cup competitions had been in England, and there was a residual feeling, in some quarters where time had stood still, that the 'colonies' might not be able to manage. As it transpired the fourth World Cup, backed by Reliance Insurance, was a resounding success. Fewer venues might have made the arrangements more practical, but none could deny that, on the whole, the tournament was a triumph. It was well organised and produced some sparkling cricket.

Botham was absent, but Gooch returned, and Eddie Hemmings and Paul Downton were also brought back. England qualified for their semi-final against India by finishing second in their group. They twice beat the West Indies and Sri Lanka and twice lost to Pakistan, who topped the group.

For the millions who watched the matches on the subcontinent, the ideal final would have featured India and Pakistan, but this dream was shattered when Australia beat Pakistan in Lahore. Two days later England beat India in Bombay to set up a final with the old enemy.

The decisive point in England's semi-final victory came when Gatting caught Kapil Dev on the square-leg boundary off the bowling of Hemmings. The Indians had been offered prize money for hitting sixes, but Kapil Dev's effort fell short.

Gooch made England's only century of the competition in the semi-final, but he, Gatting and Lamb all batted consistently. The great surprise was that Robinson was preferred to Broad in the later stages of the cup, and the selection proved costly in the final where Robinson was out first ball.

Australia made 253 for five in their fifty overs, 65 runs coming in the last five overs of their innings. Robinson was then sent back with only a single on the board. Gooch and Athey added 65 in seventeen overs before Gooch fell to O'Donnell. Athey, inevitably, did not find it easy to lift the scoring rate, but Gatting hit hard and scurried briskly. He had the facility for putting a fielding side under pressure, and after thirty-one overs England had scored 135 for two. England now appeared to be in total control. There were signs of disarray in the Australian ranks, and when Border took the ball himself it seemed as much an effort to calm his side as to break the partnership.

Border's first delivery was pitched on leg stump, and Gatting's reaction to it still haunts the memory and challenges reason: he played a reverse-sweep. Sometimes productive, never aesthetically pleasing, the shot was totally inappropriate at this juncture of the final. The area to which the ball would have been despatched was well patrolled. It was neither necessary nor wise to attempt a gesture of contemptuous authority, for England were gaining the ascendancy and nineteen overs of their innings remained. In the semi-final Gatting had swept a ball from outside off stump on to his leg stump; now his reverse-sweep succeeded only in lifting the ball on to his shoulder, from which it plopped into the wicket-keeper's gloves. It was the first of a series of

364

events which, in the coming weeks, were to suggest the decline and fall of English cricket.

There was another portent eight overs later. Athey's 104-ball innings was ended when he was run out by Steve Waugh's throw. Athey, who had made 58, chose to debate the umpire's decision, although the television replay confirmed that it had been correct.

Some brisk hitting from DeFreitas gave England hope, but Australia finished as thoroughly deserved winners by a margin of 7 runs.

The World Cup Final was played in Calcutta on 8 November. Six days later England began a tour of Pakistan with a drawn match against a BCCP President's XI. This match finished on 16 November, and two days later came the first of a three-match one-day international series that had been condensed into five days. Greed had gripped the game, for to play a one-day series ten days after a highly successful and emotionally exhausting World Cup competition seemed the height of stupidity and another attempt to kill the goose that laid golden eggs.

Javed Miandad, who had succeeded Imran as captain of Pakistan during the latter's temporary retirement, rested during the one-day series, which England won 3–0, and the great leg-spinner Abdul Qadir led the side. Three days after the last of the one-day matches the first Test match began in Lahore, where two World Cup matches had been staged in the previous three weeks.

The omens were far from good. One must remember that Botham had caused political tension by commenting that Pakistan was the type of place to send your mother-in-law. The England team had voiced displeasure over the standard of umpiring in the one-day internationals, and Sarfraz Nawaz had launched a violent attack on the English umpires Bird and Shepherd. He accused them of incompetence and bias against Pakistan in their handling of the World Cup semi-final between his country and Australia. Contrary to expectation, from then the situation deteriorated.

Gatting was happy to win the toss, and Gooch and Broad began quietly and confidently against Wasim Akram and Mudassar Nazar. Ten overs into the match, Javed brought on Abdul Qadir, who immediately bowled Gooch with a googly. Robinson groped blindly and was caught behind; two balls later Gatting swept at a ball pitched on off stump, missed and was given out leg-before. Gatting remained at the crease for several seconds and showed his obvious reluctance to accept the decision. The critics were uncertain whether the ball would have hit the stumps; but most thought Gatting deserved to be out for the grotesque shot he played.

365

England were 44 for four at lunch, and they felt more aggrieved in the afternoon when Capel was adjudged caught off bat and pad. Broad had batted with admirable concentration for nearly two sessions before falling to Qadir, but the only impetus to the England innings came from Foster, French and Nick Cook as the last two wickets added 81. England's total of 175 was meagre, but they had been the victims of what was probably the finest display of leg-spin bowling that Test cricket has seen. Abdul Qadir's nine for 56 did not flatter him. Aided by an underprepared pitch he may have been, but he gave a display of bowling that must rank alongside Laker's at Old Trafford some thirty years earlier.

England dropped catches; French had a bad time behind the stumps. The England bowlers failed to exploit the pitch as Qadir had done, runs came at 3 an over and, with Mudassar Nazar making 120, Pakistan scored 392. The innings ended in controversy. Qadir went down the pitch to Cook, missed, and French took the bails off. Umpire Shakeel Khan immediately raised his finger, although it was apparent that French had failed to remove the bails at his first attempt and that Qadir was back in his ground by the time the wicket was broken. Qadir turned to the umpire in supplication. Gatting and others laughed at the protest, and the players left the field.

England's second innings began well enough, but with the score on 23 Iqbal Qasim spun a ball past Broad's bat. Wicket-keeper Ashraf Ali caught it, and he and the close fielders leapt in appeal. Umpire Shakeel Khan immediately raised his finger. Broad spread his arms wide in indication that he had not touched the ball, shook his head in disagreement and refused to leave the crease. He stood for more than half a minute until Gooch came down the pitch and ushered him back to the pavilion.

Peter Lush, the tour manager, later issued a statement in which he condemned Broad's action and said that the player had been reprimanded, but Broad was neither fined nor punished. Lush added that the incident was a culmination of frustrations that had built up over the first three days of the match. He added that he believed that, for the benefit of the game, Test cricket should be handled by neutral umpires. This was somewhat ironic, for Pakistan and Imran Khan had advocated this policy a few years earlier, but the TCCB had been opposed to the idea.

Pakistan went on to win the Test by an innings and 87 runs. Abdul Qadir finished with match figures of thirteen for 101 from seventy-three overs, but, tragically, the unsavoury incidents are the most memorable aspects of the match. Even these events were to be overshadowed by what happened in the second Test.

Broad made 116; Gatting hit a frenetic 79 off eighty-one balls, and England were out for 292. At the end of the second day, with Pakistan on 106 for five, Gatting, at backward short-leg, gestured for a fielder to move as Hemmings was running in to bowl. Umpire Shakoor Rana invoked Law 42 on the grounds of unfair play. A confrontation, disgraceful and extraordinary, followed. Umpire and captain stood toe to toe, Gatting waving his finger and speaking vehemently, Shakoor Rana equally emphatic. Gatting insisted that he was accused of cheating; Shakoor Rana insisted that Gatting swore at him. Gatting said that the umpire swore first. The whole affair was reprehensible, and the game and the participants were sullied.

The seriousness of the situation became clear the next morning. Shakoor Rana refused to restart the game until he had received an apology; Gatting, invoking not the Laws of Cricket but Mrs Thatcher, refused to apologise. He was not for turning.

Peter Lush worked tirelessly in an attempt to bring about a solution, and received little co-operation from the Pakistani authorities. The TCCB instructed that efforts should be made to reach a compromise, but that if no compromise could be reached, Gatting should give the written apology that was requested. The England players, who were adamant that the umpire had been the first to use abusive language, issued a statement that they supported their captain and would refuse to continue the match if he did not receive an apology. When the order came from Lord's, however, they agreed to play on under protest.

Gatting gave his handwritten apology. The match, a day lost and not regained, petered to the saddest of draws. The third Test, too, was drawn.

England had lost their chance of asserting dignity, authority and diplomacy when they failed to discipline Broad for his action in the first Test. The situation was worsened by England's refusal to participate in social gatherings after that match and by Gatting's post-match statement: 'The bad decisions went against us by 10–1. I've never seen it so blatant over here. To put an inexperienced umpire into the first Test on a turning pitch, and without even first informing us, smacks of something.'

However persecuted Gatting and his side may have felt, the indisputable fact remains that the umpire is the judge. Cricket works on the principle that the umpire's decision is final and must be accepted without comment or dissent. When that principle breaks down the game ceases to exist. Shakoor Rana was wrong in his interpretation of Law 42 (of the 1980 Code)) but the law does state: 'The umpires are the sole judges of fair and unfair play.'

367

The pioneering spirit of MCC which had once won friends in many lands to which the game was taken had been forgotten. The sensitivity and respect for the customs and courtesies of others had been lost.

9

Profit and Loss, 1988–93

The events of the winter of 1987–88 left a stain on English cricket which was seen to be attended by an arrogance, a total lack of humility and self-questioning. The direction in which the game was moving was unclear, for so many paths were being suggested; there were so many committees, so many generals.

Subba Row, Chairman of the Cricket Council, Chairman of the TCCB, had authorised the payment of 'hardship bonuses' in Pakistan. Broad, whose misdemeanours we have catalogued, and Dilley, fined for swearing at an umpire in New Zealand, came home to rewards. In a previous home series Dilley had given a section of the crowd a V-sign when they barracked him. Richie Benaud had commented, 'I think you have to be a very good player before you can do that.' The gesture went unpunished.

One must not believe that England were alone in their reluctance to exert firm discipline on their cricketers. Packer had left a legacy of fear of player power. There was the constant threat that the lure of the krugerrand could, at any moment, deprive England of its better players, and May and his co-selectors were well aware that they had few men of real international class from which to choose.

Peter May had been appointed Chairman of Selectors with part of his brief being to bring a greater sense of discipline to the game. He now stood in a most unenviable position. It was he who took the brunt of criticism, invective in most cases, for England's failures. T-shirts were sold which carried slogans ridiculing May's lack of success. Micky Stewart, in contrast, escaped censure.

Stewart was confirmed as England team manager for a three-year span. It is generally thought that the job had first been offered to Ray Illingworth, but the Yorkshireman had demanded total control. Stewart was content to accept the terms that were given, but many were bemused as to what his role really was. How did captain and manager divide their responsibilities? How great a say did the manager have in selection? Certainly not as much as Illingworth had demanded. How much coaching, help with technique, was possible during the course of a five-day Test match? Whatever the answer to these questions, Stewart escaped from the debacle of Pakistan and New Zealand, where he had faced criticism for England's behaviour on the field, virtually unscathed.

May believed that one of the problems undermining English cricket was the presence of overseas players. Gatting was opposed to the inclusion of non-Englishmen in the England team, although he treated all under his command equally and fairly. Subba Row and Ossie Wheatley, Chairman of the TCCB's Cricket Committee, were convinced that the problems were in the county game, and they were prime movers in introducing four-day games into the Championship in 1988.

Of the twenty-two matches played by each county, six were of four days' duration. Some welcomed this as a step to bring county cricket into line as a meaningful preparation for Test cricket; others were convinced that it was part of a process that would ultimately destroy the domestic game in England.

Inevitably, there were greater problems facing some counties than others. There was blood-letting at Warwickshire and restructuring at Sussex. Surrey found themselves in dire straits. A ministerial promise had not been honoured, and The Oval, in the process of development, was under threat. Ultimately, the famous old ground was saved, but problems for the county club itself remained.

Over the next few years the Surrey committee was to face a series of challenges from members who questioned the county's priorities. Derek Newton, then chairman of the club, asserted that Surrey's first aim was to produce cricketers for England. Loyal members, starved of success, could not accept this as the main aim of a county cricket club. The Surrey dilemma and debate was central to the whole argument as to the future of domestic cricket in England.

In 1988 County cricket was dominated by Worcestershire. Without Ian Botham for much of the season, they came close to winning three competitions. Botham had crossed the Alps in aid of leukaemia research, got into trouble when playing for Queensland in the Sheffield Shield, and showed a total lack of form before revealing on 20 May that he was in need of a back operation to fuse two vertebrae.

That Botham was not missed was due to consistent bowling by Newport, Radford and Richard Illingworth, some astute captaincy and solid batting from Neale, reliable opening contributions from Curtis and a spectacularly successful season from Graeme Hick. Zola Budd had jettisoned her instant British nationality and returned to South Africa. Hick was still qualifying for England and giving visions of a golden future.

He had scored 827 runs in fourteen innings for Northern Districts in New Zealand and, returning to England, he hit 2,713 first-class runs, average 77.51. This placed him top of the averages, with Steve Waugh, the Australian all-rounder assisting Somerset, second, Athey third and Gooch, the only other batsman to score 2,000 runs, fourth. Gooch had given up the Essex captaincy because he felt it was affecting his batting. By the end of the season, he was captaining not only Essex but England.

The only two bowlers to take a hundred wickets were both Nottinghamshire men: Stephenson had succeeded Hadlee and completed a remarkable 'double', but Nottinghamshire only finished fifth in the Championship.

Worcestershire took the title by one point from Kent, and they also won the Refuge Assurance Sunday League. Stephen Rhodes, their Yorkshire-born wicket-keeper, established a new league record with twenty-nine dismissals. Worcestershire were also finalists in the Refuge Cup, a new competition for the top four in the league, but Lancashire were the winners.

Worcestershire were also beaten finalists in the NatWest Trophy. Middlesex won the match by three wickets. It was Gatting's fifth triumph in six years as captain, and it was a most gratifying success as Middlesex had played for nearly all the season without the aid of Wayne Daniel, who broke down early on. Dilley took five wickets, but enterprising batting by young Ramprakash complemented the early success of Fraser and Hughes for Middlesex to claim the trophy.

If Middlesex found glory without an overseas cricketer, Hampshire were most reliant on their import for winning the Benson and Hedges Cup Final. Enrolled for a season while Marshall was on duty with the West Indies, the left-arm South African seamer Steve Jefferies took four wickets for 1 run in eight balls to wreck the Derbyshire innings. He finished with five for 13 and took the Gold Award, but he owed much to the captaincy of Mark Nicholas. Nicholas insisted that Jefferies have a forward short-leg and took up the position himself. He held two catches and inhibited the Derbyshire batsmen. He later finished on 35 not out as Hampshire won by seven wickets.

Derbyshire did provide the bowler who topped the first-class averages: Ole Mortensen, 'The Great Dane'. Mortensen had been spotted playing for Denmark in the ICC Trophy in 1979, and Derbyshire had signed the tearaway fast bowler. Under the Treaty of Rome workers were at liberty to be employed in any member state of the European

Community. Mortensen, a fanatically wholehearted cricketer, was not, therefore, regarded as an overseas player. Others of the European Community followed him into county cricket. His fellow countryman Henrikksen played for Lancashire while the Dutchmen Bakker and Lefebvre assisted Hampshire and Somerset, who also recruited van Troost. Lefebvre later joined Glamorgan. The Europeans met with varying degrees of success, but none quite touched Mortensen's heights. At the end of his career he returned to Denmark as coach to the national side.

There was a lobby in favour of Mark Nicholas being appointed captain of the England side, but he was never quite of international class as a batsman, and Gatting was reappointed for the start of the 1988 season. When England beat the West Indies in all three Texaco Trophy games all seemed well again.

Gooch scored 146 in the first Test at Trent Bridge, which was drawn. This ended a sequence of ten successive defeats at the hands of the West Indies, but it meant that England had now gone fourteen Tests without a victory. Unfortunately, these statistics were the least significant facts regarding this Test match.

A month before the game, playing for Worcestershire against Somerset at Taunton, Graeme Hick had hit 405 not out in nine and a quarter hours. His innings included thirty-five fours and eleven sixes, and only Archie MacLaren had scored more runs in a Championship game. His 424 had come ninety-three years earlier on the same ground. Hick went on to become the eighth player to score a thousand runs before the end of May when he hit 172 against the West Indies in the tourists' last match before the first Test.

Hick, of course, was as yet ineligible to play for England, but his performances had heightened interest and expectation in the first Test, and that England avoided defeat was seen as some improvement. The match ended on 7 June, and the following morning the *Sun* carried a story alleging a 'sex orgy' at a Leicestershire hotel on the night of 6 June which involved two England players. On 9 June Gatting was named as one of the players involved. Other newspapers less given to scandal generally joined in the accusations. Gatting admitted that he had invited a barmaid to his room for a drink to help celebrate his thirty-first birthday, but he denied any impropriety. His explanation was accepted, but his days as England captain were over.

His position had been in jeopardy since the events in Pakistan, and he had violated his contract with the TCCB in allowing a book to be published under his name in which one chapter, appearing under the name of his 'ghost', dealt with the Shakoor Rana episode. Peter May took the role of executioner, and informed Gatting that he had been relieved of the captaincy.

There was no obvious successor and, without the pressure on him from the tabloid press and others, May would have retained Gatting. The Middlesex skipper was in the Bedser–Willis mould. He was a sergeant-major rather than a commissioned officer. He tended to bark his orders, but if he lacked distinction in the finer points of the game, he had a rugged honesty which his men greatly respected. He asked not to be considered for the second Test, and the captaincy went to his county colleague and friend John Emburey.

Once more May was vilified, yet Cornhill Insurance, the sponsors of the Test matches, made their position quite clear when they issued a statement on the eve of the second game in the series at Lord's:

> No one with the interests of English cricket at heart can take pleasure from what has happened from the first Cornhill Test, at Trent Bridge. Certainly not the sponsors, who must be as concerned as the TCCB about the image the game projects at the highest level. They support the Board in its efforts and determination to maintain standards of behaviour both on and off the field.

Cricketers of a past generation commented that Gatting's only crime was that he had got caught.

Emburey was a consistent off-spinner, accurate rather than attacking for he did not turn the ball greatly. He was a fine fielder and an effective if unorthodox batsman. He was an intelligent thinker on the game and an able leader, but when he was called upon to captain England he was totally out of form.

The first session of Emburey's leadership proved to be the highlight of England's summer. At lunch on the first day at Lord's the West Indies were 66 for five from twenty-five overs. Dilley had captured four wickets, Small one. That was the pinnacle of England's joy, although to bowl out the West Indies for 209 on the opening day was a further achievement.

England closed on 20 for one. The batsman out was Chris Broad, adjudged leg-before to Marshall. The television cameras zoomed in on Broad as he made his way back to the pavilion, and one did not have to be a trained lip-reader to decipher that he was muttering, 'That pitched outside leg stump.' He was castigated by the press, defended by Micky Stewart, who claimed that Broad was simply voicing disappointment at himself, and did not play again in the series.

Marshall went on to take six wickets, and England were bowled out for 165. Their moment had passed. Greenidge hit 103, Richards and Logie scored heavily and, in spite of Lamb's eighth Test hundred, the West Indies won by 134 runs.

John Childs made a romantic Test debut at Old Trafford at the age of 36 years, 320 days. He captured a wicket, but Gower's second-innings 34 was England's highest score, and the West Indies won by an innings.

Emburey had taken three wickets for 228 runs in three Tests and averaged under 10 with the bat. England were being annihilated. Drastic times called for drastic measures. May and his selectors reacted bravely. They brought back Jack Richards and Neil Foster and gave first Test caps to Tim Curtis, the Worcestershire opener, and to Robin Smith, the South African-born batsman whose elder brother had already played for England. Most significantly, they named Chris Cowdrey as captain for the last two Tests of the series.

This was a bold and justified move. There had not been much joy among the senior England players for some time, and the appointment of Cowdrey suggested that there would be a renewed sense of dynamism. There was a feeling that England were to be led by a man who enthused about cricket. He was leading Kent in an inspirational manner, and players and crowd were responding to him excitedly. He was a good communicator, and he was fun. In the field he was outstanding, and his enthusiasm was infectious. The problem was that he had played for England with moderate success in India, and it was apparent that he was not of Test class as a cricketer.

This much was known before Cowdrey was named as captain, but he maintains that he was told not to worry about the results against the West Indies, for the series was already doomed, and that he must try to pull the side together in preparation for taking the party to India.

England ran the West Indies close for much of the time at Headingley. Pringle had an inspired spell of three for 11 in sixteen balls and finished with five wickets. In their second innings England went from 56 without loss to 138 all out and lost by ten wickets. Cowdrey scored 0 and 5 and bowled twenty-one balls for 21 runs.

An injured foot prevented him from playing in the final Test against the West Indies at The Oval. Gooch became England's fourth captain of the summer, and the West Indies won by eight wickets.

Bailey of Northamptonshire and Maynard of Glamorgan were included in this Test, but neither of them survived for the last international game of the summer, a Test match against Sri Lanka at Lord's. Barnett of Derbyshire, Lawrence and Russell (England's third keeper of the summer) of Gloucestershire, and Newport of Worcestershire were the newcomers for this game. Tim Robinson was recalled, as was

Emburey. Robinson had threatened to resign as captain of Nottinghamshire, saying that he felt he did not have the support of the players. He was persuaded to continue, and Broad was dropped for two matches as a disciplinary measure. England's left-handed opener had not enjoyed a happy few months.

Gooch led the side to victory by seven wickets over Sri Lanka. The win ended a record run of eighteen Tests without success. England had used twenty-eight players in six Tests in the summer; nine cricketers had won their first Test caps. Cowdrey was not invited to lead the side against Sri Lanka and did not hear from the selectors again. He was shabbily treated, for nothing had been learned of him in his one Test as England's captain that had not been known before he was chosen.

Gooch was appointed captain of the side to tour India, although he had earlier stated his intention of wintering in South Africa and playing for Western Province. He was persuaded to tour as England's captain and was released from his South African contract. The Indian government refused to grant visas to Gooch and seven other cricketers whose names appeared on a list of sportsmen who had links with South Africa. The TCCB, holding to the ICC principle that no country should be allowed to influence the team selection of another, cancelled the tour. They had no option. India were held as being hypocritical in that Gooch and Emburey had been granted visas for the World Cup, but feeling was running very high against apartheid, and times were changing. England cricketers tended to remain naive or unaware. In June a crowd of more than 80,000 had attended a rally at Wembley to celebrate Nelson Mandela's seventieth birthday. The ANC leader himself had been transferred from prison to hospital for treatment for tuberculosis.

In November 1988 Peter May retired as Chairman of Selectors. The constant attacks and ridicule in the press had taken their toll on him. He was a good and conscientious man and even at the end of his all too short life – he died in December 1994 just before his sixty-fifth birthday – he was excited and delighted at the prospect of a reunion with some of his former England colleagues at a Test match. The greatest of England's post-war batsmen and a highly successful captain, May's period as Chairman of Selectors was not a happy one. The players with whom he dealt spoke a language that was different from his, and values had changed.

He was succeeded by Ted Dexter, who received a salary of £20,000 a year to compensate him for his loss of business and who was termed, initially at least, England's 'supremo'. Dexter had been neither a pop-

375

ular nor a successful captain, but he had given much thought to the game since his retirement and he was richly experienced in committee. The appointment caused the inevitable class divide, North versus South, gentlemen versus players, which constantly bubbles below the surface of English cricket and which occasionally erupts into the open.

Just as the England season of 1989 was beginning, the sporting world was devastated by the Hillsborough tragedy. The subsequent Taylor Report into stadia and its recommendations have never been fully implemented by the cricketing authorities.

Dexter's immediate problems were that he was confronted by an Ashes series and by the hottest summer for twenty years. Within a few months it was to become even hotter, but the sun was not to blame.

English cricket had suffered a grievous loss during the winter with the death in the Gambia of Wilf Slack. The Middlesex and England opener was, perhaps, just short of Test class, but his commitment to the game was exemplary. Six years before his death he had written in his coaching notes:

> There must be a deep down love for the game. The batsman must want to bat and score many runs, the bowlers must want to bowl whether or not they are getting the correct results. A deep down love for the game is a must. Without this, no amount of coaching will achieve the correct results.

Dexter had come to power in what amounted to a palace coup, and a new era was promised by the England Committee, founded on what Wilf Slack had called 'a deep down love of the game'. But it soon became apparent how limited were Dexter's powers. He, supported by Micky Stewart who now held a stronger position, wanted Gatting reinstated as captain. Ossie Wheatley, utilising a new weapon, vetoed the choice.

Wheatley and Subba Row continued to be at the forefront of those who wished to emphasise that the principal role of the County Championship was to produce Test cricketers and that the competition should be shaped to that end. Following the introduction of four-day matches and the continuing lobby to make all Championship matches four days in length came the decision to punish counties for what were considered to be substandard pitches. The uncovered pitches on which England's greatest players had learned the game were long in the past and what was now looked for, it seemed, was conformity. Whether you batted at Southport or Southend, the surface would be the same. Another essence of character was to be driven out of the game.

It was at Southend that the new law was applied with a vengeance.

376

The first match of the Australian tour had been played on a dreadful pitch at New Road, Worcester. Worcestershire stated that they had unavoidable problems, called in the TCCB's pitch adviser and thereby assured themselves of immunity for the rest of the season. When Essex came to play their second match in the Southend Festival against Yorkshire, their lead over Worcestershire, who were lying second in the Championship, was more than fifty points. Southend was always a popular venue for Essex, and 25,000 people paid for admittance during the week, in addition to members, who attended in great numbers. Essex had beaten Kent by an innings in the first match of the week with Pringle, very much in form, taking ten wickets and Hussain scoring a century. In the second match Yorkshire, bowled out for 115 on the opening day, were beaten by three wickets. It was an exciting match that was thoroughly enjoyed by large crowds on all three days. However, Carrick, the Yorkshire captain, was seen remonstrating with the umpires during a lunch interval, and the umpires duly reported the pitch. Although found guilty of no malpractice, Essex were deducted twenty-five points.

It was ironic, for Essex's first-innings score of 248 against Yorkshire was 2 runs more than Worcestershire had made in any first-class game at New Road, where only Warwickshire, at the start of the season, had passed 250. Like Essex, Nottinghamshire were to suffer a twenty-five-point penalty, but Essex's penalty was to cost them the title. They were shattered by the decision and temporarily lost form and confidence. They finished second to Worcestershire. The final difference between the two sides was *six* points.

One feels that the rule was allowed to lapse quietly in the next few seasons, or perhaps all pitches came up to standard. When Kent were involved in a thrilling game at Dartford in 1990 and the spinners Davis and Patel wrought havoc against Leicestershire, the pitch was reported, but the suggestion simply came that Kent should not use the ground for a first-class fixture the following season.

Essex and Worcestershire were also in contention in the Sunday League but both finished behind Lancashire. Essex were also runners-up in the Benson and Hedges Cup Final, where Eddie Hemmings hit John Lever's last ball of the match for four to give Nottinghamshire victory by three wickets.

The NatWest Trophy provided an equally exciting finish. Middlesex, who had acquired Desmond Haynes as their overseas player, scored 210. The last over of the match, bowled by Simon Hughes, arrived with Warwickshire needing 10 for victory and Asif Din and Neil Smith at the wicket. Smith, son of M.J.K., the former England captain, was a surprise choice, but Andy Lloyd had picked him because he was a man in form and had hit his maiden first-class century the previous day. Asif Din took a single which put the onus on the inexperienced Smith, who responded by hitting Hughes high over long-off for six. Shaken, Hughes delivered an enormous leg-side wide, and Smith drove the next ball past him for the winning runs. Dermot Reeve, once of Sussex, won the Man of the Match award, and more was to be heard of him.

These excitements and controversies in the domestic game were, inevitably, overshadowed by the Ashes series of 1989 and by other movements on the international front. Deprived of Gatting as captain by Wheatley's veto – a matter which, like government papers, was leaked when it should have remained private – Dexter decided to recall David Gower to the captaincy.

Gower, one felt, was a skipper closer to Dexter's heart than Gatting, but again he took the reins at a most unenviable time. Since winning the World Cup in 1987, Australia had been reborn and could now boast a strong side, while Gower was to remain one of England's least success-ful captains. For the Australians, by contrast, Allan Border was blos-soming into one of their most accomplished leaders.

Honours were even in the Texaco Trophy, but England went to Headingley without Botham or Gatting, both injured, and left out Emburey. An attack lacking in all variety was severely punished – Taylor and Steve Waugh got hundreds – and, in spite of Lamb's century, Australia won by 210 runs.

Steve Waugh, who averaged 126.50 in the series, looked assured of a century as soon as he took guard on the second afternoon at Lord's. He finished unbeaten on 152, and he and Lawson put on 130 in 108 minutes for the ninth wicket. Australia, 528, took a first-innings lead of 242. England were 58 for three on the Saturday evening. At the press confer-ence following the day's play Gower was being questioned about the tactics he had employed when he stormed out of the meeting saying that he had a taxi waiting to take him to see a preview of Cole Porter's *Anything Goes*. He later apologised for his action, and he hit a century on the Monday, but England lost by six wickets.

More than nine and a half hours' play were lost in the Edgbaston Test, in which Angus Fraser made his Test debut. Dean Jones hit 157, and England were thankful for the rain and the draw.

Australia regained the Ashes with a nine-wicket victory at Old Trafford. The only centuries in the match were Robin Smith and 'Jack' Russell, his first in first-class cricket, but England were still outplayed. Gower had been under increasing pressure from the start of the season, and he was being castigated daily in the press. It was believed that he would resign following defeat at Old Trafford, but on the last day of the

Botham's 100th Test wicket. Gavaskar is caught by Brearley, Lord's, August, 1979. Bob Taylor is the wicket-keeper.

Botham's unhappy period as captain against West Indies. He is caught by Gordon Greenidge for four in the fourth Test, at The Oval, 1980.

England captain Keith Fletcher with the Indian Prime-Minister Mrs Gandhi during the third Test in Delhi, December, 1981. Geoff Cook, Graham Dilley and Mike Gatting are behind Fletcher with Allott in the back row. (ADRIAN MURRELL/ALLSPORT)

England v New Zealand, The Oval, July, 1983. BACK ROW – Fowler, Marks, Tavare, Cowans, Edmonds and Lamb. FRONT ROW – Taylor, Gower, Willis (capt), Botham and Randall. Willis and Botham had been the heroes of England's 'Ashes' victory two years earlier. (ADRIAN MURRELL/ALLSPORT)

England in West Indies, 1986.
BACK ROW – Robinson, D.M. Smith, L. Taylor, Thomas, Edmonds, Ellison, Foster, Downton and French. FRONT ROW – Gooch, Botham, Gatting, Gower (capt), Lamb, Willey and Emburey. (ADRIAN MURRELL / ALLSPORT)

Richard Hadlee was a magnificent servant to Nottinghamshire and New Zealand in the 1980s. He helped his county to success in all competitions and finished with 431 Test wickets. Here, he claims Border as his 300th.

Geoffrey Boycott, one of the most prolific scorers and most consistent opening batsmen Test cricket has seen, but never far from controversy.
(BEN RADFORD/ALLSPORT)

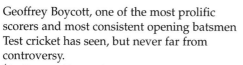

England v India, Lord's, June, 1986. David Gower sits dejected as the axe is about to fall to terminate his captaincy.
(ADRIAN MURRELL/ALLSPORT)

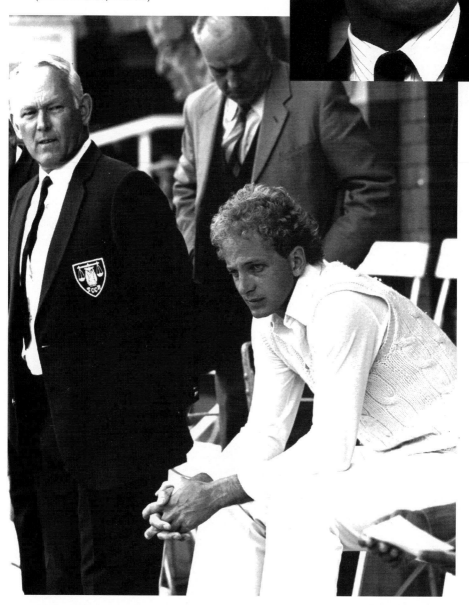

Gooch is bowled by Ellison in the Championship match between Kent and Essex, Folkestone, August, 1986. Kent went on to win and to take the title. (SIMON BRUTY/ALLSPORT)

England manager and astute marketer and public relations man, Peter Lush.
(ADRIAN MURRELL/ALLSPORT)

The year of captains, 1988. Chris Cowdrey, Mike Gatting and John Emburey pictured at Lord's. All three led England in 1988.
(ADRIAN MURRELL/ ALLSPORT)

A solid performer for England and an inspiring coach for Warwickshire in the nineties before moving to South Africa, Bob Woolmer.
(MIKE POWELL/ALLSPORT)

Alec Stewart –
good service for
England.
(GRAHAM CHADWICK
/ALLSPORT)

Dominic Cork in
exuberant appeal.
(GRAHAM CHADWICK/
ALLSPORT)

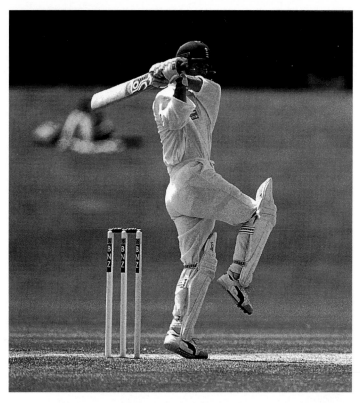

Surrey and
England –
Graham Thorpe.
(GRAHAM CHADWICK/
ALLSPORT)

Captain and vice-
captain, Mike
Atherton and
Nasser Hussain.
(GRAHAM CHADWICK/
ALLSPORT)

match news broke which changed the complexion of the season and of the future. It was learned that sixteen players had signed to tour South Africa the following winter. Nine of the men involved had represented England during the current series, and three of them – Robinson, Emburey and Foster – were playing in the Old Trafford Test. Dilley would have been in the side but for injury, and the other defectors included Gatting and Broad. Disillusioned and uncharacteristically embittered, Chris Cowdrey was also in the party.

Rarely can a decision have been so ill-judged and ill-timed. As Australia rejoiced in regaining the Ashes it appeared that many of England's top players could not care less one way or the other, nor, it seemed, could they gauge the tenor of international events as they happily accepted an automatic five-year ban from Test cricket. P.W. Botha had resigned as Prime Minister of South Africa, and the Republic witnessed its biggest anti-apartheid demonstrations for many years. F.W. de Klerk and the Nationalist Party were re-elected, but a tidal wave was already in motion.

In Eastern Europe there was ferment, and the Berlin Wall came down. Even Great Britain showed a move towards more open government with the televising of the House of Commons.

The tour of South Africa by Gatting and his men was a total disaster. There were dinners and speeches but virtually no cricket. The English party was hounded wherever it went, and there were twenty-four hours of riots in Bloemfontein. The ban was lifted on political parties with anti-apartheid policies. Nelson Mandela was released from prison, and the ANC had regained its leader and legality. By the end of 1990 South Africa had released all political prisoners.

None of this, at present, was of any help to Dexter and the beleaguered Gower against Australia. Atherton and Malcolm won first Test caps at Trent Bridge, but Marsh, 138, and Taylor, 219, scored 329 for Australia's first wicket. In contrast England were 37 for four before Robin Smith hit a century, but Australia won by an innings.

Terry Alderman brought his total number of wickets in the series to forty-one when he captured seven in the sixth match at The Oval. That England avoided defeat was due mainly to Gladstone Small, whose first-innings 59 saved the follow-on.

With Botham and Malcolm unfit, Greg Thomas, once so eager and full of ambition to play for England, was called in to play for the side only to reveal that he, too, had signed to join the 'rebels' in South Africa. His place went to Igglesden, the promising Kent bowler, who was destined to spend a great deal of his career on the physiotherapist's table rather than on the cricket field. Another newcomer at The Oval was John Stephenson, then of Essex, later captain of Hampshire. Stephenson played soundly until receiving a blow on the arm from Merv Hughes, but he was not chosen in the party to tour the Caribbean; nor was David Gower.

Following the disasters of the summer against Border's side and the defections of some of the top players, Dexter and his advisers decided to dispense with Gower altogether. It was a strange decision, for England's options were very limited. The two cricketers who had topped the national averages were both South African: Jimmy Cook of Somerset, the only batsman to score 2,000 runs; and Allan Donald, the Warwickshire pace bowler who had begun to strike fear into many county batsmen's hearts.

The problems were obvious, but the administrators did not help their cause with a succession of confusing decisions. Ian Botham had had a moderate season, and he had said that he would not tour the West Indies. The selectors set about persuading him to change his mind, and when he agreed he then was not chosen.

Botham, like Gower, had become too closely associated with recent defeats. As a captain, Gower seemed too amiable, too unwilling to assert himself. He had also never seemed totally enamoured of the county game. It was almost as if he had been born out of his time. He should have been an Edwardian amateur, playing as the mood took him and expenses allowed. He would have graced the golden age. For the time being, however, he was not wanted on the voyage. He had been the fifth England captain in two seasons. Where could Dexter turn now?

Some three or four days before the selectors met to decide who would lead the side in the Caribbean, Alan Lee, cricket correspondent of *The Times* and a journalist ever close to events, wrote that Ian Greig would be named as the new England captain. Greig had won the reputation of being a hard, fair and outstanding captain of Surrey, a position which was certainly not a sinecure. Other correspondents later supported Lee's assertion, although several questioned whether Greig was of Test standard. The echoes of Mike Brearley's captaincy were loud, and perhaps the selectors saw in Greig a way of emulating Brearley's success.

Ian Greig received a phone call from the TCCB asking him to confirm that he was available for the tour. He was then contacted by Lieutenant-Colonel John Stephenson, a splendid secretary of MCC but acting on this occasion in his capacity as Secretary of the ICC. Stephenson said that he needed clarification on four points:

1 When Greig went to Australia at the end of the 1985 season in England had he intended to stay there on a permanent basis?
2 Did he buy property in Australia?

3 Did he sell property in England?
4 Had he intended playing in England in 1986?

Ian Greig, whose transparent honesty was one of his greatest virtues, replied that he had gone to Sydney to see Peter Roebuck because he had every intention of returning to England to play in the 1986 season if it could be arranged, and he wished to discuss the matter with the Somerset captain. He had never had the money to buy property in England and therefore had never sold any, and the only one who had owned property in Australia was his wife Cheryl, who was Australian by birth.

John Stephenson was totally satisfied with Greig's responses and told the Surrey captain he would be in touch again shortly. He was, but he told Greig that the ICC had put his case to their lawyers, who had advised that he was ineligible to play for England and that he required a further four-year residential qualification period. Paradoxically, he remained recognised as an English-qualified cricketer.

Greig had appeared in two Tests for England, had attended a British university and held a British passport, but was deemed ineligible to captain England. If such confusions were rampant in the committee room, what hope was there on the field?

Certainly the counties themselves were concerned as to what was happening, and it was no surprise when Subba Row stood down as Chairman of the TCCB. There was an opinion that he had assumed too much power and that the county clubs were under threat. His successor was William Chamberlain, President of Northamptonshire, a less contentious choice.

Having sacked Gower and, for different reasons, been denied Gatting and Greig, Dexter and his men had little option but to return to Graham Gooch. Gooch had settled as a successful captain of Essex, but his form in 1989 had been indifferent, and he had asked not to be considered for the penultimate Test against Australia. Returning at The Oval, he had been leg-before in Alderman's opening over.

When Dexter announced the England squad he said that they were cricketers capable of 'fighting fire with fire'. The comment was greeted with a certain amount of contempt, for the team was raw and inexperienced. The Test careers of Rob Bailey, Angus Fraser and Devon Malcolm had barely begun, and Nasser Hussain and Alec Stewart were to make their Test debuts on the tour. Wayne Larkins, much favoured by Gooch, had not played Test cricket since 1981. Newcomers Medlycott and Lewis did not figure in the series, nor did the veteran Eddie Hemmings, recalled following the defection of Emburey.

Keith Medlycott, left-arm spinner, most capable batsman and excellent fielder, was a promising all-rounder with Surrey, but after the tour of the Caribbean his ability to spin and control the ball deserted him and he dropped out of first-class cricket.

Gooch had been nobody's first choice as captain, but he proved outstandingly successful. Dedicated to physical fitness, he was a leader by example rather than by any astute tactical awareness, but he won the respect of his men. There was an immediate common purpose, and Gooch's relentless insistence on his own physical training and practice was an inspiration.

Practice, though, was limited through circumstance. Two one-day internationals before the first Test were ruined by rain, and Jamaica fielded a somewhat weakened side in the only first-class match before the Test. Gooch made 239, and Larkins had a convenient injury which forced him to retire when he had scored 124. England were given no chance whatsoever of winning the first Test in Kingston. Nor were their chances seen to improve when they gave first Test caps to Alec Stewart and Nasser Hussain and named an eleven which included only four bowlers and no spinners. The West Indies were without Logie and Ambrose, but they could still afford to leave out Arthurton and Moseley.

Richards won the toss, and the West Indies, through Haynes and Greenidge, moved smoothly to 62 in 103 minutes. At this point Greenidge turned a ball from Fraser to long-leg. Malcolm fumbled, and Greenidge went for a second run only to be beaten by Malcolm's recovery and fast throw which left the batsman well short of his crease. Ten more runs came before the lunch interval to leave the West Indies still reasonably contented.

Capel was given the ball immediately after the break and captured two vital wickets in a fine spell: Richardson mishooked to Small at square-leg, and Capel found the edge of Best's bat. When Haynes pushed a return catch to Small the West Indies were 92 for four, and England were exultant.

Richards seemed to want to deal only in fours. He hit four of them, survived vociferous appeals for leg-before and caught behind, before playing all over a ball from Malcolm that left him plum leg-before.

All the England bowlers had bowled, maintaining a relentless off-stump line, but it was Angus Fraser who shredded the West Indian innings after tea. He took the last five wickets at a personal cost of 6 runs. The West Indies were out for 164 in sixty-four overs. England lost Gooch and Stewart, but they ended the day on 80 for two. They had enjoyed their best day's cricket for several years.

Having batted for three hours and held the West Indies at bay after the early and damaging loss of Gooch, Larkins was leg-before on the second morning, but his was the only wicket to fall before lunch, by which time England had made 132. Crucially, Lamb was dropped by Dujon immediately after the interval, and he responded by taking total command. In forty-seven overs he and Robin Smith added 172. It was a momentous stand. Lamb hit sixteen fours and faced 209 balls in his six-hour innings. The two South African-born men had put England in a very strong position.

Lamb, vice-captain on the tour, was a fine, natural player, ever eager to take the initiative and dominate the bowling. His record against pace was as good as it was brave. He was a fun player who took the game seriously; he enjoyed cricket as much as he enjoyed life, and he was a crowd pleaser. Strangely, for all his exuberance and success, he never quite captured the public imagination. He was, after all, South African, still spoke with a strong accent and had learned his cricket in the Republic. The dilemma of the South African cricketer was understood, but there was still a feeling that it was the country that taught you your cricket that should have the claim on you. The feeling increased in the next few years.

Once the Lamb–Smith partnership was broken the England innings lost its impetus, but at stumps, with 342 for eight on the board, a lead of 178 and three days remaining, England were touching dizzy heights.

The innings was extended for fifty-two balls and produced 22 runs on the third morning so that England's first-innings lead was exactly 200, an important figure psychologically. To add to West Indian woes, the ball was now keeping low. The England bowling was eager and attacking, the fielding keen and determined and the leadership positive. A fast delivery of full length soon accounted for Haynes.

Richardson and Greenidge appeared secure, but Fraser's relentless accuracy taxed them both, and Richardson succumbed when he impatiently pulled across the line. Greenidge had been at the crease for two and a half hours when he drove at Malcolm and was caught at cover. Hooper was taken at slip, the ball rebounding from Gooch to Larkins, and the West Indies were 112 for four.

Viv Richards found himself in the unaccustomed role of captain in a crisis, and he was partnered by Carlisle Best, who was batting to save his side and to save his own Test career. They added 80 and threatened to seize the initiative when Malcolm cut a ball back sharply and wrecked Richards's stumps. The West Indies were still 8 runs short of avoiding an innings defeat.

That embarrassment was avoided, but Small and Malcolm produced a spell which put the game irrevocably in England's control. Small found the edge of Best's bat and had him taken at slip. In the next over

Malcolm spreadeagled Dujon's stumps. Malcolm's pace had surprised the West Indians, and his four wickets in the innings by no means flattered him.

Bishop was caught low at slip, but, at 229 for eight, with England on the brink of victory, the umpires decided that the light was too bad to continue.

There was a little rain on the rest day, and, on the scheduled fourth day, there was a deluge. England looked on in frustration as the victory which they had earned by outplaying the West Indies in every department of the game was seemingly going to be denied them.

Thankfully for England, the sun shone on the fifth day and, although the pitch was damp, the match began on time. It took twenty balls for England to end the West Indian innings. Small knocked back Walsh's off stump in his second over, and Patterson and Marshall dithered to such an extent that Capel had time to lob the ball gently to the bowler and run out Patterson.

Needing 41 to win, England were given no easy passage. With 6 runs needed, Gooch turned Bishop to leg where Greenidge took a fine diving catch. Stewart was given a torrid reception, but survived, and Larkins ran from the field, bat held on high, when the winning hit was made.

England had beaten the West Indies for the first time in sixteen years, thirty Tests. Of the previous Tests, twenty had been won by the West Indies. Solid preparation, discipline and commitment had brought a rich reward for England. The world had been turned upside down, and the cricketing establishment was shattered.

The End of Famine
West Indies v England at Sabina Park, Kingston, Jamaica
24, 25, 26, 28 February and 1 March 1990

West Indies First Innings		Second Innings	
C.G. Greenidge run out	32	c Hussain b Malcolm	36
D.L. Haynes c and b Small	36	b Malcolm	14
R.B. Richardson c Small b Capel	10	lbw b Fraser	25
C.A. Best c Russell b Capel	4	c Gooch b Small	64
C.L. Hooper c Capel b Fraser	20	c Larkins b Small	8
I.V.A. Richards (capt) lbw b Malcolm	21	b Malcolm	37
†P.J.L. Dujon not out	19	b Malcolm	15
M.D. Marshall b Fraser	0	not out	8
I.R. Bishop c Larkins b Fraser	0	c Larkins b Small	3
C.A. Walsh b Fraser	6	b Small	2
B.P. Patterson b Fraser	0	run out	2

Extras (b 9, lb 3, nb 4)   16   (b 14, lb 10, w 1, nb 1) . . 26

Total   164 240

BOWLING	Overs	Mdns	Runs	Wkts	Overs	Mdns	Runs	Wkts
Small	15	6	44	1	22	6	58	4
Malcolm	16	4	49	1	21.3	2	77	4
Fraser	20	8	28	5	14	5	31	1
Capel	13	4	31	2	15	1	50	–

fall of wickets
1–62, 2–81, 3–92, 4–92, 5–124, 6–144, 7–144, 8–150, 9–164
1–26, 2–69, 3–87, 4–112, 5–192, 6–222, 7–222, 8–227, 9–237

England First Innings		Second Innings	
G.A. Gooch (capt) c Dujon b Patterson	18	c Greenidge b Bishop . .	8
W. Larkins lbw b Walsh	46	not out	29
A.J. Stewart c Best b Bishop	13	not out	0
A.J. Lamb c Hooper b Walsh	132		
R.A. Smith c Best b Bishop	57		
N. Hussain c Dujon b Bishop	13		
D.J. Capel c Richardson b Walsh . .	5		
†R.C. Russell c Patterson b Walsh .	26		
G.C. Small lbw b Marshall	4		
A.R.C. Fraser not out	2		
D.E. Malcolm lbw b Walsh	0		
Extras (b 23, lb 12, w 1, nb 12) . .	48	(lb 1, nb 3)	4
Total	354	for one wicket	41

BOWLING	Overs	Mdns	Runs	Wkts	Overs	Mdns	Runs	Wkts
Patterson	18	2	74	1	3	1	11	–
Bishop	27	5	72	3	7.3	2	17	1
Marshall	18	3	46	1	–	–	–	–
Walsh	27.2	4	68	5	6	–	12	–
Hooper	6	–	28	–	–	–	–	–
Richards	9	1	22	–	–	–	–	–
Best	4	–	19	–	–	–	–	–

fall of wickets
1–40, 2–60, 3–116, 4–288, 5–315, 6–315, 7–325, 8–339, 9–364
1–35
umpires – L.H. Barker and S.N. Bucknor
England won by 9 wickets

385

From this point, the tide turned against England. The second Test match was abandoned without a ball being bowled, and, before the third Test, Hussain broke a bone in his arm when he had an accident while playing tennis. The West Indies were without Richards and Marshall, but they welcomed back Ambrose.

Gooch won the toss and asked the West Indies to bat. Had Russell not missed a vital catch, the West Indies could well have been out for under 100. As it was, England were frustrated to some extent as the home side, mainly through Logie, reached 199. By the close England were 43 without loss, and Gooch and Larkins extended their partnership to 112 on the second morning. England eventually took a lead of 89.

Devon Malcolm took three wickets in an over, and the West Indian second innings was ended early on the fifth morning. Malcolm's selection for the tour had been much criticised, but, bowling very quickly, he had returned match figures of ten for 137 and was a national hero. England had virtually the whole of the last day in which to score 151 to win the match and take 2–0 lead in the series.

They began hearteningly with 25 runs in six overs. The advent of Moseley changed matters. He had Larkins caught behind and in his next over struck Gooch on the left hand. The England captain was forced to retire hurt. He had suffered a broken bone and his tour was over; this was not revealed at the time. The extent of the captain's injury was hidden from his players, who remained optimistic of victory. When rain began to fall shortly before lunch England were 73 for one.

The rain persisted, and England's chances lessened, but when play was able to resume thirty overs could be bowled, and England needed to score 78 to win. There was, of course, very little chance that the West Indian pace bowlers would get through thirty overs before the night descended.

A no-ball was added to the total before Stewart was out, caught off Walsh after hitting 31 off thirty-two balls. Bishop began to bowl but complained he could not keep his footing. By the time the second over was under way fourteen minutes had elapsed since the resumption. Wickets fell as England pressed for runs, and delaying tactics of an unforgivable nature permeated the West Indian out-cricket. In near darkness, with limb and life under threat, Gooch called the batsmen in. England were 31 runs short of victory with five wickets standing. Only seventeen of the thirty possible overs had been bowled.

With Gooch unfit, Hussain was forced into action in the fourth Test although he was still nursing a broken bone. Fraser was also unable to take his place in the side and was replaced by DeFreitas. The West Indies won by 164 runs. Best and Haynes scored centuries, and Richards launched a violent attack on Malcolm, who conceded 188 runs in the match without taking a wicket. England, guilty of using delaying tactics themselves, came close to avoiding defeat and were beaten with little more than half an hour of daylight remaining.

The game was sullied on the fourth evening. A ball from Ambrose brushed Bailey's thigh pad. Those behind the stumps (although not, initially, the bowler) appealed for a catch at the wicket. Umpire Barker turned as if to walk away in rejection of the appeal, but Richards ran from slip wagging his finger, and the umpire raised his in acquiescence.

Several construed Richards's actions as being intimidatory, and Christopher Martin-Jenkins said as much on World Service Radio. Richards's reaction was to launch a verbal attack on the BBC's Cricket Correspondent at the start of the fifth Test when he should have been leading his side out on to the field. Sadly, there were times in his career when Richards interpreted any criticism of himself as racial abuse.

The West Indies won the fifth Test by an innings and so took the series by two matches to one, but for England there was much satisfaction. Deprived by injury of a captain who had proved both capable and inspiring, they *had* met fire with fire. Lamb had hit two Test centuries, Smith had battled bravely and the bowling had shown marked improvement. Fraser, fit for only two of the Tests, had emerged as an international player of sound temperament and considerable ability. Devon Malcolm was erratic, often wayward, but he was fast and capable of turning the course of a match in a single over.

The outlook for English cricket suddenly seemed brighter, but what of international cricket? The gamesmanship, the intimidation of umpires through excessive appealing, the verbal abuse of batsmen at the crease and the general reluctance to show any form of manners now appeared to be part of the norm.

Gooch had not only established himself as England's captain without rival but had developed into a batsman mature in years and technique. The violent hitter of 1979 was still in evidence on occasions, but the hitting was now allied to intelligent selection, unwavering concentration and solidity of defence. In 1990 he led Essex to second in the Championship behind Middlesex, and he led England to series victories over both New Zealand and India.

Hussain's injury in the Caribbean was diagnosed as a broken wrist, and he did not play until June and could not recapture a place in the England side. Larkins, too, was jettisoned, and Atherton opened with Gooch. The Lancastrian scored 151 against New Zealand at Trent Bridge and was immediately dubbed 'FEC' (future England captain). Gower was recalled against India and hit 157 not out at The Oval. He replaced Neil Fairbrother, who had played in all three Tests against New Zealand without doing himself justice.

Lancashire won both the Benson and Hedges Cup and the NatWest Trophy, and Fairbrother played a major part in these successes. He was also a major player in the drawn four-day Championship match between Surrey and Lancashire at The Oval at the beginning of May.

Surrey batted first; Ian Greig, at number seven, set the pace. On the first evening he and Medlycott hit 61 runs off ten overs of the second new ball. Greig and Martin Bicknell added a record 205 for Surrey's eighth wicket, and twelve overs after lunch on the second day produced 101 runs. Of the 311 runs scored by Surrey in fifty-five overs on the second day, Greig made 235. When he was caught on the boundary attempting to hit his tenth six he had made 291 off 251 balls. His innings included twenty-five fours and nine sixes, four in the space of five balls. Michael Atherton considered it to be the most remarkable innings he ever saw. Surrey made 707 for nine declared.

Atherton himself made 191, and Gehan Mendis, a fine opener who could have played for Sri Lanka and should have played for England, made 102. The Lancashire innings was dominated, however, by Neil Fairbrother, who scored 366 off 407 balls with five sixes and forty-seven fours. This surpassed Len Hutton's Oval record of 364 made against Australia in 1938, and Lancashire were all out for 863. Surrey made 60 for one, and after four days of uninterrupted play, the match was drawn. For the statisticians, this was a marvellous game, but the supporters began to ask if this was what the TCCB really wanted the game to become – four days on a pitch so benign as to rob the game of all balance in the contest between bat and ball.

There were two other triple centuries during the season. The South African Jimmy Cook hit 313 not out for Somerset against Glamorgan at Cardiff, and Gooch made 333 against India.

The first two Tests against New Zealand were drawn, but Gooch set up victory for England at Edgbaston with an innings of 154. Hemmings and Malcolm, who helped Derbyshire to win the Sunday League, took the bowling honours. The victory brought to an end England's worst ever Test run at home. They had beaten Sri Lanka in a one-off Test in 1988, but this was their first series victory since Gower's side had won the Ashes in 1985. Now, in 1990, they had fought well in the West Indies, beaten New Zealand and were about to beat India in a marvellous match at Lord's.

Azharuddin won the toss and asked England to bat. He was rewarded with success after twenty minutes when Kapil Dev bowled

Atherton between bat and pad. Gooch, too, was troubled and, on 36, he was badly dropped by More off Sanjeev Sharma. Rarely has there been such a costly miss. At lunch England were 82 for one. In the afternoon session Gooch hit Shastri out of the attack, took total command, and England added 127 for the loss of Gower.

At tea Gooch was 117. By the close he was 194, Lamb was 104, and England were 359 for two. In the final session Gooch and Lamb had scored 150 off twenty-eight overs.

Gooch cautiously saw off the second new ball on the Friday morning, and when Lamb was caught in the gully the third-wicket partnership had raised 308. At tea Gooch was on 299, and his triple century came immediately after the break. It seemed that only tiredness could end his innings, for he looked able to score off every ball. Having batted for 633 minutes, faced 485 balls and hit three sixes and forty-three fours, he played outside the line at a ball from Prabhakar and was bowled for 333. This was the third-highest score ever made by an Englishman in Test cricket.

Gooch declared when Robin Smith reached his century and Test debutant Morris of Derbyshire had had the chance to hit a four. England's 653 for four had come off 162 overs. In sixteen overs before the end of the day India made 48.

India's opening stand was brisk and purposeful and realised 63 in seventy-six minutes before Sidhu was taken at short-leg. Manjrekar slashed wildly at Gooch's third delivery and was caught behind, but Shastri and Vengsarkar batted with calm authority. Shastri reached an admirable century before, momentarily losing concentration, he lofted Hemmings to mid-on.

Tendulkar and Prabhakar came and went, but Azharuddin played a gem of an innings, rich entertainment for a capacity Saturday crowd. He hit twenty fours and raced to his century off eighty-eight balls. He was unbeaten on 117 on the Saturday evening, and India were 376 for six.

The Indian captain's pulsating innings ended early on the Monday morning, and More and Sharma went quickly so that when Hirwani joined Kapil Dev 24 runs were still needed to avoid the follow-on. Kapil Dev contemplated the first two balls of an over from Hemmings and straight drove the remaining four into the construction work at the Nursery End for sixes. It was an astonishing feat and another record in a match of records. Hirwani fell next ball, but the follow-on was saved.

The glories of the day were far from over. Gooch and Atherton scored 204 in 150 minutes. Gooch, 123 off 113 balls with four sixes and thirteen fours, became the first batsman in Test history to hit a triple century and a century in the same match.

England scored at 5 an over, and when Gooch declared India had seven hours in which to make 472 runs to win. The loss of both openers for 57 before the close made the task more difficult.

Caution on the last day might have brought a draw, but the blades continued to flash and the edges were held. The end came when Sanjeev Sharma attempted an unwise run, and the fielder at mid-on ran him out with a direct hit on the stumps. Inevitably, the fielder was Gooch.

Gooch and the Match of Records
England v India at Lord's
26, 27, 38, 30 and 31 July 1990

England	First Innings		Second Innings	
G.A. Gooch (capt) b Prabhakar ...		333	c Azharuddin b Sharma	123
M.A. Atherton b Kapil Dev		8	c Vengsarkar b Sharma .	72
D.I. Gower c Manjrekar b Hirwani		40	not out	32
A.J. Lamb c Manjrekar b Sharma ..		139	c Tendulkar b Hirwani .	19
R.A. Smith not out		100	b Prabhakar	15
J.E. Morris not out		4		
†R.C. Russell				
C.C. Lewis				
E.E. Hemmings				
A.R.C. Fraser				
D.E. Malcolm				
Extras (b 2, lb 21, w 2, nb 4)		29	(lb 11)	11
Total for 4 wickets, decl.		653	for 4 wickets, dec. 272	

BOWLING	Overs	Mdns	Runs	Wkts	Overs	Mdns	Runs	Wkts
Kapil Dev	34	5	120	1	10	–	53	–
Prabhakar	43	6	187	1	11.2	2	45	1
Sharma	33	5	122	1	15	–	75	2
Shastri	22	–	99	–	7	–	38	–
Hirwani	30	1	102	1	11	–	50	1

fall of wickets
1–14, 2–141, 3–449, 4–641
1–204, 2–207, 3–250, 4–272

India	First Innings		Second Innings	
R.J. Shastri c Gooch b Hemmings .		100	c Russell b Malcolm	12
N.S. Sidhu c Morris b Fraser		30	c Morris b Fraser	1
S.V. Manjrekar c Russell b Gooch ..		18	c Russell b Malcolm	33

D.B. Vengsarkar c Russell b Fraser .	52	c Russell b Hemmings . .	35
M. Azharuddin (capt) b Hemmings	121	c Atherton b Lewis	37
S.R. Tendulkar b Lewis	10	c Gooch b Fraser	27
M. Prabhakar c Lewis b Malcolm ..	25	lbw b Lewis	8
Kapil Dev not out	77	c Lewis b Hemmings ...	7
†K.S. More c Morris b Fraser	8	lbw b Fraser	16
S.K. Sharma c Russell b Fraser	0	run out	38
N.D. Hirwani lbw b Fraser	0	not out	0
Extras (lb 1, w 4, nb 8)	13	(b 3, lb 1, nb 6)	10
Total	454	224	

BOWLING	Overs	Mdns	Runs	Wkts	Overs	Mdns	Runs	Wkts
Malcolm	25	1	106	1	10	–	65	2
Fraser	39.1	9	104	5	22	7	39	3
Lewis	24	3	108	1	8	1	26	2
Gooch	6	3	26	1	–	–	–	–
Hemmings	20	3	109	2	21	2	79	2
Atherton	–	–	–	–	1	–	11	–

fall of wickets
1–63, 2–102, 3–191, 4–241, 5–288, 6–348, 7–393, 8–430, 9–430
1–9, 2–23, 3–63, 4–114, 5–127, 6–140, 7–158, 8–181, 9–206
umpires – H.D. Bird and N.T. Plews
England won by 247 runs

Gooch, Atherton, Smith, Lamb, Azharuddin and Tendulkar scored centuries in the drawn Test at Old Trafford. Tendulkar, not yet eighteen years old, was brilliant, a sign of joys to come.

At The Oval England were forced to follow on after Shastri and Kapil Dev had hit hundreds, but Gower's sublime 157 not out on the final day meant England had won the series.

There was much purring contentment, which was natural after the agonies of recent years, but a glance at the averages gave cause for concern. Gooch and Hick dominated. Cook came closest to Gooch in runs, but third and fifth in the batting list were the Australians Tom Moody and Mark Waugh, neither of whom had been able to win a place in the Australian Test side. The bowling was topped by the West Indians Bishop and Marshall. Millns of Leicestershire was third, but then came Mortensen, Ambrose and the formidable Waqar Younis of Pakistan and Surrey. In real terms England's leading bowler was Neil Foster with ninety-four wickets, but he was one of those serving a five-year Test ban, and his knees were injured to such an extent as to give little hope for the future.

In spite of the continued absence of Gatting, Broad, Foster and the rest, England had reason to view the tour of Australia in the winter of 1990–91 with optimism. They had beaten New Zealand and India, and Gooch, Lamb, Robin Smith and Atherton now represented a formidable batting nucleus while the magic of Gower could still charm any match. Fraser and Malcolm formed a potent pace attack. Hemmings was an experienced spinner who had maintained form and fitness, and much was expected of Phil Tufnell, the left-arm spinner, who had done much to help Middlesex take the Championship.

Gooch was the choice of *This is Your Life* just before the team's departure, and they set off in high spirits. Three months later they were being described by Ashley Mallett, the former Australian off-spinner, as 'the worst England side to come to Australia since the Second World War'. The aspect of the side most severely criticised was the fielding which, by any standards, was very poor. Tufnell and Malcolm were the main offenders, but, in truth, England carried too many men who were not of international calibre.

There were excuses in that Gooch, Lamb and Fraser all missed Test matches because of injury, but the gap between England and Australia was enormous. Australia won the first, second and fifth Tests while the other two were drawn. England also failed to reach the final of the Benson and Hedges World Series, a one-day tournament, and the final was contested by Australia and New Zealand.

Gooch had personally argued the cases for Larkins and Tufnell and wanted them in the party. Larkins was a great fighter, but he was beyond his thirty-seventh birthday when the tour started, and England should have been looking to blood younger players. Some might argue that the younger players were the most problematical. Tufnell performed reasonably in four Test matches, but his fielding was conspicuously poor, and he quickly established himself as one who presented disciplinary worries.

John Morris, the Derbyshire batsman, could not find a place in the side, and, at Carrara, he made his one century and England beat Queensland for their solitary first-class victory of the tour. It was during this match that he and David Gower took to the air in a pair of 1938 Tiger Moths and *buzzed* Robin Smith when he reached his century. They were fined £1,000 each for their prank and for leaving a game in which they were playing without permission.

Vice-captain Lamb, too, was guilty of misdemeanours, but he was treated more leniently. The Gooch–Micky Stewart regime was one of intense practice and physical fitness, but perhaps the unrelenting demand for dedication was counter-productive. What does he know of cricket who only cricket knows? A 'new' type of war was raging in the Gulf, and contemplation of it may well have put sport in sharper perspective.

Certainly, Gower remained unrepentant regarding his flying escapade. He believed that the tour was too unremittingly serious and that an injection of levity was desperately required. Gower scored centuries in the second and third Tests, but in the first innings of the fourth he played a totally irresponsible shot to the last ball before lunch and lobbed a catch to long-leg. Gooch stood in brooding fury as Gower and the Australians left the field, and captain and former captain said little to each other for the rest of the tour.

This fourth Test match at Adelaide saw Mark Waugh's debut in Test cricket. He had looked a magnificent player for Essex in the 1990 season, and he now proved his quality at international level, beginning with a glorious century. The Australian batting, unlike England's, was totally dependable, and the bowling, spearheaded by Reid, was lethal. Border led the side with zest and intelligence, and the fielding was as good as England's was bad.

England's fielding was not helped by the fact that, following continued middle-order batting collapses, Russell was omitted for the final two Tests so that another batsman could be accommodated. It was not the last time that the specialist wicket-keeper was to lose his place because of the inadequacies of the batsmen. Stewart took over the gloves.

The collapses persisted in New Zealand, where winning positions in two of the three one-day internationals were thrown away. England returned home in disgrace. Not only had they been beaten ignominiously, but they had retreated into that sense of isolation, the siege mentality that had taken root in Pakistan under Mike Gatting. Like Britain itself, the England cricket team seemed both unwilling and unable to recognise its role in the modern world. They had forgotten how to tour.

Those in England responsible for running the game regarded the losing of a Test match as an economic threat with dreadful consequences. They snatched at short-term solutions and embraced an economic policy which, at a higher level, had already been discredited. Obsessed with the revenue derived from international cricket, they hacked away at the domestic game on which it had always been founded, claiming with every action that all was being done in order to produce better England cricketers. To this end the TCCB announced that the starting days for the majority of three-day county matches would be changed from Saturday and Wednesday to Friday and Tuesday. This would give the England team an extra day in which to prepare for Test matches.

The announcement made one wonder who was responsible for making the decisions which affected the future of cricket and, if they were ever considered, the paying customers. Ostensibly, the TCCB was presumed to be the corporate voice of the first-class counties. Those counties had rejected the proposal for a two-division Sunday League. They had also rejected the idea of four-day Championship cricket, but that was being forced upon them whether they liked it or not.

The counties would also disclaim any responsibility for the change in the starting days of matches or for the disgraceful entrance fee levied for NatWest Cup games, saying that these were decisions taken by the TCCB. One is left with the frustrations of V.S. Naipaul's narrator in *In a Free State*: 'These people here they confuse me. Who hurt me? Who spoil my life? Tell me who to beat back.'

Thankfully for the TCCB, England's disasters in Australia and New Zealand were soon forgotten. With sponsors' logos adorning the pitch, England won a memorable victory in the first Test against the West Indies at Headingley. There were new caps for Hick, now qualified, Ramprakash of Middlesex, and Watkin, the Glamorgan medium-pacer, but the honours would go to Gooch.

England had already won all three Texaco Trophy matches to lift spirits and boost confidence, but when they were put in to bat in the first Test, they were bowled out for 198. At the start of the West Indies' reply the ball was moving extravagantly, but at first the England bowlers could not control it. Then Watkin broke through, and Pringle showed admirable control. DeFreitas had learned the value of line and length and ended with four wickets as, in spite of a blistering innings from Viv Richards, the West Indies were dismissed for 173.

The lead was too slender for England to be either optimistic or complacent, and Atherton, Hick and Lamb were soon out with only 38 scored. Ramprakash made 27 in a fourth-wicket stand of 78 with Gooch, and Pringle hit 27 in a seventh-wicket stand worth 98. These were the only two batsmen other than Gooch to reach double figures. England's second innings was brought to an end late on the fourth day.

Of the 231 runs to come from the bat, Gooch had made two-thirds. His innings of 154 not out occupied seven and a half hours and was a monument of concentration, dedication and outstanding technical ability. Resolute and calm, he carried his bat, facing 331 balls and striking eighteen fours. By nature a free-scoring batsman, he had the self-discipline to become a weighty accumulator because England and necessity demanded it. This was one of the great Test innings.

De Freitas bowled Simmons with the first ball of the West Indies' second innings. Needing 278 to win, the visitors were never really in contention once Pringle had broken a dangerous second-wicket stand between Haynes and Richardson. The Essex all-rounder bowled a spell of nineteen relentlessly accurate overs, and his contribution to England's victory, with bat and ball, was immense. The man, once a figure of fun, passed into Headingley folklore as the crowd sang 'God Save Our Pring'.

With DeFreitas taking four wickets for the second time in the match, England won by 115 runs. It was the first time England had beaten the West Indies in a Test match in England for twenty-two years.

The euphoria persisted. The Lord's Test was drawn. England held their own thanks mainly to Robin Smith, who made an unbeaten 148 after five wickets had fallen for 84. Lamb and Smith had survived the axe after the Australian debacle, but Gower, now with Hampshire, had paid the full price for his levity and one rash shot.

Smith had little form to support his selection for the first Test, and Fairbrother would have been the people's choice. There was also a strong lobby for David Lawrence, the Gloucestershire fast bowler, and he did play in the third and fifth Tests.

Richard Illingworth, Worcestershire's Yorkshire-born left-arm spinner, won his first Test cap at Trent Bridge when Watkin was injured. The West Indies won by nine wickets, and they went 2–1 up in the series when they won at Edgbaston, where Hugh Morris opened with Gooch and Chris Lewis took six first-innings wickets.

Lewis was to prove one of the most frustrating of cricketers for England. An all-rounder of immense natural talent, he seemed unable to settle as he moved from Leicestershire to Nottinghamshire to Surrey. He often performed outstandingly, but then he would suffer a mysterious injury and pass into oblivion. In May he would appear to be heir-apparent to Botham's throne; by September he had disappeared.

In 1991 he did survive until the fifth Test at The Oval; Lamb, Hick, Illingworth and Russell did not. Hick's long-awaited arrival in the England side had proved a bitter disappointment. He had been heralded as the messiah who would save English cricket. The way he had thrashed bowlers in England and New Zealand suggested that this must be so, but with the Test spotlight upon him he was seen to be vulnerable to genuine pace, and his first seven Test innings produced a mere 75 runs.

The uncertainties in the England batting again caused Russell to be sacrificed, and there was consternation that the man who replaced him, Alec Stewart, was not a regular wicket-keeper. Stewart's response was to keep outstandingly well at The Oval, and it could be argued that Russell had not been in top form all summer.

Ian Botham was brought back for the final Test. He had done well in the Texaco Trophy matches before being troubled by injury. He was still a magnetic figure, but his miracles were ten years in the past.

England won the final Test to level the series and give satisfaction. Gooch and Hugh Morris began with a stand of 112, and Robin Smith hit his second century of the series. 'Bad Boy' Tufnell played his first Test of the summer and bowled splendidly to take six for 25 and help to force the West Indies to follow on. Lawrence took five wickets in the second innings, and England, facing something of a chase, won by five wickets.

This series marked the last appearance of Viv Richards in international cricket in England. It was obvious that the West Indies were a declining force, but England could be well pleased with their efforts. Not everyone, however, was pleased that the tour had taken place. The West Indies had last toured England in 1988 and the fact that they were invited back within three years was for commercial rather than cricketing reasons. Sri Lanka's pleas for a tour of England with a three–or five-Test series have been ignored for more than fifteen years, presumably on the grounds that the authorities do not consider them good enough 'box office'. Even the fact that they were to prove themselves superior cricketers to England did not help their cause. In 1991 they were recognised with the patronising single Test at the end of August. The days when MCC were dedicated to spreading the gospel of the game seemed to be a distant memory.

In spite of Stewart's maiden Test hundred and DeFreitas's seven for 70, Sri Lanka kept pace with England for much of the first two and a half days, but Gooch then hit a mighty 174, and England went on to win by 137 runs.

Gooch had a dominant summer. He was restored as a national hero, batted with total command throughout the season and led Essex to their fifth Championship title since 1979. They were a strong side, with their overseas player, Salim Malik, batting as brilliantly as Mark Waugh had done the previous season.

Nottinghamshire maintained their good record by capturing the Sunday League while, having appeared in six Lord's finals without success, Worcestershire beat Lancashire in their seventh to win the Benson and Hedges Cup. In the NatWest Trophy Final, Hampshire beat Surrey with two balls to spare.

A talented and disciplined Surrey side was taking shape under Ian Greig, but there were still hints of temperamental weakness. The young fast bowler Martin Bicknell had gone to Australia with Gooch's party but had been troubled by injury. He was a capable cricketer who should have done well at international level, but he broke down at vital moments in the season with a depressing regularity. David Ward was an exciting batsman who was never to receive the accolades he deserved, but Graham Thorpe, who made 93 in the final, was very much part of Ted Dexter's plans.

Robin Smith took the Man of the Match award in the final for his innings of 78 off ninety-four balls, which contributed a great deal to bringing Hampshire the trophy.

Smith battled bravely against Waqar Younis in the final. Other batsmen were less successful during the season. Waqar finished with 113 first-class wickets at 14.65 runs each, and, of course, he played half his matches on The Oval pitch which was less than friendly to bowlers. Neil Foster, who captained Essex with flair and intelligence in Gooch's absence, captured 102 wickets, and a third fast bowler, Allan Donald of Warwickshire, finished just above Foster and just below Younis in the averages.

It is fair to say that no better fast bowler has been seen in England since the Second World War than Waqar Younis, but, in the opinion of many, Donald runs him close. When he enjoyed his outstanding season with Warwickshire in 1991 Donald had not been seen in international cricket, but events were moving rapidly.

In South Africa in the early part of 1991 the last of the apartheid laws were abolished. Within months South Africa was welcomed back into the international sporting fold. The exile was over. Clive Rice led South Africa in a three-match one-day international series in India, and Donald began his international career with figures of five for 29. He shared the Man of the Match award with one of his victims, Sachin Tendulkar, who was about to make history by being engaged as Yorkshire's first overseas player.

Special provision was made to include South Africa in the World Cup which was to be held early in 1992 in Australia and New Zealand. Before engaging in the World Cup, England played a three-Test series and three one-day internationals in New Zealand. They won both series convincingly. Botham joined the party late, because he was appearing in pantomime at the Pavilion Theatre, Bournemouth.

Botham took the individual award in England's first World Cup match, which produced a victory over India by 9 runs. Wins over the West Indies, Australia, Sri Lanka and South Africa followed, and the match against Pakistan was abandoned after a downpour with England totally in command. Elated as England supporters were, there was a feeling that the side had peaked too soon, and, indeed, the last two matches in the qualifying group, against New Zealand and Zimbabwe, were lost. Nevertheless, England had qualified for the semi-finals and met South Africa in Sydney.

This produced a somewhat bizarre match. Hick scored 83 off ninety balls, and England made 252 for six in forty-five overs. A spectacular climax seemed in prospect when South Africa reached 231 for six with thirteen balls remaining. Rain then began to fall, and umpires Aldridge and Randell asked the batsmen if they wished to go off. They declined, but Gooch said that he did not think the conditions were fit for play and England left the field. Twelve minutes were lost, and when the players re-emerged it was announced that 22 runs were now needed from seven balls. This was then corrected, for the Australians (whose organisation was not of the best for this competition) had evolved their own system; it was announced that 21 runs were needed from *one* ball. What should have been high drama had been turned into low farce. England were booed from the field, although the fault was not theirs, and South Africa did a lap of honour.

In the final Pakistan scored 249 for five from fifty overs. This was a disappointment for England, for Pringle had given them an excellent start by dismissing both openers cheaply and taking three for 22 in his ten overs. Dermot Reeve, included as a specialist limited-overs cricketer, conceded as many runs in three overs and was wicketless.

Botham went for nought and Stewart for 7, and England struggled from then on in spite of Fairbrother's 62. Pakistan won by 22 runs.

Reasonably satisfied with their performances in the winter of 1991–92, Gooch and his men returned to England to face the side that had beaten them in the World Cup Final and to a domestic season that was facing great structural changes.

Durham had been admitted into the County Championship. They had not been unanimously welcomed, but for enthusiasm and hospitality they could not be faulted. They engaged a vast playing staff, all of whom were immediately capped, but the majority of their cricketers were imported rather than home-grown. Botham and McEwan came from Worcestershire, Larkins and Simon Brown from Northamptonshire, Hughes from Middlesex, Parker from Sussex, Bainbridge from Gloucestershire, Scott from Nottinghamshire, and David Graveney, the captain, arrived via Gloucestershire and Somerset. None of the signings was opposed, and the team sheet hinted at a list of 'golden oldies'.

398

Occasionally, young local talent came into the side, flourished briefly and disappeared. The overseas star, the Australian Dean Jones, batted well at the start of the season, but he was able to play in only half the matches, and Durham finished well adrift at the bottom of the table.

Essex retained the Championship in 1992, and Middlesex won the now sponsorless Sunday League. Hampshire added the Benson and Hedges Cup to the NatWest Trophy they had won the previous season while Northamptonshire took over as NatWest holders. All these domestic competitions produced their moments of joy, but they were played in a mood of impending change and under shadows cast by events at international level.

England had lost David Lawrence with a terrible kneecap injury in New Zealand. Indeed, the injury was so bad as to keep the fast bowler out of the game for five years. Tufnell was also injured, but neither of the newcomers to the England squad, Ian Salisbury of Sussex and Tim Munton of Warwickshire, found his way into the final eleven for the Edgbaston Test, a match which was destroyed by the weather. There was no play on the Thursday, and only two balls were bowled on the Friday. As play had officially started, the 15,000 paying customers were not entitled to compensation. There were angry scenes. As a sop, the disappointed spectators were offered free admission for the fifth day. This was an added insult, for it was obvious that the match was already dying and would be totally dead by the Monday. The debate raged for the rest of the season, but the TCCB had lost £150,000 on the first day's abandonment and was unwilling to lose another £250,000 because of the second day's almost total wash-out.

The second Test match at Lord's was won by Pakistan in a thrilling manner. England gave a first Test cap to the leg-spinner Salisbury. It was an historic selection, for Salisbury was the first specialist leg-spinner to play for England since Essex's Robin Hobbs twenty-one years earlier.

England made 255, and Pakistan took a first-innings lead of 38. Two sessions were lost on the Friday so that the Pakistani innings extended until late on Saturday. The day ended with England having scored 52 for the loss of Gooch in their second innings.

Leg-spinner Mushtaq Ahmed undermined England's innings when he sent back Hick, Smith and Lamb in twenty-two deliveries, and any hopes England had of setting Pakistan a testing target disappeared when Wasim Akram took the final three wickets in four balls. Alec Stewart confirmed his development as a Test cricketer by carrying his bat for 69, but Pakistan needed just 138 to win and had nine hours in which to get the runs.

Chris Lewis produced one of his inspired spells, and Pakistan were

399

reduced to 18 for three. England were handicapped in that neither Botham, who had equalled Colin Cowdrey's record of 120 Test catches, nor DeFreitas was able to bowl, but Salisbury took two wickets, Malcolm accounted for Mushtaq Ahmed and there was a foolish run out. Suddenly, Pakistan were 95 for eight. Seventeen wickets had fallen on the Sunday, and England scented victory. It was not to be. Wasim Akram and Waqar Younis came together in an unbroken partnership which took Pakistan to victory. They had tormented England with the ball and now proved themselves with the bat.

The third Test at Old Trafford was drawn, but it became memorable and notorious. It was memorable in that England recalled David Gower, who had been in fine form for Hampshire, and the elegant left-hander scored a dashing 73 which took him past Boycott's aggregate and gave him the record as England's highest scorer in Test cricket. It was notorious in that umpire Roy Palmer warned Aqib Javed for intimidatory bowling. An altercation followed which involved skipper Javed Miandad and even manager Intikhab Alam. Fines were levied, and there were warnings as to the spirit in which the game should be played.

The warnings had little effect. At Headingley, where England won by six wickets, the Pakistanis believed that they were the victims of a grave injustice. They felt that decisions were very much against them, and when England, needing 99 to win, had already lost two wickets for 27 they had an appeal for run out against Gooch rejected by umpire Ken Palmer. Television replays suggested that Palmer had erred and that Gooch was a yard short of the line when the wicket was broken. The rejection caused several of the Pakistani fielders to lose discipline. They believed that they were being cheated, and England moved to a six-wicket victory in an atmosphere that was highly charged. There were two major factors in England's win: the first was a magnificent first-innings century by Gooch, and the second was the splendid exploitation of the Headingley pitch by the Somerset medium-pacer Neil Mallender, who took eight wickets on his Test debut.

The teams went to The Oval on level terms, but there was a further bone of contention between them with allegations of ball-tampering against the Pakistani pace bowlers. The debate raged and has spawned several books and many articles. The acceptable fact was that the main strength of Wasim Akram and Waqar Younis was that they bowled at the stumps. They both moved the ball late, but Waqar relied far more on the yorker than the bouncer and maintained such accuracy that one felt that if the batsman missed the ball, he would be out. He gave an exceptional display at The Oval, where his five for 52 in the second innings set up Pakistan's ten-wicket victory, which gave them the series.

The ball with which Waqar dismissed Gower was a gem and showed that here was a bowler of astonishing talent. It was a very quick delivery which pitched on the line of off stump and looked likely to swing away towards slip. Gower offered no stroke, but the ball straightened and hit the top of the off stump. It was as close to being unplayable as a ball can be. Gower commented, 'You have only a split second to make up your mind whether to play the ball or leave it. I chose the wrong option, and I think I would do if I were in the same position again.'

David Gower was never to be in the same position again in Test cricket. When the party to tour India was announced his name was not among those chosen. There was a public outcry. He had averaged 50 in the three Tests and finished second only to Alec Stewart in the averages for the series. So incensed were the followers of the game that a special meeting of MCC was demanded to discuss a proposal of no confidence in the England selectors. The motion was defeated on the postal ballot, although those members who attended the meeting voted 715 to 412 in favour of the censure.

Salisbury and Russell were other omissions from the England party, but the inclusions caused as much anger as the omissions. With South Africa welcomed back into the sporting fold, an air of reconciliation prevailed, and the ban on Gatting, Broad and the other 'rebels' was lifted.

Ted Dexter refused to give any reason for Gower's omission, a stance which was regarded as arrogant, while Keith Fletcher, who was succeeding Micky Stewart as England manager, gave the reason that too many batsmen in the party would have been in their mid-thirties had Gower been chosen. Gower was two months younger than Gatting who, along with fellow recent rebels Jarvis and Emburey, was chosen. Indeed, Emburey had twice accepted the krugerrand in preference to playing for England – so what price loyalty? Even Gooch, leading the side to India, had stated that he would not be accompanying the party to Sri Lanka for the last leg of the tour. He had picked, chosen and rebelled over the years, but his every whim was accepted.

There was a sneaking suspicion that Gower, England's leading run-scorer, was too much of an individual for the new, pragmatic approach of the England team. Where once there had been a constant cry for brighter cricket there was now simply a demand for track suits, fitness and an avoidance of defeat. Gower was no pragmatic cricketer. His was the beauty that flirted with danger, the very music of the game. To deprive cricket of its music is to deprive it of the mystery which is its charm. Gower was one of the victims of an age and an administration which increasingly saw cricket as a science rather than an art and strove

401

to eradicate the human fallibility on which the game was based.

The tour of India and Sri Lanka seemed plagued from the start. When Gooch had led the side to Australia for the Ashes series he had flown out with the red book of *This is Your Life* under his arm; now he set forth for India accompanied by the startling news of his broken marriage.

As the tour progressed, confusion followed confusion. It was well known that spin would be the principal weapon in India's attack, and that pitches would be prepared accordingly, yet England chose four seamers for the first Test and then brought in Salisbury. The Sussex leg-spinner was not in the official party, but he had been taken to India as a 'net' bowler before joining the 'A' team in Australia.

Alec Stewart was chosen as first-choice wicket-keeper, and it was anticipated that he would bat in the middle order. In the first Test he opened and kept wicket. In the second he captained the side in the absence of Gooch and opened while Blakey kept wicket. Gooch returned for the third Test, Blakey was retained as wicket-keeper and Stewart opened. In Sri Lanka, Stewart captained the side, batted in the middle order and kept wicket.

The choice of Blakey, the Yorkshire keeper, was indefensible. Even the most generous of critics would not have placed him in the top ten of English wicket-keepers, and as a batsman he was an average county player. He had played for England against Pakistan in the Texaco Trophy and had not looked to be of international class. The main reason offered for choosing Blakey and Reeve ahead of Russell and Gower was the number of one-day internationals that were to be played on the tour. Reeve and Blakey were seen as 'one-day specialists'.

Such a definition only added to the confusion. When England were in Australia, Angus Fraser, the leading bowler, was included in one of the Benson and Hedges World Series games even though he was not fully fit. As one county captain angrily remarked, 'In a year's time who will even remember who won the one-day matches; in ten years' time they'll still tell you you lost the Ashes.' England and India shared the one-day series, three matches each, but the indelible record was that England became the first side ever to lose all three Tests in a series in India.

There were extenuating circumstances in that communal violence raged in India following the destruction of the temple of Ayodhya, and there was a strike by Indian airline pilots. There were changes in an itinerary that was already exhausting, but none of these frustrations could really excuse the fact that England played poorly.

Hick and Lewis scored maiden Test hundreds, but Gooch scored only 47 runs in four Test innings while Tendulkar, having had a moderate season for Yorkshire, and Kambli, making his debut, both averaged over 100.

While Kumble, Chauhan and Venkatapathy Raju, the three Indian spinners, took forty-six wickets between them, Tufnell, Salisbury and Emburey managed nine. Hick was the leading spinner: the forty-year-old Emburey played in only one Test. Opinions regarding the merits of Emburey as an off-spinner differ. The late Les Ames considered that Emburey simply rolled his fingers over the top of the ball rather than spinning it until his fingers were raw, as Laker once did; but then there have been few to equal Laker.

India won two of the Tests by an innings and the other by eight wickets. Worse was to follow. In Sri Lanka, England were beaten in both one-day internationals and lost the single Test match by five wickets. Robin Smith scored a century, but the Sri Lankan cricket was exhilarating. Ranatunga was out with only 4 runs needed for victory; Jayasuriya came in and promptly hit Tufnell for six. These were the cricketers to whom the England authorities were reluctant to give a Test tour.

There were the inevitable whinges about bowling actions and conditions which now accompanied every tour by an England side, but energy spent in excuses and irrelevant complaints is wasted energy.

At home a complaint was made by the TCCB as to the dress and appearance of the England side. Particular reference was made to what was fashionably known as 'designer stubble'. The censure was totally justified, but it came nine years too late. After the final Test against the West Indies at The Oval in 1984, a presentation ceremony was held which was an insult to the public, the sponsors and the game itself. Players lolled on the grass in various stages of casual dress, suggesting that they were doing everybody a favour by collecting their bonuses and awards.

Cricketers, like members of other professions which are constantly in the public eye and dependent upon public support, have responsibilities in appearance and behaviour. Warwickshire had set England an example in 1991. Knowing, during the last match of the season, that they had been beaten to the Championship by Essex, the eleven Warwickshire players took the field wearing their county caps. It was more than a gesture. It was a show of pride, harmony and dignity which was to bring rich dividends in the near future.

The overwhelming defeats suffered in India and Sri Lanka brought into question the judgements and positions of both Dexter and the new team manager, Keith Fletcher. The officers of the TCCB had been jubilant at acquiring the services of Fletcher. Observers were more sceptical, especially as Fletcher was given a five-year contract.

403

Fletcher had been one of the finest batsmen of his generation and had a very good Test record, although he had endured a long, hard struggle before he gained public recognition. He had really come to prominence first as captain and then as team manager of Essex, the most successful county side of the 1980s and early 1990s. The Essex tale was a fairy story come true. Having won nothing for the first 103 years of their existence, they claimed every trophy county cricket had to offer under Fletcher's leadership. He was given most of the credit for the success, although more perceptive critics would suggest that the guiding hand of Doug Insole, the exceptionally fine judgement in the recruitment of overseas players and the shrewd business sense of secretary/manager Peter Edwards were important contributory factors to the Essex golden years.

Fletcher's period as England captain had come late and was neither successful nor happy. It had ended with summary dismissal by May and with the defection of many of Fletcher's team to the rebel tour of South Africa.

As coach to England 'A' sides on tour, Fletcher was obviously being groomed for promotion and had earned respect, but his guidance of the team in Zimbabwe in 1989–90 had virtually paralysed the game. It seemed that young batsmen were encouraged to meet the off-spin of Traicos with a dead bat, and maiden had followed upon maiden.

Fletcher was a most capable adviser on technique, but he was not a disciplinarian, and the truth is that he was essentially a parochial figure far happier in the north Essex countryside than facing interviews and questions in front of a television camera.

Having suffered the indignities of being England's manager on the disastrous tour of the Indian subcontinent, Fletcher now returned home to face an Ashes series against a revitalised and rampant Australian side again led by Allan Border. It was to be Fletcher's destiny to be manager of the England side at a time when the success of that side became more important to the well-being of English cricket than ever before.

For in 1993 English cricket underwent drastic reconstruction.

10

New Structures, 1993–96

A committee, under the chairmanship of Mike Murray, Treasurer of the TCCB and Chairman of Middlesex, had been set up to report on the structure and future of English cricket. Its three main recommendations were that the County Championship should consist of seventeen four-day matches, that the Benson and Hedges Cup should become a simple knockout competition and that the Sunday League should be extended to fifty overs an innings. This new format, it was suggested, should run for an experimental period of five years. This was rejected, and the period was reduced to three years. Two of the recommendations, however – the abolition of the zonal matches in the Benson and Hedges Cup and the extension of the Sunday League matches to fifty overs – were abandoned after just one season. In 1993 coloured clothing became a feature of the Sunday League.

Four-day cricket had long been advocated by those in power, and it had long been opposed by the majority. That it was now presented as a *fait accompli* suggested that intrigue and conspiracy had been at work. Arguably, the conspiracy had started at a meeting in 1980. In 1993's *Wisden*, John Thicknesse clarified what had happened:

> Scores of retired cricketers and most spectators over 40 will be convinced there never can be a game as good as three-day county cricket. But the version that was laid to rest in August 1992 was a burlesque of the one they loved. Three-day cricket had been dying, slowly, since the winter meeting of the Test and County Cricket Board in 1980, when the switch to full covering was made. Imperceptibly at first, but unmistakably by the end of the decade, pitches lost the individuality that had made the English game unique.

Other factors were heaped upon that fatal decision made in 1980. The two-day *rest* period before a Test match and the mixture of three–and

405

four-day games had thrown the fixture list into confusion. It was insisted that every change, from pitches to starting days, had been implemented in order to produce better cricketers and a better England team. Ironically, just the opposite happened. From those heady days of Botham, Willis and Brearley in 1981, there had been nothing but a steady decline, and moderate batsmen had been flattered by the number of runs that they had been allowed to score.

In the rush for flat-earth conformity, those who ran the game – many of whom, as players, had participated when cricket came close to extinction in the 1960s – were eradicating character and uncertainty, the very life-blood of the sport. Ben Travers, who entertained millions with his plays and who watched cricket from Jessop to Gooch, reminisced on the game shortly before his death and concluded:

> The administration of the game has, of recent years, been based on a cardinal fallacy, namely that the greatest attraction cricket has to offer is easy run-getting under conditions favouring the same. This has not only resulted in the discouragement of the spin bowler; it goes deeper than that. It means that the younger generation never, or very seldom, has the chance of seeing the most enthralling spectacle cricket has to offer, the absorbing, anguishing fascination of watching great batsmanship on a ruined wicket.

Many critics suggested that the whole economic policy that was being embraced was built upon a fallacy. All income was to be generated from the centre, and the argument was that, although counties were likely to lose some £25,000 a year each from their own revenue, this would be offset by income from other areas. This placed all the emphasis on Test cricket and television receipts.

Test matches were still well supported in England. The Lord's Test had become part of the social calendar like Wimbledon, Ascot and Henley, but Tests in other countries were far less popular. Recently granted Test status, Zimbabwe had been disappointed at the size of the crowds for their inaugural match. More seriously, South Africa, after a quarter of a century in the wilderness, had been welcomed back to Test cricket with a fanfare only to find less than 5,000 people wanting to see the first match against India. India had scheduled only three Tests for England's tour in 1992–93, for they feared lack of support. As it transpired, India's dominance over England drew capacity crowds.

Cricket was looking enviously at the amount of money that soccer earned from television deals and marketing ploys, and the decision to adopt coloured clothing for the Sunday League had direct links to what was happening in soccer, where clubs like Arsenal, Liverpool and Manchester United turned over millions of pounds in merchandise. In cricket coloured clothing had become part of the one-day game in Australia, where the Benson and Hedges World Series was played under floodlights, which gave the adoption of coloured garb some relevance. On a drab Sunday afternoon at Northampton or Leicester, it had no relevance whatsoever.

Following the football pattern, the style of Sunday League shirts was changed after a couple of years, but there will never be the floods of people in red or blue choking the roads to Taunton or Hove as they do the roads to Anfield or Stamford Bridge. Cricket has missed the point that soccer's wealth stems from the fact that it is club-based, that it is harder to buy a ticket to see Newcastle United or Arsenal than it is to buy a ticket to see an international match.

In contrast, cricket in England was turning its back on the county club tradition which had been its foundation and base. There was no longer a cry for brighter cricket, and a Barrington or Boycott, both of whom had been dropped from Test sides for slow scoring, would have been welcomed into the England side with open arms and could have dictated their own scoring rates. The quality of cricket had become less important than the financial return or the way that the game was sold. The game was fattening on corporate hospitality and sponsorship, and membership of county clubs had become secondary in importance. This was quite evident from the days of the week now allotted to the first-class game. By 1997 the last day of a four-day fixture was Saturday; the day most popular among members and paying customers was now the one least likely to see a full day's cricket.

There was no hypocrisy about this. A county chairman, discussing the new format for cricket in 1993, was asked, 'What about the paying customer who is so opposed, in the main, to four-day cricket and who will now get so much less for his money?' The reply was simple and instant: 'They were not considered. They don't bring enough revenue.'

As we have noted, two of the points in the new structure were to be quickly abandoned. Realising that they could go several seasons without a home tie in the Benson and Hedges Cup or the NatWest Trophy, the counties insisted on the return of the zonal matches in the fifty-five-over competition while attendances at fifty-over Sunday League matches, now sponsored by AXA Equity and Law, fell so badly that the old forty-over system was reinstated. People wanted to eat the Sunday dinner before going off to the match.

Throughout all the changes, the arguments and passionate exchanges, cricket was fortunate in its sponsors. They have been companies who have combined generosity with sensitivity and who have asked little more of the game than a clean image.

It was not only through changes in the game's structure that the 1993 season brought down the curtain on cricket's old order. It saw the last of some great and good players. Like Gower, Pringle left the pitch for the press box while Tavaré – Jekyll in the one-day game, Hyde in first-class matches – went to pastures new. Derek Randall swooped on the ball, picked up and threw in one movement for the last time in first-class cricket. If his fidgeting at the batting crease had disturbed the purists, his vitality and athleticism in the field had brought nothing but joy and lifted the spirits. He was a strange character, so extrovert in so many ways yet never at ease with fame.

On 19 September Glamorgan won a limited-overs competition for the first time, and victory came in the most romantic fashion. By chance, the final match of the Sunday League season brought Glamorgan to play Kent at Canterbury, and whoever won the match would take the title. Some had queued from early morning to see the game, but the home supporters were disappointed that Kent, having been 168 for four with nine of their fifty overs remaining, could manage only 200 for nine.

Glamorgan lost James to Igglesden in the third over, but Hugh Morris, initially restricted, and Dale added 78 in twenty-one overs. Dale chased a widish delivery and was caught, and Maynard soon fell to Duncan Spencer, a promising quick bowler whose career was to be ruined by injury. The fall of Maynard brought Viv Richards to the wicket to play his last innings before a big crowd in England. Following his break with Somerset, Richards had played league cricket but was persuaded back to county cricket with Glamorgan in 1990. Now, in his last match, he was to share the final stand with Cottey which brought the Welsh side to victory and the title with fourteen balls to spare. He ran from the field excited and highly emotional. One of the great careers of post-war cricket was at an end.

One would not put Richards on a par with Bradman, but no man has hit the ball with more awesome power or destroyed an attack so thoroughly. He knew his worth. There was an arrogance in his batting, but then how many batsmen have ever been beaten in the flight by a spinner and been able to readjust, as Richards did, and hit the ball for six over long-on instead of long-off? He fitted the description once accorded to a film star – mean, moody and magnificent. He was a natural, and he had been touched by genius.

Richards departed in splendour, but his friend, ally and adversary had departed two months earlier in uncharacteristic, quieter style. In

July, Ian Botham had announced his retirement through injury.

Botham is certainly no exception to the general rule that the British public tends to be uncomfortable with its heroes. His hunting, shooting and fishing; his fast cars; his aeroplane; his brushes with the law and with cricket authority; his ventures on to the football field; his extravagant social behaviour; his essays on to the stage and his indication that he would like to be a film star; the claims of his one-time manager that he was bigger than the game itself; his hairstyles and his choice of clothes – all of these, from time to time, occupied more lines in the press than his activities on the cricket field.

His size and weight, symbols of strength and power when things went well, were given as reasons for failure in lesser times. His instinctive zest for the game and his innate ability, which at first excited and were touched by romance, were seen as faults when it was publicised that he did not practise enough. His capacity to eat and drink heartily, once seen as gleeful English yeoman traits, became the explanation of lack of form or fitness.

The mighty are ever prey to character assassination, and Botham's actions, on and off the field, demanded a response. His appetite for life and for cricket was unquenchable. W.G. Grace is now so distanced from us that his excesses and peccadilloes are now seen as amusing strains of character. So will it be with Botham.

When John Lever, the Essex pace bowler, first played with Botham he remarked simply, 'This bloke will rewrite all the record books.' Lever was proved correct. The world has never known a better all-round cricketer.

One thing that Botham could not manage was to bring success to Durham, who again finished bottom of the County Championship. With consistent batting and a well-balanced attack, Middlesex won the title with weeks and thirty-six points to spare. The two knockout competitions were much closer and more exciting affairs.

Derbyshire started the 1993 Benson and Hedges Cup Final as underdogs. At 66 for four, they remained so, but Wasim Akram for Lancashire, having bowled Kim Barnett early on, lost line and length and bowled poorly. The Lancashire fielding was even worse, while O'Gorman and Cork, most impressive, added 109 in twenty-eight overs. O'Gorman and Griffith fell to successive deliveries, but Cork and Krikken launched a blistering attack over the last eleven overs which produced 77 runs.

Lancashire, chasing a target of 253, were 141 for two after thirty-eight overs when rain brought a stoppage. On the resumption, Atherton's stabilising innings came to an end, and Wasim Akram and Graham Lloyd left quickly. From the last six overs, 55 were needed, and with skipper Fairbrother in full flow a Lancashire victory looked probable, especially as Cork then bowled an over which conceded 12 runs. The last over arrived with Lancashire 11 runs short of victory and the inexperienced Griffith bowling. He kept a full length and a tight line; when DeFreitas went for a mighty, hideous heave the ball spiralled and hung in the air and wicket-keeper Krikken held the catch when the ball finally came down. Derbyshire's team spirit had taken them to a brave 6-run victory.

The NatWest Final was equally thrilling. David Smith, formerly of Surrey, Worcestershire and England, hit a powerful century before being run out for 124 off the last ball of the Sussex innings. Earlier Speight had made a fifty of exotic brilliance, and with Lenham scoring 58, Sussex reached 321 for six, a record score for a NatWest or Gillette final.

Warwickshire countered with Asif Din's wristy and subtle 104 off 106 balls. Dermot Reeve's 81 off eighty-four balls then turned the match, coming, as it did, at a time when all seemed lost for Warwickshire. Roger Twose finished the job, hitting 2 off the last ball of the match to give Warwickshire victory.

Dermot Reeve had taken over from Andy Lloyd as captain of Warwickshire in rather controversial circumstances, and his county went to Lord's for the final without the outstanding pace of Allan Donald, who was required by South Africa. Reeve proved to be an innovative and inspiring captain, particularly in the one-day game, and the victory in the NatWest Trophy was but a sampler of what was to come.

Thrills galore in the domestic limited-overs game, but what of the Ashes series? The Australians warned of their strength by winning all three Texaco Trophy matches without using the leg-spinner Shane Warne, in whom there was great interest. He was to face the English batsmen for the first time in the first Test at Old Trafford. The England selectors showed some courage in naming Peter Such, the Essex off-spinner, Ilott and Igglesden in their original attack, but, inevitably, Igglesden withdrew through injury and DeFreitas was brought in to open the bowling in preference to the left-arm Ilott. This meant that there were two new caps in the England side, Such and Andy Caddick.

Such had played for both Nottinghamshire and Leicestershire before joining Essex, where his spin partnership with the veteran John Childs had proved highly successful. He was an attacking bowler, positive in approach. Fast bowler Caddick had been born in New Zealand and learned his cricket there, but, wishing to earn his living as a cricketer, he had qualified for Somerset and now for England.

Stewart kept the wicket-keeping gloves, and, to the surprise of many,

410

Gatting retained his place in the side. Gooch won the toss and asked Australia to bat first after a delayed start. Mark Taylor hit a century, and he and newcomer Slater put on 128 for the first wicket, but Such struck back with three wickets and Australia closed on 242 for five.

Such completed a memorable debut on the second day with three more wickets which gave him figures of six for 67; Australia were all out for 289. England were heartened, for they could well have expected to be facing a total in excess of 400. Gooch and Atherton kept the spirits high with a purposeful opening stand of 71 which was ended when Atherton failed to get his bat out of the way of a lifting ball from Hughes.

Gooch reached 50, Gatting was on 4 and the score was 80 when Shane Warne was introduced into the attack. His first delivery in a Test match in England pitched well outside Gatting's leg stump and hit the top of the off stump. Gatting stood dumbfounded. In every respect this was the turning point not only of the match but of the series. In his next over Warne had Smith caught at slip. Gooch's solidity was suddenly undermined. He was beaten by the leg-break and the googly before clouting a full toss to mid-on. Warne claimed four wickets; Hughes had four wickets; and England were out for 210.

Australia lost both openers to Such, but Boon, Border and the Waugh twins scored well before Healy hit a sparkling century. Border's declaration left England eight and a half hours in which to score 512 or, more realistically, to survive.

They did not. Gooch played an innings of great character, battling away for 314 minutes to score 133 before he played a ball from Hughes defensively and brushed it away instinctively with his hand before it could drop on the stumps. He realised what he had done: 'handled the ball', bathos after the heroics. Australia went on to win by 179 runs. Warne and Hughes again had four wickets each.

Astonishingly, England recalled Neil Foster in place of DeFreitas for the second Test at Lord's. The Essex pace bowler had struggled for form and fitness throughout the season, and his twelve first-class wickets had cost him 50 runs each. This was to be his last Test appearance, and, after appearing in one more county match, he was forced to retire because of his unrelenting knee problem. He was a very good bowler and a fighting cricketer, and had the whims of selectors, injury and suspension allowed, he should have played more for England.

In his last Test he was one member of an attack that was routed by Australia. Taylor and Slater began with a stand of 260. Both hit centuries. Boon made 164 not out, Mark Waugh 99 and Border 77. The declaration came when Australia were 632 for four. England were beaten by an innings and 62 runs. Atherton played two good innings, being run out for 99 in the second innings, but Warne, aided by May and Hughes, destroyed England.

The end of the match came abruptly and underlined England's dilemma. Such was bowled by Warne. The ball pitched a foot outside leg stump and turned sharply to hit the stumps. Tufnell suffered exactly the same fate next ball. Chastening for England was the fact that McDermott, Australia's main strike bowler, had been rushed to hospital during the match and had undergone an emergency operation. He had neither batted nor bowled. Victory had come with ten men.

For England, the position was now serious, and Gatting, Hick, Lewis, Foster and Tufnell were axed. Hussain was brought back after too long an absence, and Thorpe, Lathwell and McCague won their first Test caps, as did Mark Ilott. Thorpe had been almost a permanent member of the England 'A' side. He was much favoured by Ted Dexter, who greatly admired the left-hander's technique. He had not scored consistently or prolifically for Surrey, and he had been fortunate that Greig had realised his worth and kept him in the side when others might have dropped him. He was to repay the faith in him with a century in his first Test, and he was to establish a regular place in the England side in spite of having a problem in reaching three figures after that maiden Test hundred.

Lathwell, the young Somerset opener, was enjoying a fine season, but perhaps his call was premature, while the selection of McCague caused much debate. He had learned and played his cricket in Australia before joining Kent, and England now had two new-ball bowlers, Caddick and McCague, whom many thought should have been playing for other countries.

McCague had a good debut, and the match was drawn with England in the stronger position. Gooch hit a century in the second innings, and Robin Smith made 86 and 50, but the most heartening aspect of the game for England was the batting of the two young players, Thorpe and Hussain.

At Headingley, England went into the match without a spinner and gave a first Test cap to Martin Bicknell, but this was not to be a game England bowlers would want to remember. Australia made 653 for four declared, with Border, 200, and Steve Waugh, 157, sharing an unbroken stand of 332. Boon also made a century.

Warne took only one wicket in the match, but Reiffel took eight and Hughes six, and Australia won by an innings and 148 runs. Border, the Australian captain, was named Man of the Match. In contrast Gooch announced that he was resigning the England captaincy. It had been a long, sad year for him, but none could deny that he led bravely from the front with two centuries in four Tests to his credit.

Atherton, rather than Stewart, vice-captain in India and captain in Sri Lanka, was appointed England skipper in succession to Gooch. His moment had arrived sooner than expected. At Edgbaston, England recalled Matthew Maynard of Glamorgan, retained Stewart as wicket-keeper in spite of asking Russell to attend, and decided on Emburey as a second off-spinner rather than Tufnell. This time it was Mark Waugh's turn to score a century. Warne and May shared England's ten second-innings wickets, and Australia won by eight wickets. At Headingley Gooch had resigned, although he kept his place in the side; at Edgbaston Ted Dexter announced that he was to stand down as Chairman of Selectors. Nine defeats in the last ten Test matches had taken their toll.

The TCCB philosophy and the centre of their economic policy rested on a successful England team projecting the right image. Dexter had done much in his attempts to structure and reorganise committees and procedures related to selection and to the discovery and development of talented cricketers. He was not a 'hands-on' supremo, believing that once the side had been chosen the rest should be left to the captain, but he had been involved in the Gower affair, the debacle in India and the total destruction of England in an Ashes series. The British public was not willing to forgive that much.

Smith, Ilott and Emburey were omitted from the party for the sixth and final Test at The Oval. Martin Bicknell was declared unfit, and Angus Fraser returned. This was joyful news, for there had been doubts as to Fraser's future in the game following a hip injury. Fraser was a bowler of high quality, and England were not over-blessed in this area.

On the morning of the match Thorpe injured his left thumb in prac-tice, and Ramprakash was summoned from Lord's to take his place. It is unlikely that Ramprakash would have been chosen had he not been the nearest available. England left out Tufnell and so took the field with four main bowlers, three of whom – Fraser, Malcolm and Watkin – had not appeared in any of the first five Tests.

Consistent batting took England to 380, with Hick hitting a sparkling 80. Malcolm bowled quickly to take three wickets, and Fraser delighted everyone by taking five for 87 on his return. England took a first-innings lead of 77.

Their second innings was memorable in that, in the last over before lunch on the third day, Gooch drove Reiffel to the mid-off boundary to become England's highest scorer in Test cricket. His career had been scarred with wounds – most of them self-inflicted – but his dedication to the game and to batting for England and Essex had never been in ques-tion. Botham had gone, but England still had a colossus.

Ramprakash played an encouraging knock, and Watkin, Malcolm and

413

Fraser bowled out Australia for 229 to give England some consolation for the summer. Enjoying some fortune, they had won by 161 runs, and, grasping at the offered straw, the supporters were convinced that all was well again. It was England's first victory over Australia since July 1992.

The series had seen cricket moving closer to becoming a science with the introduction of the third (television-assisted) umpire. Another element of human fallibility was removed when umpires were instructed to enlist the aid of television monitors before deciding on run-outs or stumpings. At Lord's the time it took for the third umpire to give his verdict brought an impatient slow handclap from the crowd. One wondered what would happen in a NatWest or Benson and Hedges Cup final when a single run was needed off the last ball to decide the outcome. The batsman is hit on the pad; his partner calls for the quick leg-bye and dives for the crease in a flurry of dust; jubilant supporters surge on to the field; but they must still await the television replay...

For the moment there were other considerations. Atherton's first mission as captain of an England touring party was to the Caribbean in 1993–94. Gooch was not to make the tour; and of the party of seventeen, only four – Smith, Russell, Stewart and Malcolm – had reached thirty years of age. There were surprises and contradictions. Such, the most successful England bowler against Australia, was omitted in favour of the leg-spinner Salisbury, while Igglesden was chosen ahead of Martin Bicknell or Ilott. It transpired that Martin Bicknell's fitness was again in doubt, and this told against him, but then Igglesden, too, had a constant worry about fitness. Lewis earned a place simply because there seemed to be no alternative as an all-rounder.

A win in the first one-day international was followed by an eight-wicket defeat in the first Test when England selected Thorpe and Maynard ahead of Hussain and Ramprakash and were without Fraser because of injury. Stewart, now relieved of the wicket-keeping gloves, and Atherton scored 121 for the first wicket, and the West Indies were 23 for three at one time. Keith Arthurton and Brian Lara then added 144, and, in spite of Hick's 96, England crashed to defeat.

The West Indies wrapped up the one-day series and, although Atherton made 144 and Smith 84, England tumbled to an innings defeat in the second Test. The West Indian pace men again dominated, but it was the batting of Lara and Adams which caught the eye. Adams scored 137 and Lara, rapidly emerging as a batsman of exceptional aggressive talent, hit 167.

The third Test at Port of Spain saw the West Indies win again and clinch the series with two matches still to be played. Fraser and Lewis took four wickets each in the first innings, and Caddick took six for 65

414

in the second. England had taken a first-innings lead of 76 runs, and needed only 194 to win the match. Ambrose and Walsh bowled unchanged, and in 19.1 overs of the second innings England were all out for 46, their second-lowest total in Test history.

This was a great indignity. Where did English cricket go from here? Hussain and Maynard were no part of this monumental disaster, but they were included in the team to play the West Indies Board XI and batted numbers seven and eight, an indication that they were not even under consideration for the fourth Test. Hussain had reached this match at the top of the tour batting averages and had been one of the young successes of the previous summer. Now he was out in the cold, and there were suggestions that his exclusion was not related to form.

England lost heavily to the Board XI, so that it surprised all when they gained a spectacular victory in the fourth Test in Barbados. Atherton and Stewart began the match with a stand of 171; Stewart hit 118; and England were out for 355.

The West Indian first innings witnessed an outstanding bowling performance by Angus Fraser, whose eight for 75 represented not only the best bowling figures of his career but the best performance by an England bowler against the West Indies. Fraser's mighty performance took England to a first-innings lead of 51. Stewart's second century of the match, 143, and a stand of 150 for the fifth wicket with Thorpe, who made 84, assured England of a good position. Atherton's declaration left the West Indies a target of 446 in more than a day's play.

Caddick had bowled poorly in the first innings, but now he found pace and accuracy and captured two wickets before the close. He took three more on the last day, Tufnell also had three, and England won a famous victory by 208 runs. Humiliated, ridiculed and castigated in Port of Spain, England had risen from the ashes and outplayed their opponents. This was a performance of immense courage and character.

In Antigua the fifth Test was drawn. Atherton and Smith hit centuries, but Smith had had a poor tour and was the subject of much criticism. The achievements of the England batsmen were mere addenda to the tour, for, coming to the wicket on the first day with the West Indies 11 for one, Brian Lara had batted into the third day and when he was out in the last over of the morning the West Indies were 593 for five, and Lara had established a new Test record with a score of 375.

This was to be Lara's year. He had excited attention with the style of his batting performances in Australia and in the Caribbean. Warwickshire had been quick to recognise his value. With Donald unavailable for county cricket because of his commitments to the South African side, the

415

Midlands county had engaged Manoj Prabhakar, the Indian all-rounder, as their overseas player. Prabhakar had done well for India in both the Test and one-day series against Sri Lanka, but he had missed the last game through injury and suddenly became doubtful for the England season. Warwickshire withdrew their offer to him and turned instead to Brian Lara. Membership at Edgbaston increased as news of Lara's exploits came through.

In spite of the successes of men like Walsh at Gloucestershire and Hooper at Kent, not all overseas signings could be seen as satisfactory. Tendulkar, arguably the greatest of contemporary batsmen, was perhaps too young to do himself full justice with Yorkshire, while his replacement, Richie Richardson, the West Indies' captain, left after a season and a half physically and mentally exhausted by the constant round of international cricket. The Australian Michael Bevan was eventually to meet Yorkshire's needs.

At Warwickshire, Lara was an instant success. He hit 147 off 160 balls as Glamorgan were beaten by an innings in the opening Britannic Assurance County Championship match, and he followed this with a century against Leicestershire. In fairness Roger Twose, soon to emigrate to New Zealand for whom he was to play Test cricket, also did well in these matches, with a double century in the first. By the end of May, Lara had hit six first-class hundreds in seven innings. This became a record seven in eight when, against Durham at Edgbaston on 6 June 1994, he hit 501 not out. This was the highest score ever made in first-class cricket, so that the West Indian left-hander now held the two principal batting records. He finished the season as the only batsman to score more than 2,000 runs and was sandwiched between the Middlesex pair Carr and Gatting in the top three of the national batting averages. Gooch was fourth.

Warwickshire won the County Championship by a margin of forty-two points from Leicestershire and were never really threatened. They also took the AXA Equity and Law Sunday League by a margin of four points from Worcestershire, whom they had beaten in the Benson and Hedges Cup Final in spite of losing Lara cheaply. Worcestershire gained revenge in the NatWest Trophy Final. Lara hit 81 in Warwickshire's 223 for nine, and Worcestershire lost both openers for 29, but Hick and Moody came together in an unbroken stand of 198 to win the match.

So Warwickshire were denied the first ever 'grand slam', but their achievement in winning three and finishing second in the other of the four domestic competitions had no parallel. That Lara played a big part in the success cannot be denied, but there were other major factors. Warwickshire could boast few outstanding cricketers, but that they were an outstanding team was unquestionable. They were inspiringly led by both Reeve and Munton, and the captaincy of both was positive and inventive. The spirit engendered in the side was exemplary. Each man played for the others. There were no heroes. They took joy in playing county cricket, and they wasted no time or energy moaning about pitches or parking or food or too much cricket.

All this, of course, was of little use to England, who found it difficult to capture Warwickshire's enthusiasm. The England party in the Caribbean had been managed by M.J.K. Smith, and it was apparent that, in the minds of the governors of the game, he was marked to succeed Ted Dexter as England's supremo. Perhaps he was pushed too soon, for there was a late challenge against him by those who felt that an attempt was being made to perpetuate the Oxbridge dominance and that Smith should not truly appear on any honest short-list for the job. The selection fell instead on Raymond Illingworth, a successful captain of England and Leicestershire and a poor manager of Yorkshire.

Illingworth had been a respected captain of England, and men like the Lancastrian Frank Hayes stated that they had never played under a better skipper; the general opinion, however, from Botham to Bailey, was that the appointment of Illingworth had come twenty years too late. He began in an unfortunate manner, criticising some of the players appearing against the West Indies even before he had taken up his position. Illingworth's penchant for public executions was to be a consistent blight on his period in office.

Peter Such, who had done well in the Ashes series but had not been taken to the Caribbean, was an early victim, as Illingworth pronounced his long admiration for Udal as the best off-spinner in England, and the Hampshire bowler was chosen for the Texaco Trophy squad to face New Zealand. Reeve was recalled and Gough, the Yorkshire fast bowler, was included. Rhodes, the Yorkshire-born Worcestershire keeper, was preferred to Russell. Gooch came back, but Stewart continued to partner Atherton as opener.

Not only did New Zealand lose the one Texaco Trophy match that was played but they lost the services of their main strike bowler, Morrison, for the rest of the tour. In the first Test at Trent Bridge DeFreitas, his international career given a restart by Illingworth, took nine wickets. Gooch, 210, and Atherton, 101, shared a second-wicket stand of 263 as England won by an innings.

New Zealand had looked a poor side at Nottingham, but they staged a remarkable transformation at Lord's. Martin Crowe hit 142, and quick bowler Dion Nash took eleven wickets, but New Zealand were denied victory by Stewart's century and by their lack of a top-class spinner.

England, incidentally, had returned to Such for the series.

The third Test was drawn, so that Ray Illingworth could draw comfort from his first series in charge, but South Africa, charged by national pride and passion, presented sterner opposition. At Lord's they beat England by 356 runs. Gough took four wickets, Fraser three, but Wessels, the former Australian opener, hit a century, and South Africa made 357. The pace of Donald and de Villiers, backed by Jonty Rhodes's fielding (as electrifying as it was brilliant), was too much for England, who were bowled out for 180. Wessels declared at lunch on the Sunday, by which time South Africa were 455 runs ahead. England capitulated on the Sunday afternoon and were all out for 99.

The Test threw up many questions and doubts regarding Illingworth and his advisers. The left-handed qualities of Thorpe had been ignored, and Craig White hardly seemed to fit the bill as an all-rounder. Atherton appeared to doubt the latter's abilities, for he gave White one spell of three overs while South Africa scored 278 in just over a hundred overs. White had learned and played his early cricket in Australia.

There were also grave doubts as to Salisbury's quality as a Test player. Leg-spinners like Warne, Abdul Qadir and Mushtaq Ahmed are match-winners and of immense value to any side, but there is no point in including a leg-spinner if one of Test standard is not available.

The continuing debate regarding the choice of wicket-keeper erupted, for Illingworth's choice of Rhodes ahead of Russell, Marsh, Piper, Metson or a few others did not satisfy the purists. John Crawley earned his first Test cap, and his promise was obvious, although his tendency to pull across the line suggested that he had technical deficiencies to iron out.

Interesting as there issues regarding Illingworth and his judgement were, they were totally overshadowed by an incident on the Saturday. Television cameras seemed to show Atherton tampering with the ball. The England captain was pictured rubbing the ball after taking his hand from his pocket. It was later revealed to the match referee Peter Burge, although not in the initial inquiry, that Atherton had earth in his pocket on which to dry his hands and, allegedly, with which to make alterations to the surface of the ball. The England captain was twice fined, and the wealth of newsprint that was used in debating the issue must have cost a rain forest. The whole affair was conclusive proof that television was now the major authority in the rationale, organisation and judgement of cricket. To add to the public's confusion during this season, Lancashire were deducted twenty-five points for a pitch at Old Trafford on which Neil Fairbrother had scored 204.

Thorpe and Tufnell were recalled for the Headingley Test. The Surrey

418

left-hander played two good innings, Atherton hit 99 and Hick, seem-ingly growing in confidence, made a century, but the match was drawn, honours even.

The sensation came at The Oval, where Joey Benjamin won his only Test cap, chosen ahead of Fraser, and Devon Malcolm appeared against South Africa for the first time as England went into the match without a front-line spinner.

A late starter, Benjamin had enjoyed an outstanding season for Surrey and was rightly rewarded for his success in county cricket. An honest, hard-working, fast medium-pace bowler, he had joined Surrey after four years with Warwickshire where he was unable to command a regular place in the Championship side. He did well in his one Test match, but that he should later be selected for the tour of Australia ahead of Fraser was illogical, for Benjamin was not a cricketer of genuine Test quality. In Australia he would suffer a bout of chicken pox and go for weeks with-out a game of cricket.

At The Oval, Wessels won the toss, and South Africa batted and lost Gary Kirsten in the third over of the match. In his second spell Malcolm shattered Peter Kirsten's stumps. Benjamin seemed to have adopted a line that was too wide of off stump, and his pace was undemanding, yet, with his fourteenth ball in Test cricket, he trapped Cronje leg-before. On the stroke of lunch Cullinan was caught behind off DeFreitas's away-swinger, and a lively session ended with South Africa 85 for four. There had been far too many loose deliveries from England's bowlers for comfort.

Wessels batted doggedly until being clearly leg-before to Benjamin, and Rhodes seemed in no trouble before he ducked into a delivery from Malcolm and was hit on the helmet above the left ear. He was led from the field, spent the night in hospital and was patently unfit for the rest of the match.

South Africa were now in some trouble, effectively 146 for six, but Richardson and McMillan responded with a stand of 124 in thirty overs. Benjamin returned to break the stand, having Richardson caught behind, and in his next over he had Matthews taken at slip. McMillan dictated in a useful stand with de Villiers, and an eventful day ended with South Africa 326 for eight.

The second day started late because of rain. McMillan added only 2 to his overnight score before edging to slip, but there was South African jubilation when Atherton was adjudged leg-before to the first ball of the second over of the England innings. Umpire Ken Palmer raised his finger, although most believed that Atherton had edged the ball on to his pad. Atherton left the crease immediately and made no gesture to the umpire, although he shook his head ruefully and looked at his bat on the way to the pavilion. Referee Peter Burge instantly fined the England captain 50 per cent of his match fee for dissent.

This seemed rather harsh, for Jonty Rhodes had shown obvious dissent at Headingley and went unpunished, but Burge had publicly threatened Atherton after the incident at Lord's; he was, in a sense, exacting his revenge. The referee's action galvanised England, and they united behind their captain, whom they considered had been treated unjustly.

The England batting lacked consistency. Thorpe and Stewart batted well, but the cricket was sluggish with Wessels intent on holding what advantage his side had. Although play was extended until seven o'clock, the South Africans bowled their overs so slowly that a capacity crowd was robbed of fourteen overs. Contempt for the paying customer had now become one of the norms of the game. Wessels's plans were wrecked in the last twenty-three minutes of the day when DeFreitas and Gough hit 59 runs. England closed on 281 for seven.

DeFreitas, now with his third county, Derbyshire, was having a new lease of life while Darren Gough, the Yorkshire pace bowler, had emerged as the discovery of the season. He took seventeen wickets in four Tests and warmed hearts with his fiercely competent hitting. The pair extended their partnership to 70 in eleven overs before DeFreitas was run out by Cullinan. Malcolm was hit on the head by a ball from de Villiers; it was to prove a most ill-judged bouncer. England finished only 28 runs in arrears, and the game was alive.

In South Africa's first innings England's out-cricket had been ragged; now it was aflame. DeFreitas bowled a maiden, and Malcolm began the first of three spells of bowling which were to give him an indelible place in the history of cricket. His first delivery reared from a length and flew past Gary Kirsten's nose. The second was of great pace and the third saw Gary Kirsten completely undermined. He turned his back on the ball, which looped in the air of his glove. Following through, Malcolm beat short-leg to the catch.

A single by Peter Kirsten took him to face Malcolm's next over. He essayed a hook at a fast short delivery, was never in control of the shot and was caught at long-leg. Paralysed by Malcolm's speed, Cronje pushed forward and had his middle stump knocked back. After four overs South Africa were 1 for three, all three wickets to Malcolm. Having bowled five overs, Malcolm rested.

Wessels and Cullinan added 72 in twenty overs, but when Malcolm was recalled for his second spell in the afternoon Wessels slashed wildly and was caught behind. McMillan was badly dropped by Gooch at slip,

420

and he and Cullinan put on 64 in seventeen overs. Malcolm returned for his third spell shortly before tea.

Immediately, McMillan fended a lifting ball to first slip. Two overs later Richardson was beaten by a ball of full length. Matthews gloved the third ball he received to the wicket-keeper and Cullinan, who had batted with great determination and good technique, was finally caught at slip when he tried to force Gough off the back foot.

Malcolm soon finished the innings. Jonty Rhodes slashed into the keeper's gloves, and Donald was bowled off his pads. Malcolm's third and final spell had brought him five for 17 in thirty-three balls. His nine for 57 had been bettered only three times by an Englishman in Test cricket: Laker, twice, at Old Trafford in 1956, and Lohmann against the South Africans at Johannesburg in 1896.

The positive cricket which England had shown in the field was now shown with the bat. Needing 204 to win, they lost Gooch in the fifth over, by which time 56 runs were on the board. Hick joined battle, and he and Atherton left the field to tumultuous applause at the end of the day, with England 107 for one after sixteen overs.

Hick batted better than he had when scoring a century at Headingley, and he and Atherton's second-wicket stand was worth 124 in twenty-eight overs. Thorpe maintained the aggression with 15 off fourteen balls, and victory was sweet.

Devon Malcolm and the Return of South Africa
England v South Africa at The Oval
18, 19, 20 and 21 August 1994

South Africa First Innings		Second Innings	
G. Kirsten c Rhodes b DeFreitas . . .	2	(2) c and b Malcolm	0
P.N. Kirsten b Malcolm	16	(1) c DeFreitas b Malcolm	1
W.J. Cronje lbw b Benjamin	38	b Malcolm	0
K.C. Wessels (capt) lbw b Benjamin	45	c Rhodes b Malcolm . . .	28
D.J. Cullinan c Rhodes b DeFreitas	7	c Thorpe b Gough	94
J.N. Rhodes retired hurt	8	(9) c Rhodes b Malcolm .	10
B.M. McMillan c Hick b DeFreitas .	93	(6) c Thorpe b Malcolm .	25
†D.J. Richardson c Rhodes b Benjamin	58	(7) lbw b Malcolm	3
C.R. Matthews c Hick b Benjamin .	0	(8) c Rhodes b Malcolm .	0
P.S. de Villiers c Stewart b DeFreitas	14	not out	0
A.A. Donald not out	14	b Malcolm	0
Extras (b 8, lb 10, w 1, nb 18) . . .	37	(lb 5, nb 9)	14
Total for 9 wickets	332	175	

BOWLING	Overs	Mdns	Runs	Wkts	Overs	Mdns	Runs	Wkts
DeFreitas	26.2	5	93	4	12	3	25	–
Malcolm	25	5	81	1	16.3	2	57	9
Gough	19	1	85	–	9	1	39	1
Benjamin	17	2	42	4	11	1	38	–
Hick	5	1	13	–	2	–	11	–

fall of wickets
1–2, 2–43, 3–73, 4–85, 5–136, 6–260, 7–266, 8–301, 9–332
1–0, 2–1, 3–1, 4–73, 5–137, 6–143, 7–143, 8–175, 9–175
J.N. Rhodes retired hurt at 106 for 4 (first innings)

England	First Innings		Second Innings	
G.A. Gooch c Richardson b Donald		8	b Matthews	33
M.A. Atherton (capt) lbw b de Villiers		0	c Richardson b Donald	63
G.A. Hick b Donald		39	not out	81
G.P. Thorpe b Matthews		79	not out	15
A.J. Stewart b de Villiers		62		
J.P. Crawley c Richardson b Donald		5		
†S.J. Rhodes lbw b de Villiers		11		
P.A.J. DeFreitas run out		37		
D. Gough not out		42		
J.E. Benjamin lbw b de Villiers		0		
D.E. Malcolm c sub (Shaw) b Matthews		4		
Extras (b 1, w 1, nb 15)		17	(lb 6, nb 7)	13
Total		304	for 2 wickets	205

BOWLING	Overs	Mdns	Runs	Wkts	Overs	Mdns	Runs	Wkts
Donald	17	2	76	3	12	1	96	1
de Villiers	19	3	62	4	12	–	66	–
Matthews	21	4	82	2	11.3	4	37	1
McMillan	12	1	67	–	–	–	–	–
Cronje	8	3	16	–	–	–	–	–

fall of wickets
1–1, 2–33, 3–93, 4–145, 5–165, 6–219, 7–222, 8–292, 9–293
1–56, 2–180
umpires R.S. Dunne and K.E. Palmer
England won by 8 wickets

Lewis, Cork and Udal were brought back for the Texaco Trophy matches, both of which were won by England, who thereby finished the season on a note of high optimism.

South Africa's return to Test cricket in England had produced a high-charged season with a particularly emotional and nostalgic occasion at Lord's. Indeed, one could argue that much of the South African success was founded on emotion, a passionate commitment to prove their worth as cricketers and to mark the stature of a country proud to be back in the international fold. They played poorly at The Oval, but they remained less impressed by the England side than England's chairman of selectors, as they indicated when they named Malcolm as England's Man of the Series. He had appeared only at The Oval.

Illingworth, on the other hand, voiced the opinion that he now believed England to be virtually unbeatable. He had scant evidence on which to base this opinion, and if a week can be a long time in politics, three months can be a lifetime in cricket. In the words of Flanders and Swann, Illingworth was soon to realise that it was 'bloody January again'.

The most fervent of Illingworth supporters found it hard to accept the sixteen names chosen to tour Australia in 1994–95 without more than a little trepidation. The omission of Fraser in favour of McCague caused outcry, and there was little enthusiasm for the inclusion of Udal and White. The absence of Hussain and Ramprakash, two young batsmen brilliant in the field, and the presence of the two veterans Gooch and Gatting, was seen as a recipe for disaster. Both older men had served England well, but surely one batsman of such seniority would have been sufficient as support for Atherton.

Such an ill-chosen party needed luck against an Australian side strong in talent and high in morale and self-belief. It had none. Stewart, the vice-captain, broke a finger within a week of arriving in Australia. He was fit for the first Test, but sustained another break in the second Test and was out of the rest of the series. Devon Malcolm went down with chicken pox on the eve of the first Test, and the catalogue of illnesses and injuries grew to the extent that, during the course of the tour, as many as six extra players were drafted in.

Stewart was to be accompanied home by McCague, Udal, White, Gough and Hick, all of whom left the tour through injury; even one of the substitutes, Fairbrother, departed through injury. Ilott was called up, but joined the 'A' side in India without playing a match, and Russell appeared just once as a substitute. Fraser, Lewis and Ramprakash, other substitutes, played in Test matches. All this gives some indication of the atmosphere in which the tour was conducted and the series was played.

On the eve of the first Test Illingworth could not keep quiet and publicly criticised Atherton from London for not keeping him informed as to what was happening. As M.J.K. Smith was manager of the tour and Fletcher the team manager, followers of the game could be forgiven for questioning what the lines of communication between all concerned were supposed to be.

Taylor, Border's successor as captain, won the toss and Australia batted. McCague, playing in place of Malcolm, and DeFreitas were savaged for 26 in the first four overs. Slater knocked DeFreitas out of the attack in the afternoon session while McCague was punished for 29 runs in a three-over spell. Gough and Tufnell did well, but Slater made 176 and Mark Waugh 140 as Australia reached 426. They eventually won by 184 runs with McDermott taking six English first-innings wickets and Warne eight in the second and eleven for 110 in the match.

It was the same two bowlers who destroyed England at Melbourne, McDermott taking eight wickets and Warne nine. Gough and Tufnell again did well, but Steve Waugh, 94 not out, and Boon, 131, assured Australia of their 295-run victory. Warne finished the match with a hat-trick.

The third Test was something of a surprise. England scored 309, and, with Gough taking six wickets, Australia were bowled out for 116. Atherton's declaration on the fourth day left Australia a target of 449 to win, but the declaration caused debate and brought sympathy to Hick, who was 98 not out when Atherton called the batsmen in. Atherton's action caused a rift with Hick; the captain later admitted that he had been wrong in his action. Even so, team and tactical considerations must surely override individual landmarks.

Taylor and Slater looked likely to achieve the improbable with an opening stand of 208, but once they were separated the Australian batting fell apart, and they finished on 344 for seven. The draw meant that Australia had retained the Ashes, but England had regained some pride. Fraser took five second-innings wickets, and Gough was named Man of the Match, but the Yorkshireman's tour was now over, and he returned to England to have treatment for an injury sustained as he leapt into his delivery stride. He could draw much satisfaction from his contribution to the tour.

The England eleven for the fourth Test at Adelaide virtually chose itself. It was the eleven fit men. Gatting scored a sterling century, but, with Blewett making a hundred in his first Test, Australia led by 66 on the first innings. Thorpe and Crawley batted well, and DeFreitas hit a whirlwind 88 which set up a chance of an England victory. This was duly achieved thanks to the bowling of Malcolm and Lewis, who took four wickets each.

Even in victory England suffered some indignity. Atherton was repri-

424

manded for the way in which he had conducted the game, and Lewis was fined for pointing McDermott the way to the pavilion after having him caught behind. This tiresome and ignorant gesture had become almost commonplace, part of the indiscipline and loutish behaviour which had come to permeate the game. It was a gesture that engaged the attention of the beery section of a crowd. Other gestures, such as the centurion waving his bat in acknowledgement only towards his own team-mates and the dressing room, rudely ignored the existence of a crowd.

Gooch and Gatting announced that the Perth Test would be their last in international cricket. Neither had a happy ending to a distinguished career. Thorpe scored a century, but McDermott struck again, and England were overwhelmed by 329 runs. There was no consolation in the Benson and Hedges World Series. The final was contested by Australia and Australia 'A'.

In a sense England were unlucky to lose the Test series, 3–1. They recovered well after two crushing defeats and were cruelly hit by injuries. Even the depletion of the team could not hide the fact, however, that England were inferior to Australia in every department of the game, on and off the field. They were scarcely a match for state sides, losing to New South Wales and twice in limited-overs matches to the Australian Cricket Academy.

The fielding was poor, with Rhodes short of the standard required of an international keeper, and young Crawley very disappointing in this area. The attitude to practice left much to be desired, and the substance of that practice was ridiculed by the Australians as being undemanding and totally out of date. There was, too, the question of communication as, once again, England were branded as bad tourists. Illingworth's verbal attacks on the players he had selected were complemented by manager Mike Smith's reluctance to give information to anybody, and by Mike Atherton's body-language which rarely suggested happiness, on or off the field. One's mind went back to Tony Greig and the contrast he presented to Atherton. Greig's body-language suggested perpetual optimism even in the darkest of times, and he posed the question, 'Why play cricket if there is no joy in it?'

Perhaps Keith Fletcher no longer found joy in the game. A slightly stooped figure with a worried air, he gave the impression that much churned inside him that was never articulated, and he conveyed pessimism. If this had been Pooh Corner, Fletcher would have been Eeyore.

His tenure of the England captaincy had ended unhappily; now his period as England team manager was to have an equally unhappy and

425

abrupt conclusion. Within a month of the close of the Australian tour, he was informed by A.C. Smith that his contract had been terminated midway through its intended five-year course. He had been made the scapegoat for the Australian debacle. Others survived unscathed, and Ray Illingworth now took on Fletcher's job as well as that of chief selector so that he had what amounted to absolute power.

In the wake of the Australian tour there was, inevitably, a multitude of suggestions as to how to improve English cricket. Extravagant and unsubstantiated claims were made for the success of the Australian Cricket Academy, and it was demanded that England should have its own centre of excellence. There were ideas for two divisions in the County Championship, and it was posited that there were too many players, too many teams, and that the number should be reduced.

As Durham had only recently been added to the first-class counties and the number of Championship matches reduced to seventeen, this argument was hard to follow. Gooch was one of those who advocated fewer counties, but, of course, he did not suggest that Essex should be one of the counties to be sacrificed.

The top players constantly complained that their incomes were not on a par with the top golfers or tennis players; they were also critical of the amount that they had to play and the amount of travelling that they were expected to do. It was hard to find sympathy for such arguments. In an English season few players worked more than what was the equivalent of a four-and-a-half-day week with a two-and-a-half week holiday, and rest days were frequently spent in benefit ventures.

The benefit itself had become big business. Once dependent on the loyalty and generosity of county members and Sunday matches against club sides, the beneficiary now looked to involve large companies, to go beyond the boundaries of his county and to hold dinners at which an auction could raise as much as £15,000 in under twenty minutes. Ten years as a capped player will generally be rewarded by a sum in excess of £130,000, while a Gooch or a Gatting can expect half a million pounds from a lengthy career. One does not begrudge dedicated players that, but, like so much else in cricket, the system has lost touch with its roots and original intentions. This is not surprising in a society in which money and profit has become the principal reason for existence.

While many profited, for many there had been loss. The recession was taking its toll and, although it might like to think otherwise, the cricketing world could not remain unaffected. In the general turmoil that was now part of each close season Monte Lynch moved from Surrey to Gloucestershire, Roseberry left Middlesex to become captain of Durham,

426

and Essex acquired Williams from Middlesex while losing Shahid to Surrey, Stephenson to Hampshire (where he was to succeed Nicholas as captain) and Nick Knight to Warwickshire.

The movement of Knight caused much animosity, for Essex insisted they had invested much in him and did not wish to lose him. For his part, Knight felt he was undervalued at Essex and would better his chances of playing for England if he moved to Warwickshire. It was an unsavoury affair, but Knight's belief that he would win an England cap if he moved proved to be correct. He was chosen to open the England innings in the fourth Test against the West Indies at Old Trafford in July 1995. This meant that he followed in the wake of Pringle and Stephenson as the third ex-pupil of Felsted School to win an England cap in the past six years, a proud record.

Like all independent schools with high fees, Felsted had felt the impact of the recession. Unable to cope in the economic climate that persisted, several parents had been forced to remove their children from the school. They had been replaced by young people from Hong Kong, Russia, Switzerland and elsewhere; girls, once restricted to the sixth form, were admitted at all levels. The number of girls in the school increased annually and, in the lower part of the school, is now close to 50 per cent of the intake. By the summer of 1996 sports masters, of whom Frank Hayes, formerly of Lancashire and England, was one, were voicing concern that they would be unable to field two rugby fifteens in the lower school in the near future. The problem will not be restricted to rugby, nor to Felsted.

Nick Knight's move proved advantageous to him in many ways. He was a member of the Warwickshire side which won the NatWest Trophy, the only trophy to have eluded them the previous season, and he was also a member of the side which retained the County Championship after an epic struggle with Northamptonshire and Middlesex.

Led by Allan Lamb, Northamptonshire owed much to solid batting and to the wonderful bowling of the Indian leg-spinner Anil Kumble, who took 105 wickets in Championship matches alone. The meeting between Northamptonshire and Warwickshire at Edgbaston produced one of the greatest county matches in living memory. With Donald and Munton taking four wickets each, Northamptonshire were bowled out for 152. Roger Twose, in his last season for Warwickshire before emigrating to New Zealand, hit 140, and, in spite of David Capel's career-best bowling figures, seven for 44, the home side took a lead of 72.

Northamptonshire lost three wickets before the arrears were cleared, but Fordham scored a century of immense value, Warren gave excellent

427

support and the last three wickets realised 68 precious runs. Warwickshire needed 275 to win.

With Kumble mesmerising batsmen as he had done all season, Northamptonshire looked as if they would win in three days, having reduced the reigning champions to 53 for six. Neil Smith and Dermot Reeve had other ideas, and by the close they had advanced the score to 161 without further loss. They were not separated until eighty minutes into the last day when the score was 201. When Piper and, eventually, Reeve were out Warwickshire were still 47 runs short of victory with the last pair, Munton and Donald, together. They battled bravely, but, with the total at 267 and victory just 8 runs away, Capel trapped Munton leg-before with a ball of full length.

Northamptonshire won a memorable victory, but they still had to visit Middlesex at Uxbridge, where the surface would deny both sides a result, while Warwickshire won their last six matches of the season and retained their title.

The final win came at Canterbury where Kent were beaten by an innings. They also beat Kent on the Sunday to finish with fifty points, as did Kent and Worcestershire, but Kent took the AXA Equity and Law title by virtue of a faster run-rate. Ironically, Kent finished five points adrift of Durham at the bottom of the County Championship.

The Middlesex challenge came principally through the batting of Ramprakash, the only man in the country to exceed 2,000 runs, and through a balanced attack. These Middlesex virtues could not be transferred to the Test arena, where Ramprakash scored only 22 runs in four innings, Tufnell was again *persona non grata* and Fraser was treated in such a cavalier manner as to cause Patrick Whittingdale, a city business-man and generous supporter of cricket, to withdraw his sponsorship from the England team.

Illingworth had tightened his grip on affairs. He engaged Peter Lever and John Edrich to assist him in the coaching department; he delayed naming Atherton as captain, and then the appointment was for only a limited period initially.

England won the Texaco Trophy series against the West Indies by two matches to one. Atherton scored a magnificent century at Lord's, and the new medium-pace bowler, Peter Martin of Lancashire, did well in two matches. He was chosen for the first Test at Headingley, where England lost by nine wickets.

It was generally thought that this trouncing presaged events for the rest of the summer. Ian Bishop had returned after numerous injuries with a vengeance, and the manner in which Hooper and Lara had lashed the West Indies to victory was awesome.

428

Robin Smith had bizarrely been used as opener in the first Test after his period of exile from Test cricket. At Lord's, more logically, he dropped to number four. Dominic Cork came in for his first Test at the expense of DeFreitas, and Fraser returned in place of Malcolm. In spite of Fraser's five wickets, the West Indies led by 41 on the first innings, but Robin Smith played a most courageous innings of 90, and the West Indies faced a target of 296 on a pitch that was worsening. With Campbell in top form and Lara producing some sumptuous drives, they looked well capable of reaching the target. Alec Stewart, reinstated as wicket-keeper, then took a spectacular catch off Gough to account for Lara. Cork finished with seven for 43, a wonderful debut in a fine and unexpected victory.

What transpired in the next few days indicated that all was not well within the West Indies' camp. Winston Benjamin had been sent home. They had lost to lowly Sussex, who themselves were in disarray as Eddie Hemmings left them in disenchantment and Norman Gifford resigned as coach. The rumours were rife that the West Indians were rent apart by factions, with Richie Richardson's captaincy under threat.

It came as a shock to England, then, to lose by an innings inside three days on a dreadful pitch at Edgbaston. England were bowled out for 147 and 89, and the match was over after just seventy-five minutes' play on the Saturday morning. The crowd chanted, 'What a load of rubbish.' And one could sympathise with them.

England had brought in Gallian of Lancashire, who had captained Young Australia, so once more a reliance was being placed on a cricketer who was the product of another country. Not only did England lose the match, they lost Alec Stewart for the rest of the season with an aggravation of his old finger injury. Colin Croft, who had once bowled fast and threateningly for the West Indies and Lancashire, commented after the match that, as English batsmen were now playing on only the most docile of wickets, they had no idea what to do when they encountered a pitch that posed some problems.

To their credit, men like Atherton, Martin and Hick joined their counties and played in Sunday League games when they had been expecting to play Test cricket. Thorpe did not play for Surrey against Essex at The Oval. There were suggestions that he was too tired; he had been out for nought on the Friday evening.

If England could take any consolation from the Edgbaston Test, it was in the fact that Dominic Cork took four wickets. At Old Trafford he was a hero rather than a consolation.

Illingworth chose a strange side, recalling John Emburey who was only a few days short of his forty-third birthday, bringing in Knight,

White and Watkinson. Knight was to open the England innings even though before the match he had not scored a first-class century in the season.

The inclusion of both White and Watkinson gave England two cricketers whose quality as Test players was doubtful. Watkinson, the Lancashire captain, was a good, honest player who bowled both medium pace and off-spin and batted well in the late middle order; but his off-spin, for which he was primarily chosen, was in the embryonic stage. He did well, though, taking five wickets in the match and scoring a useful 37.

Fraser and Cork shared eight wickets in the West Indies' first innings, and Thorpe played one of his best knocks for England by that time in making 94. Cork hit an unbeaten 56 at number nine, and England led by 221. Lara scored his first century of the series, but he was overshadowed by Cork, who performed the hat-trick when he sent back Richardson, Murray and Hooper with successive deliveries. England went on to win by six wickets and level the series.

In 1994 Gough had been described as 'another Botham'. He was finding his second season in international cricket more difficult, and the description was now attached to Cork. Cork was his own man, full of zest and enthusiasm; he and Gough looked to be integral to any future English success, but they would be so in their own ways, not as 'new Bothams'.

Hick had been dropped for the fourth Test, and he had responded with some outspoken criticism. He made a more constructive response at Trent Bridge by hitting 118 on his recall. Atherton scored 113, and England led on the first innings in spite of another hundred from Lara. A second-innings collapse brought danger of defeat, but this was averted by Watkinson and Richard Illingworth.

The Oval pitch never looked like offering a result. Hick, Russell and Atherton all got into the 90s, but Lara made a magnificent 179, Hooper hit 127, and the West Indies reached 692 for eight. The match, and the series, was drawn.

England were entitled to be more pleased with the summer than the West Indies. Atherton, Hick and Thorpe had shown maturity in their batting. Smith had withstood a fierce battering with much courage and application while Cork, twenty-six wickets at just over 25 runs each in five Tests and some useful runs, was just twenty-four years old and had grasped his Test opportunity magnificently. England had drawn a series in spite of being deprived of the services of Stewart and Gough for much of the summer.

There were, however, worrying signs. Illingworth had arrived at no settled attack, and the spin bowling appeared well below international standard. England might well have drawn warning, too, from an innings that was played in the Benson and Hedges Cup Final.

With Carl Hooper on duty for the West Indies, Kent had engaged Aravinda de Silva as their overseas player. The Sri Lankan gave some spectacular displays of batting and helped Kent to the final. At Lord's Lancashire, wrongly put in to bat, made 274, of which Atherton scored 93. Kent's reply was almost stillborn, and when de Silva came to the wicket the score was 37 for two in twelve overs. Taylor was becalmed, and three of Austin's first four overs were maidens. This pattern was immediately changed by de Silva. He twice lifted Austin into the Mound Stand for six, dancing down the wicket and determining his own length. He flicked the ball through mid-wicket and drove regally to the cover boundary. He offered the sublime poetry of the art of batsmanship, and while he was at the crease all seemed possible.

Facing his ninety-fifth ball, he hit Austin high towards the Mound Stand yet again, but Lloyd held a fine catch on the boundary rope. De Silva had made 112, with three sixes and eleven fours, and he became the first man to win the Gold Award in a Benson and Hedges Cup Final while finishing on the losing side. Moreover, he had shown a highly appreciative capacity Lord's crowd the true meaning of greatness. More was to be heard of him in the coming months.

It had become customary to send 'A' sides on tour during the winter months in an attempt to give experience of international cricket to players who gave promise of reaching Test level. Not all these tours had been useful or successful, but Thorpe and Gough were two who had benefited. In 1995–96 a team was sent to Pakistan, and one of those invited was Andrew Symonds, who had enjoyed a sensational season with Gloucestershire which had culminated with an innings of 254 not out against Glamorgan at Abergavenny, an innings which included a world-record twenty sixes. Born in Birmingham, Symonds had been brought up in Australia and had learned his cricket there, playing for Queensland in the Sheffield Shield. He declined the invitation to tour with England 'A', and his place was taken by Jason Pooley, the young Middlesex left-hander.

Symonds's decision was to be applauded, but it heightened the problem which some regarded as the parasitic nature of the England team, relying as it did on men like Smith, Hick, Caddick, Gallian and, later, Mullally, all of whom had learned their cricket in other countries. Mike Gatting had made no secret of his opposition to the system, but it persisted and underlined England's own lack of resources.

The surprise with regard to the England 'A' team was the naming of

Nasser Hussain as captain. Hussain had been out of the England reck-oning for two years, although the suggestions were that this was because he was considered to be something of an awkward customer rather than through any lack of ability. He was not only a batsman of quality but a brilliant fielder, and, in Pakistan, he was to prove a good captain.

One 'awkward customer', Phil Tufnell, did not make any tour, however. He was omitted from the party to go to South Africa although he was unquestionably England's leading spinner. He was also, it must be said, his own worst enemy, and his career was sprinkled with misde-meanours and the occasional unsavoury episode. His absence left England's spin attack woefully weak. South Africa's was expected to be even weaker, but just as the tour began they discovered a most unortho-dox left-arm spinner: Paul Adams's action was memorably described as a 'frog in a blender'.

South Africa had another asset in that the national side was now coached by Bob Woolmer who, having achieved miracles at Warwickshire, had been wooed to the Republic.

The tour did not begin well, and it got worse. The first first-class game to be played at the new Soweto Oval was between the tourists and an Invitation XI. It was an emotional and historic occasion. President Nelson Mandela, who placed great importance on sport as a means of healing wounds and bringing the races together, was introduced to the teams and made a special point of congratulating Devon Malcolm, who was recognised as a hero and a model by the black population. Within forty-eight hours, Malcolm was pilloried in the press by Ray Illingworth and bowling coach Peter Lever, who was quoted as saying that Malcolm had pace as his only asset and that apart from that he was a 'nonentity in cricketing terms'. Illingworth's tendency towards public executions was a blight on the game, and the administrators had given further evidence of their dreadful record in man-management.

South Africa could not have wished for greater encouragement than this totally unjustified public humiliation of the bowler whom they most feared. Malcolm did not play in the first Test, which was ruined by rain and in which Hick scored 141. He returned in the second Test at Johannesburg and took six wickets. Cork took nine, but the honours went to Mike Atherton and 'Jack' Russell, who held his place as wicket-keeper throughout the tour (Stewart now being recognised as Atherton's regular opening partner).

Russell established a new Test record with eleven catches in this second Test but his heroics did not end there. Cronje set England a target of 479. They lost four wickets for 145, one of them being that of Ramprakash, whose dismal Test record continued, and although Robin Smith showed dogged resistance, when he was out the score was 232 and only Atherton of the recognised batsmen remained. Russell joined his captain in one of the great rearguard actions in Test history. The pair stayed together for the last 277 minutes of the match and earned England a draw. Atherton, having faced 492 balls and batted for ten hours and forty-five minutes, finished unbeaten on 185 while Russell, who at one time went seventy minutes without scoring, made 29. This was a triumph for tenacity, technique and temperament.

Like the first, the third Test was ruined by rain, but there was still enough time for Crawley to put himself out of the tour with a hamstring injury. In spite of Hussain's success in Pakistan, particularly in the number three spot which was England's Achilles heel, it was Gallian who was summoned to bolster the party. He played in the fourth Test, which saw the international debut of Paul Adams, and the match was drawn.

South Africa had been superior throughout the series, and their victory inside three days in the final Test at Cape Town came as no great surprise. Malcolm played in this Test, bowled a poor spell and was again publicly castigated by Illingworth. Malcolm had begun the tour as a hero and was now seen as the villain who lost a Test match.

He, Ilott and Fraser were sent back to England where, justifiably, Malcolm reacted angrily to the treatment he had received at the hands of Illingworth.

In preparation for the one-day series, England called up Fairbrother, Reeve, Neil Smith of Warwickshire, Craig White and DeFreitas. It was an inexplicable collection of what were called 'bits and pieces players'. England were beaten 6–1 and totally humiliated. There seemed to be neither rhyme nor reason in anything that had been done in South Africa, and an ill-chosen, ill-prepared squad now went off to the Indian subcontinent for the World Cup.

The competition was due to be staged in India, Sri Lanka and Pakistan. Australia and the West Indies declined to visit Sri Lanka because of recent terrorist activities and conceded their matches against the home country, who won the three games they played and qualified to meet England in the quarter-finals in Faisalabad.

England had succeeded only in beating two non-Test-playing nations, the United Arab Emirates and Holland, and they had appeared to lurch from one catastrophe and whinge to another. This was in sharp contrast to the well-prepared and well-organised South African side, who were gracious to their hosts, carried themselves with warmth and dignity and made many friends through their captain's attempts to greet his hosts in their own language.

England made 235 for eight in their fifty overs against Sri Lanka, which was by no means a bad score, but a glittering innings of 82 off forty-four balls from opener Sanath Jayasuriya left England reeling, and Sri Lanka won by five wickets with more than nine overs to spare.

Sadly, few, if any, were sorry to see England knocked out of the tournament. Lacking grace and charm, shabby in the field, constantly complaining about conditions, facilities, decisions and the amount of cricket they were being asked to play, they were often guilty of showing a lack of manners to their hosts which sometimes bordered on contempt. There had been another outbreak of siege mentality, the disease of those who believe themselves to be unloved.

Sri Lanka went on to win the World Cup with Aravinda de Silva hitting a century in the final against Australia. They had proved themselves the most exciting and entertaining team in the world, but, seemingly, no commercial reasons could be found for granting them a Test series in England. The British public were the losers.

England returned home to entertain India and Pakistan over the summer of 1996, and to welcome a new coach, David Lloyd. A patriotic optimist, Lloyd had worked with his former county Lancashire and with young England sides. A popular and witty man, he was doubted only because he had shown a weakness for temperamental outbursts on occasion, but he certainly had the ideal start.

England entered the two series unable or unwilling to call upon their best spinner and their fastest bowler; both, apparently, for reasons outside cricket. Against India, England introduced Mullally, Patel, Ealham and Irani to Test cricket and brought back Lewis and, dramatically and successfully, Hussain.

Mullally, a medium-pace left-arm seamer, enjoyed a good summer as a player for England and Leicestershire. Under Whitaker's energetic and intelligent leadership and with the West Indian Phil Simmons making vital contributions, Leicestershire proved themselves the best team in the country and won the Championship in style. Their triumph was based on the same principles as those of their predecessors, Warwickshire. They were totally committed to and supportive of each other, a team in every sense.

Patel, a slow left-arm bowler from Kent, had taken many wickets in the Championship, but he lost form during the season and did not prove himself at international level. His team-mate, the all-rounder Mark Ealham, did much better, as did the Essex all-rounder Ronnie Irani, who

434

had begun his career with Lancashire and was a cricketer much admired by Ian Botham.

The Indian party proved to be ill-prepared and in some disarray. Kambli, their established number three, was left at home for disciplinary reasons and Sidhu walked out on the tour before the Test series began. Anil Kumble never found the form he had displayed with Northamptonshire the year before. Srinath had enjoyed an outstanding season with Gloucestershire in 1995 and bowled manfully and unluckily with Prasad. Tendulkar was brilliant, and Ganguly and Dravid emerged as fine batsmen, but England took the series by virtue of winning the first Test.

Returning to Test cricket, Hussain hit a century to set up England's victory at Edgbaston. It was an innings of skill, determination and considerable character. Russell hit a match-saving 124 at Lord's, and in a high-scoring match at Trent Bridge the centuries by Hussain and Atherton cancelled out those by Tendulkar and Ganguly.

Lloyd could be well satisfied with his first series as England's coach, but then came the much stronger opposition of Pakistan, who won a resounding victory in the first Test at Lord's. The disturbing feature of the England defeat was the collapse on the final day. They were set a target of 408 and had scored 74 for the early loss of Knight by the close of play on the Sunday evening. Atherton and Stewart skilfully negotiated the morning session on Monday, but at two o'clock the leg-spinner Mushtaq Ahmed decided to bowl round the wicket and immediately pitched a ball in the rough outside leg stump. It turned sharply and had Atherton taken at slip. In his next over Mushtaq had Stewart caught off his glove. Thorpe, Hick, Ealham, Russell and Cork followed in quick succession. England went from 168 for one to 186 for eight, shattered by the pace of Waqar Younis and the spin of Mushtaq Ahmed. Hick had scored 35 runs in four Test innings against India, and now he had twice had his stumps scattered by Waqar for 4. He would return to Worcestershire and score centuries in county cricket, but, for the time being at least, his Test career was over.

The failure of Hick to realise his potential as a Test batsman after indications in India, against the West Indies and in South Africa that the worst was behind him was a grievous blow. He had long been awaited as the messiah only to prove a false prophet, and the England side was to remain unbalanced in consequence. Salisbury had again proved inadequate at Lord's, and England, with not even Hick's off-spin to call on, took the field at Headingley without a spinner, although Atherton came out of bowling retirement to send down seven overs and take a wicket. Hussain was back after injury; Stewart hit 170 and Nick Knight a maiden

Test century in a run-saturated drawn match.

A more satisfying maiden Test hundred came at The Oval, where John Crawley gave evidence that he had eradicated his technical problems in an innings of considerable charm. But it was not enough to save England from a nine-wicket defeat.

England played two spinners in this match: Salisbury was recalled but again made little impact, and Robert Croft, the Glamorgan off-spinner and a useful batsman, made his debut. Ealham, Irani, Mullally and Durham's Simon Brown were other bowlers who had been introduced to Test cricket during the summer. The search continued.

Croft did not bowl badly at The Oval, but many of his colleagues did. Lewis not only had a dreadful match but was disciplined for arriving late, not for the first time, it was learned. Once again, having started the season brightly and been offered another chance to resurrect his international career, Lewis had faltered by the time it came to September.

He did have some consolation in that his new county, Surrey, ended their barren period by winning the Sunday League. Lancashire won two trophies, the Benson and Hedges Cup and the NatWest Trophy, taking both finals with ease. Many Lancashire supporters remained unsatisfied, though, unhappy at the county's showing in the Championship. There was a call for the head of the captain, Mike Watkinson, who had to withstand attack at a general meeting.

Illingworth's reign was at an end and, at the beginning of 1997, the TCCB gave way to a new authority, the England and Wales Cricket Board (ECB), responsible for the governance of all cricket. Inevitably, problems confronted the new board even before it came into existence. There was concern that more people had attended the semi-finals of the Benson and Hedges Cup and the NatWest Trophy than had attended two days of the Headingley Test, yet there was comfort in the advance bookings for the Ashes series. There was despair at England's inept performances in Zimbabwe and in the early part of the New Zealand tour, and the management trio of Atherton, Lloyd and John Barclay – captain, coach and manager, respectively – appeared to be under threat.

Lord MacLaurin, Tim Lamb and Bob Bennett are good men and true who have the interests of the game at heart. It is to be hoped that they will keep the game close to its roots, that they are more ready to accept criticism than their predecessors, and that they can save cricket from the supermarket mentality; the paying customer should be given what he really wants rather than what the game's administrators feel he should have and what generates the most profit.

For every winner, there is a loser, and there can be no profit without loss. The profits are high and getting higher, and it would be tragic if the loss were the game of cricket itself.

Select Bibliography

The Cricketer, various editors
Wisden Cricket Monthly, David Frith, 1979–96
A History of Leicestershire CCC, Dennis Lambert
A History of Northamptonshire CCC, Matthew Engel and Andrew Radd
Wisden Cricketers' Almanack, various editors, 1940–1996
Benson & Hedges Cricket Year, 1982–1996
Pelham Cricket Year, 1979–81
Playfair Cricket Monthly
A History of Yorkshire CCC, Derek Hodgson
A History of Yorkshire CCC, Anthony Woodhouse
News Chronicle/Playfair Cricket Annual, various editors, 19?6–1996

Various publications of the Association of Cricket statisticians have proved invaluable.

Index

Abbas, Zaheer 247
Advisory County Cricket
  Committee 155
Agnew, Jonathan 341
Ahmed, Younis 215
Aird, Ronald 2, 155
Alam, Intikhab 247
Allen, Basil 37
Allen, G.O. 'Gubby' 2; Caribbean
  tour captaincy 1947–48 41–42
Alley, Bill 215
Allom, Maurice 228
Alston, Rex 190, 244
amateur–professional divide 78;
  abolition of 155
Ames, Les 6, 22, 79–80
Amiss, Dennis 254; century of
  centuries 356; Packer series
  288; rebel tour of South Africa
  328–29
Andrew, Keith 148
apartheid 44, 214, 218–19;
  Gleneagles Declaration 315;
  Peter Hain 226; India's objec-
  tions to players 325; India's
  visa refusal 375; Robin
  Jackman 315; laws abolished,
  1991 397; rebel tour of South
  Africa 328–29; rebel tourists'
  pay 329; South Africa tour,
  1989–90 379; Stop the Seventy

Tour campaign 226–28
Appleyard, Bob 82
Arlidge, Jack 290
Arnold, Geoff 208
artificial fertilisers 141
Atherton, Mike: ball-tampering
  allegations 418; England
  captaincy 413
Athey, Bill 371
attendances falling 152–54, 180
Australia: centenary Test 313;
  Test series, 1948 46–53 (statistics 53–54); 1950–51 68–75
  (statistics 74–75); 1953 91–99
  (statistics 98–99); 1954–55
  106–14 (statistics 112–14); 1956
  118–25 (statistics 124–25); 1961
  155–60; 1964 183–87 (statistics
  185–86); 1965 198–201; 1968
  216–18; 1970–71 236–44 (statistics 242–43); 1972 252; 1975
  277, 280–81; 1977 292–96
  (statistics 294–95); 1978
  300–301; 1979–80 308–9; 1981
  316–24 (statistics 320–21);
  1982–83 333–34; 1985 349–50;
  1986–87 358–59; 1989 378–80;
  1990–91 392–93; 1993 410–14;
  1994–95 423–25
Australia and New Zealand: tour,
  1958–59 136; tour, 1962–63

168–73; tour, 1974–75 271–75
Australian Broadcasting
   Company 288
Australian Cricket Board 288; and
   Kerry Packer 308
Aylestone Road 13

Bailey, Derrick 79
Bailey, Jack 296
Bailey, Trevor 7, 8, 60; farewell to
   Test cricket 137
Bakht, Sikander 297
Balderstone, Chris: farewell to
   Test cricket 284
ball-tampering 400, 418
Bannister, Alex 301
Barclay, John 324
Barlow, Eddie 248, 284; Packer
   series 287
Barlow, Graham 310
Barrington, Ken 133; death
   315–16
Bartlett, Hugh 3
Battle of Britain 3
Bedi, Bishan 283
Bedser, Alec 8–9, 20, 21, 24, 330;
   Bradman's recognition 32; last
   game against Australia 107
behaviour: of players 309, 313,
   317, 369, 425; of spectators 261,
   296, 309, 330
Benaud, Ritchie 160; dynamic
   leadership 164; Packer series,
   management of 287; shoulder
   injury 156
benefit matches 426
Benjamin, Joey 419
Bennett, Leo 18
Bennett, N.H. 17
Benson and Hedges Cup 251;
   first century in final 306;
   Somerset disqualified 304;

Somerset victory 324; structural changes 405
Berry, Les 6, 16
Bickerstaff, Anne 362
Bicknell, Martin 397
Bird, 'Dickie' 258
bomb hoaxes 258
Bond, Jack 232–35; retirement
   234
Booth, Arthur 20
Border, Allan 378
Botham, Ian 246, 284, 298, 299,
   323–24; apartheid and Indian
   government 325; bowling
   prowess 321, 355; bowling
   record 340; centenary Test 313;
   England captaincy 312, 316;
   fastest double-century 332;
   first Test century 298; Jessop
   comparison 318; knee operation 338; libel proceedings 352;
   marathon walk for leukaemia
   research 349, 353; move to
   Worcestershire 353; resignation
   of captaincy 316–17; resigns
   Somerset captaincy 349; retirement 408–9; runs–wickets Test
   double 326, 341; talent
   confirmed 298; Test thousand
   303; *Wisden* on 276; worst Test
   series 352
bouncers 284; Ewen Chatfield's
   injury 275; head gear 313
Bowes, Bill 13, 22–23, 120–21
bowling: rules change 47
Boyce, Keith 215, 222, 257
Boycott, Geoffrey 246, 270,
   291–92; century of centuries
   293–94; farewell to Test cricket
   326; farewell to Yorkshire 353;
   first Test hundred 185;
   hundredth cap 316;

Illingworth clash 325; Packer series, declines 287, 291; quirks 312; rebel tour of South Africa 326, 328–29; sacked by Yorkshire 299; Peter West on 207; withdrawal from 1974–75 tour 271; world records 326; Young Cricketer of the Year 174

Boyd, Keith 214

Bradman, Don 29–30; 'legend' 44–45

Brearley, Mike 190, 245, 310; broken arm 297; farewell to Test cricket 323; Greig replacement 291; Middlesex leadership 281–82; northern hostility 299

Brennan, Don: campaign to replace Boycott 291–92

Bridger, John 15

'Brighter Cricket League Table' 82

Brisbane 'gluepot' 70

Britannic Assurance 348

British Empire XI 2, 3

Broad, Chris 340, 359; Pakistan incident, 1987 366; South Africa tour 379

Brocklehurst, Ben 215; World Cup suggestion 228–31

Brown, Alan 161

Brown, Freddie 2, 64; Greig and the Packer series 288

Brown, Tony 216, 234, 342

Budd, Zola 341, 370–71

Buller, Syd 152

Burnet, J.R. 134, 135–36

Bustamente, Alex 103

Butcher, Roland 311

Callaghan, James: South Africa race row 227

Capel, David 360

captaincy: England's first professional 83–84; problems for English cricket 61; professionals on the increase 116; and tour managers 314

Carmody, D.K. 7

Carr, Donald 8, 230

Carrick, Phil: Yorkshire captaincy 361

Central Mediterranean Forces 22

Chalk, Frederick 1

Champion County v. Rest of England, revival of 40

Chapman, Percy 2

Chappell, Greg 215, 237, 250

Childs, John 356–57

Clark, David 79

Clarke, C.B. 2, 3

Clark, E.W. 14

Clark Report 201–2

Clay, J.C. 16

Close, Brian 58–59, 68–69, 283; end of captaincy 208; Gillette Cup 223–24; media choice for captaincy 204; Somerset move 246; sacking by Yorkshire 245–46; tactician 174

Coldwell, Len 165

Compton, Denis 2, 3, 6, 8, 23, 35, 37, 40; 'Compton knee' 43, 66; Edrich memorial service 64; finest ever innings? 48; glamour and popularity 40–41; knee operation 118–19, 123; last Test series 126; triple hundred, fastest recorded 56

Compton–Edrich batting records, 1947 40

Constantine, Learie 2, 9–10; first England black keeper 221; racialism 9 controversies and scandals 153

Cook, Geoff: apartheid and Indian government 325

Cook, Nick 335

Cornhill Insurance 289

County Championship 208–9; Clark Report 201–2; first tie 58; four-day games 370; overseas cricketers 116–17, 202, 214; reconstruction 268–69; points system 216: structural changes 405; Yorkshire's three successive wins 214

county cricket (*See also under individual county names*): clubs' financial problems 152–53, 231, 270; rising popularity of 40;

covered pitches 314

Cowans, Norman 334

Cowdrey, Chris 342; England captaincy 374; South Africa tour 379

Cowdrey, Colin 105, 164–65, 235, 246, 272–73, 361; broken arm 180–81; century of Test matches 216; farewell to Test cricket 274; foot problems 115; recognition of greatness 148; Test runs record 237; 'too nice' 165; E.M. Wellings on 182; world catch record 274

Cranston, Ken 39, 62–63

Crapp, Jack 79

Cricket Council: Packer series 288; South Africa race row 227

Cricketer 28, 82, 176, 225, 280; India/Pakistan tour, 1960–61 162–63; on George Mann 55; on New Zealand Test series, 1949 61; on sensationalism 32; on Maurice Tremlett 35; on West Indies Test series, 1953–54 102

Croft, Colin 429

Daily Express: 'better cricket' competition 173

Daily Mail: Wardle attack on colleagues 134–35

Daniel, Wayne 282, 310

Davies, J.G.W. 3

Dawkes, George 12–13

de Silva, Aravinda 431

DeFreitas, Phillip 358

Deighton, J.H.G. 45–46

Denness, Mike 259; Illingworth's criticism 271

Derbyshire: Benson and Hedges Cup 409–10

Dewes, John 8

Dexter, Ted 132, 165; Chairman of Selectors 375–76 (stands down as 413); as communicator 168–69; increased attendances 154; leg injury in road accident 194; Tory Parliamentary candidate 187, 190; tribute to May 140

Doggart, Hubert 59

D'Oliveira, Basil 188, 214–15; apartheid 214; race row 218–19

Dollery, Tom 62, 78–79

Dominions 9

Donald, Allan 397

Donnelly, Martin 9, 21

Dooland, Bruce 116, 117

Doshi, Dilip 311

Douglas-Home, Alec 218–19

Downton, Paul 298, 311

dress 403; coloured clothing 405, 406–7

drugs allegations 337; Botham's libel action 352

Duckworth, Leslie 250
Durham 398–99

Eagar, Desmond 133
early finish 77
Eastwood, Ken 240
Ebeling, Hans 285
Edmonds, Phil 280
Edrich, Bill 6, 27, 35, 37, 40,
    63–64; back problems 66; as
    bowler 36; 'exile' 66, 94;
    farewell to Test cricket 284;
    memorial service, 1986 64;
    triple-century record 195
Edrich–Compton batting records,
    1947 40
Edrich, John 141, 166–67
eight-ball over: jettisoned 12
Emburey, John: England captaincy
    373; rebel tour of South Africa
    328–29; South Africa tour 379
Emmett, George 79
Engineer, Farokh 163, 215, 232
Essex 305–8, 404; Benson and
    Hedges Cup 305–6; Border
    signing 356; County
    Championship 338, 356, 399;
    domination 303; financial
    problems 221–22; Gooch
    captaincy 371; John Player
    League 325, 338; NatWest
    Trophy 347–48; Sunday League
    348
Essex, County Championship 336
ethics 149
Evans, Godfrey 7; stumpings
    record 140
Evening News colts scheme 126

Fagg, Arthur 80, 258
Fairbrother, Neil: Hutton record

beaten 388
Fallows, Jack 17
Farnes, Ken 2
Felsted School 427
'festival of cricket' 153
financial problems 152, 221–22,
    231, 270; Green Shield Stamps
    222
Findlay Commission 4
Fishlock, Laurie 26
Fletcher, Keith 216–17, 254–55,
    312, 325, 348, 403–4; contract
    terminated 425–26; dismissed
    as captain 331
football bribery 154
Foster, Neil 335; South Africa tour
    379
Fowler, Graeme: farewell to Test
    cricket 347
Francis, Bruce 250
Fraser, Angus 413; career best
    415
Freeman, Titch 2

Gandhi, Indira: assassinated 342
Garland-Wells, Monty 17
Garner, Joel 324, 335–36, 353
Gatting, Mike 37, 310–11, 343;
    end of England captaincy
    372–73; England captaincy 354;
    Middlesex captaincy 311;
    Pakistan incident, 1987 367;
    sex allegations 372; South
    Africa tour 379
General Election, 1950 66
Gibb, Paul 22, 78
Gibbs, Lance 215, 248
Gillette: first sponsorship 155
Gillette Cup 198, 300; changes
    202; first competition 173–74;
    Lancashire 233; second compe-
    tition 188; Yorkshire's 1969

triumph 223–24
Gimblett, Harold 6
Gladwin, Cliff 20, 39, 55; first hat-trick 56
Glamorgan: County Championship, first win 54; Sunday League 408; Woolf Wooller as captain 54–55
Gleneagles Declaration 315
Gloucestershire 233–34, 247; Derrick Bailey 79; Benson and Hedges Cup 296; Gillette Cup 261
Goddard, Tom 20
Gomes, Larry 249, 282
Gooch, Graham 276; batting prowess 387; centuries record 389; England captaincy 374, 375; Essex captaincy 371; first Test century 312; rebel tour of South Africa 328–29; runs record 338; Test career on hold 280; *This Is Your Life* 392
Goodway, Cyril 248
Gover, Alf 25, 151
Gower, David 277; 'buzzing' incident 392; dropped by selectors 380; England captaincy 333, 378; England captaincy ends 354; England debut 298; first century as Captain 350; omission row 401–2; Stuart Turner on 277
Grace Road 13
Graveney, Tom 59, 187; breach of discipline 224; farewell to Test cricket 225; Worcestershire move 79
Gray, Laurie 3
Green, Geoffrey 83
Greenidge, Gordon 247, 260
Green Shield Stamps 222

Gregory, Ernie 78
Greig, Ian 324, 348, 380–81; Surrey captaincy 358
Greig, Tony 254, 255, 270, 277–79, 290–91; captaincy denied, 1977 288; epilepsy 278; farewell to Test cricket – with a duck 295; nationality wrangle 278–79; Packer series 287; Sussex contract, release from 290
Griffith, Billy 228, 230
Griffith, S.C. 2

Hadlee, Richard 297, 324, 338, 361
Hain, Peter 226
Hammond, Wally 7, 10, 14–15, 22; retirement 28–29
Hampshire 160–61, 260–61; Benson and Hedges Cup 371, 399; NatWest Trophy 396, 399
Hampshire, John: Yorkshire captaincy 292
Hardie, Brian 306
Hardstaff, Joe, Jnr 23
Harman, Roger 181
Hassan, Basharat 279
Hassett, Lindsay 7
Hayes, Frank 257; farewell to Test cricket 284
Haynes, Desmond 260
Hayter, Reg 3; on West Indies Test series, 1953–54 102
Hayward, Tom 40
head gear 291, 313
Headley, Ron 215
Hemmings, Eddie 324
Hick, Graeme 341, 371, 372, 395, 435
Higson, T.A. 16
Hillsborough tragedy 376
Hilton, Malcolm 46
Hitchcock, Ray 168

Hobbs, Jack 40
Hobbs, Robin 236
Holder, Vanburn 215
Holding, Michael 313
Hollies, Eric 9, 20–21
Holmes, A.J. 20
Holmes, Errol 17; Surrey captaincy 18
Howard, Nigel 81; MCC captaincy, India tour, 1951–52 63
Howat, Gerald 9
Howell, Denis 219
Howorth, Dick 21
Hughes, David 234
Hughes, Kim 309
Hulme, Joe 3
Humpage, Geoff: rebel tour of South Africa 328–29
Hutton: double-century first 102
Hutton, Len 2, 23, 31, 58, 279; first professional England captain 83–84; knighted 115; MCC honorary member 115; non-fraternisation tradition 103; press campaign 94; Reg Hayter on 99–100; South Africa, 1948–49 58
Hutton, Richard 246

Ibadulla, 'Billy' 215
Iddon, Jack 16–17
Ikin, Jack 24
Illingworth, Ray 132, 224, 235–36, 246; Boycott clash 325; Chairman of Selectors 417; on Mike Denness 271; farewell to Test cricket 259; Leicestershire move 244; Yorkshire team manager 292
Illingworth, Richard 395
Imperial Cricket Conference:

name change 189
Imran Khan 324
India: government's objections to Boycott, Cook 325; Jubilee Test series 309–10; Test series 1982 325–26; Test series, 1951–52 81–82; 1952 82–89 (statistics 86–89); 1959 140–42; 1963–64 181–83; 1967 207–8; 1971 247; 1976–77 284–85; 1982 331–32; 1984–85 342–46 (statistics 345–46); 1986 354; 1990 388–92 (statistics 390–91); 1992 401–3; 1996 434, 435
India and Pakistan: Test series, 1961–62 161–63; 1972 253–55
Ingleby-Mackenzie, Colin 133, 160–61
Insole, Doug 193; D'Oliveira race row 219
International Cricket Conference 189; Packer series 289; Packer series 288
Iqbal, Asif 215
Irani, Ronnie 434–35
Irvine, Lee 215, 222, 250; retirement presentation 287

Jackman, Robin 311; Gleneagles Declaration 315
Jackson, Les 64–65, 157
Jackson, Stanley 19
Jamaica: independence 155
James, C.L.R. 9
Jameson, John 246
Jefferies, Steve 371
Jenkins, Roley 55–56
Jessop, Gilbert 318
Jesty, Trevor 334, 357
John Player League 223
John Wisden's Cricketers' Almanac – See Wisden

Johnson, Keith 10
Jones, Allan 282

Kallicharran, Alvin 248–51, 362
Kanhai, Rohan 174, 215, 248;
   benefit 293; tribute from
   Duckworth 250–51
Kay, John 63
Kent 79–80, 283; Benson and
   Hedges Cup 431; County
   Championship, first since 1913
   235; Jack Martin 38; Murray-
   Wood dismissal 80; Sunday
   League 428
Kentish, Esmond 258
Kenyon, Don 167
Khan, Majid 215; Glamorgan
   captaincy 255
King, Collis 302
Kirsten, Peter 311
Knight, Barry 161, 222
Knight, Nick 427
Knight, Roger 261, 312
knock-out tournament 154, 173,
   324
Knott, Alan 208; Packer series
   287; rebel tour of South Africa
   328–29; statistics 323; wicket-
   keeper's runs record 293
Kumble, Anil 427

Lady Chatterley's Lover 154
Laker, Jim 118; farewell to Test
   cricket 137; Over to Me 153
Lamb, Allan 311, 383
Lamb, Tim 256
Lancashire 231–35, 431; Benson
   and Hedges Cup 339, 388, 396,
   436; Jack Bond 232–35; Ken
   Cranston 39–40, 62–63; Jack
   Fallows 17; Gillette Cup 233;
   Gillette Cup three-year run

231; Gillette Cup, third win
   234; T.A. Higson 16; Nigel
   Howard 63; John Player
   League 233; NatWest Trophy
   388, 436; Sunday League 377
Langridge, James 28
Lara, Brian 415–17
Larkins, Wayne: rebel tour of
   South Africa 328–29
Larter, David 166
Lawrence, David: kneecap injury
   399
laws: Law 42 367; Law 46 149
Lee, Alan 380
leg-before-wicket law 228
Leicestershire 276–77, 281;
   Benson and Hedges Cup 348;
   Les Berry 16; Grace Road
   ground 13; John Player League
   292; Stuart Symington 62
le Roux, Garth 324
Lever, John 222, 284
Lever, Peter 236, 271; bouncers
   275; rebel tour of South Africa
   328–29
Lewis, Chris 395
Lewis, Tony 224, 253, 255
Lillee, Dennis 237, 291; back
   injury 271–72
Lloyd, Andy 339
Lloyd, Clive 215, 232
Lloyd, David 232, 434; farewell to
   Test cricket 274
Loader, Peter 90; hat-trick 131
Lock, Bert 13
London Counties 2–3
Long, Arnold 290
Lord's 4; first Sunday play 193;
   war years 2
Lord's Day Observance Act 154
Lord's Day Observance Society
   153

Lush, Peter 359–60, 366

Macartney, Ian 65–66
Majendie, Nicholas 181
Malcolm, Devon 386, 432; sent home 433
Mallett, Ashley 392
Mandela, Nelson 375, 432
Mann, George 63; Test debut 55
marijuana allegations 337; Botham's libel action 352
Marlar, Robin 307
Marner, Peter: first Man of the Match award 173, 189
Marshall, Roy 116–17, 247
Marsh, Rodney 237
Martin, Jack 38
Matthews, Austin 6
Maxwell, C.R. 14
May, Peter 59, 77; century, thirteenth and last 141; Chairman of Selectors 330–31, 369 (retirement as 375); death 375; firstclass career over 160; illness and surgery 141, 147, 150; Surrey captaincy 125; tribute from Dexter 140
MCC: cricket after the war 4–6; D'Oliveira race row 218–19; no-confidence vote 401; protest over South Africa decision 226–28; TCCB 'encroachment' 361
McConnon, J.E. 105
McEwan, Ken 307
Medlycott, Keith 381–82
Melford, Michael 290
Melville, Alan 34
Mendis, Gehan 324
Merchant, Vijay 25
Miandad, Javed 311
Middlesex 35–37, 249, 428;

Benson and Hedges Cup 336; and Mike Brearley 281–82; . Compton's eccentric bowling blend 36; Compton–Edrich 'twins' 35; County Championship 348, 409; Gillette Cup 291; Laurie Gray 36; NatWest Trophy 339, 371; Robertson–Brown opening partnership 35; Jim Sims 36; Sunday League 399; Jack Young 36
Milburn, Colin: eye loss in road accident 225; farewell to Test cricket 225
Miller, Keith 7, 9
Millman, Geoff 161
Milton, Arthur 59, 132
Mitchell, Arthur 2
Mitchell, Bruce 40
Mitchell, Tommy 14
Mohammad, Mushtaq 247
Mohammad, Sadiq 247
Moles, Andy 362
Morris, John: 'buzzing' incident 392
Mortensen, Ole 371–72
Moss, Alan 100, 126
Muncer, B.L. 54
Murray, Deryck 249
Murray, John 156; farewell to Test cricket 208; operation 163; selector 291
Murray, Mike 405
Murray-Willis, Peter 18–19
Murray-Wood, Bill 79–80; dismissal by Kent 80

Nash, Malcolm 215–16
Nash. J.H. 134
NatWest Bank 324
Nawab of Pataudi 21

Nawaz, Sarfraz 247, 282, 365
Nelson, Robert 1, 3, 18–19
New Zealand: Test series, 1949
    60–61; 1958 131–32; 1965
    193–97 (statistics 196–97); 1969
    225; 1971 244; 1973 255–57;
    1983 335; 1984 337–38; 1986
    355; 1994 417–18
Newton, Derek 370
Nicholas, Mark 371, 372
Norfolk, Duke of 169
Normandy landing 6
Norris, Percy: shot dead 342
Northamptonshire 18–19, 247,
    427–28; Leo Bennett 18; Peter
    Murray-Willis 19; NatWest
    Trophy 399; overseas players
    283
Nottinghamshire 324, 361–62;
    Benson and Hedges Cup 377;
    County Championship 361;
    NatWest Trophy 361; Sunday
    League 396

Old, Chris: rebel tour of South
    Africa 328–29; second-fastest
    hundred 292
Oldfield, Norman 2
Olympic Games, London, 1948 44
one-day international born 238
O'Sullivan, David 260
Oval: Anne Bickerstaff 362; requi-
    sitioned 13
Over to Me 153
overseas players 116–17, 202, 214,
    248–51, 341, 370; Greig wrangle
    278–79; and Northamptonshire
    283; qualification change 356

Packer series 287–91; effect on
    other competitions 301, 314
Packer, Kerry 287, 288; and the

Australia Cricket Board 308;
    injunction against ICC and
    TCCB 289
Pakistan: ball-tampering allega-
    tions 400; Test series, 1954
    103–6; 1962 165–67; 1967 208;
    1968 219–20; 1971 246–47; 1978
    298–99; 1982 332–33; 1984 338;
    1987 360; 1992 399–401; 1996
    434, 435–36; tour, 1955 117–18
Pakistan and New Zealand: twin
    Test series, 1977–78 297–98
Palmer, C.H. 100
Parfitt, Peter 161, 245
Parks, Jim 6
Parslow, L.F. 3
Pataudi, Nawab of 21
Pawson, Tony 80
Pearce, Tom 41
Pepper, Cec 7
Phillip, Norbert 307–8
Phillipson, Eddie 8
Phillips, Wayne 349
Playfair Cricket Monthly 228
Pocock, Pat: farewell to Test
    cricket 347
points system for counties 216;
    rule change 126
Pollard, Dick 8
Pollock, Graeme: Packer series
    287
Pope, George 8, 14
Prabhakar, Manoj 416
Preston, Hubert 68
Preston, Norman 2, 31, 154, 186,
    199; on Brown 76; on
    Caribbean tour, 1947–48 43
Prideaux, Roger 216
Pringle, Derek 331–32; accident-
    prone 333–34
Private Eye 154
Procter, Mike 215, 216, 247;

Packer series 287
Professional Cricketers'
Association 226
Prudential Assurance Company
275
Pugh, Tom 79
Pullar, Geoff 140

racism 9–10
Radford, Neil 354
Radley, Clive 245, 310
Rainey Brown, George 362
Rait-Kerr, R.S. 2, 153
Randall, Derek 284, 324, 408
rationing 14, 33, 115
Reeve, Dermot 378; Warwickshire
captaincy 410
Refuge Assurance 354
Rhoades, Cedric 231–32
Rhodes, Harold 'Dusty' 141
Rhodesia 221
Rhodes, Stephen 371
Rice, Clive 311, 324, 361–62;
Packer series 297; sack as
Notts captain 297
Richards, Barry 215, 260, 300;
Packer series 287
Richards, Jack 358
Richards, Viv 311, 324, 336, 353,
408; last international appear-
ance in England 396
Roberts, Andy 261, 300
Robertson, Jack 4
Roberts, Ron 192
Robins, Derrick 248
Robinson, Ray 28, 173
Robinson, Tim: Nottinghamshire
captaincy 361; South Africa
tour 379
Robins, Walter 2, 20, 153, 183; on
playing the 'right way' 163–64
Roebuck, Peter: Somerset

captaincy 349
Roope, Graham 256
Ross, Gordon 193
Rowe, Lawrence 263
Rumsey, Fred 198
Russell, Eric 161–62, 245; farewell
to Test cricket 208
Rutnagur, Dicky 284–85

Schweppes 289
Sellers, Brian 20, 89
Shackleton, Derek 133
Sharpe, Phil 246
Sharp, Harry 37
Shastri, Ravi 343–44
Shepherd, David 261
Shepherd, John 214
Sheppard, David 83, 104, 165;
South Africa race row 226;
South Africa tour refusal 150
Shuttleworth, Ken 232, 236
Sidebottom, Arnold: rebel tour of
South Africa 328–29
Simmons, Jack 232
Sims, Jim 36
Singh, C.L. 142, 144
Sismey, S.G. 7
six-ball over: reinstated 12
Slack, Wilf 351; death 376
Slater, Keith 138
Smailes, Tom 22
Smith, A.C. 168, 359
Smith, Chris 335
Smith 'Collie', death in road acci-
dent 128
Smith, David 161, 351
Smith, Ian 221
Smith, Leslie 82, 149, 162–63, 172;
on Dexter 173
Smith, M.J.K. 132, 181–82; retire-
ment announcement 210
Smith, Neil 306

Smith, Peter 21; hoax 30

Smith, Ray 3

Smith, Robin 397

Smithson, Gerald 42; arm injury 43

Snow, John: farewell to Test cricket 284; Packer series 287

Sobers, Gary 101, 215; six sixes 215; stoned by youths 213; *Wisden* tribute 249–50

Somerset 15, 303–4, 348–49; Botham's departure 353; Brian Close 246; disqualification from Benson and Hedges Cup 304; Gillette Cup 305; John Player League 305, 336; NatWest Trophy 335; Richards–Garner contracts row 353; Maurice Tremlett 34–35; victory in Benson and Hedges Cup 324

South Africa 351; 1970 programme for England tour 226; black political organisations outlawed 150; declaration of republic status 155, 189; D'Oliveira race row 218–19; expulsion from Olympic movement 227; Gleneagles Declaration 315; Peter Hain 226; Imperial Cricket Conference name change 189; rebel tour 326, 328–29; rebel tourists' pay 329; Sharpeville massacre 150; Stop the Seventy Tour campaign 226–28; Test series, 1947 34, 38–39; 1948–49 55–58; 1951 76–77; 1955 115–16; 1956–57 125–26; 1960 150–52; 1964–65 189–92; 1965 193, 197–98; 1994 418–23 (statistics 421–22); 1996 432–33; tour, 1989–90 379;

welcomed back 397

Southend Festival 377

Spencer, Duncan 408

Spender, Stephen 4

Spooner, Dick 59

Springboks 221

Sri Lanka: Test , 1992 402, 403; Test, 1982 326–27; Test, 1988 374–75; Test, 1991 396; Test, 1996 435

St Hill, E. 2

Standen, Jim 187

Stanford, R.M. 7

Statham, Brian 232; farewell to Test cricket 197–98

Steele, David 279; farewell to Test cricket 284

Steele, Ray 308

Stewart, Micky 133, 166, 359; England team manager 369–70

Stollmeyer, Jeff 290

Stop the Seventy Tour Committee 226

Storey, Stewart 348

Subba Row, Raman 132, 376

Such, Peter 417

Sunday cricket 153, 154, 173; first County Championship 201; first in a Test series 322

Sunday League 223; structural changes 405

Surrey 17–18, 89–91, 247–48; Bennett Nigel 17–18; Championship record under Surridge 89, 125; Championship, seventh win 132; Ian Greig captaincy 358; Errol Holmes 18; Sunday League 436; Surridge captaincy 89

Surridge, Stuart 89–91; Championship record 89, 125

452

Sussex: first John Player League victory 331
Suttle, Ken 100
Swanton, Jim 32, 225
Symington, Stuart 62
Symonds, Andrew 431

Tallon, Don 31
Tattersall, Roy 59
Tavaré, Chris 312
Taylor, Bob 298
Taylor, Brian 126
Taylor, Clive 254–55
Taylor, Les: rebel tour of South Africa 328–29
television and sport 66, 115, 308, 330, 354, 418
Terry, Paul 340; broken arm 341
Tesco Trophy 422
Test and County Cricket Board 413; ban over rebel tour of South Africa 328–29; Botham's drug-taking 352–53; covered pitches 314; 'encroachment' accusation from MCC 361; fines for slow over rates 296; Packer series, new rule 289; Rhodesia question 221; starting-day change 394–96; World Cup 229–30
Tests: attendances down 189, 197; Australia and New Zealand tour, 1958–59 136–40; 1962–63 168–73; 1974–75 271–75; Australia, 1948 46–54 (statistics 53–54); 1950–51 68–75 (statistics 74–75); 1953 91–99 (statistics 98–99); 1954–55 106–14 (statistics 112–14); 1956 118–25 (statistics 124–25); 1961 155–60; 1964 183–87 (statistics 185–86); 1965 198–201; 1968 216–18; 1970–71 236–44 (statistics 242–43); 1972 252; 1975 277, 280–81; 1977 292–96 (statistics 294–95); 1978 300–301; 1979–80 308–9; 1981 316–24 (statistics 320–21); 1982–83 333–34; 1985 349–50; 1986–87 358–59; 1989 378–80; 1990–91 392–93; 1993 410–14; 1994–95 423–25; captain–manager quandary 314; centenary at Melbourne 285–86; centenary test against Australia 313; converging of national strengths 255; first post-war Test (statistics) 26–27; India and Pakistan, 1961–62 161–63; 1972 253–55; India, 1951–52 81–82; 1952 82–89 (statistics 86–89); 1959 140–42; 1963–64 181–83; 1967 207–8; 1971 247; 1976–77 284–85; 1979 303; 1982 325–26, 331–32; 1984–85 342–46 (statistics 345–46); 1986 354; 1990 388–92 (statistics 390–91); 1992 401–3; 1996 434; Jubilee series in India 309–10; New Zealand, 1949 60–61; 1958 131–32; 1965 193 (statistics 196–97); 1969 225; 1971 244; 1973 255–57; 1978 299; 1983 335; 1984 337–38; 1986 355; 1994 417–18; Pakistan and New Zealand, 1977–78 297–98; Pakistan, 1954 103–6; 1962 165–67; 1967 208; 1968 219–20; 1971 246–47; 1978 298; 1982 332–33; 1984 338; 1987 360, 365–67; 1992 399–401; 1996 434; South Africa, 1947 34, 38–39; 1948–49 55–58; 1951 76–77; 1955 115–16; 1956–57

125; 1960 150–52; 1964–65
189–92; 1965 197–98; 1994
418–23 (statistics 421–22); 1996
432–33; Sri Lanka, 1982 326–27;
1988 374–75; 1991 396; 1992
402, 403; 1996 435; twin tour,
1965 193; West Indies, 1950
66–68; 1953–54 97, 99–103; 1957
126–31 (statistics 129–30); 1960
142–49 (statistics 145–46); 1963
174–80 (statistics 178–79); 1966
202–7 (statistics 206–7); 1967
210–14; 1973 257–59; 1974
262–68 (statistics 266–67); 1976
283–84; 1980 312–13, 314–16;
1984 338–41; 1986 351–52; 1988
372–74; 1990 381–87 (statistics
384–85); 1993–94 414–15; 1995
427; 1996 428–31
Texaco Trophy 339, 372, 394, 417,
428
That Was the Week That Was 154
Thicknesse, John 405
third umpire 414
Thomas, Greg 351; South Africa
tour 379
Thomson, Jeff 272, 331
Thomson, Philip 102
throwing 149, 151
The Times 83
Titmus, Fred 196; boating acci-
dent 211–12; farewell to Test
cricket 274
Tolchard, Roger 284
Travers, Ben 406
Tremlett, Maurice 34–35; South
Africa Test series, 1948–49 55
Tribe, George 116, 117
Trinidad independence 155
Trueman, Fred 59, 82, 84, 91, 284;
bowling record 172–73; Reg
Hayter on 99–100; star fading

190
Tufnell, Phil 432
Turnbull, Maurice 1
Turner, David 260
Turner, Glenn 215, 235, 311;
batting record 255; century of
centuries 331
Turner, Stuart 223, 308; on Gower
277
Twining, R.H. 2
Twose, Roger 416
Tyson, Frank 105; farewell to Test
cricket 137, 140; foot problems
116

Underwood, Derek 285; Packer
series 287; rebel tour of South
Africa 328–29

Valentine, Bryan 2
van der Binl, Vincent 310
Verity, Hedley 1
Voce, Bill 27–28

W.D. & H.O. Wills 229–30
Walford, Michael 16
Walker, Max 272
war: Battle of Britain 3; declared
1; and Lords 2; Normandy
landing 6; Oval requisitioned
13; players killed in action 1–2;
war years 1–10
Ward, David 397
Wardle, Johnny 134–36; unflattering comments about Yorkshire
players 134–35
Warner, Pelham 2, 41; death 6
Warne, Shane 410
Warr, John 69
Warwickshire 15, 78–79, 248–51,
403, 415–17; Benson and

Hedges Cup 416; County
Champions 1951 78; County
Championship 416, 427; Tom
Dollery 62; NatWest Trophy
377–78, 410, 427; Sunday
League 416; tactics complaint
against Yorkshire 209
Washbrook, Cyril 6; self-selection
119–20
Waugh, Mark 393
Waugh, Steve 371
Webster, Jack 19
Wellard, Arthur 20
Wellham, Dick 349
Wellings, E.M. 181, 212; Australia
test, 1970–71 236; on Cowdrey
182
Wessels, Kepler 333
West Indies: independence 155;
Test series, 1950 66; 1953–54
97, 99–103; 1957 126–31 (statis-
tics 129–30); 1960 142–49
(statistics 145–46); 1963 174–80
(statistics 178–79); 1966 202–7
(statistics 206–7); 1967 210–14;
1973 257–59; 1974 262–68
(statistics 266–67); 1976
283–84; 1980 312–13, 314–16;
1984 338–41; 1986 351–52; 1988
372–74; 1990 381–87 (statistics
384–85); 1991 394–96; 1993–94
414–15; 1995 427; 1996 428–31
West, Peter 207
Wharton, Alan 59–60
Wheatley, Ossie 376
Whitaker, James 358
White, 'Butch' 161
White, Luke 8
Willey, Peter 283; rebel tour of
South Africa 328–29
Willis, Bob 249, 331; farewell to
Test cricket 340; injury prob-

lems 285, 319
Wilson, Don 236, 246
Wilson, Harold: South Africa race
row 227
Wilson, Vic: first-class career, end
of 167
Wisden 171, 186–87, 301; Australia
test, 1970–71 236; on Botham
276; on Brown 76; on
Caribbean tour, 1947–48 43; on
Dexter 173; on first post-war
test hundred 25; on Greig 264,
290; on poor captaincy 77; on
structural changes 405; on
Surrey's seventh
Championship title 132–33; on
Surridge 90; on throwing 149;
tribute to Sobers 249–50;
wartime obituaries 1–2
Wood, Barry 232
Woodcock, John 164, 280; on
Denness 277; on Greig 267
Wood, Graeme 349
Wooldridge, Ian 290
Wooller, Wilf 13, 54–55
Woolmer, Bob 279, 432; last Test
hundred 292; Packer series
288; rebel tour of South Africa
328–29
Worcestershire 15; Botham's
move from Somerset 353;
County Championship 371;
dominance 370; first County
Championship 187; NatWest
Trophy 416; Sunday League
371
World Cup 228–31: first competition 275–76; second competition 302–3; third competition
334–35; fourth competition
363–65; fifth competition
397–98; sixth competition

433–34, 435; growing popularity 276
World Series Cricket *See* Packer
Worrell, Frank 174
Wright, Doug 21, 23–24, 33, 80
Wright, John 311
Wyatt, Bob 4

Yardley, Norman 3, 29, 33, 46, 63
Yorkshire 133–36, 202, 208–9, 336–37; Benson and Hedges Cup 361; captaincy row 291–92; Carrick captaincy 361; 'civil war' 325; Close sacking 245–46; County Championship wins 214; farewell to Boycott 353; Gillette Cup 223–24; John Player League 336; tactics' complaint by Warwickshire 209; Wardle's unflattering comments 134–35
Young, Jack 36
Younis, Waqar 397

Zimbabwe 406